Mozart in Prague

Daniel E. Freeman

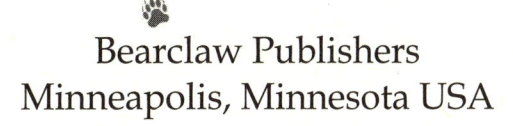

Bearclaw Publishers
Minneapolis, Minnesota USA

Mozart in Prague
©2013 by Daniel E. Freeman

ISBN-13: 978-0-9794223-1-7

Library of Congress Control Number: 2013943792

First printing 2013 in the United States of America

All rights reserved. No part of this publication may be reproduced, stored in a retrieval system, or transmitted by any means - electronic, mechanical, photographic (photocopying), recording, or otherwise - without prior permission in writing from the publisher.

Bearclaw Publishers
Minneapolis, Minnesota USA
www.bearclawpublishers.com

Editing and book design: Jamie Peterson Černá/Bearclaw Publishers, Minneapolis, Minnesota, USA

Original etchings - ©Martin Sladký, Prague, Czech Republic:
    Nerudova (front cover)
    Bertramka (back cover)
    Týn Church
    Malostranské náměstí (page 1)
    Dome and Spire of St. Nicholas, Malá Strana (page 103)

Map: The City of Prague in 1791 - Jiři Roun, Surveyor, City Development Authority, Prague, Czech Republic

Mozart
in
Prague

*It is not easy to convey an adequate conception
of the enthusiasm of the Bohemians for Mozart's music.
The pieces which were admired least of all in other countries
were regarded by those people as things divine;
and, more wonderful still, the great beauties which
other nations discovered in the music of that rare genius
only after many, many performances,
were perfectly appreciated by the Bohemians
on the very first evening.*

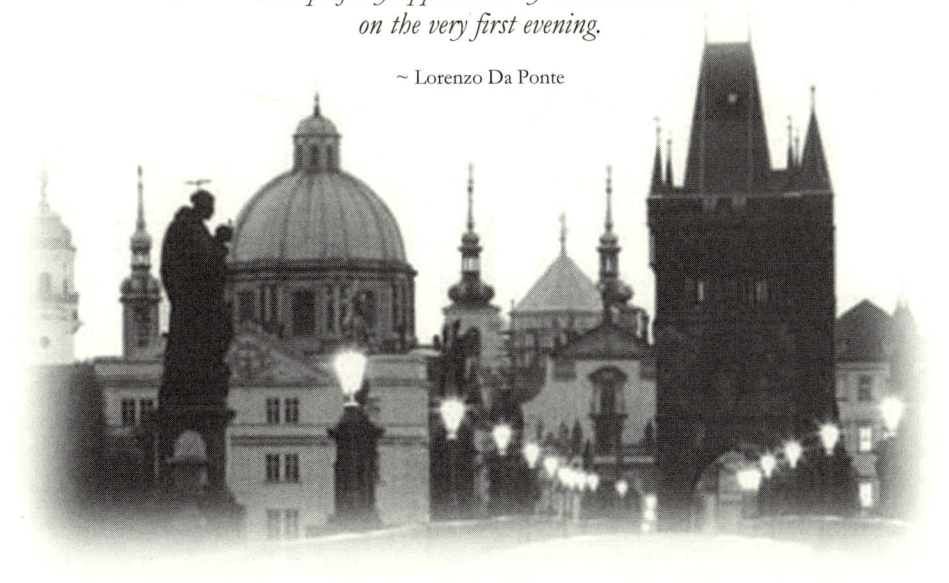

~ Lorenzo Da Ponte

Photo Credits:

Anna Chromy's "Danube," Czech Musicians - ©Carith Saranapala, Middlesex, United Kingdom
Page 4: *House of Three Violins* - ©Aris Jansons, Riga, Latvia
Page 16: *St. Wenceslas* - ©Nick Ansell, York, United Kingdom
Page 36: *Christmas Carp* - ©Petr Beránek, Teplice, Czech Republic
Page 58: *Anna Chromy's* Czech Musicians *and Jan Wagner's* Dancing Fountain; page 63: Hanácká Hospoda - ©Jason Vanderhill, Westminster, British Columbia
Prague Castle - ©Dean Ayres, London, England (www.flickr.com/photos/deano/27754933)
Page 65: *1791 Clothing of Count Jan Rudolf Černin,* (collection of chateau, Jindřichův Hradec, Czech Republic - ©Hana Běťáková, Český Brod, Czech Republic
Page 102: *Church of St. George,* - ©George Christoforidis, Athens, Greece
Page 115: *Anna Chromy's* II Commendatore - ©Jaime Silva, Lisbon, Portugal
Page 137: *Church of the Assumption* - ©Adam Smok, Wroclaw, Poland
Page 141: *Rott House* - ©Henry Ristic, Woodridge, Illinois

The publisher warrants that every effort has been made to confirm that the following and all additional graphics are in the public domain and not subject to copyright. If there are any errors or omissions, we will be pleased to insert the proper acknowledgement(s) in any future edition(s) and/or printing(s):

Title page: *Mozart* - PD1923/PD-Art, United States/European Union - Dora Stock, 1789
Table of Contents: *Edlinger Mozart* - PD100, United States/European Union - Johann Georg Edlinger, presumed 1790; Berliner Gemäldegalerie, Berlin, Germany
Page 67: *Anna Maria Mozart* - PD1923/PD-Art, United States/European Union - Rosa Hagenauer-Barducci, 1775; Mozart's Geburtshaus, Salzburg, Austria
Page 118: Giacomo Casanova - PD-Art, United States/European Union - Jan Berka, Prague, 1788
Page 1209: *Teresa Saporiti,* PD-Art, United States/European Union - Ferdinando Fambrini, 1791; Portrait Collection, Friedrich Nicolas Manskopf, Library, Johann Wolfgang Goethe-University, Frankfurt-am-Main, Germany
Page 160: *Albertine and Franz Alexander von Kleist with their children* - PD1923/PD-Art, United States/European Union - Wilhelm Jury, *Das Glück der Ehe* (*The Happiness of Wedlock*) by Franz Alexander von Kleist, 1796, Friedrich Vieweg
Page 184: *Carl and Franz Xaver Mozart* - PD1923/PD-Art, United States/European Union - Hans Hansen, 1798; Mozart Museum, Salzburg, Austria
Page 195: *Drawing of earliest known stage set for* Don Giovanni, Prague, 1790s - PD1923/PD-Art, United States/European Union
Page 260: *Luigi Bassi in the Role of Don Giovanni* - PD1923/PD-Art, United States/European Union - Medardus Thoenert

About the Author...

Musicologist Daniel E. Freeman is the world's leading authority on the musical culture of eighteenth-century Prague born outside of the Czech lands, an American who has lived and studied in Prague since before the Velvet Revolution. Besides his work with Bohemian music, he has published extensively on topics such as eighteenth-century keyboard music, eighteenth-century opera, and the music of Antonio Vivaldi, W. A. Mozart, J. S. Bach, the Bach sons, and Josquin des Prez.

Dr. Freeman gives lectures on music at the University of Minnesota and has appeared frequently as a speaker at the Smithsonian Institution in Washington, D.C. His research for *Mozart in Prague* was supported by a grant from the National Endowment for the Humanities.

Mozart in Prague is the third monograph in Dr. Freeman's eighteenth-century Prague trilogy. The other two titles in the series are *The Opera Theater of Count Franz Anton von Sporck in Prague* and *Josef Mysliveček, "Il Boemo": The Man and His Music*.

For Ruth Lillian Brummond,
the Friends of the St. Paul Chamber Orchestra,
and the musicians and music lovers of the Bohemian lands ~
Mozart's most enduring advocates

Table of Contents

Acknowledgments		*xiii*
Preface		*xv*
Map: City of Prague in 1791		*xvii*
Geneologies		*xviii*
Introduction		*1*

Part One:
THE SETTING

Chapter 1	The Passing of a "Time of Darkness": Bohemia in the Late Eighteenth Century		7
Chapter 2	Royal Capital Without a King: Prague in the Late Eighteenth Century		27
Chapter 3	"Everyone in Prague Loves Music": The Musical Culture of Eighteenth-Century Prague		44
Chapter 4	False Starts and Flirtations: Mozart and Bohemia Before 1787		61

Part Two:
MOZART'S EXCURSIONS to PRAGUE (and AFTERMATH)

Chapter 5	A Musical Oasis in Bohemia: Mozart's First Visit to Prague in 1787		83
Chapter 6	Seduction on the Mind: Mozart's Second Visit and the Première of *Don Giovanni*		104
Chapter 7	Interim Diversions: Legends, Second Departure, and the Short Visits of 1789		131
Chapter 8	Playing Second Fiddle: Mozart and the Coronation of Leopold II in 1791		148
Chapter 9	Slights Redeemed: The Reaction in Prague to Mozart's Death		178

Part Three:
MUSIC for PRAGUE

Chapter 10	Titillation Under the Guise of Condemnation: Mozart's Opera *Don Giovanni*	*193*
Chapter 11	Music for a Dirty Deal: Mozart's Opera *La clemenza di Tito*	*227*
Chapter 12	Musical Miscellany: The "Prague" Symphony & Lesser Works Written for Prague	*238*
Postscript		*258*
Appendix I	*Don Giovanni*: Survey of the Musical Numbers in the Prague Version of 1787	*260*
Appendix II	*La clemenza di Tito*: Survey of the Musical Numbers	*268*
Appendix III	Sites in Prague Visited by Mozart (that can be seen today)	*273*
Appendix IV	The Blood of the Přemyslids	*275*
Notes		*277*
Select Bibliography		*321*
Index		*323*

Edlinger Mozart
by Johann Georg Edlinger,
presumed 1790

Acknowledgments

Many individuals deserve to be singled out for their help in seeing this volume through to completion, with the most fervent expression of gratitude reserved for Jamie Peterson, its publisher and editor, whose steadfast support from the moment she learned that the manuscript was in existence has been an unflagging source of inspiration and perseverance. I met her through my connection with the opera lover Judy Berge, to whom I will aways be indebted. Hardly less critical to my ambitions for this work was funding provided by a research grant from the National Endowment for the Humanities. Three distinguished musicologists provided me with essential support in obtaining it: Michael Beckerman, John Walter Hill, and John A. Rice.

I was fortunate to be able to rely on three valued music lovers of long acquaintance to look over the first drafts of the manuscript and provide me with suggestions to improve the text: Mary-Louise Clary, Joan Gacki, and Inge Schwochau. Their excellent advice was supplemented by that of a professional musician, the pianist Stephanie Wendt, and one of my oldest friends, Remigijus Klyvis, who provided me with a particular insight about Mozart.

In addition to the contributions of these individuals, I have been favored with the kindness of a large circle of friends whose encouragement throughout the long process of preparing this volume for publication could never be forgotten. Among these, I would like to thank Josephine Bailey, Inez Bergquist, Norlin and Carole Boyum, Elizabeth Buschor, Rachelle Chase, Gisela Corbett, Patrick DeWane, Johan Dirks, Sara Donaldson, Mary Frederick, Margaret Hanegraaf, Brent Johnson, Betty Kok, James and Gail LaFave, John and Karen Larsen, Patricia Limbacher, Judie Lucchesi, Mary McDiarmid, Marc Nicholson, Carole Nimlos, Scot Pearson, Cheryl Salamanca, Christopher Schout, Stan and Connie Suchta, Carol Thomas, and Lucio Tufano. A much more extensive group of well-wishers who merit my gratitude is encompassed by the membership of the Friends of the St. Paul Chamber Orchestra, one of the dedicatees of this volume. My association with this organization has provided me with some of the most rewarding experiences of my life, musical and otherwise. No mention of its importance to me would be complete without extending due credit to Jean London, who first brought me to the attention of its administration.

Upon completing a study such as this one, I would be remiss in failing to acknowledge two members of the staff of the University of Minnesota who have been mainstays of my work with the general musical public, Anastasia Faunce and Susan Thurston Hamerski, as well as Pamela Wejman of the Smithsonian Institution, who was responsible for initiating my long association there with a lecture about Mozart in Prague. Her successor Mary McLaughlin has been no less supportive.

Many residents of Prague have offered me hospitality or specialized services that could never be overlooked in any proper expression of acknowledgment. In particular, I was privileged for many years to be able to stay in the Prague apartment of Bohumil and Helena Socha whenever I was conducting research in the city; I will always retain warm memories of their company. The Czech archivists that I worked with were very helpful to me, and I would like to draw special attention to the courtesy of Helena Sedláčková of the National Archives of the Czech Republic. I am also grateful for the goodwill of Gabriela Kalinová, a historian of the city of Prague with unusually vast knowledge and great generosity in sharing it. Czech artist Martin Sladký must be recognized for his generous contribution of original etchings to help illustrate this volume, and I am no less grateful to Jiří Roun, Surveyor for the City Development Authority of Prague, for his map depicting the geographic bounds of the city as they existed in the year 1791, and Ingrid Ledererová, Technical Director of Dial Telecom, Prague, and Dana Ruranová, broker for RE/MAX Harmony, Prague, for their ready assistance in identifying helpful resources in Prague.

Finally, I wish to express my thanks to the following photographers whose work appears in this volume: Nick Ansell, York, United Kingdom; Dean Ayres, London, England; Petr Beránek, Teplice, Czech Republic; Hana Běť'áková, Český Brod, Czech Republic; George Christoforidis, Athens, Greece; Aris Jansons, Riga, Latvia; Henry Ristic, Woodridge, Illinois; Charith Saranapala, Middlesex, United Kingdom; Jaime Silva, Lisbon, Portugal; Adam Smok, Wroclaw, Poland; and Jason Vanderhill, Westminster, British Columbia.

Daniel Freeman
Minneapolis, Minnesota
July 2013

Preface

The present volume represents the culmination of one of the author's most treasured professional goals: the completion of a series of monographs matched to each of the three topics related to the musical culture of eighteenth-century Prague that are of greatest interest to English-speaking music scholars, musicians, and music lovers worldwide: the opera theater of Count Franz Anton von Sporck (with its connection to Antonio Vivaldi), the career of the Prague composer Josef Mysliveček (with his connection to Wolfgang Amadeus Mozart), and Mozart in Prague. The need for such a series can be illustrated by the fact that the Sporck theater study, published in 1992, was the first monograph devoted to the musical life of eighteenth-century Prague ever written in English. The biography of Mysliveček was published in 2009. As the most significant component of the series, *Mozart in Prague* was always intended to be reserved for the last.

Funding from the National Endowment for the Humanities was critical to the successful completion of this study. It was awarded with a strict mandate stipulating that the text be accessible to a far broader reading public than professional musicologists, the natural interest group for the first two studies of the series. Thus the text prepared for this volume is intended to be more lively and engaging than that which is encountered in most musicological literature. There has been an attempt only to use musical terminology in the general parlance of ordinary music lovers, unless it is defined for the reader. No sophisticated discussion of music theory has been included, and - at the urging of readers who saw early drafts of the original manuscript - the flow of the main text is not interrupted by any indications of footnotes or endnotes. Rather, bibliographic citations are collected in a special section after the main text. This documentation is intended to render the study more useful for professional musicologists even aside from the commentary in the main text, which attempts to draw attention to the author's most original interpretations of the subject matter.

Always mindful of the needs of English-speaking musicians and music lovers, the bibliographic citations intentionally favor English-language musicological and historical literature, including English translations of research materials originally written in German; however, helpful resources in any language have been included when they have been deemed valuable enough. In particular, the author is eager to draw attention to the excellent entries found in the Czech theatrical dictionary *Starší divadlo v českých zemích do konce 18. století* (2007), which is much to be recommended even to scholars unable to read Czech simply for its unprecedented bibliographies. For more information concerning a plethora of minor musical figures of minimal interest to a general readership, the notes will direct those with more specialized pursuits to articles in dictionaries such as this one.

It has been a daunting task to balance the expectations of music lovers and musicologists simultaneously. There may still be professional musicians and music scholars who feel themselves patronized by parts of the text and non-professionals who may sense that parts of the discussion are over their heads or reveal too many traces of the author's academic training. For any possible shortcomings in this regard, the author expresses sincere regret. Some readers may decide to skip over the discussion of musical works, or other parts, if they are not of particular interest, in order to concentrate on the portions that satisfy the greatest personal curiosity. It can only be hoped that readers will try to appreciate the author's intention of making the information contained in this volume available and comprehensible to the largest number of readers possible.

Anna Chromy's "Danube," Czech Musicians
©Carith Saranapala

The City of Prague in 1791

Family of Maria Theresa

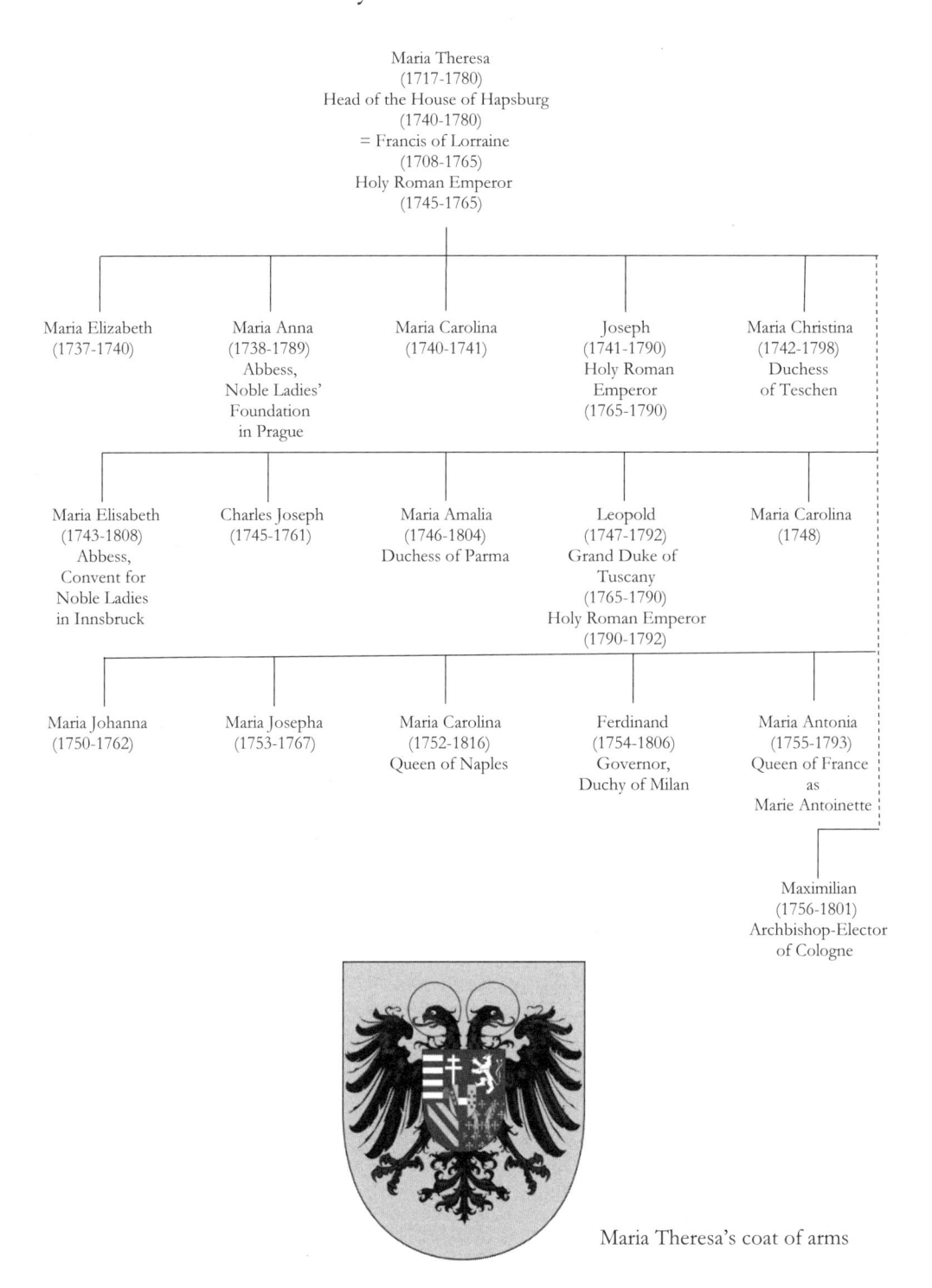

Maria Theresa
(1717-1780)
Head of the House of Hapsburg
(1740-1780)
= Francis of Lorraine
(1708-1765)
Holy Roman Emperor
(1745-1765)

- **Maria Elizabeth** (1737-1740)
- **Maria Anna** (1738-1789) Abbess, Noble Ladies' Foundation in Prague
- **Maria Carolina** (1740-1741)
- **Joseph** (1741-1790) Holy Roman Emperor (1765-1790)
- **Maria Christina** (1742-1798) Duchess of Teschen
- **Maria Elisabeth** (1743-1808) Abbess, Convent for Noble Ladies in Innsbruck
- **Charles Joseph** (1745-1761)
- **Maria Amalia** (1746-1804) Duchess of Parma
- **Leopold** (1747-1792) Grand Duke of Tuscany (1765-1790) Holy Roman Emperor (1790-1792)
- **Maria Carolina** (1748)
- **Maria Johanna** (1750-1762)
- **Maria Josepha** (1753-1767)
- **Maria Carolina** (1752-1816) Queen of Naples
- **Ferdinand** (1754-1806) Governor, Duchy of Milan
- **Maria Antonia** (1755-1793) Queen of France as Marie Antoinette
- **Maximilian** (1756-1801) Archbishop-Elector of Cologne

Maria Theresa's coat of arms

xviii

Family of Leopold II

(All living members were present for the 1791 coronation celebrations in Prague, including performances of Mozart's operas)

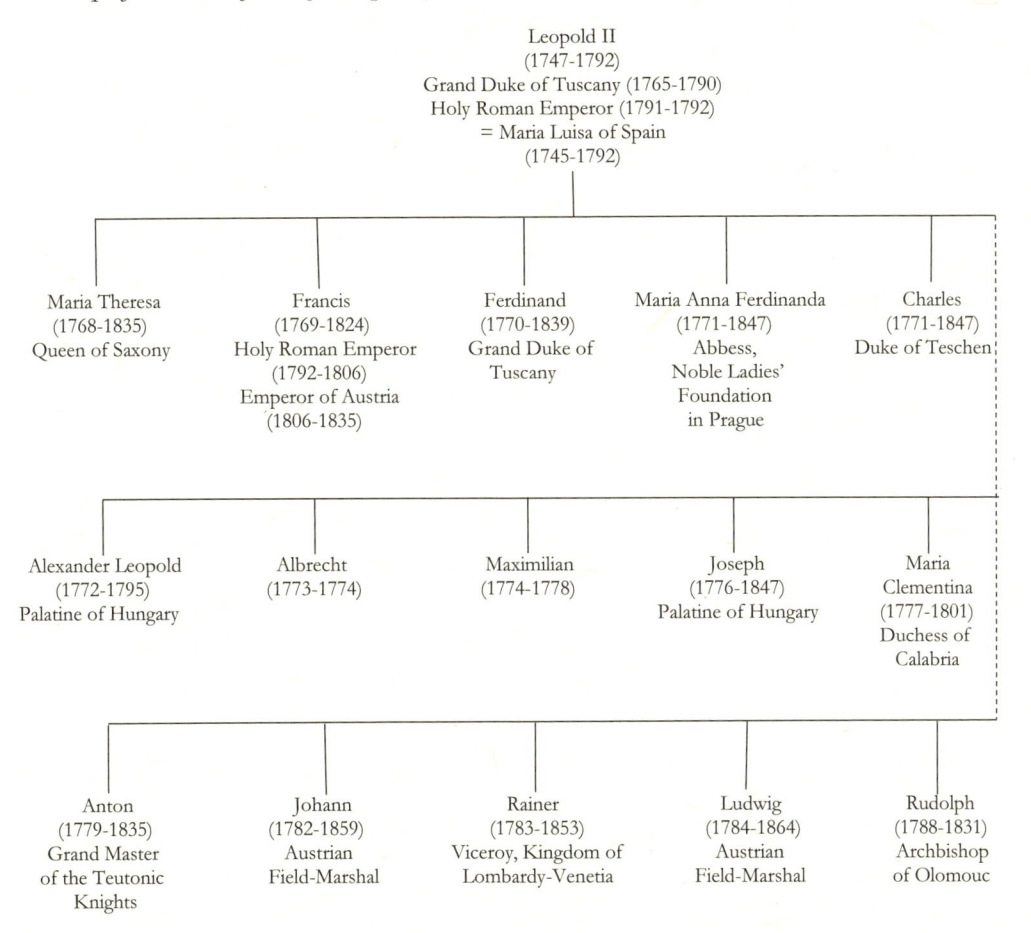

Leopold II
(1747-1792)
Grand Duke of Tuscany (1765-1790)
Holy Roman Emperor (1791-1792)
= Maria Luisa of Spain
(1745-1792)

- Maria Theresa (1768-1835) Queen of Saxony
- Francis (1769-1824) Holy Roman Emperor (1792-1806) Emperor of Austria (1806-1835)
- Ferdinand (1770-1839) Grand Duke of Tuscany
- Maria Anna Ferdinanda (1771-1847) Abbess, Noble Ladies' Foundation in Prague
- Charles (1771-1847) Duke of Teschen
- Alexander Leopold (1772-1795) Palatine of Hungary
- Albrecht (1773-1774)
- Maximilian (1774-1778)
- Joseph (1776-1847) Palatine of Hungary
- Maria Clementina (1777-1801) Duchess of Calabria
- Anton (1779-1835) Grand Master of the Teutonic Knights
- Johann (1782-1859) Austrian Field-Marshal
- Rainer (1783-1853) Viceroy, Kingdom of Lombardy-Venetia
- Ludwig (1784-1864) Austrian Field-Marshal
- Rudolph (1788-1831) Archbishop of Olomouc

Coat of arms of the
Holy Roman Empire
with Leopold II's personal blazon

Přemyslid Descent of Holy Roman Emperors Joseph II and Leopold II

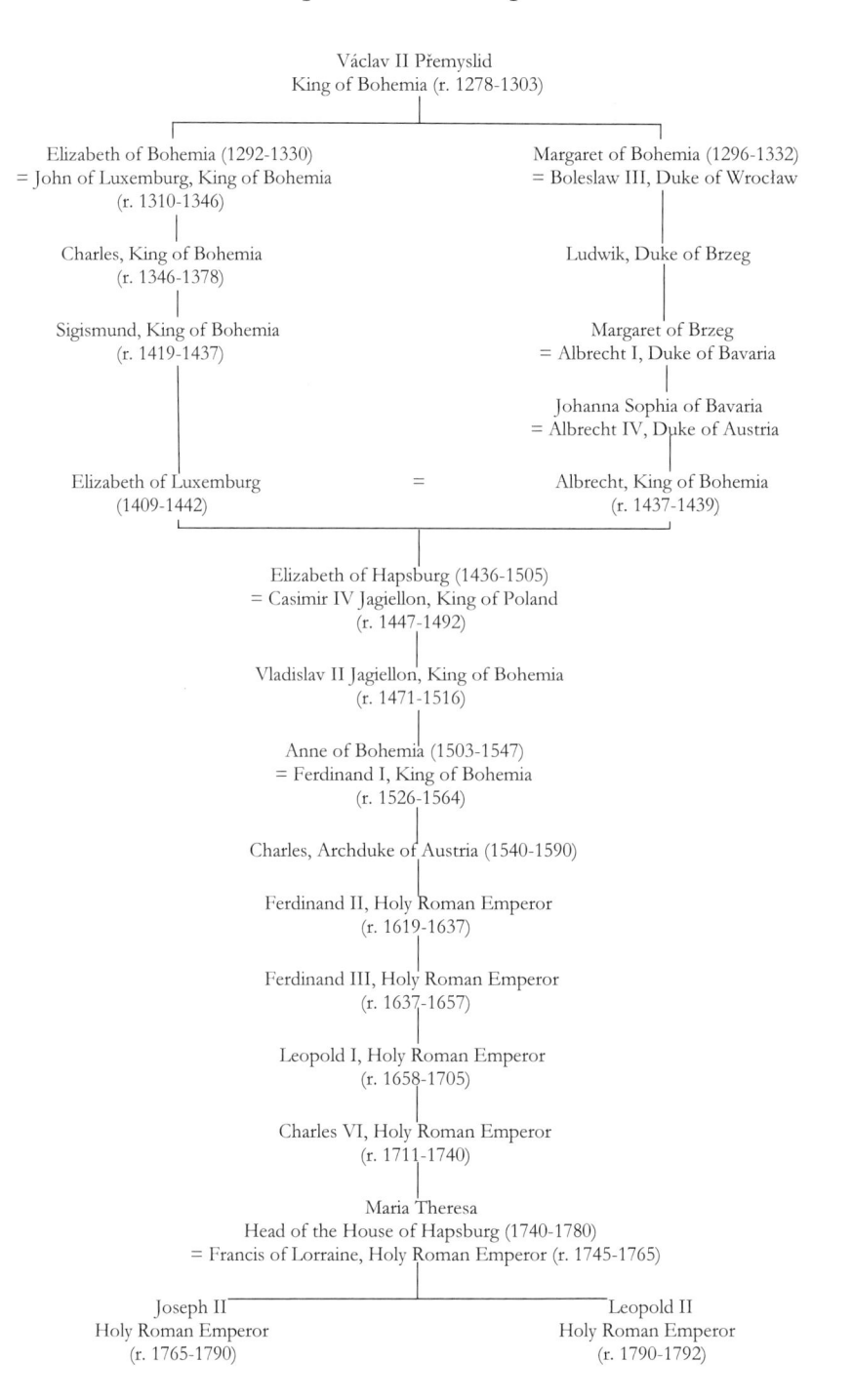

Václav II Přemyslid
King of Bohemia (r. 1278-1303)

Elizabeth of Bohemia (1292-1330)
= John of Luxemburg, King of Bohemia
(r. 1310-1346)

Charles, King of Bohemia
(r. 1346-1378)

Sigismund, King of Bohemia
(r. 1419-1437)

Margaret of Bohemia (1296-1332)
= Boleslaw III, Duke of Wrocław

Ludwik, Duke of Brzeg

Margaret of Brzeg
= Albrecht I, Duke of Bavaria

Johanna Sophia of Bavaria
= Albrecht IV, Duke of Austria

Elizabeth of Luxemburg
(1409-1442)
=
Albrecht, King of Bohemia
(r. 1437-1439)

Elizabeth of Hapsburg (1436-1505)
= Casimir IV Jagiellon, King of Poland
(r. 1447-1492)

Vladislav II Jagiellon, King of Bohemia
(r. 1471-1516)

Anne of Bohemia (1503-1547)
= Ferdinand I, King of Bohemia
(r. 1526-1564)

Charles, Archduke of Austria (1540-1590)

Ferdinand II, Holy Roman Emperor
(r. 1619-1637)

Ferdinand III, Holy Roman Emperor
(r. 1637-1657)

Leopold I, Holy Roman Emperor
(r. 1658-1705)

Charles VI, Holy Roman Emperor
(r. 1711-1740)

Maria Theresa
Head of the House of Hapsburg (1740-1780)
= Francis of Lorraine, Holy Roman Emperor (r. 1745-1765)

Joseph II
Holy Roman Emperor
(r. 1765-1790)

Leopold II
Holy Roman Emperor
(r. 1790-1792)

Mozart in Prague

Týn Church
©Martin Sladký

Introduction

The weather in Vienna on the afternoon of 6 December 1791, unseasonably mild but foggy, should have provided the perfect contemplative atmosphere for the mourners who attended the ceremony in St. Stephen's Cathedral that preceded the burial of Wolfgang Amadeus Mozart. Be that as it may, the emotions of those who did present themselves to pay their last respects can only be guessed at; there is not even a reliable record of their names. All that is known for certain is that they were few in number and the composer's widow - too distraught to attend - was not among them, nor were his two surviving children.

No friends or family members accompanied the wagon that conveyed the composer's body to its final resting place in the cemetery of St. Marx, where it was simply dumped into a mass grave. Years of financial irresponsibility had left the Mozart family nearly without funds at the time of Wolfgang's death, and his widow Constanze was able to afford only the bare essentials of a simple church service and transportation of his remains. None of the composer's many acquaintances in Vienna stepped forward to arrange anything more elaborate. As a result, one of history's greatest composers was laid to rest without any special performance of music.

Eight days later, on the morning of 14 December 1791, a group of 120 musicians assembled in one of the most beautiful churches in Prague to perform a Requiem Mass in honor of the deceased Mozart. According to a newspaper report published the next day, the church could only hold about 4,000 of the mourners who had arrived. The square in front of the church, clogged with carriages, accommodated countless more. The musical performance was judged so moving that "Mozart's soul in Elysium must have rejoiced over it." No other city could match the depth and sincerity of the grieving over Mozart's death that was witnessed in Prague, and the memorial arranged in December of 1791 was hardly the last; regular commemorations of Mozart's death continued in Prague for years to come.

It would not be accurate to say that Mozart's talents were completely unappreciated in Vienna (far from it), but it is clear that music lovers in Prague displayed a much more instinctive understanding of

Malostranské náměstí
©Martin Sladký

the merits of Mozart's music. Their level of discernment has nowhere been described with more eloquence than in the memoirs of the poet Lorenzo Da Ponte, who wrote the texts for three of Mozart's operas. In the course of relating some incidents from a visit he made to Prague a few years after Mozart's death, Da Ponte included these remarks about the reception of Mozart's music in the city:

> It is not easy to convey an adequate conception of the enthusiasm of the Bohemians for [Mozart's] music. The pieces which were admired least of all in other countries were regarded by those people as things divine; and, more wonderful still, the great beauties which other nations discovered in the music of that rare genius only after many, many performances, were perfectly appreciated by the Bohemians on the very first evening.

Many traditional notions about Mozart's personality and musical career have been modified or rejected in recent decades, but the luster of Mozart's special relationship with the musical public of eighteenth-century Prague remains undiminished. Hardly a quaint legend, its validity is well attested in contemporary accounts. For those mindful of Mozart's struggles for recognition, the tributes recorded from Prague in the 1780s and 1790s can be deeply moving as vindications of the composer's worth.

Considering the enormous interest in the city of Prague that has arisen worldwide since the "Velvet Revolution" of 1989 - to say nothing of the mystique that accrues almost automatically to any location closely associated with Mozart - it is much to be regretted that accurate and useful information about the composer's visits to Prague has been so difficult to come by for English-speaking music lovers. During the long period of Communist rule in the former Czechoslovakia, Prague and the Bohemian lands was very much *terra incognita*, if not *terra aliena*, to music researchers in western Europe and North America; few could seriously contemplate performing research in Prague or delving very deeply into the musicological literature available concerning its musical culture. Invasions over the Carpathian mountains during the early Dark Ages brought Slavic peoples well to the west of what is now Vienna and Berlin - and their descendants in the provinces of Bohemia and Moravia have been responsible for remarkable contributions to the heritage of Western art music - but their language was difficult to master. Furthermore, the political isolation of Communist Czechoslovakia poisoned intellectual exchanges and made it challenging for scholars from outside the Soviet bloc to gain access to research materials, just as it was difficult for Czech scholars to travel outside of their native country. The musical culture of the Czech people indeed formed something of a problem for historians of eighteenth-century music. It became easy to lose sight of the legacy of Czech composers who lived before the nineteenth century, and the traditional tendency of Western literati to view Slavic Europe with condescension became somewhat institutionalized among musicologists.

It is heartening to observe that a new attitude toward the musical culture of the Bohemian lands has taken hold since the fall of the Communist régime in 1989, including recognition that they were fully integrated into the Germanized cultural traditions of central Europe during the eighteenth century. Language still remains a frustrating impediment, however, and there can still be no expectation that a significant number of specialists in eighteenth-century music in western Europe or North

America will ever acquire a working knowledge of Czech, which is essential to a thorough exploration of Mozart's association with the city of Prague. Due in particular to this consideration, it is really not surprising that the last comprehensive reappraisal of Mozart's association with Prague and the Bohemian lands appeared over seven decades ago. The scholar who undertook this task was Paul Nettl, the leading German-language musicologist in Czechoslovakia at that time. Nettl took great pains to prepare his 1938 study *Mozart in Böhmen* as a resource for non-Bohemians. In the 1930s, his position as a linguistic intermediary was invaluable. At that time, German was the most important international language for musicological research, and the combination of an upbringing in Bohemia and fluency in German and Czech made him uniquely qualified to explain many of the most important issues related to Mozart's visits to the Bohemian lands to an international community of Mozart scholars and music lovers.

The completion of Nettl's work in 1938 came just in time. Czechoslovakia was abandoned to Nazi Germany by the Western powers in the autumn of the same year. As a Jew, Nettl and his family found it advisable to flee to the United States from Nazi-controlled Bohemia only a short time later, just before the outbreak of World War II in 1939. If Nettl had not been able to see his Mozart study through to publication by 1938, there would have been little likelihood that it ever would have appeared, whether or not he had been able to escape central Europe. Resident in the United States, the research materials needed to complete such a study would have been very difficult to access, at first because of the difficulties created by the Nazi occupation of Czechoslovakia, and later because of the attitude of the Communist regime that took over the country in 1948. It is almost impossible to imagine another German-speaking scholar within Czechoslovakia stepping forward to take Nettl's place, since the German community in the Bohemian lands almost completely disappeared shortly after the conclusion of World War II due to a combination of expulsion and extermination.

Paul Nettl introduced his study of Mozart as being a revision and expansion of an older study by Rudolph Freiherr Procházka, *Mozart in Prag* (1892). Nettl was rather modest in describing his work in these terms, since it contains so much new material and so many new avenues of interpretation. A few additional topics have been explored more recently by Harald Salfellner in his *Mozart und Prag* (2000), but the latter's work is essentially nothing more than a repackaging of Nettl's research. The musicological research conducted by Czech scholars since World War II only naturally tends to emphasize composers native to the Bohemian lands; thus no Czech-speaking scholar has since authored any study comparable in scope to Nettl's, nor has any scholar outside of central Europe.

It would be a great service to music lovers to simply present in this volume the principal outlines of Nettl's discussion of Mozart's visits to Prague, but taking into account the priorities of English-speaking music lovers of the 21st century, some of the arcane topics he explored in some detail seem best left to a cursory summary. On the other hand, a number of important issues that he left almost untouched beg for treatment - in particular, detailed descriptions of the masterpieces that Mozart wrote for

Prague and explorations of how the composer's contacts with the city help to illuminate his personality.

If the process of investigating issues surrounding political and social conditions in Prague at the time of Mozart's visits will assist in making the history and culture of the Bohemian lands a bit less obscure to music scholars and music lovers outside of the Czech Republic, then some of the author's most treasured aspirations will find fulfillment. It will certainly be possible to offer the reader of this volume a more complete accounting than ever before of how it was that Mozart came to visit Prague in the late 1780s and early 1790s; what it was about the Praguers that made them so receptive to his music; and what makes the compositions that Mozart wrote for Prague so unique and memorable.

House of Three Violins, Nerudova
©Aris Jansons

Part One:
The Setting

1

The Passing of a "Time of Darkness": Bohemia in the Late Eighteenth Century

The most significant cultural event that took place in Prague or the Bohemian lands during the second half of the eighteenth century was the first performance of Mozart's opera *Don Giovanni* on 29 October 1787. For the past three hundred years, music and musicians have been the most valued cultural exports of the Czech nation, and it is therefore fitting that a musical masterpiece would touch the lives of more people worldwide than any other artistic work that originated in Bohemia at the time. In addition to its position as one of the greatest operas ever written, *Don Giovanni* has become the most universally accessible portrayal of the legendary seducer Don Juan of Seville. Unlike the other literary and dramatic treatments that have appeared over the centuries, Mozart's opera has completely transcended linguistic barriers.

It would surprise many to learn that the memoirs of Giacomo Casanova form another important contribution to Western civilization from the Bohemian lands of the late eighteenth century. Written partially in an effort to relieve the tedium of a dreary appointment as librarian in a remote castle in rural Bohemia, the Casanova memoirs rival the Mozart opera for their fame, even though they are not generally known from actual reading. In the same way as the title character of the Mozart opera, the name Casanova has become a household expression to denote the persona of a male seducer. It is indeed an extraordinary coincidence that two such celebrated explorations of sexual promiscuity (one based on fiction, one based on fact) emerged almost simultaneously in a part of the world whose history in the eighteenth century is not widely known except to researchers and its native population.

As products of foreigners, Mozart's opera *Don Giovanni* and the Casanova memoirs are usually given little more than passing mention in general histories of the Bohemian lands, regardless of language, and this is quite proper; neither is very crucial to an understanding of Czech history and culture any more than the première of Handel's *Messiah* in Dublin in 1742 is very pertinent to the development of Irish civilization. Nonetheless, it will be useful to embark on a survey of the history of the kingdom of Bohemia up to Mozart's time in the interest of illuminating his association with the country. Mozart did, after all, find himself drawn into the politics of the country when he accepted money from the Estates of Bohemia to compose a coronation opera for the king of Bohemia in 1791. The task of explaining the political character of eighteenth-century Bohemia necessarily must be more prosaic than relating the exploits of Casanova and Don Juan, but the long, complicated history of the Bohemian lands is fascinating to study - and it is frequently moving.

Among the ancient non-Russian peoples of eastern Europe, there is a common historical heritage marked by periods of political and cultural greatness during the Middle Ages followed by centuries of oppression at the hands of Germans, Austrians, Swedes, Russians, or Turks. The attainment of liberation from foreign rule during the late nineteenth and early 20th centuries gratified national movements across eastern Europe, but for long stretches of time in the mid and late 20th century, the political independence that had been achieved earlier became only partial or nominal in most cases, due to the imperialist political policies of Nazi Germany and the Soviet Union. Contrary to a widespread perception in western Europe and North America today, Czechs are properly referred to as central Europeans, and not as eastern Europeans. Nonetheless, their history is similar in many respects to that of other Slavic and non-Slavic peoples who reside to the east and south. As with all the non-Russian Slavs, the legacy of foreign oppression has left a deep impression on national identity that is still perceived strongly today.

A first high point in the history of the Bohemian lands was reached in the thirteenth century under rulers from the Přemyslid dynasty, who occupy a place in Czech history similar to the Capetians of France. Both dynasties are associated with the beginning of a nation state and a national consciousness in their respective countries. The Přemyslids emerged in Bohemia in the late eighth century and became Christianized in the ninth. As with the Capetians, their male line died out in the early fourteenth century.

The Czech dynasty is named for the peasant Přemysl, chosen by the legendary princess Libuše to rule over her people. Libuše and Přemysl, figures occaionally portrayed in operas written both within and outside the Bohemian lands since the seventeenth century, may actually have lived at some point after Slavic peoples first entered central Europe, probably in the mid-sixth century, but a precise date is impossible to determine.

Josef Václav Myslbek's
Přemysl and Libuše, 1881
Vyšehrad

In the year 1212, one of the Přemyslid rulers, Otakar I, was able to negotiate an agreement from his overlord, Holy Roman Emperor Frederick II, to elevate his territories permanently to the status of a hereditary monarchy known as the kingdom of Bohemia. Earlier, they had usually been ruled by a Přemyslid "duke" of Bohemia, the most famous one St. Wenceslas (Václav), who held the title between 921 and 935. (In the well-known Christmas carol, he is notoriously misidentified as "Good King

Wenceslas"). The central European provinces of Bohemia and Moravia ruled by Otakar I still form the homeland of the Czech-speaking Slavs, and they are almost all that remain of what was once a much larger patrimony. The more populous province of Bohemia lent its name to the entire monarchical state, a circumstance that sometimes creates confusion about references to Bohemia as a province of central Europe and Bohemia as a kingdom comprised of the provinces of Bohemia and Moravia.

The reign of Otakar II (1253-1278) marked the zenith of Přemyslid rule in central Europe. For a time, Otakar was able to acquire the provinces of Austria, Styria, Carinthia, Carniola, and Istria to the south, conquests that expanded his reach to the shores of the Adriatic. But Otakar's successes built up a great deal of resentment among neighboring rulers, one of them Count Rudolf of Hapsburg, the first member of his family to control the duchies of Austria and Styria. Rudolf raised a coalition against the kingdom of Bohemia, and at the time of Otakar's death in battle in 1278, the Přemyslids were left once again with the provinces of Bohemia, Moravia, and almost nothing more. It was Otakar's son Wenceslas II (r. 1278-1305) who sought to acquire all of the province of Silesia to the north and east, a territory that would remain a component of the Bohemian crown lands for over four centuries after the process was completed in 1335. After the start of the War of the Austrian Succession in 1740, nearly all of it fell to Prussia, whose territorial possessions were incorporated into the German Empire proclaimed in 1871. Silesia remained part of Germany until the end of World War II, after which it was turned over to Poland.

A period of instability following the death in 1306 of Wenceslas III, the last Přemyslid king, was brought to an end in 1310, when the crown of Bohemia was offered to John of Luxemburg, husband of Wenceslas' sister Eliška. John was of German origin and spent much of his youth at the court of France, but his dynasty came to identify itself closely with the Czech people, in particular during the reign of his son Charles (1346-1378), who was elected Holy Roman Emperor as Charles IV in 1355.

Charles IV presided over a golden age in the Bohemian lands. As capital of the Holy Roman Empire, Prague attracted artists, scholars, clerics, and nobles from all over Europe. So charmed a period in Czech history was this that the Great Plague, which ravaged most of the rest of Europe in the late 1340s, spared the kingdom of Bohemia almost entirely.

Two sons of Charles IV, Wenceslas IV and Sigismund, were the last of the Luxemburg dynasty to occupy the throne of Bohemia. The brothers rivaled each other for ineptitude as statesmen, and neither maintained the cultural brilliance of their father's court. As a result, the Bohemian lands receded from the attention of Europe, except in one important area: religion.

The early fifteenth century saw the emergence in Prague of the theologian Jan Hus, who challenged certain tenets of Roman Catholic dogma, among them the withholding of communion wine to the laity and the insistence on a liturgy in Latin. The Catholic Church succeeded in having Hus burned at the stake as a heretic in 1415 after he was lured to the Council of Constance with a false promise of safe passage.

This outrage only emboldened his followers in Bohemia. Under the leadership of the legendary military commander Jan Žižka, the Hussites were able to defy the pope and neighboring rulers who sought to suppress their faith. All forces sent against them were beaten back, a feat remembered with great national pride long after the country was re-Catholicized in the seventeenth century.

In the end, the struggle to impose Catholicism on Bohemia was not deemed worth the effort by the rest of Europe, and the papacy agreed to tolerate the Hussite church within Bohemia only; a sanction issued at the Council of Basel in 1437 formalized its status. For centuries afterward, the kingdom of Bohemia was host to one of the most complicated religious situations in all of Christendom. The Hussites splintered into irreconcilable factions at an early stage; Lutherans and Calvinists found adherents in Bohemia almost as soon as they emerged in other parts of Europe; and there were large numbers of Roman Catholics and Jews in the country as well.

Unsympathetic to the Hussite cause, Sigismund of Luxemburg was essentially overthrown as king of Bohemia after his brother Wenceslas died in 1419. He retained his title of king, but lived most of the time outside of the country (mainly in Hungary, whose throne he had held since 1387) until his own death in 1437. Sigismund's authority was effectively supplanted by Hussite nobles through the agency of the Bohemian Estates, a sort of national assembly whose meetings were referred to as Diets. Four estates were recognized by the crown - clergy, nobles, knights, and burghers - but the Diets were always dominated by the noble estate.

The death in 1471 of the last native Czech king, George (Jiří) of Poděbrady, by no means extinguished the power of the Czech nobles or led to a suppression of native religious practices. The Polish rulers of the Jagiellon dynasty who assumed the throne of Bohemia at the invitation of the Bohemian Estates showed scant interest in disturbing the religious and political balance within the country. Indeed, they never would have been allowed into Bohemia if they had not agreed to respect the privileges of the Estates.

Three members of the Hapsburg family held the crown of Bohemia during the fourteenth and fifteenth centuries - Rudolf I (1306-1307), Albrecht (1437-1439), and the boy king Ladislav (1440-1457) - but none of them was able to establish a lasting bloodline. More permanent Hapsburg control of Bohemia began in 1526, after the second of the two Jagiellon rulers, Louis II of Bohemia and Hungary, died at the battle of Mohács against the Turks. His sister Anna was married to the archduke Ferdinand of Austria, a connection that gave Ferdinand a claim to the crowns of both Bohemia and Hungary, and he did acquire them for the Hapsburg dynasty after reaching agreements with the local nobility of each country. Ferdinand's son Maximilian and all later Hapsburg rulers of Bohemia were descended from the ancient Přemyslid rulers through Ferdinand's wife Anna. After Ferdinand assumed the imperial throne upon the abdication of his brother Charles V in 1556, the Hapsburg kings of Bohemia were almost always simultaneously Holy Roman Emperors until the dissolution of the Holy Roman Empire in 1806.

The Hapsburgs could always be counted on to promote the Catholic element in their domains, but the power of the Protestant Estates of Bohemia was little diminished after Ferdinand came to the throne, and his attempts at re-Catholicizing Bohemia were almost completely unsuccessful. For his son, Maximilian II (r.1564-1576), and grandson, Rudolf II (r.1576-1612), it also proved impossible to either strengthen the influence of the Catholic party within Bohemia or to settle disputes among the rival Protestant factions. Rudolf's apparent indifference to the outcomes of these struggles seems ironic, since he took up residence in Prague and made it once again the capital of the Holy Roman Empire.

The aloof setting of Prague Castle - perched on a hill overlooking the river Vltava - served as the perfect backdrop for Rudolf's reclusive lifestyle. For years on end, he seldom left its grounds. To assist his indulgence in a wide range of interests, among them alchemy and astrology, he surrounded himself with an international collection of some of the day's most prominent scientists, artists, and mystics.

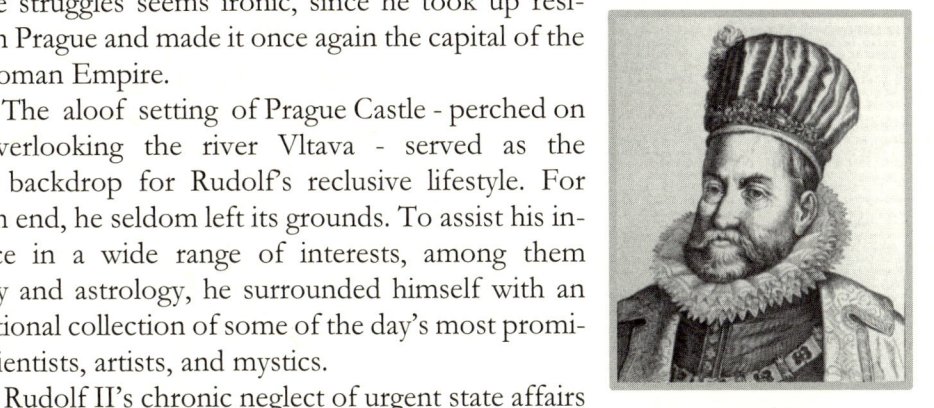

Rudolf II's chronic neglect of urgent state affairs was the cause of great concern within the Hapsburg domains, and one by one, his brother Matthias was able to wrest control of them. Matthias and some of Rudolf's other Hapsburg relatives largely succeeded in re-Catholicizing the territories that they took over, but in the province of Bohemia, there was still no success. The only way that Rudolf could retain his authority over the province in the face of attempts by his brother to oust him was to gain the support of the Protestant nobles. To this end, he issued the Letter of Majesty of 1609, which granted them complete religious toleration. It proved only a stopgap measure, however. Rudolf was overthrown by his brother Matthias as king of Bohemia in the year 1611. Until his death in 1612, Rudolf was allowed to remain in Prague as titular Holy Roman Emperor, but for the last months of his life he exercised no direct authority over any of the Hapsburg territories.

When Rudolf's brother Matthias became the new Holy Roman Emperor in 1612, he professed himself disinclined to enforce the stipulations of the Letter of Majesty. Violations of its provisions to allow the unrestricted construction of new Protestant churches precipitated a revolt of the Bohemian Estates in 1618 that was signaled by the famous Defenestration of Prague on 23 May, when a group of imperial officials was tossed from a window of Prague Castle, their lives saved only by a pile of dung that broke their fall below. The Estates then contrived to replace the Hapsburg dynasty with an elective Protestant monarchy. In 1619 they turned over the throne of Bohemia to the Calvinist Frederick, ruler of the Rhenish Palatinate.

Crowned on 4 November 1619, detractors predicted that Frederick would be able to hang on in Prague only as a "winter king," and he almost literally was. Neither Frederick nor his Czech supporters were able to replicate the military successes of the

Hussite armies two hundred years earlier. At the battle of White Mountain to the northwest of Prague on 8 November 1620, the armies of Frederick and his generals fled from the field in panic after only a few hours of fighting against the imperial forces sent to crush them. The kingdom of Bohemia was then at the mercy of the new Hapsburg emperor, Ferdinand II, who had succeeded his uncle Matthias the year before.

Consequences of the Defeat at White Mountain

The consequences of the battle of White Mountain reverberated well into Mozart's time. In fact, the defeat at White Mountain was directly responsible for creating the Germanized Catholic Bohemia that Mozart was familiar with. The eighteenth century in Bohemian history is still commonly referred to by Czech historians as part of a "post-White Mountain" period, if not actually a *doba temna* (i.e., "time of darkness" or "dark ages") that only started to lift at the end of the century.

Ferdinand II, a villain in Czech history hardly less odious than Adolf Hitler or Reinhard Heydrich, exacted a harsh retribution for the revolt of the Estates. The public execution of a group of rebellious nobles in 1621 was only a superficial humiliation. More significant punitive measures resulted from a series of imperial decrees issued in 1627 that led to the criminalization of non-Catholic worship, the expulsion and dispossession of Protestants, the neutralization of the Bohemian Estates as a nationalistic political entity, and the promotion of the activities of the Jesuit order, which was charged with proselytizing the country and supervising the educational system.

Certain other consequences of the defeat at White Mountain were catastrophic, not only for Bohemia, but for central Europe in general. Ferdinand's success at subduing the Protestants of Bohemia led him to try to confront them elsewhere in the Holy Roman Empire, an enterprise that led to the intervention of Denmark, Sweden, and France into the affairs of central Europe. The complicated series of religious and political conflicts that raged between 1618 and 1648 are known to historians today as the Thirty Years' War, but little remembered is the centrality of Prague in defining its chronological bounds. Just as the first event of the war is deemed to be the Defenestration of Prague in 1618, so the last is reckoned to be a siege of Prague by the Swedes in 1648.

In the interim, the incessant warfare that raged through central Europe had harsh effects in the kingdom of Bohemia. Its population dropped from close to three million to about a million and a half, and much of the countryside was laid waste. At the time of Mozart's visits to Prague between 1787 and 1791, Bohemia had recovered its population to a level of about four million.

After the end of the Thirty Years' War, Bohemia slid into a state of political stagnation for about a century, its role within the Hapsburg domains mainly as a source of revenue for the whole. In fact, the kingdom of Bohemia eventually became one of the most economically developed parts of the Hapsburg Empire. In the article on

Bohemia published in the famous *Encyclopédie* of Diderot and d'Alembert, special attention was drawn to the industrious nature of the Bohemians. The chief assets of the country were said to be fertile soil and an abundance of mines. Glassmaking was mentioned as a special craft for which the country was famed all over Europe. Thomas Nugent's *The Grand Tour,* a guidebook for English travelers that went through several editions after its original publication in 1749, also made mention of the excellent "strong beer" that was brewed in Bohemia, an export commodity as well-known today as the high quality glass that continues to be manufactured in the country.

The residents of Bohemia certainly would have been within their rights to complain of being cheated out of the fruits of their labors, since the country was taxed heavily in order to lessen the danger of revolt from other territories, especially Hungary, whose nobility was far more assertive. No significant opposition to Hapsburg policies, no matter how injurious to the country, was ever expected from the nobility of Bohemia, and there were no other elements within the Bohemian lands strong enough to provide alternative resistance. Periodic revolts of the peasantry were easily crushed.

The victory at White Mountain had made it possible for the Hapsburgs to uproot or neutralize the rebel nobility of the early seventeenth century entirely. Those that remained and those who were brought in from other parts of Europe to replace the dispossessed - some from as far away as Ireland and Scotland - were almost completely dependent on the Hapsburgs for their positions and fortunes. There was almost no way for a noble family in Bohemia to prosper without the favor of the Hapsburgs. Some of the greatest Bohemian noble families, such as the Kinskýs and Černíns, once had rebels in their ranks, but all those who did not prefer an impoverished exile came to terms with Hapsburg rule, a move that made possible rich rewards from lands that had been confiscated from others.

It is tempting to describe the basic political arrangement in the Bohemian lands for over a century after the defeat at White Mountain as a sort of *Ausgleich*. The latter term is frequently applied to the "settlement" or "compromise" struck by the Austrians and Hungarians in 1867, which left each group free to oppress the ethnic minorities who resided in their respective territories without interference from the other. In the Bohemian lands of the seventeenth and eighteenth centuries, this *Ausgleich* applied only to the emperor and the nobility. In return for loyalty to the Hapsburg dynasty, devotion to Catholicism, and a pliant attitude toward taxation and military service, the emperors did not interfere very much with the manorial rights of the nobles - to their immense enrichment.

Conditions started to change after 1740, when the death of Holy Roman Emperor Charles VI without a male heir created serious challenges for the Hapsburg dynasty. Charles VI's eldest daughter Maria Theresa - as a woman - was ineligible for election to the imperial throne in her own right; it was hoped that election could be secured instead for her husband, Francis of Lorraine. Charles had succeeded in gaining the assurance of foreign rulers and the nobility of his various domains to respect his daughter's succession within the hereditary Hapsburg lands. However, the weakened state of the Austrian government at the time of Charles' death and the presumed inexperience of the young new ruler led neighboring states to take advantage of her vulnerability.

The kingdom of Bohemia found itself once again at the center of European politics when Frederick the Great, in an act of naked aggression, invaded the rich province of Silesia in an attempt to augment the territories of his own kingdom of Prussia. Frederick's struggles to retain the province for Prussia, and Maria Theresa's efforts to regain it for Austria, triggered two major European conflicts: the War of the Austrian Succession (1740-1748) and the Seven Years' War (1756-1763). With the exception of a small portion of Silesia that was returned to the Hapsburgs at the end of the second conflict, Maria Theresa was unsuccessful in her efforts to reverse its acquisition by Frederick.

Maria Theresa

Warfare frequently brings unexpected results, and no contemporary observer could have guessed that the War of the Austrian Succession would help set into motion conditions that led to a revitalization of Czech national identity by the end of the eighteenth century, including a major confrontation with the Hapsburg monarchy that was patched up partially with the first performance of Mozart's opera *La clemenza di Tito*. Ironically enough, it was the Bohemian nobility that became the catalyst for a fresh reassertion of Czech nationhood after the traditional bond of trust that tied the Bohemian nobility to the Hapsburg monarchy was put to the test. It was not only foreign rulers, but also a large number of Bohemian nobles, who did not think that Maria Theresa would be able to hold the Hapsburg territories together. When Frederick the Great's ally Charles Albert, elector of Bavaria, invaded Bohemia in 1741, he was welcomed by the local nobility - in fact proclaimed king of Bohemia in Prague - and the next year he was elected Holy Roman Emperor, the first non-Hapsburg to hold the office since the death of Sigismund of Luxemburg in 1437. Charles Albert soon alienated the Bohemian populace by exacting a huge indemnity to defray the cost of his occupation, and a newly-energized Austrian military was able to dislodge him from Bohemia in short order. After Charles Albert died in 1745, Maria Theresa's husband, Francis of Lorraine, succeeded him as Holy Roman Emperor.

Maria Theresa was understandably enraged at the betrayal of so many of her Bohemian subjects. She remained suspicious of the Bohemian nobility for the rest of her life, even though certain Bohemian nobles of unquestioned loyalty - most importantly her brilliant foreign minister Count Wenzel von Kaunitz - were a part of her inner circle of advisors. There was surprisingly little retaliation against Bohemia beyond an increase in the already crushing taxation, but she did try to begin a process of weakening the authority of the Bohemian Estates within their country by setting up an administrative entity known as the Gubernium in 1751. Its officials were appointed by the Crown and were largely independent of the Estates. Efforts at centralizing the administration of all the Hapsburg domains were a hallmark of the reigns of both Maria Theresa and her son Joseph II, and entities similar to the Bohemian Gubernium were set up in other Hapsburg territories with the same intent of weakening the power of local aristocrats.

Certain policies pursued by Maria Theresa may have been irksome to the Bohemian nobility, but it was her son Joseph II who brought political conditions in the Bohemian lands to near revolt in the late 1780s. Between 1765 and 1780, Joseph ruled jointly with his mother after the death of his father Francis of Lorraine. Maria Theresa was alarmed at many of her son's progressive political and social attitudes, especially regarding religion, but she had the authority to curb many of his impulses. She did not succeed in preventing the expulsion of the Jesuits from the Hapsburg domains in 1773, however, nor was she able to persevere in the persecution of Protestants in Bohemia and Moravia who wished to practice their faith.

Joseph II

Energetic and exceptionally well-intentioned, Joseph was sadly unable to grasp the limitations of "absolute" monarchical rule in carrying out social and political reform. He was fascinated by the social experiments that could be created with the powers available to him, but learned that deeply-ingrained attitudes could not be changed by means of decree. Joseph's meddlesome, tactless nature hardly improved matters. He died a broken man, forced to rescind many of the reforms that were dearest to him, shocked at what he considered to be the ingratitude of the beneficiaries. The discontent he fostered in Bohemia was not nearly as serious as what was experienced in other Hapsburg territories, especially the Austrian Netherlands (a territory that has been known as Belgium since 1830), but it did foment a challenge to Hapsburg rule in Bohemia more serious than anything seen since the early seventeenth century.

Valuable testimony concerning the impact of Joseph's reformist political policies in Bohemia at the time of Mozart's visits in the 1780s can be gleaned from the memoirs of Count Kaspar von Sternberg, one of the most prominent cultural figures in the history of the Bohemian lands. In spite of his German-sounding name, he was actually a member of one of Bohemia's oldest noble families. A brilliant scientist and intellectual, he is chiefly remembered today as the founder and first president of the Czech National Museum. Count Sternberg's memoirs offer a rare glimpse into political attitudes from the 1780s that ordinarily could not have found their way into print due to censorship. He himself considered his memoirs so frank that he thought it best to entrust the manuscript to the Czech historian František Palacký to be published in another country after his death. Palacký waited thirty years after Sternberg's death in 1838 to publish the memoirs, by which time censorship in the Austrian Empire had relaxed considerably.

Count Sternberg left perceptive observations about both of the Hapsburg emperors whom Mozart knew personally during his adulthood - the brothers Joseph II and Leopold II - and he attended the two coronation ceremonies in honor of Leopold II for which Mozart performed or composed music (his coronations as Holy Roman Emperor in Frankfurt-am-Main in 1790 and king of Bohemia in Prague in 1791). The count, born in 1761, spent much of the 1780s traveling and studying in various parts of Europe, but visits home always prompted commentary on political affairs.

Early in 1784, he returned to Prague after an absence of four years spent primarily in Italy, a period that coincided with the first four years of Joseph II's sole rule. At this time, Sternberg remarked that "much had changed during my absence." In particular, there was considerable talk about the new government of the emperor Joseph,

Josef Václav Myslbek's *St. Wenceslas* (patron saint of the Czech Republic) in front of the Czech National Museum, Václavské náměstí (Wenceslas Square)
©Nick Ansell

which had caused a revolution in attitudes. The vagueness of Sternberg's remarks probably masked his discomfort in discussing topics such as Jewish emancipation, which Joseph had promoted courageously in the early 1780s. While describing a trip to France in 1787, he offered a more detailed view of Joseph's character and the effects of his policies in Bohemia:

> Great dissatisfaction reigned here, especially among the nobility and clergy, and there was confusion among all social classes. On his trip to Paris [in 1777], the emperor Joseph II had picked up many new ideas from the Physiocrats [a school of eighteenth century French thinkers who developed the first complete system of economics] and made note of them in his journal. Unfortunately, alongside his great native intelligence and charm, he possessed no knowledge of economics, and, distrustful of everyone, he tried to do everything in an impossibly short amount of time, without regard to custom and tradition, for example a general land register in all of the hereditary lands to be completed in two years and his desire to meld four nations into one, so that he caused general unhappiness without attaining his goals. It was not only abbeys and cloisters that were dissolved (with their mendicant friars turned out), but also a great many charitable institutions. Since Joseph had no appreciation for the arts and sciences, the dissolution of the abbeys led to vandalism, just as the old art collection of the emperor Rudolf II was sold by a court official [who disposed of one of the most valuable sculptures for only eighteen florins]. The transformation of the royal castle in Prague into an artillery barracks, as good as a

declaration that no king of Bohemia would ever live there again, incensed the entire country; the forcible removal of the noble families' foundation in the New City, which was private property, into the imperial women's foundation in the Hradčany district and its transformation into a maternity hospital, provoked the nobility. In this way, discontent spread everywhere against a monarch who wished good by resorting to ever-increasing absolutism to push things through with unseemly haste.

Count Sternberg's account of the dissolution of monastic institutions certainly offers an explanation for the anger harbored by the Bohemian clergy towards Joseph, but it seems rather suspicious that the sale of an art collection, the alleged symbolic debasement of Prague Castle, and the disruption of an obscure noble foundation would actually bring Bohemia to the brink of revolt in 1789 and 1790. For those acquainted with Joseph's policies in Bohemia, a close reading of Sternberg's remarks reveals how carefully he skirted what it was that actually provoked the Bohemian nobles. One major complaint was increased taxation, but there was another issue that Sternberg could not broach directly without revealing his entire social class in a very unflattering light: the easing of serfdom.

A dirty secret about musical patronage in central Europe in the late eighteenth century is the origins of the wealth of many nobles who supported composers such as Mozart, Haydn, and Beethoven. In fact, it had derived substantially from an economic system that forced peasants by law to perform labor on feudal manors without pay. Versions of the system in place in Bohemia also existed in Austria, Hungary, Prussia, and Russia, the further east, the more oppressive. A stark appraisal of the true nature of social conditions in eighteenth-century Bohemia was offered to English-speaking readers in Thomas Nugent's *The Grand Tour*, whose publishers in London had no fear of retaliation from the Hapsburg government. Nugent's account closely paraphrases remarks found in an account of a visit to Prague in the autumn of 1729 by the German baron Karl Ludwig von Pöllnitz:

> …The [E]states are summoned here every year to the city of Prague, and consist of the clergy, nobility, gentry, and towns. The assembly generally consents to the sovereign's demands, which frequently amount to a great sum; and yet the Bohemians would not complain of taxes were their sovereign to reside among them. Though the Bohemians are brave and good soldiers, yet the nobility and gentry are not fond of the service. The reason is, they are used to be absolute masters upon their own estates, where the peasants are their slaves, and to be respected like petty sovereigns by the burghers at Prague; wherefore they do not care to reside at Vienna, where they must be obliged, like other subjects, to pay their court to the sovereign. The peasants are all in a state of vassalage to the nobility, and are a brutish, heavy kind of people, pretty much addicted to pilfering and thieving, and the whole nation is charged with excess and intemperance in eating and drinking…

More on the conditions of the peasantry can be found in an account of a visit in the early 1780s by the German nobleman Johann Kaspar von Riesbeck:

...The constitution and manners of the country contribute much to make the Bohemians such soldiers as they are. The farmers live in a poverty which preserves them from effeminacy and luxury much more effectually than any positive sumptuary law could do. Besides this, the feudal slavery system, which obtains here in the extreme, accustoms them from their youth upwards to unconditional obedience, the great military virtue of our days.

    Their constant labor and scanty food renders them hardy, and, like the Spartans, they find the soldier's life easier than plowing the fields of their masters. I have conversed with several of them, who lamented the horrors of their situation in terms sufficiently expressive, and spoke of the cruelty of their tyrants as it deserved to be spoken of...

The peasantry of Bohemia was gradually bound to the land during the fifteenth and sixteenth centuries, and in the eighteenth century the vast majority of the residents of the provinces of Bohemia and Moravia lived in a state of serfdom. At the time of Mozart's youth in the 1760s and 1770s, the peasants of Bohemia could not enter into marriages, choose their own professions, or migrate outside the estates in which they resided, without the permission of their landlords. Their obligation of forced labor on several days of the work week was known as *robota*, a Czech word that is the origin of the English "robot." (Its use to denote a mechanized worker in human form incapable of disobedience is traceable to the 1920 play *R.U.R.* by Czech author Karel Čapek).

It was generally acknowledged at the imperial court in Vienna in the eighteenth century that the living conditions endured by the Bohemian peasants were wretched. Many landlords abused their power over the serfs, for example, by exacting *robota* in excess of legal standards, and by inflicting brutal physical punishment to disobedient serfs. Periodic attempts to compel fair application of the landlords' privileges were half-hearted and ineffective. Maria Theresa recognized very well that a productive, contented peasantry was essential to the strength of her empire, but her good intentions were not backed up with firm action. Her son Joseph II, on the other hand, sought to intervene vigorously on behalf of the peasants.

In 1771, he formed a commission to inquire into conditions in Bohemia and even visited the country himself on a fact-finding tour. The findings of the commission (shocking as far as Joseph was concerned) were issued in 1772, at the same time that a serious famine in Bohemia was leading to an immense loss of life among the peasantry. Nonetheless, Joseph's efforts to assist the serfs were blocked completely by the Bohemian nobles until outbreaks of violence erupted in the Bohemian countryside in 1775. After this, the service obligations were curtailed and means were devised to prevent landlord abuse.

After attaining sole rule upon the death of his mother in 1780, Joseph actually tried to abolish serfdom almost entirely. His first step, in 1781, was to take away the landlords' rights to restrict the movements of the serfs and determine their professions and marriage partners. Later, Joseph aimed at replacing the labor obligation with rental payments in cash and reforming the taxation of land to the disadvantage of the landlords. In 1785 he began the land register that Count Sternberg made mention of in order to end the concealment of holdings that had lessened the tax burden for many noble landlords. In 1789, he released an entire class of serfs from their obligation to render *robota* and instituted his new system of taxation.

By this time, the old *Ausgleich* that had worked so much for the benefit of the Bohemian nobility had come to an end. When Count Sternberg condemned Joseph's lack of understanding of economics, it appears that he was actually making a veiled reference to his attacks on aristocratic privilege. Joseph's efforts to aid the serfs had cost the Bohemian nobles dearly by raising the cost of agricultural labor, and his tinkering with the land tax - a legacy of his fascination with the French Physiocrats - had resulted in significant reductions in income for many noble landors. Furthermore, Joseph's attempts to centralize the administration of Austria, Bohemia, Hungary, and the Austrian Netherlands (the "four nations" that Count Sternberg said Joseph had tried to "meld into one") had come at the expense of the power of local noble families. Count Sternberg did mention that "all social classes" had been thrown into confusion by Joseph's policies, but evaded the subject of the serfs, who wanted even greater freedom and independence than Joseph had seen fit to grant. The class of peasants who had not been freed from the obligation of *robota* became restless and disobedient. At the same time that Joseph had lessened their obligations to the manor lords, he also issued decrees that stipulated strict punishments for disobedient serfs.

Leopold II

The nobility of Bohemia still would not have dared assert itself if Joseph at the end of 1789 had not gravely weakened his position by involving himself in a senseless war with Turkey and antagonizing his possessions of Hungary and the Austrian Netherlands. On 20 January 1790, the Austrian Netherlands declared itself an independent republic, while the Hungarian nobles were seriously plotting to overthrow the Hapsburg dynasty. In the midst of all of these political setbacks, Joseph became quite ill. Count Sternberg still remembered the preoccupation in Vienna with Joseph's health throughout the second half of 1789, at the same time that revolution had broken out in France. The emperor died on 20 February 1790.

Childless at the time of his death, Joseph II was succeeded by his younger brother Leopold, who had been ruling since 1765 as grand duke of Tuscany, a possession that had entered the Hapsburg patrimony from Maria Theresa's husband Francis of Lorraine. For his achievements as the ruler of Tuscany, Leopold might fairly be described as the most successful of any of the "enlightened despots" of the eighteenth century. His subjects were able to enjoy an exceptionally high standard of living and a humane government that was administered with integrity. In addition, Tuscany's subservience to Austrian foreign policy left Leopold unable to engage in the kind of aggressive militarism that marred the "enlightened" reigns of monarchs such as Frederick the Great, Catherine the Great, and his own brother.

The chief contribution of Leopold's policy-making during his brief two-year reign as Holy Roman Emperor was to pacify the Hapsburg domains and end the disastrous war with Turkey started by his brother. Because of his legacy as ruler of Tuscany, many historians have assumed that Leopold would have instituted a vast program of political and social reform much more carefully considered and skillfully implemented than his older brother had been able to do. Actually, this course would not have been assured by any means.

We do know of Leopold's suspicious nature, his attachment to absolutist government, and his vigorous deployment of the secret police. It would not be at all unreasonable to believe that he would have pursued political policies not so different from those of his son, the reactionary and indolent Francis II, especially considering the dangers posed by the political attitudes spreading through Europe from revolutionary France. His need to placate the noble communities in his various domains would never have lessened as long as there was a military danger from revolutionary France or Napoléon Bonaparte.

Count Sternberg himself left a fascinating account of the behavior that Leopold was capable of. During a trip he made to Vienna in March of 1791, the count was shocked to learn that he was being closely watched by the secret police. He was fortunate indeed to have connections at the highest level of imperial government. He discussed the matter with his uncle, Count Leopold von Kolovrat, a minister of state at the imperial court, who was able to arrange a private audience with the emperor himself.

Count Sternberg was greeted cordially by Leopold II, who told him the reason for which he had been under surveillance. Leopold said, "This happened, because you are one of the Illuminati, whom I mistrust." Count Sternberg explained that he had been a Freemason in Regensburg, but had never associated with the Illuminati, a group of intellectuals whose secret societies were considered subversive. He then asked the emperor who had denounced him.

Leopold answered, "It was a secret denunciation." The count felt strongly that the emperor should clear his name and end the surveillance, since he was completely innocent. The emperor equivocated about the intelligence he had received, saying "I cannot tell you how I came to know this, but I will look over my papers; come back in three days."

Three days later the emperor said that he had not had the time to investigate the matter and that he should come back in another three days. The next time, Count Sternberg found the emperor at a window with a list of Illuminati in his hand, saying, "I am sorry, for I have done you an injustice by confusing your name with someone else…" The obvious implication is that Leopold prevaricated in order to evade the embarrassment of having to acknowledge the excesses of the police state he relied upon.

In the winter of 1789-1790, leading Bohemian nobles met secretly to discuss what could be done to quiet the disorder in their country. Shortly before Joseph's death the meetings became public, and two weeks after his death the new emperor authorized the meeting of a "Little Diet" in Prague. It is referred to as "little" because it included only a few nobles who happened to be present in Prague at the time. On 1 May 1790, Leopold issued a patent that summoned Diets in all of the provinces of Bohemia and Austria. The Estates in these territories were permitted to submit grievances to the emperor in the manner of the famous *cahiers de doléances* submitted to the king of France the year before.

A Grand Diet of the Bohemian Estates assembled on 12 July 1790 with an attendance larger than at any Diet since the battle of White Mountain in 1620. The participants were allowed to discuss the issues of the day with great freedom. Joseph II had reduced the Diets to a state of near irrelevance in Bohemia; Leopold II was eager to listen to the complaints of the Estates, but not to accede to their demands in a way that would weaken his powers as king of Bohemia.

The deliberations of the Grand Diet dragged on into the summer of 1791, much of the time occupied with arcane discussions of constitutional privileges and procedural matters. Meanwhile, Leopold strengthened his hand by ending the war with Turkey and pacifying the Austrian Netherlands and Hungary. Leopold's method of placating the Bohemian Estates was to capitulate on all of the issues that were most important to the nobility. Leopold rejected most of the constitutional demands raised in the Diet in the interest of maintaining absolutist powers to the greatest extent he could, but he did use his power of decree to abolish his brother's obnoxious system of taxation and repeal the abolition of *robota* as of 9 May 1790. Leopold informed the Estates that he intended to devise another means of releasing the serfs from their obligation of *robota*, but at the time of his death, no new proposals had been drafted. His son Francis certainly did not press the issue. As a result, the institution of serfdom was not completely eliminated in the Hapsburg Empire until the time of the revolutions of 1848.

Lest there be any misunderstanding about the matter, the coronation ceremony arranged for Leopold II by the Estates of Bohemia on 6 September 1791 - which was followed that very evening by the first performance of Mozart's opera *La clemenza di Tito* - was anything but a celebration of Leopold's earlier record as an "enlightened" ruler of the grand duchy of Tuscany, as some Mozart scholars have supposed. It was, in fact, a ratification of an aristocratic reaction against Josephine reforms. Considering the critical issues at stake for the nobles who dominated the Estates, among them the preservation of their income and the protection of their own personal safety, it is difficult to see how the audience that gathered for the first performance of *La clemenza di Tito* in 1791 would have been thinking much about the happiness of the Tuscans. In agreeing to a coronation ceremony, Leopold was willing to take an oath to preserve the privileges of the Estates, but he made sure that the nature of these privileges was never precisely spelled out. The entire situation that led to the coronation was summed up nicely by Count Sternberg when he described the political atmosphere in Bohemia in 1790 and 1791:

> Indeed a restless time ensued. The Bohemian Estates assembled in a rather loud Diet. The emperor Leopold, who sought above all to pacify the hereditary lands at

the start of his reign, repealed the last decrees of the emperor Joseph. There were negotiations about many lapsed privileges, and much was promised to put an end to this that was forgotten in the course of time and circumstances.

Once they had obtained the political concessions needed to secure their fortunes and personal power, the Bohemian nobles lost the will to press for constitutional niceties. Within a year after Leopold's coronation, the Estates were once again docile, and they would remain so until the 1840s.

Leopold's skillful method of quieting Bohemia could not have been successful if the interests of the peasants had not been suppressed, and they suffered mightily for Leopold's shift of policy in the year 1790. Many of those who believed they would be released from the obligation of *robota* had sold the horse and cattle that were needed in order to render it. When the *robota* was reinstated, they found it difficult to purchase new livestock, due to inflation caused by the war with Turkey.

Many peasants were naturally loath to return to the old system of oppression. There were disturbances in the countryside, but whether willingly or by force, the serfs had returned to obedience by the end of Leopold's reign early in 1792. All in all, the reputation of Leopold II as an "enlightened" despot does not hold up well when it comes to the political policies he pursued in Bohemia.

The Revival of Czech Language and Czech National Identity

While describing Leopold II's coronation in Prague in 1791, Count Sternberg included a series of remarks about the brothers Joseph and Leopold that invites a discussion of the revival of Czech language and patriotism so noticeable in Bohemia at the time of Mozart's visits:

> Here [in Bohemia] the pressure brought to bear on the Estates by the emperor Joseph awakened a nationalism that had long remained dormant. The emperor Joseph, who wanted to centralize everything, even sought to suppress the Czech language; no people could allow itself to be robbed of this safeguard of nationhood. Spontaneously, Czech was heard spoken in the anterooms of the castle by all who were proficient in the mother tongue. The emperor Leopold, whose régime in Tuscany had brought him a favorable reputation, very well understood the state of affairs [in Bohemia] and showed himself willing to protect the rights of the nation.

The Bohemian nobility and intelligentsia started to embrace Czech more and more as it became clear that their interests did not necessarily coincide with those of the Hapsburg emperors. This phenolmenon was one of the most important aspects of the passing of the "time of darkness." As a result of these changing attitudes, the German community within Bohemia started to lose its prominence in the late eighteenth century, although it was still very powerful culturally, politically, and economically - and would remain so until it was expelled just after World War II.

German settlements had been numerous within the kingdom of Bohemia for centuries, especially after various Czech kings had encouraged the migration of Germans during the thirteenth century. They were especially plentiful in the cities and in certain regions that now border Germany and Austria, including the romantic "Bohemian Forest" in southwest Bohemia that was used as the setting of Carl Maria von Weber's opera *Der Freischütz*. These regions are now frequently referred to collectively as the Sudetenland, even though this term refers properly only to territories surrounding the Sudetian Mountains in northeast Moravia.

The importance of the German community in Bohemia inevitably increased after the defeat at White Mountain in 1620, partially because it had always been more reliably Catholic, and partially because new German families started to enter the country, including noble families who were given lands once held by rebellious Czechs. Gradually, the kingdom of Bohemia became integrated into a greater German-language cultural sphere. Whether of native or foreign origin, the great Bohemian noble families tended to adopt the tastes of the German Catholic nobility of central Europe, their acquaintance with these tastes refreshed by periods of residence in Vienna. As shocking as it can be today, it is ordinary to find Bohemia referred to in eighteenth-century writings as merely a region of Germany and its residents referred to as Germans.

For a time, Czech was actually threatened with extinction as a written language, and it was effectively destroyed as a literary language. There was no standardized grammar or orthography, and for many western Europeans, it did not even have a name. In the article on Bohemia in the *Encyclopédie* of Diderot and d'Alembert, the language spoken in the country was identified only as "a Slavic dialect" ("une dialecte de l'Esclavon"). In central Europe it was usually referred to as "böhmisch" ("Bohemian"). The role of the Jesuits, whom Ferdinand II gave great authority over the educational system, was critical. The Jesuits considered Czech language inextricably linked to Bohemia's Hussite religious traditions and sponsored the destruction of thousands of Czech-language books over a period of decades, an incalculable loss to the cultural heritage of the Czech people. The educated elite of Bohemian society generally regarded Czech as a language used only to communicate with servants and other social inferiors. Once again, there is important testimony about conditions in Bohemia from Thomas Nugent's *The Grand Tour*:

> ...[The language of the peasants], like that of the Poles, is a dialect of the ancient Sclavonian, and is said to be very sweet and copious. The modern Bohemians neglect the cultivating of it, and their nobility especially look upon it as beneath them to speak their native tongue, but chuse rather to use the High Dutch [i.e., German].

One of the earliest signals of efforts to revive the Czech language is recorded from Count Franz Josef von Kinský, who left this memorable observation in an educational tract of 1773: "I confess that, as a good descendant of the Slavs, I inherited the prejudice that if the mother tongue of a Frenchman is French and of a German is German, that of a Czech ought also to be Czech." Count Kinský was pleased to note that French troops who had served in Bohemia during the Seven Years' War of 1757-1763 had found the Czech language much more pleasing to their refined ears than

German. He considered the Czech language "harmonious" and attributed the aptitude of Czechs for music to the language they spoke. The 1780s saw the publication of Czech grammars both in Vienna and Prague and the famous *Defense of the Czech Language Against Its Spiteful Detractors* by Karel Hynek Thám. There was also an explosion of Czech plays within a few years after the opening of the National Theater in Prague in 1783.

Count Sternberg may well have been correct in his claim that the greatest impetus of all for the revival of Czech language was a reaction to attempts of the Hapsburg rulers to suppress it, a process that accelerated after the War of the Austrian Succession. The foundation of the Gubernium in 1751 and other attempts to set up bureaucracies intended to supplant the Estates were accompanied by the imposition of German-speaking officials in the country. The expulsion of the Jesuits from the Austrian Empire in 1773 forced decisions concerning the nature of the educational system in Bohemia that they had earlier dominated, and in 1774, German was made the language of instruction in the gymnasia instead of Latin. In 1784, classes in Czech were discontinued at Charles-Ferdinand University in Prague, and in 1788, Joseph decreed that all government communications be drafted in German only.

The emperor Joseph II knew how to speak Czech, and it is acknowledged that his attempts to suppress Czech were motivated principally by practical concerns of centralization and uniformity. Nonetheless, they prompted a sharp reaction in the context of the other political policies he pursued in Bohemia. The Diet of 1790-1792 tried to promote the use of Czech language, and it gradually returned to the schools and government. Leopold II, mindful of the newly-found identification of the nobles with Czech language, made some highly important symbolic gestures, such as founding a chair of Czech language at Charles-Ferdinand University in Prague. (There had already been one at the University of Vienna since 1775.)

Mozart's awareness of the linguistic struggles that raged in Prague at the time of his visits is open to question. As far as can be established from the surviving documentation, his attitude was likely not so far from that of the English traveler Charles Burney, who visited Bohemia in 1772. It is clear that Burney expected everyone he encountered to be able to converse in German (after all, he imagined himself to be traveling in a region of Germany), and he was irritated that so many were unable to do so. As we will see in Chapter 5, Mozart's way of dealing with the insecurity of finding himself in the midst of individuals whose language he could not understand was to mimic it.

This short sketch of the history of the Czech nation may suffice as an introduction to the political and social conditions that held sway in the kingdom of Bohemia up to the time of Mozart's visits, but it is impossible to ignore entirely the remainder of the story, however briefly it must be told.

The various compromises made with the Estates in the early 1790s succeeded in preventing revolt in the Bohemian lands until 1848, when disturbances throughout the Hapsburg domains threatened the dissolution of the Austrian Empire. In Bohemia, serfdom was finally abolished, but the Czech people failed in their attempts to secure independence. The next time the Hapsburg monarchy found itself in serious difficulties (in 1866 after a disastrous war with Prussia), Bohemia remained quiet, but Hungary was able to force the Hapsburgs to form the Dual Monarchy of Austria-Hungary in 1867. With a Hapsburg emperor at the head, the Austrians and Hungarians agreed to the infamous *Ausgleich* that allowed each group to have a great deal of freedom in dealing with the ethnic minorities who resided within each half of the new state. The Slovaks who lived in the Hungarian half of the empire received far worse treatment than did the Czechs who were ruled by the Austrian-dominated government in Vienna.

It is an interesting coincidence that so many of the important dates in modern Czech history, beginning with the Defenestration of Prague in 1618, took place in years ending with "8." After the revolution of 1848, the next critical year was 1918, the end of World War I, when the Hapsburg Empire was finally weakened so irreparably that it flew apart. With considerable backing from the American president Woodrow Wilson, a new state was created from the provinces of Bohemia, Moravia, and Slovakia to form a Republic of Czechoslovakia. Historically, the Czechs and Slovaks had had almost nothing to do with each other, but their languages were very similar, and there was a recognition by world leaders that the Slovak territories did not have enough educated people within their borders to form a viable government and bureaucracy - one of the most horrible legacies of the severe repression of Slovak culture by the Hungarian government of the late nineteenth and early 20th centuries.

Thus the Czechs were thrown together with the Slovaks, who soon began to view the government in Prague as a new source of oppression. Tensions among the Czechs, Germans, Slovaks, and Hungarians who lived in the First Czechoslovak Republic of 1918-38 nevertheless were kept under control as a result of the extraordinary leadership of its president Tomáš Garrigue Masaryk, a statesman of international stature whose prestige could be compared to that of the late Václav Havel in recent times.

Masaryk's resignation in 1935 for reasons of health was a stunning blow to Czechoslovakia. Thereafter, the "8s" came fast and furiously: the beginnings of a Nazi takeover in 1938, a Communist takeover in 1948, and a Soviet invasion in 1968. In between the events of 1938 and 1948 there were ghastly episodes of "ethnic cleansing" that nearly eliminated the presence of Jews and Germans in the Bohemian lands entirely through a mixture of extermination and expulsion (extermination the more common method for Jews, expulsion the more common method for Germans). Naturally, their rich cultural contributions were lost along with them.

The Communist regime that came to power in 1948 was ousted by means of popular revolt in 1989 ("the Velvet Revolution"), and in 1993, the Slovaks took advantage of an irresistible opportunity to achieve true independence for the first time in their history ("the Velvet Divorce"). Czechoslovakia was divided into two new countries, the Czech Republic and the Slovak Republic, a separation that eventually led to more cordial relations than had ever existed before between Czechs and Slovaks after their fortunes had been joined in 1918.

It is easy to list these key political events in quick succession, although except for the last, it cannot be emphasized enough to what extent they represented cataclysmic upheavals for the residents of the Bohemian lands. At each one of these junctures, any persons involved in politics would have found themselves in grave personal jeopardy, and the same was true for additional thousands who wanted nothing to do with politics whatsoever.

Velvet Revolution memorial
Národní třída

2

Royal Capital Without a King: Prague in the Late Eighteenth Century

The death of Holy Roman Emperor Rudolf II in Prague on 20 January 1612 was commemorated with a solemn, quiet funeral that mirrored the stiff court manners he had affected during his lifetime. Rudolf was interred in St. Vitus' Cathedral alongside his father Maximilian and grandfather Ferdinand, both of whom had also reigned as Holy Roman Emperors and kings of Bohemia. Ferdinand, who died in Vienna, and Maximilian, who died in Regensburg, had not centered their lives around Prague in the way that Rudolf had, but arrangements had been made to have them buried in the royal city of Prague. Vienna, at that time capital of a mere duchy, was deemed less attractive as a final resting place.

There was little mourning for Rudolf II in Prague. After years of living as a recluse in Prague Castle, he was barely known to his subjects, who thought of him as aloof and self-indulgent. Furthermore, he was tainted with the shame of vanquish. His brother Matthias had ousted him as king of Bohemia the year before his death, but rather charitably allowed him to remain in Prague Castle to live out his days surrounded by his beloved collections of art, furniture, books, and curiosities. Furthermore, Rudolf's efforts to guarantee toleration of the Protestant religion had been little appreciated. By 1612, the militant Protestants of Bohemia would only have been satisfied with even greater powers and privileges than he was willing to grant.

In light of the tragic events that engulfed Prague during the decades that followed Rudolf's death, it is easy for the modern historian to observe that the residents of Prague in 1612 should have mourned his passing as deeply as those who were present in 1937 for the funeral of Tomáš Garrigue Masaryk, the revered first president of Czechoslovakia. It was only the events of the Thirty Years' War that demonstrated to what extent Rudolf had been Prague's protector simply by his presence in the city. His disinterested attitude toward the administration of Bohemia was tantamount to a policy of tolerance and respect for local customs and religions, including the Jewish religion. Moreover, the cultural and economic benefits that had accrued from Rudolf's residence in Prague were enormous. The population of the city had swelled and become much more cosmopolitan than it otherwise would have been, due to the embassies sent by foreign powers and the visitors who helped Rudolf cultivate his wide-ranging artistic and intellectual pursuits. Rudolf's tastes could be eccentric - if not downright weird - but they had resulted in the arrival to Prague of intellectual figures of such eminence as Johannes Kepler and Tycho Brahe.

The departure of the imperial court for Vienna in 1612 and the outbreak of the Thirty Years' War in 1618 brought to an end an exceptionally brilliant period in Prague's history that had immediate negative effects for the cultural life of the city. The dispersal of Rudolf's art collection, which began to be plundered almost immediately after his death by members of his own household, was one of the first catastrophes. Rebel Protestants stole or sold off much more of it, and most of what remained by the end of the Thirty Years' War was expropriated by Swedes who mounted a siege of Prague in 1648. The few items left by the late eighteenth century were sold by the emperor Joseph II for a paltry sum, an incident that Count Kaspar von Sternberg found particularly distasteful. To this day, the paintings and sculpture that await the visitor to Prague are not nearly as rich and varied as the architecture, since the buildings simply could not be carted off in the way that other treasures had been.

In many respects, seventeenth-century Prague came to resemble seventeenth-century Edinburgh. After King James VI of Scotland departed his capital in 1603 to assume the throne of England, there was little left to attract foreign visitors, and the lack of government expenditure impoverished urban life. The empty residence of Holyrood was rarely visited by a royal family that centered its activities in a foreign country, just as Prague Castle was used in the later seventeenth century by the kings of Bohemia as little else than a refuge from calamities in Vienna, such as outbreaks of the plague.

In the case of Prague, severe depopulation was one of the worst consequences of the migration of the imperial court. During Rudolf's reign, the population of Prague is believed to have reached 50-60,000, the highest it ever had been. An earlier high point, attained in the fourteenth century during the reign of Charles IV, was about 40,000. Perhaps 35,000 people lived in Prague at the time of the Defenestration of 1618, and the number continued to decrease steadily due to the effects of the Thirty Years' War and epidemics that swept through the city in 1625, 1632, 1639, and 1648. It is believed that only about 26,000 remained by the end of this period. Recovery later in the seventeenth century was slow in coming. It has been estimated that there were about 40,000 inhabitants in Prague in the first decade of the eighteenth century, but roughly 10,000 of these were carried off by an outbreak of the plague in 1713-1714.

As of the 1750s, the population of Prague had increased to nearly 60,000, making it the fourth largest city in the Hapsburg domains at that time. Vienna was of course the largest, with about 180,000 inhabitants, but Vienna was only the fifth largest city in Europe (London, Paris, Naples, and Amsterdam were all more populous). The second largest city controlled by the Hapsburg rulers was Milan, capital of the duchy of Lombardy, with approximately 110,000 inhabitants. Brussels, the principal city of the Austrian Netherlands, had around 70,000. A census of 1784 revealed a population in Prague of just over 76,000 - a new record - but it took a long time for the population to grow much more than that. Epidemics in the late 1790s once again reduced it, and as late as 1850 there were less than 120,000 inhabitants within the city limits. The modern population of over one million was reached only after the annexation of suburban regions in the late nineteenth and early 20th centuries, and the establishment of Prague as the capital of an independent Czechoslovakia in 1918, which led to an influx of immigrants from all parts of the new country. Prague's rival Vienna, no longer an imperial capital at the end of World War I, suffered at the same time a sharp decline in population from which it has never recovered.

The geographic bounds of the city of Prague in Mozart's time were naturally much smaller than they are today and correspond to the four traditional divisions of the historic city center: the Old City, the New City, Malá Strana (the "Little Side"), and Hradčany (the "Castle District"), areas that are still commonly marked on maps of Prague.

Of the four, Hradčany is the oldest. In the ninth century, the Přemyslid ruler Bořivoj moved his seat from Levý Hradec, a settlement located a little further north on the river Vltava, to a plateau overlooking a bend in the river that marks the site of the modern city center of Prague. On this plateau, Prague Castle expanded to its present size over a period of centuries. For most of its history, it was a city unto itself, made up of a conglomeration of sacred and official buildings.

The castle complex looked almost the same in Mozart's time as it does today. The last major renovation of the royal residences took place under the supervision of the architect Nicolò Pacassi at the instigation of the empress Maria Theresa, who also employed him to expand and beautify her favorite palace of Schönbrunn in Vienna. Pacassi incorporated the accretions of centuries within an imposing neoclassical enclosure. The most important change within the castle complex since the eighteenth century has been the completion of St. Vitus' Cathedral, begun in the fourteenth century, but not completed until 1929. When Mozart saw it, the cathedral still had no nave.

In the ninth and tenth centuries, as many as could find protection behind the fortifications of the castle walls did, but there were also settlers beneath on the west bank of the Vltava, where the Malá Strana district would one day take shape. The eleventh century saw two important developments: the gradual settlement of a community on the east bank of the Vltava, now recognizable as the beginnings of the Old City, and the construction of a new Přemyslid residence known as Vyšehrad (the "high castle") on the east bank of the Vltava, far to the south of the Old City across the Botič brook.

The seat of the Přemyslid dukes was moved to Vyšehrad by Vratislav II (r. 1061-92), who built a residence and various church buildings there. The court moved back to Prague Castle during the reign of Soběslav I (1125-40), but Vyšehrad nonetheless acquired a reputation as a nostalgic historical monument with mythical connections to Princess Libuše. In musical circles, a certain mystique about it derives from the symphonic poem "Vyšehrad" from Smetana's cycle *Má vlast* ("My Homeland"). In Mozart's time it was remote and uninteresting - except for its magnificent view of the river.

The settlements on the east bank of the Vltava became more and more important after migration across the river was prompted by a fire on the west bank in 1142 and the completion of the first bridge across the Vltava in 1172. About 3500 people lived in what is now the Old City at the start of the thirteenth century. The modern New City of Prague was originally created on the east bank of the Vltava to the south and east of the Old City as an urban planning project sponsored by the emperor Charles IV in the second half of the fourteenth century.

The boundaries that separated the New City from the Old City are pretty much the same as they were in Charles IV's day. The outlines of the walls and a moat that surrounded the Old City can be traced on maps today by following the course of Národní třída on the west to Revoluční on the east. The ditches that formed the moat had only recently been filled in and replaced with elegant streets at the time of Mozart's visits. The eastern and southern boundaries of the New City were marked off rigidly by a system of walls, fortifications, and gates constructed in the second half of the seventeenth century on the orders of the emperor Leopold I. They extended from the Vltava at modern-day Klimentská street to Wilsonova, then down Mezibranská and Sokolská streets to Horská and Svobodova. A large gate stood at the site of what is now the National Museum.

The neighborhood beneath Prague Castle on the west bank of the Vltava started to be referred to as "Malá Strana" in the fifteenth century. "Malá Strana" does not translate conveniently into English, and in many English-language guidebooks it is identified with approximations such as the "Lesser Town" or the "Minor Town" (from the Latin "urbs minor"). The Germans prefer a literal translation: "die Kleinseite," or "the little side."

The "side" referred to is the west side (or bank) of the river Vltava, and as far as area and population are concerned, the portion of Prague that occupied the west bank was indeed small in comparison to the districts on the east bank. The wall that marked the southern boundary of Malá Strana in Mozart's day stood at the end of what is now Újezd street where it intersects Petřínská. Following Újezd north, the southern and western boundaries of historic Malá Strana can be traced by following the course of modern-day Karmelitská, Tržiště, and Vlašská. The northern limit was marked roughly by a small area known as Klárov that now leads to the Manes bridge over the Vltava.

In Mozart's day, neither the Manes bridge nor an equivalent structure had yet been constructed. Until the middle of the nineteenth century there was only one bridge over the Vltava at Prague: the stone bridge decorated with statues of saints that has been known as Charles Bridge since 1870; before then it was simply known as Prague Bridge. The original span was erected shortly after the first bridge over the Vltava was damaged beyond repair by ice floes that struck it in the year 1342. For centuries, no other bridge was much needed, since there were no significant population centers to the north of the Old City across the Vltava, or to the south of the New City and Malá Strana on its opposite banks.

The Old City, New City, and Malá Strana traditionally had their own city governments and were referred to as the "three cities of Prague" before they were united into a single civic government at the insistence of the emperor Joseph II in 1784, one case in which entrenched resistance to one of Joseph's projects was soon forgotten. The castle district (Hradčany), which was made up only of a small region of the plateau on which the Prague Castle complex was constructed, remained a separate administrative unit. Its western and northern boundaries were delineated by walls across the deep "deer ditch" ("jelení přikop"). Their outlines can be followed along the modern-day streets Mariánské hradby, Jelení, and Keplerova to Pohořelec and the Strahov monastery complex. The street now called Strahovská marked the southern and western boundaries of the walls that surrounded Hradčany.

Descriptions in English of Prague During the "Time of Darkness"

The flavor of life in Prague during the long period of recovery from the devastation of the Thirty Years' War was vividly recorded by visitors from western Europe, a number of them from England. The appetite for travelogue publications was enormous even in the those days, and press freedom in England combined with the great distance from Prague led to the publication of frank observations. Visitors from England were present in Prague to witness the splendor of the court of Rudolf II, but few made the trip to central Europe during the period of the Thirty Years' War - unless one counts mercenary soldiers. In the late seventeenth century, English tourists started to return, and two accounts of visits to the city appeared in London from traveling physicians. The first, originally published by Edward Brown in 1673, left testimony concerning the effects of depopulation:

> ...The walls of this City seem to enclose the greatest Circuit of ground of any I have seen in Germany but the Hills and void spaces within it take up a large Tract, and therein it is like the city of Lyon in France...

On a more positive note, Brown made mention of the beautiful residences in the Malá Strana district built by noble families rewarded for their service to the Hapsburgs, as well as of many notable landmarks in the city. He went out of his way to explain why he felt that Prague compared favorably in most respects to Florence, which he had also visited.

Reminiscences of a visit to the kingdom of Bohemia by the French physician Charles Patin were first published in France in 1695, and then in London in 1697 in English translation. His summation of the general state of the country is pithy and colorful:

> ...It is a very fine Country, but its intestine and foreign Wars have extremely weaken'd and depopulated it: Insomuch that it may not be unfitly compar'd to a valiant Soldier who has destroy'd his Enemies, but still languishes under the Wound he receiv'd in the Battel. I have heard say, that the Emperor's Presence wou'd in a little time restore that vigour which is now no longer to be seen there; and this puts

me in mind of some sick Persons, who recover their Health at the very sight of their Physician…

Neither the emperor in Patin's day (Leopold I), nor any later Hapsburg emperor, ever returned to work the physician's magic, but Patin did echo Brown's observations about the beauty of the aristocratic residences in the Malá Strana district:

> …That part of the City, which is situated beyond the River, and commonly call'd the lesser side, is much more delightful [than the Old City], and scarce anything else is to be seen there but sumptuous Palaces, which amount to the number of above three hundred; so that this Quarter may well be styl'd the Magazine of the Riches of Bohemia, and of his Imperial Majesty's Hereditary countries…

In the eighteenth century, descriptions of Prague in English appeared from Lady Mary Wortley Montagu, Charles Burney, and Hester Lynch Piozzi, besides reports on political and social conditions in Bohemia prepared for various editions of Thomas Nugent's *The Grand Tour*. The effects of serfdom in impoverishing the ordinary populace while enriching a tiny elite are unmistakable in all of these writings.

The inveterate traveler Lady Mary Wortley Montagu is best known today for her accounts of life in the Near East, but she also left striking impressions of Dresden, Prague, and Vienna in letters written home to her sister. On 17 November 1716 she relayed the following news from Prague:

> …The kingdom of Bohemia is the most desert of any I have seen in Germany. The villages are so poor, and the post-houses so miserable, that clean straw and fair water are blessings not always to be met with, and better accommodations not to be hoped for. Though I carried my own bed with me, I could not sometimes find a place to set it up in, and I rather chose to travel all night, as cold as it is, wrapped up in my furs, than go into the common stoves, which are filled all sorts of ill scents.
>
> This town was once the royal seat of the Bohemian kings, and is still the capital of the kingdom. There are yet some remains of its former splendour, being one of the largest towns in Germany, but, for the most part, old built and thinly inhabited, which makes the houses very cheap. Those people of quality, who cannot easily bear the expence of Vienna, chuse to reside here, there they have assemblies, musick, and other diversions (those of a court excepted), at very moderate rates, all things being here in great abundance, especially the best wild fowl I ever tasted. I have already been visited by some of the most considerable ladies, whose relations I know at Vienna. They are dressed after the fashions there, after the manner that the people at Exeter imitate those of London; that is, their imitation is more excessive than the original. 'Tis not easy to describe what extraordinary figures they make. The person is so much lost between headdress and petticoat, that they have as much occasion to write upon their backs, "This is a woman," for the information of travellers, as ever a signpost painter had to write, "This is a bear."

Lady Montagu did not seem to realize that the reason for much of the "thin habitation" she noticed in Prague was the outbreak of plague in 1713-1714. Her account unwittingly reveals the key to the later recovery of cultural life in Prague without the support of a royal court: the patronage of a vibrant aristocratic community that preferred to live in Prague rather than in Vienna either full time or part-time. The diversions typical of this social class were the central motivation in efforts to build traditions of music, theater, and opera, later strengthened by the participation of middle-class citizens as the population recovered. Some of these activities were described in Thomas Nugent's *The Grand Tour* of 1749, with heavy reliance on observations borrowed from the memoirs of Baron Karl Ludwig von Pöllnitz that were first published in 1734:

> There are few cities in Europe, where there are more gentry, or gentry more wealthy than at Prague; nor do the nobility in any part of the world keep greater state. As to company there is no town in the [Holy Roman] empire that has a greater choice. There are assemblies in the houses of quality every night, where they divert themselves with gaming, and crown the night with good cheer, as pheasants, ortolans, trouts, salmon, and crayfish, with good wine. They have a tolerable Italian opera, and but a very indifferent play-house, with wretched performers. In winter they have races in stately sledges, besides masquerading and splendid balls.

Nugent's reference to Prague's "tolerable" Italian opera is a paraphrase of Baron Pöllnitz's estimation of a production that he saw in October or early November of 1729 at the opera theater of Count Franz Anton von Sporck. The "play-house" mentioned by Nugent would have to be the Divadlo v Kotcích (the "theater in the stalls"), which first opened in 1738.

Charles Burney, the noted music critic and historian who visited Prague in 1772, witnessed the effects of a famine in Bohemia during the early 1770s and the enduring neglect of the fabric of the city of Prague after a bombardment by the Prussians in 1757. The remarkable fortune of Prague in preserving its architectural treasures through some of the most ruinous military conflicts in European history is legendary, but the Prussian bombardment had dealt the city a devastating blow. Burney's heartbreaking impressions of the suffering he witnessed in the Bohemian countryside during September of 1772 were considered so disturbing that they were suppressed from a German-language edition of his travels published in 1773:

> My journey through this country was one of the most fatiguing I ever took in my life; for though the road, in general is very good, for a German road, yet my want of time, which obliged me to travel night and day; the excessive heat and cold of the weather, occasioned by the presence and absence of the sun; together with bad horses, and diabolical wagons, used as chaises, exhausted both my spirits and my patience.
>
> The country is flat, naked, and disagreeable to the eye, for the most part, all the way through Austria, Moravia, and Bohemia, as far as Prague, the situation and environs of which are very beautiful. The dreariness and scarcity of provision, of all kinds, on this road, were now excessive; and the half-starved people, just recovered from malignant fevers, little less contagious than the plague, occasioned by bad food, and by no food at all, offered to view the most melancholy spectacles I ever beheld.

Of Prague, Burney had this to say:

> This city is extremely beautiful when seen at a distance. It is situated on two or three hills, and has the river Mulda running through the middle of it. It is divided into

three quarters, or districts, which are distinguished by the names of Alt Stadt, Neue Stadt, and Kleine Stadt, or Old Town, New Town, and Little Town; the Kleine Stadt is the most modern, and the best built of the three. The houses are all of white stone, or stucco, in imitation of it, and all uniform in size and colour…A great part of the town is new, as scarce a single building escaped the Prussian batteries, and bombardment during the blockade, in the last war. A few churches and palaces only, that were strongly built, and of less combustible material than the rest, were proof against their fury; and in the walls of these, are still sticking innumerable cannon balls and bombs…

Hester Lynch Piozzi's visit to Prague in 1786 had been occasioned by the ostracization she endured in England as a result of her marriage to an Italian Catholic of low birth. For nearly 20 years after a first meeting in 1765, she had been an intimate friend of Samuel Johnson, who adored her for her wit and vivacity and forgave her for her acid tongue. But after her first husband died in 1781, Hester fell in love in for the first time in her life with an Italian musician named Gabriel Piozzi. Everyone in her social circle was horrified, partly because the marriage threatened to deprive Johnson of stimulating companionship during his old age. Nonetheless, once the approval of her daughters was secured, she did marry Piozzi, and then left England on a Grand Tour of Europe with her new husband just before Johnson died in 1784. Her impressions were published in 1789 under the title *Observations and Reflections Made in the Course of a Journey Through France, Italy, and Germany*.

Piozzi stayed in Prague during the period 24-30 November 1786, less than two months before Mozart's first arrival, and she may have seen a performance of *The Marriage of Figaro*. She certainly did attend the opera at least once. In the winter season of 1786-1787, the only operas being performed at the National Theater in Prague were Mozart's *Marriage of Figaro* and Stephen Storace's *Gli sposi malcontenti*. Regrettably, she did not report which one she saw, since her interest in opera extended little beyond the apparel of the female spectators. Her account nonetheless offers a sampling of the conversational skills that Samuel Johnson prized so much in her:

> The inns between Vienna and this place are very bad; but we arrived here safe the 24th of November, when I looked for little comfort but much diversion; things turned out however exactly the reverse, and *aux bains de Prague* ["at the watering place of Prague"] in Bohemia we found beds more elegant, dinners neater dressed, apartments cleaner and with a less foreign aspect, than almost any where else. Such is not meantime the general appearance of the town out of doors, which is savage enough; and the celebrated bridge [Charles Bridge] singularly ugly I think, crowded with vast groups of ill-made statues, and heavy to excess, though not incommodious to drive over, and of a surprising extent. These German rivers are magnificent, and our Mulda here (which is but a branch of the Elbe neither) is respectable for its volume of water, useful for the fish contained in it, and lovely in the windings of its course…
>
> Doctor Johnson was very angry with a gentleman at our house once, I well remember, for not being better company; and urged that he had travelled into Bohemia, and seen Prague: - "Surely," added he, "the man who has seen Prague might tell us something new and something strange, and not sit silent for want of matter to put his lips in motion!" *Horresco referens* ["I dread to recall it"]; - I have now been at Prague

as well as Doctor Fitzpatrick [the guest at Johnson's house], but have brought away nothing very interesting I fear; unless that the floor of the opera-stage there is inlaid, which so far as I have observed is a new thing; the cathedral I am sure is an old thing, and charged with heavy and ill-chosen ornaments, worthy of the age in which it was fabricated!...

This truly Gothic edifice was very near being destroyed by the King of Prussia, who bombarded the city thirty-five [actually 29] years ago; I saw the mark made by one ball just at the cathedral door, and heard with horror of the dreadful siege...the whole town has, in consequence of that long blockade, a ragged and half-ruined melancholy aspect; and the roads round it, then broken up, have scarcely been mended since.

The ladies too looked more like masquerading figures than any thing else, as they sat in their boxes at the opera, with rich embroidered caps, or bright pink and blue sattin headdresses, with ermine or sable fronts, a heavy gold tassel hanging low down from the left ear, and no powder; which gives a girlish look, and reminded me of a fashion our lower tradesmen in London had about fifteen or eighteen years ago, of dressing their daughters, from nine to twelve years old, in puffed black sattin caps, with a long earring hanging down on one side. It is a becoming mode enough as the women wear it here, but gives no idea of cleanliness; and I suppose that whilst finery retains its power of striking, delicacy keeps her distance, nor attempts to come in play till the other has failed of its effect. Ladies dress here very richly, as indeed I expected to find them, and coloured silk stockings are worn as they were in England till the days of the *Spectator* [a guide to middle-class deportment originally published in 1711-1712]: - "*Thrift, thrift, Horatio*"; as Hamlet observes: for our expenses in Great Britain are infinitely increased by our advancement from splendor to neatness.

Here every thing seems at least five centuries behind-hand, and religion has not purified itself the least in the world since the days of its early struggle; for here Huss preached...

With the food, at least, she could find no more fault than Lady Montagu had:

The eating here is incomparable; I never saw such poultry even at London or Bath, and there is a plenty of game that amazes one; no inn so wretched but you have a pheasant for your supper, and often partridge soup. The fish is carried about the streets in so elegant a style it tempts one; a very large round bathing-tub, as we shall call it, set barrow-wise on two not very low wheels, is easily pushed along by one man, though full of the most pellucid water, in which the carp, tench, and eels, are all leaping alive, to a size and perfection I am ashamed to relate...

Modern-day travelers who have seen live carp purchased out of open tubs of water on the streets of Prague in the week before Christmas might well be surprised at how long this custom has endured. As for the beauties of Charles Bridge, it is very doubtful that there have been many visitors to Prague, past or present, who have shared the negative appraisal of Hester Lynch Piozzi.

Live carp for sale on Prague streets before Christmas
©Petr Beránek

Descriptions of Eighteenth-Century Prague in German

By the 1780s, it was not only in England that travelogue publications appeared with descriptions of Prague. In the German lands - which in this era could be said to encompass Bohemia itself as well as modern-day Germany and Austria - a great deal of information about Prague was being published, including two book-length treatments in 1787, the very year of Mozart's first visits.

One was the *Complete Description of Prague, the Royal Capital and Royal Residence, from the Most Ancient Times to the Present* (*Vollständige Beschreibung der königlichen Haupt- und Residenzstadt Prag, von den ältesten bis auf die ietzigen Zeiten*), which was probably the work of the Bohemian literatus Johann Ferdinand Opitz. It was a detailed guidebook "specially designed for foreigners and travelers" that was brought out simultaneously in Prague and Vienna. Living as they did in an era when titles and privileges were of such importance, the Praguers of Mozart's day clung to the prestige of the status of their city as capital of a venerable kingdom, even though it was hardly a self-ruling one in their day, and their pride is reflected in the title of Opitz's work. It is attractive to imagine Mozart purchasing a copy in Vienna before starting on one of his trips to Prague, but there is no record of it. The *Complete Description of Prague* offered its readers a wide range of information concerning the history, topography, demography, and civic institutions of Prague presented in a rather dispassionate, "scientific" manner with occasional observations that are more lively.

Overall much more readable than the *Complete Description of Prague* is the anonymous *Observations in and about Prague by a Traveling Foreigner* (*Beobachtungen in und über Prag von einem reisenden Ausländer*), written by a German who stayed in Prague during the winter of 1786-87 through the following summer. He made mention neither of Mozart's presence in the city at the same time as he was there, nor of the overwhelming popularity at that time of Mozart's opera *The Marriage of Figaro*.

The *Dictionary of Anonymous German Literature* (*Deutsches Anonymen-Lexikon*) of 1911 proposes four names as candidates for authorship. The most likely seems to be Johann Friedrich Ernst Albrecht, a prolific author of the 1780s and 1790s who wrote similar travelogue publications. Whoever the author was, he probably found it advisable to conceal his name because his account of Prague was far from uncritical. Besides drawing attention to the principal tourist attractions in a fashion similar to the *Complete Description of Prague*, the *Observations* provided its readers with sophisticated sociological analysis that could only have been published in the environment of relaxed press censorship under the emperor Joseph II. Leopold II instituted tight restrictions on Bohemian publishers almost as soon as he came into power.

Lenient as they were, the Josephine censors were still not permissive enough for Karl Heinrich Krögen, who described their policies in Prague in a fascinating collection of travel accounts published in 1785: the *Free Remarks Concerning Berlin, Leipzig, and Prague* (*Freye Bemerkungen über Berlin, Leipzig und Prag*). In his introduction, Krögen hinted that his authorship had to be suppressed for fear of legal action against him. It is recorded for posterity only in the *Dictionary of Anonymous German Literature*. Since Krögen's book could not have appeared in Austria, Saxony, or Prussia (the countries whose major cities he visited), it was published instead in distant Copenhagen. Among a number of delicate subjects, his discussion of sexual customs is astonishingly frank.

Perhaps the most important theme that emerges from the *Free Remarks*, the *Observations*, and the *Complete Description of Prague* - whether intended or not - is the marked economic and cultural recovery of the city that had taken place in the fifteen years or so since the Bohemian famines of the early 1770s and the tolerant political atmosphere fostered by the emperor Joseph II. One of the most notable developments reported in the *Observations* was Jewish emancipation. According to census results of 1784 published in the *Complete Description of Prague*, there were 7,901 Jews in Prague, almost all of them residents of the ghetto in the Old City, which maintained its own separate civic administration. The ghetto was located in the northwest corner of the Old City, its southern boundary marked by modern-day Kaprova street.

Mention of the Jews of Prague is found only occasionally in earlier travelogue publications. Usually their culture and customs are brought up delicately, without any overt anti-Semitic slurs, in much the same way that Mozart spoke of Jews in his correspondence. The further west a publication appeared, the more sympathetic the author was likely to be to their circumstances. The reign of Rudolf II in the late sixteenth and early seventeenth centuries was as much of a golden age for the Jewish ghetto as it was for the rest of the city, but after the ravages of the Thirty Years' War, the wealth and vibrancy of the Jewish community had been much diminished. The English physician Edward Brown described the ghetto in these terms in 1673:

> A part of Prague is inhabited by Jews, and called the Jews' Town; there are no small number of them, and many rich, as trading in all commodities, and have good skills in jewels, and several sorts of stones digged out of the mines in Bohemia: I bought some Bohemian topazes of them, neatly cut and well-figured, and some which were very large and clear.

These remarks about the Jewish jewelers of Prague may be contrasted with those of Brown's French counterpart, Charles Patin, whose impressions of Prague were translated into English in 1697:

> …The Jews brought Medals to me every day, but such as were of very little value; so that I was even asham'd of their Ignorance and despicable Poverty. They also shew'd me a considerable quantity of Stones which may be call'd precious; but in those kinds of Rarities I have regard to nothing but what is extreamly beautiful; neither did I there meet with any of this Nature.

Remarks of Baron Pöllnitz made after a visit to Prague in 1729 reflect anti-Semitic attitudes typical of central Europeans of his day:

> The Jews are the only sectarians tolerated in Bohemia. There are still some Hussites, but they are so much in hiding that the government pretends to ignore their existence. Someone assured me that there are 24,000 Jews in Prague alone. I am not able to say whether or not he was exaggerating a little; what is certain is that there are a great number of them. Their quarter in the Old City forms a separate little town. They are skilled in commerce and practice all sorts of professions; and since they accept payment in kind with used goods [in lieu of cash], they cut the throats of the Christian tradesmen. As these people multiply like rabbits, it was believed that the emperor was about to issue a decree stipulating that only the oldest son of a family could marry. This rumor alarmed many of the Jews; they turned over a large sum of money to ensure that the decree would never take effect.

Maria Theresa's temporary expulsion of the Jewish population from Prague in the early 1740s on trumped-up charges of treason during the War of the Austrian Succession, an incident suppressed from the history of the Jewish ghetto published in the *Complete Description of Prague*, would have been well within living memory in Mozart's day. The Englishman Thomas Nugent, in contrast, did not hesitate to draw attention to this event in *The Grand Tour*. He was certainly referring to the government of Great Britain, Austria's ally during the War of the Austrian Succession, as one of the "maritime" powers who pressured Maria Theresa in allowing Jews to return to their homes:

> Before the last war in Germany, there was a vast number of Jews who inhabited this part of the city, and gave it the name of the Jews-Town: but in the last war they were expelled from this city as well as most parts of the kingdom, for being supposed to have carried on an illicit correspondence with the king of Prussia. It is said however, that at the intercession of the maritime powers, several of them were permitted to return.

In the 1780s, as the author of the *Observations* pointed out, "one would do the Praguers a great injustice, if one maintained that under the leadership of the great Joseph they did not adopt tolerance. They are doing it with giant steps." In recognition of Joseph's efforts to lift a vast body of legal restrictions from the Jewish citizens of his empire beginning in 1781, the site of the former Jewish ghetto in the Old City was renamed Josefov in the mid-nineteenth century.

It is clear from German travelogues published in the 1780s that by this time Prague had succeeded in building up a full range of political, cultural, religious, and educational institutions commensurate with the status of a major European city. All that was lacking was a court. After his trip to Prague in 1729, Baron Pöllnitz asserted that except for Rome, Paris, and London, there were more nobles in Prague than in any other European city, and nowhere outside of the same cities was the nobility wealthier.

To Baron Pöllnitz, Prague was something of a playground for the Bohemian aristocrats, and he found their company so agreeable that he was reluctant to leave it. The ladies in Prague he found "amiable," just as a noble visitor from Germany who had passed through in 1781 - Baron Johann Kaspar von Riesbeck - found them more approachable than the ladies in Vienna and more predisposed to flirtation. According to the French military tactician Jacques Antoine Hippolyte de Guibert, who visited Prague in 1773, warfare, taxes, and a taste for luxury had impoverished many of the great Bohemian families by his day, but Baron Riesbeck still reported large numbers of hedonistic nobles in Prague in 1781, many of whom masked their indolent and self-indulgent lifestyles by trying to pass themselves off as "literati." As depicted in a series of articles published anonymously in 1787 in the Leipzig journal *German Museum* (*Deutsches Museum*) - under the title "Letters of the Wandering Hypochondriac from Bohemia, Moravia, Austria, and Hungary" ("Briefe des wandernden Hypochondristen aus Böhmen, Mähren, Oesterreich und Ungarn") - the nobles of Prague were numerous and much taken to amusing themselves with eating, drinking, hunting, gambling, and theater.

Dissipated or not, the Bohemian aristocracy had done much to beautify the city in the eighteenth century through the construction of town residences and private gardens that compensated for the old-fashioned architecture that visitors such as Guibert, Krögen, and Piozzi felt dominated the city. Some nobles even stepped forward to provide public accommodations such as the vast pleasure garden built by one of Mozart's acquaintances, Count Canal, outside the city walls in an area that corresponds to the modern district of Vinohrady. Certain nobles also promoted the enrichment of intellectual life, and it is known that a number of them maintained vast private libraries. An eminent agricultural society was founded in Prague in 1770 after the model of the learned societies encouraged by the empress Maria Theresa throughout her territories, but more influential was the Bohemian Society of Sciences.

First formed as the Private Learned Society, it began to meet in the home of Count Nostic in Malá Strana in 1769. By the time of his coronation as king of Bohemia in 1791, Leopold II had granted the society a royal charter, and it was renamed the

Royal Bohemian Society of Learning. It eventually came to function much as the royal academies that existed in other countries to foster study of the liberal arts and sciences. One of the most active members of the society was the scientist Ignaz von Born, a friend of Mozart who was a prominent Freemason and - some believe - the model for the high priest Sarastro in the opera *The Magic Flute*.

After his trip to Prague in 1781, Baron Riesbeck reported very favorably on the activities of the noble Freemasons of Prague:

> Freemasonry flourishes extremely here, and some persons…dote on it to enthusiasm. The Freemasons in general do so much good, in particular by their establishments for education, that the emperor should not be displeased with them [for their secrecy].

Ancient Masonic symbols adorn architecture and other structures throughout the city of Prague

Learned societies throughout Europe at this time tended to make up for a certain lack of intellectual vigor in universities, and this was no exception in Prague. Charles University, founded in 1348 as the oldest university in central Europe, had fallen into a lamentable state as a result of its domination by the Jesuits since the seventeenth century (who renamed it Charles-Ferdinand University to honor their patron, the emperor Ferdinand II), but it experienced a rejuvenation after the Jesuits were expelled from the Hapsburg lands in 1773. One result of this was the foundation of chairs of Czech history and language in the late eighteenth century.

The former Jesuit college in the Klementinum may not have been a great educational institution at the time of Mozart's visit, but its spectacular library was an important tourist attraction that Mozart himself did not pass up. He also saw the magnificent library at the Strahov Monastery, just completed at the time of his visits in 1787.

Music and theater flourished to a degree remarkable for a city of Prague's size, and in the 1780s the cultivation of both arts were encouraged greatly, due to the efforts of Count Nostic, who constructed a large theater at his own expense between 1781 and 1783 that could compare with the finest theaters in the major capitals of Europe. Often referred to as the National Theater, it soon became the most important venue in Prague for the performances of operas, concert music, and plays in German and Czech. It is clear that the residents of Prague aspired to a sense of courtly glamour when attending this theater. In fact, Karl Heinrich Krögen reported in his *Free Remarks* of 1785 that "the Praguers believe that their new theater is the best one in all of Germany." He did not dispute the claim. It is easy to imagine how the beautiful new structure must have helped to brighten the Old City. Krögen corroborated Piozzi's estimation of the overall "savage" appearance of Prague when he remarked that "the buildings are mostly old and black and the streets (especially in the Old City) are very narrow and dirty."

Far more interesting to certain foreign travelers than what was happening in the opera house was what was going on in the dance halls at the time. The *Observations*, for example, contains a detailed account of the social spectacle to be encountered at a pre-Lenten carnival ball in the Wussin house in the Old City, the same place that Mozart visited on the first day of his arrival in Prague in January of 1787. The author of the *Observations* devoted pages and pages to a description of the ball he had attended, more space in fact than for any other event he witnessed during his entire stay in Prague of several months. He marveled at the large attendance (around 600 persons), the social tensions created by the simultaneous attendance of nobles and commoners, and the gaudiness of the dress and decorations. By pointing out the preponderance of women at the ball (many of whom must have arrived without male relatives or companions to escort them), the author of the *Observations* left no doubt of the existence in Prague of a thriving *demimonde*. He reported that heavy make-up was an affectation of the women he had seen, and in fact he had the same impression of masking that Hester Lynch Piozzi had commented on:

> By my reckoning perhaps somewhat more than half of those present were ladies. Since I had been told beforehand that I would be able to see all of the beauties of Prague here - and as I am a great admirer of the feminine ideals - I hoped that my imagination would be considerably enhanced and delighted.
>
> But heavens! How my expectations were disappointed. Instead of seeing beautiful faces, I saw prettily painted masks. From that perspective the ball could indeed be considered a masked ball. I remember having seen only three or four unpainted faces, and I admired the good sense of those who dared oppose such generally prevalent corrupt practices, because ladies here who only sparingly use white or red make-up are considered coquettes.
>
> When here and there I took note of a pretty figure or my eyes beheld a flowing bosom, and I saw a painted head atop, I was reminded of my little daughter who often stuffed the bosoms and corsets of her dolls in order to give them appealing figures, and I became cold as ice.

The author continued on and on in the same vein, expressing his disgust with the painted ladies, their garish dress, the overpriced refreshments, and the silly, artificial nature of the whole spectacle. Disapproving as he claimed to be, he failed to conceal his complete fascination. The fondness for extravagant female dress he mentioned was noticed also by Piozzi, Lady Montagu, and the author of the *Complete Description of Prague*, who felt that the city's residents preferred a certain "grotesqueness" in apparel and furniture over comfort and utility.

For his part, Karl Heinrich Krögen in the *Free Remarks* devoted an entire subject heading to "make-up" ("das Schminken") in Prague. He reported that heavy face-painting was ordinary for ladies of fashion and that noblemen frequently observed the custom as well.

Whereas the author of the *Observations* spoke of sexual matters only with veiled references, Krögen in the *Free Remarks* was much less inhibited in his discussion of the culture of the ball houses. He mentioned the existence of no less than four that were flourishing at the time of his visit. The one described in most detail was in the inn "Zum Bade," a former bathhouse located on modern-day Lázeňská street just off Mostecká street in Malá Strana. Krögen reported that it was "quite large and splendidly decorated with many mirrors and chandeliers." He also had this to say:

> …It has a well-appointed orchestra, and on the side of it are adjoining rooms where one can eat, gamble, and make love as far as one's means permit. The style of dancing is called German dancing; English dances and contredances are rarely done, but sometimes Styrian dances and minuets are included. German dancing is a pleasure so terribly draining that many drop dead from it. It sets the passions aflame and arouses illicit desires that are generally satisfied vulgarly in secret places.
>
> The women would not deny themselves this pleasure at any cost. Beware a young man whose wife is obsessed with these pleasures. He must watch as his wife wantonly twirls around with any available man and breathlessly sinks into his arms. To calm down her husband, she tells him that the man dances quite tenderly. By the way, she pays no heed to the admonishment of her husband that she should not get so heated up: "I would rather die than not be able to dance" is the answer.

"German dances" of the late eighteenth century were the forerunners of waltzes, and no less a master than Mozart composed examples for use at Prague balls. Their reputation for licentiousness is confirmed from this account.

The author of the *Observations* provided some valuable clues about the sort of people Mozart would have encountered in Prague in 1787 in upper-class circles. The noblemen with whom Mozart would have associated are described as hedonistic. He found them proficient in French and Italian (for their love of opera), and was surprised at how many knew English. German, he said, was spoken poorly in Prague, and travelers were well advised to learn Czech. According to Krögen in the *Free Remarks*, adulterous behavior was normal for men of fashion in Prague, who neglected their wives for prostitutes and chambermaids. Krögen included a special subject heading devoted to the flourishing culture of female prostitution, and the author of the *Observations* wrote even more about it, right down to pricing and the form of payment accepted.

One of the vices of the lower classes that the author of the *Observations* found deplorable was lottery mania. He claimed that Prague citizens unable to afford bread would squander their money away in hopes of attaining riches. This failing could be related to his additional opinions about a certain civic character he claimed he found in the city:

> As a whole, it appears to me as partly good and partly bad that a pronounced sense of pride and propensity for luxury are the two primary traits of the national character of the Praguers, and perhaps all Bohemians. Every Bohemian is sensitive

and degenerates into rudeness when his pride is threatened and he is not inclined to yield his ground.

The "wandering hypochondriac," also writing in 1787, was more positive in his estimation of the character of the residents of Prague. Fresh from a visit to Dresden, he had this to say:

> …the outward appearance [that] the inhabitants of Prague form is in stark contrast to that of the inhabitants of Dresden. The latter creep along the streets with bowed heads, whereas the former skip about and have a happy, open demeanor from which it can clearly be seen that they are content with life.

For an upper-class visitor such as Mozart, there is no question that Prague was a city of plentiful diversions, delicious food, and beautiful scenery, even if its "infrastructure" had not been completely rebuilt after the destruction of the Seven Years' War. By all accounts, the nobles who resided there could offer stimulating company, and they all would have been able to speak German well. The greatest attraction for Mozart, of course, would not have been the potential for dancing, flirtation, or fresh game to eat, but rather music-making. In this respect Prague could offer something that was not merely a less glamorous version of the aristocratic culture or civic life found in greater capital cities, but something truly unique in all of Europe: an intense cultivation of the art of music by all social classes.

Jewish Cemetery, Josefov

3

"Everyone in Prague Loves Music": The Musical Cultural of Eighteenth-Century Prague

In the autumn of 1777, the 21-year-old Wolfgang Amadeus Mozart faced one of the greatest crises of his professional career. After four years of enduring restricted outlets for his talents and a lack of encouragement from his employer, the prince-archbishop of Salzburg, Mozart finally decided to quit his job as a court musician. The separation was quite an unpleasant affair that led to his father's temporary dismissal from the archiepiscopal service right along with him. Many options occurred to Mozart as alternatives to residence in his native Salzburg. He tried unsuccessfully to establish himself in Munich and Paris, for example, but one suggestion he did not act on - and it came from more than one source - was the possibility of moving to Prague. Considering the astonishing compositions that resulted from his later association with the city, it is easy to view this decision as a lost opporunity. A careful consideration of the nature of musical life in Prague in 1777 makes it clear, however, that his decision to pass up Prague at this time made perfect sense. Residence in Prague in 1777 could not possibly have led to the creation of a musical work as remarkable as the opera *Don Giovanni*, even if Mozart were as skilled a composer in 1777 as he would become by 1787.

The Foundation of a National Theater in Prague

The overriding factor that made such a difference for Mozart in later years was a single event that took place in 1783: the opening of a grand new theater in the Old City of Prague. For the first time, there was a permanent civic theater in Prague capable of mounting operatic productions commensurate with those of other major European musical centers. The composition of opera, especially Italian opera, was the most prestigious activity to which an eighteenth-century composer could aspire. Success in the opera theaters was the surest way to acquire an international reputation of the first rank, and it was generally the only means available to achieve true financial independence. As a rule, the only musicians in Europe with greater earning potential than the most successful composers of opera were the best opera singers. One of the chief motivations for Mozart's permanent move to Vienna from Salzburg in 1781 was the hope of attracting lucrative operatic commissions, and it is difficult to see how any extended visit to Prague would have been worthwhile without the prospect of seeing at least one of his operas produced in suitable surroundings. Thus the construction of this new theater was almost a precondition for Mozart's visits.

Opera was certainly not new to Prague in the 1780s. In fact, one of the earliest operas ever performed outside of Italy, an anonymous "pastoral comedy" whose title is not recorded, was presented in Prague Castle in 1627 for members of the imperial family. Later in the seventeenth century, it was customary for the imperial court to sponsor operatic performances during occasional visits of the Hapsburg emperors to Prague, and in the first two decades of the eighteenth century, traveling impresarios put on a few operas at various locations in the city.

The desirability of setting up some sort of permanent venue for a city with such a large population of nobles was driven home at the time of the coronation in 1723 of Holy Roman Emperor Charles VI as king of Bohemia. The musical entertainments that accompanied this event included a lavish performance of Johann Joseph Fux's opera *La costanza e fortezza* on the grounds of Prague Castle, an event attended by one of the largest gatherings of distinguished musicians ever assembled during the entire eighteenth century.

An opportunity to satisfy a certain demand for Italian opera among the upper classes in Prague was soon seized upon by a traveling impresario from Venice, Antonio Maria Peruzzi, who was permitted the free use of a theater in one of the Prague palaces of Count Franz Anton von Sporck. Performances began in October of 1724. Peruzzi was not an astute businessman, however, and he was quickly ousted as impresario by another Venetian, Antonio Denzio, whom Peruzzi had contracted to engage singers. As the new impresario of the Sporck theater, Denzio took care to attract some of the most talented singers in Italy to Prague, not to mention the composer Antonio Vivaldi, who visited in the early 1730s. At first, Denzio's productions were supported enthusiastically by the nobility of Prague, who viewed attendance a valuable social accoutrement, but after 1729, their interest dwindled, and Denzio started to run out of money. His venture finally collapsed in 1735 after he had served time in debtor's prison.

Once the Praguers lost their chance to see opera, they soon found that they missed it, and operatic performances resumed again after a new civic theater was opened in 1738, the Divadlo v Kotcích ("theater in the stalls"), which was constructed in a market district of the Old City. This theater was often referred to as the Royal Theater (of the kingdom of Bohemia) or informally in German as the "Kotzentheater" (from the same linguistic root denoting marketplace stalls). It is entirely unknown whether wags at the time drew attention to the meaning of "Kotzentheater" unavoidable to anyone conversant with modern German: the "vomit theater."

The Divadlo v Kotcích both struggled and flourished for over four decades. Its impresarios produced Italian opera, ballets, plays in German, and a few music dramas in German. In architectural terms, the building that housed the theater was about as attractive as a barn, and it sponsored few noteworthy operatic productions, mainly because very few operas of lasting value were being written anywhere in Europe during the mid-eighteenth century. The only work ever performed there whose title would be familiar to opera lovers today is Pergolesi's *La serva padrona* of 1733, first given in Prague in 1744.

The Divadlo v Kotcích was never capable of mounting productions as sumptuous as those seen in central European capitals such as Munich, Dresden, or Vienna, but the scope of its productions was ambitious, particularly in the 1760s and 1770s under the impresario Giuseppe Bustelli. His activities pretty much ended after 1777, however, and Italian operas ceased to be produced there entirely after 1780. Between 1781 and 1784, the principal center in the city for Italian operatic productions was a small theater built in 1779 inside a palace in the Malá Strana district owned by Count Johann Joseph Franz von Thun-Hohenstein, later a patron of Mozart in Vienna. Count Thun's theater hosted the distinguished operatic company of Pasquale Bondini and presented plays in German as well. In the early 1780s, the most common venue for performances of music dramas in German continued to be the Divadlo v Kotcích. Opera in Czech was nonexistent.

A solution to the need for a large multi-purpose public theater in Prague was presented by a single individual of immense political prominence, Count Franz Anton von Nostic (or "Nostitz" in German). After pursuing a brilliant military career during the War of the Austrian Succession in the 1740s, Count Nostic was given a series of official posts by the empress Maria Theresa. In 1782, under Joseph II, he was appointed presiding officer of the Gubernium, the council of nobles that exercised both executive and judicial government functions within the province of Bohemia.

The meaning of the unusual title attached to this post, *Oberstburggraf*, does deserve a bit of clarification. The particle "burg" ("castle") in the word refers to Prague Castle and indicates that its incumbent was a sort of superintendent of the castle during the perpetual absence of the king of Bohemia. Because of this association, it is possible to encounter the phrase "count of the castle" as a way of translating the title into English ("count" is the English rank of nobility equivalent to the German "Graf"). Another common translation is "grand burgrave," but the more literal "supreme burgrave" will be used in this volume. Count Nostic held the title *Oberstburggraf* until 1787. For all the credit he deserves as a patron of the arts, there is no denying his uncouth character. Karl Heinrich Krögen, author of the *Free Remarks about Berlin, Leipzig, and Prague*, described him as "merciless, coarse, and surly."

Count Nostic's project to build a theater in Prague at his own expense began early in the year 1781, after he had secured permission from the emperor Joseph II to start construction in the Karolinplatz, a large, empty square in the Old City that was named for the Carolinum, the historic seat of Charles University. This square is now designated officially as the Ovocný trh ("the fruit market"), a name that harkens back to a time when fresh produce was sold there. The structure built by Count Nostic, one of the finest examples of neoclassical architecture remaining in the city of Prague, can still be seen in much the same condition as when it first opened.

Count Nostic published a manifesto in 1782 that set out his goals in sponsoring the construction of his new theater. One of the chief complaints he had about the existing theaters in Prague was the shabby appearance of the Divadlo v Kotcích and the "shack" ("Bude"), as it was called, a ramshackle theater that sponsored productions of spoken drama during the summer in the Karolinplatz. Count Nostic said that he wanted Bohemians who traveled abroad no longer to arrive home in a state of embarrassment after seeing the stately theaters that graced other European cities. He felt that Prague, one of Europe's greatest capitals, should have a theater and theatrical productions that would draw attention to the city from all over Germany. As did many Bohemians of his day, Count Nostic considered himself a German and Bohemia to be a region of Germany.

Count Nostic intended to model his project on the efforts of the emperor Joseph II in the late 1770s to endow a German National Theater next to the imperial residence in central Vienna. Usually referred to by music historians as the Burgtheater (the "castle theater"), Joseph originally intended it as a place to foster productions of German drama, including attempts to revive traditions of German opera that had nearly disappeared during the mid-eighteenth century. The Nostic theater soon became one of the most successful attempts to create quasi-imperial cultural institutions in Prague. Joseph II signaled his approval of the result by attending performances at Count Nostic's theater in September 1783, while supervising military maneuvers in the vicinity of Prague. In his manifesto, the count himself stressed his desire to emulate the example of the emperor:

National Theater
of the Kingdom of Bohemia
(today the Estates' Theater)

>…How high has the National Theater in Vienna risen under the protection of His Imperial and Royal Apostolic Majesty? All residents of the hereditary German lands aspire to this exalted example; should we Bohemians alone be an exception and feel less German blood in our veins? In order to avoid reproach, national productions in our mother tongue will be given my principal attention…

Still to be seen emblazoned over the front door of the Estates' Theater today is Count Nostic's dedication "Patriae et Musis" ("to the fatherland and to the muses"), and it soon came to be called the National Theater of the kingdom of Bohemia. The first theatrical entertainment given there was a production of Gotthold Ephraim Lessing's play *Emilia Galotti* on 21 April 1783. Among the first German music dramas performed there later in the year was Mozart's *Abduction from the Seraglio*, which had received its première at the Burgtheater in Vienna in 1782.

The strong German nationalism of Count Nostic's original message seems uncompromising, but the linguistic orientation of the productions in his theater soon became more flexible, a phenomenon that ran parallel to trends at the Burgtheater in Vienna. Once the Italian impresario Pasquale Bondini was installed at the National Theater near the end of the year 1783, Italian opera became one of the principal musical entertainments presented there. Plays in Czech also began to be produced in 1785, a development that led to an outpouring of literary activity now reckoned to be one of the most important early manifestations of a revival of Czech language and literature in the Bohemian lands. Performances of Czech plays came to be regarded as unseemly, however, and they were stopped the next year - resuming again shortly at another "shack" (bude) built in the "horse market" of the New City (now Wenceslas Square). At the time of Mozart's visits between 1787 and 1791, the National Theater was the most prestigious venue in Prague for opera in German and Italian, plays in German, instrumental concerts, and ballet. Balls of the type so beloved of the city's upper classes were also held there with some frequency.

Accounts of performances in the National Theater from foreign visitors began to appear almost as soon as it opened. Hester Lynch Piozzi's description of 1786, excerpted in the last chapter, singled out the beautiful parquet floor and the gaudy dress of the female audience members. Karl Heinrich Krögen, author of the *Free Remarks about Berlin, Leipzig, and Prague* of 1785, mentioned the cost to Count Nostic of 990,000 gulden for decorations. He did complain that it was difficult to hear the actors when spoken plays were performed, and the anonymous author of the *Observations in and about Prague* of 1787 had much more to say about the matter.

In his manifesto of 1782, Count Nostic said he was determined to make his theater accessible to all social classes. The result was a division of the theater into areas intended exclusively either for nobles or commoners. According to the *Observations*, there were loges and a "noble parterre" for the aristocrats, with another parterre and gallery for everyone else. Most of the spectators present, he claimed, came to the theater only to "kill time," and they were so noisy and inattentive that spectators genuinely interested in theater could barely hear what was being said. Even the spectators in the "noble parterre" and loges were inconsiderate of the wishes of the true theater lovers and preoccupied themselves with other amusements. All in all, he believed that Italian opera was the most suitable entertainment for the theater-going public of Prague; all that was heard was the music and all that was seen was facial expressions. The text did not need to come through, since it could not be understood anyway. In fairness, it should be emphasized that complaints about noisiness in public theaters were common throughout Europe at this time.

The author of the *Observations* obviously had little appreciation for the dramatic capabilities of Italian opera, but he did have a few interesting things to say about Bondini's company. "Prague," he said, "as mentioned already, has an extraordinary taste for music, and is very satisfied with this opera company, a sign that it must be good. Herr Bondini spares no expense to obtain the best and newest scores." He reported that "connoisseurs" rated the opera productions overall more highly than what was seen at the Dresden court opera, which enjoyed the generous financial support of the government of the elector of Saxony. He noted that the "the costumes and decorations are excellent."

In fact, Prague during the 1780s was one of the most successful "provincial" opera centers in Europe. Popular new repertory was typically heard there within a few years of its first appearance in Italy or Vienna, and it was capable of mounting creative new productions of its own, the most famous one being Mozart's *Don Giovanni*. What continued to give Prague a provincial status was the lack of any talented operatic composers who chose to take up residence there (a situation that would not change until the 1860s, when Bedřich Smetana emerged as the leading composer of Czech opera) and an inability to attract the most expensive singing talent.

The subsequent history of Count Nostic's theater, known on and off as the Estates' Theater after it was purchased by the Estates of Bohemia in 1798, highlights a series of flashpoints for "culture wars" between ethnic Czechs and ethnic Germans in the city of Prague, long after performances of Czech plays were stopped there in 1786. The orientation of the operatic productions toward Italian language ended in 1806, after which German dominated. In certain periods during the first half of the nineteenth century, the Estates' Theater nonetheless became an important center for the production of plays in Czech once again. During the Communist era it was known as the Tyl Theater in honor of the most prominent playwright active at that time, Josef Kajetán Tyl.

In 1862, the régime of the emperor Franz Joseph banned productions of Czech plays in the Estates' Theater entirely, a move that had far-reaching, though unintended, consequences. A sense of outrage led to a movement to erect a new national theater for the Czech residents of Bohemia funded by the Czechs themselves without any government subsidy. While money was being raised from a general subscription throughout the Bohemian lands, a so-called Provisional Theater was built on the banks of the Vltava River in the New City so that Czech-language productions could begin as soon as possible.

The Provisional Theater flourished in the 1860s and 1870s and sponsored the first performances of Bedřich Smetana's *Bartered Bride* (*Prodaná nevěsta*), the first truly notable opera composed to a libretto in Czech. The opera orchestra of the Provisional Theater, conducted by Smetana for many years (Dvořák played the viola under him), would later become the basis of the Czech Philharmonic Orchestra.

Provisional Theater

The completed National Theater, built on the same site as the Provisional Theater, was open to the public until 11 June 1881. Just two months later, on 12 August 1881, the theater burned to the ground and had to be built again from scratch.

A new structure, still in operation, opened on 18 November 1883 after a fresh subscription for funds took only a matter of months to complete.

Not to be outdone, the Germans of Prague had a lavish new theater built to replace the Estates' Theater as the principle center for German theatrical performances. The New German Theater (now the home of the State Opera), opened in 1888 and flourished until the 1930s, when it fell on hard financial times due to depressed economic conditions and a decline in the German-speaking population of Prague. A period of particular brilliance was witnessed in the years 1911-1927, when the Austrian Alexander Zemlinsky was artistic director. Zemlinsky was responsible for introducing Prague to the avant-garde music of many early 20th-century German and Austrian composers.

New National Theater

New German Theater (today the State Opera)

The Estates' Theater continued to operate with German-speaking management and staff until November 1920, when a mob of Czechs, including personnel from the National Theater, forcibly expelled the Germans during an anti-German/anti-Jewish riot. A production of Smetana's *Bartered Bride* was mounted immediately. Czech management was dislodged in turn during the Nazi period, and then restored at the end of World War II. The theater still presents a wide variety of theatrical entertainments and remains the only building in the world where a Mozart opera was first performed that still functions as a public theater.

The Effects of the Thirty Years' War on Musical Life in Prague

Without the construction of Count Nostic's theater, it is possible that Mozart would never have come to Prague, but there were also other significant signs of recovery in the musical life of the city that would have made it a more stimulating destination in the 1780s than it had been since the reign of Rudolf II. As with so many other aspects of artistic and intellectual life in Prague, musical culture suffered immeasurably from the effects of the migration of the imperial court in 1612 and the devastation of the Thirty Years' War. It was only during the reign of Rudolf II in the late sixteenth century that Prague had established itself as a musical center of international importance for the first time.

The Netherlander Philippe de Monte, one of the most prominent composers in Europe at that time, had come to Prague about 1580 to serve as head of Rudolf's musical establishment. Another talented figure at Rudolf's court, Jacobus Gallus, was originally from Slovenia. While there were important traditions of Czech monophonic composition extending far back into the Middle Ages, it was not until the second half of the sixteenth century that the names of Czech polyphonists began to be recorded in musical sources. The most remarkable one associated directly with Rudolf's court was the nobleman Kryštof Harant z Polzič a Bezdruzič, a dashing figure to be sure. Few of Europe's composers have ever demonstrated skill at soldiering, but Harant did, and his sense of patriotism led him to join the forces of the Protestant Estates present at the battle of White Mountain in 1620. For his part in the revolt against the Hapsburgs, he was beheaded along with fellow rebels in the Old City Square of Prague in 1621.

Harant's fate was symbolic indeed. For over a century after the defeat at White Mountain, there were virtually no notable composers resident in Prague. There were periodic visits by distinguished foreigners such as Vivaldi, but the city offered almost nothing to entice talented composers to remain. For much of the "time of darkness" Prague did not exercise its later position as the musical capital of the kingdom of Bohemia. There was a great center for music-making in the Bohemian lands during the late seventeenth and early eighteenth centuries, but it was not Prague. Rather, it was the ecclesiastical court of Kroměříž (Kremsier), residence of the bishops of Olomouc (Olmütz). During the rule of Bishop Karl von Liechtenstein-Kastelcorn (1664-1695), Kroměříž was one of the most important musical centers in Europe, due mainly to the activities of distinguished foreigners. The most notable Czech composer of the seventeenth century, Adam Václav Michna z Otradovic, centered his entire life in the town of Jindřichův Hradec (Neuhaus) in southern Bohemia.

In eighteenth-century Prague, most of the composers who chose not to emigrate were employed in ecclesiastical institutions and had to double as choir directors or organists - for example, Bohuslav Černohorský, Jan Zach, Franz Xaver Habermann, Josef Seger, Jan Lohelius Oehlschlägel, František Xaver Brixi, and Jan Antonín Koželuh. The sacred vocal music of these masters, little heard today, is far from negligible in value, but ecclesiastical employment must be taken as a sign of low prestige. In the eighteenth century, employment in ruling or aristocratic households with responsibilities oriented toward secular music, was what brought the highest status to composers. For those who could cope with the responsibilities, the most prestigious musical post was *Kapellmeister* (head of a musical establishment). Only a very small group of composers could earn good livings essentially without institutional employment if they were talented enough at composing opera in major population centers.

Two Czech composers who were especially successful as opera composers outside of Bohemia were Josef Mysliveček and Christoph Willibald von Gluck. Both had left Prague at an early age, since the population was not large enough to accommodate their ambitions. It is true that wealthy aristocrats in Prague did have their own musical establishments, but none was funded to the extent that it could attract the talents of a major composer. Often the musicians in the noble households had to double as servants. What was needed was the resources of a royal court able to draw on tax revenues. Without any prospect of seeing the imperial court return to Prague, the residents of the city had to take responsibility for building civic musical traditions into their own hands, and impressive results were achieved by the end of the eighteenth century.

The Emergence of the Dušek Couple and the Conductor Strobach

It is scarcely an exaggeration to assert that the most important turning point in the restoration of Prague as a great European musical center was a wedding that took place on 21 October 1776. The groom was František Xaver Dušek, 45 years' old at the time, the son of a serf from northeast Bohemia who had been fortunate enough to find sponsorship from a noble patron to acquire a good general education in the city of Hradec Králové (Königgrätz), and then to study music in Prague and Vienna. Dušek settled permanently in Prague no later than 1770. His bride was Josefa Hambacher, a former student 23 years his junior, the daughter of a wealthy pharmacist in Prague and one of the most remarkable female musicians of eighteenth-century Europe.

After their marriage, the Dušeks became pillars of musical life in the city of Prague. František may not have been a first-rate composer, but he was primarily involved in the production of secular instrumental music instead of sacred vocal music or organ music. Although he had connections with the musical establishments of the Pachta and Clam-Gallas families, he was never active in any of the Prague churches. Acknowledged as one of the most talented keyboard artists of his day, he was also a noted teacher who trained many musicians in Prague. His wife's wealth freed them both from reliance on regular employment of any type and ensured that there was no financial incentive for them to emigrate. Their ability to cultivate international connections while based in Prague was unprecedented.

Josefa Dušek

Of her many musical connections, Josefa's most interesting one came courtesy of her mother, a native of Salzburg, whose father, a wealthy textile merchant, had once been the mayor. During a visit to relatives to Salzburg in 1777, the Dušeks came into contact for the first time with the Mozart family. Eventually, Wolfgang composed two vocal masterpieces just for Josefa to perform (and Beethoven would write one for her as well).

Josefa's singing career was built on a basis very unusual for a female artist of her day. Unlike most, she sang almost exclusively in concert settings, not in operatic roles, a circumstance that lent her an aura of respectability. In the eighteenth century, theaters were considered centers of vice and immorality. Women who chose to "represent themselves" in costume on stage (whether singers, actresses, or dancers) were relegated roughly to the same social status as prostitutes and could expect ostracism from persons who considered themselves religiously observant. The nature of their theatrical engagements meant that they traveled frequently and pursued what came to be known as a "Bohemian" lifestyle. Josefa Dušek could be accused neither of rootlessness nor exhibitionism, so she escaped the usual stigmas attached to theatrical personnel of her day. Something of a musical "Lady Bountiful," she was famed for her charity concerts. Hardly any civic musical event in Prague was considered complete without her participation.

The Dušeks had become so famous in Prague by the 1780s that they were virtually the only musicians mentioned by name in the anonymous *Observations in and about Prague* of 1787. They are brought up in a section describing concert life in the city:

> It is only occasionally that public concerts are given in the National Theater, which are held in exceptional cases for foreign virtuosos traveling through. The house is generally quite full, and the generosity of the nobility brings in a good crop of them, both virtuosos recommended by the nobles and recommended by themselves.
>
> The natives acquit themselves as well as the foreigners. This summer Madame Dušek, a beloved singer with much strength in her voice (especially in her low range) and an attractive tone that is very musical, gave a concert for the benefit of the poor. This is a noble trait of Madame Dušek, who, due to a rich inheritance, no longer requires the support of the public, and employs her talent for the benefit of the unfortunate. Herr Dušek is a great keyboard player and gives very profitable instruction in it. Herr [Vincenc] Mašek, also a virtuoso on this instrument [who studied with Dušek], plays it with great delicacy. I would like to be able to name further deserving men, whose names merit mention, if only space would permit.

Another important musician he could have written about was Johann Joseph Strobach. Born in the town of Svitavy (Zwittau) near the northern border between the provinces of Bohemia and Moravia in 1731, he pursued university studies in Breslau (now Wrocław, Poland), and then moved to Prague about 1750 to study at Charles-Ferdinand University. Strobach dropped out of university in order to start a career as a professional musician, first as a church violinist, then (after 1765) as choirmaster at various churches. In 1775, he became choirmaster at the magnificent church of St. Nicholas in Malá Strana and began his career conducting opera orchestras. This switch to secular music-making eventually made him almost as much a fixture of musical life in Prague as the Dušeks.

In his position as conductor of the orchestra of Count Nostic's theater, Strobach led the closest thing Prague had in those days to a civic orchestra. It was the orchestra he built up that played the first performance of Mozart's "Prague" Symphony. No alternative ensemble capable of playing it could have existed in Prague had the Nostic theater not opened in 1783.

After the emergence of the Dušek couple, Prague never again wanted for native Czech musicians with international connections to act as leaders of musical life.

Upon the death of František Dušek in 1799, his place was filled eventually by Václav Jan Tomášek, a composer and music critic whose prestige both within the city and abroad was even greater than Dušek's had been. In the late nineteenth and early 20th centuries, Smetana and Dvořák came to the fore, and there were many others less well known to music lovers today.

In general, the principal musical talents produced in the Bohemian lands tended to remain in the country after around 1810. Before that time, they usually went abroad. In Mozart's day, the best-known émigré was Christoph Willibald von Gluck, but there were also Josef Mysliveček, Florian Gassmann, Jan Křtitel Vaňhal, Václav Pichl, František Antonín Rössler (Rossetti), Leopold Koželuh, Pavel Vranický, and Jan Ladislav Dusík. Additional notable composers of this period of emigration were Antoine Reicha, a friend of Beethoven active in Paris during the early nineteenth century; Jan Václav Hugo Voříšek, active in Vienna at the same time as Beethoven and Schubert; and Ignaz Moscheles, one of the greatest piano virtuosos of the nineteenth century. (Moscheles had begun his life in 1794 as a resident of the Jewish ghetto of Prague. He was the first of a long series of assimilated Jews from many different countries who rose to the highest levels of European music-making as the result of an era of emancipation fostered by the French Revolution and the Napoleonic Wars.)

Accounts of the Musical Aptitude of the Czechs

Eighteenth-century European musical life was enriched by wave after wave of musical emigration out of Bohemia, but the phenomenon also points to a sad irony: Whereas it is clear that the residents of Prague were fairly mad for music, the ambitions of the large number of musicians that the country produced could not be satisfied. The author of the *Observations in and about Prague* of 1787 had several comments to make about this:

> I briefly mentioned earlier that love of the art of music is almost universal in Prague, and I must say something more about it here. Whether or not the general talent of Bohemians for music lies in the national temperament, or whether it can be attributed to the former brilliant epoch in the country's history, is just not for me to decide, at least I have no ability to do so. That it does exist, however, can be observed very easily. Nowhere else can one find so many children going about with instruments, especially the harp, and even though quite young, actually earning their bread with them. The mechanical practicing instilled during youth makes them all the more skillful if they choose to develop their talents as adults. In the great majority of cases they do. But since Bohemia has such an abundance of unneeded musicians due to the large number of dilettantes, many of them travel abroad to seek and find a living. This process of youthful instruction, refinement, and finishing renders the itinerant musicians from Prague more prominent in Germany than native German musicians, excepting only the Thuringians, who have many musicians brought up professionally among the rural people.

Other contemporary observers did try to find an explanation for the unusual musicality of the Bohemians. From England there was Charles Burney, who offered some speculation on the matter after visiting Prague and the Bohemian lands in 1772:

> I had frequently been told, that the Bohemians were the most musical people in Germany, or, perhaps, of all Europe; and an eminent German composer, now in London [probably J. C. Bach or C. F. Abel], had declared to me, that if they enjoyed the same advantages as the Italians, they would excel them.
>
> I could never suppose effects without a cause; nature, though often partial to individuals, in her distribution of genius and talents, is never so to a whole people. Climate contributes greatly to the forming of customs and manners; and, it is, I believe, certain, that those who inhabit hot climates are more delighted with music than those of cold ones; perhaps, from the auditory nerves being more irritable in the one than in the other, and from sound being propogated with greater facility: but I could, by no means, account for the climate operating more in favour of music upon the Bohemians, than on their neighbours, the Saxons and Moravians.
>
> I crossed the whole kingdom of Bohemia, from south to north; and being assiduous in my enquiries, how the common people learned music, I found out at length, that, not only in every large town, but in all villages, where there is a reading and writing school, children of both sexes are taught music.
>
> At Teuchenbrod [Havlíčkův Brod], Janich [Golčův Jeníkov], Czaslau [Čáslav], Böhmischbrod [Český Brod], and other places, I visited these schools; and at Czaslau, in particular, within a post of Colin [Kolín], I caught them in the fact.
>
> The organist and cantor, M. Johann Dulsick, and the first violin of the parish church, M. Martin Kruch, who are likewise the two schoolmasters, gave me the satisfaction I required. I went into the school, which was full of little children of both sexes, from six to ten or eleven years old, who were reading, writing, playing on violins, hautbois, bassoons, and other instruments. The organist had in a small room of his house four clavichords, with little boys practising on them all: his son of nine years old, was a very good performer.

In Prague, Burney stayed at the Unicorn Inn (or Golden Unicorn Inn), which Mozart and Beethoven one day would also visit. He was serenaded there, an incident that led to further analysis:

> An itinerant band of street-musicians came to salute me at the inn, the Einhorn, or Unicorn, during dinner; they played upon the harp, violin, and horn, several minuets and Polonoises, which were, in themselves very pretty, though their performance of them added nothing to the beauty of the compositions; and it will, perhaps, appear strange to some, that this capital of so musical a kingdom, in which the genius of each inhabitant has a fair trial, should not more abound with great musicians. It is not, however, difficult to account for this, if we reflect, that music is one of the arts of peace, leasure, and abundance; and if, according to M. Rousseau, arts have flourished most in the most corrupt times, those times must, at least, have been prosperous and tranquil. Now, the Bohemians are never tranquil long together; and even in the short intervals of peace, their first nobility are attached to the court of Vienna, and seldom reside in their own capital; so that those among the poorer sort, who are taught music in their infancy, have no encouragement to pursue it in riper years, and seldom advance further than to qualify themselves for the street, or for servitude.

> Indeed many of those who learn music at school go afterwards to the plough, and to other laborious employments; and then their knowledge of music turns to no other accounts, than to enable them to sing in their parish-church, and as an innocent domestic recreation, which is, perhaps, the best and most honourable use, to which music can be appropriated.

Only a few years after Burney's account of his musical travels appeared in Germany, a rival musical travelogue was published by the composer and literatus Johann Freidrich Reichardt. At the time, Reichardt made his home in distant Königsberg (now Kaliningrad, Russia), but later he would become a mainstay of musical life in Berlin. Reichardt's acounts, published in two parts in 1774 and 1776 as *Letters of an Attentive Traveler Concerning Music* (*Briefe eines aufmerksamen Reisenden die Musik betreffend*) were produced specifically as a means of rebutting negative remarks about German musical culture made by Burney. Reichardt's commentary on Bohemian musicians was intended explicitly to shed more light than Burney did on the reason for the remarkable musical talents displayed by the Czech people. His observations, in the form of a letter addressed to an anonymous "most valued friend," were written in 1776 from the village of Šluknov in northern Bohemia (which he referred to as "Schluckenau"). He began his discussion this way:

> What a fruitful land Bohemia is for the musical observer! I had barely crossed the border, and I came upon sights that left me amazed. When I recovered from my astonishment, I began to consider why the Bohemians are more musical than their neighbors, and sought patterns and reasons why this should be the case.

Reichardt took pains to dispute what he felt was Burney's belief that the musicality of the Bohemians was due only to the vocal training offered in primary schools. Burney did record instruction on musical instruments, but Reichardt gave him no credit for it. Instead, he faulted Burney for not recognizing that it was a combination of instruction in both vocal and instrumental music in the school system that formed one of the three principal reasons for the remarkable cultivation of music in Bohemia. The second reason, he said, was the patronage of nobles, who were usually skilled in music-making themselves, in addition to sponsoring their own musical establishments. He singled out Mozart's friend Count Thun as one who had a particularly large one. The third reason Reichardt cited was the importance of an "academy" in Prague attended by people of quality from throughout the country. In this case, he must have been referring to the former Jesuit college (or "Gymnasium") in the Klementinum, which required proficiency in at least one musical instrument, as well as the ability to sing, of all of its students.

There is no mistaking the importance of music education in creating a musically literate populace in Bohemia. The music education available in Bohemia to children of both sexes during the "time of darkness" remains a source of fascination to music educators even today and must be considered one of the most positive cultural developments that grew out of seventeenth-century Bohemia after the Thirty Years' War. It was the Bohemian nobility that took the lead in mandating music education in village schools. One noble whose regulations have been studied carefully, Count Ernst Joseph von Waldstein, issued these instructions in 1689 for all his lands in the region of Bakov in northern Bohemia: "In every village parish, children must receive instruction in the literary arts and in music" in order that they "will revere God and know how to worship." He was so eager to further this instruction that he would allow "no son of the parish to be taught any kind of trade until he at least has been aware of the music of the liturgy and can supply some contribution to the church choir." Similar decrees were issued by nobles on estates throughout the kingdom of Bohemia.

Musical training of this sort was not intended to foster professional musical careers. Yet, as anyone who works with school-aged children knows, the spark of interest created by an early introduction to music can frequently lead to extraordinary results; thus the consequence of universal music instruction was the production of many musicians able to perform on a professional level without sufficient opportunities for musical employment.

Widespread musical emigration began in the late seventeenth century, just when the impact of universal music education took hold. All types of musicians made their way to every corner of Europe and even to distant parts of the globe, but the most renowned musical skill associated with Bohemian musicians was excellence in the playing of wind instruments, especially French horn. Testimony about this is preserved from Baron Riesbeck's visit to Bohemia in the early 1780s, who had this to say about the residents:

> Their fondness for music is astonishing. I have heard several orchestras here which equalled those of Paris in brilliancy of execution, and surpassed them in accuracy and exactness of harmony. Bohemian players on the horn and harp are to be met with throughout all Germany…

Some might be surprised that young musicians did not come from all over Europe to study in Bohemia, just as they came to Italy to study in the famous conservatories there, but it must be emphasized again that the village schools of Bohemia were not designed to train musicians for professional careers. Furthermore, there was no recognizable Bohemian style of composition in the way that France, Germany, and Italy each were recognized to have talented composers and distinctive manners of writing music. One of the greatest attractions of study in Italy was the opportunity to become conversant with musical traditions that were admired and imitated throughout Europe. There was nothing in the way of musical style that Bohemia was famous for. Bohemia was a net exporter of musicians and net importer of musical style. As a musical force in Europe, it was at once powerful (for its personnel) and impotent (for the stylistic influence it exercised on foreign composers).

Setting aside all of the reasons for the musicality of Bohemians, there can be no question of how much the populace of Prague loved music. Once again, the author of the *Observations* left vivid testimony:

In general, one can find in the taverns of Prague better music than one encounters in the ballrooms of many cities. A music lover who likes to hear charming music can find himself sometimes compelled to remain standing in the street to satisfy his yearnings beneath the windows of a tavern and not just once, but frequently. And there is also ample opportunity to hear elevated, composed music. All public entertainments here are accompanied by very good music, and many of them feature virtuosos.

Everyone in Prague loves music, everyone takes part in it. The general inclination for music is so strong that the natives here cannot be happy without it. If one enters public places on days in which music is forbidden, everybody is seen looking sullen, with bowed heads. For the average man appreciation of music is not the issue. It is something of a necessity like food, and the overwhelming effect of this in his body is something one notices in all. Here music exercises a powerful attraction. Almost as soon as it is heard, people spring up and dance around. Every fiber in their bodies is in motion. Dancing especially is a favorite passion among the female sex.

Anna Chromy's *Czech Musicians* and Jan Wagner's *Dancing Fountain,*
celebrating the musicality of the Czechs
Senovážné náměstí
©Jason Vanderhill

As for explaining the particular appreciation of Mozart's music in the city of Prague, there is one last piece of evidence that should be discussed from the author of the *Observations*. Like Burney, he felt compelled to compare the Bohemians to the famously musical Italians:

> If there is anything wanting among the Bohemians in comparison to the Italians, it would be a delicacy in playing and taste. One should not enter into a dispute about superiority. In this regard the Bohemians certainly have a more regular knowledge of music, and one might say are better grounded in the art.

The operative phrase to make note of here is the Bohemians' reputed "regular" ("regelmässig") knowledge of music. It is useful in this context to draw attention to the common etymological root of the English "regular" and the German "regelmässig" in the Latin "regula" (meaning "rule"). What the author of the *Observations* was trying to convey is that the rigorous training Bohemians received as youngsters gave them a better understanding of the "rules" of music, i.e., the "nuts and bolts" of music, or simply "music theory." For performance, the "more regular knowledge of music" carries with it a connotation of greater technical precision, as noted by Baron Riesbeck. Of all the major cities of late eighteenth-century Europe, there is little question that the population of Prague was the most musically literate.

The degree to which the ordinary music lovers of Prague were musically literate is what probably provides the fundamental explanation for why they were so receptive to Mozart's musical style, which was considered extravagant and overly complex in most of the rest of Europe. The famous quip frequently repeated with slight inaccuracy about the intricacies of Mozart's music - "too many notes" - was supposedly uttered by the emperor Joseph II after he heard a performance of the opera *Abduction from the Seraglio* in 1782 (the actual phrase was "exceedingly many notes" - "gewaltig viel Noten" - as recorded by Mozart's first biographer, the Prague schoolteacher František Xaver Němeček).

It is reasonable to believe that individuals with such a good grounding in music - and fully able to practice the art themselves - would have had a better appreciation of the possibilities of musical composition, even when certain techniques were brought to a level of sophistication that was unusual for the day. It is also reasonable to believe that Mozart knew very well that the Praguers had a greater tolerance for musical complexities. He certainly knew, for example, that *The Abduction from the Seraglio* (with its "exceedingly many notes") had been a tremendous success in Prague in 1783, just as the extravagantly sophisticated *Marriage of Figaro* was in 1786. It may be that Mozart counted on the willingness of the Praguers to try a little harder than the Viennese to bring his musical vision to life, hence the unprecedented difficulty of the "Prague" Symphony and the opera *Don Giovanni*.

The extraordinarily favorable reception of Mozart's music in Prague, the technical challenges found in the music Mozart wrote for Prague, and the magnificent musical legacy left over from his association with the city may all be the result of the unique system of music education set up in the kingdom of Bohemia after the defeat at White Mountain.

St. Vitus Cathedral, Prague Castle
©Dean Ayres

4

False Starts and Flirtations
Mozart and Bohemia Before 1787

It is tempting to describe the kingdom of Bohemia in 1787 in poetic terms as a refuge for Mozart from an uncomprehending European musical public, but there was a time when Mozart's father Leopold literally did seek refuge within its borders in order to save his son's life. 20 years earlier, in September of 1767, Leopold Mozart had taken his family from Salzburg to Vienna on the chance that they might be able to earn some money during the wedding festivities planned for the archduchess Maria Josepha, a daughter of the empress Maria Theresa. By this time, at the age of eleven, Wolfgang had already performed on the keyboard with his older sister Maria Anna (Nannerl) before the ruling families of Austria, France, and Great Britain. Leopold Mozart and his children were already well known to the empress Maria Theresa and her son, the emperor Joseph II. The potential for continued patronage from the imperial family seemed promising.

Leopold Mozart

Everyone's plans were upset, however, when the archduchess Maria Josepha died during an epidemic of smallpox in Vienna on 15 October, just before she was to be married. Her intended bridegroom, King Ferdinand IV of Naples, could hardly be described as grief-stricken, however. The wedding to be celebrated in Vienna was to be merely a proxy ceremony. Ferdinand never visited Vienna in his lifetime and had never met the archduchess.

Since she still had other daughters available for dynastic alliances, Maria Theresa had no trouble replacing Maria Josepha with the archduchess Maria Carolina, who became Ferdinand's bride the next year. In the case of the archduchess Maria Elisabeth, an exceptionally beautiful young woman, the smallpox epidemic had the tragic result of leaving her facially scarred for life, thus ineligible for a dynastic marriage. Her eldest surviving sister, the archduchess Maria Anna, had been similarly stigmatized by disability, so the archduchess Maria Amalia was the only possible candidate remaining who was old enough to marry the duke of Parma in 1769 after it had been decided to offer him a Hapsburg princess.

Maria Theresa's youngest daughter, born in 1755, was too young for the duke of Parma at the time of her sister's marriage, but a few years later a more brilliant match was made for her with the heir to the throne of France, the future Louis XVI. Were it not for the smallpox epidemic of 1767 that had eliminated two sisters from competition, she likely never would have been sent to France.

As queen of France, she was known as Marie Antoinette. As the archduchess Maria Antonia of Austria, she had been an acquaintance of Mozart in early childhood. Wolfgang's boldness at the age of six had been a source of wonderment at the court of Vienna when he visited in the autumn of 1762. Not only had he jumped on the empress' lap, he actually kissed her on the neck, an astonishingly presumptuous stunt for a commoner. For her part, the little archduchess had considerately helped him up off the polished marble floor of Schönbrunn palace after a fall. Wolfgang made certain that her mother knew how much he appreciated her kindness.

The smallpox epidemic in Vienna in the autumn of 1767 naturally carried off many more victims than the archduchess Maria Josepha, and two of those in danger were Leopold Mozart's son and daughter. An extraordinary account of Wolfgang's brush with the disease is preserved in a letter written by his father from the Moravian town of Olomouc on 10 November 1767, to Johann Lorenz Hagenauer, the Mozarts' landlord in Salzburg. The letter is striking for its defensive tone. Leopold made it clear that he had been fully aware of the danger of infection in Vienna. Three children in the household in which they were staying had contracted smallpox, and he knew of several children in the city who had died from it. Leopold claimed that he had intended to flee Vienna for Moravia, the southern province of the kingdom of Bohemia, but said it was "impossible" at first to do so, because the emperor Joseph II "talked about us so often that we could never be certain when it would occur to him to summon us," a remark that reveals Leopold as perfectly capable of putting the health and lives of his children in jeopardy if the promise of financial gain were great enough. Leopold claimed that once he had heard that the archduchess Maria Elisabeth had contracted smallpox, "I let nothing more stop me, and I could scarcely wait until the hour came when I could get my little Wolfgang out of Vienna." However, the boy was already infected, and his father had come dangerously close to killing the goose that laid the golden egg.

Leopold took advantage of connections from Salzburg to find a place in Moravia for his son to recuperate. The Mozart family left Vienna on 23 October and reached Brno (Brünn), the principal city of the province of Moravia, on 24 October. There, Leopold called on Count Franz Anton von Schrattenbach, governor of the province, who happened to be the brother of his employer, Count Siegmund Christoph von Schrattenbach, prince-archbishop of Salzburg from 1753 to 1771.

In Moravia, Leopold arranged to have Wolfgang, sick as he was, perform before the Brno Count Schrattenbach, but told Hagenauer that he had changed his mind and proceeded instead to the remote town of Olomouc with all due haste. Leopold never offered a reason to explain just why he had felt it was so important to transport his children to Olomouc. Apparently he was acting on the belief that it was in Wolfgang's best interest to recuperate at a location as distant as possible from the source of infection in Vienna. From the modern perspective, however, it is clear that it would have been better to simply stay put wherever they were until the disease had run its course.

Instead, Leopold forced his children to travel for days in bumpy carriages without medical attention. Upon arrival in Olomouc on 26 October, the only lodging that Leopold could find was at an uncomfortable inn. There young Wolfgang nearly died. The only room available at first was damp and cold, and the only means for heating it generated a great deal of noxious smoke. Leopold was able to move the boy to a better room the next day, but by 28 October, he was in a state of delirium. Later the same day, Wolfgang was transferred to lodgings at the Deanery of Olomouc Cathedral after Leopold appealed personally to a local noble, Count Alois Arnošt Podstatský z Prusinovic, the brother of the Dean of the Salzburg canonry. Leopold gave Count Podstatský credit for taking in his family, heedless of the danger of infection to his own household, and was certain that his gesture assisted his son's recovery. By 31 October, Wolf-gang appeared to be out of danger. Many years later, Nannerl reported that as a result of contracting smallpox, Wolfgang had lost his eyesight for nine days and had to spare his eyes for several weeks.

Inn where Leopold Mozart lodged his family during Wolfgang and Nannerl's illness
(today Hanácká Hospoda, Olomouc, Czech Republic)
©Jason Vanderhill

His sister Nannerl's sufferings were not considered important enough to describe in as much detail, but it appears that she was never in as much danger as her brother. Considering how unflattering his own behavior had been, it is remarkable that Leopold left any account of the experience at all. Regardless, the Mozarts were back in Vienna by January of 1768 and remained another full year with Leopold's ambitions for imperial patronage for his family unfulfilled.

Mozart and the Černín Family

Another intriguing series of incidents involving Bohemian noblemen began in 1776, when Wolfgang found a patron from one of the oldest and most illustrious Czech noble families who was willing to provide him with an annual income: Count Prokop Vojtěch Černín z Chudenic. A resident of Prague, Count Černín almost certainly never met either Wolfgang or Leopold Mozart in his life. The first record of a connection with Wolfgang comes from a letter written to the count from Salzburg on

13 December 1776 by Baron Karl von Petermann, a lieutenant colonel in the imperial army who was living in Salzburg at that time as the guest of Archbishop Colloredo. Petermann was charged with supervising the education of Count Černín's son Jan Rudolf at the Collegium Virgilianum, a school for the sons of noblemen. Count Černín's first wife, Countess Maria Antonia von Colloredo, was the eldest of a family of eighteen children that included Mozart's employer, Count Hieronymous Joseph Franz de Paula von Colloredo, the prince-archbishop of Salzburg between 1772 and 1803. Count Černín had left the responsibility of educating his son to the family of the boy's mother, who died only a few months after he was born.

In the 1770s, Jan Rudolf's uncle Hieronymous (as archbishop of Salzburg) was much more powerful than any of his other relatives, including his own father, wealthy as he was. The prince-archbishops of Salzburg were the rulers of one of the largest ecclesiastical states in Europe, a domain that corresponded roughly to the boundaries of the modern Austrian province of Land Salzburg. Count Colloredo was its last independent ruler. As a result of revolutionary and Napoleonic invasions in the late eighteenth and early nineteenth centuries, the territories of all of the ecclesiastical states in the German lands were turned over to secular rulers.

Count Colloredo himself had been forced to flee French troops approaching Salzburg in 1800. He immediately took up residence in Vienna, never to return to Salzburg, and he resigned his temporal authority in 1803. (He continued to live in Vienna until his death in 1812.) The territory he once ruled changed hands several times, but was incorporated permanently into the domains of the Austrian state in 1816. While he was still prince-archbishop, Count Colloredo could draw on income from taxation to fund a court, bureaucracy, and a musical establishment. Due to his generosity, Count Jan Rudolf received an excellent musical education in addition to his general studies at the Collegium Virgilianum, and his familiarity with Leopold and Wolfgang Mozart is probably what created the opportunity to seek patronage from his father, Count Prokop. The young count was one year younger than Wolfgang, who was also well-acquainted with Jan Rudolf's older sister, Countess Antonie von Lützow, wife of the commander of the Salzburg fortress. A talented pianist, she was the dedicatee of Mozart's Piano Concerto in C major, K. 246 of 1776.

Petermann's letter of 13 December 1776 states that Mozart was to receive an annual payment of 20 ducats in expectation of musical compositions to be ordered by Count Černín and sent to Prague. Mozart had told Petermann that he would send the count a symphony and other pieces at the earliest opportunity in return for the payment of this stipend. It is not known whether or not any of Mozart's compositions were sent to Prague at this time or whether the stipend was ever paid. Mozart is certainly not known to have completed any new symphonies during the years 1775-77, and the count died in Prague on 31 January 1777, just a short time after Petermann's letter was written.

Nonetheless, Mozart did not easily forget Count Prokop. During the winter of 1780-81, a time when Mozart was once again seeking a way to escape the service of Archbishop Colloredo, he mentioned him in a letter to his father written from Munich on 19 December 1780. Mozart speculated on how agreeable it would be to find another patron such as "old" Count Černín who would be willing to grant him an annual stipend in return for composing any type of music he desired.

The "young" count, Jan Rudolf, was still very well known to both Leopold and Wolfgang Mozart in 1780. Nine letters of Leopold and Wolfgang from the years 1777 and 1778 allude to Jan Rudolf's participation in musical life at the court of Salzburg as a violinist and composer. As proficient in music as all classes of Bohemians were in Mozart's day, it is still unusual that such a talented musician could have emerged from the ranks of the upper nobility. From the 1780s until his death in 1845, Jan Rudolf was one of the most prominent nobles in the kingdom of Bohemia and one of the most generous patrons of the arts and sciences in the entire Austrian empire. A Knight of the Golden Fleece, he eventually held important posts in the imperial government, but in the late 1770s he had been little more than a court musician in Salzburg alongside Wolfgang and Leopold Mozart.

1791 clothing worn by nobleman Count Jan Rudolf
©Hana Běťáková

Letters written by Wolfgang to his father from Vienna in 1781 and 1784 confirm that Wolfgang continued to have friendly contacts with the "young" count for at least that long, but it is largely unknown to what extent he continued to use the musical training he had received in Salzburg. Regretably, no account of Jan Rudolf's impressions of the Mozart family is known to have survived.

Hradčany today

In Prague, the Černín family was famous for its palace in the Hradčany district begun in 1669 by Jan Rudolf's great-great-grandfather Count Humprecht, an imperial ambassador to the republic of Venice. Designed by an Italian architect in a style similar to the Ca' Pesaro in Venice, it was the largest private residence in Prague, regarded by many as an unsightly monstrosity. It now houses the Foreign Ministry of the Czech Republic (and as such was the venue for the famously mysterious death of Foreign Minister Jan Masaryk in 1948).

Completing and maintaining the structure nearly bankrupted the Černín family over a period of generations. Jan Rudolf had no interest in living there after his father died in 1777, but he did sponsor a major renovation in 1791 for the coronation of Leopold II as king of Bohemia. A ball held there on 10 September included lavish musical entertainments. It is unknown whether or not Mozart was invited.

Plans to Travel to Prague in 1777 and 1778

Serious attempts to attract Mozart to Prague presented themselves only a few months after the death of "old" Count Černín at a time when Mozart had made a firm decision to leave the service of the prince-archbishop of Salzburg. Put simply, the type of musical establishment the archbishop was willing to support was too small to satisfy the scope of Mozart's talents. A particular objection was the impossibility of putting on an opera with a first-rate cast and first-rate production values. Additionally, Count Colloredo was not inclined to treat the Mozarts with the same deference that his predecessor Count Schrattenbach had shown them. Count Schrattenbach, proud of his association with musicians capable of attracting attention at the leading courts of Europe, had permitted long leaves of absence that enabled Leopold to enrich himself enormously by promoting his children's talents. To Count Colloredo, the Mozarts were court musicians of low birth who had no right to expect special treatment.

Mozart's withdrawal from the archiepiscopal court in the autumn of 1777 led to travels in Germany and France in search of alternative employment. While in Paris, Wolfgang's mother died, a source of renewed tensions with his father, who had never wanted him to leave the service of the archbishop in the first place. Leopold had only let his wife accompany Wolfgang on the trip because he himself had been fired by the archbishop along with his son and could only get his job back by remaining in Salzburg for the time being. Under no circumstances would Leopold have permitted Wolfgang - at the age of 21 - to embark on such a trip unchaperoned. The result was that Leopold never saw his beloved wife again.

Anna Maria Mozart
by Rosa Hagenauer-Barducci, 1775

Two connections of the Mozart family suggested that Wolfgang might be wise to travel to Prague at this time: the singer Josefa Dušek and the composer Josef Mysliveček. Josefa Dušek and her husband František had met the Mozarts for the first time in August of 1777, when they were in Salzburg visiting Josefa's grandfather Ignaz Anton von Weiser, an acquaintance of Leopold Mozart of over thirty years' standing. Highly educated, Weiser was the author of the libretto for Wolfgang's first dramatic composition, the sacred music drama *Die Schuldigkeit des ersten Gebots* (*The Obligation of the First Commandment*), which he produced in 1767 at the age of eleven. After Wolfgang and his mother left Salzburg for Munich in September of 1777 in a vain attempt to obtain a position for him at the court of Bavaria, Josefa wrote to Leopold from Prague to extend an invitation to his son. Leopold informed Wolfgang and his mother of this in a letter of 28 September in which he explained how concerned the Dušeks were for Wolfgang's well-being after Leopold had written to them explaining his professional frustrations. Josefa did not offer a clue as to how Wolfgang, whom she referred to jokingly as a "scamp," might make a living as a musician in Prague once he arrived; thus it is no wonder that the invitation was never acted upon.

During Wolfgang's employment crisis of the years 1777 and 1778, the best practical help that either one of the Dušeks gave him was to have Josefa write a letter of introduction to the Bohemian clarinettist Joseph Beer, who happened to be living in Paris at the same time as Mozart's stay in 1778. In a letter written to his son in Paris on 29 June 1778, Leopold reported that the letter had been sent to Salzburg from

Prague, but whether it ever found its way to Paris or led to any opportunities for Mozart is completely unknown.

The Dušeks may have been ineffective at this juncture in Mozart's life, but at least they did try to help - and exactly the same can be said for Mozart's friend Josef Mysliveček. A miller's son, Mysliveček had left Prague in 1763 in order to pursue the career of an opera composer in Italy and the lifestyle of a "rake" and "adventurer." He had been an intimate friend of Leopold and Wolfgang Mozart since they had first met in Bologna in the spring of 1770 during the Mozarts' first trip to Italy. Mysliveček possessed a charming and dynamic personality that both father and son found irresistible, and he was one of the most talented composers of operas and symphonies in Europe. There is no doubt that Wolfgang was keenly interested in Mysliveček's music and as a teenager had picked up musical ideas and technical expertise from his older friend.

Late in the year 1776, Mysliveček arrived in Munich to help supervise a production of one of his operas at the court theater. He soon found himself stranded by illness (specifically, the effects of tertiary syphilis) and was unable to leave Munich until April 1778. In the autumn of 1777, he had surgical treatment for the facial disfigurement caused by syphilis, with the result that an incompetent physician burned off his nose. Mozart went to visit him in a Munich hospital in October while he and his mother were in the city, and both he and his mother fell completely under his spell. An account of the time he spent with Mysliveček is the main focus of one of the longest and most remarkable letters Mozart ever wrote to his father. For the concern it reveals for the welfare of another composer, it is unparalleled in the entire Mozart correspondence.

Josef Mysliveček

It seems that Mysliveček, who was much better established as a composer than Mozart was at the time, had been praising him everywhere in Munich, and he claimed he had two concrete proposals to assist Wolfgang in finding musical employment worthy of his talents. One was to use his influence to arrange an operatic commission for Mozart at the Teatro San Carlo in Naples, the most prestigious venue for performances of serious Italian opera in Europe. The other was to put him in touch with one of the Counts Pachta in Prague.

Neither option worked out, however. No connection with the Pachta family was established at this time, and the Naples commission hoped for by both Wolfgang and Leopold may have never even been a serious proposition. Within a few months, the only reason Mysliveček continued to string the Mozarts along was to manipulate Leopold into obtaining patronage from the archbishop of Salzburg for himself, an enterprise in which Mysliveček was quite successful. Leopold did everything Mysliveček asked of him without receiving anything in return, a rare case in which it can be established that the shrewd Leopold Mozart would be bamboozled by another musician. By the spring of 1778, both Leopold and Wolfgang had lost patience with him, and as a result, Mysliveček's friendship with the Mozarts ended.

Despite Mysliveček's urgings, a move to Prague at this point would have had made little sense for someone of Mozart's abilities. In 1777, there were no private musical establishments in Prague even as large as the one at the disposal of the archbishop of Salzburg. Furthermore, there was no court or opera theater that could compare with those in the principal capitals of Germany, and a musical public insufficiently large to support him. For years, no serious thought of visiting Prague seems to have entered Mozart's head. Until late in the year 1786, the only hint that he might have considered such a thing is found in a letter to his father written from Vienna on 16 May 1781. In the course of explaining how much more advantageous it was for him to be living in Vienna rather than Salzburg, he mentioned that it might be easier for him to travel to Prague from Vienna, should he ever want to do so.

As for Mozart's employment problems in the years 1777 and 1778, no attractive solution ever materialized. Months of travel in France and Germany failed to yield any satisfactory opportunities. All that Mozart could do under the circumstances was to come crawling back to the archbishop, who agreed to engage him as court organist. He endured this employment for only a few years. In 1781, after the successful première of his opera *Idomeneo* in Munich, Mozart once again felt ready to break with Count Colloredo. This time, he had the idea of trying to make a living as an independent musician in Vienna after Count Colloredo summoned him there in March while participating in celebrations honoring the accession of Joseph II as sole ruler of the Hapsburg domains. A very unpleasant argument with the archbishop made the final break something of a necessity.

Mozart was much more successful at supporting himself as a musician in Vienna than legend would have it. By means of teaching, composing, and performing, he was able to earn handsome incomes during the last ten years of his life, but was still unable to establish financial security for himself or the family he had started after his marriage in 1782 to the singer Constanze Weber. Employment and recognition remained chronic frustrations to the end of his days.

The Way to Prague in 1787

Prague in 1787 offered temporary solutions to both. The sequence of events that finally did bring him to the city is best traced from the first full-length biography of Mozart ever written, František Xaver Němeček's *Life of Mozart* (*Leben des K. K. Kapellmeisters Wolfgang Gottlieb Mozart*) of 1798. Němeček, born in 1766, was a secondary schoolteacher in Prague who was appointed to a chair of philosophy at Charles-Ferdinand University in 1802. He remembered many details about the reception of Mozart's music in the city and was privy to information supplied by Mozart's widow, whose orphaned children were brought to Prague after her husband's death to be cared for by Němeček and others. His biography was written in an engaging conversational style that often seems fatuous and naïve, but his reminiscences about Mozart's connections with the city of Prague are undoubtedly based on information from eyewitnesses. Regrettably, there is no denying that his biography does not satisfy modern expectations for careful factual accuracy in all respects.

According to Němeček, interest in Mozart's music in Prague began in the early 1780s, when the opera *The Abduction from the Seraglio* first became known in the city. Originally produced at the Burgtheater in Vienna on 16 July 1782, it was the first opera Mozart had completed after moving to Vienna the year before. Němeček left an amusing account of its first performance:

> Soon after Mozart took up residence in Vienna, the unforgettable emperor Joseph II had the idea, so worthy of a German emperor, of trying to push aside the taste for Italian opera by supporting German Singspiels and German singers and doing more to bolster the [musical life of the] fatherland. He therefore collected the best singers together and had Mozart write a German opera. For these virtuosos Mozart composed the renowned and universally-loved Singspiel *The Abduction from the Seraglio* in the year 1782.
>
> It caused a sensation, and the cunning Italians soon realized that such a head as his might soon be dangerous to their tinkling. Jealousy now arose with the full strength of Italian venom! The monarch, who at heart was charmed by this deeply penetrating music, nonetheless said to Mozart, "Too beautiful for our ears and exceedingly many notes, dear Mozart."
>
> "Only as many, your majesty, as are necessary," he replied with that noble pride and frankness which so well complements great minds. He realized that this was not [the emperor's] own opinion, but rather something others had said.

Němeček was hesitant to acknowledge that Mozart had any personality flaws at all - certainly not impudence in the presence of monarchs - nor did he seem to want to criticize the "enlightened" emperor Joseph either (whose memory was worshipped among Bohemian intellectuals, in contradistinction to his brother Leopold II). As far as that goes, the censorship policies of Joseph's nephew Francis II would have made it difficult or impossible to do so in the 1790s. Němeček might have pointed out that the emperor Joseph had known Mozart off and on for 20 years by the early 1780s; Mozart had first met Joseph in 1762 at the age of six. A bit of teasing familiarity from both sides would have been appropriate without either man taking offense.

Mozart's *Abduction from the Seraglio* was one of the first operas performed in Count Nostic's National Theater after it opened in Prague in the spring of 1783. An important surviving indication of the time of year comes from a contemporary German music journal published in Hamburg, the *Magazin der Musik*. In an issue from 1783, a report sent from Prague in August records all of the operas that had been performed in the National Theater since Easter of that year. There had been eight in all, some in German and some in Italian. The only one whose reception was recorded was Mozart's, which met with "extraordinary success." Němeček corroborated as follows:

> I cannot describe from my own experience the success and sensation [*The Abduction from the Seraglio*] achieved in Vienna - but I was a witness to the enthusiasm its performance in Prague aroused among connoisseurs and non-connoisseurs alike.

It was as if everything that had been heard and known here up to then was not music at all! Everyone was carried away - amazed at the innovative harmonies and the original, previously unheard-of treatment of the wind instruments. Now the Bohemians began to seek out his works, and in the same year, Mozart's symphonies and piano music were already to be heard at all the better musical concerts. From then on the preference for his works among the Bohemians was decided! All the connoisseurs and artists of our capital were Mozart's greatest admirers, the most ardent advocates of his brilliance.

Bohemia was famous for its wind players all over Europe, so it is no wonder that Mozart's imaginative treatment of wind instruments was so much admired in Prague. Although the success of *The Marriage of Figaro* is much better known today, it was *The Abduction from the Seraglio* that originally created a taste for Mozart's music in the city. He was certainly aware of its success in Prague, since he bragged about it in a letter to his father of 6 December 1783.

It is interesting to speculate on the identity of the Mozart symphonies and piano music that came to be known so suddenly in Prague. Perhaps Mozart had been asked to select pieces and sent them there himself. With regard to solo piano music, examples of one or more of the sonatas K. 284, 309-311, and 330-333 would have been good candidates. Written in Mannheim, Munich, Paris, and Vienna beginning in 1775, they set a new standard of excellence for eighteenth-century piano music. Sonatas were not usually considered suitable material for public concerts in the eighteenth century, however. More typically, sonatas were performed only for the enjoyment of their players and perhaps a small circle of acquaintances, whereas piano concertos, which required an orchestra to bring to life, were the more usual vehicles for public performance. Thus it is possible that Němeček was referring to piano concertos, instead of piano sonatas, when he spoke of Mozart's piano music being heard in the "better" musical concerts. Three of very high quality, K. 413-415, had just been composed in Vienna by 1783.

There is also another type of "piano" music that may have assisted in building Mozart's reputation as a composer in Prague: works referred to in the eighteenth century as "piano sonatas with accompaniment of violin" or "accompanied piano sonatas" that are generally referred to now as "sonatas for piano and violin." Shortly after his move to Vienna, Mozart was trying to promote a series of six "accompanied" sonatas that had been published in Vienna that year, the sonatas K. 296 and 376-380. Plans to complete and publish the set are mentioned in a letter of Mozart to his father of 19 May 1781. On 1 August 1781, Mozart reported to his father that he had sent a letter to Josefa Dušek in Prague asking her to assist him in creating an interest for the sonatas in Prague. At that time she was in Salzburg, but she was supposed to have received the letter before leaving Prague. Mozart sent greetings to Josefa in Salzburg on 8 August and 5 September 1781, but no surviving correspondence confirms whether or not she received the letter addressed to her or whether she actually did try to promote Mozart's music.

There was not much new by Mozart in the way of symphonies from which to choose during the summer of 1783. After he left Salzburg in 1781 and no longer had an orchestra as his disposal, his output of symphonies had dropped dramatically. In fact, until his death in 1791, he never wrote a single symphony with the prospect of an imminent performance in Vienna. By the summer of 1783, he had completed only one symphony since moving there, the Symphony No. 35 (the "Haffner"), which was finished in July of 1782 to be performed as part of celebrations in Salzburg to commemorate the ennoblement of his friend Siegmund Haffner, scion of a prominent merchant family. The Symphony No. 36 (the "Linz") was composed in October of 1783 only because Mozart needed some concert material in a hurry for a stop he made in Linz while traveling back to Vienna after another visit to Salzburg. Both of these symphonies may well have made it to Prague rather quickly, but there is just as much likelihood that some of the symphonies Mozart had written before moving to Vienna had arrived before them - for example, the Symphony No. 31 of 1778 (the "Paris"), the Symphony No. 33 of 1779, and the Symphony No. 34 of 1780. It is not impossible to imagine any of the symphonies written as far back as Mozart's return to Salzburg from Italy in the spring of 1773 as finding favor in Prague in the early 1780s, including the well-known Symphonies No. 25 of 1773 and No. 29 of 1774.

In time, the interest in Mozart became established enough that reports about his activities in Vienna started to appear in the Prague press. The first one that still survives comes from the 31 December 1785 issue of the principal newspaper published in Prague in the late eighteenth century - the *K. K. Prager Oberpostamtszeitung* ("the newspaper of the supreme royal and imperial post office of Prague"), which appeared twice a week on Tuesdays and Saturdays. It will be referred to from here on as the *Prague Post* (not to be confused with a weekly newspaper of the same name published in Prague today).

The notice of 31 December 1785 describes two concerts of the Viennese Musician's Society in an annual series sponsored for the benefit of widows and orphans. The first, on 22 December, featured a performance of Karl Ditters von Dittersdorf's oratorio *Esther*. Oratorios (non-staged sacred dramas) were frequently presented in Europe during the penitential seasons of Advent and Lent, when opera theaters were customarily closed. Eighteenth-century oratorios were generally divided into two "parts" (as opposed to the "acts" of an opera). In between the two parts of this oratorio was heard a violin concerto by the German violinist and composer Joseph Otter.

The *Prague Post* continued with a description of the second performance of 23 December: "On the second day Herr Wolfgang Mozart substituted [for Herr Otter] with a piano concerto of his own composition. We mention nothing about its reception, because our regard for the well-deserved renown of this esteemed master is so well known, that it is superfluous to do so." Mozart's newest piano concerto at this time was the E-flat major concerto, K. 482, just completed on 16 December, the ninth in a magnificent series of twelve written between 1784 and 1786.

According to Němeček, Mozart continued to struggle in Vienna after the première of *The Abduction from the Seraglio*, successful though it was, and he did not have the opportunity to see another full-length opera produced in the city until the spring of 1786. This was *The Marriage of Figaro*, first performed at the Burgtheater on 1 May

1786. In Vienna it was only a moderate success, a fact reported in the *Prague Post* on 20 May 1786. Its readers were informed that the play *The Marriage of Figaro*, which it assumed all the cultured populace of Prague would recognize as the scandalous work of the French playwright Beaumarchais, had been made into an opera by Mozart. In this form, it "pleased only half [of the audience]. Connoisseurs found fault with a number of things, which this clever composer has resolved to improve on."

What actions Mozart ever took to respond to putative complaints about his style of writing is unknown, but it can be said that the report of a mixed reception in Vienna for *The Marriage of Figaro* is corroborated from a number of sources. The *Wiener Realzeitung* of 11 July 1786, for example, published a telling account of the first run of the opera, explaining that "connoisseurs" generally admired it from the first, whereas less-cultivated listeners did not warm to it. This observation goes to the heart of why Mozart's music was so much loved in Prague, which had such a high proportion of "connoisseurs" among its music lovers compared to Vienna. But even some of the most astute music lovers in Vienna did not enjoy it much. One of the most famous, Count Johann Karl von Zinzendorf, an imperial official whose diaries record many events in Mozart's life, said that it bored him. Němeček offered additional reasons for a less than satisfactory first performance:

> Just at this time the French comedy *Figaro* by Beaumarchais made [Mozart's] fortune as it was, making its way through all the theaters. With the encouragement of the emperor Joseph, Mozart decided to make this play, originally intended to be an opera, famous as an Italian opera with his music. It was performed in Vienna by the Italian opera company [of the imperial Burgtheater]. If what is generally held to be true is true, and what has been asserted by so many reliable witnesses cannot be doubted, Italian singers, out of hate, envy and other base motives, tried to ruin the opera at its first performance by doing all they could to make deliberate mistakes. The reader may decide for himself how much the whole cabal of Italian singers and composers feared the superiority of Mozart's genius and how true it was what I said just a little earlier about *The Abduction from the Seraglio*. This cowardly band of undeserving people continued, until the premature death of the immortal artist, to preoccupy themselves with hating him, slandering him, and belittling his art. What a struggle Mozart's spirit had to undergo, until it triumphed completely!
>
> It is said that the singers had to be called to their duty by a stern warning from the late monarch after Mozart, full of dismay, came to the emperor's box during the first act and made it known to him what was happening.

Remarks such as this about "Italian singers and composers" are the closest that Němeček ever came to documenting anything about the legendary rivalry between Mozart and Antonio Salieri. Leopold Mozart, however, told his daughter quite directly in a letter of 28 April 1786 that he believed Salieri and his supporters would try to do everything they could to sabotage the production of *The Marriage of Figaro*. Leopold said that the Dušeks had just told him that his son's enormous talents had made him very much the object of envy.

There can be no dispute that the reception of *The Marriage of Figaro* in Prague was quite different from that which was seen in Vienna. In fact, it was the most popular opera that had ever been performed in the city up to that time. The precise date of the première has never been established, but it might have been the opera seen by Hester Lynch Piozzi during her visit to Prague during the last week of November 1786. An allusion to earlier performances comes from the first surviving documentation of its run, an issue of the *Prague Post* dated 12 December 1786 that printed the following news report dated from the day before:

> It is the general opinion here that no piece has ever made such an impression as the Italian opera *The Marriage of Figaro*, which has already been performed several times by the Bondini company of opera virtuosos with the greatest applause. Madame Bondini and Herr Ponziani excelled, especially in the comic roles. The music is by our renowned Herr Mozart. Connoisseurs who saw this opera in Vienna will assert that it turned out much better here, very probably because the wind instruments, of which Bohemians are well known to be decided masters, are used throughout the entire piece. The duets for trumpet and horn were especially pleasing. Our great Mozart must have heard this himself, because the rumor has it that he will be coming here in person in order to see the piece so wonderfully performed by a well-appointed orchestra under the direction of Herr Strobach.

The singers referred to in this notice are Caterina Bondini, wife of the impresario Pasquale Bondini, and Felice Ponziani, who performed the roles of Susanna and Figaro, respectively. The reference to "duets" for trumpet and horn is a bit puzzling, since there is really only one number in the entire opera with a duet for trumpets and horns that would have been memorable: Figaro's delightful aria from the end of Act I, "Non più andrai." Modern audiences find the martial style of the brass writing in this aria as distinctive as did the Praguers of 1786.

Another report about *The Marriage of Figaro*, this time dated 16 December, appeared in the *Prague Post* on 19 December 1786:

> Last Thursday, the masterpiece by Herr Mozard [sic] already mentioned recently was given at our National Theater for the benefit of Madame Bondini. It has not yet been heard enough, for the theater was again filled with spectators, although it was not a subscription day [the Bondini company usually did not perform on Thursdays]. This time it so-to-speak rained German poems that were thrown down from the gallery. We caught one of them with the following text: "Bondini sings and brings joy to the melancholy heart; sorrow flies away as long as Bondini sings, as long as roguish jesting resounds from her throat." To the honor of Prague's taste, it is said, it will be possible to give this opera many times still before a new one will be asked for in its place.

The doggerel written in honor of Caterina Bondini does not sound much better in the original German. In eighteenth-century musical culture, a "benefit" concert was not necessarily intended to benefit charity, but rather that it could mean that all of the profits from a performance would be turned over to a single artist - in this case Caterina Bondini - whose "roguish jesting" in the role of Susanna had amused the Praguers so much.

One last notice about the winter performances of *The Marriage of Figaro* appeared in the *Prague Post* on 9 January 1787, just before Mozart's arrival. It seems fair that Felice Ponziani was also granted a benefit performance:

> Last Thursday Mozart's beloved opera *The Marriage of Figaro* was performed once again, with the proceeds intended for Herr Ponziani, who sang the role of Figaro. The loges, nobles' parterre, and every other place in the theater were so full that one could hardly move. The only pity is that this wonderful company of singers is now breaking up, and we truly wish luck to Herr Ponziani, now engaged for another theater, this man who, here and everywhere he performs, is the favorite of connoisseurs and indeed all who hear him.

For his part, Němeček had this to say about the first Prague production of *The Marriage of Figaro*:

> Just as it was that every one of his works was recognized and esteemed at its true value in Bohemia, so it was with this opera. It was given at the [National] Theater by the Bondini company in Prague, in the year 1786, and even at its first performance encountered a reception that could only later be equaled by *The Magic Flute*. It is the absolute truth when I state that this opera was performed almost without interruption throughout the winter, and that it greatly alleviated the unhappy circumstances of the impresario. The enthusiasm it excited among the public was without precedent; it could not be heard often enough.
>
> A good piano arrangement was prepared by one of our best masters, Herr [Jan Křtitel] Kuchaz [Kuchař], and it was arranged for wind ensemble, chamber quintet, and as German dances; in short, *Figaro*'s melodies echoed through the streets and gardens; even the harpist on the tavern bench had to play "Non più andrai" if he wanted to be noticed at all. This phenomenon was of course due mainly to the excellence of the work, but only a public that had so much feeling for what is beautiful in music and that included so many real connoisseurs could have recognized immediately the merit of such art. In addition, there was the incomparable orchestra of our opera theater, which understood how to execute Mozart's ideas so precisely and diligently. On these worthy men, who for the most part were not skilled soloists, but nevertheless truly knowledgeable and capable as ensemble players, the innovative harmony and fiery passagework of the vocal pieces made a deep and immediate impression. The renowned orchestra conductor Strobach, now deceased [he had died in 1794], often asserted that at each performance he and his personnel became so excited that they would gladly have started from the beginning again in spite of the hard work it entailed.

With a reaction such as this, it is clear that the time was ripe for Mozart to visit Prague, but just how and when this trip was planned cannot be established for certain. To complicate matters, he also had plans in the autumn of 1786 to travel to London. As a boy of eight and nine, Mozart had spent a good deal of time in England, and he had always wanted to return. One of its chief attractions for him as an adult was the patronage available there from a large and prosperous middle class. He pointed out the potential to his father in a letter written from Vienna on 17 August 1782. In the same letter, he mentioned that he was studying English and expected to be able to read books in English within a few months. By 1786, Mozart apparently had the idea to take advantage of connections he maintained with some British acquaintances who were living at that time in Vienna - Nancy Storace, Michael Kelly, and Thomas Attwood.

Nancy Storace had sung the role of Susanna in the original production of Mozart's *The Marriage of Figaro*, whereas the noted Irish tenor Michael Kelly performed the roles of Don Curzio and Don Basilio, and Thomas Attwood was one of Mozart's composition students. All three of them did leave Vienna for England together late in February of 1787. It is impossible to verify what opportunities they may have promised Mozart, but correspondence from his father of March of 1787 reveals how impractical the whole idea was. There had been no attempts to contact potential patrons or concert managers in London in advance of the trip, and Mozart did not have enough money on hand to pay for the traveling expenses.

Additionally, there was a tremendous family obstacle: child care. It is known from a letter of Leopold Mozart written to his daughter on 17 November 1786 that Wolfgang had the idea of leaving two of his children with Leopold while he and his wife Constanze traveled to England. Although Leopold did not know it at the time, there would have been only one child to care for, since the infant Johann Thomas Leopold Mozart, born on 18 October 1786, had died on 15 November of the same year. Tragically, the Mozart family did not escape the high infant mortality rates common in eighteenth-century Europe.

Maria Anna Mozart, 1785 (Nannerl)

Many music lovers are under the impression that Wolfgang's older sister Nannerl was his only sibling, but actually there were five others who had not survived childhood. As the youngest in the family, Wolfgang had never known any of them. In Wolfgang's own family, Johann Thomas Leopold was the third child. The first, Raimund Leopold, was born on 17 June 1783, but lived for only two months. The second, Karl Thomas (1784-1858), survived to the oldest age. Three other children arrived later: Theresia, born on 27 December 1787, who lived for six months; Anna Maria, who died within an hour of her birth on 16 November 1789; and Franz Xaver Wolfgang (1791-1844), born 26 July 1791.

Leopold Mozart was very irritated at his son's request to leave small children in his care. He told Nannerl that he wrote to her brother at length about the matter in a letter that does not survive. Leopold was not pleased that Wolfgang had learned of a precedent for the arrangement he was contemplating. In fact, Leopold was already taking care of Nannerl's son Leopold, who had been born in 1785. After a long, frustrating period of spinsterhood, Nannerl had finally married in 1784 at the age of 32 to Johann Baptist Franz von Berchtold zu Sonnenburg, a member of the lower nobility who was eventually created a baron. Nannerl was his third wife, and she had immediately found herself occupied with the care of five stepchildren born to her predecessors.

There is no doubt that Nannerl was Leopold's favored child by that time. She had remained obedient and loyal to her father throughout the years, and at great personal cost. In her teens she had been forced to give up what had been an extraordinary career as a professional musician. She had performed everywhere that her brother had up to the year 1769. Once it was clear that she was too old to be marketed successfully as a child prodigy, Leopold was no longer willing to spend the money needed to take her along on Wolfgang's trips abroad. Perhaps worst of all, she had abandoned all thoughts of marrying her first love, Franz Armand d'Ippold, director of the Collegium Virgilianum in Salzburg, because her father had objected to the match.

Wolfgang, in contrast, had married Constanze Weber in the face of strong disapproval from his father. In the matter of Wolfgang's marriage, Nannerl had sided with her father and nearly cut off relations with her brother completely, as close as they had been throughout their childhood and early adulthood. Leopold had tried to keep his care of Nannerl's son secret, but Wolfgang found out about it from a mutual acquaintance. Leopold had no intention of caring for Wolfgang's children while he and Constanze were in England, not even with an offer of money for hiring a nanny. Leopold was afraid that he would have no control of the obligation; in other words, he feared that Wolfgang and his wife might never return, whether due to death or permanent relocation. In this case, Leopold might well have reminded his son about what had happened to his mother in Paris in 1778.

Leopold's attitude may have been the decisive factor that led Wolfgang to cancel plans to visit London, but there are hints in the Mozart documentation that it was not firmly abandoned for some time. On 26 December 1786, the *Prague Post* published a report from Vienna dated 6 December 1786, indicating that Mozart definitely would be traveling there. The same notice had appeared in a newspaper in Hamburg on 15 December and perhaps in other newspapers in Germany as well: "The famous composer Herr Mozart is preparing to travel early next year to London, where he has received most profitable offers. He will travel there by way of Paris." This must have been confusing to music lovers in Prague who had been told by the *Prague Post* on 12 December 1786 that Mozart would be coming to their city. As late as 12 January 1787, by which time Wolfgang was already in Prague, Leopold Mozart wrote to his daughter with the news that he was still receiving reports from Vienna, Prague, and Munich confirming the rumor that his son intended to travel to England. In the same letter of 12 January, Leopold provided some of the most specific information available concerning his son's immediate invitation to come to Prague:

> …His opera *The Marriage of Figaro* was performed there with such success that the orchestra and a company of distinguished connoisseurs and music lovers sent him letters inviting him to Prague and also a poem composed in his honor. I heard this from your brother, and Count Starhemberg heard about it from Prague. I will send you the poem by the next courier…

Count Josef von Starhemberg was a canon of Salzburg cathedral with family connections in Bohemia. The text of the poem in question, written by the Prague physician Anton Daniel Breicha, still survives. Much longer than the poem written in honor of Caterina Bondini, its quality is little better.

The only "connoisseur" or "music lover" who was mentioned by Němeček as having extended an invitation to Mozart was Count Johann Josef Franz von Thun-Hohenstein: "Admiration for the composer of [*The Marriage of Figaro*] went so far that one of our most prominent nobles and connoisseurs of music, Count Johann Thun, who himself maintained a first-class orchestra, invited Mozart to Prague and offered him accommodation, expenses, and every comfort in his home." This individual, referred to by Mozart as "old Count Thun," was a member of a noble family originally from the Tyrol that was one of the oldest in the Hapsburg domains. He died in 1788 just after Mozart's first visits to Prague.

Like Mozart, Count Thun was an active participant in the Masonic movement in Vienna. At one time he owned huge estates in Bohemia and several properties in Prague, but retained only one palace in Malá Strana after dividing up many possessions among his children in 1785. Mozart stayed as a guest at his palace in Linz in 1783 during the trip that resulted in the composition of the "Linz" Symphony. The count's daughter-in-law, Wilhelmine von Thun-Hohenstein, was one of Mozart's most supportive patrons in Vienna almost from the day of his arrival in March 1781.

Němeček did not mention it, but there is no doubt that *The Marriage of Figaro* was performed in the theater Count Thun maintained in his palace in Malá Strana as well as in the National Theater, since the original libretto for the Prague production indicates that it was performed "in the theaters of Prague" ("nei teatri di Praga"). The author of the *Observations in and about Prague* confirms that the Bondini company in the winter of 1786 was giving performances three times a week in the National Theater and once a week in the Thun palace (hence the plural "theaters of Prague"). With such a personal connection to the success of *The Marriage of Figaro* in Prague, it is no wonder that Count Thun took it upon himself to act as principal host for Mozart's first trip to Prague the next year.

Mozart may have tried to make contacts with other prominent Bohemian nobles in advance of his arrival in Prague, but there is only one case that can be documented. At some point Mozart requested a letter of introduction to Count Vincenz von Waldstein from one of the princes Auersperg, who obliged him and wrote a letter to the count from Vienna on January 6, 1787; it was signed "Prince Auersperg" without any Christian name. The Auersperg family is known in the Mozart documentation from a list of subscribers to a concert series in Vienna that is detailed in a letter of Mozart to his father of 20 March 1784. Two princes of the family are mentioned in the list as living in Vienna at that time: the brothers Karl Josef Anton and Johann Adam. The more likely author of the recommendation would be Johann Adam, an acquaintance of Lorenzo da Ponte who maintained a private theater in Vienna where Mozart's *Idomeneo* had been performed in 1786. Johann Adam owned an estate in Bohemia adjacent to Count Waldstein's estate of Mnichovo Hradiště (Münchengrätz).

Count Vincenz von Waldstein was a distant relative of two rather more famous personages: Albrecht von Waldstein (or "Wallenstein"), Duke of Friedland, the outstanding Hapsburg general of the Thirty Years' War (his third cousin five times removed), and Count Ferdinand von Waldstein, a friend of Beethoven immortalized as the dedicatee of the Piano Sonata in C major, Op. 53 (his first cousin once removed). He probably would have been known to Mozart as a patron of music from his old protégé Josef Mysliveček, who had benefited mightily from his generosity in the 1760s and 1770s.

From the perspective of the upper nobility of Bohemia, Mozart did not rate very highly as a social contact. After nearly six years' residence in Vienna, Mozart still had no appointment in the imperial household, nor in any other musical establishment. Prince Auersperg referred to him only as "a piano teacher in our capital city," rather than as the greatest living European musician - a more accurate description of his true status. Prince Auersperg's efforts may well have been wasted, since there is no particular reason to believe that Count Waldstein ever met Mozart. The precise nature and extent of the preparations Mozart made for his trip to Prague in the middle of winter early in 1787 will never be known, but his memorable first stay left an amazing trail of documentation.

Astronomical Clock
Old Town Square

Mozart's alleged room in the Bertramka villa

Part Two:
Mozart's Excursions to Prague
(and Aftermath)

5

A Musical Oasis in Bohemia: Mozart's First Visit to Prague in 1787

What was probably Mozart's most enjoyable stay in Prague took place in the dead of a central European winter. A brief inscription left in an album belonging to Constanze Mozart's cousin Edmund Weber indicates that she and her husband left Vienna for Prague early on the morning of Monday, 8 January 1787, accompanied by a motley group of companions. Traveling by carriage, they almost certainly would have followed the speedy "post route" through Bohemia and Moravia outlined in Thomas Nugent's *The Grand Tour*.

The first Moravian town they would have encountered was Znojmo (Znaim), the surroundings of which offer modern travelers quite a contrast in scenery after they have just seen the quaint villages of Austria. The appearance of rural Moravia is grayer and less prosperous, an impression shared by Baron Riesbeck when he traveled the same route in the early 1780s. The poverty that foreign observers found so disturbing in the countryside of Moravia probably would have been no less obvious to Mozart under cover of snow.

Using modern place names with the German equivalents in common use during the eighteenth century, the next stops in Moravia would have been Moravské Budějovice (Mährisch Budwitz), Třebíč (Trebitsch), Čechtín (Stecken), and Polná, a route quite different from what is usually taken by automobile and rail travelers today between Vienna and Prague; the existing highway and railway system more conveniently traverses the larger population centers of Jihlava (Iglau) and Brno (Brünn). The first stop in the province of Bohemia would have been Havlíčkův Brod (Deutsch Brod), known in Czech until 1945 as Německý Brod ("German ford"). From there, the route would be more familiar to modern travelers: Habry (Habern), Čáslav (Tschaslau), Kutná Hora (Kuttenberg), Kolín (Köln), Český Brod (Böhmisch Brod), and then Prague. It was customary for travelers from Vienna to enter Prague at the New Gate ("Neuthor") that skirted the walls of the New City. It was located at what is now the intersection of Wilsonova street and Bolzanova at the northern boundary of Prague's main railway station.

Mozart arrived in Prague on Thursday, 11 January 1787, as recorded in a notice in the *Prague Post* dated 12 January:

> Last night our great and beloved composer Herr Mozard [sic] arrived here from Vienna. We do not doubt that Herr Bondini will have *The Marriage of Figaro* performed in his honor, this beloved work of his musical genius, and our glorious renowned orchestra will not fail to provide fresh proof of his skill; surely the discerning inhabitants of Prague will assemble in large numbers, even though they have already heard the piece frequently. We would also like to be able to admire Herr Mozard's [sic] drama for ourselves.

The precise time of arrival recorded here is contradicted in Mozart's own account of his first day in Prague (see below), which indicates noon. The *Prague Post* may have specified a later arrival because Mozart was not seen in public until he attended a ball that evening.

Mozart probably sent several versions of his recollections to various friends and family members, but the only one that still survives was written on 15 January to Gottfried von Jacquin. The son of a distinguished botanist, Jacquin was a talented amateur singer and composer not quite 20 years' old at the time. He and his younger sister Franziska were two of Mozart's music students. The affection that Mozart expressed for Jacquin and his family is touching to read, but just what personal qualities they possessed to merit it is a mystery. In general, little is known about Mozart's relationships with the dizzying array of acquaintances in Vienna and Salzburg who are mentioned in his correspondence. Mozart's letter to Jacquin is so long and so rich in detail that it must be broken up here for the purpose of commentary. It begins innocuously enough by explaining Mozart's neglect of correspondence:

> Dearest Friend!
> At last I have found a moment to write to you. - I resolved upon my arrival to write four letters to Vienna, but in vain! - I was able to manage only a single one (to my mother-in-law) and then only half of it. My wife and Hofer had to finish it.

Constanze Mozart

Mozart's mother-in-law was Caecilia Weber, a widow and mother of two unmarried daughters at the time that Mozart sought lodging in her household in Vienna shortly after he moved there in March of 1781. Her husband had been Fridolin Weber, an uncle of the composer Carl Maria von Weber.

Before the time of her daughter Constanze's marriage to Mozart in August of 1782, it is known that Caecilia had fought with her frequently and bitterly. The precise reason for all of the conflict is not known; perhaps it had something to do with the mother's impatience to see her daughter's wedding concluded. On the evidence of veiled references found in a letter written to Leopold on 27 July 1782, there is reason to believe that Wolfgang and Constanze had initiated sexual relations before their marriage. This would have been a dangerous step for Constanze, who could easily have found herself abandoned and unmarriageable if things had not worked out as they did. A hurriedly-arranged wedding ceremony took place without Leopold's blessing on 4

August 1782, after which Caecilia's relations with both daughter and son-in-law improved enormously.

There is a strong possibility that the Mozarts' second son, two-year-old Karl Thomas, was left in the care of his grandmother Weber while his parents disported themselves in Prague. Later in the same letter to Jacquin, Mozart named all of his traveling companions, and Karl Thomas was not among them. Caecilia Weber was the child's only living grandparent in Vienna and thus a good candidate for babysitter. This could be the reason that Mozart took pains to write to her immediately upon his arrival in Prague. Whoever was caring for the child, it was clearly someone they would not have trusted to look after him during a trip as long as the one planned for London, or they would not have tried to get Leopold to take over the responsibility.

At the time of their first trip to Prague, Mozart and his wife lived in a handsome Vienna apartment building that was only a short walk away from St. Stephen's cathedral (now referred to sometimes as the "Figaro House," since they lived there during the period when the opera *The Marriage of Figaro* was composed). Their friend Franz de Paula Hofer (who helped finish Mozart's letter to this mother-in-law) was a violinist at the cathedral. His closeness to the Webers and Mozarts culminated in his marriage to Constanze's older sister Josepha in July of 1788.

Like all of her sisters, Josepha was a talented singer who in fact appeared as Queen of the Night in the original production of *The Magic Flute*. Constanze's two other sisters were Aloisia and Sophie, the latter a valued confidante to her sister Constanze who was present with her at Mozart's deathbed in December of 1791. Mozart had met Aloisia in Mannheim in 1777 during his travels that year in search of employment outside of Salzburg. He had fallen in love with her, and had even found his father's approval in courting her, but she rejected him definitively late the next year, a crushing emotional blow. No one could have imagined him later coming into such close contact with her younger sister Constanze that he would want to marry her, but this did happen once he moved to Vienna in 1781. There is no reason to believe that Mozart ever regretted his decision.

Mozart continued his account of his first day in Prague:

> ...Immediately upon our arrival (on Thursday the 11th at noon) we had to rush head over heels in order to get ready for lunch at one o'clock. After the meal old Count Thun regaled us with some music, performed by his own people, which lasted about an hour and a half. - This kind of real entertainment I could enjoy every day.

The palace of "old" Count Thun in Malá Strana was one of the most important cultural centers in the city of Prague. With a theater, musical instruments, and sumptuous accommodations, it is difficult to think of another location in Prague more ideal for a musician to pass some time during the winter months. Mozart's friends the Dušeks were out of town; Josefa had a singing engagement in Berlin, as recorded by Leopold Mozart in a letter to his daughter of 12 January 1787. Mozart would have to wait until later the same year to enjoy staying at the Dušeks' country residence, the Bertramka villa.

Paul Nettl, in his 1938 study *Mozart in Böhmen*, correctly identified the site of the Thun palace where Mozart stayed, but it has been confused in many recent guidebooks with a palace that presently houses the British Embassy in Prague. The building located at Thunovská 14, was once owned by "old" Count Thun, but he turned it over to his son Franz Josef in 1785. There is no particular reason to believe that Mozart ever set foot in it. Nearby was the one palace in Prague still remaining to "old" Count Thun in 1787, a structure that burned to the ground in 1794 after one of the actors engaged to perform in its theater had accidentally started a fire. The property remained vacant for a few years after that, and in 1801 was purchased by the Estates of Bohemia. A new neoclassical structure was soon erected on the site that has always been used as a meeting place for various types of political assemblies. Today it is occupied by the Chamber of Deputies of the Parliament of the Czech Republic and bears the address Sněmovní 4. It was in the palace that formerly stood on this site that Mozart stayed in Prague during his first visit early in 1787.

A Ball at the Wussin House

The remainder of Mozart's first day in Prague, 11 January 1787, was hardly uneventful:

> …At six o'clock I drove with Count Canal to the so-called Bretfeld ball, where the cream of the beauties of Prague is wont to gather. - That would have been just the thing for you, my friend! - I can imagine seeing you running, do you think? - no, limping - after all those pretty girls and women! - I neither danced nor flirted. - Not the former, because I was too tired, and not the latter due to my natural reserve. - But I observed with the greatest pleasure how all these people leaped about in sheer delight to the music of my *Figaro*, arranged as noisy contredanses and German dances. - For here nothing is spoken of but - *Figaro*. Nothing is played, blown, sung, or whistled but - *Figaro*. No opera is attended like *Figaro*, eternally *Figaro*. Certainly a great honor for me…

Mozart's companion Joseph Emmanuel Malabaila, Count von Canal, was something of an anomaly in late eighteenth-century Prague: a nobleman of foreign origin who had made residence there a lifestyle choice. Many foreign families came to Bohemia as a result of land grants doled out by the Hapsburg emperors in the seventeenth century for loyal service during the Thirty Years' War, but few new ones followed. Count Canal was from an Italian family, but born in 1745 in Vienna, where his father had served as ambassador to the Hapsburg court from the kingdom of Sardinia. He had moved to Prague in 1770 after leaving the service of the Austrian army and soon became prominent in upper-class social circles, particularly after he helped found a Masonic lodge in 1783. From the time of his arrival, Count Canal had started building up gardens outside the city walls in what is now the Vinohrady district. In 1787, he opened them to the public. The "Kanálka," as the gardens were called, was devoted not only to pleasure, but also to scientific research that earned the count a permanent place in the history of botany and horticulture. Since he maintained his own private musical establishment, the combination of musical interests and participation in the Masonic movement provide an easy explanation for his fast friendship with Wolfgang Mozart.

The precise location of the ball that Mozart attended has been the subject of confusion in the Mozart literature. Some sources specfy the Wussin house in the Old City, while others the Konvikt of St. Bartholomew. The latter was a religious school operated by the Jesuits in the Old City from the seventeenth century until their expulsion from the Hapsburg domains in 1773. In 1785, the remaining students were transferred elsewhere. According to an appendix in the *Complete Description of Prague* of 1787, the first public balls at the Konvikt were given that same year in the former dining hall of the school. Later, in the 1790s, it became the venue for concerts given to benefit Mozart's widow Constanze (and also a place to showcase the talents of the young Beethoven).

The Wussin house, unlike the Konvikt of St. Bartholomew, no longer stands. It was once located on a street in the Old City now known as Masná ("meat street"). In Mozart's time, there was an open-air meat market just a short distance away from it. According to the *Complete Description of Prague*, the ball at the Wussin house was the "privileged" ball during the pre-Lenten carnival celebrations. The privileged balls were regulated by the Czech Gubernium under the "ball decree" of 4 September 1780, which specified the amount of money that could be charged for admission.

Documents preserved in the National Archive in Prague confirm that the privileged balls given in the months of January and February were flourishing in the 1780s. Receipts from entrance fees multiplied several times during the period 1781-1786. The patron of the first Konvikt ball was Baron Franz von LaMotte, who came before the Czech Gubernium on 22 December 1786 for the necessary permit (granted on 1 January 1787). The sponsorship for the privileged ball at the Wussin house in 1787 is not specified in any surviving documents, but documents from the next carnival season identify Baron Joseph von Bretfeld as sponsor. His Thursday balls were famous at this time and for years to come. It is extremely unlikely that Mozart would have used the phrase "wont to gather" unless he was attending a ball that already had an established reputation. The Wussin house balls did have a reputation in January of 1787, whereas the Konvikt balls were only starting up. Many organizations in Prague still maintain the tradition of "ball season" today - although attire now ranges from casual to formal.

Mozart clearly found the ball he attended as intriguing as did the author of the *Observations in and about Prague*, but unlike the latter, saw no need to condemn the spectacle for its brazen sexuality. Rather, Mozart's love of sexual and scatological references found a suitable outlet in his description of the event. The author of the *Observations* claimed that the "painted ladies" of the balls in the Wussin house left him "cold as ice." They left Mozart weak-kneed, otherwise he would not have tried to ascribe the effects of his own sexual arousal (the "limping") to his friend Jacquin.

And where was Constanze? Apparently he had left her back at the Thun palace while he indulged his guilty pleasures with Count Canal. No matter; as enticing as the Prague beauties were, Mozart's wife would have had little to fear in the way of marital infidelity.

Fictionalized portrayals of Mozart familiar to music lovers from sources such as the film *Amadeus* make it appear as though sexual promiscuity and skill at seduction are qualities only to be expected from a musical genius. In fact, there is no reason to believe that Mozart had any accomplishments of which to boast in either area, and the "natural reserve" he mentioned in his letter to Jacquin may provide part of the explanation.

A sense of his true attitude toward sexual matters (regardless of the joking and insinuation to be found in his correspondence) can be gleaned from a letter he wrote to his father from Vienna on 15 December 1781. One of its principal aims was to explain why he was so eager to marry Constanze Weber, a choice his father found appalling. Nearly 26 years old, he said that up to that time he had had no sexual relations at all - and was eager to begin - but could not conceive of doing so without benefit of marriage, for reasons of religion and character. It is difficult, if not impossible, to imagine Mozart lying outright to his father in writing (as opposed to concealing facts from him), especially in a case in which information was volunteered and not demanded. Consistent with his strict middle-class Catholic upbringing, a sense of filial piety was instinctive in Mozart, even if he did resent his father's manipulative, controlling nature and was capable of disobeying him or ignoring his advice. Except for the possibility of premarital sex with the woman who did become his wife, there is no credible evidence to suggest that Mozart ever committed adultery in his entire life.

Was Mozart uncomfortable with dancing as well as seduction? Fatigue after a long day seems a convenient excuse for not participating. Public balls were clearly not the type of social occasion that could be counted on to show off Mozart's talents to best advantage. Not only his music, but also his music-making, would have been necessary for that. In an activity such as dancing - one that prized grace and physical beauty - the slight, stooped Mozart could not have cut much of a figure. At the Bretfeld ball, he was a wallflower.

Nonetheless, there does exist an account of Mozart's visit to the Bretfeld ball that portrays him as a skilled dancer, specifically a charming vignette found in Alfred Meissner's *Rococo Portraits after Notes from my Grandfather (Rococo-Bilder: nach Aufzeichnungen meines Grossvaters)*, a collection of stories that was first published in 1871. Meissner claimed that his work was based on voluminous notes kept by his grandfather August Gottlieb Meissner, an author and professor at Charles-Ferdinand University in the late eighteenth century. Supposedly these notes recorded a wealth of political, social, and cultural events that took place in Prague over a 20-year period before the elder Meissner's death in 1807. The grandson never specified where they were stored, and no trace of them has ever been uncovered; in fact, it is possible that they never existed. Much of the material presented in the *Rococo-Bilder* actually appears to have been drawn from the grandson's research about various notable personalities that his grandfather had known or perhaps had only heard about. In his introduction, the younger Meissner explained that he viewed his role as that of an "art restorer." In other words, he sought to "refresh the colors" of the era in which his grandfather had lived. As a result, the *Rococo-Bilder* contains suspiciously detailed character sketches of celebrities who enlivened cultural and political life in Prague and the Austrian Empire during the late eighteenth century. The lengthy dialogues that Meissner attributed to Mozart and others could not have been transcribed verbatim by his grandfather, who had not even been present to hear many of them.

Meissner portrayed the poet Lorenzo Da Ponte, author of the librettos for Mozart's operas *The Marriage of Figaro, Don Giovanni,* and *Così fan tutte*, as a visitor in Prague with Mozart at the Bretfeld ball, a detail corroborated nowhere else. In his memoirs, Da Ponte does not exactly confirm where he was throughout the months of January and February of 1787 (nor has any researcher been able to establish precisely what he was doing then), but it is improbable that he would have traveled to Prague in the middle of winter for any reason other than a professional engagement (of which there was none at this time). Another possibility is that Meissner's depictions of Mozart and Da Ponte actually derive from a ball held in the autumn of 1787, when Da Ponte was certainly present in Prague, or that they represent a conflation of remarks gathered from various places in the original notes of his grandfather. These theories of course are rather charitable toward the younger Meissner, who may simply have fabricated them entirely. Furthermore, Da Ponte's purported opinion that Mozart was "always more cheerful" when he was in Prague is certainly a strange one, since, in the carnival season of 1787, he had never even been there before. The origin of the discussion of German opera by Da Ponte and Meissner's grandfather is also suspicious. His grandfather's prediction about German opera one day taking the upper hand and actually becoming a model for Italian composers was just starting to be realized in the 1860s and 1870s, due mainly to the wide dissemination throughout Europe of the operatic music of Richard Wagner and - almost equally important - his writings about music.

Lorenzo Da Ponte
by Samuel F. B. Morse

Unreliable as they are, the *Rococo-Bilder* sketches are impossible to ignore for their humanity, entertainment value, and overall plausible evocations of the personalities that appear in them. Thus all passages relevant to Mozart's visits will be translated in full for the first time in this volume, starting with Meissner's version of the events at the Bretfeld ball of January 1787. The Italian phrases that supposedly peppered Da Ponte's conversation have been transcribed in brackets next to the English translations:

> Baron Bretfeld's balls had been famous for years, but in the winter of 1787 they were especially brilliant. Everyone conspicuous for rank, beauty, wealth, or talent was invited there. Two medium-sized halls were devoted to dancing, whereas three adjoining rooms were intended for buffets and "shadowy" activities.
>
> This time all attention was centered on two personalities - one of whom moved about with great liveliness - and the interest they infused was hardly to be suspected. On the one hand there was a thick-set man, inclined toward corpulence, who could be referred to as rather short. He was barely over 30 years' old and wore his unusually

voluminous hair tied into a thick pigtail. This was Mozart, whose *Marriage of Figaro* had recently been performed in Prague and had made a furor.

Mozart had a great need for social intercourse, and he gladly circulated among the many people present. He was not one to object to enjoying himself at the dinner table or disdain any invitation to a party that promised to meet with his idea of a good time. In Vienna it was customary for him to take part in the merry St. Bridget's day celebrations [on February 1, during the carnival season], usually dressed as [the *commedia dell'arte* character] Pierrot. [The pre-Lenten] carnival [season in Vienna] was truly a time of boisterousness for him, and here in Prague he was also not prudish.

He possessed an uninhibited and giving nature. In conversation he never revealed the genius that resided in him, and whether he was walking about with his host or when he was amusing himself with ladies, he indulged himself with harmless puns, which now and again were spiced with double meanings.

The second foreigner was a man in his forties, whom, it seemed, all the female singers paid court to. He was short, lean, moved at the speed of quicksilver, and had the black, fiery eyes of a southern European. In contrast to Mozart, he was a man who appeared to observe the effect of every glance he made. His broken German identified him as an Italian and he was addressed as Signor Abbate, even though nobody thought of him as a cleric. Everyone in France or Italy called Abbé or Abbate was either intended originally for a religious order or only had undertaken instruction in a theological institution in hopes that he would be granted a prebend, i.e., a stipend from the income of a cloister. They formed their own social class; there were rich ones and poor ones, talented and untalented, the "household friends" of families. With coiled locks of hair, and short brown, violet, or black attire, the Abbé was ready-made.

The merry Amphitryon of the gathering [in Greek mythology Amphitryon was a venerable general, stepfather of Hercules], old Baron Bretfeld, circulated untiringly through the halls as an inspector, making certain during the breaks between the dances to reinforce the cheerfulness of his guests until he called for the first chord of music in a choreographed gesture. The old man truly looked astonishingly youthful, and he accepted the compliment of my grandfather on his handsome appearance with great satisfaction.

"Is it not true," he called out, "that I do not look my sixty years of age?" (He was already in his seventies [in fact, he turned 67 years of age in 1787].) "But now I also have a new Hippocrates [i.e., a new physician]. His simple regimen serves me better than everything I required before. No more roborants - I am ruddy and plethoric enough. No more spicy foods, wine, truffles, chinoiserie, Voltaire and Crébillon and your *Alcibiades* [a literary work by A. G. Meissner] - no more of that, only calming agents: tea and lemonade along with [Christian] Gellert's poems. This calms and decreases the congestion of my still youthful blood…"

At this moment he took the foreigner with the southern eyes under his arm. "Your friend Mozart," he said, "I like very much." He is a true Viennese, always a good fellow, *bon enfant*, and besides everything else that can be said about him, an excellent minuet dancer!"

"Oh, my dear Amadeus [*mio caro Amadeo*] is always more cheerful when he comes to Prague," answered the foreigner. "Here people give him their affection. It seizes the heart and the mind [*prende cuore, piglia animo*]. He knows that he can find friends here - how can one say it? - who know how to appreciate him, esteem his talents, value him [*appressare, stimare, dare prezzo*]…"

"In fact, I do believe that the Praguers know better how to appreciate him than the Viennese," the baron said.

"Oh, in Vienna he is a buried jewel. I do what I can within my powers to promote him, to bring his genius to the light of day - but this great talent, beautiful as the day, beautiful as the sun, splendid as the star of the day [*bello come il sole, splendido come il astro del sole*], has to battle with dense air, with the fog of criticism [*colla nebbia dei giudizzi*], with stupidity and evil intentions. Oh, and that frequently discourages him!"

"You are a true friend indeed," the baron answered. "I have been told that without your energy and persistence *Figaro* never ever would have come to the stage, this *Figaro* that delights us so much now."

"Never again will this play of Beaumarchais that I laid before him be considered immoral, indecent, detestable. All sorts of cabals were arrayed against it. It took all my power and application to overcome the impediments. I arranged an audience with His Majesty, who made a personal decision - "

"A command."

"Yes, a command. An emphatic command [*A comandato a bacchetta*]."

"Surely I am not mistaken," my grandfather injected himself into the conversation, "when I presume to be speaking to the Abbate Da Ponte?"

"That is him indeed," answered the baron. "It is only my opinion that you already knew the gentleman here that is to blame for my not introducing you long ago." He introduced them.

"Have you ever directed a theater?" [Da Ponte asked my grandfather.]

"I have not done that, but when I was a young man I wrote several librettos. But I was not as fortunate as you to have a genius to write for, and therefore they are today already forgotten. You are an enviable bird of luck, Abbé; perhaps you don't realize how much so."

"Signor Professore," answered Da Ponte, "you wrote your librettos in German. As such they cannot be valued, are destined for ruin [*sono sacrati alla rovina*], they must sink to the ground. That would be called wasting talent [*spender il talento inutilmente*]."

"You believe Signor Abbate, that there is no such thing as German opera?"

"Never, never! This language is not made for music, not made for singing, and also - permit me to say it - not made for poetry. It is too clumsy, and there is something too heavy about it [*ha qualche cosa di troppo pesante*]. I know, I know, these German authors have talent and ideas, but the language! The language! To write a German opera is a waste of a lot of time and effort on a lost cause [*cosa perduta*]."

"I believe, my dear professor," the baron cut in, "I believe that the Abbate is correct! Only the Italians and the French truly have art, poetry, music, and ballet. We are still half barbarians. The palm tree of art thrives only under Hesperian skies. However - the music is starting, the dance lines are forming, people are waiting for me. Farewell, farewell!"

My grandfather, in whose chest beat a strong German patriotic heart, did not abandon the field so quickly. "Signor Abbate," he called out, "I would disagree with you in that every nationality cultivates art only for itself. If we consider our language resonant, if it sounds melodic to our ears, that is sufficient. But in fact it also has a power that no other language has: the best imagery and suppleness of form; it has an energetic beauty. Are not melodic-sounding lines already poetry? And what is poetry? The content of thought and feelings, which burn and glow in the breasts and heads of the Germans just as they do in Italians. Might it not be that the differing intonation of the Romance languages induces shallowness and triviality rather than enhancing true poetry? Truly, is it not a good thing, when the poet so to speak has the ripe grapes of rhymes hanging from his mouth! In any case German is better suited for singing than French and English, and so we will not only have an opera, Signor Abbate, we already have German theater! I can foresee the day in which French and Italians, in order to refresh the spent sources of their productions, will seize German originals."

With that he went away, leaving the Abbate to shrug his shoulders.

After the Ball

Mozart's own account of his first visit to Prague from 15 January 1787 continues as follows with reference to the events of 12 January, his second day there:

> …Now back to the course of my day. As I got home very late from the ball and moreover was tired and sleepy after my trip, nothing in the world could be more natural than that I would sleep very late, which was just what I did - Consequently the whole of the next morning was spent again without writing a line. - After lunch the Count's music must never be forgotten, and as on that very day a quite good piano had been put in my room, you can easily imagine that I did not leave it unused and unplayed for the whole evening; and that as a matter of course we would perform a little quartet among ourselves (*Und das schöne Bandl hammera*), and in this way fritter away the whole evening without writing a line; and this is just what happened. - Now you must scold Morpheus on my behalf; that deity looks down on both of us very favorably in Prague; - the reason for this I do not know; no matter, we are sleeping very well…

In ancient Greek mythology, Morpheus was the god of dreams, not of sleep (his father Hypnos was the god of sleep), but the confusion is common in writings of the day. The composition that Mozart mentioned by name as "Und das schöne Bandl hammera" ("And we also have the pretty ribbon"), K. 441, is better known by the name "Liebes Mandel, wo is's Bandel?" ("Dear husband, where is my ribbon?"). In its original form, it was a humorous piece for three voices and instruments about a real-life incident in which Mozart's wife Constanze dropped a ribbon during a stroll in Vienna, perhaps in 1783. Sometimes it is referred to as the "ribbon trio" (the "Bandel-Terzett"). The reference to a quartet here likely indicates that Mozart played a reduction of the original instrumental accompaniment on the piano while the vocal parts were performed by three of Mozart's companions - perhaps his wife Constanze, his future brother-in-law Franz de Paula Hofer, and the clarinettist Anton Stadler. The piece had a personal connection to Jacquin, who is portrayed in the text as picking up the ribbon that Constanze had dropped, but not letting Constanze have it back until she or Wolfgang could catch it from him (he was much taller than either of them). Undoubtedly that is why Mozart took such pains to make mention it.

Mozart continued his narrative with the events of Saturday, 13 January 1787:

> …Still, we managed to be at Father Ungar's already at eleven o'clock and inspected the Royal and Imperial Library and General Theological Seminary high and low; - After we had almost stared our eyes out of our heads, we thought we heard a little growling in our stomachs and thus found ourselves driving to Count Canal's for lunch…

Raphael Ungar, a member of the Praemonstratensian monastic order, was another one of Mozart's Masonic acquaintances, co-founder of the "Truth and Unity" lodge in Prague, along with Count Canal and a correspondent of members of Viennese lodges. According to Karl Heinrich Krögen, author of the *Free Remarks* of 1785, he was a stupendous glutton. The General Theological Seminary and the Royal and Imperial Library were both housed in the Klementinum, a severe seventeenth-century structure in the Old City originally built for the use of the Jesuits. Before their expulsion from the Hapsburg domains in 1773, the seminary mentioned by Mozart was known as the Jesuit College.

In addition to the books, Ungar oversaw a vast collection of scientific specimens. Mozart certainly could not have seen very many books or specimens on such a short tour, and it is more likely that the sights that led him to stare so much were actually the fascinating sacred frescoes that decorate the hallways and reading rooms. Then as now, the displaced Jesuits haunt the building through the medium of these frescoes. Mozart might also have seen two exquisitely beautiful churches within the Klementinum complex that also cause visitors to stare: the so-called Italian Chapel (in Renaissance style) and the Church of the Holy Savior (in Baroque style).

Just across Křížovnická street to the west of the Klementinum is the baroque Church of St. Francis Serafin, a traditional venue for performances of oratorios in eighteenth-century Prague. Perhaps someone pointed out the musical interest of this church to Mozart. It would have been difficult to overlook, since its dome dominates the skyline over the right bank of the Vltava. Someone might also have drawn Mozart's attention to another building just across the street from the Klementinum: one to the south, a splendid palace owned by Count (later Prince) Franz de Paula Adam Gundackar von Colloredo-Mannsfeld, the eldest brother of Hieronymous von Colloredo, Mozart's former employer in Salzburg. The palace had come to the count in 1780 as part of an inheritance received by his wife, the Countess Maria Isabella, from her father. (The countess is known to have been a patron of Mozart's English friends in Vienna. A letter of 1-2 March 1787, written by Leopold Mozart to his daughter Nannerl, mentions that the countess wrote a letter of introduction to her brother-in-law in Salzburg on behalf of the singer Nancy Storace, so that she and her friends could find hospitality there on their way back to Britain.)

According to the *Complete Description of Prague* of 1787, the palace of Count Canal, where Mozart went to lunch, overlooked a stretch of today's filled-in moat that separated the Old City from the New City. The modern name for this area is Na příkopě ("on the moat"); in Mozart's day, it was called "Der Graben" ("the ditch"). Trees were planted all along it in order to make it more attractive for strolling. On the New City side of the "ditch" was a block of residences that included the palaces of several noble families. The only ones remaining today are the Sylva-Taroucca palace and the Vernier palace, interspersed as they are among commercial buildings of varying age and beauty. The former location of Count Canal's palace corresponds to the west corner of the modern-day streets Na příkopě and Nekázanka.

An advantage of the location of Count Canal's palace was its proximity to the National Theater, where the Bondini company performed operas on Mondays, Wednesdays, and Saturdays. On this particular Saturday of 13 January 1787, a most distinguished spectator - Mozart - presented himself:

> …The evening surprised us sooner than you might believe; - enough, it was time to go to the opera. - So we heard *Le gare generose*. - What the performance of the opera was like, I cannot say anything definite because I was chattering a lot; just why I was chattering contrary to my usual habit is a subject I would like to let lie. - Enough; this evening was also frittered away as usual…

Could this passage provide evidence of a flirtation? It is difficult to imagine what other reason Mozart might have had for wanting to conceal details about whomever it was that he was chattering with. The theater piece in question is an obscure comic opera by Giovanni Paisiello that was new at the time of Mozart's visit (it had received its first performance in Naples the preceding spring, roughly the same time that *The Marriage of Figaro* was first heard in Vienna).

There is no mention in the Jacquin letter of what Mozart did on Sunday, 14 January. For those who know the city of Prague today, it is enjoyable to speculate whether or not he worshipped in one of the churches that can still be seen in the Malá Strana or Hradčany districts, in particular the exceptionally beautiful church of St. Nicholas, only a short walk from the Thun palace, where his death was commemorated with such pomp in 1791. But instead of clarifying this point, Mozart chose to devote the remainder of his letter of 15 January to flattery:

> …Today at last I have been so fortunate as to find a moment to inquire about the well-being of your dear parents and the whole Jacquin household. I hope and wish with all my heart that you are all as well as we are. - I must frankly admit that (although I have met with all possible courtesies and honors here and Prague is indeed a very beautiful and pleasant place) I long very much to be back in Vienna; and believe me, the principal reason for this is certainly your family. - When I think that after my return I will enjoy only for a short while the pleasure of your valued company and then so long - and perhaps forever - have to do without this pleasure, then I realize the full extent of the friendship and regard that I hold for your entire family; - Now farewell, dearest friend, dearest Hinkiti Honky! That is your name, just so you know. We all invented names for ourselves on our journey, and here they are. I am Punkitititi. - My wife is SchablaPumfa. - Hofer is RozkaPumpa. Stadler is Nàtschibinìtschibi. My servant Joseph is Sagadaratà. My dog Gaukerl is Schamanuzky. - Madame Quallenberg is Runzifunzi. - Mademoiselle Crux is PS. Ramlo is Schurimuri. Freystädtler is Gaulimauli. Be so kind as to tell him his name…

It is completely unknown just what Mozart meant when he referred to the short time he would be able to enjoy Jacquin's company after returning to Vienna. Of greater interest is the attitude he revealed toward Prague. For the time being, he could not wait to leave it. Even though the storybook quaintness of the historic districts of Prague would not have been such a novelty in his day as it is today, he did at least have an appreciation for the beauty of the city, and he was grateful for the hospitality he received there.

Perhaps some of the most telling evidence of Mozart's attitude about Prague and the Bohemian people can be found in his silly game of creating nicknames, a reflection of a side of his character that is much explored in the film *Amadeus* - i.e., Mozart as Peter Pan, or the boy who never grew up. Some of the names appear to be parodies of the sounds of Czech language. Indications of this come from the emphasis on stressed first syllables and the soft "s" and "c" in words such as "Nàtschibinìtschibi." In modern Czech, this might be rendered "Náčibiníčiby," but it is still a nonsense word. Many Czech words begin with the accented syllable "ná," and many Czech phrases begin with the accented preposition "ná" ("on" or "at"). Some Americans who learned the Czech folksong "Stodola Pumpa" in elementary school will recognize the similarity of the words "SchablaPumfa" and "RozkaPumpa." "Pumpa" in Czech is cognate with the German "pump" (as well as with the English "pump") and has the same meaning. The adjectival ending in the name "Schamanuzky" (which might be rendered in modern Czech as "Šámanucký") also indicates an attentiveness to the sound of Czech.

Mozart was an accomplished linguist, but mastery of Czech was not a priority for him. It is possible to interpret Mozart's nonsense words as a manifestation of the same insecurities experienced by some present-day travelers to the Czech Republic who are confronted with an unfamiliar and complex language. For those who imagine themselves experiencing the country from a position of cultural superiority, ridicule and mimicry become easy techniques for assuaging feelings of awkwardness and ignorance.

The composition of Mozart's large traveling party is partially baffling. The traveling party was in fact so large that it would have been required to hire two coachmen and at least six horses by law. Among the persons involved with the planning of the expedition, it seems that only Count Thun could have afforded the travel expenses outright. There would be no surprise about the presence of his wife, but a dog does not seem as obvious a choice as his son, who did not come along. The fact that he took a servant along is yet another reminder - if any were needed by this time - that Mozart was really not at all the starving musician of legend. True, he was frequently short of ready cash, but at no time in his life did Mozart experience anything resembling genuine poverty, which in Europe of the 1780s would have involved a basic lack of food or shelter. In an era when the vast majority of Europeans were agricultural workers or manual laborers living at subsistence level, it would be outrageous to consider anyone able to engage domestic servants as impoverished. As for the servant's name, one can hardly resist drawing attention to a remark found in the novel *The Lady of the Camellias* by Alexandre Dumas. At one point, the principal character Armand Duval mentions to the narrator that his servant was named Joseph, "just like all servants" ("mon domestique s'appelait Joseph, comme tous les domestiques").

The inclusion of Hofer, a future brother-in-law, as one of Mozart's traveling companions could also be understandable, but there is some mystery concerning Anton Stadler, one of the greatest clarinettists of the day, unless his presence can be attributed to Mozart's Masonic connections. Marianne Crux was a fourteen-year-old violin virtuoso and student of Mozart who passed herself off as a thirteen-year-old; the obscure Madame Quallenberg was her chaperone. Crux did perform successfully at a public concert at Count Thun's palace in Prague on 22 January; perhaps Mozart viewed her as a protegée and had taken her along in order to help break her in as an experienced performer. Ramlo was the very little known violinist Kaspar Ramlo, later a musician at the court of Bavaria. It would be intriguing to learn which of his companions were Mozart's guests, which ones were Count Thun's guests, and which ones (if any) had to pay their own way.

The last person mentioned as having a special nickname was Franz Jakob Freystädler, one of Mozart's pupils in Vienna. In this case, the nickname "Gaulimauli" stuck. Later in 1787, Mozart composed a canon, K. 232, on the words, "Lieber Freystädtler, lieber Gaulimauli" ("Dear Freystädtler, dear Gaulimauli"). Freystädtler's nickname has no apparent Slavic elements. Rather it appears to be based on the German words "Gaul" (horse, but more properly an old nag) and "Maul" (mouth). "Runzifunzi" is probably meant to derive from "Runzel" (wrinkle) or "runzlig" (wrinkled), perhaps an appropriate attribute for a chaperone such as Elisabeth Barbara Quallenberg.

Mozart's rambling close does reveal some additional interesting information:

> ...Goodbye now. My concert is to take place in the theater next Friday, the 19th, and presumably I will have to give a second one; unfortunately that will prolong my stay here. I ask that you give my regards to your worthy parents and embrace your brother (who could be called Blatterizi if need be) a thousand times for me - and I kiss your sister's hands (she is Signora Diniminimi) a hundred thousand times with the request that she practice diligently on her new pianoforte - but this admonition is unnecessary, for I must admit that I have never yet had a female pupil who was so diligent and who showed so much zeal as she does - and indeed I am looking forward to giving her lessons again according to my inferior ability. - By the way, if she wants to come tomorrow - I will certainly be at home at eleven o'clock. But now it is surely time to close - is it not? - You have been thinking that already a long time. - Farewell, my best friend! - Keep me in your precious friendship. - Write to me soon - quite soon - and if perhaps you are too lazy to do so, send for a scribe and dictate a letter to him - even though no letter comes as much from the heart as it does when one writes oneself; now - I will see whether you are as truly my friend as I am entirely yours and always will be.
>
> Mozart
>
> P.S: Address the letter which you might write to me at Count Thun's palace. My wife sends her best to the whole Jacquin household, and so does Hofer.
>
> NB. On Wednesday I am to see and hear *Figaro*, - if I do not become deaf and blind by then. - Perhaps I will once the opera is over - - -

It was an affectation of Mozart's era to offer "thousands," if not "millions," of kisses to female relatives and friends in correspondence. Posterity may thank the "diligence" of Jacquin's sister Franziska as a piano student, since it led Mozart to compose for her the Piano Trio, K. 498, of 1786, and the Piano Sonata, K. 521, of 1787. Why a name like "Blatterizi" would be appropriate for Gottfried's brother Joseph

Franz more than likely has to do with an interest in botany that he shared with his father: "Blatt" is the German word for "leaf."

The Mozart Concert of January 19

The concert Mozart intended to give at the National Theater was not something that could be arranged informally. For a public concert there, express permission was required from the Czech Gubernium. Whether or not Mozart himself had to undergo the indignity of making the journey uphill to Prague Castle himself for the purpose of requesting it is unknown, but permission was granted on Thursday, 28 January 1787, one day before the concert actually took place. The decree issued by the Gubernium makes no mention of Mozart's presence before it or the requirement of his signature for any purpose; everything may well have been arranged through the impresario Bondini.

There is no question that Mozart's concert, once it occurred, was an unforgettable event for many of those who witnessed it. The driest account comes from the *Prague Post*, which left this description in an issue of 23 January 1787 (the notice itself is dated 21 January):

> On Friday the 19th Herr Mozard [sic] gave a concert on the piano in our National Theater. Everything that was to be expected of this great artist he fulfilled completely. Yesterday he himself conducted the opera *Figaro*, this work of his genius.

Thus the performance of *The Marriage of Figaro* alluded to in the Jacquin letter did in fact take place. Němeček was probably referring to this performance when he remarked that "on the day of his arrival *Figaro* was performed and Mozart made an appearance. At once the news of his presence spread in the parterre, and as soon as the overture ended the entire audience broke into applause to welcome him." This would not be the only instance in which Němeček was confused about dates, since he claimed that Mozart had first come to Prague in February, not January, of 1787.

As imprecise as his memory was for dates, the sincerity of Němeček's impression of the Mozart concert can leave little room for doubt:

> In response to a general demand, he gave a grand musical concert on the piano at the opera house. Never had the theater been so full of people as on this occasion, never had there been such strong, unanimous enthusiasm as that awakened by his divine playing. We did not, in fact, know what to admire most, whether the extraordinary composition or the extraordinary playing; both together they made such an overwhelming impression on our souls that it was as if we had been bewitched!
>
> But this mood dissolved, when Mozart at the end of the concert improvised alone at the piano for more than half an hour and our delight reached the highest level in loud, overflowing applause. And indeed his improvisations exceeded anything that could be imagined in the way of piano-playing, as the highest degree of the composer's art was joined with the highest skill in playing.
>
> Certainly, just as this concert was something quite unique for the people of Prague, so Mozart counted this day as one of the happiest of his life. The symphonies

he composed for this occasion are true masterpieces of instrumental composition, full of surprising turns and exhibiting a brisk, fiery momentum, so that the soul is carried to a state of exaltation. This applies particularly to the great symphony in D major [the "Prague" Symphony], which is still a favorite of the Prague public, even though it might well have been heard a hundred times.

The opera director Bondini commissioned Mozart to compose a new opera for the Prague stage for the following winter, which he gladly undertook to do, because he had experienced how much the Bohemians valued his music and how well they executed it. He often mentioned this to his acquaintances in Prague; he was always glad to visit Prague, where he found a sympathetic public and true friends who carried him, so to speak, on their hands. He thanked the opera orchestra obligingly in a letter to Herr Strobach, the director at the time, and attributed the greater part of the positive reception his music had received in Prague to their excellent execution. This trait in his character, insignificant though it may seem, is very lovely; it shows that pride, conceit, or ingratitude were not faults of his, as is so often the case with much lesser virtuosos.

Georg Nikolaus
von Nissen

In spite of Němeček's indication, there is no reason to believe that any more than one symphony was written by Mozart specifically for this occasion - which would have been the "Prague" Symphony, of course - although it is possible that he may well have brought a preexistent symphony or two with him that had never been heard in Prague before.

Another account of the concert of 19 January survives in the Mozart biography written by Georg Nikolaus von Nissen, the wealthy Danish diplomat who happened to be Constanze Mozart's second husband. Nissen was almost as devoted to the memory of her first husband as he was to Constanze herself. The Nissen biography, perhaps begun in 1823 or 1824, was left unfinished at the time of the author's death in 1826 and had to be completed by two associates who brought it to publication in 1828. Nissen's version of what happened is a transcription of a reminiscence taken down by the incumbent director of the Estates' Theater in the early 1820s, Jan Nepomuk Štěpánek. It was embedded in a long introduction to Štěpánek's Czech translation of the libretto to Mozart's opera *Don Giovanni* that had been supplied to Nissen by a professor at Prague Conservatory. The translation with its introduction was published in Prague in 1825, but only in greatly abbreviated form. The Nissen biography is the only surviving source of what appears to be Štěpánek's full, original text (although Nissen published it in German in preference to the original Czech). Precisely from where Štěpánek got his information is a mystery. Born in 1783, he was certainly too young to have been able to record such a detailed account of Mozart's concert by relying solely on his own memory, if indeed he had even been present for it:

> ...During his stay Mozart gave a grand musical concert in the opera theater in which all the pieces performed were composed by him. How much this seized every-

one's hearts cannot be described; it could only have been felt at the time. At the end of the concert Mozart improvised at the piano for a good half an hour, and by this means raised the enthusiasm of the delighted Bohemians to the highest level, indeed so high, that as he started to inch his way through the crowd, he was forced back and had to sit himself again on the piano. The stream of this new improvesation grew with ever greater force and had the result that he was assaulted for the third time by the inflamed listeners. Mozart appeared. Inner contentment for the universal, enthusiastic acknowledgment of his artistic workmanship shone from his face. He began for the third time with even more excited inspiration, performing what had never been heard before, when at a moment of deathly silence a loud voice in the parterre rose up with the words "Something from *Figaro*!" at which Mozart started up a motive from the favorite aria "Non più andrai" and produced off the top of his head a dozen of the most interesting and artful variations. With this he brought to an end a remarkable artistic performance with the greatest rush of jubilation. For him it was certainly the most glorious day of his life and for the delirious Bohemians the most richly enjoyable.

The extraordinary nature of this event is difficult to exaggerate. The musical public of Prague witnessed something on the evening of 19 January 1787 that was unprecedented in eighteenth-century Europe. In the profession of music, adulation of the type that the ordinary music lovers of Prague accorded Mozart was generally reserved only for opera singers. For an instrumentalist to achieve it simultaneously in recognition of two distinct aspects of musical talent (performance and composition) would ordinarily have been beyond the realm of imagination. Mozart had never experienced anything like it before, and he never would again for the rest of his life. A similar scene would be inconceivable in honor of any living composer of "art" music.

Additional Activities During Mozart's First Stay in Prague

The amazing reception that Mozart was able to enjoy for his concert of 19 January may well have changed his attitude about remaining in Prague. There can be no question that he stayed longer than expected, perhaps with a view towards cashing in on his reputation. In his letter to Jacquin, Mozart said that he expected a delay for the purpose of another concert, but in spite of a claim made in the Nissen biography, no record of such an event has ever been uncovered.

Exactly what Mozart did during the last weeks of his first stay in Prague, and just how long he put off his return to Vienna, is not precisely known. All that is certain is that he must have gotten back by mid-February, or he could not have transmitted information about his trip that his English friends knew about when they visited his father Leopold in Salzburg later in the month. The possibility that he left the palace of Count Thun and stayed with the Dušeks is invited by a remark made by Leopold Mozart in a letter written to his daughter on 26 January 1787. He told her, "Herr Dušek is back in Prague. The good man! Presumably your brother will stay with him." No confirmation of a move has ever been uncovered. As pleasant as it would have been to stay just outside of Prague in the Dušeks' lovely villa, it still could not have offered the comforts of a nobleman's palace, including a working theater and a casino on the premises. As an aspect of Bondini's role in providing entertainment to the upper classes of Prague, the author of the *Observations* noted that the impresario operated a casino for the use of the nobility in Count Thun's palace. There is no way of knowing whether or not Mozart chose to sample this amusement in addition to the other amenities offered him by Count Thun. It has become fashionable recently to blame gambling as the principal cause of Mozart squandering so much of his income - even though there is no direct evidence of a gambling addiction from either his own writings or from the testimony of any individuals who knew him.

The last firm record of his presence in Prague comes from a collection of six contredanses for orchestra, K. 509, that were entered into Mozart's own catalog of compositions with a date of 6 February 1787. According to the manuscript, they were composed for one of the Counts Pachta. Their composition leaves no doubt that Mozart continued to sample the seductive culture of the carnival balls of Prague after his first taste of them in the company of Count Canal. Many were going on during the carnival season of 1787 in the Wussin house, the Konvikt, the inn "Zum Bade," and the National Theater, in addition to any number of private residences. The *Prague Post* of 20 February 1787 reported that the balls of the ongoing season had been particularly brilliant.

The identity of the Count Pachta specified in the manuscript of contredanses has always been problematic; several members of this family lived in Prague, and confusion about their identities persists because of a close similarity in Christian names among several family members. The present author was fortunate to have at his disposal information supplied by a descendant of the family, the physician Count Percival von Pachta, to help sort things out. Family legend holds that the dances were written for the long-lived Count Johann Josef von Pachta (1723-1822), a distinguished patron of music in Prague, although another member of the family, Count Johann's nephew Johann Joseph Philipp von Pachta (1756-1834), was also a friend of Mozart, as well as an acquaintance of Carl Maria von Weber and the young Richard Wagner. Count Johann Joseph Philipp was a talented musician in his own right who was exactly Mozart's age. He married a daughter of Count Canal the very year of Mozart's first visit to Prague. In consideration of that connection, it is possible that the contredanses were written for him. In sum, the most likely candidates for recipient of the contredanses, K. 509, would be either Count Johann Joseph Phillip or Count Franz Joseph, but no definitive identification is possible.

It is not certain whether or not these dances were used for the balls in one of the Pachta residences, or if so, which one. The *Complete Description of Prague* of 1787 lists three palaces owned by members of the Pachta family. The only one that is still standing today was owned at that time by Count Hubert Karl von Pachta (1755-1809), the older brother of Count Johann Joseph Philipp. This palace is located in St. Anne's square (Anenské náměstí) in the Old City. Pachta family legend has it that Mozart did visit this palace, but at present no independent documentation exists.

A more likely candidate for a visit by Mozart is the Pachta palace located on what would now be the corner of Platnéřská and Křížovnická streets in the Old City, a building so large that it is referred to as the "Pachta hotel" in the *Complete Description of Prague*. Jaroslaus Schaller's four-volume *Description of the City of Prague, the Royal Capital and Royal Residence* (*Beschreibung der Königlichen Hauptund Residenzstadt Prag*), published between 1794 and 1797, identifies it as the palace of Count Franz Joseph von Pachta (d. 1799), brother of Count Johann Joseph. This palace certainly would have been a suitable venue for a grand carnival ball. It was adjacent to a square known at that time as the "Tummel-platz" ("the playground"), now corresponding roughly to modern-day Jan Palach square.

One last incident that is a bit difficult to pin down chronologically - but which must have taken place during Mozart's first trip to Prague - was a visit to the Noble Ladies' Foundation in the New City. Readers with good memories will recall the complaint of Count Kaspar von Sternberg that this foundation, devoted to the care of destitute noblewomen, was forcibly ejected by the emperor Joseph II from its longtime location overlooking the "cattle market" ("Viehmarkt") of Prague, now Charles Square in the New City. According to *The Complete Description of Prague*, the Noble Ladies' Foundation in the New City had originally been endowed in 1705 by the emperor Joseph I as a private girls' school for daughters of the most prominent Bohemian families. Candidates for entrance had to prove several generations of noble blood from both parents. Joseph II had the structure made over into a maternity hospital, and a hospital functions on the same site even today on a street called "U nemocnice" ("At the hospital") that skirts Charles Square.

According to the first volume of Schaller's *Description of Prague*, the last residents of the New City foundation were forced to join the noblewomen housed in a similar foundation within the grounds of Prague Castle. The nominal "abbess" of that institution was none other than the archduchess Maria Anna of Austria, the daughter of Maria Theresa whose disability had rendered her unmarriageable. The foundation in the castle complex had been started in 1755 by Maria Theresa herself, just across a short lane from the medieval church of St. George. Its exterior appears today exactly as it did in Mozart's day. Schaller included an amazing list of strict regulations that the residents of the foundation had to observe in a fashion similar to the rules of monastic orders. At least they were permitted to leave occasionally to attend operas and balls (albeit "unmasked" ones only). All remaining residents of the New City foundation were moved to lodgings within the Prague Castle complex by 10 September 1787.

The evidence that Mozart visited the New City foundation comes, in fact, from a musical instrument - an eighteenth-century piano that had once belonged to it. Paul Nettl reported it in 1938 in the possession of Count Oswald Thun Hohenstein-Salm in Lipová Castle (Schloss Hainspach). During the Communist era in the former Czechoslovakia, the piano could usually be seen in the Bertramka villa, where it remained until 2005. Since 2007, after restoration, it has been on display at the Czech Museum of Music on Karmelitská street in the Malá Strana district of Prague. Nettl reported that the instrument bore an old plaque with the legend "Wolfgang Amadeus Mozart played on this piano in the year 1787." Since Mozart did not return to Prague from Vienna a second time until October of 1787, he would have had to have played the instrument for the residents of the New City foundation during his first trip in January and February of the same year, before the last residents were ejected in September 1787.

The financial success of Mozart's first trip to Prague must have been at least as gratifying as the artistic acclaim he gleaned. Details about this come from a letter of Leopold Mozart written to his daughter on 1-2 March 1787. Leopold learned a number of things about his son's affairs from the party of English musicians who were traveling through Salzburg on 26 February on their way back to Britain from Vienna that he felt should have been told to him personally. Leopold complained to his daughter that Wolfgang had never answered a letter he had sent to Prague, which was why he was relaying news about the trip to Prague gleaned from the English visitors.

The Church of St. George,
©George Christoforidis

Leopold told Nannerl that Wolfgang had earned 1000 gulden in Prague, a handsome sum of money indeed. There is no indication of precisely how he had earned all of it. On a more somber note, the strained relations between father and son meant that it was not until this time - and from strangers - that Leopold learned of the death in the previous November of his grandson Johann Thomas Leopold. Wolfgang's plans to travel to London had by no means been abandoned (nor were they even at the time of Mozart's death in December of 1791). The English visitors told Leopold that Wolfgang first wanted Thomas Attwood to arrange some type of engagement in London - especially an opera commission - before he would actually be able to go. How he could have expected an unknown musician in his early twenties to arrange such a thing is baffling, a perfect illustration of Mozart's habitual impracticality.

Leopold told Nannerl that he had already sent his son another discouraging letter about traveling to London, explaining that the whole idea was pointless without 2000 gulden in the bank for traveling expenses and the firm promise of some sort of musical employment. Apparently Wolfgang realized the sense of these arguments himself and gave up all thought of London for the time being. In a letter to his father of 4 April 1787, Wolfgang insisted that he had written to his father from Prague twice. He thought perhaps that a servant of Count Thun had merely pocketed the postage money and discarded the letters. Unfortunately, he did not choose to offer any new details about his trip that might have been contained in the missing correspondence.

If not London, there was still Prague to supplement Mozart's musical opportunities in Vienna. According to Němeček, the impresario Bondini promised an operatic commission to Mozart for the following autumn as a result of his success during the winter (see above). While all three of Mozart's extended visits to Prague resulted in the composition of masterpieces, his second trip would lead to the greatest of all: the opera *Don Giovanni*. There would also be another round of hospitality, this one involving a different circle of acquaintances even more interesting than those who had kept Mozart company the first time he had visited Prague.

Dome and Spire of St. Nicholas
©Martin Sladký

6

Seduction on the Mind: Mozart's Second Visit and the Première of *Don Giovanni*

Few Mozart enthusiasts would doubt that there have been many more fictional treatments of incidents from the composer's life than what is found in the play and film *Amadeus*, but what might come as a surprise to many is the existence of a masterpiece of German literature set around nothing more than the short trip Mozart took from Vienna to Prague in the autumn of 1787: Eduard Mörike's *Mozart on His Journey to Prague* (*Mozart auf der Reise nach Prag*).

The Mörike novella, first published in 1855, brings to life the tantalizing fantasy of what it might have been like to have Wolfgang Amadeus Mozart as a house guest. The composer and his wife are portrayed as happening upon the estate of a Moravian nobleman who decides to put them up for a short time while on their way to Prague. In return for their hospitality, the nobleman and his family are treated to some enjoyable music-making and a great deal of stimulating conversation. It is clear that Mörike studied the Mozart correspondence carefully. The dialogues he created perfectly capture the composer's sardonic sense of humor and refreshingly blunt manner of expressing himself. Mozart was nothing if not opinionated, and the topics Mörike touched upon included the composer's professional frustrations, his family relationships, his irritation with social customs of his day, and his ideas about the creation of the opera *Don Giovanni*, which was about to be performed in Prague. A particularly sensitive item of discussion was Mozart's relationship with his father, whose sudden death in Salzburg on 28 May 1787 had come as quite a shock.

What can come as a shock to readers of the Mozart correspondence is the way the composer spoke of his father in a series of letters written to his sister and brother-in-law between June and September of 1787. Wolfgang's relationship with his father had always been affected by mutual character flaws, but in earlier correspondence, Wolfgang comes off as an almost perfect son - respectful, affectionate, and obedient (at least to a point). The letters from the summer of 1787 present quite a contrast. Expressions of bereavement seem perfunctory, and the reader is left with the impression that Wolfgang's only interest in his father's death was the potential for inheritance.

In fairness, Wolfgang had good reason to concern himself so much with money. His family was not financially secure, unlike his sister's, and he must have been aware that the basis of his father's modest fortune was his own earnings as a child musician. No trust fund had even been set up for Mozart to draw upon once he reached maturity. Rather, in keeping with contemporary custom, Leopold as head of his household retained control of all the money his children earned to use as he saw fit. Parsimonious by nature, he invested it shrewdly.

In desperate need of money and without steady employment, in the spring of 1787 Wolfgang had to move his family out of the handsome apartment they had been living in (the "Figaro House") to cheaper lodgings. This bit of information was relayed to his sister Nannerl in the last letter that Leopold Mozart is ever known to have written (dated 10-11 May 1787). Apparently the thousand gulden earned in Prague had not gone very far. Wolfgang made it clear to his sister that he was eager to accept a quick settlement from his brother-in-law that would provide him with ready cash instead of waiting for probate proceedings. In return, he was prepared to relinquish all claims to his father's estate. The agreement he made with his brother-in-law is confirmed in a letter of 29 September 1787. He mentioned that he intended to leave for Prague the following Monday, 1 October.

There is no doubt that Mozart's second visit to Prague was as rich in memorable experiences as his first one had been. Unfortunately, some of the most colorful incidents repeated in the Mozart literature are based on unreliable sources of information that date from the early and mid-nineteenth century. The most reliable accounts - those that originate in Mozart's correspondence or the *Prague Post* - are disappointing for their terseness.

Reports of Mozart's name in the Prague press were sparse for months after his departure in February of 1787, other than the residual effects of the interest in his music created by the winter performances of *The Marriage of Figaro*. Arrangements of music from the opera were offered for sale in the *Prague Post* on 31 March and 3 April 1787. On 6 June, the *Prague Post* announced an upcoming performance of *The Marriage of Figaro* in German translation at the Rosenthal Theater in Prague. The Rosenthal Theater was located in a building just outside the city walls of Prague in front of the gate that lay at the end of the "Hospital Lane" (modern-day Na poříčí) on the northern and eastern boundary of the New City. According to the *Complete Description of Prague*, it was part of an area outside the city walls that contained beautiful gardens and walkways. Its productions lasted for only a few years in the 1780s; the building that housed it was demolished in 1789. The Rosenthal Theater specialized in popular entertainments in German; thus its production of a full-length opera would have been an ambitious undertaking justified only by the popularity of Mozart's music at that time.

The Praguers received no advance announcement of Mozart's return. Rather, news of his second arrival appeared suddenly in the *Prague Post* on 6 October 1787 (in a report dated 4 October): "Our celebrated Herr Mozart has again arrived in Prague, and the word since then has been that his newly-written opera *The Stone Guest* will be given here for the first time at the National Theater" (*The Stone Guest* - in Italian, *Il convitato di pietra* - was a common alternative title for Don Juan dramatizations). The date of 4 October confirms that Mozart's second trip took three days to complete, as had his first one. Pedantry need not spoil the effect of the charming fiction concocted by Eduard Mörike, but the documentation available proves that Mozart could not have tarried in Moravia as long as Mörike portrayed and still have made it to Prague in three days.

The pretext for Mozart's return to Prague had always been an operatic commission. Testimony about this from Němeček was excerpted in the previous chapter. In similar vein are some remarks of Jan Nepomuk Štěpánek that appeared in the 1828 biography of Mozart that was written by Constanze Mozart's second husband, Georg Nikolaus von Nissen. Concerning the composer's first visit, Štěpánek related:

> ...Wherever he went and wherever he was caught sight of, the inflamed Praguers greeted him with love and respect. Pleased with the drunken joy that *The Marriage of Figaro* had inspired, he said, "Since the Bohemians understand me so well, I must write an opera for them." Bondini took Mozart at his word and concluded an agreement with him for an opera - an opera for the Prague stage - for the following winter, and Mozart returned to Vienna, where he served as imperial and royal court chamber composer to His Majesty the Emperor Joseph. After his arrival he was soon mindful to keep his promise to the Bohemians, and there began to busy himself with his setting of *Don Juan*. However, in order to ensure that his work would be given with the greatest possible degree of perfection, Mozart traveled for a second time to Prague in September of 1787, where he first stayed in the Three Lions' Inn in the coal market [of the Old City], but later with his friend Dušek [at the Bertramka villa] in the orchard at Košíře, where he mainly stayed and wrote his *Don Juan*.

Three Lions' Inn
(today the pub Wolfgang)

Štěpánek apparently did not realize that Mozart had been appointed chamber composer at the imperial court in 1787, only after he had returned to Vienna from Prague the second time. Mörike's belief that Mozart left Vienna sometime in September probably derived from this passage in the Nissen biography, a bit of misinformation that colored his description of the weather that Mozart supposedly encountered in rural Moravia. Mozart's arrival at the Three Lions' Inn is also portrayed as taking place in September in Eduard Herold's *Picturesque Wanderings Through Prague* (*Malerische Wanderungen durch Prag*), a collection of historical sketches published in 1866 that probably served as a model for Meissner's *Rococo-Bilder*. The dialogue from Herold's vignette, which was intended to bring to life the joyous reaction of Mozart and his wife upon their second arrival in Prague, is not relevant enough to translate.

There is no mention of the existence of a Three Lions' Inn in the *Complete Description of Prague* of 1787. It is mentioned, however, in the third volume of Jaroslaus Schaller's guidebook to Prague, published in 1796, so it is possible that the name had been changed from something else. The *Complete Description of Prague* does specify an inn called the "Golden Wheel" ("zum Goldenen Rad"), next to the Platýs Inn in the coal market, that had just been renovated. The Three Lion's Inn was indeed very close to the Platýs Inn.

There is no reason to believe that the opera *Don Giovanni* was mainly composed in Prague itself, in spite of what Nissen believed. It is clear that it must have been largely completed before Mozart arrived in the city on 4 October, since it was originally supposed to be performed on 14 or 15 October. According to the composer's correspondence, only the logistics of arranging the production, not the completion of the music, delayed the première until 29 October.

There is considerable confusion in the Mozart literature about how the subject of *Don Juan* was chosen, due mainly to conflicting accounts preserved from the librettist Lorenzo Da Ponte, the only source of information that sheds light on the matter. Da Ponte's reminiscences make delightful reading in spite of his penchant for boasting and fictional embellishment. His love affairs rivaled those of his friend Giacomo Casanova for their passion and intensity, and his tangled financial affairs were the catalyst for amazing peregrinations that finally caused him to flee Europe entirely. For all of his many travels in Europe, Da Ponte actually spent more of his adult life in the United States than in any other country. He moved to the United States permanently in 1805 as a means to escape creditors in Europe and died there in 1838 at the age of 89.

It is still little known even to professional musicologists that there are two sets of reminiscences by Lorenzo Da Ponte that describe the events that led to the composition of the operas *The Marriage of Figaro* and *Don Giovanni*. The larger work, known as his *Memoirs*, was first published in New York City in 1823, and contains the only version of events that Mozart scholars have ordinarily made reference to until recently. An earlier shorter collection of his reminiscences, known as the *Extract from the Life of Lorenzo Da Ponte*, had been published in New York City in 1819 in response to an article that Da Ponte had seen in *Blackwood's Edinburgh Magazine* of March of the same year. Da Ponte had been outraged that a review of a production of Mozart's *Don Giovanni* in London in April of 1817 had made no mention of Da Ponte's contribution to the success of the work. In response, he related a version of the genesis of the Mozart opera that was intended to draw attention to his talents as a dramatic poet, one aspect of his nature for which his vanity seems amply justified.

In the *Extract*, Da Ponte claimed that the story of Don Juan had been suggested to Mozart by Domenico Guardasoni, the Italian singer who took over many duties from the impresario Bondini sometime during the middle months of the year 1787. According to Da Ponte, Guardasoni at first wanted Mozart simply to re-set a Don Juan libretto by Giovanni Bertati that had just been performed earlier that year in Venice with admirable success. Da Ponte claimed that Mozart would not hear of setting such an inferior libretto and insisted that Da Ponte be engaged to prepare a new one on the same subject:

> …Why did Mozart refuse to set to music the *Don Giovanni* (of evil memory) by Bertati, and offered to him by one Guardasoni…manager of the Italian theatre of Prague? Why did he insist upon having a book [i.e., libretto] written by Da Ponte on

the same subject, and not by any other dramatist? Shall I tell you why? Because Mozart knew very well that the success of an opera depends, FIRST OF ALL, ON THE POET: that without a good poem an entertainment cannot be perfectly dramatic, just as a picture cannot be good without possessing the merit of invention, design, and a just proportion of the parts…

Da Ponte's *Memoirs* present an entirely different story based on the claim that Mozart had approached Da Ponte in Vienna with a request for a new libretto on a subject of his own choosing. Da Ponte also claimed that the composers Vicente Martín y Soler and Antonio Salieri had approached him at the same time in search of librettos, and that he had written texts for all three composers simultaneously:

…The opportunity was offered me by "maestri" Martini, Mozart, and Salieri who came all three at the same time to ask me for books. I loved and esteemed all three of them, and hoped to find in each compensation for past failures and some increment to my glory in opera. I wondered whether it might not be possible to satisfy them all, and write three operas at one spurt. Salieri was not asking me for an original theme. While in Paris he had written the music for *Tarar*, and wished now to see it Italian in manner as regards both words and music. What he wanted, therefore, was a free adaptation. Mozart and Martini were leaving everything to me.

For Mozart I chose the *Don Giovanni*, a subject that pleased him mightily; and for Martini the *Arbore di Diana*. For him I wanted an attractive theme, adaptable to those sweet melodies of his, which one feels deep in the spirit, but which few know how to imitate.

The three subjects fixed on, I went to the Emperor, laid my idea before him, and explained that my intention was to write the three operas simultaneously.

"You will not succeed," he replied.

"Perhaps not," said I, "but I am going to try. I shall write evenings for Mozart, imagining I am reading the *Inferno* [of Dante]; mornings I shall work for Martini and pretend I am studying Petrarch; my afternoons will be for Salieri. He is my Tasso!"

He found my parallels very apt. I returned home and went to work. I sat down at my table and did not leave it for twelve hours continuous - a bottle of Tokay to my right, a box of Seville [snuff] to my left, in the middle an inkwell. A beautiful girl of sixteen - I should have preferred to love her only as a daughter, but alas…! - was living in the house with her mother, who took care of the family, and came to my room at the sound of the bell. To tell the truth, the bell rang rather frequently, es-pecially at moments when I felt my inspiration waning. She would bring me now a little cake, now a cup of coffee, now nothing but her pretty face, a face always gay, always smiling, just the thing to inspire poetical emotion and witty thoughts.

I worked twelve hours a day every day, with a few interruptions, for two months on end; and through all that time she sat in an adjoining room, now with a book in hand, now with needle or embroidery, but ever ready to come to my aid at the first touch of the bell. Sometimes she would sit at my side without stirring, without opening her lips, or batting an eyelash, gazing at me fixedly, or blandly smiling, or now it would be a sigh, or a menace of tears. In a word, this girl was my Calliope [muse of eloquence and epic poetry in Greek mythology] for those three operas, as she was afterwards for all the verse I wrote during the next six years.

At first I permitted such visits very often; later I had to make them less fre-quent, in order not to lose too much time in amorous nonsense, of which she was a perfect mistress. The first day, between the Tokay, the snuff, the coffee, the bell, and my young muse, I wrote the two first scenes of *Don Giovanni*, two more for the *Arbore di Diana*, and more than half of the first act of *Tarar*, a title I changed to *Assur*. I presented those scenes to the three composers the next morning. They could scarcely be brought to believe that what they were reading with their own eyes was possible. In 63 days the first two operas were entirely finished and about two thirds of the last.

Even aside from its closer chronological proximity to the actual events, the story found in the *Extract* is much more believable. It was generally the prerogative of the sponsoring theater, not a librettist solicited by a composer, to choose the subject for operatic productions in eighteenth-century Europe. In addition, there was a tradition of Prague settings of the Don Juan tale that Guardasoni was certainly aware of. Guardasoni more likely viewed the presence of Mozart in the city as a rare chance for producing a definitive Prague setting of the Don Juan tale. Da Ponte's second account - replete with pretentious literary allusions and extravagant braggadocio - is preposterous at face value. There is an easy explanation for Da Ponte's sudden recall in 1823 of Dante's *Inferno* as a supposed inspiration: He had just published a translation of Lord Byron's 1819 poem *The Prophecy of Dante* in 1822. Earlier Mozart literature - for example, Nettl's *Mozart in Böhmen* - has proposed chronologies for the completion of the libretto and the composition of the music based on clues derived from the *Memoirs*, but none of these hypotheses can be accepted as valid due to the unreliability of Da Ponte's claims. In truth, the chronology of the genesis of the libretto and score of *Don Giovanni* sometime during the middle months of 1787 is impossible to establish.

Nonetheless, there is no doubt that Da Ponte was present in Prague for the preparations surrounding the first performance of *Don Giovanni*. The *Prague Post* of 9 October 1787 reported that he had arrived in the city the previous day: "The imperial and royal poet Herr Abbé Laurenz da Ponte, a native Venetian, has arrived here from Vienna, and will remain here for a few days." The *Prague Post* was technically incorrect in identifying Da Ponte as a Venetian, even though he had spent much of his youth in Venice (in fact, he was born in 1749 in the town of Ceneda to the north of Venice). The reason for Da Ponte's presence in Prague to witness the first production of *Don Giovanni* was that it was supposed to be attended by the archduchess Maria Theresa of Austria, niece of his employer, the emperor Joseph II. Da Ponte had held the post of "imperial and royal" poet since 1783, and it was in this position that Da Ponte first made the acquaintance of Mozart as librettist for *The Marriage of Figaro* in 1786.

A persistent legend in the Mozart literature asserts that Da Ponte stayed at the Platýs Inn in the coal market - so short a distance from the Three Lions' Inn that Mozart and Da Ponte could communicate with each other from the windows of their rooms. Documentation for this charming imagery is actually very scanty. The first known published claim of Da Ponte staying at the Platýs Inn comes from Herold's *Picturesque Wanderings* of 1866. Herold said nothing about Da Ponte interacting with Mozart there and gave no indication of how he learned that he had stayed at the Platýs Inn. The idea of interaction appears to have originated in Procházka's *Mozart in Prag* of 1892. In truth, Mozart may already have transferred to the Bertramka villa by the time of Da Ponte's arrival on 8 October 1787. Regardless, no one knows for certain where Da Ponte was staying in Prague at this time.

Mozart was accompanied on his second trip to Prague only by his wife Constanze, who was pregnant at the time with their daughter Theresia. Once again, their son Karl had been left behind in Vienna, as far as can be established. In the autumn of 1787, there was nothing like the carnival celebrations in Prague to attract a party of travelers, and, for whatever reason, Count Thun's hospitality was not available. It is not known whether the count was unwilling to offer it, was out of town, or whether it had ever occurred to anyone to seek it, since the impresario Guardasoni was responsible for providing lodgings to Mozart in Prague as part of his contract to compose the opera *Don Giovanni*. Without Count Thun's generosity to draw upon, anyone who went to Prague on this trip would have had to pay his or her own way.

The most reliable descriptions of Mozart's activities in Prague in the autumn of 1787 come from two letters written to his friend Gottfried von Jacquin. The first one, completed over a period of more than a week in October, is mainly concerned with intrigues caused by the archduchess Maria Theresa. Born in Florence in 1767, she was the eldest daughter of Joseph II's brother Leopold, later Holy Roman Emperor Leopold II, who in 1787 was still grand duke of Tuscany (all of the children of the empress Maria Theresa were expected to name their first-born daughters after their mother).

The archduchess was a great nuisance to Mozart at this time, but the later course of her life does offer some cause for sympathy. As the second wife of Prince Anton, heir to the throne of Saxony, she bore her husband four children, none of whom lived to see the age of two. Her brother-in-law, the childless Friedrich August III of Saxony, lived so long that she was able to enjoy the title Queen of Saxony for only six months before her death in November of 1827. By that time, the kingdom of Saxony had been greatly reduced in size by the victorious allies at the close of the Napoleonic Wars in retaliation for the close political alliance that Frederick Augustus III had maintained with Napoléon Bonaparte.

The archduchess had already married Prince Anton by proxy in Florence on 8 September 1787. A short time later she traveled to Vienna, and then left on 10 October with her brother Francis, the future Holy Roman Emperor Francis II, to continue by way of Prague to Dresden, capital of the Saxon state, for a face-to-face marriage ceremony on 18 October. The archduchess, her brother, and Prince Anton all stayed in Prague Castle. They were supposed to have seen the first performance of the opera *Don Giovanni* on 14 October, just as they had seen the first performance of Martín's *L'arbore di Diana* (also on a text of Da Ponte) on 1 October in Vienna. Assuming that it took the wedding party three days to travel from Vienna, just as it did for Mozart, they probably stayed in Prague for less than 48 hours, arriving sometime during the day on 13 October and departing early on the morning of 15 October.

According to a letter of Countess Caroline von Waldstein written to her father Vincenz von Waldstein from the castle of Loučeň on 5 October 1787, the opera *Don Giovanni* was supposed to have been given on 15 October. Without specifying a title, she said that Mozart's opera was generally expected to be "most promising." Mozart's first letter to Jacquin, however, clearly indicates a date of 14 October as the intended date for the première. The itinerary of the archduchess Maria Theresa and her husband Prince Anton probably explains the discrepancy. It is known that the National Theater in Prague in 1787 usually gave operatic performances only on Mondays, Wednesdays, and Saturdays. Since 15 October fell on a Monday, it is likely that this was indeed the date originally intended for the première. It seems the date was changed to accommodate the traveling plans of the wedding party.

Difficulties described by Mozart made it impossible to present the new opera on time, even though librettos had been printed in Vienna announcing that it was to be produced in Prague just for the visit of the archduchess and her bridegroom. In place of *Don Giovanni*, Mozart's opera *The Marriage of Figaro* was given instead, with Mozart himself conducting. According to an account of this event left by Štěpánek in Nissen's biography of Mozart, the composer's style of conducting caused the singing of a certain female singer "M * *" (probably Caterina Micelli) to be a "little forced." By way of apologizing to her, Mozart called out "just two words" to her at the conclusion of her final aria: "Bravo, Donnella!" ("Bravo, little lady!"). Mozart's own amusing account to Jacquin of this unusual revival of *The Marriage of Figaro* reads as follows:

Dearest Friend! -
   You presumably think that my opera is already over by now - on the contrary - you are a little mistaken; in the first place, the theatrical personnel here are not as skilled as those in Vienna when it comes to rehearsing an opera of this kind in such a short amount of time. Secondly, I found on my arrival that so few preparations and arrangements had been made that it would have been absolutely impossible to present it yesterday on the 14th; - So yesterday my *Figaro* was performed in a fully illuminated theater and I conducted it myself. - Concerning this occasion I must tell you a joke. - Some of the leading ladies here (especially a particularly illustrious one) were pleased to find it very ridiculous, improper, and whatever else, that *Figaro*, or "The Crazy Day" (as they chose to call it) should be given for the princess [Maria Theresa]. They did not realize that no opera in the world can be exactly suitable for such an occasion if it was not carefully written just for it; and that it is immaterial whether this or that opera is given, as long as it is a good one that the princess has never seen before; and *Figaro* at least was certainly that. - In short, the ringleader through her eloquence took things so far that the impresario was forbidden by the government [i.e., the Czech Gubernium] to produce this opera on that day. - And so she triumphed! - - "Ho vinta" ["I've won"], she called out one evening from her box; - She certainly never suspected that the "ho" might be changed to a "sono"! [to make the phrase "sono vinta," - "I've been beaten"] - But the next day Le Noble came - he brought a command from His Majesty saying that if the new opera could not be given, *Figaro* had to be performed! - If you, my friend, had only seen the beautiful, magnificent nose of this lady! - Oh, it would have amused you as much as it did me! - *Don Giovanni* is now intended for [Wednesday] the 24th.
   October 21st. It was intended for the 24th, but the illness of one of the female singers caused a new delay; - since the company is so small, the impresario is always in a state of anxiety and has to spare his people so much that if he did not, by means

of some unexpected indisposition he would be placed into the most critical of all critical situations and not be able to put on any production at all! - So everything dawdles along here because the singers (out of laziness) will not rehearse on opera days [Mondays, Wednesdays, and Saturdays] and the impresario (out of timidity and anxiety) will not force them, but what is this? - Is it possible? - What do my ears see, what do my eyes hear? - A letter from - I am almost rubbing my eyes sore - it is - the devil take me † God be with us † actually from you; - in fact, it is; if winter were not approaching, I would smash the stove. But since I am already frequently using it now and intend to use it even more often in the future, you will permit me to express my surprise in a somewhat more moderate fashion and merely tell you in a few words that I am extraordinarily happy to receive news from you and your precious family.

October 25th: - Today is the eleventh day that I have been scrawling out this letter; - You will see from this that I am not lacking in good intentions - whenever I can find a moment, I daub on another little piece - but indeed I cannot stay at it very long, because I belong too much to other people - and too little - to myself; - that this is not my favorite way of living I hardly need to tell you; - my opera will be performed for the first time next Monday, October 29th; - you will receive an account of it from me a day or two later; - as for the aria, it is absolutely impossible to send it to you (for a reason I will tell you in person). I am delighted to hear what you say about Katherl [Mozart's dog], that is, that she commands the respect of cats and knows how to retain the friendship of dogs. If your Papa, to whom I send most cordial greetings, likes to keep her, well, let us pretend that she never belonged to me. Now, farewell. Please kiss your gracious mama's hands for me, give my best greetings to your sister and your brother and rest assured that I shall ever be your true friend and servant
W. A. Mozart

Leopold Le Noble von Edlersberg was the imperial court quartermaster, present in Prague to help arrange festivities for the wedding party both in Prague and Dresden. The identity of the "aria" promised to Jacquin is mysterious. Surely the only individual aria that originated from Mozart's pen at this time was "Bella mia fiamma, addio," K. 528, specified in Mozart's own catalog as being written for Josefa Dušek in Prague. In a letter to Jacquin of 4 November, Mozart did make reference to a completed aria. Perhaps this one, entered in Mozart's catalog as completed on 3 November, was the one he was referring to, although it is difficult to fathom what use Jacquin would have had for it.

As for the identity of the "illustrious" lady who tried so hard to cancel the production of Mozart's *Marriage of Figaro*, there is some room for speculation. It seems doubtful that anyone capable of shouting with impunity from a box at the opera and influencing the policy of the Gubernium could not have held a very high noble rank. Since there was no queen of Bohemia resident in Prague (nor any vicereine), the highest rank available for a woman would have been *Oberstburggräfin*, the consort of the supreme burgrave. Count Franz Anton von Nostic, who had just relinquished that title on 9 September to Count Ludwig Franz Xaver von Cavriani, was of course the founder and owner of the National Theater. His wife, Countess Maria Elisabeth, since birth a member of the upper nobility of Bohemia, should have fulfilled every qualification for haughtiness and outlandish behavior in her own husband's theater. While no positive identification is possible, Countess Nostic must be considered the best available candidate for this "illustrious" lady.

The production of Mozart's *Marriage of Figaro* witnessed by the archduchess' wedding party satisfied the terms of an imperial decree of 1785 that forbade performances of the original play of Beaumarchais in the Hapsburg domains. Only performances of the play adapted for the operatic stage were permitted. According to the memoirs of Lorenzo Da Ponte, the ban on the play had nothing to do with what many modern scholars (and the film *Amadeus*) portray as subversive political content; rather, it was banned for its "licentiousness." Indeed, the sexual references and puns in the play are unremitting. Da Ponte toned down the sexual content of the play considerably in its adaptation as an operatic setting. The issue of the ban never seems to have come up in Prague during the winter of 1786-87, but with members of the imperial family present at the National Theater in October, there apparently was a sense that legal niceties had to be respected. For the benefit of a performance in the presence of the emperor's niece, a fresh issuance of his decree, dated 11 October 1787, was prepared by the Prague magistracy, just in time for the production given on 14 October. It stipulated that the Beaumarchais play "could also be performed in Prague not as a play, but as an Italian opera, just as it had been presented on the Vienna court stage."

On 16 October, the *Prague Post* published the following description of the performance of *The Marriage of Figaro* on 14 October that glossed over all scandal and unpleasantness in the days preceding:

> ...At half past six o'clock they [Prince Anton of Saxony, the archduchess Maria Theresa, and the archduke Francis] presented themselves at the Nostic National Theater, which for this occasion was decorated and illuminated in a very distinguished manner. The theater was so much glorified by the finery of the numerous guests that one must acknowledge never having seen such a magnificent spectacle before. Upon the arrival of Their Highnesses they were welcomed with public expressions of joy by the whole audience. By command [of the emperor Joseph II], the renowned opera *The Marriage of Figaro*, generally acknowledged to be so well performed here, was given. The zeal of the musicians and the presence of Maestro Mozart awakened a general approbation and satisfaction in Their Highnesses. After the first act, a sonnet ordered by several Bohemian patriots for this festivity was publicly distributed. Due to their early departure [the next day], Their Highnesses left for the royal castle even before the conclusion of the opera.

The *Prague Post* was probably not exaggerating when it drew attention to the glamour that attended this occasion, graced as it was by the presence of members of two of the most illustrious ruling families in Europe - and in fact, the highest-ranking collection of aristocrats ever to set foot in the theater up to that time. The production was significant enough as a social event to be reported in the *Wiener Zeitung* in Vienna on 20 October, its announcement (dated Prague, 15 October) partially repeating remarks already published in the *Prague Post*:

...the afternoon of the day before yesterday [13 October], Her Imperial Highness the archduchess Maria Theresa, accompanied by her exalted brother, the archduke Francis, arrived at the royal castle here. The next day they attended high mass at the Metropolitan Church [of St. Vitus on the grounds of Prague Castle]. They took lunch alone in the company of their high stewards. At 5 o'clock there was a reception, at which all the local nobility as well as the generals, their staff, and other officers were present. The presentation was performed by the consort of the High Steward for Bohemia, Count [František Xaver] Věžník [a member of the Gubernium].

In the evening Their Highnesses presented themselves in Count Nostic's National Theater, which was illuminated in a very beautiful manner for the occasion. At their entry, Their Highnesses were welcomed with public expressions of joy by the whole audience. The renowned opera *The Marriage of Figaro* was given. After the first act a poem written for this festivity was distributed publicly. Early this morning Her Imperial Highness departed for Dresden accompanied by blessings and good wishes.

It is notable that the *Wiener Zeitung*, not to mention Mozart himself in his letter to Jacquin, chose to suppress news of the failure of "Their Highnesses" to attend the performance of *The Marriage of Figaro* until its conclusion. Observers must certainly have taken this gesture as a snub. Considering the intrigues involved, it is not difficult to imagine them leaving the opera for reasons much less practical than having to wake up early the next morning. Count Johann Karl von Zinzendorf, the inveterate diarist who left volumes of commentary on events associated with the imperial court of Vienna in the late eighteenth century, wrote on 19 October 1787 that neither *L'arbore di Diana* nor *The Marriage of Figaro* could be deemed appropriate entertainments for a newly-married woman. Opera lovers will remember that *The Marriage of Figaro* contains a poignant illustration of the way that marriages can deteriorate over the years due to infidelity, as well as a portrayal of the emotional distress caused by the possible assertion of the *droit du seigneur* (the right of a feudal lord to sleep with a bride before her wedding night). Furthermore, three of the four principal characters in the opera were clearly born out of wedlock (the only exception being the Count of Almaviva). The "illustrious" lady may have had just the right idea in trying to suppress the production after all. The report in the *Wiener Zeitung* is also notable for its suppression of Mozart's name and the patriotic nature of the poetry distributed to the audience members.

More news from Prague came to Jacquin in a letter of 4 November 1787:

Dearest, best friend!

I hope you received my letter; - my opera *Don Giovanni* went into production on October 29th with the greatest applause. - It was performed yesterday for the fourth time (indeed for my benefit); - I am thinking of leaving here on the 12th or 13th - upon my return, you will receive the aria at once; NB: between ourselves - how I wish that my good friends (especially Bridi and you) were here just for one evening in order to share my pleasure! - but perhaps my opera will be performed in Vienna? - I hope so. - People here are doing everything possible to persuade me to remain on for a couple of months and write another opera, - but I cannot accept this proposal, however flattering it may be...

"Bridi" is probably a reference to Giuseppe Antonio Bridi, an Italian singer who appeared in a performance of Mozart's opera *Idomeneo* in Vienna in 1786. Considering the richness of the stories preserved in other sources about the first performance of *Don Giovanni*, this account is frustratingly brief, but the most important point - the success of the production - was soon corroborated in the *Prague Post*. On the very day that it was to be performed, a brief announcement was prepared for publication the next day, 30 October:

> The director of the Italian company here yesterday issued news of the opera *Don Juan*, or, *Debauchery Punished*, which was intended to be performed in the presence of the exalted Tuscan guests. Its author is the court theater poet Abbé Da Ponte, and is to be performed for the first time today, the 29th. Everyone takes pleasure in the excellent music of the great master Mozart. The next issue will have more to say about this.

After the first performance had taken place, there was indeed more to say in the issue of 3 November (a report dated 1 November):

> On Monday the 29th the Italian opera company gave the longingly awaited opera by Maestro Mozart, *Don Giovanni*, or, *The Stone Guest*. Connoisseurs and musicians say that nothing like it had yet been performed in Prague before. Herr Mozart conducted himself; when he entered the orchestra he was given three cheers, which happened again when he left it. The opera, by the way, is extremely difficult to perform, and everyone was amazed at the good performance in spite of such a short period allotted for rehearsal. Everyone, both on the stage and in the orchestra, offered his full abilities to thank Mozart by rewarding him with a good performance. There were also many additional costs caused by several choruses and changes of scenery, which Herr Guardasoni presented brilliantly. The extraordinarily large attendance attests to a unanimous approbation.

The same news was reported in Hamburg on November 9 and in Vienna in two different newspapers on 10 November and 14 November. František Xaver Němeček, who was probably present for the event, included his own version of events in his 1798 biography of Mozart:

Anna Chromy's tribute to the première of *Don Giovanni - Il Commendatore*, Estates' Theater
© Jaime Silva

> Toward the winter of the same year 1787, Mozart came to Prague again by reason of his contract, and completed there the crown of all his masterpieces, the opera *Debauchery Punished*, or, *Don Giovanni*.
> The Bohemians are proud that by creating this exalted music from the depth of his genius he recognized and esteemed their good taste in this art. "Don Giovanni was written for Prague" - no more needs to be said to prove what a keen understanding Mozart had for the musical sense of the Bohemians. He succeeded

completely in striking this sense and stirring it; for no opera has retained its popularity on the stage here as long as *Don Giovanni* has. It has now been ten years since it was first given - and it is still heard with pleasure and still attracts large gatherings in the theater. In short, *Don Giovanni* is the favorite opera of the better classes of Prague. When Mozart himself appeared at the first performance at the piano in the orchestra, the entire theater, so crowded that people were almost crushed to death, welcomed him with a general, enthusiastic applause. Mozart indeed received in Prague at every opportunity great and undoubted proof of respect and admiration, which were certainly sincere, since neither prejudice nor fashion, but rather pure feeling for his art was responsible for it. His beautiful works were loved and admired; how could anyone remain indifferent to the person of this great creative figure?

Latter-Day Legends about the First Performance of Don Giovanni

It is at this point that eyewitness accounts of the first performance of Mozart's opera *Don Giovanni* must come to an end. Additional details are plentiful, but they were set down on paper only decades after the fact. From Lorenzo Da Ponte, who did not stay in Prague to witness the event, there is commentary about the première in both sets of his memoirs. The *Extract* of 1819 offers this information:

> …I will say…that Mozart, either because he considered me till the last moment of his life, the promoter of his musical glory, or because he was too well pleased with the words and success of *Le nozze di Figaro*, to try another vehicle to his notes, would never have set to music the verses of another poet, when he could have had those of Da Ponte. "Our opera of *Don Giovanni*" said he in a letter written to me from Prague "was represented last night to a most brilliant audience. The princess of Tuscany [Maria Theresa], with all her company, was present. The success of our piece was as complete as we could desire. Guardasoni came this morning almost enraptured with joy, into my room. 'Long live Mozart, long live Da Ponte,' said he: 'as long as they shall exist, no [theater] manager shall know distress.' Adieu! My dear friend. Prepare another opera for your friend Mozart." I was so happy for the opportunity, that although I had on hand at that time two other dramas, nevertheless I did not neglect my favorite Mozart, and in less than three months I gave a tragicomic drama, entitled *Assur re d'Ormus*, to Salieri, who, in spite of his first assertion, had begun to have a relish for my dramatic verses, an heroicomic to Martini, called *L'abore di Diana*, and a comic opera to Mozart, with the title *La scuola degli amanti* [*Così fan tutte* of 1790], which was represented in Vienna, in Prague, in Dresden, and for several years in Paris, with unbounded applause.

There is no possibility that Da Ponte could have been quoting a genuine letter of Mozart directly, since the archduchess Maria Theresa was in Dresden at the time of the first performance of *Don Giovanni*, nor is there any reason to believe that Da Ponte supplied Mozart with the libretto to *Così fan tutte* two years in advance of its first performance. Da Ponte's *Memoirs* contain another version of the events surrounding the first performance of *Don Giovanni* in which he explained his need to leave Prague early:

> …Only the first performance [in Vienna] of [Martín's opera *L'arbore di Diana*] had been given [on 1 October 1787], when I was obliged to leave for Prague for the

opening of Mozart's *Don Giovanni* on the occasion of the arrival of the Princess of Tuscany in that city. I spent eight days there training the actors who were to create it; but before it appeared on the stage, I had to hurry back to Vienna, because of the fiery letter I received from Salieri, wherein he informed me, truly or not, that *Assur* had to be ready at once for the nuptials of Prince Francis [brother of the archduchess Maria Theresa], and that the Emperor had ordered him to call me home [Francis was in fact married to Princess Elisabeth of Württemberg in Vienna on 6 January 1788].

In returning to Vienna, I traveled day and night; but finding myself very tired at the midway I asked permission to go to bed for a couple of hours. I lay down, and, when the horses were ready, they came to call me. I leapt from the bed, half asleep, ran down the stairs, entered my carriage, and departed. Some distance along the road we reached a toll-gate and I was asked for a small sum to pay the toll. I searched in my pocket and what was my surprise to find not a cent in my purse, where I had placed fifty sequins that morning - money which Guardasoni, the Director at Prague, had paid me for that opera. I thought I might have lost them on the bed where I had lain down in my clothes. I returned at once to the inn; there was not a pfennig to be found. The innkeeper and his wife, polite, well-bred people, called all the servants, hunted, searched, threatened; but no one would confess having touched that bed. However, a little girl of five or more who had seen one of the servants remake the bed for another guest piped up: "Mama, mama, Catherine made the bed over when the gentleman went away."

The innkeeper's wife, thereupon, made "Catherine" undress, and found my fifty sequins in her corsage. I had lost two hours' time in the business, but happy to have found my money, I begged those good people to forgive their maid.

I went on without stopping, save to change horses, and I arrived the following day in Vienna. I sent for Salieri, and went to work. In two days *Assur* was ready. It appeared in due time and such was its success that I was long in doubt as to which of the three operas was the most perfect, whether in the music or in the words.

I had not seen the première of *Don Giovanni* at Prague, but Mozart wrote me at once of its marvelous reception, and Guardasoni, for his part, these words:

"Long live Da Ponte! Long live Mozart! All impresarios, all virtuosi should bless their names. So long as they live we shall never know what theatrical poverty means!"

The emperor sent for me, and overloading me with gracious felicitations, presented me with another hundred sequins, and told me that he was longing to see *Don Giovanni*...

Far more detailed than any of the accounts excerpted thus far are passages in Meissner's *Rococo-Bilder*, which explores not only the intriguing combination of Mozart and Da Ponte together in Prague, but also the introduction of Giacomo Casanova into the mix. The simultaneous presence of Mozart, Da Ponte, and Casanova in Prague in October 1787 must be regarded as one of the most extraordinary coincidences in the history of European music and theater. As far as modern reputations are concerned, the three most famous Europeans living in 1787 (at least, those who had already reached adulthood) were Marie Antoinette, Giacomo Casanova, and Wolfgang Amadeus Mozart. Casanova and Marie Antoinette never met, but Mozart encountered each of them at different times in his life.

It was only through improbable means that Casanova had found himself in Prague in October of 1787. In recent years it has started to become better known that Casanova was a resident of the kingdom of Bohemia for the last thirteen years of his life (he died in 1798). In 1785, down and out in Vienna at the age of 60, the only acceptable offer of employment that had come his way was from Count Joseph Karl Emanuel von Waldstein, brother of the dedicatee of Beethoven's famous "Waldstein" Piano Sonata, Op. 53, who hired him as librarian at his castle of Duchcov (Dux) in rural Bohemia. Casanova was never happy in these dreary surroundings. The count did not treat him with much deference and there was little useful work as a librarian that needed to be done. The memoirs responsible for Casanova's notoriety as a great lover were written mainly out of boredom; if he had not moved to Bohemia they probably would never have been written at all.

Giocomo Casanova, 1788
by Jan Berka, Prague

Occasionally he did have the opportunity to travel to Prague, and his presence there in October of 1787 is not merely an incident concocted by Meissner for the *Rococo-Bilder*. Paul Nettl discovered a letter dated 4 November 1787 that was written from Brno by Count Max von Lemberg to Johann Ferdinand Opitz (presumed author of the *Complete Description of Prague*), in which the count reported receiving a letter from Casanova in Prague dated 25 October. Apparently he was there in order to arrange for the publication of his (rambling and unsuccessful) novel *Icosameron*. It would have been very odd for Casanova not to have stayed in Prague just a few more days for the production of *Don Giovanni*, considering his love of opera and the lack of intellectual stimulation in Duchcov.

Not until the 20th century did any commentator speculate on Casanova's possible reaction to seeing sexual behavior similar to his own held up to moral scrutiny in Mozart's opera - since it took quite a long time for Casanova to acquire a reputation as the world's greatest lover and to achieve the status of a household name. The process began only with the publication of his memoirs, an occurrence that took place many years after his death. To his friend Lorenzo Da Ponte, Casanova was simply a literatus with exalted international social connections and a passionate interest in Italian poetry - who happened to share the experience of many years of residence in Venice - and this is how Meissner portrayed him (with just one subtle reference to sexual prowess).

Meissner began his account of Mozart's stay in Prague in the autumn of 1787 by explaining how warm and beautiful the weather was that season. He also had much to say about the pleasantness of the Bertramka villa and its grounds. According to Meissner, the charms of the estate were enhanced by significant subsidies from "Count Clam," presumably Christian Philipp Clam, Count von Gallas, a talented amateur pianist and one of the most generous patrons of music in late eighteenth-century

Prague, whom he referred to as Josefa Dušek's "professed lover." It is clear that this characterization derives from Mozart's biographer Otto Jahn, the author of a monumental four-volume treatment of Mozart's life and works published between 1856 and 1859. In the last of these volumes, he quoted excerpts from a letter supposedly written by Leopold Mozart to his daughter Nannerl in which Clam is described as Josefa's "professed lover" responsible for supplying all of her "equipage." Jahn specified neither a date nor a source for this letter; no original has ever been found, although a letter of Leopold written to his daughter on 14 October 1785 records a visit to Salzburg of Dušek and Clam, whom he did refer to simply as her "lover." According to Jahn, Leopold described the count as "a handsome, friendly, dear man without the nobleman's pride."

Whatever happened to the couple is unknown. A piece of information that may have some bearing on the issue is found in the correspondence of Friedrich Schiller. During a visit to the ducal court of Weimar in May of 1788, Schiller reported the impression of the dowager duchess Anna Amalia, who observed that Josefa appeared to her "not unlike a mistress who had bowed out of a relationship." It is intriguing to imagine just what it was about her demeanor that would have left this impression with the duchess.

Meissner's full account of the days preceding the first performance of *Don Giovanni* begins with these remarks:

> As we know, Mozart had already been in Prague in January of this year and remained until February. He was there again from the middle of September, for his new opera *Don Giovanni* was the next one to go into production.
>
> Mozart already knew the Dušeks back in Salzburg and made it a point to socialize with them whenever he came to Prague. The impresario [Guardasoni], who was obliged by custom at that time to provide lodging to the composer of an opera until a production had ended its run, arranged quarters for the composer in the Three Lions' Inn in the coal market, but Mozart used them only infrequently and preferred instead to stay [at the Bertramka villa] in the orchard in Košíře, where he was provided with two small rooms in which he was not infrequently in the habit of staying overnight.

Meissner continued with an amazing reconstruction of a social gathering at the Bertramka villa on 27-28 October 1787. Those present included Mozart, Da Ponte, Casanova, František Dušek, and most of the members of the original singing cast of the opera *Don Giovanni*. The participation of Da Ponte in the dialogues contradicts a claim made in his *Memoirs* that he stayed in Prague for only eight days after his arrival on 8 October. Other suspicious details include the claim that a duke of Mantua known to Da Ponte's mentor, the bishop of Ceneda, once married the daughter of a baker. No such event is recorded for any duke of Mantua, and as far as the duchy of Mantua is concerned, it was simply ruled directly by the Hapsburg emperors after 1708 without a separate duke ever reigning again. Further, the tavern in Templová lane cited by Meissner was not famed as a "night spot" until a later time. The one accomplishment of Casanova that was only beginning to make him famous in 1787 was his account of an escape from the state prison of Venice ("The Leads"), and Meissner did draw attention to it. He also seemed to want to go out of his way to expose the Jewish origins that Da Ponte himself made every effort to conceal:

> ...A couple of days before the announced première [of the opera *Don Giovanni*] a large gathering of people assembled at the country house in Košíře. Two carriages dropped off the impresarios Bondini and Guardasoni and the singers Luigi Bassi, [Teresa] Saporiti, [Caterina] Bondini, and [Caterina] Micelli, the last of these with her mother; Da Ponte also came, and he brought along with him a certain Signor Casanova.
>
> After the guests had finished drinking afternoon coffee in the large room on the ground floor, the mood became as cheerful as can be. Mozart, conscious that he had created an immortal work and certain of its success, moved about with an Olympian freedom and candor. Not a cloud of doubt blemished the clear horizon of his soul. He was an optimist in the purest sense of the word, full of naïve joy in the world and all that is beautiful in it, without malice, as he had no rivals. Mozart looked forward to the day of the opera's performance as if it were a holiday, with almost childlike exuberance. Boisterously merry, he flirted with the ladies, played pranks, and spoke in rhymes (which was particularly amusing for him). Everyone was delighted with everything he did, just as if he were a child or very young adult.
>
> Those present were so carried away by his mood that nobody was concerned about the performance to come. Only the young baritone Bassi [the original Don Giovanni] - an astonishingly handsome but utterly stupid fellow - was unhappy that in the entire opera he had not been given one great aria worthy of his talents. The impresarios Bondini and Guardasoni had voiced concerns that the overture had not yet been committed to paper and Mozart was evading the task from day to day like a careless schoolboy. Both had already conveyed to Mozart the most serious consequences of this delay, which Mozart brushed off half laughingly, half angrily. Now they said nothing more, but frequently mimicked his gestures behind the backs of the ladies hoping thus to persuade Mozart to withdraw and start working. Maestro Amadeus, however, seemingly pretended not to notice these hints and listened attentively to the conversation between Signor Casanova and the Abbé Da Ponte on the one hand and [František] Dušek and the singers on the other.
>
> Signor Casanova was presented to the company as librarian of Count Waldstein of Duchcov and Litvinov; he was a man in his sixties of Herculean stature and rigid self-control. He wanted to put his mysterious past behind him, a past that appeared to be known to all the world. A short time before he had published in Prague a booklet in French that described his amazing escape from The Leads of Venice, but now he was preparing to publish a three-volume novel in the same language with the title *Icosameron*. In Casanova and Da Ponte there stood face-to-face two men with great similarity to each other. Both had spent their youth in Venice, both wandered restlessly in the world, and both acquired an unmistakable trait of vanity. Both of them loved to boast with friendly airs and loved to mention the potentates with which they had come into contact. The first had encountered Frederick [the Great] of Prussia and Catherine the Great [of Russia], just as the other would soon be hobnobbing again with Joseph II. But Da Ponte had the decided advantage. He could tout Jo-

Teresa Saporiti, 1791 (Donna Anna in the original cast of *Don Giovanni*) by Ferdinando Fambrini

seph's continuing favor, whereas with Casanova it was evident that the monarchs who once found him so pleasing and so estimable had distanced themselves from him. Da Ponte, as the incumbent "theater poet" in Vienna, merited the special amorous attention of the women, all of whom had the ambition of departing Prague for the premier stage of the German empire.

"Did you know, dear Abbé," said Micelli's mother, a Neapolitan and true stage mother (with the ulterior motive of angering Signora Saporiti, who had never been so fortunate as to appear on a court stage), "did you know, dear Abbé, that my daughter is intended for an engagement at one of the great court theaters?"

"Well, well," said Da Ponte. "Guardasoni will not take kindly to that! At which court theater then, if I may ask?"

"I do not know that yet myself! But we will not have to wait much longer to find out. Perhaps you have already heard of the famous fortune teller in the square at Pohořelec [in the Hradčany district of Prague]? Her cards have already revealed three times that my Maria is intended to be a court chamber singer, and this woman has had incredible predictions come true!"

"But worthy lady," Da Ponte retorted, "this is not an incredible prediction! Why should Signora Maria not suitably fill a place at a court stage? Indeed it would be better to seek assurance from a court Kapellmeister, since playing cards are mere paper and a proper contract would be better in any case - however just the expectation of such a prophecy is nonetheless something."

Signor Casanova was listening with a serious look on his face. He made certain that he was given the precise address of the fortune teller without delay. He explained that he had often been a witness to the fact that the prophecies of good old women such as this one do come true and finally offered his opinion that fortune tellers are clairvoyant women who place themselves in a hypnotic state by means of shuffling, cutting, and dealing the cards.

"Even more has been prophesied for my daughter," Mama Micelli continued like someone who could not keep a secret to herself. "A crowned head - a sovereign!"

"Not another word, dearest mother!" shouted the daughter to the old woman as she sprang up and covered her mouth with both hands.

"What's wrong? Why should I not say it?" the old woman said as she freed herself, "my daughter would bring a great deal of luck to a great lord or sovereign."

"Look here!" shouted out Saporiti while laughing. "I always thought that Signora Micelli would only pay attention to somebody who actually had the intent of marrying her."

"And would a wedding ring on her left hand be so impossible?" the old woman asked indignantly.

"Or at least on the little finger of her left hand!" said Madame Bondini.

"Idiocy! I certainly do not believe that such weddings could take place!" said Saporiti.

"Then you are wrong, fair Signorina," said Da Ponte. "Weddings like that really do take place, but it is only a figurative expression to say that the bridegroom gets married just like everybody else. When my good uncle, the bishop of Ceneda, married the duke of Mantua to a baker's daughter, he also used the expression of getting married on the left hand."

"Oh mama, now everyone will laugh at me!" cried Micelli, "and I certainly do not believe in such things and put no faith in prophecies."

With small talk like this the group embarked on a tour of the gardens. "Herr Abbé Da Ponte appears to be a man of high birth," Micelli remarked to Casanova. "He speaks of his good uncle, the bishop."

"Oh you should not pay any attention to that!" retorted Casanova. "You must understand that he is of Jewish origin! When he was a young Jewish boy, he lost his parents at an early age and was placed in a seminary overseen by the bishop of Ceneda. Ever since then he has been accustomed to referring to him as his uncle."

"What are you saying then? So he was a baptized Jew? But he has a spiritual dignity nonetheless…?"

"I would not advise about that if you are considering marrying him," Casanova remarked with a raised finger. "I fear that he would take marriage vows no more seriously than the thought that I myself could give up copulation."

"Signor Casanova appears to be a dignified old gentleman," Saporiti said to Da Ponte, "and he must have held several high positions at various courts."

"In that you are terribly mistaken!" Da Ponte protested. "He is an adventurer who relies on cards, potions, and fortune telling to get through life. He is a clever man, to be sure, with remarkable knowledge. Ever since the last time I saw him, he has been raised to a noble state, and there is no doubt in my mind that he awarded the patent of nobility himself."

"You Italians always say the most terrible things about each other!" interjected Dušek, who had been listening to the conversation.

"There are Italians and then there are Italians!" retorted Da Ponte. "Can I say of [Giovanni Battista] Casti [the imperial court poet] that he is an honest man? Can I say of Salieri that he can be trusted? Casanova says that he practices cabala. Out of love for him could I consider cabala to be a serious science? Dear friend, one can travel out to the countryside, but among my countrymen one must always be on guard. I have not always done so and have come to misfortune due to a lack of caution. Italians, dear Dušek, are far too clever, and that is why they are masters in the art of deception. I trust nobody, I like nobody.

"As regards Salieri - I am merely a dramatist, and I give my librettos to him just as readily as I do to Mozart, but Mozart is the only one I am truly attached to. I have the feeling that only those operas set to music by him will be known to posterity. To him I also send the texts that are closest to my heart."

"Now I will tell the coachmen that they should prepare to leave," Guardasoni called out. "It is four o'clock, and the sun will set soon. We will drive back [to Prague] and leave Mozart alone. I have no idea whether or not the overture will be finished by tomorrow."

"Can you assure us that the last rehearsal will take place tomorrow and the performance the day after tomorrow?" asked Micelli.

"What does the maestro think?" asked Guardasoni.

"By all means you can be certain of it!" Mozart responded. "Otherwise there would have to be a delay for All Saints' Day [November 1] and All Souls' Day [November 2]. And by the way, Da Ponte and I have been tormented by all of you quite enough. I had my fill of rehearsing long ago. All of you know what trouble there was with [Caterina] Bondini [as Zerlina] producing the cry for help in the finale for the first act. And for you, dear ladies, things have still gone comparatively well. As for Bassi, I have often wished him to go to the same hell into which he must ultimately descend."

"And I still say that I have no true arias in the whole opera," Bassi retorted defiantly.

"You are a stupid young man, Bassi," answered Mozart. "Everything is fine the way it is, just sing and act your part, and let the music be my concern."

And he said to the departing ladies: "You still have a little room for me in the carriage, don't you?"

"What, Mozart, you still want to ride back to Prague today?" Bondini asked horrified, as if it were the worst thing he could have heard. "Certainly. I promised to go out with a couple of friends [to a tavern] in Templová lane [in the Old City of Prague]."

"Good heavens! In Templová lane! Where you never return before midnight! But Mozart, be sensible. - The overture…"

"As a matter of fact it is finished…"

"I know you! Finished in your head, but nothing put down on paper yet. Look here, Mozart - it has to be written out by noon tomorrow - the parts have to be copied - the overture has to be rehearsed."

"Of course! I will finish it, even if I have to do it in the middle of the night. My friends are waiting for me."

"This is terrible!" cried Bondini as the female singers and even the Dušeks flocked around him. "There has never been such frivolity in the history of the world. Friends, friends," he said in a muffled voice, "he won't change his mind. Something has to be done."

"But what? What?"

"We will have to lock the bird up."

"Excellent. But how can we get him into a room?"

"Child's play!" cried Madame Bondini. "Dear maestro, I left my gloves on the piano. Would you be so kind as to fetch them for me?"

"Very gladly!" answered Mozart, and he went into the house. But after a few minutes he appeared at the window and called out: "I can't find them."

"Then I'll have to look for them myself!" answered Madame Bondini, and immediately the whole group of people went up the steps to the house. "There they are!" cried the singer, who was pretending to search under the sheet music. She opened the piano and pleaded: "Mozart! Just a few chords from the overture, just a few chords!"

Mozart sat down and played some loud, long-resounding chords. He did not have a clue that there was a conspiracy at work against him. Everyone stepped back behind him on their tiptoes, one of them opened the door without a sound, and then one after another they all left the room.

Mozart only became aware of the prank after the door had closed behind him. He sprang to his feet. "What is this? What is the meaning of this?"

"It means that you're locked up and confined here for the evening instead of going out to Templová lane."

"What have I done?"

"Hear the judge's sentence!" cried a merry Saporiti. "Wolfgang Amadeus Mozart, who as a debtor in arrears for owing us the overture to his opera so long already and putting his own interests and ours gravely in danger, is sentenced to confinement for a period of hours until his debt is paid."

"But ladies, will you still favor me with your company for a while?" cried Mozart appearing from the window, below which the entire group had assembled. "How can I write without light, food, or drink?"

"That won't help; consider yourself imprisoned! If you want to be free soon, you had better get to work right away. Yes, you shall have light, also wine and a big cake. Nothing you require will be lacking."

"That is treachery!" cried Mozart. "I cannot endure solitude. What if I take my own life out of despair - maybe jump out the window - ? "

"Really, that is nothing to be concerned about. You love life far too much, little Amadeo!" cried Micelli.

"And you, Dušek, will you put up with this?" Mozart began, turning to his friend, who had concealed himself behind the group.

"This is well-intentioned! Really, really!" Dušek said.

"Then one should always say yes to good intentions, even when it involves treachery!" cried Mozart, now truly concerned that he was being held prisoner. Nonetheless his face, which had been serious, started to turn to laughter, when he saw the ladies march away in single file.

They divided the long stems of grape vines stored in the corner of the courtyard among themselves and tied them to the items needed by the prisoner for the night.

"Here are two lamps - Here a few bottles of wine from Mělník! - Here some cakes and candies!" cried the ladies holding up these items at the window sill. Da Ponte, however, more boisterous than the others, appeared with a rake to which one bottle was tied, as necessary as it was unaesthetic.

He cried, "You will also need this overnight. Take it, divine master."

"Unfortunately it's empty!" answered Mozart, "otherwise it would do you ill," and he stood there among the items that had been sent up half delighted, half annoyed. "And you, Signor Casanova," he cried, "you, who were confined in The Leads of Venice, and are familiar with the ways prisoner are tormented, want to leave me here to languish? You don't want to steal the key that was taken away so scornfully? No, you were never in prison!"

"Patience, dear maestro!" the old man answered.

"At least let me have my wife with me in prison!" cried Mozart. "Do I have to sing for you the plea to the demons from Gluck's *Orfeo*? Don't be crueler than they."

"The end justifies the means!" cried Guardasoni. "Good night, Mozart. All of us will return quite early tomorrow morning to find out whether the overture is finished."

"Yes, yes, all of us!" cried the ladies. "Good night, sweet Amadeo! Good night! Get straight to work!"

In this way a boisterous gang joked around with an immortal genius. The genius came down to earth in human form, in most respects more modest than other people, and only at times could be seen the crown on his head shining like a flame of fire.

But Mozart was in no way pleased with the prank that had been played on him. He was even less in the mood to write down the overture. He walked to and fro, bit his lips, and finally sat down discontented on the sofa.

Then the key turned in the lock, the door opened, and the imposing figure of Casanova appeared at the threshold.

"Maestro," he said. "Excuse the joke in which this overly-merry band indulged itself. Your goodness and forbearance made them overconfident. They intended everything to come out well. These people believe that you will compose only when you are first made to sit down and do not suspect that perhaps your displeasure would scare away all of your inspiration. Mozart has the best understanding of his talent; he knows best what he needs to do. That is why I took the key from Bassi and freed you from your confinement."

"You appear to me to be the most sensible of all," answered Mozart, putting out his hand, "I thank you."

"The joke will be on the ladies," said Casanova. "Appear among them unexpectedly and steal a kiss from each; that will be the best punishment for them."

"Thank you, Signor Casanova," Mozart answered, "for doing this for me. I will remain here. And tomorrow I will make sure the world will have the overture."

He kept his word. When Guardasoni, who could not sleep all night for his feverish restlessness, drove out already at 4 to the Dušek villa, he saw a light on, a sign that he was still writing. At 7 the overture was finished. It was immediately given to several copyists in order to write out the individual parts.

On the morning of 29 October 1787, it was announced from the street corners that *Don Giovanni* really was going to be performed that evening, since there was doubt about it the day before...

It would seem that some of the ideas developed by Meissner came from Eduard Herold's *Picturesque Wanderings Through Prague* of 1866. Herold had his own version of Mozart's close call in completing the overture to *Don Giovanni*, including concocted dialogues that are not as well-crafted as Meissner's. He claimed that Mozart was playing billiards at a tavern near the National Theater known as the "Blue Grape" the night before the first performance of the opera. Mozart's skill at playing billiards is indeed well attested. But Herold got the date of the première wrong; he specified 3 November 1787 as the date of the evening before. Herold had Mozart reminded of the necessity to complete the overture by his friends at the tavern, who got him to finish it in one of the rooms at the tavern during the night - precisely when is not revealed.

Mozart's wife Constanze is not mentioned as being a party to any of these remarkable incidents. If a reminiscence recorded by her second husband Nissen is to be trusted, she must have emerged from somewhere to join him late during the evening of 27 October to help him finish the overture to *Don Giovanni*:

> Mozart's widow related the incident as follows: Two days before the performance, after the dress rehearsal was over, he told her in the evening that he wanted to write the overture that night. She wanted to make him some punch and stay with him in order to keep him awake. She did this by telling him light, stimulating stories that he requested, for example Aladdin's Lamp, Cinderella, etc., which made him laugh to the point of tears. But the punch made him so sleepy that he nodded off whenever she stopped, and he was only able to work as long as she was telling stories. The strain of his sleepiness along with his frequent nodding off and reviving again made the work so difficult that his wife persuaded him to take a nap on the sofa with the promise that he would wake up in an hour. But he slept so soundly that she did not have the heart to wake him, and he did not get up again for two hours. This was about 5. At 7 the copyist was summoned and about the same time the overture was finished. It was only with difficulty that the copyists finished their work in time for the performance. The opera orchestra, whose skill was already known to Mozart, performed it superbly at first sight.

In the same biography of Mozart by Nissen, Štěpánek offered yet another version of the events surrounding the last few days before the performance of *Don Giovanni*. In this case, there is a contradictory claim that the overture was finished only on the morning of the first performance, October 29, not the day before, as specified by Mozart's wife. Mozart himself recorded the completion of *Don Giovanni* in his own catalog of compositions on 28 October 1787, a piece of evidence that helps confirm the accuracy of what Mozart's wife remembered. Almost certainly, the version of events found in the Nissen biography is the most reliable one presently preserved. Nonetheless, other accounts have come down with a similar aura of sincerity. After listing the original cast members of the opera, Štěpánek left additional testimony about the composer's playfulness:

> Out of this entire company [i.e., the original cast of *Don Giovanni*] only two are still living: Herr [Luigi] Bassi [Don Giovanni], Vice-Director of the royal Italian opera in Dresden, and Herr [Giuseppe] Lolli in Vienna [who sang the roles both of the Commendatore and the peasant Masetto]. Mozart himself coached each role with every member of the cast. Once at the first rehearsal of this opera inside the theater, Signora Bondini (as Zerlina) after several tries was not properly able to scream at the moment at the end of the first act where Don Giovanni grabs hold of her, so Mozart got up out of the orchestra, went onto the stage, had the scene repeated again, waited for the right moment, then grabbed her so suddenly and with such force that she let out a quite terrifying scream. "That's right," he then said, praising her for what she did, "that's how you have to scream."
>
> The opera was now rehearsed and had to be performed, but Mozart still had not finished the overture by the evening of the day before the performance and was out so late in the company of his friends, whose anxious concern about this seemed to displease him. Finally one of his intimates said to him: "Mozart, *Don Giovanni* is to be performed tomorrow, and you still haven't finished the overture." Mozart got a hold of himself, as if he were a little embarrassed, went into an adjoining room, where he was supplied with music paper, pen, and ink, began writing at midnight and by early in the morning completed within a few hours one of the most excellent overtures of his own or of all time. At 7, when the opera was supposed to begin, the copyists were still not ready with the parts, and it was not until a quarter of 8 that the orchestral parts, still full of the sand needed to dry the ink, were brought to the orchestra, at which time Mozart himself entered to conduct the first production. All of the very large audience received him with general applause.
>
> The overture, which never had the chance to be rehearsed beforehand, pleased the audience ever more and ever more and finally climaxed into loud cheers of praise. During the Introduction [i.e., the first scene of *Don Giovanni*] Mozart said to someone who was standing next to him, "Many notes fell under the desks, but the overture went quite well anyway."

In a special section of his biography devoted to musical anecdotes associated with Mozart's stay in Prague, Nissen included this account of a rehearsal of the opera, probably based on information supplied by Mozart's widow:

> When Mozart held the first rehearsal of his opera *Don Giovanni* in 1787, he had the rehearsal stopped at the place [in Act II] where the Commendatore sings "Di rider

finirai," etc., and "Ribaldo audace," etc., which was accompanied by three bare trombones, because one of the trombonists did not execute his part correctly. When it still did not go any better after repeated attempts, Mozart conducted himself to the trombonist's desk and explained to him how he wished it to be performed. The trombonist answered quite dryly, "it cannot be played that way, and I will not learn how to do so for the first time from you." Mozart responded laughing, "God preserve me from wanting to teach you how to play the trombone; just hand over the parts to me and I will change them." He did just that and added in this place two oboes, two clarinets, and two bassoons.

For his part, Němeček included an account of the composition of the *Don Giovanni* overture in a section of his biography that was devoted to a description of Mozart's compositional processes and the amazing speed with which he was capable of writing music. Němeček's version also assumes that the overture was completed on October 29, the same day as the first performance of the opera:

> We have already seen this facility with which Mozart composed even when he was a boy, proof that it was the product of genius. But how often in his later years did he surprise even those who believed in his talents? The overture to *Don Giovanni* is a remarkable example of this. Mozart wrote this opera in October 1787 in Prague; it was completed, rehearsed, and was to be performed in two days, only the overture still lacking.
>
> The anxiety of his friends, which increased by the hour, seemed to amuse him; indeed, the more embarrassed they became, the more lighthearted Mozart made himself. At last, on the evening before the day of the first performance, when he had been joking long enough he went to his room towards midnight, began to write, and in a few hours completed the admirable masterpiece that connoisseurs value even higher than the overture to *The Magic Flute*. It was only with difficulty that the copyists were able to finish before the performance, and the opera orchestra, whose skill Mozart was already acquainted with, executed it excellently prima vista ["at first sight"]. Němeček even added a special footnote to confirm that "this occurrence is common knowledge in Prague."

Still more details about hasty preparation of the overture to *Don Giovanni* are recorded in the reminiscences of Wilhelm Kuhe, a nineteenth-century pianist from Prague who claimed to have heard them from an obscure string bass player named Václav Svoboda, a member of Strobach's orchestra in the National Theater at the time of the première of the opera:

> The conceit (as I may term it) of the good people of my native city was increased a hundredfold when Mozart, in a speech delivered at a banquet in his honor, declared (so Svoboda told me) that the citizens of Prague were the only people in the world who understood his music. Had he lived longer he might have modified this opinion. Speaking of Mozart, I am reminded that my friend Svoboda used also to refer to the pleasure evinced daily by the great master in the game of billiards. He would also from time to time recall Mozart's habit of laying aside mere speech in favor of musical recitative, which even in public he would use as a means of making remarks and conveying requests to his circle of friends. From the same authority I learned the positive truth of the story (often told and as frequently denied) that on the night be-

fore its production the overture to *Don Giovanni* had not even been sketched. The impresario, said Svoboda, was in despair. Mozart's wife, however, undertook that the overture should be finished in time. She accordingly sat up all night with her husband, although she found it difficult to keep him awake. As he wrote, the sheets of the score were passed from his desk to those of a little army of copyists who were in attendance to transcribe the instrumental parts. Again and again was the great maestro overpowered by sleep, and every time he was aroused by his vigilant helpmate he broke into song as follows: [At this point Kuhe quoted the first two measures of the "second theme" of the fast section of the overture, a unison passage that can be found at measures 77-78 of the score.] These two bars continually recurred to him, and were as often written down.

The ink, Svoboda recalled, was hardly dry on some of the pages when they were placed on the desks of the orchestra. A rehearsal was impossible. Nevertheless, the overture was played with a spirit which not only roused the enthusiasm of the audience to the highest pitch, but so greatly delighted the illustrious composer that, turning to the orchestra, he exclaimed, "Bravo, bravo, meine Herren, das war augezeichnet!" (Bravo, bravo, gentlemen, that was admirable!).

At the end of that memorable first night Mozart declared that such a performance at sight was an extraordinary feat, "obschon manche Noten unter die Pulte gefallen sind" (although several notes had tumbled under the desks).

And now another of Svoboda's reminiscences:

At the final rehearsal of the opera Mozart was not at all satisfied with the efforts of a young and very pretty girl, the possessor of a voice of greater purity than power, to whom the part of Zerlina had been allotted [Caterina Bondini]. The reader will remember that Zerlina, frightened at Don Giovanni's too pronounced love-making, cries for assistance behind the scenes.

In spite of continued repetitions, Mozart was unable to infuse sufficient force into the poor girl's screams, until at last, losing all patience, he clambered from the conductor's desk on to the boards. At that period neither gas nor electric lights lent facility to stage mechanism. A few tallow candles dimly glimmered among the desks of the musicians, but over the stage and the rest of the house almost utter darkness reigned. Mozart's sudden appearance on the stage was therefore not noticed, much less suspected, by poor Zerlina, who at the moment when she ought to have uttered the cry received from the composer a sharp pinch on the arm, emitting, in consequence, a shriek which caused him to exclaim: "Admirable! Mind you scream like that tonight!"

The opera, as at first written, did not terminate with the carrying off of Don Giovanni by the Furies. This episode was followed by four additional numbers, including a quartette by Donna Anna, Elvira, Zerlina, and Ottavio. After the first night, however, these pieces remained unheard until the jubilee performance of the opera at Prague in 1837, on which occasion I was present. They were then voted exceedingly dull…

Meissner also contributed some information about the first performance of *Don Giovanni* after the completion of the overture:

The opera was to open the winter season under the most brilliant auspices, since it was known that Mozart had composed his work with special regard for Prague. The carriages began to drive up already at half past 5, and their passengers were soon dropped off on the ground floor. In spite of their careful grooming, the clean ladies who got out of the carriages had to make their way to the entrance through a sea of mud. Entering the hall, they found the galleries and parterre already filled. The appearance of the gallery was utterly frightening. There were people crowded head to head, and the last row of spectators clinging to the iron railings in between the columns appeared to be on the verge of falling down into the rows below. Through the buzz of the agitated crowd it was hardly possible to hear the cries of the servants who were circulating around and still offering "beer and fresh sausages" to satisfy the irrepressible appetite of the spectators in the gallery, whereas in the lower areas the call "lemonade, almond-milk" rang out.

The rumor about the lateness of the overture broke through to the audience, but nobody could comprehend how Mozart could have written down a work to the last note that was simply worked out and carried about in his head. It was let out that he had sat up the entire night working on it so that the copyists thought they would hardly be able to finish their work in time and the musicians at 4 still did not have their parts, so that they would have to play from sight. In the worst case, it was said, the overture to *Idomeneo* would have to be substituted.

The agitation of the audience increased, since there was in fact a particular unease to be noticed among the members of the orchestra. The time for the curtain to rise had already passed by several minutes. Then came the theater attendants with pages of music in their hands to distribute them on the desks. And like impatient children who cannot wait for the end of a long prayer at table before a holiday meal, so the audience waited for the parts to be distributed. Already by the time Mozart appeared at the conductor's podium, a thousand hands were raised up to welcome him. He acknowledged them thankfully in all directions, then gave the signal to begin and the overture rang out with such force as if it were coming out of the spirit world. The three chords [at the start], which are so to speak the opening gates of the composition, stirred up all men's hearts…

Three hours later, this opera, the likes of which the world of music had never seen before, finished its first run over the stage. The reckless heathen [Don Giovanni], in defiance of God and all his angels, was dragged down to his eternal grave of flames. A world of desire, wantonness, terror, lament, and despair that only Mozart could depict was displayed before the listeners and the reward was boundless applause.

On this evening Mozart spoke the words that would become famous: "My Praguers understand me," a phrase that would be passed down to every generation with honor.

Mozart immediately sent word of the success of his *Don Giovanni* to Da Ponte in Vienna, who was busy with his *Assur*, and Guardasoni wrote the following in his pathetic way: "Long lives Da Ponte, long live Mozart! Impresarios and musicians may wish you good fortune! As long as they live, there need never be a worry about venturing into the theater."

One last quotable reminiscence with information similar to what Meissner recorded about the first performance of the opera *Don Giovanni* originates from the German actor Eduard Genast in a collection called *From the Diary of an Old Actor* (*Aus dem Tagebuche eines alten Schauspielers*), published in Leipzig in 1862. Genast's father Anton, also an actor, had been brought up in Silesia and came to Prague in 1786 to be a member of the theatrical troupe of Karl Wahr. Since he had been trained to speak several foreign languages, including Italian, he soon made the acquaintance of the Italian singers associated with the Bondini and Guardasoni companies. He became a particularly good friend of Luigi Bassi, who was almost exactly his age (Genast was born in 1765, Bassi in 1766). From Bassi, Eduard Genast claimed, his father learned a great deal about the "immortal" Mozart. In his collection of reminiscences he included in quotation marks the following story, which he said was told to him directly by his father:

> The opera *Don Giovanni* was ready to be rehearsed, but there was still no overture ready, and it was even lacking at the rehearsal before the dress rehearsal, so that Guardasoni was earnestly reproaching the composer with the warning that the opera would probably have to be given without an overture. Mozart, however, quite undisturbed about this, went to supper the day before the dress rehearsal at a clergyman's house, a supper to which Bassi, Guardasoni, Wahr, and I were invited.
>
> The gathering was very enjoyable; the clergyman, a bon vivant, regaled us with excellent food and even more excellent Hungarian wine, which Mozart drank vigorously and in great quantity. The conversation, which became ever more lively, was spoken partly in Italian and partly in Latin. After the clergyman gave us a sharp tongue lashing, the party broke up shortly after 1. Wahr and I undertook to bring Mozart home, and on the way he continually sang tunes from *Don Giovanni*, but always came back to "Finch'han dal vino calda la testa," the "Champagne Aria." The sharp October air and the singing completely drained his energy by the time we got him home. Fully clothed, he threw himself on his bed and went to sleep immediately. Because we were also tired and wanted to avoid the long drive home, we sat down on an old feather sofa and Morpheus likewise took us in his arms. We were suddenly awaken from our deep sleep by loud sounds and were astonished when we got up to see Mozart sitting and working at a desk by a dim lamp. None of us dared to say a word and with true reverence listened as his immortal ideas developed. Without ever closing our eyes again, we remained completely still.
>
> After 9 he sprang up with the words: "There! That's it!" We did something like that as well and with astonishment he called out: "Hah, what devilry! How did you get here?" We kissed his beautiful white hands with enthusiasm. He let go of the score to us and asked us to turn it over to four copyists at the [opera house's] office right away. "Now we will want to sleep a bit," he said. In the evening the written-out parts, still partly wet, were laid on the desks.
>
> I did not neglect to attend any of the earlier rehearsals, so that the impression the overture made on me was even greater. Bassi was unsurpassable as *Don Giovanni*! At this time in Prague there prevailed in everyone who was concerned with music a discerning judgment that was in advance of all the German cities, and so this masterpiece found enormous success already at its first performance. The opera was given 20 times in succession to packed houses.

The success of *Don Giovanni* at its first performance in Prague cannot be questioned, although perhaps not the precise chronology of its completion nor Mozart's activities in the city during its preparations. There is much more to make note of during his trip to Prague in the autumn of 1787, including some amazing incidences to be detailed in the next chapter, but unfortunately nothing that led the composer to remain permanently in the city, as he was urged to do.

7

Interim Diversions:
Legends, Second Departure, and the Short Visits of 1789

Possessed as he was of an outgoing personality - and always in need of "society" - there can be no doubt that Mozart enriched the musical and social life of Prague in one way or another almost every day he was present in the city. Operatic productions may have been the principal focus of Mozart's visits to Prague between 1787 and 1791, but there was also more informal music-making and less ambitious composition projects undertaken for the benefit of musicians and music lovers who resided there. Stories that survive about these incidents are rich in human interest and attractive as legends, but they are frequently lacking in reliable documentation. All that can be done for the most part is to report their sources and leave it to the reader to decide whether they ring true or not.

One Harpist, Several Inns and Coffeehouses

Mozart appreciated musical talent wherever he found it, including places that would now be considered venues for the performance of popular music. An unusual incident related to this type of music-making has to do with a humble harpist in Prague whose contacts with Mozart are preserved in multiple accounts. The harpist in question lived in circumstances quite different from those enjoyed by the privileged Mozart. He genuinely was a "starving musician" dependent on a precarious livelihood, someone who could never hope to experience the glamorous music-making that Mozart had been accustomed to since early childhood. If the legends about him can be trusted, it is clear that Mozart took sincere interest in the abilities of this individual and supported his career to the extent he was able, including a means to cash in for decades on the fruits of a brief encounter.

The first published account of the legend of Mozart and the harpist is found in the Nissen biography of 1828, based on unidentified sources. Němeček made no mention of it in his biography, although he did illustrate the enormous popularity of the opera *Marriage of Figaro* with the remark that "even the harpist on the tavern bench had to play 'Non più andrai' if he wanted to be noticed at all." Nissen brought up the harpist in a section devoted specially to anecdotes about Mozart's visits to Prague:

When Mozart stayed in Prague at the inn called Das Neue Wirtshaus ["The New Inn"], he heard an accomplished and universally-loved harpist who took it upon himself to entertain guests with favorite selections from the beloved opera *The Marriage of Figaro* as well as his own improvisations, even though he did not play from notes. Mozart had him come to his room, played him a theme on the piano, and asked him whether he could produce variations on it off the top of his head. The harpist thought for a while, requested Mozart to play the theme one more time, and then produced a number of variations on it. Mozart pronounced himself satisfied with this and rewarded him handsomely. Since this theme, which Mozart probably made up on the spot, had never been committed to memory up to then by anyone other than this aged harpist, a zealous admirer of Mozart's transcribed it into notes for fear it would be forgotten, and thereby secured its existence forever. The owner protected it as we would the most costly jewel.

Nissen never mentioned the harpist's name, but he is identified in another account of the legend published in 1887 by Rudolf von Freisauff in his book *Mozart's Don Juan*. Freisauff claimed that a civil servant in Prague named Edmund Schebek shared with him a letter written on 29 October 1827 by Friedrich Wilhelm Pixis, a violin teacher at the Prague conservatory, to his brother Johann Peter Pixis, a piano virtuoso in Paris. Friedrich Wilhelm told his brother that his version of the encounter between Mozart and the harpist originated from Friedrich Dionys Weber, the first director of Prague Conservatory, who knew the harpist personally:

When Mozart came to Prague with the intention of hearing and conducting his opera *The Marriage of Figaro* (which had been performed time after time with unheard-of success), he became accustomed to seeing in the hotel he was staying at the accomplished and beloved harpist Josef Häusler, who entertained the guests at the tables with his playing. This harpist, who did not even have a pedal harp at this disposal, and did not know how to read notes, distinguished himself for the improvised fantasies he played that were based on the best-loved motives from the celebrated opera *The Marriage of Figaro*. They were performed with such a high degree of skill that they excited the attention of Mozart, who was seated at a table.

After the end of a meal, Mozart had him come to his room and played a theme for him on the piano and asked him whether or not he would like to be entrusted with improvising variations on it. The harpist thought about it a little while and requested Mozart to let him hear the theme once more, then began to produce variations one after another. Mozart expressed himself much delighted and the harpist acknowledged that he rewarded him richly. Gratified and encouraged by the approval of this great man, he retained this theme in his memory, and when he noticed connoisseurs among the listeners he was playing for, created new variations every time he played it.

He remembered the theme even as he advanced toward old age. In order that the theme would never be forgotten, an admirer of Mozart's genius in the same inn took it down in notes as best he could while the old harpist was going around the guests at the tables. In all probability this charming melody is an improvisation of the immortal Mozart, since nothing like it has been found after this long time. Its possessor, who guards it until today as a valuable keepsake, found the occasion to share it with his friend [myself] to be turned over to the pianist and composer of genius J. P. Pixis as material for a new, delightful artistic creation.

At the end of the letter, Pixis expressed his admiration for the theme and recommended it to his brother as the basis of composed variations for violin and piano. He included a transcription of what is now known as the "harpist's theme" ("Harfner-Thema"), a curious little composition in D minor.

Pixis never made mention of the "New Inn" specified by Nissen, an omission that points to the confusion concerning the chronology of the incident and its venue. It was assumed in earlier literature that this meeting would have taken place during Mozart's first visit to Prague in January and February of 1787, when *The Marriage of Figaro* was particularly popular in the city, but during that trip he was staying at the palace of Count Thun. In the autumn of 1787 Mozart supposedly stayed at the Three Lions' Inn in the Old City in alternation with the Bertramka villa.

A piece of information that may have some bearing on this question comes from a decree discovered by the present author in police records preserved in the National Archive in Prague. Signed by supreme burgrave Ludwig von Cavriani and issued on 27 September 1787, it granted permission for harpists to perform in inns, but not in the streets. If Němeček's indication that "the harpist on the tavern bench" was playing excerpts from *The Marriage of Figaro* early in 1787 is accurate, it would appear that harpists had earlier played both in inns and in the streets. Regardless, the decree intended to remove them from the streets in the future. It is possible that the sight of harpists playing inside inns was something new to Prague at the time of Mozart's second trip in the autumn of 1787. Even if they had performed in the inns earlier, there would have been more of them all of a sudden, since they were no longer supposed to play outside.

The "New Inn" mentioned by Nissen can be identified with certainty as the same building that once housed an inn known as the "Golden Angel" since the nineteenth century. A restaurant with that name ("U zlatého anděla") was in operation until recently on the corner of Celetná and Templová streets in the Old City of Prague. The old building has now been completely replaced by new construction. The "New Inn" is mentioned in the third volume of Jaroslaus Schaller's guidebook to Prague, published in 1796, though not in the *Complete Description of Prague* of 1787. It was located close to the National Theater and would have been the perfect location to have a meal. Mozart could have heard the harpist there even if he did not actually stay overnight. Surely *The Marriage of Figaro* would still have been an attractive source of melodies during Mozart's second trip. It is also possible that when Mozart invited Häusler back to his room, it was not a room in the "New Inn," but his room at the Three Lions' Inn, which would not have been a long walk away. Few innkeepers in Europe provided pianos for their guests, but the standing arrangement for lodgings with the impresario Guardasoni may have made this a standard accommodation at the Three Lions' Inn. It is even possible that Mozart took Häusler back to his room at the Thun palace during his first trip to Prague, where we know he had a piano, and not to any inn at all. Of course this incident may have occurred during the last trip to Prague in 1791 - no one knows where Mozart stayed at that time - or it may never have occurred at all, as disappointing as that thought may be.

In his 1892 study, Rudolph Freiherr Procházka transcribed an account from the Prague bookseller Joseph Max Schenk that claimed that the harpist in question actually performed in an inn right around the corner from the "New Inn" known as the Inn "Zum Tempel" ("U templu") for its location on "Temple lane" (Tempelgässchen/Templová), a narrow street named for a cloister once located in the vicinity that had been operated by the Knights Templar centuries before. The harpist in Schenk's version of the legend, which dates from 1842, is identified as "Hofmann," not Häusler, without any indication of a given name. In his *Rococo-Bilder,* Meissner included a colorful description of this "Hofmann," who went through the streets of Prague with very old-fashioned clothing, including knee breeches and a pigtail:

> The harpist Hofmann, to whom Mozart dedicated a theme and variations suitable for his instrument, was a unique fixture to be seen in the streets of Prague up to the year 1843: an ancient, short, weather-beaten little man wearing the clothes of a lost era. He tripped over himself, carrying around his harp with difficulty, from inn to inn, bare-headed wearing a powdered wig with a well-braided pigtail, in knee breeches, stockings, and buckled shoes. The street urchins were in the habit of running after him and calling him "pigtail." The showpiece of this old virtuoso, who seemed like a counterpart to the harpist in [Goethe's] *Wilhelm Meister*, was always the composition of Mozart's once dedicated to him, which he only played on special request.

Procházka believed that Schenk confused Häusler with a peddler named Hofmann who was well known in Prague in the 1830s. The identification provided in the Pixis letter was strengthened in 1912, however, when a lithograph now in the possession of Prague Conservatory was published that actually depicted the harpist Josef Häusler (identified as "Josef Haisler") as he looked in the year 1834 at the age of 80. The lithograph does show him sporting old-fashioned knee breeches and a pigtail consistent with the description of the harpist provided by Schenk and Meissner. It included another version of the "harpist's theme," a short minuet in F major.

The Inn "Zum Tempel" is surrounded by enough Mozart legend that it does deserve special discussion. An interesting description of it is found in Herold's *Picturesque Wanderings* of 1866, perhaps the basis of Meissner's story in Chapter 6 about how Mozart's friends were worried about him leaving late to join his friends in Templová lane rather than finish the overture to *Don Giovanni*:

> Here he sat often in the company of his admirers, merry and jovial, until late into the night. For this reason the inn was known for some time as "Mozart's Cellar" ["Zum Mozart Keller"] and the table at which this famous man sat and was frequently in the habit of using his knife, could be found in the inn for some time until the location was remodeled for use as a factory for locks and engines (by the court locksmith Janaušek). Since this time the table was transferred to the residence of the owner of the building.

Paul Nettl learned that the building that housed the inn was demolished in 1911, but there is photographic record of an inscription once found on one of its interior walls that states that "Mozart ate, drank, and composed here, for example, sausages, wine, and *Don Giovanni*." No such inn is mentioned in the *Complete Description of Prague* of 1787. The third volume of Jaroslaus Schaller's *Description of the City of Prague* (1796) does mention that the church of St. Paul the Apostle, which once belonged to the Knights Templar, was converted to private ownership in 1787, but there is no indication that the building was being used as an inn or coffeehouse in his time. Guidebooks from the 1820s, however, attest to its popularity - for example, August Griesel's *Newest Portrait of Prague* (*Neuestes Gemälde von Prag*) of 1823, and Wolfgang Gerle's *Prag and Its Landmarks* (*Prag und seine Merkwürdigkeiten*) of 1825. The unavoidable inference to be drawn is that the legends about Mozart accrued over the years in order to help enhance the mystique of this establishment.

Nettl also uncovered stories about Mozart's visits to another coffeehouse near the National Theater, the "Grape" ("Zur Traube"), where he supposedly enjoyed playing billiards. The earliest known source that matches the inn to reports of Mozart's billiard-playing in Prague is a book published in 1835 with the title *Prague in Its Present State* (*Prag in seiner jetzigen Gestalt*). In the *Complete Description of Prague* of 1787, the coffeehouse (or tavern) is referred to as the "Blue Wine Grape" ("Blaue Weintraube"). The guidebooks of Griesel and Gerle confirm its continued popularity in the 1820s. It is probably from the guidebook of 1835 that Eduard Herold got his idea for Mozart completing the overture to *Don Giovanni* at the "Grape" tavern (mentioned in the preceding chapter). Herold reported that it closed in 1865 after a long run as a favored meeting place for musical, theatrical, and artistic personnel. It was once located in the Karolinplatz, now the "Fruit Market" (Ovocný trh), the same square that encompasses the Estates' Theater (known in Mozart's time as the National Theater). The ultimate origins of anecdotes concerning billard-playing in Prague, however, is Nissen, who related a story that has to do with Mozart's activities during the coronation festivities of 1791. In this account, a coffeehouse is mentioned, but there is no indication of which one:

> While Mozart was writing his coronation opera, *La clemenza di Tito* in 1791, he visited a coffeehouse not far from where he was staying almost every day with his friends to distract himself with billiard-playing. For several days it was noticed that he sang a motive quite softly to himself, *hm, hm, hm*, while he was playing, and sometimes while the others were playing, he took a book out of his pocket, glanced at it briefly, and then started playing again. How astonished one was when Mozart once played for his friends on the piano at Dušek's house the beautiful quintet from *The Magic Flute* for Tamino, Papageno, and the Three Ladies ["Wie? Ihr an diesem Schrecksort?" from Act II], which begins with just the same motive that preoccupied Mozart so much while he was playing billiards.

Mozart had to interrupt his progress on *The Magic Flute* in order to write *La clemenza di Tito* for Prague. He had to wait until his return to Vienna to finish *The Magic Flute,* thus it is no wonder that he had his mind on it while visiting Prague. Meissner claimed that this incident took place at a coffeehouse known as the "Storm" ("zum Sturm"), whose location is not presently identifiable.

Herold's *Picturesque Wanderings* of 1866 includes its own version of the harpist's legend, one that is less flattering about Mozart's motivations in composing the "harpist's theme" and contradicts the accounts of Nissen and Pixis concerning the harpist's lack of musical literacy:

> The composer of *The Marriage of Figaro* - Mozart - often visited the guestroom of the "New Inn." A little man who played the harp also came there. Mozart expressed himself dissatisfied that he would hear the same pieces played every time he came, furthermore executed in a not very masterful way. One time he turned to the little man and asked him if he could play something different.
>
> "Oh yes," answered the one who was questioned, and he began to play another song.
>
> "Oh, I know that one already," Mozart called out, "that one also - and this one as well."
>
> The little man was at a loss, for he did not have a large number of selections to play, but undeterred, he grabbed the strings of his instrument in order to satisfy this gentleman who was unknown to him.
>
> "Be still," Mozart now requested, "don't touch a single string, I will write something for you."
>
> After these words he sat down in a corner, took out a piece of paper from his pocket and in the timespan of barely a quarter of an hour he wrote a little piece of music that he gave to the perplexed harpist with the instruction to study it.
>
> As soon as the bystanders around the little man took note of Mozart's attention to him they acquired enthusiasm for the good-natured musician.
>
> He then hurried home and practiced day and night until he knew the melody intimately, then as soon as he returned to his famous guest room to perform Mozart's little melody for curious patrons, everyone remarked "that this melody of the great Mozart was written for him alone."
>
> The little man wandered the streets of Prague vigorously with his harp into the 1840s, to the general delight of merry youths, who teased him with the cry of "pigtail" for strutting around in rococo-era dress with a pigtail, knee breeches, etc.

There can be no reasonable expectation that the true story of Mozart and the harpist will ever be known.

A Visit to the Strahov Abbey

A more reliable incident of Mozart's informal music-making in Prague comes from an eyewitness account of a visit he made to the Strahov abbey with Josefa Dušek. Its source is a reminiscence preserved from the priest and musician Norbert Lehman, who was active at the Strahov from 1772. Decades after the event, on 1 May 1818, Lehman wrote a letter about it to František Xaver Němeček, whose biography of Mozart had appeared long before. Lehman mistakenly remembered the incident as happening in June of 1787, a time when Mozart was certainly in Vienna. It must actually have taken place in October or November of the same year. It is not likely to have taken place during Mozart's first trip to Prague, a cold time of year when the Dušeks were mainly absent, nor could it have taken place after 1787, since the choir director Jan Lohelius Oehlschlägel, also described by Lehman, died in 1788.

It is easy to imagine Mozart and his hostess taking a pleasant afternoon stroll (or ride) from the Bertramka villa to the Strahov. Even at a leisurely pace, it would have taken less than an hour and a half to walk there (some of the stretch a daunting hike uphill), but the truth of the matter is that Mozart would have been more the sort of person to take a carriage. Dušek may have made it a point to take him to the Strahov to observe its architectural wonders - for example, the Philosophical Library, just completed in 1784 - or just to see the beautiful hills and orchards that surround it. Lehman had the amazing good fortune to witness Mozart improvising on the organ in the Church of the Assumption within the grounds of the abbey. He transcribed as much as he could of what he heard Mozart play as he was being interrupted by Oehlschlägel. Lehman sent Němeček his transcription of the improvisation along with this description of its inception:

Church of the Assumption,
Strahov Monastery
©Adam Smok

I am most desirous here to hand down to you the Mozart improvisation along with its history. This virtuoso did the city of Prague the honor of visiting in the month of June 1787, in order to become acquainted with the musicians of this capital city and see its landmarks. One day at about 3 o'clock in the afternoon he arrived at the Strahov church with Frau Dušek and expressed his desire to hear the organ. As assistant to the organist, this task was assigned to me by the gracious prelate Herr Wenzl Mayer. I was certainly not pleased with this charge to have my playing heard by such a great musician and composer; still it was up to me to execute my orders.

Mozart sat in the nave of the church near the pulpit. I let him get an appreciation of the full strength of the organ and performed a theme of pathetic character. When this was finished, this virtuoso asked who was playing the organ. One of the clerics accompanying him said, "A clergyman from our abbey."

Then he asked, "There are organists among the clergymen here?"

"Yes," answered Herr Matthias Ehrlich, at that time a teacher at the Gymnasium in Malá Strana.

Now Mozart wanted to play the organ himself. He sat on the bench and casually played masterful progressions of block chords for four minutes and by this means demonstrated to every connoisseur that he was more than an ordinary organist. After this he wanted to play the manual without Brustpositiv or Rückpositiv [specialized organ ranks]. All four of the reed stops were too loud for him. Besides the usual pedal without Mixtur [added stops] he selected the eight-foot trombone stop. Then he started up a four-voice fugue theme that was particularly difficult to perform, because the theme and its development included distinct ornaments which were extraordinarily difficult to execute on an organ with such a hard action. Everyone was astonished that the fourth and fifth fingers of both his left and right hands were as strong as his thumbs, index fingers, and middle fingers.

I fixed my complete attention on the working-out of the fugue theme and intended to stand still until its conclusion; but then came the late choir director Father Lohelius alone into the choir of the church. He distracted me so much with his questions that I completely lost my thread of concentration, and indeed at the spot where it was most necessary to pay attention. Mozart had ascended so far from G minor in the pedal bass that he had progressed to B minor. Then the late Lohelius disturbed me by asking how he could get to E-flat major so quickly from there.

Now Mozart wanted to end in this key and he let out a pedal point. He held B-flat as the fifth of the key, started to play with both hands on the two highest octaves of the manuals, went through so many keys and accumulated so many suspensions and resolutions, that he was playing splendidly in B major and had to change the pedal note to F-sharp. All of his fingers were moving so quickly, partly because of the ornaments, partly because of the busywork in the middle voices, that none of them rested for a moment. It was his intention that nothing could be heard from the pedals.

Hardly was I finished answering the first question of the late Lohelius, when he had a bunch of others to be answered. He said: "Brother." (Answer): "What is it?" - (Question) "He's holding a B-flat pedal." - (Answer): "Yes indeed." (Question): "He wants to break into the key of E-flat." - (Answer): "Certainly." - (Question): "But he's playing in B major." - (Answer): "I know that." - (Question): "How can that sound good?" - (Answer): "But it does sound good." (Namely, because so many notes in the two higher octaves made such a miserable racket, that all four of the ranks could not have been heard [in the pedal]. His ten fingers skipped around those two octaves so busily, it was like ants scattering about when their anthill is being attacked.) In the midst of so many questions like these it was revealed to me in the best and most artistic manner how Mozart betrayed his strengths as a composer.

Then he performed the theme of a fugue from the Brixi mass in C minor in such a completely transformed style that hearing it was like being petrified. He gave each voice that carried the theme at a different pitch level its due, which was a wonderment mainly in the tenor voice. When the bass went too low and the tenor line could not be reached with the left hand, the right hand had to help out with various pitches and fingers…

The C-minor mass of Brixi mentioned in this letter must refer to one of the dozens of masses composed by František Xaver Brixi, the head of the musical establishment of the Cathedral of St. Vitus from 1759 until his death in 1771. Clearly his theme could never have sounded better than in Mozart's hands.

The Composition of the Aria "Bella mia fiamma, addio"

With regard to the lesser compositions Mozart wrote in Prague during the autumn of 1787, there are specific indications of dates in Mozart's own catalog of compositions. The most substantial one is the magnificent concert aria "Bella mia fiamma, addio," K. 528, which appears in the catalog on November 3 as being composed for "Madame Duschek in Prague." It is a worthy successor to his earlier concert aria for Dušek, "Ah, lo previdi," K. 272, which was written at the time of her first acquaintance with Mozart in Salzburg in 1777. In the case of "Bella mia fiamma, addio," a story about its origins survives from the composer's son Karl, only three years' old at the time of its composition and not present in Prague. He did, however, live in Prague after his father died in order to receive an education under the supervision of František Xaver Němeček. On 4 March 1856, Karl Mozart wrote from Milan, where he had worked as a civil servant in the Austrian administration of the Italian province of Lombardy, to the owner of the Bertramka villa at the time, one Adolf Popelka, with reminiscences of the villa and the city of Prague as he had known it in the 1790s. He included a story about Josefa Dušek locking Mozart up in a pavilion while the composer was going for a walk on the grounds of the Bertramka estate:

> On the peak of one of the hills belonging to the villa there stood a pavilion. One day the singer Frau Dušek locked up the great Mozart in a cunning way, then prepared ink, pen, and music paper and let him know that he would not be able to regain his freedom unless he composed for her the aria he promised with the words "Bella mia fiamma, addio!" Mozart yielded to necessity, but in order to avenge the prank that Frau Josepha Dušek had played on him, he introduced into the aria various passages that were difficult to perform and threatened his despotic friend that he would immediately destroy the aria if she could not perform it successfully at first sight.

This anecdote might well have been the inspiration for Meissner's little story about Mozart being locked up in the Bertramka villa, then freed by Casanova, in order to get him to finish the overture to *Don Giovanni* (transcribed in the previous chapter). Two episodes of confinement at the Bertramka villa seem rather suspicious.

The idea for the setting of the aria "Bella mia fiamma, addio" might well extend much farther back than the time of Mozart's second visit to Prague in 1787. On 15 December 1780, Leopold had written to his son Wolfgang, who was staying in Munich at the time for the première of his opera *Idomeneo*, with news that Josefa Dušek had sent him a text that she hoped Wolfgang could set as an aria. Leopold told her that nothing could be done about it before the new year. On 19 December, Wolfgang mentioned to his father in a long letter that indeed it would be impossible for him to compose an aria for her until he was finished writing *Idomeneo*. Nothing more about the aria is ever mentioned again in the surviving Mozart correspondence, but the story of the text sent to Leopold could have been the reason for the allusion to a "promised" aria in Karl Mozart's story. One reason to believe that the text set by Mozart was the one sent to Salzburg in 1780 is its age. It is taken from an opera by Niccolò Jommelli composed in 1772, *Cerere placata*. It might be reasonable to imagine Josefa Dušek attracted to a text from an opera that was eight years' old in 1780. It is not so likely that she would have been newly attracted to an opera text that was fifteen years' old in 1787. Still, if Mozart intended the composition as a "farewell" aria, deliberately set to a text that expresses the pain of departure (a possibility discussed in Chapter 12), it would be quite a coincidence if the text of the aria she had been carrying around for so long would just happen to be one with a text suitable for parting sentiments, as this one certainly was.

The Second Departure from Prague and Events Soon After

The only specific indication of when Mozart departed Prague for the second time comes from his letter to Gottfried von Jacquin of 4 November 1787 (excerpted in the previous chapter). Mozart told Jacquin that he expected to leave Prague on 12 or 13 November. Two tributes to Mozart in Prague are recorded in his own album of autographs from 11 and 12 November 1787. The earlier one was penned by Adelheid Weber, an older sister of Fridolin and Franz Anton Weber (thus an aunt of the composer Carl Maria von Weber), the other one by Josef Hurdálek, rector of the archiepiscopal seminary in the Klementinum. Clearly Mozart returned to the Klementinum on at least one occasion after his brief tour in January of 1787. It makes sense to believe that if Mozart intended to leave Prague on 12 or 13 November, he would not have done so on the same day as a visit to the Klementinum. Rather, an early morning start without distraction makes more sense. Assuming a journey of three days' duration beginning on 13 November, he would have been back in Vienna by 16 November.

The first documentary confirmation of Mozart's return to Vienna comes from a request of the imperial high chamberlain, Count Franz von Rosenberg, to appoint Mozart a chamber musician to the imperial court. An opening for such a position was created by the death of Gluck on 15 November 1787. The request on Mozart's behalf is dated 6 December 1787. According to Rosenberg, the emperor Joseph II had already expressed his desire to see Mozart appointed to this post. The appointment was made official on 7 December 1787 at an annual salary of 800 gulden for a part-time job, far less than the 2000 gulden per year that Gluck had been paid. The duties involved nothing more than the composition of dance music for imperial balls.

Mozart wrote to his sister from Vienna on 19 December 1787. Precisely how long she had been waiting for an answer to her last letter to him is not known:

Dearest Sister,
I most humbly beg your pardon for having left you so long without an answer. Of my writing *Don Giovanni* for Prague and of the opera's triumphant success you may have heard already, but that His Majesty the Emperor has now taken me into his service will probably be news to you. I am sure you will be pleased to hear it…

As humble as this appointment may seem, it ensured that Mozart would never consider living in Prague on a permanent basis. The value of a court appointment can hardly be overemphasized. Besides its intrinsic prestige, it also brought the hope of greater responsibility and higher rank. Prague could never have competed with Vienna as a place of residence for Mozart without a court. To a large extent, Mozart could take Prague for granted. He knew that anything he wrote would be adored there, so he might as well compose in Vienna in order to try to build his reputation in that city. The importance of the court appointment was soon noted in Prague. An announcement appeared in the *Prague Post* on 29 December 1787, although it reported his salary incorrectly as 600 gulden per year and that his new employer would be the archduke Francis, not his uncle the emperor Joseph.

On 11 December 1787, the *Prague Post* reported that a mass of Mozart had been performed in the church of St. Nicholas in Malá Strana in honor of the feast day of the saint (6 December). Without so much as an indication of a key, there can be nothing more than speculation about which mass was performed, perhaps the one he had finished most recently, the Mass in C minor, K. 427, of 1782 or 1783, in fact the only mass he had completed since leaving Salzburg in 1781. The *Prague Post* reported of Mozart's abilities as a composer of sacred music that "everyone avowed that in this specialized style of composition he was also a complete master."

In the same month a remarkable tribute to Mozart's abilities as a composer of opera was sent to Prague from none other than Joseph Haydn. Secure in his position as the most respected composer of instrumental music in Europe, as well as a successful composer of dramatic vocal works, Haydn could always be relied upon to promote the talents of the struggling Mozart, consistent with his generous nature. František Xaver Němeček was in possession of a letter written by Haydn to Franz Rott, a government official in Prague whose family residence, the Rott House, can still be seen in the "Little Square" (Malé náměstí) of the Old City of Prague, magnificently decorated with murals added during the late nineteenth century. (As of this writing, it is the home of the Hard Rock Cafe of Prague.) Rott was a patron of music who owned a large music library. It is not known exactly when or why he decided to approach Haydn about sending music for a comic opera to be performed in Prague, nor is it known precisely when in December of 1787 Haydn penned his response. Nonetheless, it makes remarkable reading:

Rott House
©Henry Ristek

> You request of me an opera buffa; it would be my pleasure indeed, if you wish to possess some of my vocal compositions just for yourself. But if the opera is to be performed on the stage in Prague, I cannot be of service to you, since all of my operas are too much too bound up with our own personnel [at Eszterháza in Hungary], and moreover would never produce the same effect as when I tailor them to local conditions. It would be quite a different matter to have the inestimable fortune to be able to set an entirely new libretto for your theater. But even I would be putting myself at great risk in that it would be difficult for anyone to be compared side-by-side with the great Mozart.
>
> For if I were able to impress on the souls of every music lover, particularly the great ones, the incomparable works of Mozart, so profound and with so much musical

intelligence, as much feeling as I sense and comprehend in them, then the nations would compete with each other to possess such a jewel within their borders. Prague should hold on to this precious man - but also reward him, for without that, the story of great geniuses is sad indeed, and gives their successors little encouragement for further exertions. For lack of this, unfortunately, so many hope-filled spirits have been defeated. It makes me furious that this unique Mozart has not yet been engaged by an Imperial or Royal Court.

Excuse me if I have gone off-track - I love the man.

Some Events of the Year 1788

Mozart's activities in Vienna were occasionally reported in the *Prague Post* until his death in 1791. One of the most interesting bits of news came on 8 April 1788:

> Some friends of the famous Mozart wished to hear something new by him, but they were quite surprised when he put together a serenade ["Nachtkassazion"], which was a mixture of all kinds of little beer hall melodies; thus he demonstrated his knowledge of the *stilo curiae*.

It is unclear exactly what meaning the odd Latin term at the end is meant to convey. The only two serenades that Mozart wrote in the preceding year were the famous "Eine kleine Nachtmusik," K. 525, and the less well-known "Musical Joke," K. 522, completed on 14 June 1787, an amusing parody of serious composition that is more likely the work referred to here.

The spread of performances of the opera *Don Giovanni* was not of much interest in Prague, as far as surviving issues of its newspapers reveal, but its momentum was unstoppable. The opera was performed in several German cities before Mozart's death (although never with the enthusiasm it received in Prague). The reception of the opera in Vienna at its first performance in 1788 has always elicited the most commentary in the Mozart literature. Meissner had some remarks about it to make, but much of what he had to say about this matter was paraphrased from the Da Ponte memoirs. The Hibernian Theater he mentioned was founded in the year 1789 in a building that once belonged to an order of Franciscan friars that had been expelled from Ireland in the sixteenth century. The emperor Joseph dissolved their order and ejected them from their abbey in the New City. The building that housed the Hibernian Theater can still be seen overlooking Republic Square (Náměstí Republiky), which was known as Josephplatz in Mozart's day:

> From this time forward (1787-1789) *Don Giovanni* was sometimes performed in the Estates' Theater, sometimes in the Thun Theater, and sometimes in the royal and imperial Hibernian Theater. Even the emperor Joseph was not unmoved by its success. He called for Da Ponte, sent him a hundred ducats and told him that he was burning with desire to hear the work. Da Ponte wrote to Mozart to get him to come back. He arrived and gave up the score to be copied immediately, and Joseph's imminent departure [to the war front] hastened the preparations for the production - but *Don Giovanni* did not please the Viennese at its first performance on May 8, 1788. Everyone, Mozart alone excepted, was of the opinion that the work should be revised.

Mozart and Da Ponte made additions and changes, the opera was performed for a second time and it still did not please. Only the emperor Joseph had the courage to say, "This work is heavenly, it is even more beautiful than *The Marriage of Figaro*, but it is no morsel for the Viennese." "Great art," said Da Ponte quite rightly, "is in general too high for the masses, it can take a century, even two, to build a reputation for genius, which finally is recognized as a fact without question and decided for all time."

In his *Memoirs*, Da Ponte told the following story about returning to Vienna from Prague. *Don Giovanni* was first performed in Vienna on May 7, 1788:

> The emperor sent for me, and overloading me with gracious felicitations, presented me with another hundred sequins, and told me that he was longing to see *Don Giovanni*. Mozart returned, and since Joseph was shortly to depart for the field [he left to pursue a campaign against the Turks on February 28, 1788], hurried the score to the copyist, to take out the parts. The opera went on the stage and…need I recall it?…*Don Giovanni* did not please! Everyone, except Mozart, thought that there was something missing. Additions were made; some of the arias were changed; it was offered for a second performance. *Don Giovanni* did not please! And what did the emperor say? He said:
>
> "That opera is divine; I should even venture that it is more beautiful than *Figaro*. But such music is not meat for the teeth of my Viennese!"
>
> I reported the remark to Mozart, who replied quietly: "Give them time to chew on it!"
>
> He was not mistaken. On his advice I strove to procure frequent repetitions of the opera: at each performance the applause increased, and little by little even Vienna of the dull teeth came to enjoy its savor and appreciate its beauties, and placed *Don Giovanni* among the most beautiful operas that have ever been produced on any stage.

The Viennese reception of *Don Giovanni* is not addressed in the Da Ponte *Extract*. There is considerable reason to believe that in this case Da Ponte's memory was more reliable than in other matters. One sign of this is the fact that he remembered correctly the payment he received from the imperial court for his efforts as librettist. Pay records preserved in the Vienna State Archives confirm that Da Ponte was paid 100 ducats for his poetry and Mozart 225 ducats for the music that performed in Vienna for the first time on 7 May 1788. Da Ponte's account of the mediocre reception of *Don Giovanni* at its first run in Vienna in 1788 is corroborated by other contemporary sources. The first reaction of Count Zinzendorf was positive, however; he wrote in this diary that "Mozart's music is agreeable and very varied." But on 12 May 1788 he reported the opinion of Countess Henriette Luisa zur Lippe, the wife of an imperial court official, who found the music "learned, little suited to the voice." The archduchess Elisabeth Wilhelmine, wife of the archduke Francis, who was fighting with his uncle in the Turkish campaign, wrote to her husband from Vienna on 15 May 1788 to report that "in the last few days a new opera composed by Mozart has been given, but I was told that it did not have much success." The emperor himself wrote to Count Rosenberg, the director of the imperial theater, on 16 May 1788 to complain that "Mozart's music is certainly too difficult for the singers," even though he was at the Turkish front and could not have heard the opera. A decade after the fact, the music critic Friedrich Rochlitz provided a more detailed explanation for the failure of *Don Giovanni* in Vienna in the *Allgemeine Musikzeitung,* after recording Mozart's opinion that the opera "was not written for the Viennese, rather for the Praguers, but most of all for myself and my friends":

> *Don Giovanni* did not especially please in Vienna at first. When it was performed there the first or second time, the famous music-loving Prince R---- had a numerous company of people with him. Most of the music connoisseurs in the capital city were present, including Joseph Haydn. Mozart was not in attendance. Much was said about this new production. After the fashionable ladies and gentlemen formed their opinions, the word was out among the connoisseurs. It was generally acknowledged that it was an estimable work of a rich genius of inexhaustible imagination, but for one it was too full textured, for another too chaotic, for a third too unmelodic, for a fourth of uneven quality, etc. In general there was no dispute that there was some truth in all of these judgments. Everyone expressed his opinion - only Father Haydn did not. Finally this unassuming artist was asked to offer his judgment. With his usual caution he said, "I cannot settle the dispute, but this I do know" - he added with great animation - "that Mozart is the greatest composer in the world today!" With that, all the ladies and gentlemen went silent.

Two Short Visits to Prague in 1789

All of Mozart's personal contacts with Prague after the original production of the opera *Don Giovanni* could be described accurately as anticlimactic, including the two short visits he made in the year 1789 on his way to and from Dresden, Leipzig, and Berlin. Mozart was traveling this time with Prince Karl von Lichnowsky, a prominent patron of music in Vienna who presumably paid all of his expenses while they were together. Mozart's wife, for whatever reason, did not come along. The most important musical legacies of this trip were string quartets and a piano sonata written for members of the royal family of Prussia. The king of Prussia at that time, Frederick William II, was a noted amateur cellist who also maintained contacts with Joseph Haydn. Mozart probably could not have passed up a trip with Prince Lichnowsky as a means to seek income and exposure for his talents after the Turkish war had caused a disruption in patronage in Vienna. Mozart and the prince separated in May after they arrived in Berlin. Where the prince was going and why he was in such haste (according to Mozart's letter to his wife of 23 May 1789) is a mystery. Interestingly, Prince Lichnowsky took Beethoven on a similar trip in 1796, and they stopped at the same inn in Prague - the Unicorn Inn - that Mozart had visited. Beethoven's stay is commemorated to this very day with a handsome plaque (whereas there is no plaque to commemorate Mozart's earlier visit).

The first stop in Moravian territory after Znojmo was Moravské Budějovice, and Mozart wrote to his wife from there on 8 April 1789. His touching affection for her as usual found ample expression:

Dearest little wife:

    While the prince is bargaining for horses, I am delighted to seize this opportunity to write a couple of words to you, dearest little wife of my heart - How are you? - Do you think of me as often as I think of you? - Every moment I look at your portrait - and weep - half out of joy, half out of sorrow - Look after your health, which is so precious to me, and fare well, my love! Do not worry about me; on this journey. I know nothing of discomfort - nor of annoyance - nothing other than your absence - which, since it cannot be helped, cannot be changed; - I write this note with eyes full of tears - Adieu - I will write a longer and more legible letter to you from Prague, because I will not have to hurry so much - Adieu - I kiss you millions of times most tenderly and am yours forever, true until death.

    Stu - stu - Mozart

As promised, Mozart wrote to his wife from Prague as soon as he arrived (on Good Friday, 10 April 1789):

Dearest, most beloved little wife!

    We arrived here safely today at half past one in the afternoon; meanwhile I certainly hope that you will have received my little note from Budějovice. - Now comes my account of Prague. - We dropped ourselves off at the "Unicorn Inn"; - after I had been shaved, had my hair done and got dressed, I drove out with the intent of having a meal at Count Canal's; but since I had to pass the Dušek residence, I called there first - but was told that Madame had traveled to Dresden yesterday!!! - So I will meet her there. [František] Dušek was eating at Leliborn's, where I also used to eat often; - I drove straight there, - I had Dušek called out (as if it were just anyone who wished to speak to him), so you can imagine our delight. - So I also lunched at Leliborn's. - After the meal I drove to see Count Canal and Count Pachta, but nobody was at home; - so I went to see Guardasoni - who has practically arranged to give me 200 ducats next autumn for the opera and 50 ducats for travelling expenses. - Then I went home to write all of this to my dear little wife - there is something else - eight days ago Ramm left Prague to return home. He came from Berlin and said that the king had frequently and insistently asked whether it was certain that I was coming to Berlin, and since I had still not come he said again: "I am afraid that he will not come at all."

    Ramm became quite uneasy and tried to convince him to the contrary; - Judging from this, my affairs should not be going badly. - Now I am driving the prince to see Dušek, who is expecting us, and at nine o'clock we are departing for Dresden, where we hope to arrive tomorrow evening. - Dearest little wife! I am longing so much for news of you. - Perhaps there will be a letter for me in Dresden! Oh God! Make my wish come true! Once you receive this letter you must write to me general delivery at Leipzig; adieu - I must close, or I will miss the post. - Kiss our Karl a thousand times and I, who kiss you from my whole heart, remain ever your faithful Mozart.

    This letter is remarkable for the number of activities crammed into a few hours. Judging from Dušek's surprise, there must have been no advance announcement of Mozart's visit to anyone in Prague; there was certainly no mention of it in the Prague press. The Unicorn Inn was one of the most luxurious in all of Prague, housed in a handsome building that still graces the Malá Strana district on Lázeňská street near Charles Bridge. It is singled out twice in the *Complete Description of Prague* of 1787. The first notice describes it as "a very spacious building that can well be overlooked for stays by notable travelers for its concealed location." Indeed it overlooks an almost hidden square just off a thoroughfare now called Mostecká. Later it is described as "one of the most famous inns in Prague which has established an ever-growing reputation for a long time after becoming known to many distinguished travelers who have passed through. It is very spacious, comfortable, and well-appointed." Yet Mozart never slept there. He only stayed to "freshen up."

The reference to "Leliborn's" is obscure. There is no mention of this name in any guidebooks to Prague from the late eighteenth century or early nineteenth century. Most likely, Leliborn is the name of an owner of one of the coffeehouses that Mozart frequented. There are legends surrounding his visits to the "Blue Wine Grape" in the Old City near the National Theater. He might have been referring to it. Considering its proximity to any of the possible residences of the Counts Pachta, Count Canal, and Domenico Guardasoni, it seems likely that wherever "Leliborn's" was, it would have had to have been near the National Theater.

The location of Domenico Guardasoni's residence can be confirmed from the earliest surviving opera bill that advertises a performance of *Don Giovanni* in Prague, one preserved in the Memorial of National Literature in Prague that was printed for a run that began on 23 September 1788. Among other things, it records the beginning of the production at 7:00 PM and its conclusion at 9:30 PM, which means that there could only have been a very short intermission between the two acts, probably just enough time to accommodate a change of scenery. Copies of individual arias and musical numbers were advertised for sale at the residence of Domenico Guardasoni ("across from the theater"), whose address is given as the "Bergmandl" house, No. 285 in the Old City. The building was long ago replaced by a more modern structure, but at that time was located on the corner of streets now named Rytířská and Na můstku. Guardasoni's idea to put on a new opera by Mozart for the autumn of 1789 must be regarded as one of the great missed opportunities for music lovers worldwide, an opportunity lost because of the impresario's travels. Guardasoni left Prague later in the year 1789 for Warsaw, not to return until the spring of 1791. The impresario Bondini left Prague permanently for Italy in the summer of 1789, but died during his journey. No new Italian operas are known to have been produced in Prague again until after Guardasoni's return in June of 1791, a sad reminder of how precarious theatrical life was in Prague when it depended on private support for its survival in the absence of government subsidy.

Friedrich Ramm, the next individual mentioned in Mozart's short letter, was an oboist whom Mozart had met in Mannheim in 1777 while searching for a court position there. He would run into Mozart from time to time until 1790. Exactly what he was doing in Berlin and Prague at this time is not known.

The novelty of traveling seems to have worn off once Mozart actually reached Berlin. The letters that survive from his trip there are mainly devoted to how much he missed Constanze and how quickly he wished to return to her. Already in a letter written from Leipzig on 16 May 1789, he said that he was glad there would be no more need to bother with letters, since they would be able to see each other again soon (but in the meanwhile, he advised her to send her answer to the letter to Dušek in Prague for greater security). By the end, he ceased to include detailed accounts of his activites; all he wanted to do was get back home to his wife. In a letter written from Berlin on 23 May 1789, he told Constanze that he intended to stay overnight in Prague on 1 June, then reach Vienna by 4 June. This plan is confirmed in the last surviving letter ever written by Mozart from Prague, in this case little more than a few instructions laid out for his wife on 31 May 1789. He did not say a word about where he was staying or whom he met while he was there:

> Best, most beloved little wife!
> I arrived this very moment. - I hope that you received my last letter of the 23rd. Everything will stay as planned; - I will arrive on Thursday, June 4th, between eleven and twelve o'clock either at the last or the first post station, where I hope to meet you; do not forget to bring someone with you who can drive to the customs instead of me. Adieu. God, how delighted I am to be seeing you again; - In haste. Mozart

An opera commission from Guardasoni could have made all the difference for the Mozarts during the financially dismal year of 1789, but it never materialized, and there were no significant connections with Prague again until a few months before the composer's death in 1791. Still, it is likely that Mozart's music continued to be performed frequently in the city. One notable confirmation of this comes from a placard that survives from a concert given in the National Theater on 26 April 1791 that featured the singing of Josefa Dušek. Of the seven selections on the program (a mix of vocal and instrumental music), there were three compositions by Mozart: a piano concerto whose identity cannot be identified; a "grand scene" for voice "quite recently completed" that is also impossible to identify securely; and a "rondò" for voice with basset horn that was probably identical to the vocal piece "Al desio di chi t'adora," K.577, of 1789. Very few such placards survive; if the preservation were greater, it is likely that there would be more evidence of the permanent place Mozart had established for himself in the musical life of Prague. Although the affection that the Praguers felt for Mozart would be somewhat obscured during his last visit to their city (due to the unusual circumstances that occasioned it), its depth was revealed again when the news of his death reached them, and it became clear that the impact made by his visits from Vienna could never be repeated.

Tomáš Seiden's *Mozart*
Bertramka

8

Playing Second Fiddle: Mozart and the Coronation of Leopold II in 1791

Although it may be difficult for the modern music lover to comprehend, Wolfgang Amadeus Mozart was not always the center of attention wherever he appeared. In Europe of the eighteenth century, a musician of low birth could never hope to be. At the coronation of Leopold II as king of Bohemia in Prague in 1791, Mozart was not lionized in Prague the way he had been during his two earlier extended stays. The Prague press was only naturally drawn to the activities of Leopold, who was at that time the most exalted ruler in Europe for his title of Holy Roman Emperor. How ironic it is to observe today that he is not only much less famous than Mozart, but not even the most famous monarch who bore the name Leopold II; that distinction now belongs to Leopold II, king of the Belgians, whose brutal exploitation of the native population of the Belgian Congo in the late nineteenth century has received considerable attention from historians in recent decades. Outside of specialized circles, interest in Mozart's Leopold II now pales in comparison.

The events that led to Mozart's last trip to Prague can be traced to tensions between the Estates of Bohemia and the king of Bohemia that were described earlier in this volume. Mozart was brought in to help prepare an operatic production commissioned by the Estates of Bohemia that was meant to ratify a fresh political arrangement between the two parties. The most important issues were settled when Leopold agreed to force the Bohemian serfs freed from the obligation of *robota* by Joseph II back into servitude and rescind Joseph's attempts to impose higher taxation on the Bohemian nobility. In return, the nobles abandoned their attempts to assert political privileges that had lapsed since the defeat of the Estates of Bohemia at White Mountain in 1620. No composition of Mozart was ever more explicitly pressed into the service of a political agenda than the opera he wrote for the Estates, *La clemenza di Tito*. The money for his fee came from the Estates, not the imperial court; thus he was working as an agent of their interests, whether he realized it or not. The true nature of the political agenda he was serving has never been fully explained in the Mozart literature before, and it belies commonly-held assumptions that Mozart was deeply interested in the political events of his day and was sympathetic to the ideals of Enlightenment philosophy.

In fact, Mozart's political convictions are not known. In all of his correspondence and all of the reminiscences about him that survive, not a single opinion about political affairs is recorded. The closest he ever came to taking a clear stand on any issue related to the progressive intellectual movements of his day is found in a letter to his father written from Paris on 3 July 1778. Mozart happened to be there at a time when the philosopher Voltaire had just died. His only reaction was to go out of his way to condemn Voltaire for his poor character and atheism. Clearly the impression of atheism was formed only from what Mozart had heard about Voltaire, not from any actual reading of his writings. (If Mozart had ever read Voltaire, he would have learned that he had never espoused atheism.) The common-sense way to interpret Mozart's general silence about politics and philosophy is of course to take it as an indication that they did not interest him very much. Furthermore, it is revealing to note that no one who ever knew him thought it important enough ever to mention anything about his political views after he died, a clear indication that they were rarely expressed while he was alive.

It is little emphasized in the Mozart literature how limited the composer's education really was. He never attended a day of school in his life, and there is no evidence that he had any ability to understand sophisticated discussions of politics, economics, philosophy, or theology. In fact, Mozart's educational background was something that his first biographer Němeček was very defensive about. It is clear that Mozart had a reputation in his own time for a lack of education, as Němeček revealed:

> In an issue of a Berlin music journal a few years ago, it is asserted that he really had no higher education. It is difficult to ascertain what the author meant by the words "higher education." What does one expect of an artist?
> Should be also be an author, journalist, and politician?

Certain Mozart scholars in modern times have indeed expected him to be a politician, to the point of imagining that he carefully considered the political implications of any operatic projects he agreed to undertake, and that he tried to introduce political messages into his musical settings, always with a view toward promoting the Enlightenment in any way he could. Němeček took a more reasonable view of Mozart as a very ordinary man who happened to possess a single extraordinary talent - the ability to compose and perform music. He certainly did not think of Mozart as an ignoramus, but as far as education is concerned, the best he could say was that Mozart had at least as much general knowledge "as was necessary for a cultured man." He also noted that "music was his main and favorite preoccupation throughout his life; it motivated all of his thoughts and feelings, and the entire focus of the powers that make up the genius of an artist were devoted to it. Is it surprising if he devoted less attention to other matters?" Rather impatiently, Němeček summarily dismissed other expectations with these words: "He was an artist, to a complete and admirable degree: that is enough!" Modern Mozart scholars would be well advised to take this admonishment to heart.

In the absence of any direct documentation to support their view, those who do believe that Mozart was sympathetic to progressive political movements cling to his involvement in the Masonic movement as indirect evidence (he had become a Mason in 1784). Although it is true that many persons attracted to Enlightenment philosophy belonged to the Masonic lodges of late eighteenth-century Europe, the common notion that these organizations somehow functioned mainly as intellectual discussion societies or "political action committees" is mistaken. Rather, the Masonic lodges of central Europe in Mozart's time operated primarily as exclusive social clubs (even though Napoléon Bonaparte's glib characterization of Masons as "a set of imbeciles who meet to have a good time and perform some ridiculous fooleries" surely understates their significance). There is no record of anyone being rejected for admission (or ejected from membership) on the basis of political views. The qualities prized among candidates for admission were elite social status, an agreeable personality, and a willingness to uphold the secrecy of Masonic rituals. The promotion of virtue within the Masonic movement was typically not directed toward political policy, but rather toward the refinement of personal behavior, including philanthropic activities. Nonetheless, there can be no dispute that the imperial Hapsburg government viewed Masonic lodges with great suspicion because of the secrecy that created such a mystique for them.

The reactionary political stance of one of Mozart's Masonic "brothers" in Prague helps to make this point. Count Kaspar von Künigl, a devoted Mason, was also one of the most prominent leaders of the Bohemian Diet, and he did everything in his power to advance the interests of his social class by exploiting the peasantry in his country. In Vienna, Prince Eszterházy was an equivalent sort of Mason, the oppressor of untold numbers of Hungarian and Slovak serfs.

It is only natural to want to believe that Mozart was attracted to liberal political views of his time. Admiration for the abilities of a musician frequently inspires a yearning to draw him or her into the personal identity of the admirer. Music lovers and music scholars want to believe that Mozart was a nice person, and that he shared their own social, political, and religious values. But in the absence of firm evidence, no one should try to claim to know what he believed in. Anyone who does assert that Mozart was passionately devoted to the ideals of the progressive political movements of his day would have to acknowledge that in accepting payment for a coronation opera in honor of Leopold II with money supplied by the Estates of Bohemia, he betrayed deeply-felt principles for quick cash. A more sensible way to interpret his agreement to write the music for the coronation opera is to recognize that there is no evidence of his political opinions; that he could not refuse any attractive offer of work when his family was in such need of money; that he could not pass up an opportunity to curry the favor of a patron as important as the Holy Roman Emperor; and that the social status of musicians in central Europe of Mozart's day was so low that their participation in an event such as a coronation (which simply accompanied the accession of any new ruler automatically) should not be taken as an endorsement of a political agenda - any more than the participation of the emperor's footmen or the empress' maids. What Mozart knew (or chose not to learn) about the internal political affairs of the kingdom of Bohemia in 1791 is anyone's guess.

Preparations for the Coronation Opera

The events leading to the composition of *La clemenza di Tito* unfolded quickly and haphazardly; the original planners were not even certain that it would be possible to arrange for a coronation opera on such short notice. Almost miraculously, Mozart produced a new masterpiece just in the nick of time.

The idea for a coronation took hold among the nobility of Bohemia in 1791 after the resignation of supreme burgrave Cavriani, governor of the Bohemian Diet, who proved himself incapable of managing its deliberations. His replacement as of 27 January, Count Heinrich von Rottenhan, pushed for a coronation ceremony almost immediately upon taking up his post. By 2 March, the imperial court issued instructions specifying that if a coronation were to take place, the celebrations were to include theatrical entertainments, fireworks, and balls. On 20 April 1791, the Estates issued a memorandum resolving to put one on just after Count Rottenhan returned from a trip to Vienna that is recorded in the *Prague Post* of 19 April. A committee was requested to study the celebrations that attended the magnificent coronation of the emperor Charles VI in Prague in 1723. On 29 April the committee issued a report that envisioned a celebration lasting three days that would include ceremonies of allegiance and coronation accompanied by German plays and Italian operas.

Rottenhan must have been discussing the possibility of a coronation with the imperial court while he was in Vienna, since the court soon took actions itself to prepare for such an event. There is record that Antonio Salieri, the head of the court musical establishment, was ordered on 1 May to draw up a list of musical personnel who would be required. He responded by saying that he would need, along with an organist, a bass singer, a tenor, two contraltos, and two sopranos. He felt that instrumentalists could be obtained locally. With these requirements, it is clear that Salieri was thinking only of the performance of the sacred music needed to accompany a coronation ceremony in the Cathedral of St. Vitus, not an opera.

A memorandum of the Estates issued on 25 May set a target date of 6 September for the coronation (a date that was met) and had a "festivities committee" set up to coordinate a wide range of entertainments. On 4 June, the *Prague Post* reported that the court quartermaster Leopold Le Noble von Edlersberg had arrived the day before and would remain until mid-July, obviously to assist with preparations (in fact, he left Prague already on 17 June, then came back again on 20 July, according to subsequent issues of the *Prague Post*). On 8 June, the imperial court in Vienna informed Wenzel von Ugarte, the *Hofmusikgraf* (keeper of the court music) of a proposed schedule. The emperor Leopold was supposed to leave Vienna for Prague on 27 August, attend an arrival ceremony on 31 August, open a session of the Bohemian Estates on 3 September, hold a service of allegiance on 4 September, and be crowned king of Bohemia on 6 September. This schedule was also largely followed. The most important deviation was created by Leopold's meeting with the king of Prussia in Saxony in late August to discuss a variety of international problems, the result of which was the issuance of the Declaration of Pillnitz. Instead of traveling to Prague from Vienna, the emperor came from Saxony. The imperial court appropriated money as an allowance for Salieri and the seven musicians who were to accompany him (precisely the number he had requested).

In spite of the intentions of the Estates, no opera could have been performed in Prague without the availability of an impresario and suitable singers. Whether by coincidence or from negotiations initiated by the Estates, the impresario Domenico Guardasoni returned to Prague from Warsaw with all his company on 10 June, according to an issue of the *Prague Post* of 14 June. Arrangements for an opera would have been much more difficult without his presence. Interestingly enough, the Seconda company of actors arrived in Prague from Dresden exactly one week before the Guardasoni company (according to an issue of the *Prague Post* of 7 June). Together, the Guardasoni and Seconda companies would be chiefly responsible for the theatrical entertainments enjoyed by visitors to Prague for the coronation in September.

In order to proceed with arrangements for a coronation opera, the first task faced by the Estates was to secure the permission of Count Franz Anton von Nostic to use his theater. By 1791, there was no need to erect a temporary structure suitable for putting on operas in the presence of monarchs. Count Nostic's National Theater was large enough and elegant enough for royalty, even if it would still need to be spruced up for this particularly brilliant occasion. It had just been leased to the impresario Guardasoni, however, so the precise terms under which it could be used for the coronation had to be made clear. Count Nostic's response to Count Rottenhan, preserved in the National Archive in Prague, is dated 1 July 1791. He professed himself delighted to put his theater at the disposal of the Estates.

On 8 July, the impresario Guardasoni signed a contract with the Estates that carefully detailed his obligations in producing a coronation opera. This contract, written in Italian, was obviously prepared by Guardasoni himself, not the Estates, whose officers could not possibly have been conversant enough with operatic customs to know precisely what was involved in planning such a project, nor conversant enough in Italian to prepare a legal document in that language. The text of the contract, preserved in the National Archive in Prague, has been transcribed several times before and translated into English. Due to its dryness and obscure references, it will not be transcribed once again here, but only summarized.

The Guardasoni contract assumed the performance of a coronation opera during the "first days" of the month of September. As of 8 July, it was not certain that there would even be a coronation, much less a coronation opera, since Leopold had not yet been formally invited by the Estates to be crowned, so the contract included a provision for a reduced payment to Guardasoni if the opera were canceled within 14 days of the impresario's departure for Italy to engage singers. Funds for a deputation of the Estates to travel to Vienna and present the emperor with a formal invitation were not appropriated by the Estates until 17 July.

Two singers outside of Guardasoni's own company in Prague were to be contracted for the opera, clearly in the interest of attracting musical figures of the greatest prestige possible for the event. Particular care was taken in discussing the engagement of a male soprano who would perform the lead role (whatever it would be). In 1791, a coronation opera had to present serious action, and serious operas in Italian demanded soprano voices for the romantic male leads. The castrated males who sang them were the costliest singers to engage if first-rate talent was desired. Guardasoni sought the sum of 6000 gulden to help arrange the coronation opera, including all traveling expenses, although if the incomparable Luigi Marchesi were to be hired, Guardasoni demanded an extra 500 gulden. It is not known whether Marchesi was ever approached. In the spring of 1791 he had been appearing in Siena, then traveled to Livorno to appear in three operas during the autumn of the same year. It is not likely that Guardasoni ever contacted him, since he was probably never able to travel as far as Tuscany to look for singers. Other male sopranos mentioned as possibilities for the principal role were Giovanni Maria Rubinelli, Girolamo Crescentini, and Valeriano Violani. Regardless, Guardasoni did promise to locate someone of "leading quality." He expressed no opinion about who might be engaged to sing the lead female role - the *prima donna* - but did promise that she would also be of "leading quality."

It appears that Guardasoni found himself restricted to searching for singers who happened to be available in northeast Italy - as close to Prague as possible - during the months of July or August of 1791. A document of 10 July 1791 preserved in the National Archive in Prague records that the sum of 1000 gulden was appropriated ("if need be") for travel only as far as Bologna. For the male lead, Guardasoni settled for Domenico Bedini, an aging star in his late forties who happened to be in Padua that summer. The *prima donna* he engaged, Maria Marchetti Fantozzi, was appearing at the same time in nearby Vicenza with her husband Angelo. She could hardly have been considered a disappointment. Still, the original cast of Mozart's *La clemenza di Tito* cannot be regarded as anywhere near as luminous as the one assembled for the coronation opera of 1723. For whatever reason, Giovanni Maria Rubinelli was not engaged, even though he was in Vicenza at the same time as the Fantozzis. Violani had been singing in Florence and was on his way to Lisbon; Crescentini appeared that autumn in Bologna, but his whereabouts during the summer are unknown. As far as can be determined, all of the rest of the original cast members for *La clemenza de Tito* were already attached to the Guardasoni company, including Antonio Baglioni, the original Don Ottavio in *Don Giovanni*, who had accompanied Guardasoni to Warsaw in 1789. Guardasoni never had to travel as far south as Bologna; he found both singers he needed of "leading quality" in the northern Italian cities of Padua and Vicenza.

As for the subject matter of the opera, Guradasoni promised to commission a new libretto on one of two unspecified subjects suggested to him by the supreme burgrave if there was time to have a new libretto written. If not, the Estates were to settle for a fresh setting of Metastasio's *La clemenza di Tito*. Likely the latter suggestion originated with Guardasoni, who would have had a much quicker grasp of the themes explored in the best-known Italian librettos of the day than the officers of the Bohemian Estates. *La clemenza di Tito* is based on a story about a magnanimous Roman emperor who pardons rebellious nobles for the crime of treason. There could not have been a better allegory for political events in Bohemia during the years 1790 and 1791.

The remaining provisions in the contract are mundane. Guardasoni promised to create sets accommodating two changes of scenery, have new costumes made up, and to provide suitable illumination and decoration for the theater. One performance of the opera was to be presented free of charge to spectators. As for the payment of his fee, Guardasoni demanded an advance of 600 gulden for a trip to Vienna to start, then 2000 more if the singers to be engaged required an advance payment of their own. Documents preserved in the National Archive in Prague record the authorization of payments to Guardasoni in the amount of 600 gulden on 9 July for the trip to Vienna, then 1000 more (on 10 July), as just mentioned, to get him as far as Bologna, if needed. The rest of his fee was to be paid on the day of the première of the opera. Three provisions were added against the possibility that the entire project would never materialize. If the opera were to be canceled within 14 days of Guardasoni's departure to Italy, then only the expenses of the trip would be paid. If a singer had left Italy for Prague after the announcement of a cancellation, the singer was to be reimbursed only for his or her travel expenses. Guardasoni was to retain items purchased in preparation for the production even if it never took place and was to receive extra remuneration if he could prove that his traveling expenses exceeded the sum advanced to him.

At the time that his contract was concluded, Guardasoni specified nobody as a good candidate to compose the music for the coronation opera. According to an issue of the *Prague Post* of July 12, Guardasoni had passed the New Gate, the usual departure point for travelers bound for Vienna, already on 10 July. In search of a composer, it made sense for Guardasoni to attempt to contact the head of the musical establishment of the monarch who was to be honored. Leopold II's *Kapellmeister* was none other than Mozart's famous rival Antonio Salieri, and Guardasoni did offer him the chance to compose the music for the coronation opera. In a letter believed to have been written at the end of August 1791, Salieri told Haydn's employer Prince Anton Eszterházy that Guardasoni had traveled from Prague to Vienna five times in order to offer him 200 ducats to compose it. Salieri refused the commission on grounds of overwork. His assistant at the imperial court theater, Joseph Weigl, was occupied in August of 1791 with supervising musical entertainments to celebrate the installation of Prince Esterházy as the lord-lieutenant of the county of Sopron, Hungary. Weigl was the unofficial conductor of the court theater in Vienna, and in his absence, Salieri had to take over his duties.

Whether Mozart was Guardasoni's second or even third choice is unknown, but he must have received the commission for the opera sometime before mid-August for there to have been enough time to mount the production with adequate rehearsals. The precise dates of Guardasoni's trips to Vienna and Italy are unknown, but it is almost inconceivable that he could have found the time to travel to Vienna from Prague on five occasions in order to persuade Salieri to take on the coronation project. As we know from Mozart's travels, each trip back and forth from Vienna would have consumed three days' time.

Precisely when Guardasoni and the Estates gave up on the idea of commissioning a new libretto and decided to use Metastasio's *La clemenza di Tito*, a text originally set to music by Antonio Caldara for the imperial court of Vienna in 1734, is also unknown. It would not have been acceptable to use Metastasio's original text unaltered, since operatic customs had changed significantly since the 1730s. A new setting of the complete original drama would have been far too long to please audiences of the 1790s, and certain alterations were needed to accommodate the latest aria types and heighten the dramatic impact of the actions of the principal character, the Roman emperor Titus, as a means of drawing attention to his similarity to Leopold II.

It is tantalizing to imagine Lorenzo Da Ponte being contacted in Vienna, although this was impossible in July of 1791, since he had been forced to leave the imperial service after antagonizing the emperor. His departure, given out as a resignation, was reported in the *Prague Post* on 19 April. Guardasoni turned instead to Caterino Mazzolà, a poet who was experiencing some quick employment turnover of his own just at this time. In the spring of 1791, he was serving as court poet at the court of Dresden, but he was hired to replace Da Ponte as the poet for the imperial court almost as soon as Da Ponte had been dismissed. He traveled to Vienna from Dresden through Prague, where he arrived on 6 May (according to an issue of the *Prague Post* of 10 May).

Mazzolà served as imperial court poet only until the end of July 1791, when he was replaced by Giovanni Bertati. It was most likely during the second half of July in Vienna that Mazzolà was approached by Guardasoni with the idea of refurbishing Metastasio's *La clemenza di Tito* for the coronation of Leopold II as king of Bohemia.

While Guardasoni was busy trying to engage singers, a poet, and a composer for the coronation opera, the Estates were busy trying to secure Leopold's agreement to show up to see it. On 17 July, funds were appropriated to fund a delegation, which arrived in Vienna on 22 July to make a formal request for Leopold's appearance. It was soon agreed to, since the invitation had been expected for some time. All during the remainder of the summer, the Estates supervised arrangements for balls, banquets, and the logistics of hosting an imperial entourage, the progress updated regularly in the *Prague Post*. One of the most important symbolic events reported there was the return of the Bohemian crown jewels from Vienna along with the deputation of the Estates that invited Leopold to Prague (in an issue of 13 August). The cost of putting on the coronation was astronomical. A memorandum prepared by Count Jan von Chotek on 5 August for the benefit of the supreme burgrave Rottenhan complained that the expenditures had become alarming. The Estates were forced to borrow 300,000 gulden from bankers in Frankfurt in order to underwrite the coronation celebrations.

Disputed information about the preparations Mozart made for the opera *La clemenza di Tito* and his last trip to Prague originates mainly from his biographer Němeček, almost certainly based on information from Mozart's widow Constanze, whom he knew well. The music was written at a time when Mozart was also preoccupied with work on his opera *The Magic Flute* and his Requiem. The commission came so suddenly that he had to interrupt plans to complete both. Němeček described events from the year 1791 in these terms:

> ...the music for the opera *La clemenza di Tito* had been commissioned by the Bohemian Estates for the coronation of emperor Leopold. [Mozart] began the latter in his traveling coach on the journey from Vienna, and he finished it in the short time span of eighteen days in Prague.
>
> The story of his last work, the Requiem Mass mentioned above, is as mysterious as it is remarkable.
>
> Shortly before the coronation of the emperor Leopold, even before Mozart had received the commission to travel to Prague, a letter without signature was brought him by an unknown messenger, which contained an inquiry with many flattering remarks as to whether he would be willing to undertake the composition of a Requiem Mass, at what price, and how long it would take before it was delivered.
>
> Mozart, who was not accustomed to taking the slightest step without his wife's knowledge, told her of this odd commission, and at the same time expressed his desire to try out this genre of composition, all the more so since the higher pathetic style of church music had always been well suited to his genius. She advised him to accept the commission. He therefore wrote back to his anonymous patron to say that he would complete a Requiem for a set fee; he could not specify precisely how long it would take to finish; nonetheless, he wished to know where the work should be delivered when it was ready. In a short time the same messenger appeared again, and not only brought the stipulated fee, but also the promise that he would receive a considerable bonus when the work was received, since his asking price had been so low. Moreover, he should write according to the mood and humor of his genius, but should take no pains to learn the identity of his patron, since the effort would certainly be in vain.
>
> In the meantime he received a prestigious and advantageous request to write the serious opera for the Prague coronation of emperor Leopold.
>
> It was too much of an enticement for him to refuse to go to Prague to write for his beloved Bohemians!
>
> Just as Mozart and his wife were getting into their traveling coach, the messenger stood before them like a ghost, pulled at Constanze's coat, and asked: "What about the Requiem?"
>
> Mozart excused himself by explaining the necessity of the trip and the impossibility of informing his anonymous patron; in any case it would be the first task on his return, and it was only a question of whether the stranger would wait so long. The messenger was completely satisfied with this answer.

If this incident really did ever happen, it probably took place on 25 August 1791. The *Prague Post* of 30 August reported that Mozart had passed through the New Gate on 28 August (as we have seen, it usually took travelers from Vienna three days to reach Prague). Němeček made no mention of Mozart's pupil Süssmayer joining the Mozarts in their carriage to Prague, even though it is now believed that he was with them, as was the clarinettist Anton Stadler. The decision to take Constanze along meant that there was nobody in Vienna that Mozart needed to write to urgently, thus there is no record of any correspondence from Prague during his last trip.

Mozart certainly did not begin his opera on the coach from Vienna to Prague, and it is difficult to understand how much could have been written down satisfactorily in a bumpy carriage. The opera would have to have been pretty much completed at the time of his arrival in Prague in order for it to be rehearsed adequately for a performance only eight days later, and analyses of the paper types found in the original score confirm that only a small portion of it was actually composed in Prague. If eighteen days were needed to write it, it would have had to have been started by mid-August. Its completion is recorded in Mozart's own catalog of compositions on 5 September, the day before the first performance. Attempts to settle on a chronology of the composition of the opera cannot account for how long it might have taken Mazzolà to revise Metastasio's libretto and just when it was that Mozart was contracted to provide music. The immensely complicated researches of Sergio Durante led him to the conclusion that the music was begun at the end of July 1791. It is not possible to establish with certainty precisely how long it took Mozart to complete *La clemenza di Tito*. What can be asserted, however, is that the short amount of time available to Mozart to complete *La clemenza di Tito* rivals that available to Rossini for his *Italian Girl in Algiers*, *Barber of Seville*, and *Cinderella*. Of the all the operas most commonly performed today, these were the four that appear to have been prepared in the shortest amounts of time. Legends that the recitative for the opera was actually written by Mozart's pupil Süssmayer are impossible to verify.

Mozart's arrival for the coronation ceremonies was not recorded in the journals that were published to commemorate the event, although this information was provided for dozens of dignitaries who attended them. As head of the emperor's musical establishment, Salieri was the only court musician whose presence in the city was noted by name in the coronation journals. During the celebrations, he was housed in along with the emperor's entourage. In one of the journals, seven other court musicians are specified as being housed in Prague, but only their places of residence are given, not their names, although one of them is believed to have been the organist Johann Georg Albrechtsberger. According to another journal, Salieri left Vienna for Prague on 19 August in a carriage that was also supposed to transport the court physician and the court apothecary.

Mozart apparently was not traveling with other members of the imperial chapel. No one knows for certain where he stayed during his last visit to Prague. Meissner claimed in one spot that he stayed with František Dušek (but whether in the Bertramka villa or the Dušek town house he did not specify), and in another spot indicated that Mozart left Prague from a house known as the "Three Axes." In a letter to the Leipzig publisher Breitkopf & Härtel written in 1799, Němeček claimed that Mozart "stopped off at" the Dušek "house" on a daily basis, but said nothing about staying with them. The context of the remark indicates that Němeček was referring to the period of the coronation ceremonies, not the visits of 1787. If Mozart was "stopping off" on a daily basis, it was most likely not at the remote Bertramka villa, but rather at the Dušek town house. The story from Nissen's biography about Mozart's billiard-playing, quoted in the previous chapter, indicates that he would have been staying in some sort of lodging near the National Theater, and not at the Dušek town house or Bertramka villa.

Leopold II and the Declaration of Pillnitz

In contrast to Mozart's unobtrusive entry into Prague for the coronation ceremonies, Leopold made an entrance befitting the emperor he was. His movements are of course much easier to trace. Leopold had been party to a political event of tremendous importance just a few days before he appeared in Prague for his coronation. During the late summer of 1791, the rulers of central and eastern Europe were very nervous about events in revolutionary France. In June, the French royal couple had fled Paris in order to seek refuge in the Austrian Netherlands (modern-day Belgium), which Leopold controlled as one of the hereditary domains of the Hapsburg dynasty. Famously, the royal family was arrested on 21 June at Varennes and escorted back to Paris into much closer confinement than they had previously endured. The queen of France, Marie Antoinette, had been only ten years' old in 1765 when her brother Leopold left Vienna to serve as grand duke of Tuscany. They never saw each other again in their lives, but Leopold did feel it important to uphold monarchical institutions and express concern for the personal safety of a family member, even if he was not eager to start a war to secure it.

Marie Antoinette's brother-in-law, the Count of Artois (the future King Charles X of France), was an uncompromising royalist ("more royalist than the king," as the phrase went) who wandered the courts of Europe in hopes of organizing military opposition to the French Revolution. The Count of Artois had reason to expect hospitality in Dresden, since the local ruler, Frederick Augustus of Saxony, was his first cousin. In the summer of 1791, with a large body of French émigrés, he urged Leopold to plan firm action against the revolutionaries in France. As confirmed in the *Prague Post* of 27 August (which records his arrival in Prague on 23 August), and the Albrecht coronation journal, the Count of Artois passed through the city on his way to meet with Leopold at Pillnitz Castle. It was at this time that he would have gotten his first glimpse of Prague Castle. In the 1830s, after he had been deposed as king of France for his repressive political policies, the Emperor Francis of Austria permitted him refuge there for a period of years.

The result of the deliberations of the crowned heads was certain language found in the Declaration of Pillnitz, issued jointly with the King of Prussia, Frederick William II, on 27 August 1791. To his credit, the host for the occasion, Frederick Augustus, did not sign it. The French émigrés who clung to Leopold's court were more than anything else a nuisance, but Leopold did feel that he had to placate them in some way. The Declaration dealt with several foreign policy matters. In regard to France, it intended to direct a cautious threat to revolutionary political figures. Any further infringement on the political privileges of King Louis XVI or violation of his personal safety was held to be grounds for military intervention. Austria resolved to go to war only if the other major European monarchies agreed to do the same. Leopold knew that Great Britain, at least, had no intention of doing so, thus the threat was hollow. He was not prepared to go any further in satisfying the belligerent stance of the émigrés, and he would have been perfectly justified in viewing the Declaration as a restrained response to events in France.

The revolutionary leaders in France, however, regarded the Declaration as a direct and immediate challenge. The long-term effect of the Declaration was to radicalize the revolutionary government in France to the point where it sought a "preemptive strike" against the monarchical European states. Bordering as it did on the Austrian Netherlands, France felt that Austria constituted the greatest threat to the security of the revolutionary government, and so the National Assembly declared war on Austria on 20 April 1792, just a month and a half after Leopold's death. From then on, warfare in Europe was almost constant until the surrender of Napoléon at Waterloo in 1815. In the shorter term, the tone of political discussions in France became ever more strident and, under cover of war, the French revolutionary government was able to introduce terror as a political tool. The standing of the French royal family soon deteriorated to the point where the king was deposed and executed. In sum, the Declaration was a catastrophic diplomatic blunder.

Events Surrounding the Coronation Ceremony

None of the ghastly consequences of the Declaration of Pillnitz could have been foreseen at the time of Leopold's coronation. Instead, the glittering celebrations masked the dangers faced by the Austrian state and the plight of the Bohemian serfs who had no hope of seeing the celebrations that their feudal obligations funded. But not all observers were taken in by the splendor. In particular, there was one who left a detailed account that eloquently exposed Leopold and the émigrés around him for their policies of political oppression. This was Franz Alexander von Kleist (1769-1797), a young German poet and essayist who should not be confused with the much more eminent literary figure Heinrich von Kleist (1777-1811), also a member of a prominent Prussian noble family.

As holder of a minor government post in the Prussian bureaucracy, Franz Alexander von Kleist traveled to Prague to witness Leopold's coronation in an official capacity. In the tradition of German writers who concealed their authorship of provocative material, his observations were published anonymously the next year as *Impressions on a Trip to Prague (Fantasien auf einer Reise nach Prag)*. Kleist genuinely was what some music scholars would have Mozart be: a sensitive and dedicated intellectual who was passionately devoted to the ideals of Enlightenment philosophy. He revered the memory of the progressive monarchs Joseph II and Frederick the Great, viewed Leopold II as a reactionary tyrant, and was sympathetic to the goals of the revolutionary government of France as it existed in 1791, struggling as it was to establish a working constitutional monarchy and still unsullied by the excesses of state terror.

Franz Alexander
von Kleist
and family

Kleist did not share the high estimation of Leopold's character that is found in the works of worshipful latter-day biographers, nor did he view Leopold's coronation in the way it is portrayed in some Mozart literature as a sort of "celebration of the Enlightenment," based partially on the mistaken notion that the Estates of Bohemia somehow desired to recognize Leopold for his progressive rule as grand duke of Tuscany (as if the rulers of the kingdom of Bohemia were only notable to its residents for policies they pursued in other countries). The well-known dictum of Thomas P. O'Neill had been ignored - i.e., "all politics is local." There is no reason to believe that the reactionary nobles who arranged Leopold's coronation had done so in order to congratulate him for the way that he had ruled Tuscany. The preservation of wealth and power within their own country was what chiefly motivated them. In any case, conditions in Tuscany of the 1770s and 1780s would have been ancient history for political observers trying to catch up with the swift-moving events of the early 1790s.

Kleist departed from Potsdam on 16 August and left extensive descriptions of what he saw in Leipzig and the countryside of Saxony. He did not travel to Prague by way of Dresden, the most direct route from Potsdam, but rather took a detour through northwestern Bohemia to visit the spa town of Karlovy Vary (Karlsbad) and the nearby castle of Krásný Dvůr (which he knew as "Schönhof"). After his arrival in Prague on 28 August, he complained bitterly about events he witnessed during the coronation celebrations. His first observance of the imperial entourage is recorded in a chapter called "The King's Entrance" ("Der Königseinzug"). The formal "entrance" procession for the imperial couple had been arranged for 31 August.

Leopold originally intended to leave Vienna for Prague on 27 August, but changed his plans in order to meet with the rulers of Saxony and Prussia at Pillnitz. Instead, he left Vienna on 20 August with the archduke Francis, Leopold's heir, and arrived in Prague on 23 August on the way to Dresden for a very brief stay. In the meantime the empress Maria Luisa left Vienna on 27 August, following the original plan, and arrived on 30 August to stay in Libeň Castle (Schloss Lieben), a small castle that belonged to the city government of Prague. Before the unification of the "three cities of Prague" in 1784, it was the summer residence of the mayor of the Old City. Libeň Castle can still be seen in the Libeň district of Prague. In Mozart's time, Libeň was a rural area to the northeast of the city, a short distance downstream on the Vltava river. Leopold left without pomp to be present at Libeň Castle to greet his wife with suitable courtesies. Prince Anton of Saxony and his wife, Leopold's daughter Maria Theresa, the original dedicatees of the libretto for Mozart's opera *Don Giovanni*, had accompanied Leopold from Dresden to Prague and were present. The idea of staying in the outskirts of Prague was to assist with the preparations for the ceremonial entrance of the entrance to Prague that took place the day after the empress' arrival. The imperial party started out from the Invalidovna (Invalidenhaus), a dormitory for veterans that was located just to the east of Prague (now in the Prague district of Karlín). From there the procession entered Prague through the "Hospital Gate" ("Spitalthor") at the northeast boundary of the New City (corresponding to the eastern end of the modern street Na poříčí), and then made its way up to the cathedral for a grand service. It took hours to reach the cathedral, since many ritual greeting ceremonies on the way were performed by various civic officials.

The modern observer cannot help but note the absurdity of the emperor and his court surreptitiously leaving just for the purpose of re-entering it ostentatiously. Kleist made no mention of this foolishness in order to concentrate on the larger picture. Indeed, Kleist considered the panoply that accompanied it a disgraceful extravagance intended to mask the emperor's distasteful authoritarian policies. The Jews who had benefited so much from the rule of Leopold's brother Joseph were not even permitted to witness it. A decree from the supreme burgrave Rottenhan that was published in the *Prague Post* on 30 August ordered them to remain within the ghetto throughout the day. There could be no clearer confirmation of the anti-Enlightenment atmosphere that fell over Prague during Leopold's coronation than this insult to the Jewish community:

> The great spectacle of the king's entrance is over. The city is richer a king, and its inhabitants are poorer a million thalers! - I will not say more about this royal entrance, where enslavement paraded about in its most splendid garments, and the crowds stared at it blindly, without realizing that a gilded yoke presses down as hard as any other, and that these gleaming liveries, these gold-covered vessels, were purchased with their own drops of sweat. One of the residents said to me, "Joseph never wanted to make this sort of an entrance in order to spare us the money, and we grumbled; Leopold enters like a king; we squander thousands that we cannot do without; we offer up the last resources that war taxes have left us for a glittering spectacle - and do we appear content?" This man was right! With childlike blindness the people ran after the glitter that deceived them splendidly, and they did not see at their backs the weeping reality that limped behind and sighed after necessities. And still this splendor could be pardoned, if the great citizens of this country had purchased its instruments in their own fatherland: rather they sent hundreds of thousands abroad,

and what the hard work of their subjects provides has been consumed by the manufactures of a Briton or a Frenchman.

Kleist vividly documented the sense of a victorious aristocratic reaction in Prague during the time of Leopold's stay in the city. It "incensed" him that the Seconda company of actors was presenting the play *The Ladies' Jacobin Club* (*Der weibliche Jakobiner-Club*), a vicious satire of French revolutionary political culture written by August von Kotzebue, one of the leading anti-Enlightenment intellectuals of Mozart's day in the German-speaking lands (who was assassinated in 1819 by a young theology student who regarded him as an enemy of social and political progress for the German people). The play *The Ladies' Jacobin Club* was obviously being produced in the National Theater in order to appeal to the sympathies of the Bohemian nobility and the French émigrés who had followed Leopold's court from Saxony. Its most striking political message is a reinforcement of the view that French aristocrats really were a superior class of human beings, not only wealthy and refined, but affable, attractive, and virtuous. Two other plays of Kotzebue were also produced in Prague that week.

Kleist's estimation of the false spectacle of Leopold's coronation was hardly unique. The composer Václav Jan Tomášek, living in Prague as a teenager, actually boycotted it. Similar to many central European intellectuals of the day, Tomášek viewed the emperor Joseph with great affection and nostalgia. As a child in Jihlava sometime in the 1780s he had the opportunity to see him on the very day that he saw his first *Singspiel*:

> At the same time I had the good fortune to see the emperor Joseph accompanied by the [military] hero [Field Marshal Ernst Gideon von] Laudon, surrounded by young and old alike, who was visiting the construction site of a military hospital and giving out orders for its extension.
>
> The monarch, for whom the welfare of his people lay closer to his heart than anything else, forbade any type of reception ceremonies. The physiognomy of these two notable men left me with such an impression that if I were a painter, I certainly would have produced the most finely executed portrait of these unforgettable personalities.

The way he spoke of Leopold's coronation provides a striking contrast and emphasizes how Joseph's lack of ostentation found so much favor among his subjects:

> During the school recess of 1791, the magnificent coronation of emperor Leopold took place. With secret sadness I saw all the extravagant preparations for the celebration. In order to spare my father the unnecessary display, I decided to forego the approaching pomp of the coronation.

Instead, Tomášek went with his father to visit his brother in the countryside.

Kleist left detailed accounts of only a few of the many remaining social, political, and religious events that took place in September of 1791 as part of the coronation celebrations. These events, lasting between 1 September and 22 September, are neatly summarized in a journal of 1791 whose author is identified only with the surname Albrecht (perhaps the same Johann Friedrich Ernst Albrecht who may have been the author of the *Observations in and about Prague* of 1787). Four key ceremonies formed the central focus of the celebrations: a "mass of allegiance" (Huldigungsmesse) at St. Vitus' Cathedral on 4 September in honor of Leopold II; his coronation as king of Bohemia in the same church on 6 September; the installation of his daughter, the archduchess Maria Anna Ferdinanda of Austria, as abbess of the Noble Ladies' Foundation in Prague Castle on 8 September; and the coronation of Leopold's wife Maria Luisa as queen of Bohemia on 12 September. The archduchess Maria Anna Ferdinanda had succeeded her disabled aunt Maria Anna as abbess of the Noble Ladies' Foundation after her death in 1789.

Rehearsals were held on the two days preceding the two coronation ceremonies (5 September and 11 September). These were the only days during the period of coronation celebrations in Prague that did not include official midday banquets or entertainments in the evening. As the coronation festivities wound down beginning on 19 September, the banquets were the only public events held. The imperial court sponsored banquets in Prague Castle on 1-4, 6-10, 12-13, and 15-17 September, but the imperial family did have the opportunity to enjoy more private meals after each of the two coronations and on 14 and 18 September (as well as a private reception for select dignitaries held at Prague Castle during the evening of 1 September). Midday banquets were sponsored by the archbishop of Prague (Count Příchovský) on 19 September; the archbishop of Olomouc (Count Colloredo-Waldsee) on 20 September; the supreme burgrave (Count Rottenhan) on 21 September; and the supreme chancellor of the Czech Gubernium (Count Leopold von Kolovrat) on 22 September (as the last official event of the coronation festivities). The private reception of 1 September was the first entertainment for which there is clear confirmation of the inclusion of Mozart's music, in this case from the diary of Count Zinzendorf, who was permitted to attend. He reported dining with 100 guests and listening to excerpts from *Don Giovanni* (that were probably played by a wind ensemble).

A variety of entertainments were organized for the evenings. Balls sponsored by the imperial court were held in Prague Castle on 3, 7, 15, and 18 September, whereas balls were also hosted by the supreme burgrave on 8 September; Count Černín (Mozart's erstwhile friend from Salzburg) on 10 September; the Estates of Bohemia on 12 September; the supreme chancellor of the Gubernium on 13 September; and the archbishop of Prague on 17 September. A display of fireworks was organized for the evening of 4 September and military reviews for 14 September (both during the day and the evening). Operas of Mozart given in the National Theater were the only other entertainments sponsored by the court or the Estates in the evenings, specifically a performance of *Don Giovanni* on 2 September and performances of *La clemenza di Tito* on 6, 9, and 16 September.

Selective accounts of these events provided by Kleist are of course much more interesting and insightful than those found in the official coronation journals. His next report of what was going on in the city comes from Thursday, 1 September, a day when no public events were sponsored by the Estates or the imperial court except for a midday banquet. Kleist chose instead to report his impressions of a performance of the play *Bruder Moritz* by Kotzebue as presented by the Seconda company. In this case, the play was not so controversial, and his description of the production is rather bland. Kleist was not invited to the private reception hosted by the imperial family.

In contrast, Kleist's scintillating description of a performance of Mozart's *Don Giovanni* in the National Theater on 2 September in a chapter called "The Opera Gathering" ("Die Opergesellschaft") must form the centerpiece of his work for music lovers and historians of European social life. Kleist drew special attention to several audience members associated with the royalist party in France, among them the dashing Swedish nobleman Count Axel von Fersen.

Of all the persons of both sexes whom Marie Antoinette has been accused of taking as lovers, the only one who may actually have filled that role was Axel von Fersen. Until her death, their liaisons were never suspected by any of the queen's enemies. Exactly the same age as Marie Antoinette, there is no question that Fersen had achieved the status of her "special friend" in the 1780s while serving as a diplomatic representative of the king of Sweden in France. His lifelong loyalty to the queen was unshakeable. It was he - a foreigner in France - who was mainly responsible for planning the ill-fated Flight to Varennes of 20-21 June 1791, and he personally accompanied the royal family as far as Bondy. If he had been in a position to guide decision-making later in the journey, the plot might well have succeeded. In February 1792 he was able to penetrate the Tuileries Palace unobserved - at the risk of his life - in order to spend a few hours with the queen (the last time he ever saw her). His participation in the political intrigues of his native country led to his murder in Stockholm in 1810 by an angry crowd who mistakenly thought him responsible for the death of the popular Prince Karl August.

Kleist's impression of Fersen was highly negative. He probably could not have known about Fersen's long history of sexual conquests, but he had no trouble detecting his licentious nature merely from observing him from afar that one evening. It is as enjoyable to speculate on Fersen's reaction to seeing behavior similar to his own held up to moral scrutiny at a performance of Mozart's *Don Giovanni* as it would be for Casanova, who may also have been present for the coronation ceremonies. Fersen was considered so handsome in France that he was referred to as "le beau Fersen," but Kleist found him unattractive and offensive, partly for his sporting of the French royalist white cockade.

The duke of Polignac observed by Kleist was the husband of Gabrielle de Polastron, Marie Antoninette's closest confidante during the 1780s and former governess to her children. Jules de Polignac owed his title of duke to her influence on the queen, and indeed her entire family benefited enormously from the queen's favor. Gabrielle was widely despised in France for the huge sums of money showered on her family, and she found it expedient to leave France with her husband shortly after the fall of the Bastille in 1789. Gabrielle died in Vienna in 1793, having escaped the fate of another of Marie Antoinette's favorites, the princess de Lamballe, who was brutally murdered by a revolutionary mob in 1792. There would have been nothing unusual about Gabrielle not being present with her husband in Prague at this time. The product of an arranged marriage, their relationship had never been close.

Kleist's greatest condemnation was reserved for François Claude Amour, the marquis de Bouillé (1739-1800), a prominent general in France both before and after the fall of the Bastille. He was hated in France for his brutal suppression of military uprisings precipitated by the conduct of noble officers in his position as a provincial governor and fled France after the Flight to Varennes, which he had helped to plan. Bouillé's activities as a counter-revolutionary were actually quite well known in central Europe at this time; the *Prague Post* reported on them extensively during the month of July 1791. Bouillé holds the distinction of being the only individual mentioned by name in the original version of the French national anthem, the *Marseillaise*, which was composed in April of 1792 shortly after the National Assembly declared war against Austria. In one of the verses, foreign "despots" opposed to the French Revolution are referred to as the "accomplices of Bouillé."

Kleist could be said to express modern sensibilities in referring to Mozart as the true outstanding personality in the opera theater that night. He claimed that the reception Leopold received from the Bohemians was forced and insincere. He was indifferent to the other members of the imperial family except for the archduke Francis, whom he imagined to have been brought up in the mold of Joseph II (how disappointed he probably was to see what sort of a ruler he became after the death of his father in 1792). The true promise should have been recognized in the archduke Karl, later one of the few Austrian generals who ever succeeded in defeating the French before Napoléon's withdrawal from Russia in 1812.

It is enjoyable to speculate on the interesting conversations that could have been shared among the individuals present for the performance of *Don Giovanni* that evening who had connections to Marie Antoinette. A large selection of her relatives were there, a former lover, the husband of one of her closest companions, a former official in her husband's military establishment, and a casual acquaintance from early childhood: Wolfgang Amadeus Mozart. The rigid social barriers of eighteenth-century Europe unfortunately would have prevented any intimate gathering of this motley group of people who had something quite interesting in common. Kleist's account of their activities that evening is fascinating:

> I was never so rewarded by leaving an opera house as today, where I saw in one hall so many notable people in such varied circumstances. The emperor with his family was to come to the opera today, and the entire route from the castle to the opera house swarmed with people who were curious to see how an emperor travels to a theatrical performance. In the opera house all of the boxes and the pit were filled with people, and when the emperor finally entered, he was greeted with a three-fold applause and a cry of "Vivat!" ["long live the emperor!"] in which it was possible to number and distinguish each individual voice even without the hearing of an Indian. Some even asserted that the Vivat must have been whipped up by police agents.
>
> The emperor seemed to be satisfied with his welcome and bowed several times to the audience. However I must rise to protest that in spite of the applause and in spite of the clanging of tympani and trumpets, this entrance did not have the slightest

celebratory character because it was entirely lacking in his case of the enthusiasm needed to inspire a gathering of people if the expression of their joy was to be sublime and beautiful. Here the upward-surging expression of inspired souls was completely silent; there was a feeling that the sense of joy was a child of convenience, and it was feared from the start that its continuation would falter, since the joy of the citizens of Prague would go only so far. Surely there is much good in the custom of Indian princes who only reveal themselves to their people behind veils. Most people think of their rulers, their hereditary monarchs, as higher beings, or at least as very beautiful, wise, and perfect people. If the monarch is veiled, this is the image that he impresses, and curiosity about him leads him to be imagined as even more beautiful than he is; but when he steps out from behind the veil, he unfortunately appears only too often in an imperfect form in which nothing about him can be imagined as great or elevated. A disappointment of this sort is counteractive and leaves behind preconceptions about the character of such a man that require tangible deeds to overcome.

The archduke Francis [oldest son of Leopold II, later Holy Emperor Francis II] has much in common with Emperor Joseph and great things from him are promised. His face, even if not expressive, nonetheless demonstrates already something noble, strong, and determined that is not contradicted in his manner of behavior. Right after his arrival, the first thing he did was have the court bookseller fetch for him all the newest literature and maps. I was also told a story about the love he had for his deceased wife [Elisabeth Wilhelmine of Württemberg], whose picture was hanging over his writing table across from where the portrait of his next wife would be placed. The empress, who did not like this arrangement, once had the picture hung elsewhere during his absence. The archduke noticed the change upon returning, but said nothing about it. But after a few days he ordered his valet to place his writing desk under the picture of his dead wife and thereby achieved his purpose without changing the placement of the picture in contradiction to the order of the empress. This little incident appears noteworthy to me, because it demonstrates the principle of achieving fixed goals without disturbing preexisting order. The brothers of the archduke Francis all look the same; the most handsome and best brought up is the Palatine [viceroy] of Hungary [the archduke Alexander Leopold, who was burned to death in a fireworks accident in 1795]. I know that I really should not say anything more about them, if I do permit myself to say that I could discover nothing more about the empress than she was simply the wife of the emperor.

More noteworthy to me were the people of the second social stratum, those not surrounding the emperor, whose life stories could be seen in their facial expressions. The sight of General Bouillé below in the pit was moving; and even though the fate he bore at present was so well deserved, I was not able to repress all feelings of sympathy for him. His misfortune was written in a legible code on his brow, and worry appeared to diminish gradually the fire in his eyes. But wisdom and courage still spoke from his glances, and everyone recognized that he was destined to be nothing more than a deserted refugee. I have still never seen a face that had so much grief impressed on it as his; and I can imagine what dreadful feelings pierce his heart. By indulging a passionate moment blinded by sweet delusions about the future, he made it his goal to overturn the temple of freedom and institute despotism. He abused the trust of the National Assembly to become a traitor to his fatherland and his people. He went from being one of the most prominent French citizens to being a beggar abroad, and now sees himself feared by no one, esteemed by few, and despised by most. How repentance must torment him and how the thought must shock him that in order to justify his misjudgment he perhaps can be held responsible for shedding the blood of many thousands! How completely impoverished of great and beautiful feelings his soul must be, since it is lacking in the pride of independence; for it was slack enough to indulge in self-interest, to follow its signs, and to renounce the blessed fruits of liberty! How deserted he must feel, for his nation runs away from him, his fatherland spits him out as a monster, and no heart approaches him that is harmoniously composed, surging with the virtues of the human race for liberty and love! He stands there alone like a poison plant that no friendly animal will go near, a plant in front of which the wanderer will pass over without looking at it and only scorpions will gather around it!

How laughable do the other French émigrés appear next to this bewitched, unfortunate man! Especially the unattractive Fersen, who appears to be looking everywhere for his Amanda [i.e., a woman "deserving of love"], pointlessly playing with the white [royalist] cockade in his hat, and running from one group of people to another for no reason! He does not find her, and hopes against hope that the spectators will take note of what he is searching for. Bouillé's son and the duke of Polignac are so insignificant that one can close the book on their merits by recording only their names.

Away with these people! I am beckoned to finer remarks by a little man over there in a green coat, whose eye betrays what his modest condition hides. It is Mozart, whose opera *Don Giovanni* will be given today, who has the pleasure of seeing with what delight his beautiful harmonies fill the hearts of all the spectators. Who in the whole opera house can be prouder and more happy than he? Who could be more satisfied with himself than he? In vain would monarchs squander their fortunes, in vain the riches of the nobleman proud of his ancestors; he cannot purchase a tiny spark of the feeling with which art rewards those it favors! Joys bought with gold are the tolerable pastimes of a sick person; the pain only comes back again more fiercely. How else can an artist find delight except by producing an immortal work? His joy is like an intoxication, but its effects are eternal; it continuously brings forth new beauty and endows dead people with the attributes of creators. Everyone must fear death; the artist fears it not. His immortality is not hope, it is certainty! It is the more beautiful part of his self, the legacy of blessed hours of labor; that is what he leaves for posterity. It reaches to future generations after the bodies of kings have long rotted. And with all those persuasions Mozart could witness how a thousand ears listened to every string vibration and every whisper of the flute, and how throbbing breasts and quickly beating hearts revealed the holy sensations that his harmonies awoke. This awakening of dark feelings is the special capability of music among the fine arts. By means of the indefinite character of its expression it flatters the peculiar sensations of the heart, follows in silent agreement the secret course of our fantasies, and weighs the grief in sorrow, and the happiness in joy! Whether it be idolization or a proper human feeling, enough, at this moment I would have wished to be Mozart rather than Leopold; and if our German listeners lack a high susceptibility for enthusiasm in the way that the British admired Handel and the French admired Gluck, so the non-arbitrary expression of less intense feelings must still be a beautiful, heavenly reward for the artist who is able to evoke the music of the spheres and understand how to delight the soul with musical sounds!

On Saturday, 3 September, Kleist attended the first of the balls sponsored by the imperial court at Prague Castle, this one in the magnificently decorated Spanish Hall, whose name harkens back to the Spanish upbringing of the emperor Rudolf II.

The *Complete Description of Prague* confirms that it was known by this name in Mozart's time. Kleist's basic attitude toward such an event was that it was a sop intended to distract people's minds from the ideas of freedom and personal pride. The sumptuousness of the banquet he was willing to concede, and also his amazement that it was open to anyone who arrived decently dressed.

A police regulation still preserved in the National Archive in Prague carefully stipulates which dignitaries were allowed to attend without a ticket (including everyone present at the private reception of 1 September), where they were to gather beforehand, and which ordinary male citizens were allowed to purchase tickets (spouses were permitted to come along, but not children, due to space constraints). A brief decree issued on 6 September stated that the same rules would be followed for the ball to be given in the castle on 7 September. The emperor mixed with remarkable freedom among those who attended, according to Kleist, in a "kindly and condescending" manner. Nonetheless, Kleist reported the opinion of many that the rougher affability of Joseph II was preferred to the version of it experienced from Leopold.

The "mass of allegiance" on Sunday, 4 September, was a religious ceremony that Kleist (with his Protestant anticlerical views) found intolerably elaborate to be conducive to proper religious worship. From the standpoint of the imperial court, the purpose of the service was to pin down the Bohemian nobility to a firm oath of allegiance to Leopold as their sovereign. A service of this importance would be expected to include lavish performances of sacred music organized by the personnel brought to Prague by Salieri. Earlier literature reports that the mass setting used for this ceremony was written by Jan Antonín Koželuh, the choirmaster of the cathedral and one of the most prominent musicians in Prague.

It can be established from a musical score preserved in the collection of the Cathedral of St. Vitus, however, that the mass featured for this ceremony was actually by Leopold Hofmann, the head of the musical establishment at St. Stephen's Cathedral in Vienna. Hofmann has an interesting place in discussions of Mozart's musical career. Arrangements had been made as of 9 May 1791 for Mozart to replace the ill Hofmann should he die, but it was Mozart who died first (Hofmann died in 1793). H. C. Robbins Landon, in his book *1791: Mozart's Last Year*, was eager to believe that the service of allegiance also included a performance of Mozart's Offertorium *Misericordias Domini*, K. 222, but offered no documentation to support his hypothesis. The authors of the settings of the gradual *Veni, sancte spritus* and an offertory that Salieri conducted for this ceremony are not known.

On 5 September, the day of the rehearsal for Leopold's coronation, Kleist reported as his most interesting activity the chance to make the acquaintance of August Gottlieb Meissner, grandfather of the author of the *Rococo-Bilder*, who met regularly with a circle of acquaintances on a beautiful island in the Vltava that was then known as "Little Venice" (Klein-Venedig); it is now known as "Střelecký Ostrov" ("the riflemen's island"). Kleist found Meissner thoroughly erudite and agreeable and engaged him in a lengthy discussion of the contemporary state of German literature.

No one could have been disappointed by the spectacle witnessed the next day, Tuesday, 6 September, during the actual coronation ceremony. The procession of carriages alone would have been unforgettable. The royal entourage followed a traditional route that is still marked in the streets of Prague. It originated at the Powder Tower at the eastern boundary of the Old City, then proceeded to the Old City Square, then over Charles Bridge to Malá Strana, and up the hill on which Prague Castle is built. This "royal route" even today provides a basic tour of the city that includes many of the most beautiful churches and palaces to be seen there (it is easier of course to walk it backwards, downhill from the castle). Perhaps the most interesting part to observe in the eighteenth century would have been the sight of carriages being forced to negotiate a hairpin turn at the top of the steep street now known as Nerudova (see front cover), but was then called the "Spornergasse" (the lane of spurs). Indeed, judicious application of spurs would have been needed in Mozart's time, either up the street or down it by horseback.

Kleist himself was unaffected by the political theater that he saw that day, even though he did record the beauty of the interior of the Cathedral of St. Vitus. He found the sight of Leopold II bedecked in coronation regalia (with his crown, orb, scepter, and sword) rather comical. The strongest impression left on him by the coronation ceremony itself appears to have been the strange circumstance that Leopold found himself in, having to humble himself before clergyman. In this unique situation, the greatest monarch in the world had to prostrate himself before individuals of lower birth than himself. This was especially striking when the archbishop of Prague followed the curious (but age-old) custom of baring Leopold's left shoulder during the service, dripping oil on it, and after a blessing, wiping off the oil with bread and salt. In general, Kleist found it dangerous that a monarchical authority is not legitimate unless ratified by clergymen. As always, Kleist felt that Joseph, who had chosen not to put himself in the same position, had been the monarch with superior principles. He reported considerable nostalgia for Joseph not only among the peasants, who had benefited most from his policies, but also from the nobility and bourgeoisie.

The music for this ceremony was also expected to be quite lavish. A mass preserved in the music collection of the Cathedral of St. Vitus by the local composer Jan Antonín Koželuh bears an inscription that says it was composed expressly for the coronation ceremony, "even though it was never performed" ("benchè non prodotta"). What was performed instead is open to question. H. C. Robbins Landon was eager to believe that the coronation ceremony was graced with music by Mozart. In his book *1791: Mozart's Last Year*, he even claimed (without documentation) that Salieri had definitely brought three of Mozart's masses and other Mozart sacred works with him to Prague from Vienna. The basis of this speculation is an assertion of Salieri's nineteenth-century biographer Ignaz Franz von Mosel that almost the same music was used for each of three coronation ceremonies that Salieri was responsible for organizing: Leopold II as Holy Roman Emperor in Frankfurt-am-Main in 1790; Leopold II as king of Bohemia in Prague in 1791; and Francis II as Holy Roman Emperor in Frankfurt-am-Main in 1792.

The idea was that Salieri arrived in Prague with what could be described as a musical "coronation kit," a series of sacred compositions suitable for incorporation into coronation ceremonies. Landon wanted to believe that the masses used for Leopold's coronation celebrations were K. 258 of 1776 (a "short" mass, or *missa brevis*), K. 317 of 1779, and K. 337 of 1780, all of them masterpieces written during Mozart's residence in Salzburg. In the realm of sacred music, new creations were never as much insisted upon as they were in the realm of secular dramatic music. Landon also asserted that the Offertory used for the service was an arrangement of a chorus from Mozart's music to the play *Thamos, König in Ägypten,* written in the late 1770s.

The performance of these works was never publicized or attributed to Mozart, but there is room for conjecture. In spite of Landon's overreaching speculation, it is possible that the mass performed for Leopold's coronation ceremony on 6 September was either K. 317 or 337, and that a "short" mass performed on 8 September to commemorate the installation of the archduchess Anna Maria Ferdinanda as the abbess of the Noble Ladies' Foundation in Prague was the *Missa brevis*, K. 258. However, no one knows for certain whose music was used for either of these ceremonies, only that Koželuh's mass was rejected.

The First Performance of La clemenza di Tito

Mozart's *La clemenza di Tito* was performed for the first time during the evening of 6 September. Police decrees still preserved in remarkably pristine state in the National Archive in Prague offer a taste of how carefully controlled its performance was intended to be. Such regulations naturally did have to be issued in order to avoid chaos when so many visitors were in the city. Admission was free of charge, in accordance with the original contract that the Estates had made with the impresario Guardasoni, but tickets were compulsory for entrance.

One of the decrees printed for general distribution set forth highly-detailed procedures for their issuance. Priority was given first to members of the imperial entourage and foreign nobles, then to native nobles, then to foreign and native dignitaries not of noble rank. The citizens of Prague were to give up the best seats to foreigners as a courtesy (the experience of Czechs being relegated to the status of second-class citizens in their own country has been a familiar situation for centuries). Dignitaries who had been present for the private reception in honor of the emperor, given at Prague Castle on 1 September (along with certain other classes of dignitaries who were not there), were to pick up their tickets at an office of the Czech Gubernium within the castle complex at designated times. They were also instructed to indicate the names of servants who would be attending them. Whatever tickets that were left, after the most favored classes of spectators were guaranteed comfortable accommodation, were to be distributed among lesser dignitaries who were supposed to obtain them from their appropriate government superiors. These ticket holders were permitted to be accompanied by wives and one "grown" daughter. There was no provision made for general admission. The ordinary citizenry of Prague was not allowed to see the first performance of *La clemenza di Tito*. Attendance was restricted only to favored nobles, bureaucrats, military officers, academics, and clergy - plus a few prominent bankers and merchants - and it is doubtful that even the lower ranks of dignitaries were actually able to obtain many of the tickets made available, since demand for them was so high. The audience that assembled for the opera on 6 September 1791 was one of the most exalted and exclusive that was ever brought together for a performance of a dramatic work by Mozart.

The traffic regulations distributed by the Prague police for the coronation opera are equally remarkable for their precision. In this case, the decree was issued both in German and Czech, undoubtedly because it did contain certain regulations that were to be followed by the common people in Prague who would not have been allowed into the theater. In order that the opera begin promptly at 7:00 PM - so that the emperor and the highest dignitaries would not be annoyed by latecomers - ticket holders were instructed to leave in their carriages from wherever they were staying at about 5:00 PM. All carriages that originated from the Old City, New City, and Malá Strana were to line up first in what is now called the Old City Square, then follow a path through the "Iron Lane" (modern Železná street) that would permit ticket holders to be dropped off in front of the National Theater. Carriages that originated in Malá Strana were to return by way of the coal market in the Old City (modern Uhelný trh), then down either the "Dominican Lane" (modern Jilská street) or the "Post Lane" (modern Karoliny Světlé). Either would have led logically to the bridge over the Vltava now known as Charles Bridge. Carriages originating in the Old City and New City were to drive first to the "old moat" (modern Na přikopě) before returning to their point of origin. According to the Albrecht journal, many houses in Prague were specially illuminated throughout the evening of the coronation ceremony. The same journal also reported that the tickets for the event were collected personally by members of the Estates of Bohemia to help ensure that nobody who did not have one would be allowed in.

It must have taken hours for all of the spectators to be picked up and driven home. The carriages that had left were supposed to return to pick up their passengers the same way they had gone home, then travel down the "Iron Lane" to disperse their passengers after waiting in certain designated areas. Street traffic and pedestrians not involved with the coronation opera were prohibited from entering the lanes around the National Theater, the square behind it (the "Karolinplatz," now known as the Ovocný trh), and the pavilion that had been built to accommodate a ball on 12 September between the hours of 5:00 PM and midnight. If the opera had started on time, its performance would have been finished well before 10:00 PM, but it did not start on time. Count Zinzendorf and the Albrecht coronation journal reported that the court did not arrive until 7:30 PM, but one of the coronation journals (probably basing its information on a report in the *Prague Post* of 10 September) claimed that the court did not arrive until shortly after 8:00 PM. The Czech press reported that the main streets of Prague from the Castle to the theater were completely full of people from

6:00 PM, that the court did not arrive until 8:00 PM, and that spectators were unable to leave the theater until 10:30 PM.

Kleist had disappointingly little to say about *La clemenza di Tito*, but what he did say was highly complimentary:

> In the evening a very beautiful new opera, *La clemenza di Tito*, was given by the Estates free of charge. The music is by Mozart, and quite worthy of its composer. Here it pleased especially with the Andante [perhaps a collective reference to several of its musical numbers in Andante tempo], in which the melodies were beautiful enough to entice the gods down from heaven. It is impossible for me to express my opinion about it, since I heard the opera only once, seated among a great crowd.

Famously, the general reaction to *La clemenza di Tito* was either muted or negative. The *Prague Post,* in its issue of 10 September, simply reported that the event had taken place, and that it was mainly attended by the numerous nobles who happened to be in town. Not a word was said about the quality of the music. Of course, the *Prague Post* had no basis to offer a firsthand judgment, since no representative from the newspaper would have been able to gain admittance. Count Zinzendorf thought it a "tedious spectacle," even though the emperor was very pleased with the singing of Maria Marchetti Fantozzi. In recent years, the legendary negative opinion of the empress Maria Luisa has been reinforced with documentary proof that she considered the music "very bad so that almost all of us fell asleep." The more quotable observation of hers - that the opera was nothing more than "German swinishness" ("una porcheria tedesca") - does not predate the Meissner *Rococo-Bilder* of 1871. Since his account of the coronation has never been translated into English before, it will be excerpted here in order to provide the precise context in which the empress' famous denigration was brought up.

Meissner's work reinforces the highly negative view of Leopold II's character that was common in the Bohemian lands. He was determined to besmirch Leopold's reputation by any means, and always compared him in unflattering terms to his brother Joseph. It is obvious that Meissner prepared his remarks with reference to Kleist's impressions, and even ascribed to his grandfather quotations that are actually paraphrases of remarks attributable to Kleist:

> Joseph had himself crowned neither in Hungary nor in Bohemia. On the one hand this was due to the Josephine concept of a unified empire, in which the pretensions of individual provinces and regions were not to be encouraged. On the other hand, his liberal intent was to not grant to the clergy the appearance of supremacy over the monarchical principle. A ceremony such as a coronation is ultimately an acknowledgement of the power of priests over the monarch, who receives the crown from their hands. A consequence of this is the popular belief that the king is put in place by priests and thus could be deposed by them
>
> Whereas Joseph sought to uphold the concept of a unified empire and the principle of world supremacy, and at the same time save the money of the people, Leopold II, his opposite in anything and everything, did nothing with urgency other than to have himself crowned and to use whatever was left over from the war taxation to be sacrificed on a glittering, but inwardly shallow, theatrical performance. When he

had been grand duke of Tuscany, he had been beloved of his subjects. Florence was quite content to have him as its lord for so long. During the 27-year rule of [his father] Francis I, about 30 million Tuscan florins left the country every year, a circumstance that nearly repressed all commercial activity. Now, suddenly transferred from the Arno to Vienna, he started off by breaking up Joseph's Privy Council and dismissing those sympathetic to Josephine ideals. It is true that he found the empire in extreme jeopardy, the Netherlands in rebellion, and Hungary, Bohemia, and Austria discontented. He gave back to these lands everything they had had under the rule of his mother [Maria Theresa]; above all he sought to appease the Netherlands. A general amnesty was proclaimed and the Belgian aristocrats gladly returned to the indulgent Austrian scepter from the rule of clerics and lawyers under [Hendrik] van der Noot and [Jean André] van der Mersch.

Leopold was emotionally and physically exhausted and gave the impression of premature aging to those who had the opportunity to see him in the hallways of Prague Castle. His memory was so weakened that he could not even remember recent events or recall conversations from the day before. During audiences at which ambassadors from foreign powers were present (and were not concluded quickly), he would pace back and forth in the room. On his table lay rolls of white wax that he was accustomed to biting in order to soothe spasms in his jaw. The pieces he would spit out on the parquet floor. When he was finished with these audiences, whether he was alone or with others, he was never seen to leave walking out in a straight line; rather he would walk along the walls and touch the high valances and windows for support.

This premature state of exhaustion can be attributed to his extraordinary passion for the fair sex, whose company he would not give up even after his health had been seriously damaged. There was no limit or moderation shown to those women who offered him the favor of their love. When he was having a love affair with Lady Cowper [née Hannah Anne Gore, wife of the third Earl Cowper, a noted patron of the arts in Florence], he had his brother Joseph name her husband a prince of the Holy Roman Empire, a distinction that had never been granted to an Englishman since it had been bestowed on John Churchill, duke of Marlborough [in 1707 during the War of the Spanish Succession]. For Countess Wolkenstein he assumed debts in the amount of 200,000 gulden. Now he preferred the merry Polishwoman Prohaska, and among the innumerable lovers he had discarded was the Italian singer [actually dancer] Donna Livia [Raimondi]. His wife since 1763, Maria Luisa, daughter of Charles III [of Spain], a pale, skinny, frail, and in no way graceful woman, was indulgent of her husband's weaknesses in accordance with the prevailing custom of the time.

On 2 September the emperor was to appear in the opera house with the imperial family. Curiosity seekers swarmed the entire path from Hradčany to the theater. Inside the opera house all of the loges were occupied and the parterre was overflowing. When the emperor finally appeared, he was greeted with three rounds of applause and cries of "Vivat" that he responded to by bowing to the audience. In spite of all the noise created by trumpets and tympani, this entrance did not in the slightest have an enthusiastic character.

In the parterre there were three celebrities associated with [French] legitimism: old General Bouillé with a white cockade in his hat; the duke of Polignac; and Count [Axel von] Fersen. The last of these, the fair Fersen ["le beau Fersen"], was the young Swede gallantly devoted to the unfortunate queen of France. It was just eleven weeks before, on the memorable evening of 20 June, that he escorted the royal family out of Paris dressed as a coachman. After reaching the town of Bondy his mission came to an end. Another guide was waiting. Silently he bowed wearing his coachman's clothing, while a little hand waved inexpressible thanks to him. He traveled north to flee from France, but soon turned up again in order to bring those languishing in the Temple [where the French royal family was imprisoned in Paris] relief from their suffering. But a fourth celebrity present in the theater was more noteworthy than all of these. He was a short man wearing a greenish-colored coat who glanced around with fiery dark eyes and was identified at the beginning of the performance in this way: Mozart, imperial chamber composer since 7 December 1787 at a salary of 800 gulden a year. His opera *Don Giovanni* was to be given.

On 6 September the coronation took place in the splendidly decorated Metropolitan Church [of St. Vitus]. It was an empty formality. The archbishop uncovered the emperor's left shoulder and poured oil on it, which was rubbed with salt and bread after the completion of the consecration. Then the crown of St. Wenceslas was placed on his head, in his hands he was given a scepter and the imperial orb, and a sword fastened onto him. It was only to be expected that the sound of tympani and drums and the thunder of cannons broke out at the oath, and that the emperor would take his supper and celebrate a sumptuous high mass. Even so, the entrance and exit of the imperial entourage and guards were magnificent.

In the evening *La clemenza di Tito* was performed, the libretto commissioned from the Bohemian Estates from Metastasio. Mozart began the work in his carriage on the way from Vienna to Prague and completed it in Prague, where he once again stayed with Dušeks, within eighteen days. The work was commissioned so late, with so little time permitted to complete it, that Mozart had the unaccompanied recitative written by his student Süssmayer, and he had to copy out the completed musical numbers into parts as well. And while Mozart was composing so strenuously, he was getting continually sicker, taking medicine, and his coloring was pale, his face mournful. He not only had to compose, he also had to rework the libretto completely. In order to make an opera out of it, it had to be shortened and focused. Nonetheless portions of this work are masterful - for example the finale of the first act, a composition of terribly emotional grandeur. "It contains melodies," my grandfather wrote in his diary that evening, "that are beautiful enough to entice deities down to earth! If we Germans are lacking in the susceptibility and enthusiasm for intellectual heroes that Handel, for example, found among the English and Gluck among the French - who would not prefer to see Mozart crowned today rather than Leopold?"

La clemenza di Tito did not receive a favorable reception overall. The emperor spoke of it disdainfully and the empress referred to the music as a "porcheria tedesca." The audience had been oversaturated with balls, dances, entertainments, and spectacles of all kinds in order to enjoy the great charm of these melodies, which were conceived with a pure soul. Mozart received 200 ducats from the Estates. That he was given no consideration from the crowned heads is obvious, otherwise they would not have been behaving as Austrians.

Another report of the first performance of *La clemenza di Tito* only tends to heighten the lack of consensus about its success. A very interesting account of it is preserved from an anonymous author in a journal article that appeared in Brno in December 1794 in the *Allgemeines europäisches Journal* (the *General European Journal*), under the title "Some Reports About the State of Theater in Prague." This author reported the opinion of "connoisseurs" in general that *La clemenza di Tito* was a masterpiece at the same level as (or higher than) *Don Giovanni*. However, like Meissner, he attributed the indifferent reception it received to the distraction caused by the magnificent balls, banquets, etc. that competed with it for the attention of the public. In addition, he blamed the inadequate performances of the two lead singers. - The male soprano Bedini he considered "wretched." The emperor Leopold may have been taken with Maria Marchetti Fantozzi, but this observer reported that she sang "more with her hands than with her throat" to the point that she resembled a madwoman. Certainly, the impresario Guardasoni lost money; otherwise he would not have had to petition the Estates for an enhanced subsidy. His request was supported by comments from Count Rottenhan, who also indicated that the opera attracted sparse crowds after its first performance due to the competing coronation events. Additionally, he claimed that the imperial court harbored a "preconceived aversion" to Mozart's setting (for reasons unspecified).

The Remaining Coronation Events

Kleist left no impression of the installation of the archduchess Maria Anna Ferdinanda as abbess of the Noble Ladies' Foundation on 8 September and may not have attended the ceremony. He did record another long discussion with August Gottlieb Meissner the following day (this time on the subject of theology) at the "Grape" tavern close to the National Theater. In spite of legends that Mozart appeared there frequently and loved to play billiards inside, Kleist did not report seeing him on that day, 9 September, which closed with a performance of *La clemenza di Tito* at the nearby opera theater. On the day of the rehearsal of the queen's coronation (11 September), the last day when no official events were scheduled, the French balloonist Jean-Pierre Blanchard took advantage of the lack of competing attractions to fly over the city as an exhibition of his abilities. Blanchard was in the middle of a tour of continental Europe, where he introduced the art of flying in balloons to many countries. The *Prague Post* of 27 August recorded his arrival from Vienna on 23 August. Kleist was fascinated by Blanchard's technological achievement and left a long description of the spectacle he saw and the construction of the apparatus used to create it.

Kleist's last substantial account from the coronation celebrations was a description of the ball sponsored by the Estates after the coronation of the queen on Monday, 12 September. 2400 people were invited to this event according to the Albrecht coronation journal. Once again, Kleist found both the ceremony and the ball a stupendous waste of money - and took pains to record the sums spent on them - but his account of the ball in particular demonstrates that it must have left a dazzling impression. A special pavilion had been built onto the rear of the National Theater to accommodate all of the guests who danced that evening. The illuminations in particular, and also the refreshments, were clearly as magnificent as any court in Europe experienced in that day. Kleist had little to say about the cantata of Leopold Koželuh performed that evening in the National Theater (whose text was prepared by his new friend Meissner). He concluded with a brief description of the last ball given in the castle under the sponsorship of the court (on 15 September). With that, his narrative abruptly ends without explanation.

Mozart's Last Departure from Prague

The circumstances of Mozart's final days in the city of Prague are recorded nowhere in contemporary documents, nor is there any record of how he might have tried to participate in the non-operatic events going on in Prague in September of 1791. It is known from one of the coronation journals, however, that Salieri left on 15 September (the empress left on 1 October 1 and the emperor on 2 October). All that can be said for certain about Mozart is that he must have been back in Vienna within a reasonable amount of time to assist with the preparations for the première of his opera *The Magic Flute* on 30 September. The completion of the latter work was recorded in Mozart's own catalog of musical compositions on 28 September.

A clue about the time of Mozart's departure can be gleaned from a letter that he wrote to his wife in Baden on 7-8 October 1791, one of his last. Constanze was absent from Vienna in order to take a cure. Mozart relayed to her a report about the last performance of *La clemenza di Tito* in Prague that came courtesy of the clarinettist Anton Stadler, who remained in the city longer than Mozart did. Based on the list of coronation events set forth in the Albrecht journal, the only possible dates for subsequent performances of *La clemenza di Tito* would have been 9 and 16 September; thus Mozart must have left before 16 September, and in all had spent less than three weeks in Prague. Stadler's report was heartening to Mozart, who told his wife that the last performance had been met with extraordinary success, just as *The Magic Flute* was enjoying immediate popularity in Vienna. Mozart learned from Stadler that all of the vocal pieces were applauded and that the duet from Act I, "Ah, perdona al primo affetto," had to be repeated. The rondò from Act II, "Non più di fiori," would also have been repeated if the audience had not wished to spare the singer Maria Marchetti Fantozzi. He added that the male soprano Bedini sang better than ever. Stadler reported that the Dušeks were well, but Mozart complained that they had not written to him since he had left Prague. As for Stadler himself, he used a Slavicized version of his name to tell Mozart how "Stodla" was enthusiastically applauded for his playing (undoubtedly the basset horn solo in the rondò "Non più di fiori") and how much he deserved it. This led Mozart to remark to his wife what a "jackass" Stodla was. If Stadler's reports were accurate, it must be regarded as rather curious that subsequent performances of *La clemenza di Tito* were completely ignored in the Prague press.

There is little likelihood that he would have had to witness the overwhelming success of Koželuh's cantata as performed on 12 September at the ball given at the National Theater or its repetition on 23 September with Josefa Dušek singing. The patriotic nature of the composition and the pride of showcasing local talent led Mozart to be overshadowed during the coronation celebrations even in the realm of music. As for Mozart's unobtrusive "French leave" from the city, Meissner did have a good story prepared that would be enjoyable to believe - but it cannot be true. One of the factual errors easiest to expose is the presence of Pasquale Bondini (who had died in 1789) for the final farewells. To see Mozart off for the last time, it would seem that Meissner simply tried to include every non-nobleman he could think of who was friendly to him. Meissner included his own version of the story about billiard-playing that is quoted in the previous chapter from the Nissen biography, and he drew on a passage from Němeček's biography quoted in the next chapter to concoct his account of Mozart's last moments with his friends in Prague:

> During this time, his last stay in Prague, Mozart, an ardent Mason, appeared many times at the "Truth and Harmony" lodge. The last time he came, he had the lodge brothers arrange themselves in two rows and at his entrance was received with the cantata "Mauerfreude," which was composed in 1785 in honor of [Prague resident Ignaz von] Born. This distinction stirred Mozart deeply and to express his thanks for it he said that next time he would bring along a better homage to Freemasonry. He was referring to *The Magic Flute*, which was already ruminating in his imagination. Already while he was at work on *La clemenza di Tito*, his friends who came to play billiards with him in his lodgings next to the coffeehouse "zum Sturm" noticed that during the course of the games he would softly sing or whistle a motive, take out a book from his pocket, glance at it, put it back, and them resume his game. The book was Schikaneder's libretto [for *The Magic Flute*]. How astounded his friends were when Mozart was once sitting at the piano at Dušek's performing a composition in which the motive he had been whistling appeared again worked out most excellently. It was the quintet for Tamino, Papageno, and the Three Ladies ["Wie? Ihr an diesem Schreckensort?" from Act II].
>
> In fact, perhaps while he was by necessity pressing on with the work on *La clemenza di Tito*, he was continuing to carry around in his head Papageno's pranks and the secret trials of Tamino and Papageno. Part of the overture and the march of the priests [in Act I] was likewise created at this time. Then came the day of his departure. Mozart's carriage was waiting quite early in front of the house "at the Three Axes," packed not only with luggage and boxes, but also with baskets, since Frau Constanze would never undertake the journey to Vienna without taking care to bring along the delicacies that the noble country of Bohemia offered in the way of foodstuffs, in particular, ham, pheasants, and stuffed geese. The Dušeks came, as did Kapellmeisters Kuchař and Strobach (with a big bouquet of flowers) and the impresarios Guardasoni and Bondini - the last with his wife and daughter - besides a crowd of others standing in the background. Quite bashfully approached also the little harpist Hofmann, a master of his instrument, who was still so poor, that he had to play in inns and often had to perform for nothing more than a pair of groschens. But the good Mozart respected him and had even composed for him the theme and variations that was never published and remained the exclusive property of this little man until he died. Now everyone said goodbye and Mozart embraced the ladies. He had often left Prague before, but never did a departure have the same character as this day. Mozart was peculiarly sentimenttal and wistful and shed many tears. Could he already have been feeling a premonition of his death? He would never see the new year, because he would pass away on 5 December 1791.

It would take the shock of the composer's death to make the residents of Prague fully realize the treasure they had lost - and perhaps also to regret the lack of attention he had been accorded during his last visit to the city.

9

Slights Redeemed:
The Reaction in Prague to Mozart's Death

The degree to which Mozart might have felt a lack of attention from the music public of Prague during his last visit will likely never be known, but at least one thing is certain: No one could have predicted at the time of his departure how little time left there would be for him to live. It is well known to music lovers that the events surrounding Mozart's death and the precise reason for it remain stubbornly resistant to clarification. Němeček reported that "the doctors did not agree on the cause of his death," a finding just as valid today as it was in 1791. A basic scenario of an ill Mozart leaving Prague after the coronation of Leopold II, then recovering somewhat during the following autumn, and then dying suddenly in December of 1791, originates in the Mozart literature principally from remarks found in Němeček's biography. His complete account follows, based on information he received from Mozart's widow Constanze:

> While he was in Prague, Mozart became ill and was continually seeing doctors. His complexion was pale and his expression was sad, although he often demonstrated his lively humor in the company of his friends with merry jokes. While saying farewell to his circle of friends, he became so melancholy that he shed tears. An ominous feeling that his life was going to come to an end seems to have produced this dreary mood - for already at that time he carried in him the germ of the illness that would soon dispatch him.
>
> Upon his return to Vienna he started work right away on his Requiem Mass and worked at it with great intensity and keen interest, but his indisposition increased visibly, and it sent him into a dark melancholy. His wife realized the seriousness of this with sadness. One day when she was driving in the Prater with him in order to cheer him and give him some diversion, and they were sitting by themselves, Mozart began to speak of death and declared that he was writing the Requiem for himself. Tears came to the eyes of this sensitive man: "I feel all too much," he continued, "that I will not last much longer; surely somebody has given me poison. I cannot shake myself loose from this thought."
>
> This sort of talk fell on his wife's heart like a heavy load. She was hardly in a position to comfort him, or to convince him that his melancholy delusions were without foundation. Since she felt that he was coming down with an illness, and that the Requiem was upsetting his sensitive nerves too much, she called a doctor and took the score of the composition away from him.

His health actually did improve somewhat, and during this time he was able to finish a small cantata that had been commissioned by a society for a celebration. The good performance of the composition and the great amount of applause it received gave his spirit a new impetus. He became more cheerful and repeatedly said that he expected to continue and finish his Requiem. His wife could no longer justify any reason not to give him his music back.

This hopeful state of affairs did not last long, however. In a few days he fell back into the melancholy he had experienced before, becoming ever more listless and weak, until he finally sank back in his sickbed from which, alas, he never rose again!

On the day of his death he had the score brought to his bedside: "Did I not say before that I was writing this Requiem for myself?" This is just what he declared, and then he looked through the whole composition with tears in his eyes. This was the last sad look of farewell that he had of his beloved art - a punishment of its immortality!

The sad circumstances of Mozart's funeral in Vienna were described in the introduction to this volume: a pathetic service in St. Stephen's Cathedral attended by few mourners without any special performance of music. Although his death was reported with appropriate regret, and there was recognition of his talents in the Vienna press, there was nothing like the spontaneous outburst of grief that was witnessed in Prague by the general populace. The Viennese certainly did not erupt in mourning in the way that the Praguers had. In the years just after Mozart's death, no one in Vienna ever arranged a public tribute for him commensurate with his artistic stature, a shortcoming that has left music historians searching for excuses and rationalizations for decades. For a lifetime of inadequate recognition and comparatively tawdry commemorations of his musical legacy, all the slights of Europe were redeemed in Prague in December of 1791. No admirer of Mozart could read the account that appeared in the *Prague Post* of 17 December 1791 without being profoundly moved:

The solemn exequies of Wolfgang Amadeus Mozart, the Kapellmeister and royal and imperial court composer who died in Vienna on 5 December, were held on 14 December at 10:00 AM in the parish church of St. Nicholas in Malá Strana; it was a commemoration quite worthy of the great master and did the greatest honor to the Prague orchestra of the National Theater, under the direction of the most distinguished and renowned Herr Joseph Strobach, who organized it, and all the famous musicians here who took part in it.

The previous day a printed announcement was distributed to the upper nobility and the general public; on the day itself all the bells in the parish churches rang out for half an hour; almost the entire population of the city streamed by; the carriages needed to transport the roughly 4000 people accommodated by the church for the veneration of the deceased assembled in the Italian Square [modern-day "upper" Malá Strana Square in the front of St. Nicholas Church]. The Requiem was by the renowned Kapellmeister Rosetti, whom we designate patriotically with the name Rössler; it was so beautifully performed by 120 of the best musicians, the beloved singer Dušek at their head, that Mozart's great soul in Elysium must have rejoiced over it.

In the middle of the church stood a magnificently illuminated mourning platform, three choirs of tympani with trumpets sounding solemn tones. The service was led by His Eminence the parish priest Rudolph Fischer with assistants; twelve students from the Malá Strana Gymnasium carried small torches crosswise with mourning bouquets hanging over their shoulders and white handkerchiefs in their hands; solemn silence hung over everywhere, and a thousand tears were shed everywhere for our Mozart, who was so often the cause of the most tender feelings in our hearts by reason of his heavenly music!

It is fitting that his merit be recognized in Prague after his death. His loss is irreplaceable; there are now and will be ever after preeminent masters of the art of music, but it would take centuries for nature to produce another Mozart. His original genius permeates his work; how could his enemies not fail to suffer in comparison when confronted with his unattainable artistic greatness? Yet they could find only one fault in him, as much as they envied him, and that was that he was too full of musical ideas; nonetheless his friends preserved the most unforgettable examples of this failing for posterity!

What he wrote bears the unmistakable impression of classical beauty, which pleases more with each new hearing, because one beauty evolves from the ones before. That is why his music will be enjoyed eternally, because it will always sound fresh. Is this not a mark of every classicist, or are his operas not evidence of this? Does one not hear them for the eightieth time with any less pleasure than the first? And oh, how we pity those who do not like them! Alas, Mozart the One and Only is no more!

The exceptional character of this intense demonstration of grief and gratitude is hardly to be believed. It was all organized for the memory of a cultural hero, rather than of a political figure or military commander - and furthermore, one who was a foreigner. But then, Prague was a city of practicing musicians unlike any other in Europe. The high level of musical literacy in the city in comparison to Vienna provides the surest means to explain the instinctive sense of loss that the citizenry of Prague felt at Mozart's passing. The accuracy of the anonymous journalist's estimation of Mozart's talents seems obvious to music lovers in modern times, but it was only in Prague that they were articulated so clearly very soon after his death.

Lavish commemorations of Mozart's death hardly ceased in Prague on 14 December 1791. Already on 13 January 1792, the Praguers put on a fresh musical tribute for the benefit of Mozart's widow and orphaned sons that was almost as touching as the one the month before, as described in the *Prague Post* of January 21. Among other things, this account reveals that the service of 14 December was put on at the expense of the musicians themselves, without subsidy from any noble patron or civic institution:

> Yesterday Mozart's memory was commemorated here in the Royal National Theater in a manner worthy of a great and deserving man who died so prematurely, by a public that recognized his talents and knew how to honor him. The entire undertaking was organized by a group of local friends of Mozart for the benefit of the family he left behind. Herr Graf Franz von Sternberg and Herr Dr. von Vignet, who were mainly responsible for the event, earned from it a new claim to the honor and attention that they are in deserving possession of. The generous support that our illustrious nobility in particular encouraged for this undertaking - the theater was filled with persons of all stations and classes - the noticeable level of participation, and the

unquestionable conspicuous success that lasted from the beginning to the end, proved how large the number of Mozart's admirers is in this capital city.

Because of the extent of output of this genius, there could be nothing more appropriate than selecting among Mozart's own masterworks the flowers for the wreath, with which one could adorn the urn. The vocal pieces were taken from the great opera *Idomeneo*, still never performed here. Fräuleins von Vignet and von Mariani, along with Herr Ramisch, joined in the performance and supported the recognized talent of our beloved virtuoso. Mme. Dušek, who, inspired by the beautiful and moving occasion, could not have offered a stronger rendering or received more recognition for the lively, unqualified success from connoisseurs.

Herr [Jan August] Vitásek, a worthy pupil of our distinguished Herr Dušek, played a new grand Mozart concerto on the piano with great success, which did him as much honor as was commensurate with the occasion. Already some weeks ago we reported in this newspaper in what glorious style our musicians put on at their own expense a commemorative service for the deceased Mozart. With the same nobility of intention they used their talents and efforts to put together yesterday's commemoration, without any other claim to reward than to honor a genius of such rare greatness in his art with repeated proof of their admiration.

The "grand new" piano concerto in question was undoubtedly K. 595, which had just been published in Vienna as Mozart's Op. 17. This immediate gesture of assistance to Mozart's widow and orphaned children is touching indeed. The extent to which Mozart's friends in Vienna offered similar aid to his survivors remains very much open to question. Eventually, Mozart's widow and children moved to Prague, obviously because they were more welcome there and could count on more generous support. Until Constanze and her children left Prague permanently in 1797, the Prague press reported on many events of interest having to do with Mozart's music or his family. The Prague première of *The Magic Flute,* on 25 October 1792, for example, was described in the *Prague Post* on 27 October. Performed in German by the Mihule theatrical company in the National Theater, it met with predictable success:

> On Thursday, 25 October, *The Magic Flute*, a grand opera in two acts, was performed for the first time by the Mihule theatrical company in the National Theater in the Old City. The libretto is by Herr Schikaneder, and the excellent music by the renowned and eternally unforgettable maestro Wolfgang Mozart. Herr Director Mihule, along with all his company, made every effort, through lengthy rehearsal and great expense, to present the true effect of this celebrated and excellent opera, which earned the most conspicuous success in a full opera house, and earned the unfeigned praise of everyone there. On Sunday, October 28, *The Magic Flute* will be given for the third time at 7 o'clock.

The year 1793 saw the appearance of a fresh source of news in the city of Prague, the *Prager Neue Zeitung (The New Prague Newspaper)*. It was published for only six years, but with a sense of discernment and detail in the reporting of musical events that was unprecedented in Prague - and exceptional in central Europe at the time. The bourgeoning of journalistic activity in Prague in the 1790s had sadly come too late to illuminate Mozart's personal visits in greater detail. On 24 January 1794, the *Prager*

Neue Zeitung reported on the first performance of *The Magic Flute* in Prague by the Guardasoni company in Italian. It was ecstatically received:

> On Wednesday, 22 January, the Prague public experienced a great delight for its artistic tastes. Mozart's last masterpiece, the admirable *Magic Flute*, was given in Italian translation by the opera company of Herr Guardasoni. The public, which had heard this opera so often in German, eagerly awaited the result of the effort and cost that the impresario expended on it - and its expectations were completely satisfied, indeed exceeded. Everything came together perfectly to set off the composition. One cannot say what should be praised more, whether the splendidly refurbished theater decorations, the suitable costumes - or the pomp of the choirs, the hard work and competitiveness of the singers, and the quite superb playing of the opera orchestra. The latter performed its obligations so well that connoisseurs could not have wished for more. Mozart's spirit was certainly not understood as well by any other orchestra, nor so accurately executed, as by this one! Everything was so generally satisfactory that everyone wished to congratulate Herr Guardasoni personally after the performance. The theater was already full of people an hour before the beginning of the opera. For Mozart's genius still hovers over us; even though he has certainly long passed away, his heavenly harmonies still delight us! Peace and joy to his ashes!

Among Mozart's other operas, *Così fan tutte* received its first performance in Prague in November 1791, just over a year after its première in Vienna, and only a matter of weeks after Mozart's last departure from the city. The Guardasoni company revived it in 1794 along with the production of *The Magic Flute* in Italian just mentioned, and they also revived *The Marriage of Figaro, Don Giovanni,* and *La clemenza di Tito* that year - an extraordinary series of productions that may have been prompted by visits of Constanze Mozart.

One of the most poignant accounts of the impact of this festival of Mozart operas in Prague in the year 1794 comes from the autobiography of the composer Václav Jan Tomášek that was published in the journal *Libussa* in serial form between 1844 and 1849. Tomášek became a towering figure in the musical life of Prague for half a century after the death of Mozart's friend František Dušek in 1799, but in 1844 he described his attendance as a young person at a performance of *Don Giovanni* from the perspective of a humble student trying to learn about the great masterpieces available to audiences of his day.

Earlier literature has claimed that his account derives from a performance of *Don Giovanni* that took place in Prague shortly after Tomášek had arrived there from Jihlava to study at the Malá Strana Gymnasium in 1790. Actually, Tomášek was not specific about what year he had seen it. Since he reported that the performance was given by the Guardasoni company during a cold part of the year, there is no possibility that it could have been so early; there is no record of a performance of it during a month in which it would be necessary to wear coats inside the theater during the first years after his return to Prague in 1791. Placards and lists of performances surviving from the National Theater in 1794, however, indicate productions in November and December of that year. Furthermore, Tomášek indicated that he saw the soprano Teresa Strinasacchi in productions of the Guardasoni company at about the same time (although not necessarily in this one), and she was present in Prague only between the years 1793 and 1797.

The sophisticated impressions that Tomášek recorded would be much more plausible from a 20-year-old than a sixteen-year-old. He attended the opera with his older brother Jakub, who was at that time a cloth merchant in the city of Prague:

> In the evening I visited the theater in order to hear the opera *I filosofi imaginari* by Paisiello. It made an inextinguishable impression on me, more for the musical-dramatic effect rather than Paisiello's abilities as a composer. At the same time I was playing my spinet very diligently, but mostly compositions by [Ignaz] Pleyel, whom I considered at that time to be the greatest living composer for his naturally-flowing melodies. His compositions were much celebrated in those days, only so soon to be driven out of the picture by the colossal specter of Mozart. My brother was displeased with my excessive reverence for Pleyel. Himself a decent piano player; he was keen to introduce me to music of better taste. In order to make this come about, he truly could have done nothing better than take me to the theater where Mozart's *Don Giovanni* was being given. We sat next to each other bundled up in our coats while awaiting the beginning.
>
> The overture began. Its magnificent ideas and quicker-moving, richly orchestrated continuation (in sum, the noble life blood of that organic work of art) seized me to such an extent that I sat there like a dreamer, barely breathing, and in my heavenly joy I saw a sunrise, which, lighting up something darkly imagined in me, warmed my whole soul with a magical force. With each moment, my interest grew in the whole work, and during the scene in which the ghost of the Commendatore enters, my hair stood on end from terror. On the way home I thanked my brother with tears in my eyes, pressed his hand, and left him without being able to say a word. Undeniably, this evening had the most decisive influence on my musical career…

Although he said that he continued to play the music of Pleyel, Tomášek claimed that he was now addicted to attending operatic performances:

> …for nothing but the finest could be expected, especially when the singers were electrified by such an excellent orchestra as that one was…Mozart, who knew precisely the capabilities of all the orchestras in Germany, was always in the habit of saying, " My orchestra is in Prague."

Other reports from the Prague press in the 1790s concentrate on the fate of Mozart's widow and children. On 17 December 1791, in the same issue that describes the commemoration of 14 December, the *Prague Post* published an announcement "from the Danube" with the bare facts of Mozart's passing:

> Mozart died in the prime of life at the age of 36 years with little means and two children left behind who faced the prospect of having to grow up wretchedly. Only the unforgettable genius of their father has made it possible for the orphans to acquire a benefactor who has taken them completely under his protection. This is someone generally known to the public by reason of his fine character and admired as the former president of the [Imperial] Court Education Commission, namely Herr von Swieten, who has clearly stepped forward to assume paternal responsibility for the orphans and care for them.

There is still much that is very obscure about the immediate fate of Mozart's wife and children in the first several years following his death. Many reports in the press of Vienna and other cities make mention of the generosity of Mozart's steadfast patron Baron van Swieten in coming forward to help care for the composer's sons, even to the extent of adopting them. Whatever assistance he did provide, he certainly did not adopt them. It is also clear that he did not take responsibility for the education of Mozart's sons for more than only a couple of years. This is clearly demonstrated by their move to Prague no later than 1794.

In reminiscences dating from a much later period, the eldest son Karl indicated that he believed he had come to Prague already in 1792 to continue his education with Němeček, but Němeček himself indicated that Karl stayed with him for a period of three years that would have had to have ended in 1797, when Constanze and her sons left Prague permanently. Němeček expressed this in a letter to the Leipzig publisher Breitkopf & Härtel written in 1799. Němeček's recollection, which dates from so much closer to the events in question, probably exposes Karl Mozart's recollection from the 1850s as faulty.

Two sons of Wolfgang and Constanze Mozart - Karl and Franz Xaver by Hans Hansen, 1798

Němeček had met Mozart at the time of the coronation ceremonies of 1791, and actually permitted Karl to live in his household while he was being educated in Prague. Whatever assistance Baron van Swieten may have provided at first was apparently insufficient to ensure an adequate education for the boy, so he was sent to Prague, as specified in the *Prager Neue Zeitung* of 7 April 1794 (see below). There is no way that Karl's transfer to Prague could be interpreted any other way than as an economy measure. There was certainly no lack of adequate educational institutions available to boys of his social class in Vienna at which he could study, and it is not likely that they would reject his enrollment for any reason other than the inability of his mother to pay tuition. The training Karl received in Prague was probably not inferior, in particular because it was so personalized under Němeček's auspices, but there would have been much more prestige in keeping him in Vienna to be educated. In the year 1800, in a letter to Breitkopf & Härtel, Němeček indicated that he had never received the smallest reimbursement for any assistance he provided to the Mozart family, in spite of "fine promises" and "sweet letters" that came to him from Baron von Swieten.

Constanze obviously realized in the mid-1790s that she could rely on the populace of Prague to alleviate her vulnerable position with unique generosity. In contrast to what Praguers provided her family, none of Mozart's former patrons in Vienna are known to have stepped forward to provide significant sustained assistance to his family. Equally disappointing was the attitude of Wolfgang's own sister Nannerl, who lived comfortably at the time married to a member of the lower nobility of Salzburg, yet never even met either of her two surviving nephews until her old age, much less contributed to their upbringing.

It seems that Mozart's widow Constanze soon exhausted the options available to her in Vienna to support her family adequately. Before she met her second husband, the Danish diplomat Georg von Nissen, later in the 1790s (perhaps in Vienna in late 1797), she had to try to collect as much money as she could to provide for herself and her sons, and she had few options available to her, left as she had been with no inheritance - only debts - from her husband. Furthermore, she was not talented enough as a singer to pursue a successful professional career in that field of endeavor. The paltry pension she received from the imperial court was only a fraction of what had been a small salary drawn by her husband for a part-time position. Within the constraints of the social customs of her day, charity, menial labor, or remarriage would have been her only alternatives (and eventually the last of these options did indeed solve her financial problems permanently).

However Constanze Mozart was viewed in Vienna in 1794, she was unquestionably welcome in Prague, and it was there that she began a career of several years' length organizing musical concerts in various cities whose proceeds were made over to her. The relationship that she began with the wealthy nobleman Georg Nissen (probably in Vienna at the end of the year 1797) enabled her to cease this activity. An issue of the *Prager Neue Zeitung,* of 10 February 1794, describes a concert organized for the benefit of Mozart's widow on 7 February, by the law faculty of Charles-Ferdinand University. It is not clear whether she was in the city to reside, simply dropping off her son Karl, or perhaps visiting him at the time:

> A monument of gratitude for Mozart. Nothing demonstrates the true taste and feeling heart of a nation better than the admiration and gratitude it shows for individuals of great accomplishments and talents. Bohemia has always done this; it has always recognized accomplished and talented individuals, justly evaluated them, and with the noblest gift - by rewarding them with admiration and respect! Prague set down a new demonstration of this on the evening of February 7. The law faculty of the local university, which has already supported for the second year at its own expense a musical concert of very fine taste for the education of prospective professional musicians and the pleasure of the residents of Bohemia, dedicated a concert to the memory of the greatest musical genius, Mozart, on the occasion of the presence of his widow in Prague. The gesture earns their hearts much honor, just as the performance is a credit to the taste of the select committee that organized it. The concert hall was brightly illuminated. In the background above the orchestra Mozart's name flamed in a sort of temple, on both sides of which stood two pyramids with the inscription "Gratitude and Pleasure" illuminated in transparent letters. Mozart's best works were chosen for this evening. A symphony in C formed the introduction, then Herr Vitásek, a very promising young Bohemian, played Mozart's magnificent concerto in D minor on the piano with as much precision as feeling. Then, Bohemia's beloved singer Frau Dušek sang Vitellia's heavenly rondò from Mozart's opera seria *La clemenza di Tito*. Her artistry is generally known everywhere; here she was inspired by her love for the great

deceased and his widow who is with us at present, whose warm friend she always has been!

The concluding item was one of the best symphonies that there is, the D major Symphony by Mozart. The music went very well - even though the works were difficult to play and mainly in concertante style, for it was the Prague orchestra that was playing and they are devoted to Mozart! It is easy to imagine how full the hall was, if one knows Prague's artistic feeling and its love for Mozart's music. Mozart's widow and son both broke down in tears of grief at the memory of their loss and in thanks towards a noble nation!

Thus this evening was fittingly and admirably devoted to a fine expression of homage to merit and genius; it was a rewarding feast for sensitive hearts - and a small tribute to the unspeakable delight that Mozart's heavenly sounds frequently elicited from us! From many a noble eye there flowed a silent tear for this well-loved man! It is as though Mozart had composed especially just for Bohemia; nowhere was his music better understood and better executed than in Prague, and even in the countryside it is universally loved. This is how a brave nation holds genuine merit in esteem - this is how a brave nation locates and supports its promising youths - and so many hearts were won by Mozart's great genius!

A fatuous poem in praise of Mozart by the locally renowned poet Joseph Georg Meinert followed the announcement. The musical selections featured the "Prague" Symphony (surely the D major symphony cited), the piano concerto in D minor, K. 466, Vitellia's rondò "Non più di fiori" from the opera *La clemenza di Tito*, and a symphony in C major that may be identical to the "Jupiter" Symphony, the "Linz" Symphony, or the Symphony No. 34.

Just three weeks later, more documentation of the esteem with which Mozart was held in the city appeared in the *Prague Post* of 4 March 1794. The occasion was an address in honor of Franz Xaver Süssmayer that was delivered in recognition of his composition of the music for a song in praise of Bohemia performed on 24 February for the birthday of the emperor Francis II (which actually fell on 12 February). It was accompanied by a wind ensemble. The address was prepared by the Rector of Charles-Ferdinand University, Egid Chladek, and quoted in condensed form:

> Worthy friend and worthy pupil of a great Salieri and the unforgettable Mozart! …If you should one day have the fortune to catch up with your renowned teacher, the immortal Mozart, what might not be expected from your diligence and ability? Just do not forget that Bohemia…a nation so famous for its excellent native musical genius, knows, I say, very well how to foster your talent.

The next mention of the Mozart family in the Prague press details a strange incident involving his son Karl that was reported in an issue of the *Prager Neue Zeitung* of 7 April 1794:

> The esteemed Prague public, which knows how to honor the name of Mozart, is owed an explanation made necessary by the last two opera notices. The boy Mozart, son of the immortal man whose heavenly harmonies will delight us forever, was sent to Prague to obtain his education and upbringing at the instigation of his noble benefactor, His Excellency Baron van Swieten, with confidence in the spirit of the

Bohemian nation. This nine-year-old boy, full of fire and vivacity, was to have appeared publicly on the stage in the opera *Axur* [by Antonio Salieri] in the role of a boy offered for sacrifice, according to the wish of several friends of the name of Mozart. What harmful effect this might have had on the development of this young person can only be evaluated by those to whom the supervision and care of the boy has been handed over. The children of great men belong to the public to some extent; and the boy's guardians have too high a respect for [Mozart] and too much love for the wellbeing of the boy to have permitted it. As these are also the convictions of his noble benefactor and of his mother, so there was all the less hesitation in preventing the boy's appearance. Had the opera announcements not revealed the matter to the public prematurely, this explanation would not have been necessary; but a person informed according to the latest opera bill might easily think the widow Mozart, who is full of respect and gratitude towards the Prague public, of a willfulness [on the part of others] of which she knew nothing.

In the years 1794-97, Constanze Mozart was involved in organizing many memorial concerts in the principal cities of German-speaking Europe. It is possible to interpret their sudden frequency a result of a successful model for such events that she had pioneered in Prague with the concert of 7 April 1794. At the end of 1794, Constanze put on a similar concert in Vienna, and in 1795 there were concerts for her benefit in Vienna, Graz, and Leipzig. 1796 was her most successful year, with concerts given in Berlin, Leipzig, Dresden, Linz, and Graz. In some of these, she would perform herself as a singer. During part of this time, she was also resident in Prague with her sons.

The last record of the Mozarts participating in a benefit concert in Prague took place on 15 November 1797. Apparently Constanze was present in the city at the time to collect her sons Karl and Wolfgang to take back to Vienna. Whether or not she had met Nissen by this time is uncertain. The driest notice of the concert comes from the *Prague Post* of 7 November:

> The widow Mozart, who is here in Prague at present, will put on a grand musical concert for her benefit in the great National Theater on the 15th of the month, next week Wednesday. Some of the best pieces from the Mozart estate will be performed. The artistically discerning public here in Prague will surely hear of this announcement with pleasure.

Another announcement appeared in the *Prager Neue Zeitung* of 10 November that really only adds the detail that pieces never heard before in Prague would be included. It refers to Constanze as the "departing widow Mozart." The program of the concert survives, although the indications of compositions performed are too vague to permit positive identification of most of the pieces included. One was an unspecified chorus from *La clemenza di Tito* that was so familiar to the audience, the program stated, that it was hoped that the audience would join in singing it. Likely there would have been no other place in Europe at the time in which ordinary audience members for a concert of Mozart's music would have been able to participate in the performance (and in Italian language). All the other compositions on the program were billed as never having been heard before in Prague, including a piano concerto, two soprano arias, a vocal trio, a bass aria, a "quartet finale" (perhaps from *Idomeneo),* and an overture with subsequent quartet from an "unfinished" opera (undoubtedly *Zaide* of 1780). In spite of the indication that nothing else had been heard before, the program does indicate that Mozart's younger son, Wolfgang, aged six years, would sing the song "Der Vogelfänger bin ich ja" from *The Magic Flute*. This would have been one of the child's first public performances. Later, he would be able to pursue a respectable musical career, although nothing as extraordinary as his father's had been. The result of the concert of 15 November was described in the *Prager Neue Zeitung* of 17 November:

> On the 15th a musical concert was given for the benefit of the widow Mozart in the National Theater in the Old City. The very numerous attendance, with loges and parterre filled, demonstrated the admiration for Mozart's art and genius. Madame [Antonia] Campi, whose singing is as melodious as it is artistic, appears to have surpassed herself. In general everyone [performing] was eager to honor Mozart's memory through their artistic exertions. Herr Vitásek from Prague proved himself a promising developing musician through his composition, which deservedly earned the approval it met with.

These reports mark the end the immediate period of close connections between the Mozart family and Prague that appeared in the Prague press. The concert of 15 November was not Constanze's last opportunity to glean income from her supporters in Prague, however. As amazing as it seems, there is record that her friend Josefa Dušek mortgaged the Bertramka villa on 22 November 1797 for a substantial sum that was turned over to Constanze. There is no record that any of it was ever paid back, but rather that the debt seems to have been cancelled when Josefa Dušek sold the Bertramka villa at the death of her husband in 1799.

There is just one other recorded newspaper report from eighteenth-century Prague that concerns Constanze, an advertisement she took out that appeared in the *Prague Post* on 4 May 1799:

> I would be immensely obliged if those who are in possession of original scores of Mozart's unpublished compositions will please be so gracious as to lend them to me very soon. Herr Professor Němeček at the Malá Strana Gymnasium will have the goodness to take care of them, and I will pay to have them returned myself. By the way, my address is known at the post office. Vienna, 1 May 1799, the widow Mozart.

What response she may have gotten is unknown, just as it is unknown whether she attempted anything similar in other cities. There is no record that anyone in Prague or elsewhere came forward with manuscripts and no record of whether or not she ever returned items that may have been sent to her. What is known today is that she was selling unpublished Mozart works at the time to the publishers Breitkopf & Härtel in Leipzig and Johann André in Offenbach. Obviously she had no intention of sharing fees from these publishers, although she was willing to to return manuscripts to their owners at her own expense. There can be little doubt that Němeček knew what she was doing.

Clearly, the Mozart family always felt that it could rely on the goodwill of the residents of Prague. The city had provided shelter and sustenance for Constanze and her sons, education for one of her sons, and the start of a career arranging commemorative concerts in her deceased husband's honor that brought her considerable income.

Bridges over the Vltava

Philosophical Library, Klementinum

Part Three:
Music for Prague

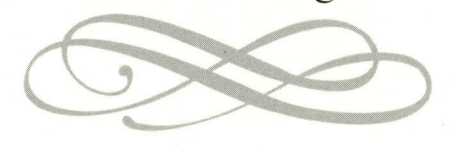

10

Titillation Under the Guise of Condemnation: Mozart's Opera *Don Giovanni*

The composition of the opera *Don Giovanni* was the crowning achievement of Mozart's association with the musical public of the city of Prague. Some enthusiasts consider it to be the greatest opera ever written, but a more common opinion is that it is simply Mozart's greatest opera. As a work with an Italian text written for the appreciation for spectators who were much more comfortable speaking in German or Czech, *Don Giovanni* is perhaps the most outstanding example in the eighteenth century of a strange cultural anomaly that music scholars take for granted: an extravagant admiration for Italian opera all over Europe that was so strong that opera in any other language was frequently dismissed as deficient, even when it was sung for the benefit of native speakers. Italy in the eighteenth century was so secure in this position of dominance that the opposite anomaly of German operas composed to German texts performed in Italy was absolutely beyond the realm of imagination. Modern opinions about the relative merits of the leading composers of eighteenth-century Italian opera yield a similarly peculiar irony. The comparative excellence of Italian operas by composers who grew up in territories controlled by German and Austrian rulers is unmistakable to modern listeners, who recognize the greatest composers of eighteenth-century Italian opera to be Handel, Gluck, and Mozart. For the typical opera lover of modern times, Italian opera written by Italians began with Rossini in the 1810s.

Undeniably, the combination of an outstanding libretto with music of intense emotional impact marks Mozart's *Don Giovanni* as a rare opera that has the power to compel spectators to reevaluate their personal views about religion and morality, in addition to offering them the opportunity to enjoy a dazzling array of musical ideas and share the unfolding emotions of an exceptionally interesting cast of characters. Regrettably, a thorough discussion of its dramatic poignancy and the ingenuity of its musical setting is not possible for a study of this scope, only a survey of selected topics of interest to a general readership, with a view toward highlighting what the author hopes will be perceived as the most original findings.

The Tradition of Don Juan Operas in Prague

It has become clear in only the last few decades that Prague was the musical center that introduced adaptations of the Don Juan tale to the operatic stages of eighteenth-century Europe. The city sponsored productions of the first one, the second one, and the greatest one. Prague's cultural connections with Venice were critical in bringing this about. The first libretto to employ the original Spanish character names and post-classical chronological setting descended from Tirso de Molina's prototype Don Juan play *El burlador de Sevilla* (*The Trickster of Seville*), was written by Antonio Denzio, the Venetian impresario who supervised productions in the Sporck theater between 1724 and 1735. Denzio came up with the title *La pravità castigata* (*Depravity Punished*) for his work, and he had it performed in Prague during Lent of 1730. It is true that the libretto for the opera *L'empio punito* (*The Sinner Punished*), produced in Rome in 1669 with music by Alessandro Melani, incorporated certain incidents and character types derived from the tradition of Don Juan dramas as they existed in the seventeenth century, but it is set in ancient Greece (consistent with operatic conventions of its day) without Spanish character names. It was soon forgotten after its original run and failed to initiate lasting interest in the Don Juan tale as an operatic subject.

The conception for the Denzio adaptation likely arose from the impresario's pressing financial difficulties. For the first five seasons of its productions, the Sporck theater flourished, but by 1729, interest had started to wane. As a result, the impresario began to take extraordinary steps to attract audiences and lower operating costs. One of the things Denzio tried to do was offer productions during Lent in order to lengthen the operatic season - a drastic move, since theatrical productions of all types were widely prohibited in Europe during the penitential seasons of Advent and Lent. In order to put on an opera during Lent in Prague, special permission was required from the archbishop himself.

Denzio's first Lenten production, a *Sansone* given in 1729, was a staged oratorio based on the Old Testament story of the lovers Samson and Delilah. For his second Lenten drama, Denzio tried once again to exploit an alluring mix of sex and religion by putting together an opera based on the Don Juan legend. He came by the music haphazardly and surreptitiously. Denzio was expert at assembling operatic pastiches by fitting new poetry of his own onto whatever preexistent music of high quality he could gather. Most of the music for the first Don Juan opera was written by Antonio Caldara, the most prominent composer at the imperial court of Vienna. With his authorship concealed in the published libretto distributed to audience members, Caldara probably never knew that his music was ever used for that purpose - and neither did Antonio Vivaldi, the likely author of the music for at least one of the arias.

The vulgarity associated with popular adaptations of the Don Juan story as performed by professional comedians all over Europe should have made this an astonishing idea for a Lenten operatic production. But in seeking the permission of the archbishop of Prague to put on his production, Denzio took advantage of the fact that Don Juan entertainments traditionally concluded with the spectacle of divine retribution for sin, a miracle that can be described as something of an individualized manifestation of the Last Judgment. Salacious as Don Juan entertainments could be, there was no argument that they depicted a ghastly penalty for the remorseless sinner: immediate consignment to hell at the behest of the spirit of an elderly man whom Don Juan has murdered. To make his case about the redeeming nature of his libretto, Denzio referred to it as a *rappresentazione morale* (morality play) in his application to the archbishop. His ploy was to present sexual titillation under the guise of condemnation, a hallmark of Don Juan entertainments throughout the ages, and thereby find a means to compete with the popular comedians in Prague for theatrical audiences.

Precisely how difficult it was to obtain the assent of the archbishop of Prague, Count Ferdinand von Khünburg, is unknown. Denzio frequently had to come before the reigning archbishops, but they always agreed to do whatever was asked of them without providing a written explanation for their decisions. Count Khünberg merely issued a curt decree permitting the production. A surviving copy of the libretto records it to have been a success.

In 1734, the Denzio libretto was re-set with music by Eustachio Bambini for a production in Brno. Bambini's setting was revived at least one time (in Strasbourg in 1750), but no new Don Juan librettos are known to have been produced anywhere in Europe until 1776, when another one appeared in Prague under the title *Il convitato di pietra* (*The Stone Guest*), a collaboration between the poet Nunziato Porta and the composer Vincenzo Righini, both minor figures in their 20s who happened to be attached to the opera company of Giuseppe Bustelli at the time. The title is borrowed from the prototypical Italian Don Juan dramatization, the play *Il convitato di pietra* by Giacinto Andrea Cicognini, believed to have been written ca. 1632.

Drawing of the first known set for *Don Giovanni* - Prague, 1790s

The Porta libretto was based principally on a Don Juan play written in Venice in 1736 under the title *Don Giovanni Tenorio* by the great comic playwright Carlo Goldoni, although it clearly was prepared with reference to the Denzio libretto as well. Nothing is known about the reception of Porta's collaboration with Righini except that it was successful enough to see revivals in Prague, Vienna, and Braunschweig in 1777, as well as in Eszterháza in 1781 under the supervision of Haydn.

A greater legacy of the production could be its role in starting a trend for new Don Juan operas in Italy. The first one was a setting with music by Giuseppe Calegari that appeared in Venice under the same title early in 1777. If the idea for the Calegari production of 1777 came from Prague, there is no documentation to confirm it, but it would be a remarkable coincidence indeed if there were no connection at all. A number of other settings soon followed in Italy, although most of them were not of much lasting importance. Early in 1787, however, a new Don Juan setting with music by Giuseppe Gazzaniga appeared in Venice. It was an immediate hit whose text by Giovanni Bertati became the principal model for Mozart's librettist Lorenzo Da Ponte.

The Genesis of the Da Ponte Libretto

The reason for the choice of the Don Juan legend as the subject matter of the Mozart opera to be given in Prague in the autumn of 1787 is open to question, due to conflicting accounts left by Lorenzo Da Ponte. As detailed in Chapter 6, Da Ponte's memoirs of 1823 supply the story that has been repeated most frequently in the Mozart literature. In this work, Da Ponte claimed that Mozart asked him for a new libretto of his own choosing at the same time that the composers Antonio Salieri and Vicente Martín y Soler came to him with similar requests, and that he himself chose the subject of Don Juan for Mozart. Da Ponte also claimed that he wrote all three librettos simultaneously, devoting evenings to *Don Giovanni* while thinking of Dante's *Inferno*, mornings to Martín thinking of Petrarch, and afternoons to Salieri thinking of Tasso.

It is tempting to dismiss this story summarily as the product of the same vanity, boastfulness, and simple delight in entertaining his readers that run through the Da Ponte memoirs generally. But more convincingly, it is flatly contradicted by Da Ponte's own words in his earlier collection of reminiscences, the *Extract from the Life of Lorenzo Da Ponte*, published in 1819. In the *Extract*, Da Ponte reported that the idea for the subject of Don Juan came from the Prague impresario Domenico Guardasoni, who took over from Bondini at some point during the year 1787. Specifically, Da Ponte claimed in the *Extract* that Guardasoni originally desired from Mozart a fresh setting of the libretto by Giovanni Bertati that had been performed in Venice earlier that same year. Da Ponte went on to explain that Mozart recognized the inferior quality of the Bertati libretto and insisted that a new one be prepared by his friend Lorenzo Da Ponte.

There are a number of reasons to believe that the earlier account is likely the accurate one, or at least more accurate than the later one, even aside from the fact that it is closer chronologically to the events in question. First and foremost, it must be kept in mind that it was customary in the eighteenth century for the subject matter of operatic productions to be chosen by theater managers. It was they who typically made the decision to commission a new libretto or revive an old one, select a poet if one was desired, engage all the singers, and then bring in a composer to be handed the libretto and told to write well for the singers others had selected. This is precisely how Mozart's second Prague opera, *La clemenza di Tito*, came into being at the same theater under the same impresario. The account in the Da Ponte memoirs of 1823 presupposes that Mozart was given free rein to treat any subject he cared to and seek out a poet himself without prior consultation. For an operatic production sponsored by an eighteenth-century public theater, such a scenario would have been highly exceptional indeed. A likely explanation for Da Ponte's suspicious change of recall with regard to Dante in the *Memoirs* of 1823 was his publication in New York City in 1821 of an Italian translation of Lord Byron's poem *The Prophecy of Dante*.

Another consideration that would lead one to believe that the idea for a Don Juan opera came from the impresario - and not from the librettist - is the care taken to engage the tenor Antonio Baglioni, who appeared in the original Venetian production of Bertati's libretto. Guardasoni clearly went out of his way to ensure that this key member of the Venetian cast would be present in Prague in addition to the standing members of his own company.

By 1787, the impresarios Bondini and Guardasoni had each been resident in Prague for many years. Both of them certainly would have known about the Don Juan opera staged in 1776 and 1777. It is less likely, but still quite plausible, that they also knew of the Denzio production from 1730. Each of the two opera principal theaters that preceded the National Theater as standing opera theaters in Prague had sponsored its own Don Juan production. It could be that the management of the National Theater felt that it was time to do the same. After all, the Don Juan tale was becoming more and more popular as an operatic subject in Italy, and there was now a musical genius available to them to bring the subject matter to life in an extraordinary manner. Reliable documentation to settle the matter completely will probably never be found, but this scenario is surely a more convincing explanation for the selection of the Don Juan legend for Mozart's opera than the tall tale told in the Da Ponte memoirs of 1823.

Historical Context of the Da Ponte Adaptation

For those accustomed to the maddening complexities of eighteenth-century operatic plots, the story of Mozart's drama *Don Giovanni* is refreshingly easy to follow, its basic outlines so clearly and forcefully presented that it can be followed almost as a pantomime. The opera opens with the spectacle of the seducer Don Giovanni trying to ravish a young noblewoman who has allowed him into her bedchamber at night.

He has arrived disguised as her betrothed, a ruse that she does not see through at first. When she discovers that the disguised man in her bedchamber is not the man she thinks he is, she escapes into the street outside.

After hearing a commotion, her father, a military officer referred to as the *Commendatore* (Commander), challenges Don Giovanni to a duel to defend her honor. The much younger Don Giovanni has no trouble besting the Commendatore and soon kills him - to the horror of his daughter. Most of the rest of the drama takes the form of an elaborate character sketch that illustrates Don Juan's odious personality traits - and not only his shameless lasciviousness - until he is finally held accountable for the murder by the Commendatore himself, who comes back to life in the form of a stone statue erected in his memory. All attempts of ordinary humans to bring him to justice fail. Invited to dinner after a confrontation with Don Giovanni in the graveyard in which he was buried, the Commendatore appears at Don Giovanni's lodgings to urge him to repent his crimes or face eternal damnation. Don Giovanni, too proud to bow to any external force, refuses to repent and is dragged down to hell by spirits summoned from the depths.

By the time that Lorenzo Da Ponte was writing, the prototypical Spanish drama *El burlador de Sevilla*, believed to have been written by Tirso de Molina about 1620, would not have been available for consultation as a literary model to any but the most determined devotees of Spanish literature. Nonetheless, it had an enduring impact filtered through generations of adaptations and popularizations.

Tirso's original emphasis was never intended to be sexual titillation, but rather the weighty theological issue of whether one could find salvation when repentance for a lifetime of misdeeds is sought only just before death. Tirso's Don Juan does repent his crimes when confronted by the resurrected military officer, but his repentance is held to be too late and too convenient, so he is dragged down to hell anyway.

Other features of the Tirso drama found more lasting influence. Two of the most important ones are the basic techniques of seduction employed by the title character (i.e., the "tricks" - *burlas* - alluded to with the designation *burlador*): irresistible promises of marriage in the case of lower-class women, disguise in the case of upper-class women. Each method is explored in the Da Ponte libretto. As important as it was as a prototype, the drama of Tirso de Molina was largely forgotten after the 1620s, even in Spain itself. As a literary model for Don Juan dramatizations, it was soon supplanted by Cicognini's *Il convitato di pietra*. The Cicognini play was famed for its coarseness, and it initiated a tradition of scenarios that was taken up by the *commedia dell'arte* all over Europe. The new emphasis was far more on the amusement elicited from sexual "tricks" than the edifying spectacle of eternal damnation for the sinner Don Juan. Erudite observers in Da Ponte's time tended to look askance at the appeal of the popular dramatizations of their day.

Da Ponte of course would have had the instincts of a literatus, but he clearly sensed the importance of incorporating popular elements in his libretto for the sake of achieving a theatrical success, as confirmed by his friend, the New York physician

John W. Francis. In a compilation of memoirs published in 1858 entitled *Old New York: Reminiscences of the Past Sixty Years,* Francis complained of not being able to learn more from Da Ponte about his relationship with Mozart, but was pleased to pass along as much as he could:

> The opportunities which presented themselves to me of obtaining circumstantial facts concerning Mozart from the personal knowledge of Da Ponte, were not so frequent as desirable, but the incidents which Da Ponte gave were all of a most agreeable character. His accounts strengthened reports of the ardent, nay, almost impetuous energy and industry of Mozart; his promptness in decision, and his adventurous intellect.
>
> The story of Don Juan had indeed become familiar in a thousand ways; Mozart determined to cast the opera exclusively as serious, and had well advanced in the work. Da Ponte assured me that he remonstrated and urged the expediency on the great composer of the introduction of the via comica, in order to accomplish a greater success, and prepared the role with *Batti, batti, Là ci darem,* etc. How far he influenced Mozart in the composition, *Nozze di Figaro,* I am unprepared to say; but the libretto of these two works, from the testimony of the best judges, enhanced the renown already widely recognized of Da Ponte as a dominant genius in his profession, enabling melody to possess its fullest expression in facile language, and with delicacy, simplicity, and exquisite tenderness.

This account implies a close collaboration between poet and composer of a type that was very atypical of eighteenth-century operatic culture, but similar to the one likely shared between Da Ponte and Mozart during the preparation of *The Marriage of Figaro* (at least if Da Ponte's reminiscences can be believed). If Da Ponte was indeed responsible for ensuring the inclusion of comic action into Mozart's opera *Don Giovanni,* operatic audiences should be eternally grateful for his shrewdness. By depicting the richness of human experience, Da Ponte created a drama of great subtlety that has ensured its interest to audiences worldwide. The genius of Mozart's music would still excite admiration at least as great as what audiences presently feel for the music written for the serious operas *Idomeneo* and *La clemenza di Tito,* but a purely serious presentation would never have created an opera that seizes the imagination in the way that *Don Giovanni* does. The portrayals of serious characters in eighteenth-century opera now strike audiences as stilted, with musicologists left searching for ways to justify their dramatic worth.

Da Ponte was never honest in his writings about who his true principal model was for the creation of the *Don Giovanni* libretto. There is a good chance that Da Ponte knew both of the notable adaptations of the Don Juan tale by Molière and Goldoni, but no reason to believe that he made close reference to any other dramatization than the libretto of Giovanni Bertati. The low opinion of the Bertati libretto expressed in Da Ponte's *Extract* of 1819 is not unjustified. By any measure of skill in developing operatic characterizations and setting up emotional situations suitable for musical treatment, the Bertati libretto falls short. In comparison, Da Ponte's adaptation is dazzling for its style and imagery.

Bertati nonetheless did put forward some effective dramatic strategies that Da Ponte had the good sense to copy. It would be pleasing to report that Bertati's best innovations were the product of a superior inspiration, but they may have been mandated by nothing more than the necessity of concentrating all of the action into a single act by the management of the theater he was writing for. The unexpected result for posterity was a judicious condensation of incidents explored in earlier Don Juan dramatizations that became the basis for brilliant new techniques of expansion in Da Ponte's hands. In general terms, Da Ponte mainly preserved Bertati's scenarios for the first act up until the beginning of the "buffo finale" (described below) and the second act beginning with the graveyard scene. Da Ponte was responsible for what falls in between.

The ingenious crafting of the *buffo finale* may be contrasted with the confusing and implausible incidents portrayed at the beginning of Act II, which feature the device of disguise so beloved of eighteenth-century librettists (and indeed many eighteenth-century dramatists in general). Disguise was an almost indispensable element in Italian comic opera of Da Ponte's time, but opera audiences today have little patience for it. They find it impossible to believe that the disguises could not be seen through easily, with the result that the intrigues that result from them seem ridiculous. It can also be difficult to remember who is supposed to be disguised as whom when the faces of performers are clearly recognizable to the audiences from their original guises. If *Don Giovanni* can be faulted for anything as an operatic entertainment for the enjoyment of modern audiences, it would be Da Ponte's introduction of weak comic scenes at the beginning of Act II that feature Leporello and Don Giovanni in disguise, even though they can be interpreted as an attempt to depict Don Giovanni's personality in a more comprehensive way. The quality of Mozart's music, of course, cannot be faulted at any point.

The most important feature of the Bertati libretto that was picked up on by Da Ponte was the strategy of opening the drama with the incident that leads to the murder of the Commendatore. The librettos of Bertati and Da Ponte both open with a special section designated the "introduction" that depicts Don Giovanni's servant complaining about his master's behavior while he waits in the street for Don Giovanni to finish his attempt to seduce Donna Anna. The failed attempt soon leads to murder. In earlier plays and librettos, this murder is always found somewhere in the interior after extensive explorations of dramatic episodes that are comparatively uninteresting. The Don Juan ballet composed by Gluck for a performance in Vienna in 1761 also begins with the depiction of Donna Anna's attempted seduction and the Commendatore's murder, but whether Bertati knew of this work or drew inspiration from it cannot be established. It is certainly possible, since the Gluck ballet was widely performed throughout Europe in the late eighteenth century (in fact, more frequently than any operatic adaptation). Naturally a balletic presentation would also require a scenario that is more concise than what would be encountered in a multi-act play or opera.

It is exceptional in an eighteenth-century Italian opera to encounter violence portrayed on stage (unlike operas from later centuries). Violence could frequently be threatened, alluded to, or taking place off-stage, but an actual depiction of brutality in front of the eyes of the audience was not common at all. For spectators in Venice and Prague in 1787, an overt act of violence in the very first scene of an opera would have been a stunning novelty. Throughout the remainder of the Bertati and Da Ponte dramas, during all of the comic banter and sexual tomfoolery, the shock of the murder is something that cannot be completely forgotten, no matter how hard Don Giovanni tries to get everyone's mind off of it, nor can the certainty that he must somehow be held accountable for it. The way that the opening murder casts a pall over the entire drama sets the Bertati and Da Ponte librettos very much apart from earlier literary treatments of the Don Juan tale.

But stark violence is hardly the only exceptional feature of Mozart's *Don Giovanni*. Indeed, the plot laid out in Da Ponte's libretto defies some of the most deeply-entrenched operatic customs of its day. One is the inevitability of marriage. To condense the stories of the vast majority of eighteenth-century operas to the simplest terms possible, they are love intrigues that resolve into happy marriages. The stories are about couples whose attractions for one another clearly identify them as individuals who should be joined in wedlock (with the implication of eternal happiness), but they cannot be (not until the end of the opera, anyway), due to obstacles (often ridiculous ones) devised by librettists. This is true of both comic and serious opera in any language. A closely-related variant on the conclusions with happy marriages is the reaffirmation of conjugal love, either after a long separation (as in Metastasio's *Semiramide riconosciuta*) or due to a temporary estrangement (as in *The Marriage of Figaro*).

For an opera with as many characters as *Don Giovanni* has, there would ordinarily have to be two happy marriages to conclude the opera satisfactorily. In Act I, two pairs of lovers are introduced who would ordinarily marry by the end, one aristocratic (Donna Anna and Don Ottavio) and one peasant (Zerlina and Masetto). But due to the pernicious influence of Don Giovanni, the relationships are disrupted. In the case of the peasant couple, Masetto learns that Zerlina would have willingly slept with Don Giovanni (and gladly abandon Masetto) if the process of seducing her had not been interrupted at the last moment by Donna Elvira (one of the ironies about *Don Giovanni* is that in a theater piece devoted to the portrayal of sexual "tricks," there are no successful seductions, just as there are no happy marriages). Zerlina and Masetto do make up at the end, but there is no more talk of an imminent marriage.

Like Masetto in the lower-class pairing, Don Ottavio of the upper-class pairing sees his marriage prospects dim. In love with Donna Anna, he desperately wants to marry her, but Donna Anna learns in the course of the drama that her idea of a "real man" is actually Don Giovanni. She can see that he is sexy, intrepid, and invincible as far as earthly powers are concerned. Her lover Don Ottavio suffers in comparison. He makes great noises about bringing Don Giovanni to justice, but drops his pursuit when it becomes clear that he is completely inadequate to the task.

Donna Anna loses interest in him in the face of endless protestations of love and devotion that become tiresome to her. By the end, she appears to postpone her engagement for the express purpose of finding somebody else who will conform better to her conception of virility.

The choice of the Don Juan legend in itself leaves little choice but to depart from the rationalist conventions of Italian opera in Mozart's day. One of the most significant anomalies is the intervention of supernatural forces in the lives of ordinary mortals. Most Italian operas, whether comic or serious, avoid depictions of supernatural elements, although they are certainly not unheard of. Generally the great exception is only serious Italian operas whose subject matter is derived from the Greek myths favored in French serious opera, such as Mozart's *Idomeneo* of 1780, which belongs to a special type of Franco-Italian fusion that was never dominant. But even here, supernatural interventions are experienced only by deities, mythological beings, or humans of exalted station.

The supernatural elements introduced in *Don Giovanni* unavoidably raise theological issues that are otherwise little dealt with in eighteenth-century Italian opera. It was customary simply to avoid them entirely and concentrate instead on amorous intrigues. Furthermore, most characters in Italian serious opera of the eighteenth century were pagan. Following traditions that extend back to the birth of opera itself, in Florence in the 1590s as a modern reinterpretation of ancient Greek drama, the plots of eighteenth-century Italian operas in serious style are typically set in the distant past, centuries - even millennia - before modern times, typically in pre-Christian eras or among non-Christian peoples who once resided in Europe, North Africa, or Asia. The pagan status of the characters would have been known to operatic audiences, but there was no reason to explore their religious beliefs in detail.

The explicit invocation of Christian teaching was something that Da Ponte did not introduce in his setting of the Don Juan tale, nor would this be expected; eighteenth-century librettists avoided mention of Christian teachings generally. Even though the tone of the Don Juan story immediately reminds spectators of the admonitions of Christian clergy, Da Ponte himself approached Christianity quite gingerly in his libretto for *Don Giovanni*. At best, it is only implied that a Christian God is overseeing events, even though the original operatic spectators surely believed that the story unfolds in a modern European era populated mainly by devout Christians.

Read literally, the Da Ponte libretto is almost exclusively a pagan document. There is no mention of Christ at any point, nor is there any mention of Christian clergy, feast days, liturgy, or places of worship. Contrary to the widespread mistranslation of one of Da Ponte's lines, Donna Elvira at the end never announces that she will withdraw for the rest of her life to a "convent"; rather, she refers only to a "retreat" (*ritiro*), following Bertati's precedent. Instead of the pleas for guidance from a Christian God that were a staple of the conversation of eighteenth-century Europeans, one finds instead the sort of polytheistic exclamations typical of distressed characters in serious opera, for example "Oh dei" ("Oh gods"), as if the cast members of *Don Giovanni* were members of one of the imperial families of ancient Rome. The monotheistic "Oh Dio" ("Oh God"), is never encountered literally, only in a dialectical form that divorces it from religious expression.

It is true that among a certain class of Europeans familiar with classical studies (a central component of formal education in Mozart's day), it would not be unusual to affect pagan expressions such as "By Jove," but pagan references in Da Ponte's libretto extend even to the lower-class characters, who in eighteenth-century Spanish society were typically illiterate or only minimally literate. For Don Giovanni's traditionally erudite servant, this might not be so surprising, but it is extraordinary indeed to witness Zerlina and Masetto joining him at the end to proclaim how Don Giovanni will now be residing in the domain of Pluto and Proserpina, the rulers of the underworld in ancient Roman mythology. It is just as arresting to hear the peasant girl Zerlina exclaim "Oh gods, I am betrayed," near the end of Act I when Don Giovanni is trying to assault her.

References to "heaven" (*cielo*) or the "heavens" (*cieli*) are also difficult to reconcile with Christianity in the way they are brought up in the Da Ponte libretto. As a rule, appeals to "heaven" serve as a substitute for what most Europeans of Da Ponte's time would direct towards "God." Examples are found in the finale to Act I, when Donna Anna, Donna Elvira, and Don Ottavio ask for the protection of "heaven" in their quest to bring Don Giovanni to justice, and in the ending of Act II, when Don Ottavio announces that "we are vindicated by heaven" ("vendicati siam dal cielo") after he learns of Don Giovanni's fate. At another point in Act II, Don Ottavio seems to try to excuse his failure in apprehending Don Giovanni by telling Donna Anna that, "We had better bow our eyes to heaven's will" ("Convien chinare il cigilio ai voleri del ciel"). Similar remarks are also a commonplace expression of serious Italian librettos set in pagan times, including *La clemenza di Tito*; they do not necessarily indicate a heaven ruled by the Christian God. A certain vagueness may have been deliberate.

The prominence of polytheistic utterances in the Da Ponte libretto (which were blasphemous by definition in eighteenth-century Christian Europe) strengthens a pagan interpretation of Don Giovanni's damnation. There is no precedent in the Bible or Christian legend for any type of agent acting independently from God who is invested with the authority to condemn a sinner to hell, as the Commendatore does, nor of a human resurrecting from the dead in an altered form. There is also no precedent for a personalized consignment to hell by demons, devils, furies, or "spirits" (as Don Giovanni refers to them). The impossibility of explaining the resurrected Commendatore's existence in terms of Christian teaching is confirmed in the graveyard scene of Act II, when the servant Leporello remarks to Don Giovanni that they have just heard speaking "what must be a spirit from another world" ("qualche anima sarà dell'altro mondo"). Considering Da Ponte's thorough instruction in Catholic theology as a seminary student in his youth, it is reasonable to conclude that he crafted his pagan libretto precisely because the Don Juan tale could not be reconciled with traditional Catholic teaching. The only way that it can be related to

Catholicism is through its inculcation of moral values common to all major world religions.

Whether or not the Da Ponte libretto is best interpreted as a studied pagan drama only approximately relevant to Christian teaching and European culture of its day, the result for posterity is the basis for a musical setting that can leave only a dispassionate spectator immune to a reevaluation of one's personal beliefs concerning the consequences of sin and sexual behavior, the imperative of repentance for immoral conduct, and the accountability of personal behavior before God, even if this reevaluation leads merely to an attitude of skepticism and defiance similar to Don Giovanni's own. This is far more than a typical audience member of the eighteenth century would have bargained for in attending an operatic production, which typically would offer no more challenges than experiencing vicariously the emotions of love as enhanced by an attractive musical setting. The Da Ponte libretto ably serves the function of a morality play, true to its ultimate origins in the original operatic version of the Don Juan tale performed in Prague in 1730, by conveying to the audience the certainty that there will be a reckoning one day for all reprehensible behavior. The punishment is made to fit the crime, of course; Don Giovanni's seductions are treated as deplorable, but not in themselves deserving of capital punishment. It is only a pitiless act of murder that merits a penalty so severe.

The Mixing of Comic and Serious Action

The sudden vogue in Italy of Mozart's day for operas in Italy based on the Don Juan tale was facilitated by a more flexible approach to the mixing of comic and serious action than was ordinarily permitted in operatic conventions that reigned in the early and mid-eighteenth century. This was something not at all unusual in the seventeenth century, but a "reform" movement among the leading Italian librettists around the turn of the eighteenth century insisted on the removal of comic scenes from serious operatic entertainments in order to "elevate" them. Intimidated as they were by classical culture, Italian literati felt that the introduction of comic action within an overall serious dramatic presentation was distracting and flew in the face of one of the "unities" of Greek drama: the "unity of action." In the early eighteenth century, comic scenes were generally banned from librettos for multi-act operas, a practice that created the genre of *opera seria* (serious opera). Comic vignettes were not necessarily banned from an evening's entertainment, however. It was possible to perform comic love intrigues with no relation to the main action of the opera between the acts, a genre referred to as *intermezzo*. Operatic works with purely comic action also existed, and they became more and more prominent and more and more sophisticated after the middle of the century.

The development in the second half of the eighteenth century of a new type of operatic genre that combined serious and comic action - the *dramma giocoso* - made it much easier for librettists to adapt the Don Juan tale to contemporary operatic customs. The libretto distributed to the original audience in Prague in 1787 explicitly designates the work a *dramma giocoso*. In the context of an eighteenth-century operatic libretto, the word *dramma* is meant to refer specifically to serious action. The word *giocoso* is cognate with the English "jocular," and the way that librettists such as Da Ponte used the designation for his version of the Don Juan tale, the qualification *giocoso* has the meaning of a serious drama enlivened with "jesting" or "witticisms." The *dramma giocoso* was set in contemporary times, just as a comic opera would be, whereas a serious opera in Italian would be set almost exclusively in the distant past.

But perhaps the libretto for *Don Giovanni* started out as a serious work and was made "mixed" only at some later point. This is what the reminiscences of Da Ponte's friend John Francis seem to indicate. If this account can be trusted, Da Ponte's evasiveness about the setting makes perfect sense. Contrary to assertions found in many modern opera guides, Da Ponte never specified Seville as the setting of the opera, rather only a "city in Spain," and there is no chronological designation either. For the portions that depict serious action, the city in question might just as easily be Hispalis in the Roman province of Hispania Baetica as Seville in modern Andalusia. In general, the most important references in the libretto that tie the serious portions of its text to the modern Christian era in Spain are simply the use of the noble titles "Don" and "Donna" and the traditional Christian saints' names used for the characters Don Giovanni and Donna Anna.

In contrast to the serious scenes, there are references in the comic scenes specific to eighteenth-century culture consistent with operatic customs of the day, which usually set comic operas in modern times. In the "Catalog Aria" of the servant Leporello, which includes the traditional "list" of Don Giovanni's sexual conquests, there are references to women using modern titles of nobility (countesses, baronesses, marchionesses, and princesses) and the modern names for the geographical regions of Spain, France, Germany, Italy, and Turkey in which Don Giovanni seduced hundreds of women (famously the most - 1003 - in his native Spain). Near the end, Leporello mentions that he chases anything in skirts (using the term *gonnella*, a rare specific reference to modern dress in the libretto). Following Bertati, the scene before the "Catalog Aria" mentions Donna Elvira's native city of Burgos, the only Spanish city ever referred to in the Da Ponte libretto by name. The ballroom scene at the end of Act I makes mention of coffee, chocolate, sorbet, and confetto - as well as Don Ottavio's drawing of a pistol. The scenes at the beginning of Act II, in which the servant Leporello tries to seduce Donna Elvira disguised as his master, also include references to a pistol, a shotgun (*schioppo*), and the modern currency of doubloons. Scenes with serious action contain no such references. Even in the Introduction, is it merely implied that Don Giovanni and the Commendatore duel with swords - there is no indication of any specific weapon that could be tied to a chronological framework. These distinctions simply cannot be coincidental.

Characterization and Dramatic Incidents

One of the most important customs respected in the preparation of *drammi giocosi* was the division of roles into categories of serious (the *parti serie*) and comic (the *parti buffe*), a distinction usually reinforced by gradations of social class. The serious characters in a typical *dramma giocoso* are aristocratic (certainly upper-class), just as members of royal, imperial, and aristocratic families from antiquity who populated Italian serious opera. Modern audiences often perceive them to be stiff and pompous, perfect embodiments of virtue within conventional sex roles. Isolated characters capable of evil or error were admitted in order to create dramatic conflicts, but any characters engaged in questionable or discreditable behavior were expected to experience a fundamental moral rehabilitation before the end of the drama. If they did not, they usually had to be killed off. By the end of an opera, it was customary for all the principal characters introduced to the audience either to be virtuous or dead. The comic characters in *drammi giocosi* were generally of low birth, just as they would be in operas of purely comic action (with some exceptions made to ridicule the pretenses of certain upper-class characters, especially upper-class men).

In *Don Giovanni*, there are eight characters whose personality traits are explored with some degree of sophistication: five nobles (Don Giovanni, Donna Anna, Donna Elvira, Don Ottavio, and the Commendatore) and three commoners (Leporello, Zerlina, and Masetto). An insistence on moral rehabilitation or death is one convention that the Da Ponte libretto respects faithfully. Four characters indulge in evil or questionable behavior: Don Giovanni, his servant Leporello (who is complicit in all of his master's misdeeds), Don Giovanni's abandoned lover Donna Elvira (who would be classified as an adulteress for engaging in premarital sex), and the peasant girl Zerlina (who wants to engage in premarital sex). Don Giovanni is irredeemably evil and killed off, whereas the others achieve moral redemption. The servant Leporello vows to seek a better master; Donna Elvira voluntarily decides to withdraw from society and live out her life in a "retreat"; Zerlina promises fidelity to her boyfriend Masetto.

Since social class and gender were by far the most important determinants of the life course of all eighteenth-century Europeans, it comes as no surprise that social status is key to understanding the way that the characters in *Don Giovanni* are depicted, and what style of music is given to them to sing. Still, the libretto does offer a refreshing flexibility related to the interaction of certain characters of unequal social station. Setting aside the unique character of Don Giovanni, the dialogue crafted for the various character types normally reflect rigid segregation by social class. When upper-class characters address social inferiors, there would ordinarily be almost no interaction that transcends the class barrier, but in Da Ponte's libretto, there are two important exceptions involving the servant Leporello and the noblewoman Donna Elvira, in addition to subtleties here and there. The first time they meet, they converse almost as equals in a scene in Act I that precedes the "Catalog Aria." This more flexible interaction would mark Donna Elvira's role as *mezzo carattere* ("middle character") capable of bridging the gap between serious and comic action. Leporello (in perfectly sympathetic terms) advises Donna Elvira to abandon her pursuit of Don Giovanni, who has discarded numberless lovers just like her. Later, in Act II, Leporello actually tries to seduce Donna Elvira himself dressed as his master Don Giovanni, and he tries to speak to her just as nobles would speak to each other.

As interesting as these interactions are, the title character Don Giovanni is accorded a special status even more fascinating to observe, a very special type of *mezzo carattere*. Don Giovanni mingles with everyone, regardless of social class, and although he is a nobleman, he participates in both comic and serious action. Fully capable of affecting the manners and speech prized by the aristocrats he encounters, he can also be quite vulgar (and quite brutal) when dealing with social inferiors. The richness of such a character, who seems so lifelike in comparison to most nobles portrayed in eighteenth-century opera, contributes greatly to the appeal of *Don Giovanni* for modern audiences. Much of the ingenuity of the Da Ponte libretto derives from the way that the title character's behavior appears to be patterned on day-to-day incidents observed with great perception by the poet, perhaps from witnessing the conduct of genuine personages of less exaggerated lasciviousness than Don Giovanni (maybe even his own or that of his friend Casanova).

The persona of the seducer Don Juan has fascinated audiences and literary critics for centuries, and his very name has become a byword. For scholars attracted to his portrayal in dramatic works, there is frequently a tendency to seek out an explanation for his sexual addiction - in other words, to psychoanalyze Don Juan. This is never attempted in the earlier dramas, however, and there is no basis from their texts to draw firm conclusions about the reasons for his behavior. Generally all that the eighteenth-century dramatists did was describe, condemn, and insist upon the remedy of moral reform with the implication that a fundamental transformation of basic character traits need only be demanded as imperative to be put into effect instantaneously.

The depiction of Don Juan in eighteenth-century dramas is actually little more than an extravagant and improbable male fantasy. It is not only the number of his sexual conquests that at once elicits fascination and envy (regardless of how unbelievable it is), but also the way that he evades certain disagreeable consequences of promiscuous sexual behavior (with equally unbelievable luck). His ability to elude discarded lovers is not the only example. Others are implied. It is extraorinary in particular that Don Juan dramatizations of the seventeenth and eighteenth centuries never portray the title character as impregnating any woman - in spite of hundreds of sexual encounters - or contracting venereal disease. For all of the clever dialogue concocted to illustrate his skills at seduction, Don Juan himself remains a simplistic caricature, but it is this very quality that contributes to the clarity of the overriding moral lesson of the Don Juan tale, which is that individuals who appear to escape earthly consequences for their misdeeds will one day be held accountable.

The upper-class characters of Donna Anna, Don Ottavio, and the Commendatore are based on conventional representations of European aristocrats that can be traced as far back as the original play of Tirso de Molina, although the precise form of the characters' names could vary from dramatization to dramatization. The name Donna Anna for the Commendatore's aggrieved daughter was transmitted with great stability from the Tirso play to Da Ponte's setting, whereas the name Ottavio for her betrothed generally stuck from the precedent of Cicognini. These two characters would find themselves quite comfortable in a conventional *opera seria* set in antiquity for their virtue and conventional behavior matched to sex roles. The same can be said of the Commendatore, the courageous defender of his daughter's honor who is later transformed into the ultimate avenger of moral failing. Because he is too old to be involved in love intrigue, his personality is rarely explored much in depth in operatic treatments.

The name for Da Ponte's Donna Elvira was copied from Bertati, who obviously picked it up from the play of Molière, which includes the portrayal of an abandoned wife named Done Elvire. Bertati also Italianized Molière's name Mathurine for the peasant girl who is the equivalent of Da Ponte's Zerlina (Bertati's form is Maturina). In the drama of Bertati, Donna Elvira is a noblewoman who pursues Don Giovanni in order to compel him to respect a promise of marriage used to seduce her. The technique of promising marriage as a means to seduce women was reserved for lower-class women in the dramas of Tirso and Cicognini. It was Goldoni who provided the important precedent of using the same technique for noblewomen. Probably basing his characterization on Molière, Bertati has Donna Elvira resigning herself to rejection, but imploring Don Giovanni to mend his ways before it is too late, a scene set to music in a very touching way by Mozart in the Da Ponte setting. The equivalent character in the Goldoni play (Donna Isabella) is unremittingly bitter.

Among the lower-class characters, the most memorable one is Don Giovanni's servant, designated Leporello by Da Ponte without authority from any earlier dramatization. This character originates in the Tirso drama, which set the basic portrayal as a servant who ostensibly resents his master and condemns his lifestyle, but actually envies him in many respects, in particular for his abilities as a seducer. Leporello is certainly well educated for a servant. Beginning with Molière, the character of Don Giovanni's servant is frequently depicted as being quite erudite (even beyond the level of the well-read Figaro of the Beaumarchais plays), conversant with classical mythology, classical philosophy, and other intellectual interests, depending on who treats him. But for all his accomplishments and perceptive insights, he fails miserably to live up to his model when Da Ponte gives him the chance to "trick" Donna Elvira by dressing up as his master.

The lower-class lovers Zerlina and Masetto conform to character types that can be traced to the earliest Don Juan dramatizations, but Da Ponte obviously based them directly on the characters Maturina and Biagio from the Bertati drama. Masetto's unwillingness to forgive Zerlina without qualification seems to be related to Da Ponte's unwillingness to conclude with happy marriages. Overall, Zerlina may be described as stereotypically naïve, while Masetto is jealous, suspicious, and resentful.

Da Ponte's treatment of his characters highlights his greatest gifts as an operatic dramatist. While respecting traditions that existed in his day for the depiction of character types, he still found room for innovation with a view towards making his dialogues more representative of ordinary life. One of the greatest tests of his skill was improving on the inferior Bertati libretto. To help prepare the libretto for *The Marriage of Figaro*, there could be no more perceptive observer of human behavior than Beaumarchais, author of the play on which it is based, which gave him an excellent head start. *Don Giovanni* provides the more reliable proof of Da Ponte's own talents as a dramatic poet.

The Musical Setting

It is probably accurate to assert that Mozart's opera *Don Giovanni* it is more difficult to perform with proper technical accuracy than any opera written before it. One wonders whether the composer indulged himself with complexities knowing full well that the work would be performed by a company of musicians eager to bring his vision to life for the benefit of an audience that was unusually sympathetic to his talents. But in spite of the intricacies that provide such wonderment for musicologists and professional musicians, one of the joys of Mozart's operatic music is its potential for appreciation by listeners with varied backgrounds in music. There are many gestures intended to be understood by listeners with little or no formal training in music at all, but also nuances that can be recognized only by listeners with advanced training in music theory, vocal production, text setting, and dramatic criticism, some only after careful study of the libretto (and if possible) the musical score. No level of musical understanding can offer a complete explanation, however, of what it was about Mozart's inspiration that led to the imagination of such distinctive musical ideas or their uncanny success in enhancing dramatic action. There are still vast areas of music criticism that must bow to the ineffable.

Some of the greatest contributions Mozart himself made to the process of bringing the Da Ponte libretto to life as a dramatic entertainment invite a continuation of the discussion of characterization - for example, Mozart's care to match character types to vocal ranges. In fact, Mozart was the earliest great composer of opera to intimate a system of casting by voice type that was standard during most of the nineteenth century. The presence of comic action in *Don Giovanni* goes far toward explaining Mozart's practice in that particular opera. By the 1780s, if an Italian opera contained any comic action at all, it would not include roles performed by castrated males who sang in soprano, mezzo-soprano, or alto range. Male singers of this type were used almost exclusively in Italian serious opera - not even in the serious opera of any other national tradition. With comic action included, *Don Giovanni* includes parts for natural male singers only, the ranges carefully coordinated with character types.

One of Mozart's greatest achievements as a composer of Italian opera was to create outstanding music for baritone roles. During the period of Mozart's training as a composer of Italian opera in the 1760s and 1770s, the division of natural voice types for males was generally not much more sophisticated than high voice (tenor) and low voice (bass). The idea of a strongly-defined middle range for men (baritone) was not an important part of operatic composition in Italian language. Mozart, however, used the baritone range skillfully to sharpen the portrayal of the Count of Almaviva in *The Marriage of Figaro* and the title character of *Don Giovanni*.

In the conception of the nineteenth century, a tenor role would ordinarily need to embody three important characteristics: youth, beauty, and virtue. This same rule is evident in *The Marriage of Figaro* and *Don Giovanni*. In the former, its application denies the status of tenor to Figaro and the Count of Almaviva. Almaviva is certainly intended to be physically attractive, but his moral character is dubious, and he is not young by operatic standards, which favor lovers in their teens or early twenties. In spite of the preferences of modern operatic directors, it is also clear from a close reading of the original *Marriage of Figaro* play of Beaumarchais (which Mozart certainly knew) that Figaro was not young (he would have to be at least as old as Almaviva). The play also contains subtle signals that he was not intended to be attractive either.

Like the Count of Almaviva, Don Giovanni is physically attractive, but neither young nor virtuous, thus Mozart did not conceive music for him in tenor range (similar to the denial of the status of soprano to his female counterpart in nineteenth-century opera, the mezzo-soprano Carmen in the opera of Bizet). Gazzaniga, in contrast, cast him as a tenor in the Venetian production on which the Da Ponte libretto is based. As far as modern audiences are concerned, the darker timbre of the baritone voice is much more effective in evoking the virile and sinister qualities of Don Giovanni's character, just as tenor range is more appropriate for the effete Don Ottavio. The spectacle of an Italian opera with a baritone as the title character would have been just as unusual for the original audience of *Don Giovanni* in 1787 as would an overt act of violence in the opening scene or the absence of happy marriages at the conclusion.

The soprano and bass roles in *Don Giovanni* are of more conventional types. Donna Anna, Donna Elvira, and Zerlina - all sopranos - clearly conform to the ideal of young, beautiful, and virtuous women. The quality of virtue as portrayed in eighteenth-century opera always includes indulgence for error (as opposed to malice), and Donna Elvira and Zerlina both err seriously by allowing themselves to be attracted to Don Giovanni. In both cases, they repent of their indiscretions and achieve moral rehabilitation.

The bass roles in *Don Giovanni* also conform to standard types familiar both from serious and comic opera of the eighteenth century. In serious operas, bass roles were generally assigned to the parts of venerable older men ineligible for amorous intrigue. If married, the implication is that the time for conjugal relations has passed. The Commendatore embodies this persona quite well, one that is also typical of serious bass roles in nineteenth-century operas. In general, sex is forbidden to basses, to the point where the spectacle of a married bass may be taken as a sign of a lack of intimacy between childless marriage partners (for example King Philip II in Verdi's

Don Carlo, Hunding in Wagner's *The Valkyrie*, and Gremin in Tchaikovsky's *Evgeny Onegin*).

Although the basic portrayal of the Commendatore is thoroughly conventional, there is an added dimension to his persona that derives from the god-like characteristics he acquires after he transfigures as a stone statue. For reasons explained earlier, the spectacle of the resurrected Commendatore is incompatible with Christian teaching, but Mozart definitely made use of gestures from traditional Christian sacred music (the only type of religious music he knew well) to evoke his status as a special type of clergyman. In the graveyard scene of Act II, his first appearance after being murdered at the beginning of Act I, his singing reminds one of priestly recitation.

To accompany this recitation, Mozart chose a scoring with a unique combination of instruments: two oboes, two clarinets, two bassoons, three trombones, and cello with string bass. The overall sonority was obviously intended to resemble the sound of a church organ accompanying liturgical singing. It is of great significance that this ensemble includes two trombones. Trombones were never widely used in the orchestras for eighteenth-century Italian operas in Mozart's day. They were a staple of central European Catholic church music of Mozart's time, however, especially in large-scale settings of texts from the mass. Of the other operas written by Mozart after his move to Vienna in 1781, *The Abduction from the Seraglio*, *The Marriage of Figaro*, and *Così fan tutte* each have no parts for trombones. *The Magic Flute* does, but it includes depictions of pagan clergy and pagan religious ceremonies. In *Don Giovanni*, trombones are used nowhere else except when the Commendatore is present on stage as a stone statue. The opera *Idomeneo*, first performed in Munich in 1781, uses trombones only to accompany the recitation of the Roman god Neptune in Act III (three of them, just as in *Don Giovanni*).

Leporello and Masetto are comic basses of a type for whom attempts at love-making are usually portrayed as ridiculous or foredoomed, the most humiliating demonstrations of their ineffectuality being Masetto's failure to maintain Zerlina's interest in him in the face of Don Giovanni's advances and Leporello's failure to seduce Donna Elvira in disguise, even after years of observing his master's techniques. These character also fail to conform to the qualifications of youth, beauty, and virtue that mark tenor roles, either due to age or lack of sex appeal. The music written for comic basses frequently features a quick lighthearted style referred to as "patter" (or *buffo patter*), which is marked by a rapid vocal declamation that can often be difficult to understand - in fact sometimes impossible when the tempo is quick - and frequent repetition of words, often to the point of silliness. Among the vocal pieces in comic style in *Don Giovanni*, the sound of patter is one of the most effective means of suggesting the facetious tone of Leporello's "Catalog Aria" in Act I.

Besides choices in voice types, the differentiation of characters by social class has important implications for the musical style used to portray their actions and emotions. Music written for lower class characters is typically much simpler to sing and much more direct than the music written for the upper-class characters, which imitates the florid, dignified style cultivated in Italian serious opera to match the high-flown rhetoric used to evoke the speech of the upper classes. In *Don Giovanni*, the most extravagant vocal virtuosity of all is heard in Donna Anna's aria in Act II, "Non mi dir, bell'idol mio." This can be compared to Zerlina's exquisitely uncomplicated "Batti, batti, o bel Masetto" from Act I (as horrifying as it is to modern sensibilities in requesting Masetto to beat her as punishment for her indiscretions with Don Giovanni).

Don Giovanni, as usual, is accorded special treatment. In Act I, he is given the brief aria "Fin ch'han dal vino" (known as the "Champagne Aria" even though it makes no mention of sparkling wine), a favorite of baritone recitalists. As a vocal piece, it is more typical of comic opera for its wordy text full of silly rhymes and its quick declamation. It is used merely to invite the revelers at a party to enjoy themselves with drinking and flirtation, If Don Giovanni does have one saving grace, it is his desire to make everyone have a good time and to be free of irksome moral restrictions. Even though Don Giovanni is a noble, there is no technical display in the vocal line of this aria at all, nor is there in the simple *canzonetta* (little song) "Deh, vieni alla finestra" in Act II, used to assist Don Giovanni's continued efforts to trick Donna Elvira, or the aria "Metà di voi qua vedano," sung in mock pursuit of his own servant Leporello in the same act. Don Giovanni is more characteristically heard weaving artfully in and out of conversations as a means to evoke the character's impulsiveness and dynamism. One of the best examples comes from Donna Elvira's aria "Ah, chi mi dice mai" in Act I. While complaining of her abandonment, yet still unidentified to Don Giovanni, he actually interrupts her singing (though not her attention) by explaining to Leporello that she must be somebody in need of his type of consolation. The effect is to broaden the dramatic capabilities of a conventional aria considerably by including action to which the main character singing the aria is not a party to. Generally, the character singing an aria in an opera of Mozart's time would have the full attention of the audience and the other characters, and his or her expression would never be interrupted. Arias are generally intended to convey a quality of emotional reflection, but Don Giovanni is a man of action - in Da Ponte's hands, he does not ponder, and he does not regret. Arias thus are not the most memorable vehicle for his character's sentiments.

It is well known that eighteenth-century composers frequently tailored vocal parts and character roles to the capabilities of the singers engaged for the first performances of their operas. There is good reason to believe that the role of Don Giovanni was carefully crafted to highlight the strengths and mitigate the weaknesses of Luigi Bassi, the first interpreter of the role. Bassi, a native of Pesaro, was a mainstay of operatic life in Prague from the time that he entered the Bondini company in 1782 (at the age of sixteen), until the death of Guardasoni in 1806 caused an interruption of Italian operatic production in Prague that led him to find fresh opportunities in Vienna and other cities (he died in Dresden in 1825). Mozart probably met him during his first trip to Prague in January 1787. That winter, Bassi had been performing the role of the Count of Almaviva in *The Marriage of Figaro*, the role in that opera that would approximate the persona of Don Giovanni the best (anotherthwarted seducer).

At any rate, the anonymous author of "Some Reports About the State of Theater in Prague" in December 1794 asserted that "Herr Bassi is quite a fine actor, but no singer, since he does not possess the most important prerequisite - a voice!" Nonetheless he said that nobody could have wished for a better Don Giovanni, Count of Almaviva, or Axur (in Salieri's *Axur*); he played these roles "incomparably" and was well-deserving of the affection of the Prague public. A little later in the same discussion, the author of the "Reports" back-tracked a bit about Bassi's poor singing abilities when he praised him again for his excellent portrayal of Axur ("the role that appears to have been made for him!"). He went on, "Among the numerous mob of Italian opera singers he is a rare phenomenon in that he is a good actor and knows not only how to sing his roles, but how to act them." This characterization of Bassi marks him as perfect for an effective portrayal of Don Giovanni, a role which does emplasize acting ability over vocal display, besides which his famous looks would have been an asset as well.

As far as the overall design of the dramatic presentation is concerned, some of the most basic expectations are mandated by what is commonly referred to as the "numbers" conception: the idea that an opera is made up of a series of self-contained musical "numbers" that have a clear beginning and ending that can be detached, if desired, from the opera for concert performance, and also deleted or substituted if doing so made sense to theater managers. The actual numerals for each of these musical "numbers" were frequently entered into musical scores and published by music editors. The customary numberings for the various sections of *Don Giovanni* are included in Appendix I.

In Mozart's day, the makeup of the musical "numbers" was still influenced by practices that extended back to the seventeenth century. There was a sense that operas should be made up of sections of music intended to relay a story line and that were followed by sections of music devoted to the expression of emotions suggested by the story line in vocal pieces referred to as "arias" (for solo singers) or "ensembles" (for groupings of singers). The musical style of the sections that function primarily to relay the story line was referred to in the late eighteenth century as "recitative." This style is intended to sound like an approximation of human speech in song. Although many opera-goers today imagine that operatic texts are in prose, the texts of recitatives were generally conceived in irregular lines of blank verse. The music for the recitatives is formulaic and not intended to be memorable; it does not feature "catchy" melodies. Also, there are few, if any, repetitions of words. Considering this style of presentation, it is no wonder that Lorenzo Da Ponte, in his *Extract* of 1819, did not even recognize the execution of recitative as "singing" (see below).

The most common type of recitiave is often referred to as *secco recitative* (dry recitative), but many music historians prefer to use the less pejorative (and more authentic) term *simple recitative*. All that composers notated for simple recitative was the vocal line plus a bass line. A keyboard instrument (harpsichord or piano) was expected to improvise a full accompaniment for both hands just from seeing the bass line, and a bass instrument (typically a cello in modern practice) would play the bass line along with the keyboard player as written. Simple recitative was rarely crafted with great attention to the dramatic effect of whatever action it conveyed; it was simply intended to put forth the plot quickly and directly. A more sophisticated type of recitative that does approximate the feeling of a fluid unfolding of dramatic action with orchestral accompaniment is referred to as "accompanied recitative." Recitative accompanied by the full orchestra was intended to enhance the presentation of emotionally intense portions of the drama, and it could be quite sophisticated. There could be orchestral introductions to the vocal portions, extended interludes, and imaginative orchestral effects intended to evoke emotional states and natural and supernatural atmospheric phenomena. Mozart's skill at composing accompanied recitative is one of the areas that marks him as the great operatic genius of his age.

The vocal pieces referred to as arias were used to explore emotional states set up by the sections in recitative. In contrast to recitatitve, the poetry for arias is cast in rhymed verse. Usually there were only two stanzas of poetry. The arias are the component of early eighteenth-century operas that were supposed to present distinctive melodies and memorable virtuosity (or distinctive amusement in comic style) - what Da Ponte considered the "real" singing. Most spectators of his day expected the most poignant expression of emotion to be found in the arias, and they were considered the backbone of a typical operatic entertainment. In order to drive home the impact of the emotions experienced by the characters, the arias would include frequent repetition of words, a very helpful aid in an age without titles over the stage.

The music for the arias relies on standard techniques pioneered in the seventeenth century that mandate the selection of evocative words or phrases to spin out an entire musical setting based on an emotional state of mind. This study will adopt the modern phrase "keyword" to denote a word of text that composers use as the basis of their inspiration for large-scale vocal structures. The keywords that the author believes were at work in the settings of the vocal pieces from *Don Giovanni* and *La clemenza di Tito* are listed in Appendices I and II.

In the early eighteenth century, the two stanzas of aria text were rigidly segregated in the musical setting. A first musical section was devoted entirely to setting the first stanza of text with its own keyword to inspire the musical setting. After the first section was heard, a second section devoted entirely to the second stanza of text would be heard. Often it would feature a completely different keyword and contrast highly in musical setting. Once that section was finished, there would be a direction for the singer and instrumentalists to start from the beginning of the first section and end the aria at the entire composition at the end of the first section, in other words, to progress *da capo al fine* (from the beginning to the end). The term *da capo aria* is derived from this short phrase often added to the end of the second section of the arias as a direction (sometimes abbreviated further just to *da capo*).

In Mozart's time, strict *da capo* arias made few appearances in operatic works, but the practice of using contrasting keywords drawn from both stanzas of the customary two-part poems endured. One of the best examples in *Don Giovanni* is Donna

Anna's aria "Or sai chi l'onore" from Act I. In this vocal piece, the keyword *vendetta* ("vengeance") is drawn from the first stanza of text to generate parts of the musical setting and the keywords *rammenta la piaga* ("remember the wound") are drawn from the second stanza for the same purpose. The choice of a keyword affects all musical elements: tempo, vocal style, the choice of instruments in the accompaniment, the amount of emotional excitement in the melodic lines and accompaniment, etc.

Another way to evoke the poetic texts is the device of "text painting," a means of introducing extra-musical depictions into a musical setting. This device was a famous technique of early eighteenth-century composers of operatic music that many critics feel degenerated into silly gimmickry (even in the hands of Handel), but it endured well into Mozart's time. One of the most imaginative effects is found in Donna Elvira's aria "Ah, chi mi dice mai." In this vocal piece there is an interesting musical enhancement of the character's anger at Don Giovanni, when Donna Elvira says that she wants to "carve out his heart" *(vo' cavare il cor)*. These words prompt a sweeping motive in the strings that is supposed to sound like a knife thrusting into Don Giovanni's body.

It is also common to switch from major to minor key when a sad thought is introduced into a text of overall optimistic or heroic nature. An excellent example of this effect is heard in Donna Anna's "Or sai chi l'onore" in Act I. The overall mood suggests resolve to punish Don Giovanni, a sentiment perfect for major key, but when she remembers the image of her wounded father surrounded with blood, the music swtiches to minor key.

Italian serious operas of the early eighteenth century consisted almost entirely of solo singing with rigid alternations of sections in recitative style followed by arias, an alternation that many listeners in modern times find monotonous. One or two love duets were frequently incorporated, but usually no other ensembles, except for a final chorus sung by the principal characters that explained the moral lesson that had been learned or expressed the general joy signaled by the joining of couples in marriage. After the middle of the century, there was a trend to add more ensembles and choruses in serious opera in order to vary the presentation.

In duets and ensembles, it is instructive to observe how the musical motives of the characters can be related to their emotional agreement or emotional conflict. When characters are in emotional synchronization, they typically sing together in parallel motion. When they are in conflict, they tend not to sing together at all, or else sing in counterpoint when they are heard together. This is a technique shared by all major operatic composers of Mozart's time. One of the most effective treatments of this technique is found in the duet "Là ci darem la mano," for many the best loved number of the entire work. The duet is intended as an intensified depiction of Don Giovanni's attempt to seduce the peasant girl Zerlina with a promise of marriage. In the opening line, he invites her to let him join hands with her and carry her off. At the start of the duet, she wavers. Her indecision is depicted in the musical setting by having her sing first in dialogue with Don Giovanni, then in counterpoint. She has many reasons to spurn Don Giovanni's advances, but in the end she relinquishes her will to his. This surrender of will is depicted musically, when on the line "Let's go, my beloved" *Andiam, mio bene)*, they begin to sing in parallel motion after Zerlina's last, half-hearted efforts to resist him are abandoned. The keywords "innocent love" *(innocente amor)* that they use to evoke their motivations form the basis of the musical setting of a second section, a signal that Don Giovanni now completely controls the mood and has completely fooled his victim Zerlina. Later, the joining of hands as a technique of seduction is seemingly mocked when the Commendatore joins hands with Don Giovanni just before he is condemned to eternal damnation, also a signal of one character ceding control to another.

In larger ensembles, there can be opposing camps of characters who sing in parallel motion with each other. The most exciting example of this technique is seen in the *buffo finale* (a type of musical structure described below), in which Don Ottavio, Donna Anna, Donna Elvira, Masetto, and Zerlina are all arrayed against Don Giovanni in their pursuit to bring him to justice. Don Giovanni has no one on his side except his servant Leporello, whose loyalty is paid for, but he does sing in parallel motion with Don Giovanni against the others.

One of the most welcome special styles that can be sampled in Mozart's operas is sections that can be referred to as "scenes" in which dramatic action is depicted in a fluid manner without abrupt starts or stops. In these sections, the musical materials are much more varied and interesting than what is heard in sections of recitative with their spare accompaniment, and the dramatic stagnation that usually accompanies arias is also avoided. Perhaps the best examples in *Don Giovanni* would be the Introduction, the buffo finale at the end of Act I, and the scene that precedes Don Giovanni's damnation. In each, musical styles unfold spontaneously as the dramatic action suggests various moods that are brought to life in the orchestral accompaniment. Characters enter and exit conversations at will. Such a treatment intimates the approach to operatic dialogue later favored by Wagner and Puccini, among others, in the nineteenth century, and modern audiences are instinctively appreciative. A type of presentation that approximates a play with music of strikingly distinctive character is what they consider normal - yet in the eighteenth century, this approach is generally exceptional.

Even in an abbreviated presentation such as this, it should be mentioned that one of the most important qualities of Mozart's operatic writing that can be appreciated without professional musical training is his tendency to reserve the most interesting musical materials in many of the vocal pieces not to the singer, but rather to the orchestra. In some of the vocal pieces, such as Don Ottavio's "Il mio tesoro intanto" from Act II, a typical tender aria for tenor lovers, the singer's vocal line clearly does include the most interesting musical ideas. Elsewhere, however, such as in the aria *"Ah, che dice mai"* of Donna Elvira from Act I, the orchestra is given the most distinctive music, and the vocal part for the most part resembles a recitation that would not be very interesting at all if it were heard separately. It can be a perpetual source of fascination to observe how Mozart hands off the musical interest from the vocalists to the orchestra and back again throughout the opera *Don Giovanni*. This habit of Mozart is another trait that distinguishes him from most of his contemporaries, who generally favored textures in which the vocal line was much more consistently the center of musical attention, and the orchestra was mainly present first to introduce an emotional state, and then to provide an unobtrusive support for the vocal expression. The music for Martín's *Una cosa rara*, for example, performed in Prague during the same operatic season, offers a much more simplistic relationship between vocalist and orchestra than Mozart does in *Don Giovanni*.

Probably the best known vocal pieces from *Don Giovanni* have been drawn attention to in the text above: Leporello's "Catalog Aria," Don Giovanni's "Champagne Aria," Donna Anna's "Or sai chi l'onore," and Don Ottavio's "Il mio tesoro intanto." All of these are staples for vocal concerts that feature the four voice types they represent (bass, baritone, soprano, and tenor, respectively), but none is as famous as the instrumental minuet from the *buffo finale*, which is frequently given to beginning music students to play in the form of arrangements (beginning pianists in particular). It will be convenient here to provide special descriptions of some of the other notable musical numbers from the work, specifically the overture and a few of the particularly memorable vocal sections that are not usually performed except during actual productions of the opera.

The Overture

The uniqueness of Mozart's musical setting of *Don Giovanni* is signaled from the very beginning by its overture, one of the three opera overtures by Mozart that have been staples of orchestral repertory since the nineteenth century (the others, of course, are the overtures to *The Marriage of Figaro* and *The Magic Flute*). In format, it is quite conventional for its time, a single movement that incorporates a slow introduction, yet it is boldly innovative for something that listeners accustomed to opera overtures from the nineteenth century today take for granted: the quotation of musical passages that will be heard later in the opera as a portent of the dramatic action. Opera-goers who are mainly acquainted with nineteenth-century operatic repertory are often surprised at how alien this concept was to most eighteenth-century composers. In Mozart's time, overtures for Italian operas were essentially interchangeable as long as they were matched either to comic or serious action, a basic principle that held true as late as the era of Rossini; opera audiences of Mozart's time could easily have accepted the overture to *The Marriage of Figaro* as the overture to *Così fan tutte* (or vice-versa), and he could easily have reused the overture to *Idomeneo* for *La clemenza di Tito*.

The overture to *Don Giovanni*, on the other hand, is much more specifically matched to the individual dramatic action of the opera that follows it. In this case, the eerie opening in minor key foreshadows the fate of Don Giovanni (as all audience members familiar with the Don Juan tale would have known), and it actually quotes the music from the Commendatore's appearance at Don Giovanni's supper directly. The much more lighthearted fast section in major key offers a taste of of the amusing *burlas* (sexual "tricks") that are to come. The quotation in an opera overture of musical material to be heard later in the opera was something completely normal in the nineteenth-century Italian opera, but not generally expected in the eighteenth century. Typically, an eighteenth-century Italian opera overture would not include any musical motives heard later in the opera (as can be seen, for example, in the overtures for *The Marriage of Figaro* and *Così fan tutte*). In German opera, this was not so unusual, and indeed the overtures to Mozart's *The Abduction from the Seraglio* and *The Magic Flute* each put forward some music that is heard later in these works.

One possible explanation for Mozart's departure from conventional practice is simply the pressure of time. As detailed in Chapter 6, there can be little doubt that the overture had to be prepared much more quickly than was usual even for Mozart. One means of making things easier was to reuse some of the music that was already written, in this case with superb results for dramatic integration. Essentially no new music had to be written for the slow section at all. Motives heard just after the arrival of the Commendatore at Don Giovanni's supper served perfectly to fill out the space. It is quite possible that Mozart used this music strictly as an expedient, and that he had no intention of using the fast section to suggest anything to the audience about dramatic action; a fast section of similar light character would be expected as a matter of course in any overture or symphonic movement that began with a slow introduction. An overture in slow-fast format with a serious fast section in minor key would have been something almost unimaginable for Mozart to attempt.

Mozart's slow introduction for the overture to *Don Giovanni* closely resembles the slow introductions of symphonies of his day in presenting an array of moods and musical ideas that are intended to be unpredictable, including sudden and surprising shifts of direction in both melody and harmony. The beginning of the fast section brings the unsettled character of the slow introduction to an immediate stop. To the experienced listener, this offers a welcome relief from melodic and harmonic instability.

Mozart's fast section is quite conventional in structure, but extraordinary for its musical materials. Just as in first movements of late eighteenth-century symphonies that begin with slow introductions, the opening theme of the fast section is soft instead of loud. The remainder is cast in a standard version of what is known as "sonata form" to music theorists, musicologists, and professional musicians. The concept is not easy to grasp for ordinary music lovers, but the three main sections ("exposition," "development," and "recapitulation"), along with certain internal musical events to be expected in each, can be heard reliably with some guidance and experience. This type of formal organization is shared with the opening fast movements of symphonies in Mozart's time, the only important alteration when adapted for overtures being the avoidance of the repeats of the exposition and the development and recapitulation together that were customarily indicated in symphonic scores (modern conductors often regard these repeats as optional).

In opera overtures, brevity was always an important consideration in the eighteenth century. If too long, the overture could threaten to detract attention from the main drama. In Mozart's hands, the brevity of the overture satisfies both opera-goers and symphony audiences with a work of unusual emotional power and variety of musical materials that takes less than six minutes to play. Even with the expedient of using preexisting material from the main drama, the achievement of creating such a masterpiece within the time frame of hours stands as one of the greatest *tours de force* in the history of European music.

The Buffo Finale

In the 1780s, a so-called *buffo finale* would be expected as a matter of course to appear at the end of an interior act of an opera with comic action to highlight the dramatic conflicts among the principal characters. To most modern listeners, the *buffo finale* is generally more exciting than the actual ending of the opera, and the reason lies in the emotional tensions that are brought into such sharp relief. The concluding scenes of eighteenth-century operas are usually supposed to celebrate the joyous resolution of all dramatic conflicts and the announcement of happy marriages, thus they exude a sense of repose and emotional relaxation. In operas such as *The Marriage of Figaro* and *The Magic Flute*, many audience members perceive the ending to be somewhat anticlimactic as a result. Once again, *Don Giovanni* is exceptional. The consignment of Don Giovanni to hell creates the perfect type of exhilarating close that modern audiences favor, especially when the final scene of the original score (which has Don Giovanni's victims congregate to express their reaction to his death) is omitted, as was customary until recent decades.

The *buffo finales* of *The Marriage of Figaro* and *Don Giovanni* represent a culmination of the late eighteenth-century version of this operatic event, whereas Rossini in the early nineteenth century was able to achieve effects of similar dramatic impact in comic operas such as *The Italian Girl in Algiers*, *The Barber of Seville*, and *Cinderella*. The basic strategy for all of these finales is to divide the characters into two opposing camps whose interests and goals are seemingly irreconcilable. Tensions only escalate as the finale unfolds, and by the end, a state of excitement is achieved in which the characters are capable of doing little else except to scream invectives at each other. In *The Marriage of Figaro*, the numbers in the opposing camps are nearly evenly matched (the "good" side consisting of Susanna, Figaro, and the Countess of Almaviva against the "bad" side of the Count, Marcellina, Don Basilio, and Dr. Bartolo). In *Don Giovanni*, the title character and his servant Leporello are the "bad" side pitted against everyone else (Donna Anna, Donna Elvira, Don Ottavio, Zerlina, and Masetto). Leporello is at Don Giovanni's side, of course, only because he is a paid retainer.

The proper makeup of an eighteenth-century *buffo finale* is nowhere better explained than by Lorenzo Da Ponte in his *Extract* of 1819. It is easy to see how he crafted the finale of the second act of *The Marriage of Figaro* and the first act of *Don Giovanni* along the same lines he used to describe the design for the *buffo finale* he prepared for Antonio Salieri's opera *Il ricco d'un giorno* of 1784:

>...This Finale in Italian comic operas, though strictly connected with the other parts of the drama, is a kind of little comedy by itself; it requires a distinct plot, and should be particularly interesting: in this part are chiefly displayed the genius of a musical composer, and the power of the singers, and for this is reserved the most striking effect of the drama.
>
>Recitativo is entirely excluded from this division of the piece. The whole of it is sung, and it must contain every species of melody[:] The *adagio*, the *andante*, the *cantabile*, the *armonioso*, the *strepitoso*, the *arcistrepitoso*, the *strepitosissimo*, with which last every act commonly ends. It is a theatrical rule, that in the course of the Finale, all the singers, however numerous they may be, must make their appearance in solos, duets, trios, quartetos &c. &c. And this rule the poet is under the absolute necessity of observing, whatever difficulties and absurdities it may occasion...

One would love to learn what other theatrical rules had to be observed by librettists and composers of Da Ponte's day. Unfortunately, very few are recorded in such an explicit manner - most have to be divined from intensive study of scores and librettos. An extraordinary distinction made here between passages of an opera in *recitativo* and passages that are "sung" highlights the stark differentiation in the vocal style between recitative and that which is heard in arias, choruses, and ensembles. For Da Ponte, recitative was clearly understood to be nothing more than a special form of human speech.

Since late eighteenth-century operas were constructed as successions of self-contained musical "numbers" with easily-recognizable starts and stops, it is not difficult to identify where Mozart's *buffo finale* begins. It is usually labeled "No. 13" in scores with Mozart's own designation *Finale,* and the same spot was identified exactly the same way in the libretto distributed for the first performance (the first words heard are Masetto's line "Presto, presto, pria ch'ei venga"). Nothing similar is found in the Bertati libretto, which only had one act, thus no spot for a *buffo finale*.

As Da Ponte prescribed, the *buffo finale* of *Don Giovanni* does have its own plot, and it even accommodates a scene change from a garden to the illuminated hall where a ball is to be held. Overall, the story can be interpreted as an extension of the failed attempt at seducing the peasant girl Zerlina that is depicted earlier in the act around the famous duet "Là ci darem la mano." In the *buffo finale*, Don Giovanni hosts a ball for the residents of the city at which he is staying and uses it as an opportunity to seduce Zerlina once again. Her fiancé Masetto is present, just as jealous as he was before. The merry-making during the ball comes to a sudden halt when Zerlina screams for help after being assaulted by Don Giovanni, at which point the mood transforms instantly into chaos. Three masked guests who had arrived at Don Giovanni's ball reveal themselves as Don Ottavio, Donna Anna, and Donna Elvira. Along with Masetto, they attempt to protect Zerlina from Don Giovanni in the same way that Donna Elvira had earlier done alone, this time in a very threatening way now that Don Giovanni has been exposed to them not only as a seducer, but as a murderer. Their intent is to have him arrested and executed. As Da Ponte specified, all the characters assemble for this *buffo finale* (all the living ones, that is, since the

Commendatore has died). After a harrowing confrontation, Don Giovanni succeeds in eluding capture along with his servant Leporello.

It is possible to identify with remarkable precision the various "species of melody" that Da Ponte said must appear in a *buffo finale*. It starts with a quick *allegro* (actually, *allegro assai*) that changes into the slow *andante* that Da Ponte indicated must be present (beginning with the words "Tra quest'arbori celata," as sung by Zerlina). The "harmonious" (*armonioso*) portions are built around the famous minuet from *Don Giovanni* (the most familiar musical excerpt from the entire opera), which is supposed to be the basis of ballroom dancing among the assembled guests. Leporello's announcement to Don Giovanni of the arrival of masked guests ("Signor, guardate un poco, che maschere galanti") marks the start of the vocal portion of this section. When these three guests (Donna Anna, Donna Elvira, and Don Ottavio) speak among themselves and request the "protection of heaven" in their quest to bring Don Giovanni to justice, the music switches to the slow *adagio* tempo that Da Ponte claimed had to be a component of all proper *buffo* finales. The vague requirement of *cantabile* style (which simply denotes an expressive singing style in slow or moderate tempo) is easily satisfied in this slow section and the *andante* that came earlier. The "adagio" section for the three nobles is followed by another fast section, which includes Don Giovanni's famous toast to "liberty" ("Viva la libertà"), after which the *armonioso* mood returns with the music of the minuet heard once already.

The section that is clearly intended to conform to Da Ponte's indication *strepitoso* (uproarious) is preceded by one of the most clever musical enhancements of dramatic action ever devised by Mozart. For some time after the music of the minuet returns, the *armonioso* mood reigns. However, remarkable transformations of the prevailing mood were written into the parts that were supposed to be played by musicians on stage to accompany the actual dancing of the guests at Don Giovanni's party (in modern productions, the music for this section almost always come from the orchestra pit; at best only mock musicians appear on stage at this point anymore). When the minuet starts up again at the conclusion of Don Giovanni's command to Leporello "Tu accopia i ballerina" ("You, have the dancers pair off"), the orchestral musicians on stage play in complete synchronization, with the down-beat falling in the same place in all parts. A second orchestra starts to play on stage when Don Giovanni pressures Zerlina to dance with him. What they are supposed to be dancing to has a completely differently melody and meter from the minuet still playing simultaneously for the other guests, with the result that there is an audible feeling of uneasiness that heightens the sense of danger into which Zerlina has been plunged. This feeling is intensified when a third dance is introduced on stage when Leporello engages Masetto in order to distract him from Don Giovanni's designs (he has just led Zerlina away to an exit). The chaotic sound of three dances heard in different meters consecutively and simultaneously suggests that the *armonioso* mood breaks down in stages as a portent of an imminent event of disturbing and shocking nature. There is a palpable feeling that the chaos built up by this means somehow has to be broken through.

The way it is done is to have everyone's attention instantly shifted to the plight of Zerlina when she cries for help with the words "Gente ajuto, ajuto gente!" ("Help, good people, help!"). The mood of *strepitoso* is confirmed by the stage direction "Di dentro ad alta voce; strepito di pedi a destra" (which indicates that her cry is to be heard "from behind the stage in a high-pitched voice" while the "clatter of steps is heard from the right"). Zerlina's attempt to free herself from Don Giovanni's clutches silences the dance orchestra on the stage immediately. The pit orchestra takes over completely with a new musical section in quicker tempo to match the excitement on stage.

The masked characters then reveal themselves as avengers. After temporarily slowing down the tempo to allow the party of nobles and Don Giovanni to express their hostility to one another (which leads Don Giovanni to draw out a sword - and Don Ottavio a pistol), a new, even more exciting section (the *arcistrepitoso*) is introduced. Dramatically, it consists of little more than the three aggrieved nobles tossing out threats and insults at Don Giovanni, who can only wonder with his servant how best to extricate himself from the situation. The first line of text heard in this section is "Trema, o scellerato" ("You had better tremble, you scoundrel") as sung by the five characters in pursuit of Don Giovanni. Wide quick leaps in the vocal lines literally force the characters to screech their denunciations.

The audience may think at this point that the tempo could never get faster, but Da Ponte insisted that there must be one more quickening of tempo (the *strepitosissimo* or "most uproarious"), and so it does appear with the indication "faster" (*più stretto*) on the line "Odi il tuon della vendetta" ("Listen to the sound of vengeance") from the singers arrayed against Don Giovanni, who escapes their trap quite handily. By the end, one would think that "the most striking event of the drama" had just been witnessed, but those who have never seen the opera before learn that something even more remarkable awaits them at the end of the second act.

Mozart's Joke

Mozart's genius as a musical dramatist and proven interest in spoken theater has always made it tempting to imagine him writing dialogue for an opera of his own. Nonetheless, no evidence of any significant activity as a librettist as has ever emerged. But in the opera *Don Giovanni*, it can be established that he did contribute a small bit of dialogue himself in the service of a clever musical pun.

The passage in question is found in Act II, scene 13, near the beginning of the section labeled by Mozart as the Finale of Act II (no. 24 in most scores). Don Giovanni has ordered a banquet to be prepared and the dining is to be accompanied with music in the background (on stage, just as in the ballroom scene of Act I). The way Mozart chose to depict the music-making for this banquet was to evoke the style of wind ensemble music scored for pairs of oboes, clarinets, bassoons, and horns, a combination that was then very common at the time in Vienna. Considering the reputation of Bohemian wind players, Mozart probably imagined this option to be particularly suitable for local resources. Operatic excerpts arranged for wind ensemble were one of the most popular offerings of this type of ensemble in Vienna, and Mozart came up with the idea of having his ensemble first perform two operatic excerpts by other composers, and then one of his own.

There are three sources of text for the opera *Don Giovanni* associated with its first performance in October 1787: a libretto printed in Vienna (perhaps in the summer of 1787) that records the use of the production to help celebrate the wedding of Prince Anton of Saxony and the archduchess Maria Theresa of Austria; a libretto printed in Prague that retracts the dedication (since the National Theater in Prague failed to produce the work in time for their visit of 13-15 October 1787); and the autograph score of the opera preserved in the music collection of the National Library in Paris. Certain lines in the score at the spot where the wind ensemble plays do not appear in either libretto; they appear only in Mozart's score. Since they are not part of larger poetic structures and specifically have to do with musical references, there can be no reasonable doubt that Mozart concocted the lines himself.

In the libretto printed for the original Prague performance, the finale for the second act begins with five lines of Don Giovanni sung at the banquet table: "The meal is ready./Make music, dear friends!/Since I spend my money so freely,/I want to be amused./Leporello, come to the table right away [to serve me]." ("Già la mensa è preparata./Voi suonate, amici cari!/Giacchè spendo i miei danari,/Io mo voglio divertir./Leporello presto in tavola.") Leporello responds, "I am quite ready to obey" ("Son prontissimo a ubbidir"), and the wind ensemble starts to play an arrangement of the aria "O quanto un sì bel giubilo" from the opera *Una cosa rara* by Vicente Martín y Soler (the title refers to that "rare thing," a woman who is both beautiful and virtuous).

The Spanish composer Martín was one of the popular operatic composers in Europe, and his *Cosa rara* of 1786 was one of the most frequently performed comic operas of the second half of the eighteenth century, far more successful internationally than any of Mozart's Italian operas ever were until the nineteenth century. Mozart certainly would have known that it was being performed during the same autumn season at the National Theater as his own *Don Giovanni*. It is also set in Spain and has a character named Don Giovanni, a virtuous tenor who does not resemble the wicked baritone of Mozart's opera. When Mozart's Don Giovanni recognizes the melody of Martín, he exclaims to the musicians in Mozart's own words, "Bravi! *Cosa rara*!" after which Da Ponte's words resume with Don Giovanni asking Leporello if he is enjoying the music: "What do you make of this lovely concert?" ("Che ti par del bel concerto?"), to which Leporello answers, "It is worthy of you" ("È conforme al vostro merto").

As Don Giovanni is enjoying his meal, he requests more food to be served: "Another plate" ("Piatto"), to which Leporello responds, "At your service" ("Servo"). At that point, the music changes to an arrangement of the aria "Come un agnello" from Giuseppe Sarti's opera *Fra i due litiganti il terzo gode* (When two people quarrel, a third one enjoys it). Sarti's opera was first performed in Milan in 1782 and was last heard in Prague in the spring of 1783 in the theater of Count Thun in Malá Strana. It is doubtful that Mozart knew of that performance, but he could rely on the fame of the opera for Don Giovanni's exclamation "Long live *I litiganti*" ("Evvivano i litiganti") to make sense to opera-goers in many parts of Europe. The inclusion of the arrangement of the aria "Come un agnello" may derive simply from Mozart's familiarity with it rather than its familiarity to the music public in Prague (he composed a variation set for piano based on the melody a few years earlier, K. 460/454a of 1784).

Da Ponte's dialogue is interrupted for a third time when Don Giovanni remarks to himself that Leporello is eating some of the food that is supposed to be reserved for him: "That rogue is eating [my food]; I'll pretend not to notice"("Sta mangiando quel marrano; fingerò di non capir"). Then the music played by the wind ensemble changes for a second time to an arrangement of "Non più andrai" from *The Marriage of Figaro*, the very music that Němeček reported as being so popular in Prague during the winter of 1786-87 that "even the harpist on the tavern bench" had to play it if he were to be noticed (see Chapter 4). Upon hearing it, Don Giovanni could have been echoing the entire assembled audience at the first performance by exclaiming in Mozart's words, "This one I know all too well" ("Questa poi la conosco pur troppo").

Most critics view this pun as rather benign, but for the author, its importance was articulated best by a friend of the author, the singer Remigijus Klyvis. The series of excerpts was clearly intended as nothing less than an assertion of superiority, a demonstration of the excellence of Mozart's music in comparison to his rivals. The point is made very well indeed. For the modern listener, the impact left of the excerpts by Martín and Sarti pales in comparison to the richness of Mozart's inspiration. One almost regrets having the Mozart excerpt come to a close, so lovely it is to hear it played by the wind ensemble. In comparison, the Sarti selection is so bland that it almost goes by unnoticed. The Martín selection may actually have been chosen deliberately for the way that its insipid melody is drummed into the audience's head in the original opera. In sum, there could be no better confimation of Mozart's supremacy as a composer of opera than this comparative selection of musical themes, and no better illustration of his love of witticisms, both ribald and clean.

The "Final Scene"

For most of the performance history of the opera *Don Giovanni*, the original ending conceived by Mozart and Da Ponte was not used. The finale of the second act encompasses Don Giovanni's last meal, the entrance of the statue of the Commendatore to the dining hall, Don Giovanni's condemnation, and commentary from Don Giovanni's victims after his death (as set forth by Bertati). According to the nineteenth-century memoirist Wilhlem Kuhe, the last of these events, labeled the "final scene" *(scena ultima)* in the score and libretto, was only presented at the very first performance in Prague, then never heard again during the original run. The libretto printed for the first Vienna performance of 1788 does not include this scene at all, and it was customary to omit it from productions until the late 20th century. The spectacular scene in which Don Giovanni is dragged to hell was considered a perfectly satisfying way to end the opera, and the preference is still understandable.

Mozart must have approved of the omission, since he was intimately involved with both of the first two productions of the opera and in Prague especially should have been able to exercise considerable artistic control. Audiences in recent time certainly find the original finale satisfying, and the present author prefers its inclusion for the way that it rounds out the characterizations and provides emotional recovery from the shock of the damnation of Don Giovanni. The music for the final scene of course is ravishingly beautiful and worth hearing simply for its own sake.

The original final scene exemplifies a few elements from Da Ponte's description of a *buffo finale* - for example, the requirement to hear from all singers left on stage and the inclusion of several types of singing, a series of duets and ensembles, and changes in tempo. The overall structure consists of three musical sections. In the first, set to fast tempo, Don Giovanni's victims ask the servant Leporello what has happened to his master. Musically, the victims form a unified bloc just as they did in the finale to the first act, but now Leporello must sing against them alone, since his one ally (his master) is now dead. Once the victims are satisfied that Don Giovanni is no more, there is a slow section in which the remaining characters explain how they intend to carry on with their lives. This section is dominated musically and dramatically by the pairing of lovers. Donna Anna and Don Ottavio mainly sing in contrary motion or in alternation, a portent of a break-up. Zerlina and Masetto sing in parallel motion, a sign that they will reconcile permanently, although there is no confirmation of this in the text. The importance of social class and right of precedence is clearly reflected in the expressions of love presented in this section. It is Donna Anna and Don Ottavio who express their feelings first and far more exhaustively; in comparison, Zerlina and Masetto's sentiments are brushed over almost as an afterthought, and even at that are heard only after the noblewoman Donna Elvira explains that she will enter a "retreat" for the rest of her life.

The last section, once again in fast tempo, fulfills a function common in eighteenth-century opera in any language to conclude with some type of choral singing that is supposed to explain the overriding moral lesson learned by the audience or else to proclaim general rejoicing after couples have overcome seemingly insurmountable obstacles in their quest to join in marriage. *Don Giovanni* concludes with no marriages, and so the moral lesson derived from its basic function as a morality play must dominate: "This is the end that awaits evildoers; and for the wicked, the means of death is always matched to the way that they lived their lives" ("Questo è il fin di chi fa mal; e de' perfidi la morte alla vita è sempre ugual").

Since all characters are in emotional synchronization, they mainly sing together with the same rhythms, but class distinctions still exert themselves. This is seen most clearly at the start, which is a *fugato*, i.e. a musical passage that intimates the beginning of a fugue, but is not actually followed by a fully-developed contrapuntal fugue. In a proper fugue by composers such as J. S. Bach, one would expect a melodic idea referred to as the fugue "subject" to be introduced at the beginning without accompaniment of any type. Mozart chose to begin with his "subject" with the sparse accompaniment of violins. Of more significance is his decision to start the *fugato* with the two noblewomen Donna Anna and Donna Elvira pronouncing the judgment "This is the end that awaits evildoers." The peasant Zerlina is excluded. As a lower-class character, she is expected to follow the lead of the noblewomen, and so she does by repeating their line in the customary "answer" to the fugue "subject," which is supposed to be in a different key. In this case, her subservience is symbolized not only by her echo of the noblewomen's line, but also by its repetition at a lower pitch level. Thereafter, class distinctions are blurred, except in the downward drop described below. The use of the *fugato* at this spot becomes an agreeable device that signals emotional agreement not only by having all singers declaim an idea at the same time with identical rhythms, but also to sing the same motive in alternation.

The original finale to the second act serves an important dramatic function in tying loose ends concerning the remaining characters on stage and in easing the emotional tension experienced by the audience (besides permitting the audience to listen to an extra dose of exquisite music by Mozart). The consignment of Don Giovanni to hell does provide an acceptable ending to the work, but it is very abrupt and shocking. In musical terms, the original finale includes three passages in particular that assist in creating a feeling of reflection, repose, and resolution. The slow middle section is the first one. It is preceded by a pause that is approached by a long falling melodic line in Donna Anna's part on the words "Ah, certo è l'ombra che l'incontrò" ("Ah, it must have been the ghost that she [Donna Elvira] encountered"). In general, downward motion in music contributes to a relaxation in mood, the perfect preparation for the contemplative nature of the slow section (in contast, upward motion tends to create emotional excitement). Later, on the last line of the opera, "For the wicked, the means of death is always matched to the way they lived their lives," there is a section in which all the voices of the noble characters fall precipitously in tandem. Singing in unison, Donna Anna and Donna Elvira gradually drop a full octave and a half before the final condemnation of evildoers is set forth. This passage is one of the most striking examples of "text painting" in Mozart's operas in the way it symbolizes Don Giovanni's descent into hell as a warning to all. At the very end, when all the remaining characters have said their peace, there is a whimsical flourish for instruments alone that includes a miniature version of the same downward-moving gesture, but this time it is far less stinging, and its admonition sounds almost halfhearted or facetious. Mozart seems to tell everyone not to take too seriously the very weighty theater piece just seen, but rather to go home and get on with the business of enjoying everyday life.

11

Music for a Dirty Deal: Mozart's Opera *La clemenza di Tito*

La clemenza di Tito retains its reputation as a lesser masterpiece of Mozart, even though the number of performances worldwide has grown considerably in the last few decades. In particular, what held back a wider appreciation of this work for so many years is its adherence to the rarefied conventions of eighteenth-century Italian serious opera and the diminished inspiration of its music in comparison to other operatic masterpieces by Mozart. The haste in which Mozart was forced to compose the music for *La clemenza di Tito* goes far toward explaining his impaired creative efforts. As explained in Chapter 8, he undertook the task at short notice from the Estates of Bohemia sometime during the summer of 1791 in order to help them ratify a reactionary political settlement: submission to the authority of the emperor in return for a reduction in taxation and greater control over the peasant population.

In comparison to *Don Giovanni*, the opera *La clemenza di Tito* conforms to a much purer operatic tradition: the eighteenth-century Italian *dramma per musica*, also referred to as *opera seria*. For many modern listeners the dramatic presentation offered by *opera seria* is serious to the point of tedium - and sometimes quite capable of eliciting unintentional laughter - even though it was widely regarded as a thrilling spectacle in its day. Gluck's *Orfeo ed Euridice* and Mozart's *Idomeneo* and *La clemenza di Tito* would be the serious operas in Italian from the eighteenth century that find most favor today, but there is no likelihood that any of them will ever supplant the popularity of works such as *The Marriage of Figaro*, *Don Giovanni,* or *The Magic Flute*, much less the beloved operas of the nineteenth century that exhibit more nuanced stories and character types. The plot of *La clemenza di Tito*, similar to many serious operas in Italian from the eighteenth century, strikes many opera lovers today as artificial, unmoving, and unbelievable.

Many outdated customs conspire to make successful revivals of eighteenth-century serious opera elusive in modern times. For example, it was normal in Mozart's time for singers to perform their arias standing in place with almost no motion on stage. Modern audiences accustomed to the continuously unfolding dramatic action of movies, plays, and television programs frequently find immobility of this type tiresome. The gimmickry concocted by many modern opera directors to mitigate this failing, however, often seems forced and ridiculous. The spectacle of male lovers singing in soprano range is another convention that modern audiences find very difficult to come to terms with. The instinctive distaste felt by many spectators is compounded by the unavoidable necessity in modern times of casting women dressed as men to perform such roles. In general, serious operas from the eighteenth century find complete acceptance only from audience members who have taken the trouble to acquire a special appreciation of their modes of expression. For these individuals, the aesthetic rewards can be enormous. For the rest, it is usually only the presence of music of surpassingly fine quality that can sustain any interest at all.

Conventions of Metastasio's Serious Dramas

The text of *La clemenza di Tito* originates from a unique period of opera history in which the librettos of a single poet were set by dozens of composers time and time again throughout Europe. The dominance in the mid-eighteenth century of Pietro Trapassi, known as Metastasio (1698-1782), a brilliant Italian literatus who served at the Hapsburg court in Vienna from 1729 until his death, has never been equaled. His verse is still remembered in Italy today (and even taught to schoolchildren), but it is difficult for non-Italians to understand the exalted reputation he enjoyed during his lifetime. His most popular operatic texts were written between the 1720s and 1740s in Rome and Vienna. *La clemenza di Tito* - not one of the most favored Metastasian librettos - was first set to music in 1734 by the imperial court composer Antonio Caldara. A fresh setting of one of his librettos in 1791 for a coronation ceremony would have helped lend an aura of verability to the occasion for which it was matched, since his texts by that time had lost much of their attraction as the basis for new operatic works.

Metastasio's text for *La clemenza di Tito* perfectly exemplifies an array of conventions that constitute something of a defining standard for his work as a librettist. On a broad level, his stories can be described as formulaic contrivances that are used to set up emotional situations conducive to the musical setting of love poetry. They have little attraction as pure literature, in spite of the beauty of many of the verses.

The stories usually involve two sets of lovers who deserve to be joined together in wedded bliss, but face seemingly insurmountable obstacles to marriage that are miraculously resolved just before the end. Their tribulations invite the depiction of emotions suitable for a wide variety of musical styles. The characters are typically based on incidents from the lives of genuine personages who once lived in the ancient Mediterranean world, a trait that reflects broad operatic trends in Italy after the appearance of the first operas there in the late sixteenth and early seventeenth centuries.

Conceived in the simplest terms as an attempt to recapture the emotional power of ancient Greek drama using contemporary modes of musical and poetic expression, the earliest operas were usually based on stories derived from Greek mythology. As leadership in operatic style shifted away from Florence and Rome to Venice in the mid-seventeenth century, the typical subject matter for operatic work expanded to include historical figures, even though the chronological settings were usually still confined to the distant past. In the later seventeenth century, the settings were often more recent than what is now recognized as ancient times, but generally not later than the Dark Ages.

In the eighteenth century, serious opera in Italian was ordinarily set no later than the era of the Crusades of the late Middle Ages. However, settings in Asia could be more recent without violating a sense that it was the opera of "long ago and far away" (as opposed to the "here and now" of comic opera). The farther away from Europe the setting was, the more recent the chronological setting could be. Thus it was possible to build up a certain tradition for librettos based on the life of Timur (Tamerlane), the Turkic ruler of vast arias of Central and Western Asia who died in 1405, and the early sixteenth-century Aztec ruler Montezuma, who died very far from Europe indeed.

Metastasio's choices for principal characters were usually quite conventional, including the Roman statesman Cato the Younger (d. 46 BC) for *Catone in Utica* (1728); the Roman general Flavius Aetius (d. 454 AD) for *Ezio* (1728); Alexander the Great for *Alessandro nell'Indie* (1729); Semiramis, a queen of Assyria in the ninth century BC, for *Semiramide riconosciuta* (1729); Artaxerxes I of Persia (d. 424 BC) for *Artaserse* (1730); Demetrius II Nicator (d. 125 BC), a ruler of the Seleucid Empire, for *Demetrio* (1731); the Roman Emperor Hadrian (d. 138 AD) for *Adriano in Siria* (1732); and the Roman general Marcus Atilius Regulus (d. ca. 250 BC) for *Attilio Regolo* (1750). In contrast, the mythological settings favored by the earliest librettists in Italy continued to be favored in France after operatic traditions started in that country during the second half of the seventeenth century. Thus the choice of the mythological settings of Gluck's *Orfeo ed Euridice* and Mozart's *Idomeneo* can be attributed to a deliberate incorporation of French traits into the conception of the dramatic spectacle.

Eighteenth-century librettists used specific historical incidents only as kernels to help spin out their improbable tales of love intrigue. There was never any attempt to recreate the culture of the various historical periods and locations authentically, merely a feeling that the dramas unfolded in a mystic, hallowed past in which the fate of peoples and nations hung on the outcome of love affairs. In the case of *La clemenza di Tito*, it was the reputation of the emperor Titus for leniency during his short reign of two years (79-81 AD, almost exactly the same length as the reign of Leopold II) that provided the necessary grist for Metastasio's treatment.

Although Titus was involved in a brutal subjugation of the Roman province of Judea during the First Jewish-Roman War of 66-73 AD, in addition to other ruthless behavior, he immediately established himself as a just and virtuous ruler when he acceded to the imperial throne in the year 79 upon the death of his father Vespasian. According to the Roman historian Suetonius, he was renowned for his extravagant generosity and his suspension of the arbitrary trials for treason that marred the reigns of his predecessors. A specific act of "clemency" that may have provided Metastasio with the idea for the title of his libretto is recorded by the Roman historian Cassius

Dio: his forbearance on learning that his own brother Domitian was plotting against him. References in Metastasio's libretto to the burning of the Roman capitol and a search for those responsible are based on incidents related to a real fire that swept Rome in the year 80 (one not nearly as destructive as the famous Great Fire of the year 64).

The six principal characters found in Mozart's *La clemenza di Tito* would be a typical number for a Metastasian drama, including two sets of lovers who marry at the end; one character whose principal function is to serve as a confidant for one or more of the others; and another character who is not shown to find a marriage partner by the end, even if he or she is involved in love intrigues during the course of the drama. This is about all the characters that an opera of Metastasio's era could accommodate if each singer were to be given a sufficient number of arias to delineate characterization properly. The operatic poet of the eighteenth century always found his or her work constrained by customs governing the placement and number of arias. Scenes were supposed to end with a character expressing his or her feelings in the musical setting of an aria and then leave the stage. No character was supposed to be given two arias in a row. The more important the character, the larger number of arias he or she was given to sing - often in a hierarchy predetermined by contractual obligations negotiated by the singers.

With their historical subject matter, the Metastasian librettos are typically rationalist; in other words, they do not emphasize the depiction of supernatural effects, nor are the characters possessed of supernatural powers, eternal life, or eternal youth. In general, Metastasio's characters embody exemplary virtue within conventional sex roles. This trait was a legacy of a major "reform" of operatic librettos that took place in Italy under Venetian leadership at the turn of the eighteenth century. There was a feeling that the operas produced for the public theaters of Venice had become morally degenerate in the service of attracting audiences for public theaters that operated on a profit-making basis. The only opera somewhat familiar to modern audiences that exemplifies this trend is Claudio Monteverdi's *Coronation of Poppea* (first performed in 1642). There was a feeling in the late seventeenth century that too much sexual prurience had been introduced in operatic entertainments and that evil characters too frequently received no punishment for their misdeeds. The trend in the early eighteenth century to make operatic characters morally pure and ensure that immoral behavior be rectified is one of the reasons that Italian serious opera of the era has fallen into disfavor in modern times. Today the characterizations seem uninteresting and the outcomes too predictable.

In Metastasio's librettos, there is usually only one character who is allowed to pursue fundamentally evil personal goals, and this character typically experiences a spectacular moral rehabilitation to ensure that all characters remaining on stage at the end of the opera are virtuous. Except for the machinations surrounding this one evil character, it was Metastasio's habit to depict his casts as living in sanitized worlds free of moral corruption. Though violence is often referred to, Metastasio's dramas avoid distasteful depictions of violence on stage. Usually his characters are merely threatened with death and physical violence, but not actually subjected to it.

It seems clear that Metastasio recognized the necessity of introducing at least one evil character in order to lend more dramatic interest to his stories and to create a means to propagate moral lessons effectively, but his texts also introduce dramatic conflict by presenting virtuous characters with the dilemma of having to choose between competing virtues. In Metastasio's *Artaserse*, for example, a character is torn between friendship and filial devotion. In *L'olimpiade*, a character faces a similar dilemma about whether to favor platonic friendship over carnal love. The most striking moral dilemma in *La clemenza di Tito* is faced by Sesto, a close friend of the Roman emperor, who is forced to decide whether to remain loyal to him or to follow the wishes of his beloved. However, by the end of most of Metastasio's dramas, whatever dilemmas that had been vexing the characters for so long turn out not to be dilemmas at all - by whatever means, they are miraculously resolved. The emotional needs of all parties are satisfied along with the conclusion of happy marriages.

It took a surprisingly long time before there was a significant reaction to the basic conception of love intrigues ending in happy marriages. Even before Metastasio's death in 1782, there was a trend among some librettists to increase the content of violence and relax the strictures of conventional sex roles (for example, by introducing warrior females as principal characters), but happy endings were still the norm. Then, in the era of the French Revolution, there was a sudden shift in taste in Italy that paralleled the political and ideological turmoil felt throughout Europe. The lead female singer in *La clemenza di Tito*, Maria Marchetti Fantozzi, appeared in three operas in Italy whose titles drew attention to the death of the main character just before she was engaged to sing in *La clemenza di Tito*.

A temporary vogue for tragic endings endured for years, although the only opera representative of this trend that is at all well known today is Cherubini's *Medea* of 1797. By the end of the Napoleonic era, opera librettos had experienced a period of reaction against tragic endings that ran parallel to reactionary political developments in Europe. In the 1810s, when Rossini first rose to fame, this was so pronounced that the composer actually found it necessary to acquiesce to a happy ending for an adaptation of Shakespeare's *Othello*. In the late 1820s, tragic endings came back into vogue for serious operas, and they continued to be normal for the remainder of the nineteenth century.

Notes on Plot and Characterizations

Metastasio's *La clemenza di Tito* is completely conventional in being conceived for six characters, four of whom are involved in successful attempts to secure ideal marriage partners after seemingly insoluble difficulties have been put in their way. The title character is involved in love intrigue, but as part of the selflessness drawn attention to in the title of the opera, he finds himself graciously renouncing all thoughts of marrying a woman who is not in love with him. The sixth character, who is portrayed as a commander of the Praetorian Guards, is a standard elderly confidant too old to be eligible for love affairs and too unobtrusive to be given very much music to sing. The one character in Metastasio's *La clemenza di Tito* who is allowed to harbor evil intentions for a time is Vitellia, a pseudo-historical figure concocted by Metastasio. Without historical foundation, she is introduced into the drama as the daughter of the dethroned and murdered Emperor Vitellius (r. 69 AD), who fell from power in the aftermath of a *coup d'état* headed by Titus' father Vespasian. Vitellia contrives to murder Metastasio's Tito out of spite, not only in revenge for the murder of her father, but also for being passed over as a marriage partner in favor of Berenice, the daughter of the king of Judea, thereby depriving her of the potential for considerable political influence. Vitellia tries to manipulate her lover Sesto into carrying out the murder of Tito as a test of love. Sesto does participate in a plot to assassinate Tito, but the plot fails. Sesto is caught, yet he refuses to reveal Vitellia's complicity; instead, he confesses sole responsibility and awaits execution.

At this point, with Sesto destined to be executed for treason, there seems little hope of a marriage with Vitellia. However, in an extraordinary gesture of magnanimity, Tito pardons Sesto in consideration of their long-standing friendship. As a result, Vitellia becomes so overcome with guilt that she confesses her role in the plot to assassinate the emperor. The emperor is so impressed by her forthrightness that he decides to pardon her as well, and thus she is free to marry her beloved Sesto. Earlier, it is understood that Vitellia's distress derives from the anger and hatred she feels for Tito, whereas Sesto's anguish derives from the moral dilemma he faces in being expected to betray his friend Tito in order to placate Vitellia.

The two other characters in Metastasio's *La clemenza di Tito* who find themselves in love are Annio and Servilia, a close friend and sister, respectively, of Sesto. Annio would like Sesto to use his influence with the emperor to obtain his consent to his marriage to Servilia. It is soon learned, however, that Tito has decided to give up all plans to marry Berenice. Instead, he wants to marry Servilia himself. The marriage prospects of Servilia and Annio appear to be as hopeless as those of Vitellia and Sesto, but Tito is so touched by a declaration of love for Annio that he permits Servilia to marry him anyway.

The participation of Caterino Mazzolà in the preparation of the final libretto for Mozart's *La clemenza di Tito* is best described as an attempt to condense Metastasio's text and enhance its value as an allegory of the virtues of Leopold II. Mazzolà added no new scenes except for the formal "finale" of Act I. It would be inaccurate to claim him as the "author" of the libretto, as is sometimes done, since there is very little of the text that actually originated with him - essentially none of the recitative, which takes up the vast majority of the text of any opera of his period, and less than a dozen sets of verses that were used as the basis for arias and other types of vocal numbers. The coronation opera of 1791 was still Metastasio's drama in almost every important respect.

Regarding the portion of the text that would be set musically as recitative, Mazzolà saw fit to delete vast amounts of it. The spectacle of Italian serious opera became ever more daunting as the eighteenth-century wore on, and long before the time that Mozart's setting of *La clemenza di Tito* was written, it was customary to cut out large portions of any of the principal Metastasian librettos whenever they were set anew. It was particularly common to abbreviate the third act, which in Metastasio's day was about the same length as the first two, but later only about half as long as either of the first two acts. Mazzolà cut material out of all three of the original acts, but his most extensive cuts were from the text of Metastasio's second act, which was eliminated almost entirely. The result was a streamlined presentation that defined the dramatic conflicts more sharply and barely told the distracting subsidiary love story of Annio and Servilia.

The final result provides an excellent demonstration of the way that eighteenth-century opera could be pressed into the service of a political agenda if desired. It has been little noticed that one of the most important alterations made by Mazzolà was the deletion of the portion of the text near the end of the original drama by Metastasio in which Titus declares that he will have no wife except Rome and invites Vitellia and Sesto to marry along with Annio and Servilia. Mazzolà rejected these sentiments entirely. Rather, in his hands, all of Rome rejoices in wonder at Tito's sense of generosity and forgiveness. Thus the marriages usually proclaimed at the end of a Metastasian opera are suppressed, lest they would distract attention from the flattery of Leopold II. As strong as the convention was to end eighteenth-century Italian operas with happy marriages, none are portrayed in either of the two operas that Mozart composed for Prague.

Notes on the Musical Setting

It was not only the libretto of *La clemenza di Tito* that would have had to be altered significantly to suit audiences of 1791 as compared to audiences of 1734, but also the manner in which the music was presented. Appendix II lists all of the musical numbers of the opera with indications of how they were incorporated into the drama. At the time that Antonio Caldara was writing, audiences could expect a regular succession of sections in recitative style alternating with arias. The first stanza of the customary two-stanza arias would be the basis of the first section of a so-called *da capo* aria, and the text of the second stanza would be reserved for the second section. In Caldara's day, the length of these arias was restricted, and their instrumentation was simple in comparison to later eighteenth-century operas: usually just strings alone without any wind or brass instruments. Because the arias were limited in length, many of them were presented during the course of an opera. In the case of the original *La clemenza di Tito*, there were 25 of them in all.

As the eighteenth-century wore on, the number of arias heard in a typical *opera seria* was reduced significantly. In Mozart's setting, for example, there are only eleven. The length of the arias that were included continued to increase until they reached a practical limit by the 1770s (sometimes around ten minutes). The increased length was one of the most important factors that mandated a lesser number of arias per opera.

In addition to their expanded length, it was also common to expand the size of the accompanying ensemble to include wind and brass instruments. During Mozart's youth, the standard accompaniment for a serious Italian aria was strings plus French horns and oboes, but parts for flutes, clarinets, bassoons, and trumpets were also added more and more. A specialty of the vocal pieces in *La clemenza di Tito* are settings that include solos for clarinet and basset horn originally performed by Mozart's friend Anton Stadler.

The monotonous presentation of arias cast in *da-capo* form was done away with gradually over time. Beginning in the 1760s, the *da-capo* format (and variants) began to disappear in favor of other formats that did not exhibit such a rigid sectional structure. In the 1770s, a new type of format that found great favor among audiences in Italy was the rondò, a vocal piece cast in two sections (slow-fast) that was usually composed to a text of three stanzas instead of the two stanzas that were standard in "arias." In a rondò, the most common way of distributing the text would be to reserve two stanzas for the slow section, and then use the third one as the basis for the musical setting of the fast section, allowing for the possibility that text from the slow section could be brought back in the fast section. Rondòs were never the most numerous of the vocal pieces to be found in serious operas, but they often made the most striking impression for their stirring fast sections, which tend to generate applause even today. The rondò for Vitellia in Act II of *La clemenza di Tito*, "Non più di fiori," is a fine example. The prestige of the rondò was so great that arias of two stanzas were frequently adapted to accommodate their slow-fast structure.

Almost all of the vocal pieces found in an opera from the 1730s would be for solo singers. By 1791, however, it had become more and more common to include duets, trios, and other ensembles. The large number of vocal pieces for more than one singer in *La clemenza di Tito* is unusual even for an Italian serious opera for Mozart's day, and they may reflect the experience he had just had of composing a rich array of cleverly-crafted vocal ensembles for the opera *Così fan tutte* of 1790. He even went so far as to re-cast Metastasio's text "Ah, perdona al primo affetto" for treatment as a duet, which appears in the original setting as an aria. The variety created by these ensembles is very pleasing to modern audiences, not only for the variation in the number of characters who sing at once, but also for the lighter and more direct vocal style used for their settings. The increased prestige of comic styles may also have been an impetus to incorporate a larger proportion of ensembles, and there is no question that the addition of formal "finales" at the end of both acts of *La clemenza di Tito* was a response to the popularity of the "buffo finales" pioneered in comic opera. The original setting of the opera by Caldara simply featured unremarkable arias at the end of the first two acts and the customary simple chorus at the end of the third act.

There can no denying that Mozart's music for the opera *La clemenza di Tito* shows many signs of hasty preparation. One of the best ways to get a sense of this is simply to compare the lean size of the published score with that of the much more substantial *Don Giovanni*. While listening to the music, it becomes all too clear that Mozart "repeats himself" in ways that can only be attributed to the press of time, not to dramatic effect. In the case of the chorus "Serbate, o Dei custodi" and the orchestral march of the first act, the music for each is repeated in its entirety at spots never indicated in the original libretto, a wonderful expedient to help flesh out the score. It had been almost obligatory to include marches in *opera serie* for decades before Mozart's setting was written, but verbatim repeats of the sort he used for *La clemenza di Tito* were not common. Additionally, the aria "Ah, se fosse in torno al trono" from Act I incorporates an instrumental flourish that is heard in the march before it. Sesto's aria "Parto, ma tu ben mio" in Act I borrows a musical idea from the overture to help spin out the setting, obviously without the intent of the audience recalling it directly or inferring any dramatic significance to its reuse.

On the subject of the overture, it must be pointed out regretfully that the status of *La clemenza di Tito* as a lesser masterpiece of Mozart is presaged already for audience members when it is heard. In recent decades it is probably accurate to describe it as the most frequently-performed overture from any eighteenth-century Italian opera in serious style, but its emotional power pales in comparison to the overtures to *The Marriage of Figaro*, *Don Giovanni*, and *The Magic Flute*. It is more on the level of the overtures to *The Abduction of the Seraglio* and *Così fan tutte*, if even that interesting. The melodies are attractive and well-crafted, but they are lacking in the distinctiveness to be sampled in the composer's greatest symphonies and ovetures. The pleasing mix of serious and comic style found in the overture to *Don Giovanni* is absent from the overture to *La clemenza di Tito*, which by necessity had to maintain a uniformly serious tone to match the action of the drama and the formality of the occasion for which it was written. Mozart's ingenuity at showcasing orchestral colors is hardly to be found at all.

The most striking musical feature in the overture for ordinary listeners is a technique heard in two spots in which a short musical motive introduced at a soft dynamic level is augmented in stages by piling on instrument upon instrument until a temporary climax is reached. It is this downward-moving motive (heard against a "sweeping" figure in the bass) that is used later in the opera as a resource for a passage in Sesto's aria "Parto, ma tu ben mio." At first hearing, one wonders how far Mozart will take the gesture. The sure demonstration of his skill is found in his decision to enhance the final statement of the motive with a passage in the violas and oboes in contrary motion that competes with the downward-moving motive on which the instrumental augmentation is based. A lesser composer would simply have continued to build up sound without including this surprising turn. The technique of piling up instruments onto short repeated motives was first popularized in Italian opera overtures in the 1770s, and a variation of it, referred to commonly as a "crescendo," was still deployed frequently by Rossini in his overtures from the early nineteenth century. A more tasteful and subtle adaptation is also found in the overture to *The Magic Flute*, the opera Mozart temporarily set aside in order to work on *La clemenza di Tito*.

The choice of vocal ranges for the characters reflects long-standing customs of at least a century's standing at the time that *La clemenza di Tito* was written. The over-all balance of the voices is unusually high in comparison to the nineteenth-century operas that most modern listeners prefer. All four of the characters who are supposed to be joined in marriage in the original drama of Metastasio (Vitellia, Sesto, Servilia, and Annio) sing in soprano range, regardless of sex. The virtuous Tito, in contrast, is perfectly cast as a tenor. It would have been highly unusual to cast the elderly confidant Publio, ineligible for love intrigue, as anything but a bass, and Mozart in this case saw no reason for innovation.

The vocal numbers of *La clemenza di Tito* are interspersed with far more "simple recitative" than is heard in *Don Giovanni*. When all that needs to be composed for these passages is a voice line with simple formulaic melodic content and a spare bass line, far less time and skill is needed than for recitative accompanied by a full orchestra. Legend asserts that Mozart left the task of writing it to his student Süssmayer, certainly a plausible expedient, but one that is still lacking in reliable documentation. *La clemenza di Tito* is much like the old-fashioned serious operas written before the 1770s in which there are only a few formal sections of accompanied recitative at points in the drama of intense emotional outpouring. This would have been more in line with the aura of venerability presented by the occasion for which it was written.

The arias and ensembles of *La clemenza di Tito* are of varying musical quality, some of them among the finest vocal compositions in serious style ever composed in the eighteenth century, but most of less fine quality. Certain ones are as bland as anyone would imagine a mature vocal piece of Mozart could be, for example, "Del più sublime soglio" and "Ah, se fosse in torno al trono," both written for the title character. Regardless of their intrinsic quality, none of the vocal pieces composed for *La clemenza di Tito* has achieved the immediate recognition among opera lovers that greet the most popular arias from *Don Giovanni*. Perhaps the finest of all is Sesto's aria "Parto, ma tu ben mio" from Act I, one of the two numbers which feature a florid solo part written for the clarinettist Anton Stadler. The other is Vitellia's rondò "Non più di fiori" (in this case with basset horn, i.e., a tenor clarinet). Both vocal pieces include effects that are strikingly reminiscent of passages from Mozart's famous Clarinet Concerto, K. 622, also written for Stadler. Vitellia's rondò, however, is not nearly as fine as the earlier aria.

Each of the vocal pieces written to showcase the talents of Anton Stadler are cast in slow-fast format. Audiences then and now find much favor in the strategy of beginning in a contemplative manner, watching the character whip himself or herself into a state of excitement that calls for a spectacular close. Many audience members feel no choice but to applaud at the end as vigorously as the bustling orchestral accompaniment that is customarily matched to the emotional excitement of the fast sections. Sesto's aria actually contains two changes of tempo in order to progress gradually to this frenzied state. Two other arias that the employ the slow-fast format are Vitellia's "Deh, se piacer mi vuoi" from Act I and Sesto's "Deh, per questo istante solo" from Act II.

It would be gratifying to report that the ensembles of *La clemenza di Tito* were capable of eliciting the same emotional response that listeners derive from those of *The Marriage of Figaro* or *Don Giovanni*. They consistently fall short, however, partly because the emotions of all the characters are not as intensely expressed. At the end of Act I, with concealed sentiments at work in the case of the characters Vitellia and Sesto, it was simply not possible to portray opposing camps of characters hurling insults at each other in the way depicted in the two earlier operas. Rather, all the characters share their horrified reactions to the political revolt they see unfolding and the danger caused by a fire that has started in Rome. The practice of segregating characters by emotional agreement is nonetheless very much in evidence in the trio "Vengo, aspettate" in Act I, in which Vitellia is notably isolated both musically and emotionally against Annio and Publio. The simple emotional agreement between Sesto and Vitellia is suitably evoked in the duet "Come, ti piace, imponi" in Act I, as well as in the simple parallel motion expressed between Annio and Servilia in the beautiful duet "Ah perdono al primo affetto" from the same act. For ensemble singing, it is the choruses that are the most impressive musical numbers in *La clemenza di Tito*. They do approach the emotional power of the best choral writing found in the two great masterpieces that Mozart was preparing at this time, *The Magic Flute* and the Requiem, although they never equal it, much less exceed it.

For a study of this scope, nothing more needs to be said about *La clemenza di Tito* except to emphasize that the adaptation of Metastasio's libretto by Caterino Mazzolà did result in a version of the story that is more attractive to modern audiences than any version that preceded it. But even with the enhanced qualities of a condensed presentation that makes the opera less daunting to sit through and much easier to follow as a lesson in morality, it is still only the genius of Mozart's music, albeit diminished, that has enabled it to achieve the exposure it enjoys today.

12

Musical Miscellany:
The "Prague" Symphony and Lesser Works Written for Prague

Mozart's impromptu encounters with the residents of the city of Prague undoubtedly would have led to constant demonstrations of his skills as a musician and stimulating conversations about music. Probably many more examples of Mozart's inspiration were produced than those that were actually written down and preserved for prosperity, but those few pieces definitely known to have been composed for Prague - in addition to his two operas - unquestionably form an impressive musical legacy. To be described here is a collection of non-operatic works of undisputed authenticity that can be confirmed to have an association with the city: the "Prague" Symphony, a series of ballroom dances for orchestra; the concert aria "Bella fiamma, addio"; and two short *Lieder* (i.e., songs in German for voice and piano). The goal is to offer the reader some idea of what to expect from these works as a listening experience, as well as set forth what information is available concerning the circumstances of their composition.

The "Prague" Symphony, K. 504

There is no dispute that the musical public of Prague was privileged to hear the first performance of one of the greatest symphonies ever written on 19 January 1787 in an extraordinary concert given at the National Theater (see Chapter 5). There is still some question, however, as to whether or not the symphony heard that evening was actually conceived for Prague, or whether it was originally intended for another musical center (perhaps Vienna or London), more than one, or none at all in particular. In the Mozart documentation, nothing is recorded about the genesis of the "Prague" Symphony except for the date of its completion, as noted in Mozart's own catalog of compositions: 6 December 1786. Even though the symphony was performed in Prague less than six weeks later, any assumption that it was written specifically for an upcoming performance with Prague in mind is open to question. Contemporary accounts indicate that it was the success of *The Marriage of Figaro* that brought Mozart to Prague (see Chapter 4), and newspaper reports of the overwhelming success of the opera date only from later in the month of December 1786 (the first one on 12 December).

A letter of Mozart's father of 12 January 1787 may help to explain how the symphony could have been completed so early, yet still with the intent of using it for a first visit to Prague. As mentioned in Chapter 4, the letter states that musicians in the opera orchestra of Prague, and not just music lovers, were among those who invited his son to the city, an observation that clearly leaves open the possibility that plans to come to Prague could well have preceded the newspaper reports of the success of *The Marriage of Figaro*. Precisely when performances of *The Marriage of Figaro* started is not possible to establish, although it is known with certainty that the winter season of the National Theater began no later than November, since the English traveler Hester Lynch Piozzi was present for a performance that month. Taking into account the necessity of sending a score of *The Marriage of Figaro* to Prague long in advance of any performances for the purpose of planning the production and rehearsing it, the musicians at the National Theater could easily have come into contact with its music many weeks before 6 December 1786. It is also possible that attempts to lure Mozart to Prague began at the time that *The Marriage of Figaro* was first proposed as a work to be performed there, considering the high regard that musicians and music lovers in the city are known to have already had for his music. The opera never would have been considered for the stage of the National Theater if that had not been so.

As a rule, eighteenth-century symphonies were composed for specific events, locations, and bodies of musicians for what would now be considered immediate performance. They generally were not created out of an impulse to express something in symphonic style that would be set aside indefinitely in hopes that an ensemble capable of realizing the music would eventually materialize. It is true that Mozart did compose his last three symphonies of 1788 in this way, but no earlier symphonies are known to have been written in similar circumstances; usually there was an ensemble waiting that Mozart could rely on to perform whatever new symphonies he was composing - though not in Vienna (at least not after he moved there permanently in 1781).

The lack of such an ensemble in Vienna was actually a major impediment to Mozart's production of symphonies. In Salzburg, the court orchestra of the prince-archbishop was ready to play new works of his at all times, and his own father was a member of that orchestra. In Vienna, Mozart was never was able to take advantage of a similar arrangement. In fact, he never produced a single symphony after his move to Vienna that he could expect to be performed shortly after its composition by an orchestra in the city. The orchestra of the National Theater in Prague, however, did take up his new symphony of December 1786, just six weeks after its completion.

This circumstance alone strikes one as something more than coincidental, but there are also two important clues having to do with the musical style of the "Prague" Symphony that seem to indicate that the work as we know it was indeed crafted to suit the tastes and capabilities of the music lovers and musicians of Prague. One is its three-movement format (fast-slow-fast), which would have been highly exceptional for a symphony written in Vienna in 1786. It is true that symphonies cast in the fast-slow-fast format were common for decades after they started to appear in large numbers in Italy in the 1730s. In fact, they were the norm in many parts of Europe before the 1760s. Originally based on the model of three-movement Italian opera overtures, the three-movement plan for symphonies was standard in Italy through the 1770s, but in the north, four-movement symphonies of the pattern fast-slow-minuet-fast were decisively favored already by the 1760s. Joseph Haydn, who was considered the most influential composer of symphonies in Europe during Mozart's lifetime, ceased writing three-movement symphonies entirely after the late 1760s. The very limited number of symphonies in the standard repertory that are cast in three movements has actually led to an alternative traditional nickname for the "Prague" Symphony in German-speaking countries: "Die Symphonie ohne Menuett" (the symphony without a minuet). In fact, there are no other three-movement symphonies from the eighteenth century that are still played with any regularity except for Mozart's own Symphony No. 31 (the "Paris" Symphony of 1778) and the Symphony No. 34, which was written in Salzburg in 1780.

Unlike Haydn, who never visited Italy in his lifetime, Mozart traveled there extensively as a teenager, and he wrote many examples as a boy and young man of Italianate symphonies with three movements, most of them in Salzburg (after Haydn had given up writing them). Mozart never wrote three-movement symphonies for Vienna, however, not even in the 1760s as a child, a time when three-movement symphonies were commonly being written in many parts of Europe. In Vienna, three-movement symphonies were simply not favored at any period during Mozart's creative career. The choice of the three-movement format for a symphony composed in Vienna in 1786 would have been so unusual that any theory for the origins of the "Prague" Symphony should attempt to offer some explanation for it. In 1786, there was not a single eminent symphonist in all of Europe who continued to cultivate the three-movement format on any sort of regular basis.

One plausible theory to account for Mozart's eccentric turn toward the archaic Italianate three-movement format lies in his acquaintance with the Prague composer Josef Mysliveček, who was the only composer from Prague that Mozart ever knew well as a symphonist. Mysliveček moved to Italy from Prague in 1763 and soon established himself as the most talented composer of symphonies resident in the country. As an exponent of Italianate style, Mysliveček's symphonies were almost invariably cast in three movements, fast-slow-fast, the same format as in the "Prague" Symphony.

Mozart had met Mysliveček on all three of his trips to Italy in the early 1770s and carefully studied his music. An encounter in Munich in 1777 renewed their acquaintance. There is no question that Mysliveček's symphonies were known at the court of Salzburg, since the archbishop actually commissioned some from him. Mysliveček's personal contacts with the Mozart family and the infusion of his symphonic works into the repertory of the court orchestra of Salzburg offer the most likely explanation for Mozart's attachment to three-movement symphonies long after most composers had discarded them. It is reasonable to speculate that if Mozart were writing a symphony for Prague, he might assume that its musical public would be receptive to a symphony compatible with the style of Josef Mysliveček, the greatest symphonist the city had ever produced, or perhaps recognize a three-movement work as a sort of tribute to Mysliveček. The use of Mysliveček's music as a source of inspiration would have been no novelty for Mozart in 1786, since he had already turned to his music for many years as a point of departure for helping create masterpieces in a wide variety of genres.

It is true that the use of three-movement format could also be compatible with theories that the "Prague" Symphony was actually composed with a performance in London in mind. As pointed out in Chapter 4, there was serious discussion in the Mozart correspondence during the winter of 1786-87 about a possible trip to London, and there were even announcements of it in the press. If the "Prague" Symphony was originally written for London, the three-movement format might harken back to the style of the composer Johann Christian Bach, the youngest son of Johann Sebastian Bach, a prominent symphonist active for many years in London until his death in 1782. Consistent with his Italian training, J. C. Bach also wrote many symphonies in three-movement format after most other European composers had ceased doing so.

But in spite of Bach's exaggerated reputation as a lifelong mentor to Mozart, there is no reason to believe that Mozart had as much access to Bach's symphonies in the 1770s as he had to those of Mysliveček, and the closeness of personal contacts cannot even be compared. Mozart had met J. C. Bach only twice in his life, first as a child in London at the ages of 8 and 9, and then once very briefly in Paris in 1778. Unlike Mysliveček, who is one of the composers most frequently mentioned in the Mozart correspondence, Bach is not known to have corresponded with any member of the Mozart family at any time in his life. Mozart reported that the one encounter he had had with him as an adult was intensely disappointing, due to Bach's unconcealed indifference towards him.

For a musical culture as rich as the one that flourished in London, it probably would not have been as obvious to music lovers that Mozart might be trying to evoke the style of a master who had recently died there. Bach could never be described as being an overriding figure in the way that was Mysliveček's unrivaled preeminence as a symphonist among composers who had worked in Prague. Bach's close friend and collaborator Carl Friedrich Abel, for example, who was still living in London in 1786, had no predilection for the three-movement format. In any case, Mozart's plans to visit London were so tentative that it is hard to see the sense of writing a symphony for London before he had any idea of whether or not a performance could be arranged or what kind of musicians would be playing it.

It is instructive to compare Mozart's situation in 1786 with a similar situation faced by Joseph Haydn in 1782, when he composed a series of three four-movement symphonies (Nos. 76-78) for London as part of a planned trip that never materialized. In a letter to a Parisian music publisher of 15 July 1783, Haydn pointed out that the symphonies were easy to play and did not contain difficult wind solos. This of course would be a sensible precaution for a composer who had no idea what sort of musicians would be performing his work in a distant city. In contrast, Mozart did know what sort of musicians were available in Prague, and the symphony they were given to perform may well be described as the most difficult one to play that had ever been written up to that time. Furthermore, it made a specialty of boldly original writing for wind instruments that few European ensembles of the time would have been able to play successfully.

This treatment of wind instruments is in fact the other important stylistic clue that tends to identify the "Prague" Symphony as a work written expressly to appeal to the musical public of Prague. It has already been pointed out several times in this volume that one of the achievements of Bohemian musical culture best known to the general European musical public was the excellence of wind players from the Bohemian lands. Also, the popularity of Mozart's operas in Prague was partly attributable to the skillful writing for wind instruments that was noticed by the musical public in Prague. The elaborate passages for wind players in the "Prague" Symphony thus strike one as a deliberate attempt to exploit what Mozart would have believed to be the greatest strength of the musicians available in Prague, as well as a stylistic feature that his admirers in the city would appreciate greatly.

There is no question that the writing for winds in the "Prague" Symphony represents a landmark in the history of symphonic writing. Traditionally, the string section completely dominated the textures of most earlier eighteenth-century symphonies, and indeed, many of the earliest symphonies were scored for stringed instruments only. As time went on, winds, brass, and tympani became more and more common, but their use was governed by sterotypical procedures. Winds were generally used only to highlight certain themes by doubling the string parts, and brass instruments and tympani were generally used only to enhance the brilliance of loud passages.

Overall, Mozart's earlier symphonies were no exception. The solos and ensembles for winds that appear in the "Prague" Symphony are more frequent, intricate, and extended than in any symphonic work that Mozart had written up to that time. The way that the winds interact with the strings, weaving in and out of the textures in unpredictable ways, is much more imaginative than the solos for individual players that can be found in earlier symphonies by any composer that made a specialty of highlighting the talents of featured virtuosos (many of a special type referred to as "concerted" symphonies). In regard to the third movement of Mozart's "Prague" Symphony, it would be difficult to identify any earlier symphony with strings that contains so many passages in which no stringed instruments play at all.

It is true that imaginative experiments with the treatment of wind instruments were a hallmark of the great series of twelve concertos for piano and orchestra that Mozart wrote for his own use in Vienna during the years 1784-86, but transfer of the same sort of techniques to a symphony seems a challenge that would have been invited by some sort of new opportunity. An invitation to Prague would certainly qualify. As with the exceptionally difficult opera *Don Giovanni*, it is possible that Mozart recognized in the orchestra of the National Theater in Prague an ensemble not only staffed by excellent musicians, but one that was willing to exert extra efforts to bring his vision to life in consideration of the unique regard that its members had for his music.

In spite of all the clues that stand out to the researcher, it is also possible that the "Prague" Symphony was never conceived as a work for Prague, that the chance to have it performed there for the first time so soon after its composition was merely a stroke of luck, and that the inclusion of features that might have appealed to the musical public of Prague was coincidental. The choice of the highly exceptional three-movement format may have been nothing more than an impulsive whim, and Mozart may actually have decided to take a chance that an ensemble capable of playing the most difficult symphony ever written up to that time could be assembled somehow for his benefit in London.

It would be pleasing to report that the handling of wind instruments in the "Prague" Symphony that influenced not only Mozart's last symphonies, but also later symphonies of Haydn, Beethoven, and Schubert, was one of the greatest legacies of the famed Bohemian wind players of Mozart's time. However, it is possible that Mozart would have adopted a similar path for his last symphonies regardless of whether or not they were first introduced into the "Prague" Symphony as a means to please his admirers in Prague. His instincts might have found full realization in any case, only at a later time.

A final determination about the circumstances of the genesis of the composition unfortunately must hope for the appearance of additional new evidence. All that can be said with certainty is that the "Prague Symphony" was finished just two days after the Piano Concerto No. 25, K. 503, the last of the great series of twelve piano concertos he began in 1784. It is possible that it was to be performed as part of the same Advent concerts in Vienna that the concerto was planned for, even though no opportunity to see it performed in Vienna presented itself at that time.

Regardless of how the "Prague" Symphony came into being, the final result occupies a unique place in the history of the eighteenth-century symphony. On the broadest level, it can be described as the apotheosis of the three-movement symphonic writing that gave the genre its start in Italy in the 1730s in the hands of composers far less talented than Mozart. It is also the culmination of Mozart's own contribution to the repertory of three-movement symphonies that extends back to his childhood in the 1760s. The imaginative effects introduced for wind instruments constitute only a portion of its ingenuity. Another distinguishing feature is the depth and sophistication of its final movement, representative as it is of a trend in the 1780s to make final movements more substantial than the pleasant trifles common in symphonic works from earlier decades.

A specialty of the finales in Italianate three-movement symphonies was dance-like melodies and rhythms, especially those evocative of rollicking jigs. The final movement of the Symphony No. 34, written in Salzburg in 1780 represents the most advanced stage of development for this sort of finale. The last movement of the "Prague" Symphony, in contrast, owes little or nothing to dance rhythms, and while it is lighter in tone than most first movements written by Mozart and Haydn in the

1780s, it does exemplify an intensity of expression and sophistication of technique that would be taken to greater and greater lengths in the hands of Beethoven and his successors in the nineteenth century.

Of the two important musical traits of the "Prague" Symphony that tend to relate it to the musical culture of Bohemia - the three-movement format and the lavish treatment of winds - it is the latter that endears the work most to modern audiences, who generally favor rich orchestral colors in line with the standards of the beloved repertory of ninetheenth-century symphonic music. The presence or absence of a minuet, on the other hand, is something that neither attracts nor repels and is actually barely noticed by most ordinary music lovers today. It is difficult to find listeners today who single out the minuets of late eighteenth-century symphonies as their favorite parts. Constrained as they are by tradition to be made up of mechanical repetitions of short musical sections, minuets admit little scope for the sweeping gestures possible in the fast outer movements or the opportunity to sample the various expressive moods that are evoked in slow movements. In modern times, the charm of the repetition of stylized dance melodies fades quickly.

For the purpose of crafting a symphony compatible with late eighteenth-century stylistic norms, however, minuets do take up space, and Mozart seems to have been aware of a need to compensate for the lack of a minuet by augmenting the length of the "Prague" Symphony somehow in other places, specifically by fashioning an exceptionally expansive slow introduction. That way, the total length of the work was brought into close alignment with typical four-movement symphonies of the 1780s even without a minuet. The slow introduction of the "Prague" Symphony is probably the longest and most sophisticated one ever written up to that time - certainly more substantial than anything written by Mozart earlier or later, or anything written up to that time by Haydn. The fast section that follows the slow introduction is also unusually spacious. As a result, the first movement of the "Prague" Symphony is substantially longer than any other ever written by Mozart, and the only other symphony by Mozart that takes somewhat longer to play in its entirety is his last one: the Symphony No. 41, K. 551 (the "Jupiter").

Slow introductions were an element of symphonic style that was being cultivated intensely in the 1780s for the first time. Their presence lends an extra dimension of grandeur and seriousness to an entire composition - and also the potential for a pleasing sense of unpredictability. The listener is never quite certain how long slow introductions will last, and since they are usually unstable harmonically and melodically, they build up a craving for the stability with which the fast portion of the opening movement always begins - usually at a soft dynamic level. The soft "first theme" that follows the slow introduction of the "Prague" Symphony is one of the most memorable in the entire repertory of late eighteenth-century symphonies, renowned for the way that what is perceived as the melody line shifts from the second violins at the start of the first phrase of music to the first violins by the end of it. The flourish for wind ensemble without strings that follows this "first theme" was probably unprecedented.

The internal structure of slow introductions, unlike that of the fast sections that follows them, is completely unstructured. Composers intensified the effect of surprise with stark contrasts of loud and soft and the sound of the full orchestra alternating with delicate solos and ensembles for various instruments. The harmonic progressions are free-flowing, also with the intent to surprise and amaze. The adventurous harmonic excursions and unusual rhythmic syncopations in the slow introduction to the "Prague" Symphony were unprecedented, and operatic techniques of drawing out the emotional tension are unmistakable. At some points, one can imagine the emotional struggles of a character on stage being acted out, and the intensity of emotions it creates for the listener can create an indescribable sensation of sweet anguish that is only extinguished with the entrance of the "first theme" of the fast section.

All three movements of the "Prague" Symphony were fashioned along the basic standards of sonata form, the complicated means of organizing the internal structure of the movements of instrumental compositions in late eighteenth-century Europe (and frequently vocal pieces as well). The use of sonata form was more or less obligatory in the first movements of any composer's symphonies in the 1780s, and it was frequently the basis of subsequent movements.

Most listeners today (including many passionate devotees of Mozart's music) have little or no idea what implications this has for the way that the musical ideas are arranged. What listeners do notice is a satisfying succession of musical ideas that flow into each other smoothly and logically. Alternations of stable and unstable areas in the musical presentation lend variety and drama.

Those with a minimum appreciation of sonata form recognize the overall two-part construction in which a first section is repeated, then a second section that may or may not be repeated. In the "Prague" Symphony, Mozart indicated repeats for each of the first sections, but none for the second sections. Connoisseurs recognize a standard series of harmonic and melodic events that are carefully crafted to heighten the effect of a grand harmonic adventure in which the listener savors at first the stability of a home key at the beginning, then unsettling excursions into new key areas, then sweet relaxation in a formalized return to the original key. All of the melodic material is carefully designed to heighten the feeling of departure from the comfort of the original key and the feeling of relief when it returns permanently in the middle of the second section.

The results of Mozart's inspiration as revealed in the "Prague" Symphony offer ample rewards for listeners at any level of comprehension: the perfect mix of musical variety and thematic unity. For those mindful of the sound of symphonic works that have been written since, the impact of the various orchestral effects and shifts of moods and styles on audiences in Mozart's time unfortunately could never be replicated today, since they seem rather restrained to most listeners in comparison to works by the leading nineteenth-century masters. Furthermore, in an era when recordings are so widely available, few can imagine anymore what a rare and special opportunity it was in Mozart's time to be able to hear orchestral music at all. It was the privilege of only a very small elite of music lovers who happened to reside in select musical centers of Europe - or who had the opportunity to visit them on occasion. All there is today to offer some idea of the effect of Mozart's innovations on the first audience for the "Prague" Symphony is the rapturous reaction recorded in the contemporary accounts.

Six German Dances for Orchestra, K. 509

Similar to the "Prague" Symphony, almost all that is known for certain about the origins of Mozart's six contredanses (German dances) for orchestra, K. 509, is that they are listed as being completed in his catalog of compositions on a certain day: 6 February 1787. As mentioned in Chapter 5, the manuscript of the score indicates that they were written in Prague and dedicated to one of the counts Pachta. It is possible that they were intended to be performed at the Tummel-Platz pleasure hall. These compositions were conceived as genuine ballroom dance music and consequently are very simple in structure and style, indeed so simple that one could hardly imagine Mozart stooping to writing such trivial novelties.

Nonetheless, Mozart composed many such collections of dances. One of the most important reasons for this was his part-time appointment to the imperial musical establishment in Vienna in 1787, which mandated the composition of dance music for imperial balls. The simplicity of the German dances was an absolute necessity, since they were intended for the enjoyment of non-professional dancers. All of them consist only of series of repeated eight-bar phrases, each phrase divided into subphrases of four bars, with a coda at the end to let the dancers know when to stop. The completely rigid and predictable phrasing provides the only means for non-professional dancers to stay together with the orchestra and with each other. This mechanical consistency unfortunately makes the dances monotonous to listen to only as music, and the only thing about them that has led to them being recorded commercially is Mozart's name on the score.

The generic designation "German dances" indicates pieces somewhat in the style of the folk music of Germany or Austria that were the precursors of nineteenth-century waltzes. Larger and better known collections of this type of dance music for piano are preserved from Franz Schubert in the early nineteenth century. Although in triple meter, Mozart's German dances do not exhibit the "oom-pah-pah" waltz accompaniment that Schubert generally adopted. They are about as imaginative and sophisticated as ballroom dance music of Mozart's time could be.

The orchestration of the six German dances was a prototype that Mozart continued to cultivate after his appointment to the imperial household in Vienna. The dance orchestra he wrote for in Prague was a large one that included piccolos in addition to flutes, and also oboes, clarinets, bassoons, horns, trumpets, and tympani, besides the usual complement of stringed instruments. Mozart never used piccolos in dance orchestras before he composed this set of dances in Prague, but after his appointment to the imperial household, it became standard procedure, and he usually included the same wind, brass, and percussion instruments as were used in Prague. One only wishes that such a clear precedent from musical life in Prague could have been associated with a more substantial musical genre.

The Concert Aria "Bella mia fiamma, addio"/"Resta, o cara," *K. 528*

As one of the most beautiful concert arias ever composed in eighteenth-century Europe, Mozart's "Bella mia fiamma, addio"/"Resta, o cara," K. 528, represents the culmination of his artistic relationship with the singer Josefa Dušek. Since she did not customarily appear in operatic productions, there would have been no other outlet for Mozart to produce a substantial vocal piece with orchestral accompaniment other than a "concert aria," i.e., a work for voice and orchestra intended to be performed as an independent selection in public concerts along with other vocal or instrumental pieces. Operatic excerpts were also performed in the same context. "Bella fiamma, addio"/"Resta, o cara" was not the first concert aria that Mozart wrote for Dušek. That was rather "Ah, lo previdi/Ah, t'invola agl'occhi miei," K. 272, which was composed for Dušek during a visit to Salzburg in 1777 (when she advised him to move to Prague as a solution to his frustrating employment situation at the time). Mozart's growth as a composer between 1777 and 1787 is abundantly evident from a comparison of the two settings.

In spite of its excellence as a vocal composition, Mozart's second aria for Dušek is little known to modern audiences, even to listeners who consider themselves Mozart enthusiasts. Much of this has to do with the fact that concert arias from the eighteenth century are little favored any more as concert material. It is difficult to appreciate the emotional transformations being expressed in concert arias when the dramatic situations from which they originate cannot be witnessed. Even when the texts are transcribed and translated in programs with detailed explanations of dramatic context, audiences still find it a challenge to appreciate them, and few but professional musicians and musicologists are able to remember the complicated Italian titles usually attached to them when they come in the form of complete dramatic scenes. Typically, the titles come in two parts, the first one to record the first line of the recitative text, the second one to record the first line of the aria text that follows the recitative. As difficult as it is to follow the meaning of the texts in the present day, it would have been even more difficult for eighteenth-century audiences in central Europe who heard them in Italian, since translations were not customarily provided. Then, as now, audience members would mainly be listening to the selections as if they were instrumental pieces, simply an array of pleasing musical ideas in various tempos, moods, and styles. Most listeners would be lucky to pick up on the meaning of more than just a few words or phrases that were used as the basis of the musical inspiration.

The date of completion for the concert aria "Bella fiamma, addio"/"Resta, o cara" can be verified in Mozart's catalog of compositions as 3 November 1787, in Prague. The entry includes an annotation that it was prepared specifically for Josefa

Dušek. It appears to belong to the tradition of "farewell arias" that Mozart occasionally wrote for female singers whose company he was leaving (such as Dorothea Wendling in Mannheim in 1778 and Nancy Storace in Vienna in 1786), in each case with words that draw attention to the sadness of departure. The fanciful legend about its origins, recorded by Mozart's son Karl in the 1850s, is discussed in Chapter 7. His reminiscence is short enough to justify a second quotation, even though he was not present in Prague in 1787 to witness the incident he described:

> On the peak of one of the hills belonging to the villa there stood a pavilion. One day the singer Frau Dušek locked up the great Mozart in a cunning way, then prepared ink, pen, and music paper and let him know that he would not be able to regain his freedom unless he composed for her the aria he promised with the words "Bella mia fiamma, addio!" Mozart yielded to necessity, but in order to avenge the prank that Frau Josepha Dušek had played on him, he introduced into the aria various passages that were difficult to perform and threatened his despotic friend that he would immediately destroy the aria if she could not perform it successfully at first sight.

Entrance gate to Bertramka

It is difficult to know what to make of the purported threat to destroy the music. Mozart was just about to leave Prague when he finished Dušek's aria, and it seems highly unlikely that a performance with a full orchestra could have been arranged while he was still there. He may have tried it out by accompanying her with a reduction of the orchestral part on piano, of course, but regardless of how her sight-reading went the first time around, the music for the piece was certainly never destroyed, even with its devilishly contrived vocal part.

It has been known for a long time that the text Josefa Dušek supposedly wanted Mozart to set for her was not a new one. Rather, it had been prepared by the obscure Neapolitan librettist Michele Sarcone for the opera *Cerere placata* (Ceres appeased) by Niccolò Jommelli, which was performed in Naples in 1772 in a lavish production intended to celebrate the birth of the princess Maria Theresa Carolina Giuseppina, a daughter of the Neapolitan royal couple. She was their eldest child, and as an adult, she was present at the coronation of Leopold II in Prague in 1791 as the wife of the archduke Francis, heir to the throne of the Holy Roman Empire. How the text and music of Jommelli's original aria came to the north, and what interested Dušek about it in 1787, remains a matter of conjecture. No performances of the Jommelli opera in question are known to have taken place anywhere north of the Alps. There is also a question about whether or not the text of the Jommelli aria was identical to a text that Leopold Mozart reported to his son in a letter of 15 December 1780 as one that Dušek hoped Mozart would set for her. It is possible that her meeting with Mozart in Prague in 1787 finally offered her the chance to have it set, but if the aria were really intended as a "farewell," it would be quite a coincidence if the aria carried around so long just happened to be set with a text concerned with the pain of departure.

The story that Sarcone concocted for *Cerere placata* is a free adaptation of ancient myths associated with Ceres, goddess of agriculture, and her daughter Proserpina, who was abducted by Pluto to reign as queen of the underworld. In order to make the libretto more suitable for a celebration of the royal family of Naples, the setting was carefully matched to ancient equivalents of the territorial possessions of the Neapolitan ruling house. The king of Naples at the time, Ferdinand IV, ruled the island of Sicily as part of his patrimony; thus Ceres is portrayed as a mortal queen of Sicily and a number of Sicilian towns are referred to. Ferdinand's father Charles was a former king of Naples who was the ruler of Spain in 1772 as Charles III. His presence was frequently felt at the court of Naples not only because he was the father of the ruling monarch, but also because of the political influence he wielded as patron of a client state. That is why another leading character, Titan (Titano), is portrayed as the "king of Iberia" (a title that never existed) to evoke this Spanish connection.

The attempt to make the drama so specific to the circumstances of the court of Naples is one of the most important reasons why Jommelli's opera was not attractive for revival. The text is also much shorter than what was usual for Italian serious operas of the 1770s - cast in two acts instead of three. The designation "festa teatrale" ("theatrical entertainment") in the libretto instead of "dramma per musica" (the usual designation for a serious opera of the type that Metastasio cultivated) denotes a "fancy" opera with dancing and choruses included. This would create a type of operatic spectacle familiar to the queen of Naples at the time, Maria Carolina, who had grown up at the court of Vienna, which made a specialty of them in the eighteenth century as a part of celebrating events such as births, marriages, birthdays, and name days. The use of mythological characters and supernatural effects was a feature of "feste teatrali" that distinguish them from most Metastasian dramas. The very personalized manner in which the Neapolitan royal family is flattered in the libretto for Jommelli's opera *Cerere placata* may be contrasted with Mozart's *La clemenza di Tito*, which was produced by a political entity (the Estates of Bohemia) that did not have the time or financial resources to sponsor a lavish new work prepared with specific references to Leopold II and his accomplishments. The Estates were content with the implied flattery of a preexistent text.

In Sarcone's drama, at the point when the text used by Mozart is introduced (Act II, scene 5), Ceres learns that Proserpina has contracted marriage with the mortal Titan, who abducted her from the kingdom of Sicily and took her back to his kingdom of Iberia. She had fallen in love with him long ago, and she is perfectly content to marry him. While traveling together on the Mediterranean Sea off the coast of Sicily, a storm raised by the god Neptune causes the boat in which they are sailing to capsize. They find themselves shipwrecked on the island of Sicily, certain to be discovered by representatives of the queen. When they are caught, they are brought into her presence. Ceres wants Titan imprisoned and executed, and is shocked that her daughter would want to marry him. A contemporary spectator would be able to know merely from the cast list of the libretto that Proserpina and Titan would be joined in marriage by the end of the opera, since they are identified as being in love - it would only be a question as to how this would come about.

Although Sarcone could certainly boast of many skills as a poet, his technique of bringing about the expected denouement does not demonstrate the ingenuity typical of Metastasio, who likely would have come up with an extraordinary contrivance to make it possible for Titan to escape the sentence of death imposed by Ceres. Sarcone's solution is quite abrupt and unimaginative: In his drama, the god Jove simply appears suddenly to announce that the gods unanimously wish to see Proserpina and Titan joined in marriage. No reason is given, though Jove does proclaim that the descendants of the couple will include the glorious rulers Charles and Ferdinand, along with the newborn princess Maria Theresa.

Titan expresses despair at having to give up Proserpina in the vocal piece composed for the scene by Jommelli and Mozart, but he faces death bravely, thinking only of her interests when he is gone. The original character who sang the text was male, and the passionate sentiments it contains were intended to be sung to a woman. When performed outside of the context of an operatic production, however, gender identification in concert vocal pieces was meaningless in late eighteenth-century European musical culture. They were simply performed by members of either sex who were capable of singing in the proper vocal range. Even in Mozart's time, the expectation usually would have been that this vocal piece with its passionate expression of love addressed to a woman would also be sung in public by a woman. The dramatic context would have been left a mystery to most audience members.

It is impossible to imagine anyone truly understanding the emotional transformations at work in Sarcone's scene without a thorough knowledge of the dramatic incidents that precede it, as hopeless as that prospect would have been to audiences hearing Dušek sing Mozart's version of it in the late eighteenth century. The scene actually involves five characters who appear in the original opera. Titan expresses his feelings to Proserpina directly, but he also addresses Ceres, his friend Alpheus, and a pagan priest. The portions of text addressed to each of the latter characters were never indicated by Mozart in his score, and it is possible that he never knew about the indications found in the original libretto. The music for the aria could have come up from Italy to Dušek with no indication of who was addressing whom and no clear idea of dramatic context except that it records an outpouring of emotion from an infatuated male lover. A vocal piece of this sort would resemble what is referred to in spoken drama as a soliloquy, and the progression from recitative to aria is in the musical section is typical of an operatic scene of the late eighteenth century, which would use recitative to set up an emotional state amplified by the musical setting of an aria text. The original text of Sarcone reads as follows with indications of who Titan is supposed to be speaking to on stage:

Recitative

To Proserpina:

Bella mia fiamma, addio!	My beauteous flaming love, farewell!
Non piacque al cielo di renderci felici.	Heaven is not pleased to grant us happiness.
Ecco reciso, prima d' esser compito,	Now cut before its effect was ever realized,
Quel purissimo nodo, che strinsero	A knot of purest intent was meant to tighten
Fra lor gl'animi nostri con il solo voler.	Our spirits into a single will.
Vivi: Cedi al destin, cedi al dovere.	[I say] Live: Yield to destiny and to duty.
Della giurata fede la mia morte t'assolve.	My death absolves you from your oath to me.
A più degno consorte...O pene! ...	To a more worthy consort...Oh misery! ...
Unita vivi più lieta e più felice vita.	You will be joined to live a happier life.
Ricordati di me, ma non mai turbi	Remember me, but do not ever permit
D'un felice sposo la rara	The prized remembrance of your happy lover
Rimembranza il tuo riposo.	To disturb your composure.

To Ceres:

Regina, io vado ad ubbidirti	Oh queen, I leave in obedience to you,
Ah, tutto finisca il mio furor col morir mio.	My death will bring all my raving to an end.

Ceres, Alpheus, and Proserpina:

Cerere, Alfeo, diletta sposa, addio!	Ceres, Alpheus, beloved betrothed, farewell!

Aria

To Proserpina:

Resta, o cara, acerba morte,	Stay, my dearest, bitter death
Mi separa, oh Dio, da te.	Separates me, oh God, from you.

To Ceres:

Prendi cura di sua sorte,	Take care of her destiny,

To Alpheus:

| Consolarla almen procura. | At least try to get consolation for her. |

To Proserpina:

Vado, ahi lasso, addio per sempre.	I leave, alas, farewell forever.
Quest'affanno, questo passo	This anguish, this step
È terribile per me.	Is terrible for me.
Ah! Dov'è il tempio, dov'è l'ara?	Ah! Where is the temple, where is the altar?

To a priest:

| Vieni, affretta la vendetta! | Come, hurry up with the retribution! |

To Proserpina:

| Questa vita così amara | A life as bitter as this one |
| Più soffribile non è! | Is no longer bearable! |

Karl Mozart's account implies that Josepha Dušek was primarily attracted to the text of the aria, and not its music, but there can be no question that Mozart knew the music for the Jommelli aria very well; he clearly used some of Jommelli's musical motives as a point of departure to create his own setting of the text. Dušek must have had the original setting of Jommelli with her, since there is very little likelihood that Mozart would have had easy access to such an old and obscure aria by any other means. Throughout his career as a composer, Mozart had a tendency to use musical ideas conceived by other composers to produce extraordinary new compositions, and his ability to improve on the modest inspiration exhibited in the Jommelli aria is typical of his work. The overall situation resembles an incident in the year 1781, in which Mozart composed a fresh setting of the text "Misera, dove son/Ah, non son io che parlo," K. 369, for the Bavarian Countess Baumgarten as a replacement for one that she already possesed by Josef Mysliveček.

One of the most obvious signs of Mozart's reference to the original setting by Jommelli is the slow-fast structure of the aria that begins with the text "Resta, o cara." As mentioned in previous chapters, vocal pieces cast in this overall format were much favored in European opera theaters of the 1780s, and Mozart himself had written a series of magnificent examples just in the few years before this one was completed, including "Vorrei spiegarvi, oh Dio," K. 418, of 1783, and "Ch'io mi scordi di te/Non temer, amato bene," K. 505, of 1786. Modern audiences continue to be attracted to the slow-fast format. The strategy of starting out in a soft, contemplative manner and finishing with a brilliant close after a character looks at his or her situation in a different light is just what modern music lovers savor, partly because it is so compatible with similar types of vocal pieces from the nineteenth century that conclude with spectacular vocal display in fast tempo. The slow-fast format provides a very satisfying way to follow a singer through a long, involved emotional transformation that begins with the simplicity of recitative style.

One might think that a text as maudlin as the one Sarcone wrote for "Bella mia fiamma, addio," might be suitable for a setting in minor key, but "bravura" arias with virtuoso passagework were almost never set in minor key in the late eighteenth century. Neither Jommelli nor Mozart chose minor key for his setting. In Mozart's aria, the dark character of minor key is only temporarily invoked for certain evocative words.

Overall, the expansive character of major key is needed to enhance the excitement of the stirring fast section. As one alternative to minor key to help suggest the deflated emotions of the character Titan, Mozart introduced downward-moving stepwise motives in the bass (and sometimes other parts) in the slow section. As mentioned in Chapter 10, this is a device that tends to suggest draining emotional energy - the perfect means to evoke Titan's dejection. This mood could not be expected to be maintained throughout the setting. Rather, the slow-fast format mandates a sudden change of emotional perspective to accommodate a brilliant musical close. In this case, Titan recovers his composure for the fast section by resolving to face his fate with courage and resignation. His exclamation "Vieni, affretta" ("Come, hurry up"), addressed to a priest in reference to his imminent execution, is the key phrase that spurs the musical excitement of the fast section.

Throughout his setting, Mozart expoits the common device of highlighting key words and phrases with special musical treatment and repetition. For the slow section, the key phrase is clearly "terribile per me" ("terrible for me"), which is repeated over and over again in order to stick out to the audience. Luckily for English-speaking Mozart enthusiasts, it is a phrase whose meaning is not difficult to pick up, much easier than the phrase "acerba morte" ("bitter death"), which is singled out prominently for minor-key coloring in the slow section. In the fast section, it is the word "amara" ("bitter") and the phrase "più soffribile non è" that are singled out for similar minor-key coloring and repetition.

Intricate harmonic inflections are prominent throughout the setting, and this is what seems to have provided the principal element of difficulty that would have presented a special challenge for Dušek in sight-reading, if Karl Mozart's indication can be accepted as valid. The virtuoso passagework Mozart crafted for Dušek is not simple to sing, but there is nothing about it that would have been especially difficult for a vocal artist as experienced as she was. Overall, it is based on rather conventional patterns. The adventurous harmonic transformations, in contrast, are very daring for Mozart's time, and it goes without saying that there was no other composer in Europe capable of fashioning them with such logic and seamlessness. In this regard, one may recall that it was that very autumn of 1787 that Norbert Lehman witnessed an extraordinary improvisation by Mozart on the organ of the Strahov Abbey that was also marked by unusual and extravagant harmonic progressions. This improvisation was witnessed by Josefa Dušek, and it seems that Mozart found an outlet for the same sort of harmonic extravagance in a composed piece at the same time in a genre that highlights all of Mozart's strengths as a composer of vocal music accompanied by orchestra.

The Lieder "Des kleinen Freidrichs Geburtstag," K. 529, and "Das Traumbild," K. 530

The two *Lieder* Mozart is known to have completed just before the end of his second visit to Prague, were both entered into his catalog of compositions on 6 November 1787. The names of the poets for the texts - Johann Eberhard Friedrich Schall for "Des kleinen Friedrichs Geburtstag" ("What little Friedrich's birthday was like") and Ludwig Heinrich Christoph Höltz for "Das Traumbild" ("The dream-vision") - are known, but how Mozart came across them or what use he had in mind for them can only be guessed at, unless they were also intended as "farewell" compositions for unknown recipients.

The choice of the first text, which refers to the birthday of a "little Friedrich," is particularly puzzling. It is known that the poem on which it was based was originally written in 1778 for the ninth birthday of Friedrich, hereditary prince of Anhalt-Dessau, who died in 1814 without ever reigning. It is possible that Mozart's setting was intended to celebrate the birthday of some other child named Friedrich, or "Fritz," to use the nickname by which the child is identified in Mozart's catalog, even though some characteristics of the text are appropriate only in the context of celebrating the birthday of the child of a ruler (or perhaps a large estate owner). The opening line that addresses a group of "good people," for example, and the last line of the eighth stanza, which ends with the exhortation "Heil unserm Friederich!" ("Hail to our Friedrich!"), would only make sense in that type of context.

This particular *Lied* is not much favored either by vocal artists or audiences, and it is not difficult to see why. Both interpreters and connoisseurs of vocal music in all styles generally seek vivid expressions of physical love to help drive inspiration and glean appreciation. This poem contains nothing of the sort and very little of interest as a substitute. The fatuous praise of the behavior of a little boy from an obscure ruling family - obviously motivated by outdated political considerations - would never likely catch the attention of modern music lovers:

Es war einmal, ihr Leute,	There was once, good people,
Ein Knäblein jung und zart,	A young and kind little boy
Hiess Friedrich, war daneben	Named Friedrich, who, besides that,
Recht gut von Sinnesart.	Possessed a pleasant disposition.
War freundlich und bescheiden,	He was friendly and modest,
Nicht zänkisch und nicht wild,	Not quarrelsome or wild,
War sanft wie kleine Schäfchen,	He was as gentle as a little lamb,
Und wie ein Täubchen mild.	And as tender as a little dove.
Drum gab auch Gott Gedeihen,	It was also God who helped make him thrive
Das Knäblein wuchs heran,	The little boy grew up,
Und seine Eltern hatten	And his parents were
Recht ihre Freude dran.	Justly overjoyed with him.

Zu Schul' und Gotteshause	To school and church
Sah man es fleissig geh'n,	He was seen to go diligently,
Und Jedem, der es grüsste,	And everyone he greeted on the way
Gar freundlich Rede steh'n.	Received friendly words.
Auch war ihm in der Schule	And also at school itself
Ein Jeder herzlich gut,	Everyone loved him dearly,
Denn Allen macht es Freude,	For he gave joy to all,
Und Allen war es gut.	And he was kind to everyone.
Einst hiess es:	One day there was an announcement:
Brüder, morgen fällt	Brothers, his birthday
Sein Geburtstag ein!	Falls tomorrow!
Gleich riefen All' und Jede:	One and all exclaimed
Der muß gefeiert sein.	That everyone must celebrate.
Da war des Wohlbehagens	Then there was a feeling of well-being
Und jeder Freude viel;	And joy for everyone;
Und wo man sah und hörte,	And wherever anyone looked and listened,
War Sang und Tanz und Spiel.	There was singing, dancing, and games.
Denn alle, alle freuten	Then everyone rejoiced
Des frohen Tages sich,	The whole day through,
Und alle, alle sangen:	And everyone sang:
Heil unserm Friederich!	Hail to our Friderich!
Und Gott im Himmel oben	And God in heaven above
Erhörte ihr Gebet;	Heard their prayer;
Sein Segen folgt dem Knaben,	His blessings follow the boy,
Da wo er geht und steht.	Wherever he might be.

The nature of the text for "Das Traumbild," on the other hand, is much more suited to the tastes of modern singers and music lovers. In this case, the sentiments are those of a man singing to a woman:

Wo bist du, Bild, das vor mir stand	Where are you, vision, that stood before me
Als ich im Garten träumte,	As I was dreaming in the garden,
In's Haar den Rosmarin mir wand,	And wound into my hair the rosemary
Der um mein Lager keimte?	That sprouted around my resting place?
Wo bist du, Bild, das vor mir stand	Where are you, vision, that stood before me
Mir in die Seele blickte,	That looked into my soul,
Und eine warme Mädchenhand	And pressed a warm maiden's hand
Mir an die Wangen drückte?	Against my cheeks?
Nun such' ich dich, mit Harm erfüllt,	Now I search for you, filled with apprehension,
Bald bei des Dorfes Linden,	Right by the linden tree in the village,
Bald in der Stadt, geliebtes Bild,	Right in the city, beloved vision,

Und kann dich nirgends finden.	But unable to find you anywhere.
Nach jedem Fenster blick' ich hin,	I peek into every window
Wo nur ein Schleier wehet,	Where I see just a curtain fluttering,
Und habe meine Lieblingin	But my beloved
Noch nirgends ausgespähet.	I have never spied.
Komm selber, süßes Bild der Nacht,	Come, sweet vision of the night,
Komm mit den Engelsmienen,	Come with your angel's face,
Und in der leichten Schäfertracht,	And in the same light clothes of a shepherdess
Worin du mir erschienen!	In which you appeared to me before!
Bring' mit die schwanenweisse Hand,	Bring with you that swan-white hand
Die mir das Herz gestohlen,	That stole my heart,
Das purpurrote Busenband,	That purple-red band around your bosom,
Das Sträußchen von Violen.	That little bouquet of violets.
Dein großes blaues Augenpaar,	Your large blue eyes,
Woraus ein Engel blickte;	From which an angel looks out;
Die Stirne, die so freundlich war,	Your brow that was so congenial
Und guten Abend nickte;	And nodded good night;
Den Mund, der Liebe Paradies,	Your mouth, that paradise of love,
Die kleinen Wangengrübchen,	The little dimples in your cheeks,
Wo sich der Himmel offen wies:	That threw open the gates to heaven:
Bring' alles mit, mein Liebchen!	Bring all of it with you, my beloved!

Late eighteenth-century German *Lieder* functioned as household music and were intended to be performed in intimate surroundings either by amateur performers or professional musicians engaged in informal music-making. Connections with folk culture are frequently obvious. The very word *Lied* derives from a type of folk poetry on which many song settings of the late eighteenth century were based, and the music is often based on folk idioms as well. The genre did not yet exhibit the sophistication so noticeable in the work of the best nineteenth-century composers, except occasionally in Mozart's hands. "Song recitals" performed by vocal soloists with the accompaniment of a piano before hundreds of people were nonexistent in Mozart's time - as were recitals for solo pianists. In the late eighteenth century, if singers or pianists performed before large audiences, they were accompanied by an orchestra. In general, song settings with accompaniment for piano from the eighteenth century were kept deliberately simple so that technical demands would be well within the reach of amateur performers. Nothing like the virtuosity of a concert aria was ever encountered. Individual songs could be performed successfully by members of either sex, just as they are today.

In order to help start the singer out (and partly to give him or her the proper pitch), a typical song setting by Mozart would begin with an introduction for the piano alone (the *Vorspiel*), and there would be a postlude (*Nachspiel*) at the end of each stanza (or pairings of stanzas). The same music would be used for each, a type of setting that is referred to as "strophic" ("strophe" is a synonym for "stanza"). In the case of "Das Traumbild," the strophic procedure applied to its eight stanzas of text is absolutely rigid; each pairing of two stanzas is heard with precisely the same music. For "Des kleinen Friedrichs Geburtstag," eight of the nine stanzas are set in the same rigid pattern. An extra ninth stanza by Joachim Heinrich Campe is treated musically as a coda with only some of the musical motives heard earlier used to create a pleasing ending.

"Das Traumbild" is nonetheless a more satisfying composition, in spite of its rigidity. The greater intensity of emotion is adequately mirrored in the musical setting, and its harmonic profile is also much more interesting. When the singer ends each stanza of text, there is a special interlude or postlude that begins with an impulsive syncopation to suggest that the emotions involved are so intense that even the accompanist cannot wait to get in his or her take on the matter, a clever detail that would not likely have occured to lesser masters of the day.

Connoisseurs are grateful for such subtleties, but even when they are present, Mozart's songs in German usually appeal only to listeners with specialized tastes. They are difficult to appreciate for music lovers without an intimate knowledge of the German language and receptive to the informal style of music-making that was a part of their inception. Regretfully, to most listeners outside of the German-speaking lands, they are little more than pleasing examples of what Mozart was capable of producing when little was expected of him.

Postscript

Some of the tributes to the musicians and music lovers of Prague ascribed to Mozart are poignant indeed - for example, his remark that "the Bohemians understand me" (with the implication that the Viennese did not, along with residents of other cities). But the truth of the matter is that none of this generous praise can be traced directly to Mozart himself; it has only come down second-hand (or even third-hand). The phrase about being understood in Bohemia is first recorded in the biography of Georg Nikolaus von Nissen in the 1820s, but it was not even Nissen himself who claimed that Mozart had said it. Rather, Nissen quoted the theater director Jan Nepomuk Štěpánek, an individual whom Mozart likely never even met. True, the sentiment of the remark (if not the exact phrase) is corroborated in the reminiscences of the Prague pianist Wilhelm Kuhe, published in 1896, who claimed that a friend he had known decades before, the elderly string bass player Václav Svoboda, had told him that he had heard Mozart give a speech at a banquet in his honor in which he declared that "the citizens of Prague were the only people in the world who understood his music," but this hardly constitutes an eyewitness account. Similarly complicated circumstances typically accompany other expressions of praise and gratitude attributed to Mozart, such as the letter of thanks that Němeček claimed was written by Mozart to the conductor Strobach for the contribution his orchestra had made to the success of the first performance of *Don Giovanni*. Němeček clearly indicated that he had seen the original letter. Still, he never specified its whereabouts - and whoever might have possessed it at one time, it has not survived to the present day.

At least there can be no doubt of the appreciation for Mozart's music by the residents of Prague, and in this case, there is the direct testimony of a very important witness, Lorenzo Da Ponte, whose remarks about the matter are quoted in the introduction to this volume. What Mozart mainly did in his surviving correspondence was to express gratitude only for the kindness of individual music lovers in Prague. No documentation survives in which he expresses any particular fondness for the city of Prague or its civic culture, and there is no evidence of praise for the orchestra of the National Theater in Prague or the singers permanently attached to the Bondini and Guardasoni operatic companies. On the other hand, there is no criticism of anyone's playing or singing in Prague (although Mozart did complain about the reluctance of the original cast members of *Don Giovanni* to attend rehearsals as much as he thought proper). The total amount of time he actually spent as a visitor to the city was only about three months - spread over a period of four and a half years.

When all is said and done, Prague of the 1780s and 1790s simply did not have sufficient population or a wealthy enough noble community to support the talents of Wolfgang Amadeus Mozart, hence his clear preference for residence in Vienna, with its imperial court, diplomatic community, flourishing noble community, and much larger population to draw upon for patronage. The court appointment that Mozart received at the end of 1787 left very little likelihood that he would ever leave Vienna, and there would have been even less reason for doing so if he had lived to assume the post of director of the musical establishment at the Cathedral of St. Stephen in Vienna upon the death of Leopold Hofmann in 1792. Without a court or opportunities for lucrative employment, in addition to having a precarious operatic culture, Prague could not have been considered a strong base of operations for Wolfgang Amadeus Mozart. His employment problems could not have been adequately solved in Prague unless a group of nobles had stepped forward to provide him with some sort of annuity, as certain nobles in Vienna later did with Beethoven. As of now, there is no evidence to suggest that the nobility of Prague was ever prepared to do the same for Mozart.

As regrettable as it is to say, Mozart had the luxury of taking the Praguers for granted. They simply loved his music for its own merits, without imagining that Mozart needed to visit them often or cultivate their musicians personally. Their only expectation was a continued supply of masterpieces to enjoy, and their gratitude for that alone was manifested in an extraordinary manner in their commemorations of Mozart's death and the generosity they extended to his surviving family members. The greatest legacy of their adulation, of course, is the musical masterpieces that were first performed in Prague, especially the opera *Don Giovanni* and the "Prague" Symphony.

The visits to Prague that led to these premiéres were the result of a remarkable set of circumstances that happened to come together at the time that Mozart reached maturity as a composer: the opening of the National Theater in 1783 that was staffed by an orchestral ensemble of unusual skill; the presence of a musical public of exceptional musical literacy; and the goodwill of certain musicians and noble patrons who lived in Prague, but who had first met Mozart in other cities. As long as there are orchestras capable of playing the "Prague" Symphony and singers capable of bringing *Don Giovanni* to life, every performance of these works will endure as a monument to Mozart's association with the city of Prague.

Appendix I

Don Giovanni:
Survey of the Musical Numbers in the Prague Version of 1787

Characters:

Don Giovanni - nobleman and seducer of women [baritone role], identified in the original libretto as an "extremely licentious young gentleman" [baritone role]

Donna Anna - a noble victim of one of Don Giovanni's "tricks" engaged to Don Ottavio [soprano role]

Don Ottavio - a nobleman engaged to Donna Anna [tenor role]

Commendatore - Donna Anna's father [bass role]

Donna Elvira - a noblewoman from Burgos abandoned by Don Giovanni [soprano role]

Leporello, Don Giovanni's servant [bass role]

Masetto, a peasant engaged to Zerlina [bass role]

Zerlina, a peasant girl engaged to Masetto [soprano role]

Original Cast:

Luigi Bassi (Don Giovanni)
Teresa Saporiti (Donna Anna)
Antonio Baglioni (Don Ottavio)
Caterina Micelli (Donna Elvira)
Giuseppe Lolli (Commendatore and Masetto)
Felice Ponziani (Leporello)
Caterina Bondini (Zerlina)

Luigi Bassi in title role of *Don Giovanni*

According to the original libretto used for the Prague première, written by Lorenzo da Ponte, the action takes place "in a Spanish city"; in spite of frequent indications in modern opera guides, there is no indication that the city is Seville (the only Spanish city mentioned in the libretto is Burgos, the native city of Don Giovanni's discarded lover Donna Elvira).

Short Synopsis:

The plots of most operas in Mozart's day can be devilishly complex, but although there are many intricate turns of action in *Don Giovanni*, the basic storyline and moral lessons are refreshingly simple and direct. The seducer Don Giovanni, seemingly immune to all earthly justice, is subject to divine retribution for a crime far more serious than his numberless sexual conquests: the murder of an elderly gentleman who tries to defend the honor of his daughter. The fatal act is portrayed at the very beginning of the drama. The main portion of the opera is taken up with a sort of prolonged character sketch that demonstrates what a thoroughly contemptible creature Don Giovanni really is; his punishment is reserved for the very end. Don Giovanni's victim the Commendatore comes back from the grave in the form of a living stone statue. The statue arrives at Don Giovanni's house for a dinner that is never actually eaten and condemns Don Giovanni to eternal damnation after he refuses to repent for his sins. He is then dragged down to hell by a band of "spirits." Don Giovanni's victims are left to explain to the audience what they will do with their lives now that his pernicious influence is gone.

Musical Numbers

Overture:
One of the most beloved concert overtures in the symphonic literature, the overture to *Don Giovanni* was hurriedly prepared just in time for the première. It is unusual in the eighteenth century for an Italian opera overture to feature melodic materials that are also found in the body of the main drama. In this case, however, the slow introduction utilizes some music from the eerie passages heard in the finale of Act II, when the Commendatore speaks to Don Giovanni and confronts him with his crimes. It is possible that the borrowings were a compositional "shortcut" to help get the overture completed more quickly. They certainly presage the action to follow in an effective manner. The forbidding slow introduction is followed by a fast section in comic style that might have been intended to hint at the mixture of comic and serious elements so characteristic of the opera as a whole. For the connoisseur, the form of the fast section is sonata form without repeats.

ACT I

No. 1 - *Introduzione*
The opera opens with a "scena" (scene) that presents a fluid musical depiction of dramatic action. The first thing to be heard is the grumbling of Don Giovanni's servant Leporello, who resents his menial duties and would like to be a gentleman himself. Here, as in common in passages written for comic basses throughout the eighteenth century, the vocal part is dominated by a style of singing referred to as "patter" (a rapid declamation within a narrow vocal range that can sometimes be very difficult to understand). When Leporello is finished with his complaints, we see the murder of the Commendatore by Don Giovanni. In eighteenth-century opera, violent acts are frequently threatened and alluded to, but rarely acted out on stage, which is what would have made this incident particularly shocking and memorable to contemporary audiences. Donna Anna, daughter of the Commendatore, has narrowly escaped a sexual assault planned by Don Giovanni. He was able to gain her trust by entering her apartments disguised as her fiancé Don Ottavio (in most of the earlier Don Juan dramas, disguise was the preferred method of seducing noblewomen). After Donna Anna is able to escape into the street, her father tries to apprehend Don Giovanni and defend his daughter's honor. The Commendatore

challenges Don Giovanni to a sword fight. Since Don Giovanni is much younger, he easily prevails over the Commendatore and kills him. He then flees with his servant Leporello.

No. 2 - Recitative and Duet for Donna Anna and Don Ottavio, "Fuggi, crudele"
After the Introduction concludes, the listener hears examples of the two principal types of recitative used in eighteenth-century Italian opera. "Recitative" is an approximation of human speech in song - there are no "catchy" melodies and none of the music or text is repeated in the way that it would be in an aria or ensemble. Most of the action in any given opera would be presented in the style of "simple" recitative accompanied only by cello with a keyboard instrument adding chords. For moments of intense emotion, the "accompanied" style with full orchestra would be deployed. One can hardly think of a moment riper for setting as accompanied recitative than the grief felt by Donna Anna after the murder of her father before her own eyes, and an unusual poignant example is heard after the opening section of simple recitative in this number. Donna Anna seeks comfort from her ineffectual fiancé, Don Ottavio. In their duet, Donna Anna implores Don Ottavio to do everything he can to bring Don Giovanni to justice. Don Ottavio swears that he will. Duets in eigthteenth-century Italian opera usually come in two parts. In the first part, the singers express their feelings separately; then, in the second part, they sing together to signify their emotional synchronization. In the first part of this duet, Donna Anna pressures Don Ottavio into promising to avenge the murder of her father. Until it is certain that he will do as she wishes, the two do not sing together. When Don Ottavio gives in to her demand, the two sing together, proof that he has surrendered to her will. He now "sings her tune," so to speak. Overall, the keywords for this duet are the countless emotions "ondeggiando il cor" ("rocking their hearts").

No. 3 - Aria of Donna Elvira, "Ah, chi mi dice mai"
The scene changes to a street near an inn while the night turns to dawn. After Leporello summons the courage to berate Don Giovanni for living the life of a scoundrel, a woman comes along. The two hide for a time, all the better to "check her out." They do not recognize at first that the woman is Donna Elvira, one of Don Giovanni's many abandoned lovers seduced with a false promise of marriage. In her aria (in serious style), Donna Elvira pleads rhetorically for assistance from anyone who can help her find Don Giovanni. The keywords are "vo' cavare il cor" ("I want to carve his heart out"). "Thrusting" motives are quite prominent in the orchestral accompaniment.

No. 4 - Aria of Leporello, "Madamina, il catalogo è questo"
After a most unpleasant exchange between Don Giovanni and Donna Elvira, Don Giovanni slips away, leaving Leporello to console Donna Elvira with some prudent advice in a famous comic aria known as the "Catalog Aria." He advises Donna Elvira simply to forget Don Giovanni, who has done the same as he did to her to countless other women. He assures her that further efforts to pursue him will bring her nothing but frustration. In this two-part aria, Leporello first takes out the famous "list" (a tally of Don Givoanni's amorous conquests) and enumerates exactly how many women were seduced in each of the countries that Don Giovanni has visited (640 in Italy, 230 in Germany, 100 in France, 91 in Turkey, and already 1003 in Spain). In patter style, he explains that Don Giovanni has seduced women of all shapes, sizes, ages, and social classes. In the second part, Leoporello describes how Don Giovanni uses flattery to seduce them. The keywords for this section are "gentilezza" ("gentleness") and "dolcezza" ("sweetness"). Donna Elvira is not mollified, however, in fact more determined than ever to pursue Don Giovanni.

No. 5 - Chorus with Zerlina and Masetto, "Giovinette, che fate all'amore"
The scene now changes to the countryside. A chorus of peasants enters to begin a celebration that has been planned in the town. Zerlina exhorts the women to enjoy themselves, then Masetto exhorts the men. The keywords are "che piacer" ("what a pleasure").

No. 6 - Aria of Masetto, "Ho capito, signore"

Happily rid of Donna Elvira, Don Giovanni happens upon the merry peasants in the countryside. He immediately fixes his gaze on the peasant girl Zerlina as a good candidate for amorous conquest. Don Giovanni tells her fiancé Masetto that he is going to take Zerlina away with him for a while, and that he should not be concerned about his intentions, since Don Giovanni is a gentleman. As he declares in his aria, Masetto knows full well why he is expected to make himself scarce. He feigns willing submission, since he really has no choice but to obey the commands of a nobleman. In an aside, Masetto insults Zerlina; he is uncertain of Zerlina's willingness to resist Don Giovanni's advances. The vocal line is made simple and direct to match Masetto's social class.

No. 7 - Duet ("Duettino") for Don Giovanni and Zerlina, "Là ci darem la mano"

As a means of seducing Zerlina, Don Giovanni promises to marry her on the spot (a promise of marriage was the preferred means of seducing lower-class women in the earlier Don Juan dramas). The opening melody of their duet is one of the most famous duet melodies in all opera. In the first part, Zerlina's resistance to Don Giovanni's advances is depicted by having her sing separately from him, or in counterpoint. When she finally consents to the seduction, a new section of the duet begins in which the two sing in parallel motion to signify Zerlina's surrender to Don Giovanni's will. There are easily recognizable keywords only for the second part: "innocente amor" ("innocent love").

No. 8 - Aria of Donna Elvira, "Ah fuggi il traditor"

Out of nowhere, Donna Elvira appears to interrupt Don Giovanni's attempt to seduce Zerlina. In her aria, Donna Elvira advises Zerlina to get away from Don Giovanni and pay no attention to his lies. The keyword is "fuggi" ("flee"), and Zerlina does soon flee after Donna Elvira grabs her by the hand.

No. 9 - Quartet for Donna Anna, Donna Elvira, Don Ottavio, and Don Giovanni, "Non ti fidar, o misera"

Donna Anna and Don Ottavio now enter. At first they do not recognize Don Giovanni, who had been visible to them at the time of the Commendatore's murder only in disguise, but they soon are able to identify him. The quartet is a fluid depiction of the unfolding emotions of the various characters. Generally the only ones who sing in parallel motion are Donna Anna and Don Ottavio, who form sort of a "team" that shares the same feelings about most everything. Donna Anna, Donna Elvira, and Don Ottavio mainly try to accuse Don Giovanni of various crimes and character flaws. In response, all that Don Giovanni can do is implore them to keep quiet, lest they all become a public spectacle.

No. 10 - Accompanied recitative for Donna Anna and Don Ottavio and Aria for Donna Anna, "Or sai chi l'onore"

This accompanied recitative is occasioned by Donna Anna's double distress at remembering her father's death and being confronted with his murderer. Donna Anna relates to Don Ottavio the grisly particulars of the manner in which her father died. In her aria, Donna Anna asks her fiancé once again to avenge her father's death and further describes the bloody scene she witnessed. The keyword is "vendetta" ("vengeance") and the setting is marked by a florid vocal style appropriate for noble characters.

No. 11 - Aria of Don Giovanni, "Fin ch'han dal vino"

Leporello argues with Don Giovanni about his misdeeds. Don Giovanni is determined to put them out of his mind and enjoy himself by flirting with peasant girls. In his aria, Don Giovanni orders his servant to prepare a grand banquet. He is certain that it will lead to at least ten seductions. This vocal piece at this spot is often referred to as the "Champagne Aria," even though there is no mention of sparkling wine in the text. Rather, the aria does refer to wine that "sets heads whirling" ("calda la testa" in Italian). This phrase appears to be the basis of the musical setting. It is one of the most favored vocal pieces performed in concert settings by operatic baritones.

No. 12 - Aria of Zerlina, "Batti, batti, bel Masetto"

Masetto is understandably upset with Zerlina (only the intervention of Donna Elvira prevented her from being unfaithful to him). For her part, Zerlina feels terribly guilty. To assuage her guilt, Zerlina invites Masetto to beat her (!). Zerlina's aria features a beautiful solo for cello; the vocal style is simple and tuneful, a perfect reflection of the character's social class. "Come agnellina" ("like a little lamb") are the keywords - Zerlina says that she will submit to Masetto's every blow as humbly as a lamb.

No. 13 - Finale of Act I

It was customary for a comic opera in Mozart's day to include a "buffo finale" at the end of one of the interior acts. By the end, all of the outstanding dramatic conflicts are aired, and two groups of opposing characters finish off by screaming at each other at the top of their lungs. The setting for this finale is a lavish party that Don Giovanni has ordered to be prepared for everyone in the town. At the start, Don Giovanni tries once more to seduce Zerlina, but when Masetto confronts him, he gives up and invites both of them to join the celebrations. Donna Elvira, Don Ottavio, and Donna Anna arrive at the party masked, so that Don Giovanni will not recognize them. Their goal is to have Don Giovanni arrested and brought to justice. Don Giovanni sees them and invites them to come and dance in his ballroom along with the other guests. The dancing is accompanied by the famous "Minuet" from *Don Giovanni*. Incorrigible, Don Giovanni persists in his attempts to seduce Zerlina. At last, Zerlina screams in terror. Donna Elvira, Don Ottavio, and Donna Anna immediately reveal themselves and try to let Zerlina know that they intend to protect her. Donna Elvira, Don Ottavio, Donna Anna, Zerlina, and Masetto form one of the two opposing groups in the buffo finale, and by the end, they all threaten and scream at Don Giovanni. The second group is made up only of Don Giovanni and Leoporello, who say nothing more than they are confused and do not know what to do. But as usual - regardless of the danger posed by mere mortal forces - Don Giovanni is able to escape. He pushes his way through the crowds and reaches safety with Leporello.

ACT II

No. 14 - Duet for Don Giovanni and Leporello, "Eh via, buffone, non mi secar"

At the beginning of this act, Don Giovanni and Leporello are shown in a street in the middle of the night. They sing a short comic duet in which they argue about whether Leoporello should remain in Don Giovanni's employ. Leporello disapproves of Don Giovanni's lifestyle and is tired of being put in danger because of him.

No. 15 - Trio for Leporello, Don Giovanni, and Donna Elvira, "Ah taci, ingiusto core"

Don Giovanni succeeds in mollifying Leporello by giving him some money and offering to lend him his clothes in order that Leporello might try to seduce Donna Elvira's maid disguised as a nobleman. At the beginning of the Terzetto, Donna Elvira is seen in her house and talks down to the dark street from a window. As a joke, Don Giovanni tries to rekindle their romance. Leporello is horrified to see that Donna Elvira still remains responsive.

No. 16 - Song ("Canzonetta") for Don Giovanni, "Deh, vieni alla finestra"

In calling out to Donna Elvira from the street, Don Giovanni's plan was to have Leporello make love to Donna Elvira while still wearing Don Giovanni's clothes, thus freeing him to try to seduce Donna Elvira's maid. Indeed Donna Elvira is fooled by the imposture, and she comes down from the window and leaves with Leporello, believing he is Don Giovanni. Then, Don Giovanni, disguised as Leporello, serenades Donna Elvira's maid, who is still at the window. Don Giovanni's "canzonetta" ("little song") is accompanied by mandolin, considered at the time to be a typically Spanish musical instrument, which makes it one of the most distinctive and well-known set pieces from any Mozart opera. The designation "canzonetta" indicates that the musical setting must have a simple, tuneful vocal line and a "strophic" musical setting. "Strophic" means that the exact same music is repeated for each stanza of text (in this case there are two). The keywords are "consolar il pianto mio" ("console my lament").

No. 17 - Aria of Don Giovanni, "Metà di voi quà vadano"
Don Giovanni, disguised as Leporello, encounters Masetto and a group of peasants who are searching for him in order to kill him. Don Giovanni talks to them as Leporello, and even gives them advice about how to catch "Don Giovanni" (that is, Leporello disguised as Don Giovanni). In his aria, he tells them exactly what their prey will be wearing and what he will be doing.

No. 18 - Aria of Zerlina, "Vedrai carino"
Don Giovanni continues his imposture. He succeeds in taking some weapons from Masetto, starts beating him, and then leaves. Masetto is left to lick his wounds. Zerlina enters to console Masetto. The keywords for her aria are "Che bel rimedio ti voglio dar" ("What a good cure I want to give you"). The vocal style is crafted with the usual simplicity and directness considered suitable for low-class characters.

No. 19 - Sextet for Donna Anna, Donna Elvira, Don Ottavio, Zerlina, Masetto, and Leporello, "Sola, in buio loco"
The scene now changes to a dark courtyard in Donna Anna's house. The listener hears a short recitative and then a long "scena" (the sextet) in which the music depicts the action very closely. At the start, Donna Elvira is still with Leporello, whom she believes to be Don Giovanni. Leporello is tired of pretending, however, and wants to slip away. Donna Anna and Don Ottavio enter, still terribly distraught at the death of the Commendatore. Masetto and Zerlina also appear as Leporello tries to escape quietly. Naturally, Don Giovanni's victims believe that they have found him, and they wish to kill him. Don Ottavio even draws his sword, but in order to save himself, Leporello removes his disguise. The others are thrown into confusion. They have failed once again to apprehend Don Giovanni.

No. 20 - Aria of Leporello, "Ah pietà, Signori miei"
After Leporello reveals himself, Zerlina is angry with him, because she believes he has just beaten Masetto (actually is was Don Giovanni in disguise who did it). For her part, Donna Elvira is angry with Leporello because he tried to make love to her disguised as Don Giovanni. Don Ottavio and Donna Anna believe that the only possible reason for Leporello's disguise is some sort of crime or mischief. All of them want to punish him. In his aria, Leporello pleads for mercy and explains that Don Giovanni put him up to everything.

No. 21 - Aria of Don Ottavio, "Il mio tesoro intanto"
Leporello flees; the others are frustrated, but more certain than ever of Don Giovanni's despicable character. In his aria, Don Ottavio promises Donna Anna once again to bring Don Giovanni to justice. "Consolar" ("console") is the keyword. This vocal piece is one of the greatest Mozart arias written for tenor voice.

No. 22 - Duet for Don Giovanni and Leporello, "O statua gentilissima"
At night, Don Giovanni finds himself hiding in the cemetery where the Commendatore is buried. An equestrian statue of the Commendatore is standing there. Leporello is also present, furious that Don Giovanni's escapades nearly got him killed. Don Giovanni is indifferent; he merely wants to relate more stories about his attempted seductions. Suddenly, the voice of the Commendatore is heard telling Don Giovanni to leave the dead in peace. Leporello and Don Giovanni are confused at first, but then realize that the statue has come to life. In their duet, Leporello expresses fear, Don Giovanni defiance. To prove that he is not afraid of the statue, Don Giovanni asks the statue to come and dine with him. The statue answers, "Yes." Since Don Giovanni and Leporello are never in emotional synchronization, they never sing in parallel motion.

No. 23 - Accompanied recitative and Aria for Donna Anna, "Non mi dir, bell'idol mio"

In a room in Donna Anna's house, Don Ottavio tries to persuade Donna Anna to forget her dead father and concentrate instead on their future happiness together. Donna Anna does not like this idea, nor is she pleased with Don Ottavio for calling her cruel after she objects to the way he has minimized her emotional struggles. In her aria, she tells Don Ottavio not to accuse her of cruelty and reminds him both of her suffering in this difficult time and her love for him. The aria is cast in slow-fast format and contains the most extravagant passagework of any vocal piece in the entire opera as a vehicle for a serious noble character. The keywords in the first part of this aria are "Calma, il tuo tormento" ("Calm your torment"). In the second part, the keyword is "pietà" ("pity"). Donna Anna hopes that heaven will have pity on her one day, so that she might find emotional peace.

No. 24 - Finale of Act II

The finale of this act takes place in a room in Don Giovanni's house. A table has been prepared for supper just in case the statue of the Commendatore does decide to show up.

Don Giovanni has hired a wind band to play music during the supper. He commands the musicians to play, and they respond with a famous series of excerpts of arias from popular comic operas of the 1780s. The first one is a bit of the aria "O quanto un sì bel giubilo" from *Una cosa rara* by Vicente Martín y Soler. Next, the wind band plays a bit of the aria "Come un agnello" from Giuseppe Sarti's *Fra i due litiganti il terzo gode*. These two excerpts are the only music by Martín and Sarti that are ever commonly heard by ordinary opera-goers today. The last excerpt played by the wind band is a section of the aria "Non più andrai" from Mozart's own *Marriage of Figaro*. The quality of the music in the first two excerpts pales in comparison to that from the Mozart aria, and one suspects that the whole point of the idea to include these excerpts was to demonstrate how superior Mozart's music was to his leading rivals.

Don Giovanni and Leporello talk while the music plays. The mood changes when Donna Elvira enters unexpectedly. By this time, Donna Elvira has given up all hope that Don Giovanni will marry her. All that she wants, she says, is for Don Giovanni to change his ways before it is too late. Don Giovanni dismisses her suggestion disdainfully. Donna Elvira prepares to leave, but suddenly she screams, as she has been frightened by the sight of the statue walking towards Don Giovanni's house for supper. Leporello goes to see what made her scream, and he screams himself when he sees the statue coming to the door. He returns to Don Giovanni's house for safety, but there is a loud knock on the door. Under pressure from Don Giovanni, Leporello answers the door to let the statue in. The statue says that he has come for dinner, as he said he would, and that he would like to reciprocate by inviting Don Giovanni to dine with him (the second gesture of the "double invitation" common to many Don Juan dramas). Don Giovanni, who as yet betrays no fear, asks the statue for his hand on it. Once the statue has grasped Don Giovanni's extended hand, it will not let go. The first sign of fear comes when Don Giovanni feels how cold the hand is. Suddenly, the statue tells Don Giovanni to repent his sins. Don Giovanni refuses to do so, even after he is given several opportunities to do so. The statue tells Don Giovanni that his time is up. Flames surround Don Giovanni and a chorus of "spirits" drag him down to hell. The music used to accompany this section is the most characteristic of the opera, brilliantly enhancing the supernatural effects, the sternness of the statue, and Don Giovanni's intransigence. Through it all, Leporello cowers in fear.

The last portion of the Finale was performed only on the opening night in Prague in 1787 and was customarily omitted from productions of the opera until the late 20th century. It was felt that this last portion was overly long and an unnecessary anticlimax after the spectacular scene that precedes it. It does contain beautiful music, however, and it helps to tie up some dramatic loose ends. Once Don Giovanni has been dragged to hell, the flames subside and the other principal characters enter. Not knowing what has just transpired, they arrive at Don Giovanni's house determined to have Don Giovanni arrested. They ask Leporello where he is. Leporello responds by describing the macabre scene he has just witnessed. The other characters conclude that Don Giovanni is now out of their lives, and they explain how they intend to carry on in the future. Don Ottavio wants to marry Donna Anna right away, but Donna Anna tells him that she wants to delay the marriage for a year (apparently

Don Ottavio's earlier attempts to minimize her grief at the death of her father had irritated her more than she let on). Donna Elvira declares that she will retire to a "retreat." Zerlina and Masetto resolve to get along better. Leporello says that he will try to find a better master. At the very end, all together, Don Giovanni's victims fulfill the usual function of final operatic chrouses: they explain the lesson of the drama, which in this case is that evildoers will be punished. The opera concludes with some trifling (but very charming) motives that seem to say to the listener that although some very weighty issues have been explored in this drama (adultery, seduction, rape, murder, and eternal damnation), the audience members should remember that this is merely a theater piece not to be taken *too* seriously.

Interior of the Estates' Theater

Appendix II

La clemenza di Tito:
Survey of the Musical Numbers

Characters:

Tito (Titus) - emperor of Rome [tenor role]
Vitellia - daughter of the emperor Vitellius [soprano role]
Sesto (Sextus) - Vitellia's lover, a friend of Tito [soprano role]
Servilia - Annio's lover, sister of Sesto [soprano role]
Annio (Annius) - Servilia's lover, friend of Sesto [soprano role]
Publio (Publius) - Commander of the Praetorian Guards [bass role]

Original Cast:

Antonio Baglioni (Tito Vespasiano)
Maria Marchetti Fantozzi (Vitellia)
Signora Antonini (Servilia)
Carolina Perini (Sesto)
Domenico Bedini (Annio)
Gaetano Campi (Publio)

The text is a revision by Caterino Mazzolà of one of the less popular librettos of Pietro Metastasio; the original musical setting was composed by Antonio Caldara for the imperial court of Vienna in 1734. The action takes place in Rome in the year 79 AD (the dialogues suggest that the events depicted take place at the beginning of the reign of the emperor Titus).

Short Synopsis:

The dramatic tension in a typical Metastasian libretto is usually created by a single character acting out of evil or out of error. The actions of this character create seemingly insoluble moral dilemmas for the others that are miraculously resolved before the end. Since no evil characters are permitted to remain on stage by the end of a Metastasian drama, the evil character must either be killed off or morally rehabilitated. Moral rehabilitation is infinitely preferred over extermination. Among the standard six principal characters, at least two (and preferably four) are involved in love intrigues that resolve into happy marriages by the end.

    The evil character in *La clemenza di Tito* is Vitellia, daughter of the dethroned and murdered emperor Vitellius (r. 69 AD). Vitellia contrives to murder Tito, a character based on the Emperor Titus (r. 79-81 AD). What motivates Vitellia is a burning desire to avenge her father's death, pursue her own ambitions to rule Rome, and punish Tito for planning to marry Berenice, the daughter of the king of Judea, instead of her. She tries to manipulate her lover Sesto (Sextus) into doing the dirty work for her as a test of love, and Sesto does participate in a plot to assasinate the emperor Titus. When the plot fails, Sesto is caught, but he refuses to reveal Vitellia's complicity. Instead, Sesto confesses sole responsibility and awaits execution. In an extraordinary gesture of magnanimity, Tito pardons Sesto in consideration of their long-standing friendship. As a result, Vitellia becomes so overcome with guilt that she confesses her role in the plot to assassinate the emperor. The emperor is so impressed by her moral rehabilitation that he decides to pardon her as well. In the original drama by Metastasio, marriages are proclaimed at the end for two couples (Vitellia and Sesto/Servilia and Annio), but there is no reference to their marriages in this version in order to focus all the attention on the "clemency of Titus" (in other words, the "clemency of Leopold II").

Musical Numbers

Overture:

Not nearly as popular (or distinctive) as the overtures to *The Marriage of Figaro*, *Don Giovanni*, or *The Magic Flute*, the overture to this opera is frequently performed as a separate concert piece nonetheless. The most interesting motives are some rushing scales that appear in all the parts near the beginning (actually the "transition" of the "exposition" in the sonata-form structure). Connoisseurs notice that it is cast as a sonata form without repeats. A complication that confuses novices is the reversal of the ordering of themes in the "recapitulation": the "second theme" begins the "recapitulation"; the "first theme" is not heard until the interior of the "recapitulation."

ACT I

No. 1 - Duetto for Sesto and Vitellia, "Come ti piace, imponi"
Under pressure, Sesto tells Vitellia that he will do as she wishes regarding her plot to assasinate the emperor Tito. In this two-part duet, the opening slow section depicts Vitellia's bullying of Sesto and his abject submission to her will. In the fast section, the lovers express their emotional anguish together. It is understood that Vitellia's distress derives from the anger and hatred she feels for Tito, whereas Sesto's anguish derives from the moral dilemma he faces in being expected to betray his friend Tito in order to placate Vitellia. The keywords for the musical setting are "un'alma lacerata" ("a wounded soul").

No. 2 - Aria of Vitellia, "Deh, se piacer mi vuoi"
Vitellia hears that Tito no longer plans to marry Berenice, the daughter of the king of Judea, and asks Sesto to postpone the assasination plot against Tito. Sesto is confused and suspicious, uncertain of what to do. The musical setting of Vitellia's aria is cast in two parts. The keywords for the slow section are "lascia i sospetti tuoi" ("cast aside your suspicions"), a soothing admonition to Sesto. The keyword for the fast section is "ingannar" ("to betray"): Vitellia warns Sesto of the consequences of betraying her.

No. 3 - Duettino of Sesto and Annio, "Deh, prendi un dolce amplesso"
After Vitellia departs from the stage, Sesto's friend Annio requests Sesto's aid in order to obtain the emperor's consent to a marriage between Annio and Servilia, Sesto's sister. Sesto replys that he will try. In this small-scale "duettino," there is not enough time to accommodate sections in which the characters sing both separately and together. In this vocal piece, there is only one section in which the two men sing together to intensify the effect of the keywords "dolce amplesso" ("sweet embrace") that evokes the closeness of their friendship.

No. 4 - March
Hardly any eighteenth-century Italian opera in serious style was complete without a march for instruments alone. This one accompanies a ceremony in which Tito is greeted by the populace of Rome and envoys from subject provinces. It is repeated after the chorus that follows.

No. 5 - Chorus, "Serbate, o Dei custodi"
In this simple declamatory chorus, the Roman people hail Tito as a strong and just ruler. It is repeated after Annio and Publio (the commander of the Praetorian Guards) heap praise and flattery upon the emperor.

No. 6 - Aria of Tito, "Del più sublime soglio"
At this point, Tito has decided to marry Servilia (Sesto's sister and Annio's lover) and raise Sesto to the highest office possible within the empire. Sesto protests that Tito is too generous, but Tito in his aria replies that generosity is the "sole fruit" of his "sublime throne." "Sublime" is the keyword for the musical setting.

No. 7 - Duetto of Servilia and Annio, "Ah, perdona al piano affetto"
Since Tito has decided to marry Servilia, she can no longer hope to marry her lover Annio. The duet expresses the emotional distress felt by the two lovers who must abandon all prospect of sharing their lives together. The keywords are "mia dolce, cara speme" ("my sweet dear hope"). The structure is typical: first the lovers sing separately, then together.

No. 8 - Aria of Tito, "Ah, se fosse intorno al trono"
Tito is so moved when Servilia tells him of her love for Annio that he permits them to marry after all. In his aria, Tito tells Servilia that ruling an empire would bring him nothing but happiness if only all of his subjects were as honest and sincere as she is. The keyword is "felicità" ("happiness").

No. 9 - Aria of Sesto, "Parto, ma tu ben mio"
Unwilling to wait and see whether Tito will marry her now that Servilia has been released from her obligation to do so, Vitellia ruthlessly pressures Sesto to assassinate the emperor. In his aria, Sesto declares the he will do whatever she wishes and hopes that by doing so he will create more peace between them. The aria is cast in slow-fast format with an elaborate solo for clarinet that was played in the original performance by Mozart's friend Anton Stadler. The keywords for the slow section are "ritorna in pace" ("return in peace"), "vendicarti io volo" ("I fly to avenge you") for the fast section.

No. 10 - Terzetto of Vitellia, Annio, and Publio, "Vengo, aspettate"
Vitellia has learned from Publio and Annio that Tito is coming to inform her that he has decided to marry her. Horrified, she realizes that it is too late to stop Sesto from setting in motion the plot to assassinate the emperor. In the terzetto, Vitellia is so emotionally distraught that she can barely formulate a complete sentence. Annio and Publio, who do not know the real reason for her distress, attribute it to her anxiety on being chosen empress. The disconnect between the feelings of Annio and Publio and those of Vitellia is depicted by having Annio and Publio sing in parallel motion with motives appropriate for the keyword "contento" ("content"), whereas Vitellia's vocal part is a counterpoint based on the keywords "O insano mio furor" ("O, my insane fury").

No. 11 - Accompanied recitative for Sesto, "Oh Dei, che smania è questa"
Sesto's emotional pain at having to grapple with conflicting loyalties at this point in the drama was deemed sufficiently significant to warrant a section of accompanied recitative. There is no overall form; rather the ever-changing emotions of the character are depicted in a fluid way as the text unfolds. While Sesto sings, a fire in the Capitol is noticeable, an indication that a revolt against Tito is underway.

No. 12 - Finale with Chorus, "Deh, conservate, oh Dei!"

This finale was introduced in imitation of the finales that typically appear at the end of interior acts of comic operas. All characters participate except for Tito, whose whereabouts and survival are uncertain. Confusion reigns in everyone's thoughts, except those of Sesto, who is responsible for putting the revolt into motion; nobody else knows who had the fire started or the reason why it was done. The only thing the others can think of is the need to flee for their lives. The keywords for the entire finale are "giorno di dolor" ("day of sorrow").

ACT II

No. 13 - Aria of Annio, "Torni di Tito a lato"

Annio tells Sesto (to his amazement) that the emperor Tito has not died in the revolt against him. Sesto now reveals to his friend Annio that he was the instigator of the plot. In his aria, Annio advises Sesto to make amends with Tito and renew his vows of loyalty. "Emenda" ("make amends") is the keyword.

No. 14 - Terzetto for Vitellia, Sesto, and Publio, "Se a volto mai ti senti"

Vitellia advises Sesto to flee Rome in order to save his life and keep her own complicity in the plot to murder the emperor secret. Although he is willing to keep her secret, Sesto refuses to leave Rome. Publio soon arrives to arrest him. In the terzetto, there is no singer whose emotions are in synchronization with those of any other character, except at the very end, when Vitellia and Sesto accuse Publio of cruelty in having Sesto arrested. In the earlier portions of the terzetto, Sesto expresses his undying love for Vitellia; Vitellia tortures herself for putting Sesto in jeopardy and taking no blame for her own actions; Publio regrets that he must do his duty and arrest Sesto.

No. 15 - Chorus, "Ah, grazie si rendano al sommo fattor"

In another simple declamatory chorus, the Roman populace rejoices that Tito has been delivered from harm. Tito expresses his gratitude.

No. 16 - Aria of Publio, "Tardi, s'avvede d'un tradimento"

Tito cannot believe that Sesto would betray him. In this aria, Publio comments on Tito's gullibility, remarking that one who has never betrayed anyone himself would never expect to be betrayed by another. This modest aria, sung by the least important character, has a very simple vocal part without a strong keyword.

No. 17 - Aria of Annio, "Tu fosti tradito"

Annio begs mercy from Tito on behalf of Sesto once it is learned that Sesto has confessed his guilt. In his aria, Annio expresses his hope that Tito will not insist on the death penalty for his friend. "Sperar" ("to hope") is the keyword.

No. 18 - Terzetto of Sesto, Tito, and Publio, "Quello di Tito è il volto"

Shocked at Sesto's betrayal, Tito decrees that he must die. In the terzetto, the emotions of the characters unfold in a fluid way, with fresh musical depictions appearing in turn (first Sesto's fear, then Tito's anger, and finally Publio's recognition of how difficult it must be to have one's friend executed). By the end, Tito and Publio are in emotional synchronization, observing how frightened Sesto seems.

No. 19 - Rondò of Sesto, "Deh, per questo istante solo"

Sesto tells Tito that he is deserving of death, but he hopes that Tito will remember their former love for one another. This vocal piece is set as a slow-fast rondo. "Duolo" ("grief") is the keyword for the slow section, "tormenta" ("torments") the keyword for the fast section.

No. 20 - Aria of Tito, "Se all'impero, amici Dei"
Tito decides to tear up the warrant for Sesto's execution. He is too kind-hearted to carry out the sentence, but is still not prepared to announce his decision publicly. In his aria, Tito emphasizes the need for ruthlessness in a ruler, but recognizes that he does not embody this quality. He asks the gods either to take away his empire or change his clement nature. The keywords are "severo cor" ("a hard heart"). The aria is cast in a three-part form with a slow middle section that sets the second stanza of text in which Tito claims that he would rather earn loyalty from love than from fear.

No. 21 - Aria of Servilia, "S'altro che lagrime"
Servilia observes that Vitellia has the power to save Sesto's life by appealing to Tito, who is about to make Vitellia his empress. In her aria, Servilia urges Vitellia to intercede with Tito; tears alone will not help Sesto. The keyword is "piangere" ("to weep").

No. 22 - Accompanied recitative for Vitellia, "Ecco il punto, o Vitellia"
In this emotionally charged musical section, Vitellia decides to confess her role in instigating the plot against Tito, even though her confession will make it impossible for her to become empress.

No. 23 - Rondò of Vitellia, "Non più di fiori"
Vitellia laments the loss of a throne and her likely imprisonment and execution. There is no obvious keyword for the slow section of her rondò, but in the fast section, "pietà" ("pity") seems the obvious choice. This vocal piece includes a magnificent solo for basset horn (tenor clarinet) that was performed by Mozart's friend Anton Stadler at the première.

No. 24 - Chorus, "Che del ciel"
This chorus takes the form of a hymn of praise for the deliverance of Tito heard at the public ceremony in which the fate of Sesto is to be announced.

No. 25 - Accompanied recitative for Tito, "Ma, che giorno è mai questo"
After Vitellia publicly confesses her guilt to the Roman populace, Tito decides to pardon all conspirators, so impressed is he by the honesty of Vitellia and the willingness of Sesto to conceal Vitellia's guilt even under threat of execution.

No. 26 - Sextet and chorus, "Tu, di ver, m'assolvi Augusto"
It was traditional to end eighteenth-century Italian serious operas with a chorus that expresses joy at the resolution of the outstanding dramatic conflicts, often with an explanation of the moral lessons learned along the way. Sesto vows never again to betray the sovereign's trust; Tito singles out Sesto for his extraordinary repentance; Vitellia, Servilia, and Annio are amazed at the magnanimity of the emperor of Rome. The chorus invokes the gods to protect Rome and its emperor. No marriages are proclaimed so as not to detract from the attention drawn to Tito's generosity.

Appendix III

Sites in Prague Visited by Mozart
(that can be seen today)

Estates' Theater/Stavovské Divadlo, Ovocný trh 1, Old City (Staré Město, Prague 1), across from the Carolinum at the west end of the Ovocný trh ("the fruit market"). This theater, also known as the Nostic (Nostitz) Theater, the National Theater, and the Tyl Theater (during the Communist period), was the center of musical life in Prague in Mozart's day. It was built in 1783 at the expense of Count Franz Anton von Nostic, who wished for Prague a civic theater as grand as those he had seen in other great European cities. A plaque on the façade proclaims its dedication "Patriae et Musae" ("to the fatherland and the muses"). This handsome building was constructed in a distinctive neo-classical style that is a bit rare for Prague. In Mozart's day, it featured performances of plays, operas, and instrumental music; it remains the only theater in the world in which a Mozart opera was first performed that still operates as a public theater. One of the first operas ever performed there was Mozart's *The Abduction from the Seraglio*, the very work that stimulated the first great interest in Mozart's music in Prague. Late in 1786, *The Marriage of Figaro* was performed there with extraordinary success, and subsequent performances in January and September of 1787 were attended by Mozart himself. It was the site of the first performances of the "Prague" Symphony (in January of 1787), the opera *Don Giovanni* (in October of 1787), and the opera *La clemenza di Tito* (in September of 1791).

Bertamka, Mozartova 169 (Smíchov, Prague 5). In Mozart's day, this villa was owned by the composer František Dušek and his wife, the singer Josefa Dušek (who had just purchased it in 1784), and it remained in their possession until František's death in 1799. It is named for a previous owner, one František Bertram. Originally built in the seventeenth century by a wealthy brewer, it has undergone several renovations, one necessitated by the near complete destruction of the building by fire in 1871. In Mozart's day, it was outside the city walls of Prague and considered a country residence. Now it is located in a traditional working-class district of Prague. Much Mozart literature and many Prague guidebooks seem eager to assert that Mozart stayed there habitually while in Prague (some with the claim that he spent at least some time there during all three of his extended visits), but in fact, Mozart himself never mentioned staying there, and there are no eyewitness accounts of anyone ever seeing him there. No claim that he ever stayed there dates from before the 1820s. The most reliable evidence that Mozart did visit the Bertramka villa at least once comes from a description of the circumstances of the composition "Bella mia fiamma, addio"/ "Resta, o cara," K. 528, for Josefa Dušek during the autumn of 1787, left by his son Karl (see Chapters 7 and 12). Even if Karl Mozart's story is not accurate in all respects, it is very unlikely that he would have been mistaken in reporting that his father at least visited the villa, considering the close ties to the Dušek family that his mother cultivated in the 1790s (a time when he himself was resident in Prague). The present site is taken up entirely by a museum devoted to Mozart that includes many fascinating exhibits and the beautiful grounds that surround it.

Strahov Abbey, Strahovské nádvoří 132 (entrance also at Pohořelec 8), Hradčany (Castle District, Prague 1). The Strahov Abbey was originally founded in the twelfth century, but the present structure was built in the late seventeenth century. It now houses the Památník Národního Písemnictví (Memorial of National Literature), the Church of the Assumption, and the magnificent Philosophical Library. Mozart visited the Church of the Assumption in the autumn of 1787 with

Josefa Dušek and performed an extraordinary improvisation on its organ that was partially transcribed by the canon of the church, Norbert Lehmann (see Chapter 7).

Inn "Zum Goldenen Einhorn" ("Golden Unicorn Inn"/"U zlatého jednorožce"), Lázeňská 11, Malá Strana (Lesser Side, Prague 1). Mozart visited this inn (but did not stay overnight) in April of 1789 during his trip to Berlin and Dresden with Prince Karl von Lichnowsky. It was considered at the time to be the finest inn in the city (see Chapter 7). In 1796, Beethoven stayed there, also in the company of Prince Lichnowsky. A plaque commemorates Beethoven's visit, but not Mozart's.

Klementinum, Mariánské náměstí 5, Staré Město (Old City, Prague 1). The former Jesuit college in Prague erected in the mid-seventeenth century. On 14 January 1787, Mozart visited the Royal and Imperial Library (now the National Library) and the General Theological Seminary. Most of the building is now used by the National Library and is not open to the general public. Without special arrangements, it is possible to see little else of the interior than the beautiful Church of the Holy Savior (Svatý Salvátor) and the Hall of Mirrors (Zrcadlová síň), where musical concerts are frequently given.

Amazing as it may seem, the five structures listed above are the only ones remaining in Prague that Mozart certainly visited (and Bertramka might best be excluded by the list since there are few traces of the structure from Mozart's time remaining). In spite of many reports in musicological literature and guidebooks to Prague, there is no proof that Mozart ever stayed in the Inn "Zu den Drei Goldenen Löwen" ("Three Golden Lions' Inn"/"U tří lvičků"), Uhelný trh ("coal market") 1 in the Old City. There is no reason to believe that an inn with that name even existed in Prague in 1787, and no assertion that Mozart stayed there dates from before the 1820s (see Chapter 7). Reports that Lorenzo Da Ponte stayed at the Inn "Zum Platteis," Uhelný trh 11, in the Old City, are completely unreliable, none dating from before the 1860s (see Chapter 6). As documented in Chapter 5, the carnival ball that Mozart attended in January 1787 almost certainly took place in the Wussin house in the Old City (long ago demolished), and not the Konvikt, Bartolomějská 11 and Karmelitská 24 in the Old City. There is also no particular reason to believe that Mozart ever visited the Pachta Palace in the Old City (Anenské náměstí 5), for reasons discussed in Chapter 5. It is true nonetheless that Mozart would have shown a remarkable lack of curiosity had he never visited sites such as Prague Castle and the Church of St. Nicholas in Malá Strana, as well as many other beautiful buildings in the city that were already in existence in Mozart's day.

Among structures no longer in existence, there are only nineteenth-century legends to suggest that Mozart frequented the "Neues Wirtshaus" ("New Inn", later called the inn "Zum goldenen Engel"/"The Golden Angel"/"U zlatého anděla"), until recently located on Celetná 29 in the Old City, and a tavern on Templová lane in the Old City that was once fashionable (see Chapter 7). One of the most frequently-encountered errors in guidebooks to Prague is the claim that Mozart stayed in the Thun Palace at Thunovská 14 in Malá Strana (presently the site of the British Embassy). This palace once belonged to the host for Mozart's first stay in Prague in 1787, Count Johann Joseph von Thun-Hohenstein, but he no longer owned it by that time (see Chapter 5). The site of the Thun palace that Mozart did stay at in January of 1787 is now occupied by an early nineteenth-century palace at Sněmovní 4, Malá Strana; the original palace was destroyed by fire in 1794. The site of the Noble Ladies' Foundation in the New City (Na nemocnice 2) has been extensively remodeled since Mozart's putative visit to the site in 1787 (see Chapter 5). It is completely unknown what parts (if any) of the existing structure Mozart may have entered, and one might question the accuracy of claims that he actually did play on a piano once owned by the foundation. There is no reason to believe that he visited the Noble Ladies' Foundation in Prague Castle.

Appendix IV

The Blood of the Přemyslids

Considering that there has been no native Czech king in the Bohemian lands since 1471, it may well come as a surprise to readers of this volume that the blood of the rulers of the original medieval Czech state runs through the veins of all seven of the remaining European monarchs. Royal genealogists are well aware of how durable a number of exotic and obscure royal blood lines are, but the extent to which the blood of the Czech Přemyslid dynasty permeates the royal houses of Europe remains almost completely unacknowledged.

Ruling houses all over Europe during the Middle Ages used marriages to cement military alliances or ease political tensions with neighboring political entities. Occasionally, however, matches were made with brides from very distant locations when certain rulers felt that the possibilities with neighboring powers were exhausted or that completely new blood was needed to revitalize a dynasty. One of the most extraordinary matches ever made was between King Henry I of France and Anna Yaroslavna, daughter of Yaroslav the Wise, Grand Prince of Kiev. Anna's marriage to Henry in 1052 brought a dose of Slavic blood into the lineage of all later French rulers. Princesses from western Europe could also find their way east. Princess Gytha of Wessex, for example, the daughter of King Harold II of England (defeated and killed at the Battle of Hastings by William the Conqueror in 1066), married into the same Kievan dynasty that Anna Yaroslavna came from.

The establishment of a Czech state in the late ninth century AD by Duke Bořivoj I, the first Přemyslid ruler known by name to emerge in the Bohemian lands, created similar opportunities for his descendants as soon as it became clear that military alliances with the duchy of Bohemia could be advantageous. The political importance of the Czech state was enhanced when the Přemyslid duchy was raised to the rank of a kingdom by the Holy Roman Emperor, first on a non-hereditary basis during the reigns of Vratislav II (1085-1092) and Vladislav II (1158-1172), and then on a permanent hereditary basis during the reign of Otakar I (1198-1230). The direct male line of the Přemyslid rulers died out in the year 1306, but the blood of Přemyslid princesses continued to disseminate among the royal houses of Europe. Under two dynasties of foreign origins (the Luxemburgs between 1310 and 1437 and the Jagiellons between 1471 and 1526), the royal family of Bohemia was also considered a prime source for dynastic alliances. The most famous marriage that resulted from negotiations with the kings of Bohemia was that between King Richard II of England and Anne of Bohemia, the daughter of Charles IV, king of Bohemia and Holy Roman Emperor, in 1382. Her husband was emotionally devastated when she died in 1394, and the affection showed her by the English people was reminiscent of that accorded her predecessor Princess Markéta in early thirteenth-century Denmark (with whom Anne shared an inability to continue the dynasty into which she had married). Princesses from the powerful kingdom of Bohemia were so desirable for so many centuries that even a daughter of George of Poděbrady, the last native Czech king (r. 1458-1471), could be married off to Matthias Corvinus, an illustrious king of Hungary, even though George was a "heretical" Hussite of non-royal birth.

The most enduring Přemyslid blood lines were founded by Princess Doubravka of Bohemia (d. 977), a great-granddaughter of Duke Bořivoj I and niece of the childless Duke Václav I (r. 921-935), the famous "Good King Wenceslas" of the Christmas carol. Princess Doubravka was married off to a neighboring ruler, Mieszko I, Duke of Poland, in 965. The descendants of Mieszko and Doubravka mainly married into neighboring ruling families for generations, and the connection with the Přemyslids was strengthened by the marriage in 1080 of Princess Jitka of Bohemia, daughter of Vratislav II, to Duke Władysław I of Poland, a great-great-grandson of Mieszko and Doubravka. But in the year 1152, Princess Richeza, daughter of Duke Władysław II of Poland and great-granddaughter of Władysław I, was married to the very distant King Alfonso VII of León and Castile. This alliance did the most to plant the blood of the Přemyslids into western Europe. Richeza's daughter Sancha of Castile is a direct ancestor of Queen Elizabeth II of the United Kingdom and the Scandinavian monarchs

Margrethe II of Denmark, Carl XVI Gustaf of Sweden, and Harald V of Norway through Sancha's great-great-grandson King Philip IV (the Fair) of France (r. 1285-1314) and his grandson King Edward III of England (r. 1327-1377). King Juan Carlos of Spain is descended from Sancha through many Iberian lines, as is Philippe, King of the Belgians, a great-great-grandson of the Infanta Maria Josepha of Portugal.

The Přemyslid descent of King Willem-Alexander of the Netherlands comes courtesy of Princess Ludmila of Bohemia, a daughter of Duke Bedřich (d. 1189) and direct descendant of Dukes Bořivoj I and Boleslav the Cruel. Her marriage to Ludwig I, Duke of Bavaria, in 1204 eventually brought Přemyslid blood into the house of Hohenzollern, and from there into the ruling families of the Netherlands and Russia, besides Brandenburg, Prussia, and Germany.

The Hapsburg emperors who are remembered as the oppressors of the Czechs were descended from the Přemyslids in several lines, the closest ones through two daughters of King Otakar II (d. 1305): Alžběta and Markéta. The first Hapsburg king of Bohemia who was able to establish a lasting blood line, Ferdinand I (r. 1526-1564), was not descended from them (rather from Sancha of Castile), but his wife, Anne of Bohemia, sister of the last Jagiellon king of Bohemia, was descended from them through her grandmother Elizabeth of Austria, the wife of King Casimir IV of Poland. She also transmitted the blood of the Luxemburg rulers of Bohemia from her great-grandmother Alžběta, who was one of the granddaughters of Charles IV. Ferdinand's son Maximilian and all later Hapsburg rulers were thus descended from Otakar II - and ultimately, the ninth-century Duke Bořivoj.

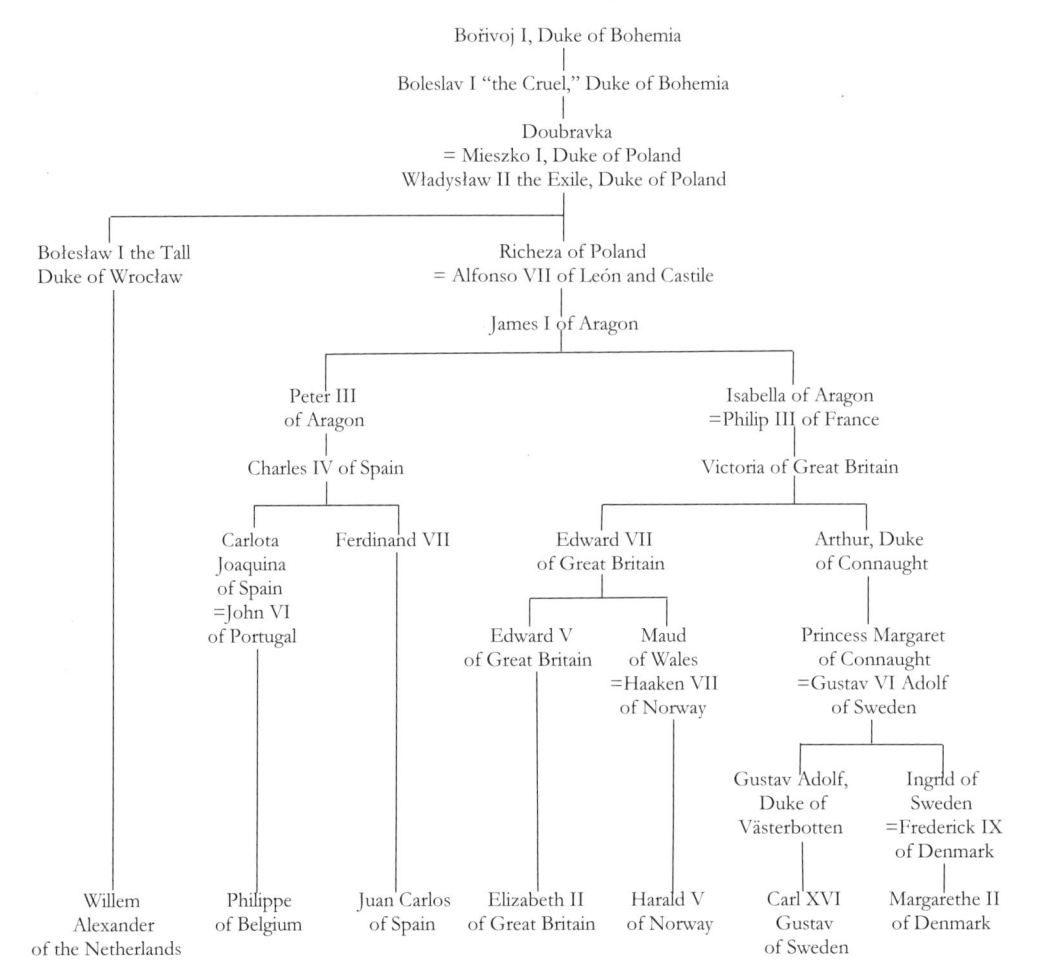

Bořivoj I, Duke of Bohemia
|
Boleslav I "the Cruel," Duke of Bohemia
|
Doubravka
= Mieszko I, Duke of Poland
Władysław II the Exile, Duke of Poland

Bolesław I the Tall
Duke of Wrocław

Richeza of Poland
= Alfonso VII of León and Castile

James I of Aragon

Peter III of Aragon

Isabella of Aragon
=Philip III of France

Charles IV of Spain

Victoria of Great Britain

Carlota Joaquina of Spain
=John VI of Portugal

Ferdinand VII

Edward VII of Great Britain

Arthur, Duke of Connaught

Edward V of Great Britain

Maud of Wales
=Haaken VII of Norway

Princess Margaret of Connaught
=Gustav VI Adolf of Sweden

Gustav Adolf, Duke of Västerbotten

Ingrid of Sweden
=Frederick IX of Denmark

Willem Alexander of the Netherlands

Philippe of Belgium

Juan Carlos of Spain

Elizabeth II of Great Britain

Harald V of Norway

Carl XVI Gustav of Sweden

Margrethe II of Denmark

Notes

Introduction

P. 1 - Good resources in English for concise information about the circumstances surrounding Mozart's death and burial include H. C. Robbins Landon, *1791: Mozart's Last Year* (New York: Schirmer Books, 1988), 148-71, and Maynard Solomon, *Mozart: A Life* (New York: HarperCollins, 1995), 483-502. A much more comprehensive consideration of the matter is found in William Stafford, *Mozart's Death: A Corrective Survey of the Legends* (London: Macmillan, 1991). The most important source that establishes weather conditions in Vienna on the day of Mozart's burial is the diary of Count Johann Karl von Zinzendorf (who recorded daily weather conditions wherever he was). His observation of "mild weather and frequent mist" in Vienna on 6 December 1791 is recorded in Otto Erich Deutsch, ed., *Mozart: A Documentary Biography*, translated by Eric Blom, Peter Branscombe, and Jeremy Noble (Stanford: Stanford University Press, 1965), 418. Deutsch's original German version of this compilation is entitled *Mozart: die Dokumente seines Lebens* (Kassel: Bärenreiter, 1961). For the benefit of the English-language readers of this text, citations in later chapters will be provided only for the English translation (subsequent editions published after 1965 preserve the original pagination). Count Zinzendorf's report contradicts later legends that held the day of Mozart's burial in Vienna to be a rainy day.

The most detailed information concerning the first commemoration in Prague of Mozart's death derives from the leading newspaper in the city at the time, the *K. K. Prager Oberpostamtszeitung* ("the newspaper of the supreme royal and imperial post office of Prague"), which is referred to informally throughout this volume as the *Prague Post*. Most of the passages in this newspaper that mention music and music-making in the eighteenth century are transcribed in Jiří Berkovec, *Musicalia v pražském periodickém tisku 18. století* [Musicalia in Prague periodical publications of the eighteenth century] (Prague: Státní Knihovna ČSR, 1989). The report of Mozart's memorial on 14 December 1791 is transcribed on pp. 77-79; it is reproduced in facsimile in Tomislav Volek and Ivan Bittner, *The Mozartiana of Czech and Moravian Archives* (Prague: Interior Ministry, 1991), 17-19.

P. 2 - The quotation of Da Ponte about Prague is drawn from his second collection of memoirs (the memoirs of 1823) and appears in the *Memoirs of Lorenzo Da Ponte*, translated by Elisabeth Abbott (Philadelphia: J. B. Lippincott, 1929; repr. New York: Da Capo Press, 1988), 231-32.

At least one example of the patronizing attitudes about cultural life in eighteenth-century Prague and the Bohemian lands from the days before the Velvet Revolution is called for. In Andrew Steptoe's *The Mozart-Da Ponte Operas* (Oxford: Clardendon Press, 1988), 116-17, the author took no trouble to investigate the nature of musical life in Prague in explaining the circumstances of the first performance there of the opera *Don Giovanni*. Rather, he relied on two sketchy accounts of general conditions in the city written by eighteenth-century English travelers (John Moore and Hester Lynch Piozzi) who were not interested in music or theater, to propagate a supercilious and uninformed characterization of Prague as a provincial backwater for whom the vulgar traditions of the Don Juan tale were perfectly suited. In fact, Prague in the 1780s was host to a wealthy and cultivated social elite, could boast the highest level of musical literacy of any major city in Europe, and supported one of the finest opera orchestras ever assembled up to that time. A view of Prague as culturally backward - while its residents exhibited a unique understanding of the merits of Mozart's music - forms an inherent incongruity in Steptoe's study that seems never to have occurred to the author. Although Piozzi's fascinating account of a visit to Prague in 1786 is transcribed nearly in full in Chapter 2, the account of Steptoe's other informant, John Moore, in his *A View of Society and Manners in France, Switzerland and Germany*, vol. 2 (London, 1779), 290-99, has not been excerpted, since it is so uninteresting in comparison to those of many other observers. It neither contradicts nor supplements their testimony in any significant way.

P. 3 - The full bibliographic citation for the Nettl study is Paul Nettl, *Mozart in Böhmen* (Prague: Neumann, 1938). In spite of its usefulness as a source of information about Mozart's connections with Prague, it has never been reprinted in German or translated into English.

Paul Nettl was a distinguished musicologist about whom personal information can be found in standard music dictionaries such as the revised *New Grove Dictionary of Music and Musicians* (London: Macmillan, 2001) and its online equivalent *Oxford Music Online*. Additional information about his family recorded here originates from Paul Nettl's son, the renowned ethnomusicologist Bruno Nettl, who was one of author's teachers.

The full bibliographic citations for the studies by Procházka and Sallfellner are Rudolph Freiherr Procházka, *Mozart in Prag* (Prague, 1892), and Harald Salfellner, *Mozart und Prag* (Prague and Furth im Wald: Vitalis, 2000).

One should not be fooled by the titles of two works in Czech that appear to offer comprehensive treatments of the topic Mozart in Prague: Karel Koval, *Mozart v Praze: Hudební kronika z let 1787-1791* [Mozart in Prague: a musical chronicle from the years 1787-1791] (Prague: Svobodné Slovo, 1957), and Tomislav Volek, *Mozart a Praha* (Prague: Editio Supraphon, 1973). The latter is merely a short illustrated handbook, the former a work of fiction.

Chapter 1

P. 7 - The authors of most biographies of Casanova have not been comfortable working with the research materials needed to evaluate the last years of his life in Bohemia, including two recent ones in English: Derek Parker, *Casanova* (Stroud: Sutton, 2002) and Ian Kelly, *Casanova: Actor, Lover, Priest, Spy* (New York: Jeremy P. Tarcher, 2008). Earlier studies such as J. Rives Childs, *Casanova: A New Perspective* (New York: Paragon House, 1988), and Thomas Schäfer, *Casanova: Magier, Gelehter, Abenteuer* (Leipzig: Militzke Verlag) are no better in this respect. There is a Czech biography, however, that fully illuminates his life in rural Bohemia: Josef Polišenský, *Casanova a jeho svět* [Casanova and his world] (Prague: Akademia, 1997). Nettl, *Mozart in Böhmen*, makes a specialty of highlighting Casanova's connections to the cultural life of Prague, including his presence in the city in October 1787 during the preparations for the première of Mozart's *Don Giovanni*. A short separate study by Paul Nettl in English is "Casanova and *Don Giovanni*," *Saturday Review* 39 (21 January 1956): 44-45, 55-56. Nettl discovered drafts of unproduced scenes for *Don Giovanni* written by Casanova that are transcribed in *Mozart in Böhmen*, 146-48. There is no reason to believe, however, that Casanova worked closely with Da Ponte in crafting the libretto for *Don Giovanni*. A recent discussion of these drafts is provided in Hans Ernst Weidinger, "The Dux Drafts: Casanova's Contribution to Da Ponte's and Mozart's *Don Giovanni*," *Maske und Kothurn* 52/4 (2006): 95-130.

P. 8 - Good summaries of the history of the Bohemian lands in English have long been scarce, although two useful studies have appeared in the last decade: Hugh Agnew, *The Czechs and the Lands of the Bohemian Crown* (Stanford: Hoover Institution Press, 2004), and William M. Mahoney, *The History of the Czech Republic and Slovakia* (Santa Barbara: Greenwood, 2011). The latter concentrate their coverage on Czech history after the eighteenth century, which is of far greater interest to a general readership than events that took place in earlier periods. Still valuable is a much older study in English: R. W. Seton-Watson, *A History of the Czech and Slovaks* (London and New York: Hutchinson, 1943), which provides more coverage to the period discussed here than the surveys of Agnew and Mahoney. A notable study in English of the Hapsburg monarchy during the time of Mozart's visits to Prague is Charles Ingrao, *The Hapsburg Monarcy, 1618-1815* (Cambridge: Cambridge University Press, 2000). Recent surveys of the history of the Bohemian lands in Czech include Otto Urban, *České a slovanské dějiny do roku 1918* [The history of the Czechs and Slovaks to the year 1918] (Prague: Nakladatelství Aleš Skřivan, 2000) and Jaroslav Pánek and Oldřich Tůma, *Dějiny českých zemí* [The history of the Czech lands] (Prague: Karolinum, 2008). In German, there is Jörg K. Hoensch, *Geschichte Böhmens* (Munich: C. H. Beck, 1987). Larry Wolff, *Inventing Eastern Europe: The Map of Civilization on the Mind of the Enlightenment* (Stanford: Stanford University Press, 1994) treats the Bohemian lands as part of eastern Europe for the purpose of evaluating the attitudes of western European literati towards the Slavs.

Although the earliest rulers of the Bohemian state are referred to as "dukes" in most English-language literature, the title used by the Czechs themselves is "prince" ("kníže"); thus the political entity they ruled is more properly referred to as a "principality" rather than a "duchy."

Duke Wenceslas was a grandson of Bořivoj I, the first documented ruler of a Bohemian state, who lived in the second half of the ninth century AD. It is little known among royal genealogists that Bořivoj was one of the great progenitors of Europe; all of the monarchs of the seven remaining European kingdoms are descended from him (see Appendix IV).

P. 13 - Agnew, *The Czechs and the Lands of the Bohemian Crown*, 72, provides these statistics concerning population loss for the province of Bohemia: a drop from about 1.7 million in 1618 to about 950,000 in 1650; for Moravia, a drop during the same period from about 900,000 to 600,000. Josef Petráň, *Počátky českého národního obrození: společnost a kultura v 70. až 90. letech 18. století* [The beginnings of the Czech national revival: society and cultural from the 1770s to the 1790s] (Prague: Academia, 1990), 12-15, provides a detailed breakdown of population information for all the territories of the Bohemian crown.

The remarks about Bohemia in the *Encyclopédie* are found in vol. 2 (Paris, 1751), 294, col. 2.

Quotations from Nugent in this volume are drawn from the second edition (London, 1756): *The Grand Tour: Containing an Exact Description of Most of the Cities, Towns, and Remarkable Places of Europe*. The section devoted to Bohemia, Moravia, and Silesia is found in vol. 2, 12-18; beer is praised on p. 13.

A unique study in English devoted to political conditions in the Bohemian lands during the eighteenth century (with special emphasis on the events of the brief reign of Leopold II) is Robert Kerner, *Bohemia in the Eighteenth Century* (New York: Macmillan, 1932; repr. Orono, Me: Academic International, 1969). A recent study in Czech somewhat equivalent to Kerner's is Roman Vondra, *České země v letech 1705-1792: věk absolutismu, osvícenství, paruk a třírohých klobouků* [The Bohemian lands in the years 1705-1792: an age of absolutism, enlightenment, periwigs, and three-cornered hats] (Prague: Nakladatelství Libri, 2010).

P. 14 - The character of the Bohemian nobility of the eighteenth century and its relations with the Hapsburg rulers is explored extensively in a recent study in English: Rita Krueger, *Czech, German, and Noble: Status and National Identity in Hapsburg Bohemia* (New York: Oxford University Press, 2009). Vondra, *České země v letech 1705-1792*, 289-300, offers a more concise discussion, whereas Ivo Cerman, *Šlechtická kultura v 18. století: filozofové, mystici, politici* [Aristocratic culture in the eighteenth century: philosophers, mystics, politicians] (Prague: Nakladatelství lidové noviny, 2011), is far more detailed. A companion in English to Cerman's study is a series of essays: Ivo Cerman et al., eds., *The Enlightenment in Bohemia: Religion, Morality, and Multiculturism* (Oxford: Voltaire Foundation, 2011. All of these studies (except Vondra's) generally ignore musical patronage, which was one of the most significant cutural activities of eighteenth-century Bohemian nobles.

P. 15 - Eduard Maur, *12.5.1743, Marie Terezie: korunovace na usmířenou* [Maria Theresa's critical date of 12 May 1743: a coronation of reconciliation] (Prague: Havran, 2003), is a study devoted to the political events surrounding Maria Theresa's coronation as Queen of Bohemia in 1743, which was tainted by an atmosphere of suspicion and ill will. Eila Hassenpflug-Elzholz, *Böhmen und die böhmischen Stände in der Zeit des beginnenden Zentralismus* (Munich: R. Oldenbourg Verlag, 1982) offers a very detailed profile of the Bohemian nobility of the mid-eighteenth century.

Hapsburg policies concerning the taxation of the Bohemian lands during the eighteenth century are documented in detail in Kerner, *Bohemia in the Eighteenth Century*, 226-272. Vondra, *České země v letech 1705-1792*, 78-86, also provides documentation concerning the heavy taxation imposed after the War of the Austrian Succession and the effects of Maria Theresa's administrative reforms.

The reform policies pursued by Joseph II in Bohemia are described in Kerner, *Bohemia in the Eighteenth Century*, 22-52 and 226-361; Seton-Watson, *The History of the Czech and Slovaks*, 147-59; Agnew, *The Czechs and the Lands of the Bohemian Crown*, 90-92; and Vondra, *České země v letech 1705-1792*, 97-131.

P. 16 - The memoirs of Count Kaspar von Sternberg were published in Prague in 1868 under the title *Leben des Grafen Kaspar Sternberg*. In his preface, Palacký included a biographical sketch and an explanation of how the memoirs were written in stages.

The original text of the passage translated from the Sternberg memoirs is found in the *Leben des Grafen Kaspar Sternberg*, 27-28.

P. 17 - The quotation from Nugent is taken from *The Grand Tour*, 2nd ed., vol. 2, 14-15. Baron Pöllnitz's observations from his visit of 1729 are set forth in the *Mémoires de Charles-Louis, baron de Pollnitz, contenant les observations qu'il composent les principales cours de l'Europe*, 2nd ed., vol. 1 (Amsterdam, 1735), 197-213.

P. 18 - The Riesbeck quotation is taken from John Pinkerton, ed. *A General Collection of the Best and Most Interesting Voyages and Travels, in All Parts of the World*, vol. 6 (Philadelphia, 1812), 158 (in a section entitled "Riesbeck's Travels through Germany").

The institution of serfdom as it existed in the kingdom of Bohemia before the nineteenth century, is described in detail in Kerner, *Bohemia in the Eighteenth Century*, 273-306; Emil Niederhauser, *The Emancipation of the Serfs in Eastern Europe*, trans. Paul Bődy (Highland Lakes, N.J.: Atlantic Research and Publications, 2004), 68-98; and Vondra, *České země v letech 1705-1792*, 167-78.

Strictly speaking, the Čapek play merely introduced the term "robot" to the public. It was actually coined by his brother Josef, who suggested the term informally while Karel was planning his play. Karel's recollection of how the term was suggested to them was published in an issue of the Czech newspaper *Lidové noviny* of 24 December 1933. Reports that Josef earlier used the term in a short story are false. For further information, see the article "Who did actually invent the word 'robot' and what does it mean?" by Dominick Zunt on the Czech website capek.misto.cz.

P. 19 - Count Sternberg's reminiscences from the year 1789 are recorded in the *Leben des Grafen Kaspar Sternberg*, 30-32.

P. 20 - The account of Sternberg's encounter with Leopold II is found in ibid., 36-37.

P. 21 - The proceedings of the "Little Diet" of 1790 and "Grand Diet" of 1790-91 are detailed in Kerner, *Bohemia in the Eighteenth Century*, 82-95 and 99-164, and Cerman, *Šlechtická kultura v 18. století*, 512-36. A more concise discussion of Leopold's policies in the kingdom of Bohemia at this time is found in Vondra, *České země v letech 1705-1792*, 131-40.

Leopold's distasteful role in enabling landlords to continue to demand forced manual labor from Bohemian serfs is often suppressed in biographies, for example, Adam Wandruszka's seminal study *Leopold II., Erzherzog von Österreich, Grossherzog von Toskana, König von Ungarn und Böhmen, Römischer Kaiser*, 2 vols. (Vienna: Verlag Herold, 1963-65), and Helga Peham's *Leopold II., Herrscher mit weiser Hand* (Graz: Verlag Styria, 1987). In Harke de Roos, *Mozart und seine Kaiser* (Berlin: Ries & Erler, 2005), 41-54, a sketch of Leopold's reign as Holy Roman Emperor confirms that he made "concessions" to the Estates of Bohemia, but does not specify what they were. A view of Leopold's rule in Bohemia as a period of political reaction is confirmed in Agnew, *The Czechs and the Lands of the Bohemian Crown*, 92-95, and Jana Machačová and Jiří Matěček, *Nástin sociálního vývoje českých zemí 1781-1914* [Outline of social developments in the Czech lands, 1781-1914] (Prague: Nakladatelství Karolinum, 2010), 378-92, but most strikingly of all in Cerman, *Šlechtická kultura v 18. století*, 509-81, which uses the chapter heading "Velká stavovská revoluce (1790-1791)" ["the great revolution of the Estates" (1790-1791)"] to evoke the character of political events in Bohemia immediately following the accession of Leopold II as Holy Roman Emperor in 1790. Jiří Beránek, *Absolutismus a konstitucionalismus v Čechách doby Velké francouzské revoluce* [Absolutism and constitutionalism in Bohemia at the time of the French Revolution] (Prague: Academia, 1989) sums up in its very title the basic political struggles between the aims of the Habsburg monarchy and the Bohemian Estates after the death of Joseph II (additionally, it is very useful for its indications of source materials now housed in the National Archive in Prague).

The terms of the Patent of 9 May 1790 are detailed in Kerner, *Bohemia in the Eighteenth Century*, 92, 283-91, and Cerman, *Šlechtická kultura v 18. století*, 516-17. The patent technically instituted a system of "free bargaining" between serfs and landlords to replace the obligation of *robota* with cash payments, but in practice, most landlords considered the substitution to be entirely at their discretion, and many peasants did not have the resources to make cash payments.

One of the best examples from the Mozart literature that falsely characterizes the coronation ceremonies of 1791 in Prague as a celebration of Leopold's political policies in countries outside of Bohemia is found in H. C. Robbins Landon, *1791: Mozart's Last Year* (New York: Schirmer Books,

1988), 100, in which it is suggested that the coronation was intended to flatter him for abolishing torture in Tuscany, among other measures.

P. 22 - The quotation of Sternberg is taken from the *Leben des Grafen Kaspar Sternberg*, 34.

The burdens endured by serfs expecting release from the obligation of *robota* are detailed in Kerner, *Bohemia in the Eighteenth Century*, 284-85.

The second quotation of Sternberg is taken from the *Leben des Grafen Kaspar Sternberg*, 38.

A valuable study in English that documents the resurgence of Czech nationalism beginning in the late eighteenth century is Hugh Agnew, *Origins of the Czech National Renascence* (Pittsburgh: University of Pittsburgh Press, 1993), something of an equivalent study to Petráň, *Počátky českého národního obrození*.

P. 23 - Hans Rothe, *Deutsche in den böhmischen Ländern*, 2 vols. (Cologne: Böhlau, 1992-93), is an excellent resource for the history of German culture in the Bohemian lands.

Variants of the phrase "Sclavonian dialect" to refer to the language spoken by the Czech residents of Bohemia date back at least to Edward Brown, *A Brief Account of Some Travels in Divers Parts of Europe*, first published in London in 1673.

The quotation from Nugent is taken from *The Grand Tour*, vol. 2, 15.

P. 24 - The quotation of Kinský, along with his opinions about the beauty of the Czech language and the favor that it found with French soldiers, is found in Franz Josef Graf von Kinský, *Erinnerung über einen wichtigen Gegenstand von einen Böhmen* (Prague, 1773), 131-36. The new cultivation of Czech language in the kingdom of Bohemia during the late eighteenth century is documented in English in Agnew, *The Origins of the Czech Renascence*, 51-92.

The full citation for Karel Hynek Thám's "defense" is the *Obrana gazyka českého protí zlobiwým geho vtrhacům* (Prague, 1783).

In addition to extensive discussion in Agnew, *Origins of the Czech Renascence*, the educational system of late eighteenth-century Bohemia and the revival of Czech language is also described in Kerner, *Bohemia in the Eighteenth Century*, 344-363, and Seton-Watson, *The History of the Czechs and Slovaks*, 160-63.

Charles Burney's frustration with the prevalence of Czech language in Bohemia is expressed in *The Present State of Music in Germany, The Netherlands, and United Provinces*, vol. 2 (London, 1773), 14.

Chapter 2

P. 27 - Accounts of the funeral of Rudolf II can be found in Karl Vocelka, *Rudolf II. und seine Zeit* (Vienna: Hermann Böhlau, 1985), 212-15, and Josef Janáček, *Rudolf II. a jeho doba* [Rudolf II and his times] (Prague: Nakladatelství Svodoba, 1987), 493-506. Information concerning the burial places of Bohemian monarchs of the House of Hapsburg (and many other personal details about them) can be found in Ivana Čornejová et al., *Ve stínu tvých křídel ... Habsburkové v českých dějinách* [In the shadow of your wings ... the Hapsburgs in Czech history] (Prague: Grafoprint Neubert, 1995). Biographical sketches of all monarchs who ruled over the Bohemian lands since the Přemyslid Bořivoj I in the ninth century AD are available in Marie Ryantová and Petr Vorel, eds., *Čeští králové* [Czech kings] (Prague: Paseka, 2008).

A concise appraisal in English of the achievements of Rudolf's reign is Josef Válka, "Rudolfine Culture," in Mikuláš Teich, ed., *Bohemia in History* (Cambridge: Cambridge University Press, 1998), 117-42. Peter Demetz, *Prague in Black and Gold* (New York: St. Martin's Press, 1997), 171-223, also offers a good summary of the highlights, including a description of the brilliant Jewish culture that flourished in Prague under Rudolf's protection.

P. 28 - Janáček, *Rudolf II. a jeho doba*, 507-17, provides a detailed explanation of the fate of the emperor's various collections after his death.

In recent years, there has been great improvement in the availability of information about the history of Prague in English and Czech. Much to be recommended for its engaging writing style is Richard Burton, *Prague: A Cultural History* (Northampton, Mass.: Interlink Books, 2009). Demetz, *Prague in Black and Gold*, is not as well written, but it does offer more coverage of the earliest centuries of the history of the city for those who are attracted to that subject matter. The chapter devoted to Mozart's association with the city, however, is factually unreliable. Some of the most useful surveys of the history of Prague in Czech include Josef Janáček et al., *Dějiny Prahy* [The history of Prague] (Prague: Nakladatelsví politické literatury, 1964); Pavel Bělina et al., *Dějiny Prahy*, 2 vols. (Prague: Paseka, 1997-98), and Václav Ledvinka and Jiří Pešek, *Praha* (Prague: Nakladatelství lidové noviny, 2000).

Detailed population statistics for the periods and cities cited can be found in Bělina, *Dějiny Prahy*, vol. 1, 125, 391-92, 411-12, and 462-64, and vol. 2, 24-25 and 308-9.

The article on Prague in Cliff Eisen and Simon P. Keefe, eds., *The Cambridge Mozart Encyclopedia* (Cambridge: Cambridge University Press, 2006), 397, incorrectly identifies the city as the second most populous city in the Austrian Empire of Mozart's day.

P. 29 - See Demetz, *Prague in Black and Gold*, 30-117, for an overview in English of the development of each of the principal districts of Prague during the Dark Ages and Middle Ages.

The renovations carried out by Pacassi are detailed in Václav Ledvinka et al., *Pražské paláce: encyclopedický ilustrovaný přehled* [Prague palaces: an illustrated encyclopedic survey] (Prague: Akropolis, 1995), 237-38.

P. 30 - The exact geographic bounds of the city of Prague during Mozart's visits are described in detail here using information prepared by Jiří Roun that marks the boundaries of Prague in 1791 (see Map, p. xvii) and a map provided in the anonymous guidebook *Vollständige Beschreibung der königlichen Haupt- und Residenzstadt Prag: von den ältesten bis auf die jetzigen Zeiten, besonders für Fremde und Reisende bearbeitet* (Prague and Vienna, 1787), perhaps written by Johann Ferdinand Opitz.

P. 31 - Vincy Schwarz, *Město vidím veliké...cizinci o Praze* [I see a great city... foreigners on Prague] (Prague: Fr. Borový, 1940), is a compilation of accounts of foreign visitors to Prague over the centuries. It includes many excerpts translated into Czech.

The quotation from Brown is taken from *A Brief Account of Some Travels in Divers Parts of Europe*, 2nd ed. (London, 1685), 162-63.

The quotation from Patin is taken from *Travels Thro' Germany, Swisserland, Bohemia, Holland, and Other Parts of Europe* (London, 1697), 272-73.

P. 32 - The quotaton from Lady Montagu is taken from *The Letters of the Right Honourable Lady Mary Wortley Montague* (London, 1793), 32-33.

P. 33 - The quotation of Nugent is taken from *The Grand Tour*, 2nd ed., vol. 2, 256. It relies on older information that can be found in the *Mémoires de Charles-Louis, baron de Pollnitz, contenant les observations qu'il composent les principales cours de l'Europe*, 2nd ed., vol. 1, 197-213. The opera Pöllnitz saw in the autumn of 1729 would have had to have been the anonymous pastiche *Roderico*; see Daniel E. Freeman, *The Opera Theater of Count Franz Anton von Sporck in Prague* (Stuyvesant, N.Y.: Pendragon Press, 1992), 256-57.

The dates for the beginning of operations in the Divadlo v Kotcích vary in the scholarly literature between 1737 and 1739. As far as opera is concerned, the first one performed there was *La fede tradita e vendicata* of Santo Lapis in 1738, as confirmed in Pravoslav Kneidl, "Libreta italské opery v Praze v 18. století" [Librettos of Italian opera in Prague in the eighteenth century], *Strahovská knihovna* 2 (1967): 121.

The quotations from Burney are from *The Present State of Music in Germany*, 1-2, 6-7; the German edition that suppresses his account of the poverty in the Bohemian countryside is *Carl Burney's der Musik Doctors Tagebuch seiner musikalischen Reisen durch Flandern, die Niederlande und am Rhein bis Wien* (Hamburg, 1773).

P. 34 - The quotation from Piozzi is taken from *Observations and Reflections Made in the Course of a Journey through France, Italy, and Germany* (London, 1789; repr. Ann Arbor: University of Michigan Press, 1967), 382-85.

The performance of Storace's *Gli sposi malcontenti* during the "winter" season of 1786 (whatever its chronological bounds were) is confirmed from a libretto cited in Kneidl, "Libreta italské opery v Praze v 18. století," *Strahovská knihovna* 4 (1969): 192.

P. 36 - The contents of Mozart's library as it existed at the time of his death is known. It consisted of only 41 titles, none of which is a guidebook to Prague. See Deutsch, *Mozart: A Documentary Biography*, 587-89, 601-2, for a listing of the titles.

P. 37 - Candidates for the author of the *Beobachtungen* (which was published in Prague in two volumes in 1787) are listed in Michael Holzmann and Hanns Bohatta, eds., *Deutsches Anonymen-Lexikon*, vol. 6 (Weimar: Gesellschaft der Bibliophilen, 1911; repr. Hildesheim: Georg Olms Verlag, 1961), 82.

For book censorship in eighteenth-century Bohemia, see Claire Madl and Michael Wögerbauer, "Censorship and Book Supply," in Cerman, *The Enlightenment in Bohemia*, 69-87.

The *Freye Bemerkungen über Berlin, Leipzig und Prag* is available in the form of a reprint (Leipzig and Weimar: Gustav Kiepenheuer Verlag, 1986) that adopts modern German spellings and a slight alteration of the original title: *Freie Bemerkungen über Berlin, Leipzig, Prag*. The authorship of Karl Heinrich Krögen is asserted in the *Deutsches Anonymen-Lexikon*, vol. 6, 81.

The statistics for Jewish residents are found in the *Complete Description of Prague*, vol. 1, 220.

P. 38 - The quotation of Brown is taken from his *Brief Account*, 2nd ed., 164; the quotation of Patin is taken from his *Travels*, 273-74.

The quotation from the *Mémoires* of Baron Pöllnitz is found in vol. 1, 204.

A history and description of the Jewish Quarter of Pragus is found in the *Complete Description of Prague*, vol. 1, 202-8.

The quotation of Nugent is drawn from *The Grand Tour*, 2nd ed., vol. 2, 251.

P. 39 - The quotation from the *Observations* is found in vol. 1, 73.

A discussion of the Jews in Prague is found in vol. 1, 103-121 of the *Observations*. The striking remark concerning the tolerance in Prague evident in the 1780s in vol. 1, 73, is clearly meant to be a reference to Jewish emancipation fostered by Joseph II (as well as the tolerance of Protestants, whom Joseph's mother Maria Theresa also persecuted).

It is very odd that H. C. Robbins Landon, in his *1791: Mozart's Last Year,* 102, expressed such certainty that Mozart was intimately familiar with the same landmarks of Josefov (the Jewish Quarter) that tourists visit so often today. Landon seemed unaware that Josefov underwent a very ambitious urban renewal project in the late nineteenth and early 20th centuries that created the exceptionally beautiful neighborhoods that can be seen there today; it was not an attractive destination for tourists in the eighteenth century. Unless Mozart had an interest in the culture of unassimilated Jews who lived in squalid ghettos that is not established in existing documentation, it is actually not so certain that he ever set foot in the Jewish Quarter of Prague. Mozart never would have had to traverse the ghetto to reach any location that he is known to have visited.

The remarks of Baron Pöllnitz concerning the noble community of Prague are found in the *Mémoires*, vol. 1, 205; remarks about women are found in vol. 1, 211, as is his remark that "I find the Bohemians the best people in the world."

Riesbeck's opinion about the women and indolent nobles of Prague is found in his *Travels*, 142.

The opinions of Guibert are taken from Jacques-Antoine-Hippolyte de Guibert, *Journal d'un voyage en Allemagne, fait en 1773*, vol. 1 (Paris, 1803), 257. Guibert shared Piozzi's impression of Prague as being dominated by old-fashioned architectural styles.

Information from the "Wandering Hypochondriac" is taken from the "Briefe des wandernden Hypochondristen aus Böhmen, Mähren, Oesterreich und Ungarn" in *Deutsches Museum* 1 (January-June 1787): 588-94, and 2 (July-December 1787): 53-61.

The foundation and development of Count Nostic's society is discussed in Agnew, *The Origins of the Czech Renascence*, 30-36, and Rita Krueger, "The Scientific Academy and Beyond: the Institutions of the Enlightenment," in Cerman, *The Enlightenment in Bohemia*, 39-53.

P. 40 - Biographical notices for Ignaz von Born in English are available in Peter Clive, *Mozart and His Circle: A Biographical Dictionary* (London: J. M. Dent, 1993), and the *Cambridge Mozart Encyclopedia*. Throughout these notes, page numbers for the latter two resources will be considered superfluous for biographical entries, since each one arranges them in strict alphabetical order.

Riesbeck's opinions about Freemasonry are found in his *Travels*, 140.

See Ivo Cerman, "The Enlightenment Universities," in Cerman, *The Enlightenment in Bohemia,* 55-67, for information about university reform in Bohemia in the late eighteenth century.

Agnew, *The Origins of the Czech Renascence,* 128-170, documents the revival of theatrical traditions in the Bohemian lands during the late eighteenth century.

The quotations from Krögen are taken from the *Free Remarks,* 183 and 205 (reprint, 120 and 134).

P. 41 - The description of balls in the *Observations* is found in vol. 1, 121-29, the quotation about "painted ladies" on pp. 122-23.

The opinions of the author of the *Complete Description of Prague* concerning apparel and furniture is found in vol. 2, 217.

The quotations and observations from Krögen are taken from the *Free Remarks,* 198, 203-4, and 223 (reprint, 131, 133, and 148). The author of the *Observations* also described the use of heavy make-up in Prague in vol. 1, 159.

P. 42 - A notice for the inn "Zum Bade," including mention of its famous carnival balls, is found in the *Complete Description of Prague,* vol. 1, 19.

A critique of the character of the Bohemian nobility is found in the *Observations,* vol. 1, 153; remarks of the author of the *Observations* concerning language proficiency are found in vol. 2, 127-28.

Krögen's discussion of adultery and prostitution in Prague is found in the *Free Remarks,* 198 and 224-25 (reprint, 131 and 148-49); the author of the *Observations* describes the same phenomena in vol. 1, 174-78, to a degree of detail that suggests he experienced it personally.

The condemnation of lottary mania in the *Observations* is found in vol. 1, 99; the quotation about the pride of the Bohemians is found in vol. 1, 172.

The observation of the "wandering hypochondriac" concerning the character of the residents of Prague in comparison to the residents of Dresden in found in the *Deutsches Museum* 2, 57.

Chapter 3

P. 44 - For an overview of the events surrounding Mozart's departure from the court of Salzburg during the year 1777, see Salomon, *Mozart: A Life,* 161-76, although connections with Prague at this time are neglected.

For an overview in English of the history of opera in Prague until the foundation of the Sporck theater in 1724, see Freeman, *The Opera Theater of Count Franz Anton von Sporck in Prague,* 17-22, and Angela Romagnoli, "From the Hapsburgs to the Hanswursts: the Slow Progress of Italian Opera on the Bohemian Scene," in Melania Bucciarelli et al., eds., *Italian Opera in Central Europe* (Berlin: Berliner Wissenschafts-Verlag, 2006), 67-97. A much older study, Oskar Teuber's monumental *Geschichte des Prager Theaters,* 3 vols. (Prague, 1883-88), has never been superseded as a comprehensive survey of the history of theater and opera in the city up to the mid-nineteenth century; its discussion of the earliest period of Prague opera is found in vol. 1, 32-59. For eighteenth-century musical life in the city of Prague in general, there is also Otakar Kamper, *Hudební Praha v XVIII. věku* [Musical Prague in the eighteenth century] (Prague: Melantrich, 1935). A survey of theatrical life of all types in the Bohemian lands up to 1945 is František Černý, ed., *Dějiny českého divadla* [The history of Czech theater], 4 vols. (Prague: Academia, 1968-77).

P. 45 - For the Divadlo v Kotcích, a specialized collection of essays is available in Czech: Josef Balvín and František Černý, eds. *Divadlo v Kotcích: nejstarší pražské městské divadlo* [The Theater in the stalls: the oldest municipal theater in Prague] (Prague: Panorama, 1992). The discussion of the operation of this theater in Teuber, *Geschichte des Prager Theaters,* is found in vol. 1, 157-279.

Operatic productions in Prague from the period of the Divadlo v Kotcích are recorded in Pravoslav Kneidl, "Libreta italské opery v Praze v 18. století," *Strahovská knihovna* 2 (1967): 115-88. Considerable information on operatic productions from Prague of the same period is also found in Claudio Sartori, *I libretti italiani a stampa dalle origini al 1800,* 6 vols. (Cuneo: Bertola & Locatelli, 1990-94). *La serva padrona* was repeated in 1747. Strangely enough, the opera *Orfeo ed Euridice,* which captured the imagination of Europe in the 1760s and 1770s, was never performed in Prague in the eighteenth century, even though its composer Gluck was a Czech who spent much of his youth in the city.

P. 46 - The productions of the Thun theater are described in Teuber, *Geschichte des Prager Theaters*, vol. 1, 354-58, and vol. 2, 127-56, but much information about them may also be gleaned from Kneidl, "Libreta italské opery v Praze v 18. století," *Strahovská knihovna* 3 (1968): 190-201.

Still a valuable resource for biographical information about prominent eighteenth-century Bohemian nobles is Constant von Wurzbach, *Biographisches Lexikon des Kaisertums Oesterreich*, 60 vols. (Vienna, 1856-91; repr. New York: Johnson Reprint, 1966-1973); a speciality of this dictionary is biographies of prominent nobles and genealogies of aristocratic families. A biographical sketch of Count Franz Anton von Nostic family is found in vol. 20 (1869), 397-98, with considerable additional infor-mation on his family on adjacent pages; his activities are also featured prominently in Cerman, *Šlechtická kultura v 18. století*, esp. 494-99. The remark about Count Nostic's personality is found in Krögen, *Free Remarks*, 251 (repr., 166).

A concise list of the holders of the title *Oberstburggraf* in Prague in the late eighteenth century is foiund in Vondra, *České země v letech 1705-1792*, 356, but Jaroslaus Schaller, *Beschreibug der königlichen Haupt und Residenzstadt Prag*, vol. 2 (Prague, 1795), 155, lists their tenures to the day.

P. 47 - For theater on the Karolinplatz and the "shack," see Teuber, *Geschichte des Prager Theaters*, vol. 1, 359-363.

Count Nostic's manifesto is transcribed in Teuber, *Geschichte des Prager Theaters*, vol. 2, 93-95.

Joseph's visit to the National Theater shortly after its opening is decscribed in ibid., vol. 2, 120-21.

P. 48 - For the revival of Czech theater, see Teuber, *Geschichte des Prager Theaters*, vol. 2, 157-72, and Agnew, *The Origins of the Czech National Renescance*, 128-48.

At present, the best reference source concerning the activities of the Prague impresario Pasquale Bondini is the dictionary Alena Jakubcová et al., *Starší divadlo v českých zemích do konce 18. století: osobnosti a díla* [Older theater in the Bohemian lands to the end of the eighteenth century: personalities and works] (Prague: Divadelní Ústav - Akademia, 2007), 67-71.

A little-known announcement of the opening of a theater for Czech plays was made in the newspaper *Schönfeldské c. k. pražské noviny* [Schönfeld's imperial and royal Prague newspaper] in an issue of 16 September 1786. The announcement is transcribed in Berkovec, *Musicalia*, 62. According to Teuber, *Geschichte des Prager Theaters*, vol. 2, 171, this small theater, devoted to Czech-language repertory, was visited by none other than Holy Roman Emperor Joseph II on 19 September 1786, who offered his support to the project. Additional information about the early productions of the "shack" in the "horse market" are found in Teubert, *Geschichte des Prager Theaters*, vol 2, 245.

Krögen's comments about the Nostitz theater are found in the *Free Remarks*, 205-6 (reprint, 134-35); remarks from the *Observations* are found in vol. 1, 131-33.

P. 49 - Interesting information on the theatrical "culture wars" and the history of the theaters in Prague is provided in Burton, *Prague: A Cultural History*, 71, 100-115; Teuber, *Geschichte des Prager Theaters*, never addresses Czech nationalist aspirations.; For Czech operatic life of all periods, see John Tyrrell, *Czech Opera* (Cambridge: Cambridge University Press, 1988).

P. 50 - No adequate survey of the history of music in the Bohemian lands exists at present in English in any form; an excellent introduction in Czech is *Hudba v českých dějinách* [Music in Czech history], 2nd ed. (Prague: Suprahon, 1989). Earlier studies useful for the eighteenth century include Jan Němeček, *Nástin české hudby XVIII. Století* [Outline of eighteenth-century Czech music] (Prague: Státní nakladatelství krásné literatury, hudby a umění, 1955), and Jan Racek, *Česká hudba: od nejstarších dob od počátku 19. století* [Czech music: from the most ancient times until the beginning of the nienteenth century] (Prague: Státní nakladatelství krásné literatury, hudby a umění, 1958).

P. 51 - The dominance of ecclesiastical institutions as sources of employment for eighteenth-century Bohemian musicians is emphasized in Paul Nettl, "The Czechs in Eighteenth-Century Music," *Music & Letters* 21 (1940): 362-70. Additionally, this article documents patterns of cultural bias among German-speaking music scholars who sought to disparage the importance of eighteenth-century Czech musicians on the basis of ethnicity - and with a frankness that modern journal editors generally would not permit.

P. 52 - No significant augmentation of biographical documentation concerning the Dušek couple has appeared since the publication of Václav Jan Sýkora, *František Xaver Dušek: život a dílo* [František Xaver Dušek: life and works] (Prague: Státní nakladatelství krásné literatury, hudby a umění, 1958). Josefa Dušek's avoidance of stage appearances has had the unfortunate consequence of rendering her ineligible for inclusion in the biographical dictionary *Starší divadlo*. *Oxford Music Online* is a good resource for English speakers seeking information about the Dušek couple. Among other reference resources on Mozart, Clive, *Mozart and His Circle*, is more useful than the *Cambridge Mozart Encyclopedia*, but a much more detailed consideration of their biographies and relationship with the Mozart family, including historical data concerning their country house, the Bertramka villa, is found in Nettl, *Mozart in Böhmen*, 27-55, based on Procházka, *Mozart in Prag*, 1-16 and 54-65. The most detailed study devoted specifically to the Bertramka estate is Jaroslav Paterna, *Bertramka v Praze: Mozartovo památné sídlo* [The Bertramka in Prague: Mozart's memorial site] (Prague: Hudební matice Umělecké besedy za účasti Mozartovy obce v ČSR, 1948). Bertramka was new to the Dušeks at the time of Mozart's visits; it had only been acquired in 1784 (and purchased by Josefa and not František, an indication for some that it was actually bought for her by Count Clam).

Josefa's surname would be spelled "Dušková" in modern Czech - and her given name spelled as "Josefina" - but these spellings have been suppressed here, since they could create confusion with readers familiar with Mozart literature originating outside the Bohemian lands. In addition, it must be acknowledged that she was not ethnically Czech. Though born in Prague in 1754, her father, Anton Adam Hambacher, came from the town of Sušice (Schüttenhofen) in the Germanized Plzeň (Pilsen) region of Bohemia close to the Bavarian border (see Sýkora, *František Xaver Dušek*, 31-32). Her mother, Maria Domenica Colomba Weiser, was from Salzburg.

The aria Beethoven wrote for Dušek is "Ah, perfido," Op. 65; the Mozart arias are "Ah, lo previdi," K. 272, and "Bella mia fiama, addio," K. 528.

P. 53 - The currency of the term "Bohemian" to refer to rootless wanderers in the eighteenth century is confirmed in the *Encyclopédie* of Diderot and d'Alembert (see vol. 2, 294-295). It is clear that the reference here is actually to Romani ("gypsies"). The use of the term to denote urban artistic and intellectual personnel originated in the nineteenth century.

The remarks concerning the Dušeks in the *Observations* are found in vol. 2, 71-72.

The best source for information on Strobach at present is *Starší divadlo*, 585-86. There is an entry for Strobach in Clive, *Mozart's Circle*, but he is ignored in the *Cambridge Mozart Encyclopedia*.

P. 54 - The quotation from the *Observations* is taken from vol. 2, 68-69.

P. 55 - The first quotation from Burney is taken from *The Present State of Music in Germany*, vol. 2, 3-5, the second one from ibid., vol. 2, 10-11.

P. 56 - The observations of Reichardt are taken from the *Briefe eines aufmerksamen Reisdenden die Musik betreffend*, part 2 (Frankfurt and Breslau, 1776; repr. Hildesheim and New York: Georg Olms, 1977), 123-34.

The best documentation in English for the role of the nobility in promoting music education in seventeenth-century Bohemia is found in Barbara Ann Renton, "The Musical Culture of Eighteenth-Century Bohemia, with Emphasis on the Music Inventories of Osek and the Knights of the Cross" (Ph.D. dissertation, New York University, 1990); the quotations of Count Waldstein are taken from pp. 79-80.

Observations about eighteenth-century Czech musical culture are expanded in Daniel E. Freeman, *Josef Mysliveček, "Il Boemo"* (Sterling Heights, Mich: Harmonie Park Press, 2009), 105-09.

P. 57 - The quotation from Riesbeck is taken from his *Travels*, 140.

On the subject of "conservatories," there have been persistent reports in musicological literature since World War II that Charles Burney referred to the Bohemian lands as the "conservatory of Europe" for all the prominent musical émigrés that originated there. In fact, no writing of Charles Burney employs that quotable phrase.

P. 58 - The quotation from the *Observations* is taken from vol. 2, 69-70.

P. 59 - The quotation from the *Observations* is taken from vol. 2, 70.

As well established as it is in Mozart literature originating outside the Bohemian lands, the awkward eighteenth-century German transliteration of Němeček's surname (Niemetschek) will not be countenanced in this volume. Němeček is a common Czech name (meaning "little German"), and the archaic spelling encourages mispronunciation (*NEE meh check* instead of *NYEH meh check*). Němeček's biography of Mozart was published as *Leben des K. K. Kapellmeisters Wolfgang Gottlieb Mozart, nach Originalquellen beschrieben* in Prague in 1798; a second edition with additional remarks appeared in 1808. In addition to being the first biography of Mozart, it is a pioneering example of the literary genre of composer biography in general. English speakers often turn to the *Life of Mozart* as translated by Helen Mautner (London: Leonard Hyman, 1956), which has been reprinted in facsimile under the title *Mozart: The First Biography* (New York: Berghahn Books, 2007). Mautner's translation is not satisfactory, thus fresh translations have been provided in this volume with references to Němeček's biography taken from a facsimile edition of the 1808 version edited with an introduction by Claudia Maria Knispel (Laaber: Laaber Verlag, 2005). The title of this version is the *Lebensbeschreibung des K. K. Kapellmeisters Wolfgang Amadeus Mozart*. The remark of Joseph II concerning "exceedingly many notes" is found on p. 34.

Most Mozart literature identifies the 1798 edition of Němeček's biography as the first version; however a more complicated chronology is detailed in Georges Favier's *Vie de W. A. Mozart* (Sainte-Étienne: Université de Sainte-Étienne), 68-69. This latter is a transcription and translation into French of Němeček's biography and a brief biographical sketch of Mozart by the German scholar Friedrich von Schlichtegroll that was published in 1793, along with extensive introductory material. Favier points to evidence that a version of Němeček's biography brought out by the publisher Caspar Widtmann circulated privately in Prague based on the testimony of Georg Nikolaus von Nissen, Constanze Mozart's second husband and her first husband's second biographer. In a letter written to Albert Stadler in Linz of 28 September 1825, Nissen revealed the sources of information he had available to him for his own biography, one of which was a Mozart biography published anonymously by Widtmann in Prague. According to a letter of Friedrich Dionys Weber, the director of the Prague Conservatory, that was written to Constanze Mozart on 8 April 1826, this biography was identical to the biography of Němeček published in Prague in 1798. No trace of a Widtmann edition of the Němeček biography has ever been located. The letters of Nissen and Constanze Mozart cited here are transcribed in in Wilhelm A. Bauer and Otto Erich Deutsch, *Mozart: Briefe und Aufzeichnungen*, vol. 4 (Kassel and New York: Bärenreiter, 1963), 466-67 and 486-89.

In case the reader is curious, the biographical sketch of Schlichtegroll, known as the *Nekrolog*, will not be referred to further in this volume for the simple reason that it reports nothing at all about Mozart's connections with Prague. The reason is that Schlichtegroll relied principally on information supplied by Mozart's sister Nannerl, who had had only limited contact with Wolfgang from the time of his marriage in 1782. Nannerl was simply not knowledgeable about her brother's activities in Prague, nor were other contacts in Salzburg. Schlichtegroll's biographical sketch was prepared with the intent of including it as part of a vast series of obituaries devoted to notables from many different fields. He himself was not a musician or music lover (as far as is known), so he could not add information about Mozart's activities from his own experience of musical life in central Europe of his day

Chapter 4

P. 61 - For Mozart's trips as a small child, the best survey in English is Solomon, *Mozart: A Life*, 40-66.

A concise presentation of the vital statistics associated with the imperial House of Hapsburg of the period encompassing Mozart's lifetime is found in *Burke's Royal Families of the World*, vol. 1 (London: Burke's Peerage, 1977), 18-27.

P. 62 - For Marie Antoinette and the family members who shared her childhood, the most frequently consulted biographical source at present is Antonia Fraser, *Marie Antoinette: The Journey* (New York: Doubleday, 2001); the incident concerning Mozart's encounter with Maria Antoinette is mentioned on pp. 19-20. The source of the incident is Němeček (see the *Lebensbeschreibung,* 9-10). Němeček's informant was likely his good friend Constanze Mozart, who possibly would have heard it from her late husband. The source of the story of Mozart jumping on the lap of the Empress Maria Theresa is a letter of Leopold Mozart written from Vienna on 16 October 1762 to Johann Lorenz Hagenauer in Salzburg.

The correspondence of the Mozart family is transcribed in German in Wilhelm A. Bauer and Otto Erich Deutsch, *Mozart: Briefe und Aufzeichnungen,* 4 vols. with additions and supplements (Kassel and New York: Bärenreiter, 1962-75). The only comprehensive translation into English of the Mozart correspondence was prepared by Emily Anderson in the earlier part of the last century, originally published in three volumes under the title *The Letters of Mozart and His Family* (London: Macmillan, 1938). At present, English speakers usually consult the third edition in one volume (New York: W. W. Norton, 1985). The translations from the Mozart correspondence used in this volume have been prepared with reference to Anderson's work, but are original. Since both the German and English editions of Mozart's letters are arranged in perfect chronological order, no page references are included in this volume, unless special circumstances invite them.

An oft-repeated variant of the story of Mozart meeting Marie Antoinette is found in the second biography of the composer (with a large portion of its text plagiarized from Němeček): Georg Nikolaus von Nissen, *Biographie W. A. Mozarts* (Leipzig, 1828; repr. Hildesheim: Georg Olms, 1984), 30-31. In this version, the child Mozart slipped onto the floor in front of two archduchesses, the other one unnamed (perhaps Maria Carolina, who was closest to Marie Antoinette in age and infamous in adulthood for her haughtiness). The other archduchess was quite indifferent to Mozart's mishap, but to Marie Antoinette he said, "You're nice; I want to marry you." He told the story to the Empress Maria Theresa, who asked him just how he had come to that decision. He answered, "Out of thanks; she was good to me, while her sister didn't care about me at all." The reliability of this anecdote is highly questionable, especially since Nissen did not specify where he had learned about it.

The incident of Mozart's illness in Moravia is generally brushed over by Mozart biographers, including Solomon, *Mozart: A Life,* 69-70, without a sense of how close Mozart came to dying. Rudolph Angermüller, *Mozart auf der Reise nach Prag, Dresden, Leipzig und Berlin* (Bad Honef: Verlag K. H. Bock, 1995), 17-28, provides a very detailed chronology of the Mozarts' travels in Moravia during the period of Wolfgang's illness.

Information about the Schrattenbach family can be found in Wurzbach, *Biographisches Lexikon,* vol. 31, 263-72; Clive, *Mozart and His Circle*; and the *Cambridge Mozart Encyclopedia.*

P. 63 - Nannerl's account of Mozart's illness in Olomouc at this time is preserved in a memoir published in the Leipzig journal *Allgemeine musikalische Zeitung* of 22 January 1800. It is translated into English in Deutsch, *Mozart: A Documentary Biography,* 494. An account of a concert given by Wolfgang and Nannerl in Brno on 30 December 1767, long after they had recovered from their illness, is translated in ibid., 77-78. Information on the obscure Podstatsky family can be found online from the websites genealogy.euweb.cz/bohemia/podstat1.html and genealogy.euweb.cz/bohemia/podstat2.html.

P. 64 - Mozart's relationship with Count Prokop von Černín is detailed in Deutsch, *Mozart: A Documentary Biography,* 157-58; there is also a notice for the Černín family (and for Countess Antonie von Lützow individually) in the *Cambridge Mozart Encyclopedia.* A sense of the prominence of the Černín family in Bohemia and the Hapsburg Empire (Count Jan Rudolf in particular) can be gauged from entries in Wurzbach, *Biographisches Lexikon,* vol. 3, 101-6. Besides its lack of recognition of how eminent a statesman Count Jan Rudolf would one day become, the notice for him in the *Cambridge Mozart Encyclopedia* is marred by the exaggerated claim that Count Jan Rudolf was "sometimes scorned by the Mozarts for his poor violin-playing and his general ineptness." In fact, Leopold complained about his musical abilities in connection with only one incident (that Wolfgang did not witness). In a letter of 11 June 1778 to Wolfgang in Paris, Leopold noted that a serenade was planned for Countess Lodron that was to be held on the Feast of St. Anthony of Padua (13 June), which was her nameday. Since Wolfgang was gone (he had organized serenades for her on 13 June the previous two years), it was to be organized instead by Count Jan Rudolf and another Salzburg musician named Kolb. Leopold feared that what was planned was too ambitious for them, and in a letter to his son of 29 June 1778 (that is not translated in its entirety in Anderson, *The Letters of Mozart and His Family*), he reported that the serenade was a disaster. Wolfgang's reaction to this news (in a letter written from Paris on 9 July 1778) was hardly "scornful" with regard to Count Jan Rudolf. He merely pointed out that that count was young and inexperienced and that the annual nameday concerts were not likely to continue (after all, he himself did not expect to return to the court of Salzburg at that point).

The Petermann letter is reproduced in facsmile in Volek and Bittner, *The Mozartiana of Czech and Moravian Archives*, 17-19.

Biographical notices for Count Colloredo are found in Clive, *Mozart and His Circle*, and the *Cambridge Mozart Encyclopedia*. Entries for members of several branches of the Collorado family are found in Wurzbach, *Biographisches Lexikon*, vol. 2, 416-39.

P. 65 - Specifically, Count Jan Rudolf is mentioned in letters of Leopold Mozart dated 20 September 1777, 4 December 1777, 12 April 1778, 13 April 1778, 28 May 1778, and 11 June 1778, and and 29 June 1779, and letters of Wolfgang of 26 November 1777 and 9 July 1778.

P. 66 - The best reference resource presently available for information on the history of palaces in Prague is *Pražské paláce*; the history of the Černín palace is presented on pp. 91-96 with the ball of 1791 mentioned on p. 96. In the *Journal der doppelten böhmischen Krönung Leopolds des Zweiten und Marien Luisens, Infantin von Spanien, in Prag im Jahre 1791* (Prague, 1791), perhaps by Johann Friedrich Ernst Albrecht, this ball is listed as one of the principal coronation events in a résumé found on pp. 304-7.

It is fanciful indeed to imagine the illustrious Count Jan Rudolf von Černín inviting Mozart to his magnificent palace in Prague for old time's sake in 1791 among a large gathering of nobles, but in fact, Mozart could pass himself off as nobility (albeit of very low rank) by reason of the knighthood conferred on him by Pope Clement XIV in Rome in 1770 (in the Order of the Golden Spur).

P. 67 - There is a notice for Weiser in Clive, *Mozart and His Circle*, but not in the *Cambridge Mozart Encyclopedia*.

There is a notice for Beer in Clive, *Mozart and His Circle*, but not in the *Cambridge Mozart Encyclopedia*.

P. 68 - For information about Mysliveček, Freeman, *Josef Mysliveček*, supersedes all previously published resources.

The letter of Wolfgang in question, which includes Mysliveček's recommendations for the professional advancement of his younger friend, was written in stages to Mozart's father from Munich on 11 October 1777; his mother also contributed to it. Mysliveček's interactions with the Mozart family during the crisis of 1777-78 are carefully documented in Freeman, *Josef Mysliveček*, 69-86.

Without the specification of given names, maddening difficulties prevent the definitive identification of which Count Pachta Mysliveček was trying to recommend to Mozart. A discussion of the possibilities is found in Freeman, *Josef Mysliveček*, 27 and 77. Likely candidates are Count Johann Joseph (1723-1822) and Count Franz Joseph (1710-1799), more likely the former.

P. 69 - The period of Mozart's break with the archbishop of Salzburg and move to Vienna is summarized in Solomon, *Mozart: A Life*, 221-51.

There are biographical notices for Němeček in Clive, *Mozart and His Circle*, and the *Cambridge Mozart Encyclopedia*, but the most detailed resource available at present concerning Němeček's movements and activities is Walther Brauneis, "Franz Xaver Niemetschek: Sein Umgang mit Mozart - Eine Legende?" in Ingrid Fuchs, ed., *Internationaler Musikwissenschaftlicher Kongress zum Mozartjahr 1991*, vol. 2 (Tutzing: Hans Schneider, 1993), 491-503.

P. 70 - The quotation of Němeček is translated from the *Lebensbeschreibung*, 33-34.

For the first performance of *The Abduction from the Seraglio*, see Carl Friedrich Cramer, *Magazin der Musik*, Jahrgang I, part 2 (Hamburg, 1783; repr. Hildesheim: Georg Olms, 1971), 999-1000. The notice about Mozart's opera is translated in Deutsch, *Mozart: A Documentary Biography*, 219. Procházka, *Mozart in Prag*, 17-18, excerpts an article of Oskar Teuber, "Prager Mozartpremièren," from the journal *Bohemia* of 23 October 1887 that proposed the names of singers who appeared in the original, not Italian singers from the Bondini company, but German actors from the theatrical company of Karl

Wahr. The Teuber excerpt is also cited in Nettl, *Mozart in Böhmen*, 68. Besides Teuber's *Geschichte des Prager Theaters*, the activities of Karl Wahr are described in *Starší divadlo*, 648-54. A libretto from the first Prague production of *The Abduction from the Seraglio* survives, but it does not indicate singers or a precise date of performance. The original article of Teuber claims that *The Abduction from the Seraglio* was performed in Prague in 1782. This is clearly a mistake, as explained in Horst Lederer, "'Meine teutsche opera … ist in Prag und Leipzig - sehr gut - und mit allem beyfall gegeben worden': Fakten und Hypothesen zur Prager Erstauffürung von Mozarts *Entführung aus dem Serail*," in Milada Jonášová and Tomislav Volek, eds., *Böhmische Aspekte des Lebens und des Werkes von W. A. Mozart: Bericht über die Prager internationale Konferenz 27.-28. Oktober 2006* (Prague: Etnologický Ústav AV ČR and Mozartova Obec v České Republice, 2011), 21-37. There is no claim for the year 1782, only 1783, in Teuber, *Geschichte des Prager Theaters*. From Procházka and Nettl, the mistaken claim of 1782 as the year of the first performance of *The Abduction of the Seraglio* in Prague was repeated in Deutsch, *Mozart: A Documentary Biography*, 219, and many other places, including the article on Prague in the *Cambridge Mozart Encyclopedia*.

The quotation of Němeček is translated from the *Lebensbeschreibung*, 34-35.

P. 71 - Specifically, Wolfgang remarked to Leopold in his letter of 6 December 1783, "My German opera *The Abduction from the Seraglio* has been performed very well in Prague and Leipzig and with great applause. I know both of these things from people who saw them there."

Mozart lovers are well acquainted with the "K." numbers that are used to identify his compositions, the most famous catalog numbers used for the works of any composer. The initial is taken from the surname of the Austrian botanist Ludwig von Köchel (1800-1877), who published a catalog of Mozart's works in 1862 under the title *Chronologischthematisches Verzeichnis sämtlicher Tonwerke Wolfgang Amadé Mozarts*. Sometimes one encounters the abbreviation "KV" instead, which stands for "Köchel-Verzeichnis" ("Köchel Catalog"). The Köchel catalog has been revised many times; the last published version appeared in 1964. A fresh revision in online and print formats to be brought out by the original publisher (Breitkopf & Härtel) is expected to appear soon.

The standard reference work in English for information on the chronology of the Mozart symphonies is Neal Zaslaw, *Mozart's Symphonies* (Oxford: Clarendon Press, 1989).

P. 72 - The report from the *Prague Post* of 31 December 1785 is transcribed in Berkovec, *Musicalia*, 138. It paraphrases a description of the same concert in the *Wiener Zeitung* of 24 December 1785 that is translated in Deutsch, *Mozart: A Documentary Biography*, 259.

The opinion of Němeček regarding Mozart's struggles at this time is expressed in the *Lebensbeschreibung*, 35-36.

P. 73 - The notice from the *Prague Post* of 20 May 1786 is transcribed in Berkovec, *Musicalia*, 139.

The notice from the *Wiener Realzeitung* is translated in Deutsch, *Mozart: A Documentary Biography*, 278-79.

Count Zinzendorf's bored reaction to *The Marriage of Figaro* is translated in ibid., 274.

The quotation of Němeček is translated from the *Lebensbeschreibung*, 36-37.

P. 74 - Piozzi's visit to the National Theater is Prague is recorded in her *Observations and Reflections*, 383.

The report from the *Prague Post* of 12 December 1786 is transcribed in Berkovec, *Musicalia*, 63, and translated in Deutsch, *Mozart: A Documentary Biography*, 280-81.

The best biographical summaries presently available concerning the singer and impresario Pasquale Bondini and his wife Caterina are found in *Starší divadlo*, 66-71. There are also notices for each in Clive, *Mozart and His Circle*, and the *Cambridge Mozart Encyclopedia*. Ponziani is accorded an entry in Clive, *Mozart and His Circle*, but not in the *Cambridge Mozart Encyclopedia*.

The report from the *Prague Post* of 19 December 1786 is transcribed in Berkovec, *Musicalia*, 63, and translated in Deutsch, *Mozart: A Documentary Biography*, 281.

P. 75 - The report from the *Prague Post* of 9 January 1787 is transcribed in Berkovec, *Musicalia*, 64, and translated in Deutsch, *Mozart: A Documentary Biography*, 282-83.

The quotation of Němeček is translated from the *Lebensbeschreibung*, 37-39.

Jan Kuchař was a Prague musician of great interest to earlier scholars such as Paul Nettl, but he merits little attention in a study of this type. There is a detailed biographical notice for him in *Starší divadlo*, 327-28.

P. 76 - All of the personalities involved with this discussion of Mozart's possible trip to London in 1787 have been accorded biographical notices in the *Cambridge Mozart Encyclopedia* and/or Clive, *Mozart and His Circle*.

P. 77 - The report from the *Prague Post* of 26 December 1786 is transcribed in Berkovec, *Musicalia*, 140, and translated in Deutsch, *Mozart: A Documentary Biography*, 282.

P. 78 - Breicha's poem is translated in ibid., 282-83.

The passage from Němeček's biography is translated from the *Lebensbeschreibung*, 39.

The best survey of Count Thun's activities as a patron of music and theater in Bohemia is found in *Starší divadlo*, 610-13, whereas the history of the various palaces of the Thun family in Prague is detailed best in *Pražské paláce*, 320-30. Wurzbach, *Biographisches Lexikon*, vol. 45, 8-66, provides an immense amount of information concerning the Thun and Thun-Hohenstein families. Members of the Thun-Hohenstein families are also accorded entries in Clive, *Mozart and His Circle*, and the *Cambridge Mozart Encyclopedia*.

A description of the theater in the Thun palace is found in the *Observations*, vol. 2, 138-39; the author describes it as very elegantly appointed. Bondini's activities are described in vol. 1, 137-38. The title page of the original libretto of the Prague *Marriage of Figaro* is transcribed in Sartori, *I libretti italiani*.

Count Vincenz von Waldstein was a Bohemian patron of the arts not known to have a direct connection with Mozart. His connections with Mozart's friend Mysliveček are documented frequently in Freeman, *Josef Mysliveček*, with some general information about his family on pp. 24-25. Wurzbach, *Biographisches Lexikon*, vol. 52, 207-42, documents the history of family in detail.

The letter of Prince Auersperg is reproduced in facsimile in Eva Mikanová, "Neznámá mozartská bohemika" [Unknown Bohemian Mozartiana], *Hudební rozhledy* 41 (1988): 181-85, which includes information about family history, and in Volek and Bittner, *Mozartiana*, 26-28. Prince Johann Adam is mentioned in Sheila Hodges, *Lorenzo Da Ponte: The Life and Times of Mozart's Librettist* (New York: Universe Books, 1985), 105-6, and Rodney Bolt, *The Librettist of Venice* (New York: Bloomsbury, 2006), 207-13.

Chapter 5

P. 83 - The album notation is translated in Deutsch, *Mozart: A Documentary Biography*, 283.

The route from Prague to Vienna is specified in detail in Nugent, *The Grand Tour*, 2nd ed., vol. 1, 218. The course of all of Mozart's trips to Bohemia and Moravia are diagrammed on a map in the illustrated booklet Alexander Buchner et al., *Mozart und Prag* (Prague: Artia, 1957).

Baron Riesbeck's impression is recorded in his *Travels*, 131.

The report from the *Prague Post* of 12 January 1787 is transcribed in Berkovec, *Musicalia*, 64, and translated in Deutsch, *Mozart: A Documentary Biography*, 284.

P. 84 - Biographical notices for the Jacquin family can be found in Clive, *Mozart and His Circle*, and the *Cambridge Mozart Encyclopedia*, as well as for all of Mozart's close family members.

P. 85 - The history of the palace that Mozart stayed in during his first trip is described in *Pražské paláce*, 320-22. The building that now occupies the site bears the street address Sněmovní 4 and the "descriptive number" (usually abbreviated in Czech as č.p., i.e., "číslo popisné") 176-III. All of the buildings in the historic districts of Prague are identified both by conventional addresses, plus "descriptive numbers" that were assigned to each one beginning in the eighteenth century. Over time, the "descriptive numbers" have proven much more stable than the street addresses. The Roman numeral for each "descriptive number" denotes the Prague district in which it is located (I for the Old City; II for the New City; III for Malá Strana; IV for Hradčany). The Thun Palace on Thunovská 14 (now the British embassy in Prague) is identified as č.p. 180-III.

P. 86 - See Nettl, *Mozart in Böhmen*, 88-89, for his correct identification of the Thun palace in which Mozart stayed. *Pražské paláce*, 322-25, presents all the evidence needed to confirm that the Thun palace on Thunovská could not possibly have been the palace in which Mozart stayed, yet still perpetuates the incorrect identification.

A biographical notice for Count Canal is found in Wurzbach, *Biographisches Lexikon*, vol. 2, 247-48. He was not accorded biographical entries in Clive, *Mozart and His Circle*, or the *Cambridge Mozart Encyclopedia* (understandably, since his association with Mozart was so brief and casual). His family is also listed in Roman Freiherr von Procházka, *Genealogisches Handbuch erloschener böhmischer Herrenstandsfamilien* (Neustadt an der Aisch: Verlag Degener, 1973), 53-54. Additional information about Count Canal can be found in Nettl, *Mozart in Böhmen,* 88-89.

P. 87 - For the ball of 1787, see the *Complete Description of Prague,* vol. 2, 285; the earlier history of the Konvikt is summarized in vol. 1, 145; the balls in the Wussin house are described in vol. 1, 133. At present, the Konvikt of St. Bartholomew is identified as č.p. 291-I; it lies between two lanes with adresses posted on both ends: Konviktská 24 and Bartolomějská 11. Near the portal on the Bartolomějská side there is a plaque recording a visit of Beethoven in 1796.

Documentation concerning the regulation of public balls in Mozart's time is preserved in the National Archive (Národní Archiv) in Prague, fund ČG (České Gubernium) - Publicum, document fascicle 33/5. The amount of money brought in by patrons of the Wussin house ball between 1781 and 1786 is recorded in document No. 2 with reference to the stipulations of the "ball decree" of 4 November 1780; documents Nos. 1 and 5 record the request and approval from the Gubernium to put on the first Konvikt ball; No. 6 records the permission for the Bretfeld ball of 1788. The culture of balls in Prague is described in the anonymous *Observations* in vol. 1, 121-29. A less vivid description is found in Krögen, *Free Remarks*, 203-4 (reprint, 133).

At the time of Mozart's visits to Prague, Baron Bretfeld owned one of the most beautiful palaces in Malá Strana (č.p. 240-III), now identified with the address Nerudova 3 and famed for its placement on a steeply-angled corner. Its history is detailed in *Pražské paláce*, 71-73. It would have been a shame if Mozart had never been able to visit it, but there is no evidence that he did; the Bretfeld balls were never held there, and he was not known to have made Baron Bretfeld's acquaintance.

Paul Krasnopolski, *Joseph Bretfeld* (Prague: Gesellschaft Deutscher Bücherfreunde in Böhmen, 1931), is an informative biography of the baron, but it does not shed any light about his possible connection with Mozart.

P. 88 - Alfred Meissner's *Rococo Portraits* were first published in Gumbinnen in 1871. This study relies on the text of the second edition (Lindau and Leipzig, 1876). The "colors" of Mozart's first visit to Prague are "refreshed" on pp. 74-80. The veracity of Meissner's vignettes was strongly questioned in the Mozart literature already in Procházka, *Mozart in Prag*, 34-35.

P. 89 - Neither Hodges, *Lorenzo Da Ponte,* nor Bolt, *The Librettist of Venice*, positively confirm Da Ponte's whereabouts during the carnival season of 1787.

Meissner's description of the ballroom attended by Mozart and Da Ponte appears to paraphrase remarks from the Krögen *Free Remarks* made about the inn "Zum Bade" that are translated in Chapter 2.

P. 93 - Ungar is featured in Krögen, *Free Remarks*, 250 (reprint, 163). Krögen's impression of Ungar as being overweight is corroborated in the travel diaries of the German scholar Georg Forster, who visited Prague in July 1784. For Forster's account, which merits little special attention for the purpose of this study, see *Georg Forsters Tagebücher*, eds. Paul Zincke und Albert Leitzmann (Berlin: B. Behr, 1914; repr. Nendeln, Liechtenstein: Kraus Reprint, 1968), 125-142. The library of the Klementinum is also described in the *Complete Description of Prague*, vol. 2, 93, 95, and 317.

For the history of the Colloredo-Mannsfeld palace (č.p. 189-I), Karlova 2 in the Old City, see *Pražské paláce,* 85-89.

For the former location of the palace of Count Canal, see the *Complete Description of Prague*, vol. 1, 162.

For the history of the Sylva-Taroucca and Vernier palaces, see *Pražské paláce*, 298-98, 357-63.

P. 94 - The performance days for opera productions of the Bondini company in the National Theater at the time of Mozart's visits are confirmed in Teuber, *Geschichte des Prager Theaters*, vol. 2, 188.

Mozart's letter provides the only documentation for this production of Paisiello's *Le gare generose*; no libretto is known to survive, although Otakar Kamper, in his *Hudební Praha v XVIII. věku*, 250, claimed to have seen one.

P. 95 - Wolff, *Inventing Eastern Europe*, 106-115, offers a summary of Mozart's relationship with the Bohemian lands, including a special section devoted to the nicknames he formed for his traveling companions on his trip to Prague during January 1787. Wolff also interprets them as a sign that Mozart found the Czech language he heard along the way to be puzzling and inconvenient and his superficial attempts to imitate the sound of it a confirmation that he had no interest in learning the language more carefully. The image of Mozart as having a perpetual childlike persona is the subject of at least one scholarly essay: Peter Kivy, "Child Mozart as an Aesthetic Symbol," *Journal of the History of Ideas* 28 (1967): 249-58.

The need to hire two coachmen and six horses is explained in Volkmar Braunbehrens, in his study *Mozart in Vienna*, trans. Timothy Bell (New York: Grove Weidenfeld, 1986), 299.

The observation about servants being named Joseph is found in the 1848 novel *La dame aux camélias* by Alexandre Dumas *fils* near the beginning of Chapter 14.

Most of the members of Mozart's party have been accorded biographical entries in Clive, *Mozart and His Circle*, or the *Cambridge Mozart Encyclopedia*.

P. 96 - In order to perform publicly in the Thun palace, permission was required from the Czech Gubernium; the decree of 16 January 1787 granting permission for Crux to do so is preserved in the National Archive in Prague, fund ČG - Publicum, document 34/47.

P. 97 - The original document requesting permission from the Czech Gubernium to allow a concert of Mozart's music to be given on 19 January 1787 is preserved in the National Archive in Prague, fund ČG - Publicum, document 34/49. A facsimile is found in Volek and Bittner, *The Mozartiana of Czech and Moravian Archives*, 29, and a partial translation in Deutsch, *Mozart: A Documentary Biography*, 285.

The report from the *Prague Post* of 23 January 1787 is transcribed in Berkovec, *Musicalia*, 64, and translated in Deustch, *Mozart: A Documentary Biography*, 285 (with the date of the issue recorded incorrectly as 25 January 1787).

The first passage from Němeček is translated from the *Lebensbeschreibug*, 39-40, the second from ibid., 40-42.

P. 98 - Němeček, in a footnote in ibid., 41, claimed to have seen the letter to Strobach (in his opinion, "very well written"), although its text does not survive.

The original passage from Nissen biography can be found in the *Biographie W. A. Mozarts*, 516-17. The entire translation of Štěpánek's text into German from Czech is found in ibid, 515-23; the abridged original was published as the introduction to Štěpánek's translation *Don Juan: Zpěwohra we dwau gednánjch* [Don Juan: an opera in two acts] (Prague, 1825), unfortunately with the account of Mozart's concert of 19 January 1787 left out.

P. 99 - Nissen's indication of a second concert in Prague during Mozart's first visit to Prague is found in a footnote attached to Štěpánek's account of the concert of 19 January (see the *Biographie W. A. Mozarts*, 517): "A second concert was demanded of Mozart soon after this, which had the same glorious success."

Leopold Mozart's letter of 26 January 1787 is not included among the letters translated by Emily Anderson in *The Letters of Mozart and His Family*.

P. 100 - Mozart's own catalog of compositions, the "Verzeichnüss aller meiner Werke," was begun in February 1784 and maintained until 15 November 1791, less than four weeks before the composer's death. The entries (with musical incipits) are transcribed in Bauer and Deutsch, *Mozart: Briefe und Aufzeichnungen*, vols. 2 and 4, interspersed in chronological order among the letters of the Mozart family. The completion of the contredanses is recorded in vol. 4, 21. Anderson, *The Letters of Mozart and His Family*, does not make note of these catalog entries.

The casino in the Thun palace operated by Bondini is documented in the *Observations*, vol. 1, 138.

The relevant passages from the *Prague Post* of 20 February 1787 are excerpted in Nettl, *Mozart in Böhmen*, 93-94. They are not transcribed in Berkovec, *Musicalia*.

The marriage of Count Johann Joseph Philipp is recorded in Procházka, *Genealogisches Handbuch*, 54. The bride was Countess Maria Josepha von Canal.

P. 101 - The *Complete Description of Prague* lists the Pachta palaces in Prague in vol. 1, 120 (on Anenské náměstí), 126 (overlooking the "Tummelplatz"), and 161 (near the Canal palace on modern Na přikopě). The history of the palace with the modern address Anenské náměstí 5 (č.p. 2018-I) is set forth in *Pražské paláce*, 222-24.

The location of the palace of Count Franz Joseph von Pachta is identified in Jaroslaus Schaller, *Description of the City of Prague*, vol. 3 (1796), 661-62; an eighteenth-century illustration of it is found in Nettl, *Mozart in Böhmen*, between pp. 88 and 89. Nettl's information on the Pachta family (pp. 98-100) is not precise enough to make positive identifications due to the confusion with Christian names. The Canals, Pachtas, and Mozart all shared participation in the masonic movement. The principal lodges in Prague were "The Three Crowned Stars" and "Truth and Unity," which was founded by Count Canal himself in 1783.

Count Hubert Karl may be the "Count Karl" Pachta listed in the *Jahrbuch der Tonkunst von Wien und Prag* of 1796 as being a talented violinist, thus a potential acquaintance of Mozart. See Johann Ferdinand von Schönfeld, *Jahrbuch der Tonkunst von Wien und Prag* (Vienna, 1796; repr. Munich: Emil Katzbichler, 1976), 129.

Whichever Pachta it was who received the contredanses, there is an anecdote about how they were commissioned that is found in the Nissen biography, but not translated here, since it is so unreliable. Nissen's *Biographie W. A. Mozarts*, 561, claims that Mozart wrote four contredanses for full orchestra for the count in less than a half an hour before a dinner to which the count had invited him. Mozart had been asked to come an hour earlier than was usual, apparently in hopes that the count could have him write the music before the dinner would start.

The Noble Ladies' Foundation is described in the *Complete Description of Prague*, vol. 1, 71-74 (for the branch in Hradčany), and vol. 1, 155-56 (for the branch in the New City). Schaller's description of the administration of the foundation is found in his *Description of the City of Prague*, vol. 1 (1794), 457-62. The entire Prague Castle complex (which contains dozens of buildings) is designated with the same "descriptive number" (č.p. 1-IV). The site of the branch in the New City presently bears the street address Na nemocnice 2 (č.p. 499-II). The building is still used as a medical facility, and a plaque on the front records its conversion for that purpose by Joseph II.

See Nettl, *Mozart in Böhmen*, 173, for the indication of the earlier ownership of the piano from the Noble Ladies' Foundation.

Chapter 6

P. 104 - Eduard Mörike's novella was first published in Stuttgart in 1856; an easily accessible translation into English by David Luke as *Mozart's Journey to Prague* has been available since 2003 from Penguin Books.

Literary treatments based on the subject of Mozart in Prague are collected in Vladimír Kovářík, *Literární toulky Prahou* [Literary wanderings through Prague] (Prague: Albatros, 1988), and a special section of the *Cambridge Mozart Encyclopedia*. Probably the most important literary work of this type produced in the last century is a series of thirteen poems ("rondels") by the Czech writer Jaroslav Seifert first published in 1938 under the title *Mozart v Praze*.

P. 105 - Reports from the *Prague Post* from 31 March, 3 April, and 12 June 1787 are transcribed in Berkovec, *Musicalia*, 65-66. The foundation and early operation of the Rosenthal Theater is detailed in Teuber, *Geschichte des Prager Theaters*, vol. 2, 243-44. The theater and the neighborhood around it are mentioned in the *Complete Description of Prague*, vol. 2, 327.

The report from the *Prague Post* of 6 October 1787 is transcribed in Berkovec, *Musicalia*, 66, and translated in Deutsch, *Mozart: A Documentary Biography*, 299.

P. 106 - The passage from the Nissen biography is translated from the *Biographie W. A. Mozarts*, 518.

For mention of the Three Lions' Inn, see Eduard Herold, *Malerische Wanderungen durch Prag* (Prague, 1866), 564-65. It is also cited in Schaller's *Description of the City of Prague*, vol. 3 (1796), 608. The modern address of the inn is Uhelný trh 1, Old City.

The "Golden Wheel" inn is cited in the *Complete Description of Prague*, vol. 1, 245.

P. 107 - The most frequently consulted edition of the Da Ponte memoirs of 1823 is cited in the notes for the Introduction. The Da Ponte *Extract* is available in modern edition as the *Estratto delle memorie*, ed. Lorenzo della Chà (Milan: Edizioni Il Polifilo, 1999); the excerpt quoted here appears on p. 58. The article on *Don Giovanni* in the *Cambridge Mozart Encylclopedia* tries to reconcile the two versions of the genesis of the opera, even though they are clearly mutually exclusive.

Although Guardasoni is referred to as the director of the National Theater in Da Ponte's reminiscences of the first production of *Don Giovanni* (besides several contemporary sources), the Czech Gubernium still recognized Pasquale Bondini as the impresario at the time. It was Bondini who came before the Gubernium to request permission to mount theatrical and operatic productions in Prague in 1787. Requests are preserved in the National Archive in Prague, fund ČG - Publicum. The last having to do with performances in 1787 is document 34/32 of 11 October 1787, which gives him permission to put on performances of *The Marriage of Figaro* as an opera, but not as a play. Document ČG 34/80 renews permission for Bondini to produce operas in Prague as of 23 October 1787, obviously in response to the renewed effort to put on *Don Giovanni* after the original production was cancelled.

P. 108 - The account of Da Ponte writing three librettos simultaneously is found in the *Memoirs*, 174-76.

P. 109 - In fact, there is a very good chance that Guardasoni actually appeared as Don Giovanni in the second Don Juan opera given in eighteenth-century Prague, Vincenzo Righini's *Il convitato di pietra* of 1776. The precise dates of its performance and the precise dates of Guardasoni's movements are not known that year, but it is known from Righini's score that the role of Don Giovanni was cast for tenor range. Considering Guardasoni's residence in Prague for at least some parts of the year, it is impossible that he did not at least know of the success of this production and its revival in Prague in 1777. An excellent summary of Guardasoni's biography is found in *Starší divadlo*, 208-12. Additional information about his movements and a precise listing of all known productions in which he can be confirmed positively as participating either as singer or impresario is presented in Pierluigi Petrobelli, "Domenico Guardasoni: Italia, Dresden, Praha," in *Böhmische Aspekte*, 187-211.

Nettl, *Mozart in Böohmen*, 118-19, believed that the composition of *Don Giovanni* began as far back as the spring of 1787.

The report from the *Prague Post* of 9 October 1787 is transcribed in Berkovec, *Musicalia*, 66, and translated in Deutsch, *Mozart: A Documentary Biography*, 299. A facsimile of the issue is reproduced in Nettl, *Mozart in Böhmen*, between pp. 112 and 113.

For Da Ponte's stay at the Platýs inn, see Herold, *Malerische Wanderungen*, vol. 1, 564. Rudolf von Freisauff, in his *Mozarts Don Juan, 1787-1887: ein Beitrag zur Geschichte dieser Oper* (Salzburg, 1887), 21, also claims that Da Ponte stayed in the Platýs inn. Procházka, *Mozart in Prag*, 82, adds the detail that staying in such close proximity made it possible for Mozart and Da Ponte to colloborate better. Nettl, *Mozart in Böhmen*, 129, adds the detail that Mozart and Da Ponte were able to communicate with each other from the windows of the inns, but neither he, Procházka, nor Freisauff provide any documentation to confirm that Da Ponte ever stayed in the Platýs inn at all. The inn still exists with the address of Uhelný trh 11, Old City.

P. 110 - The outlines of the visit to Prague of the Saxon couple are detailed in Deutsch, *Mozart: A Documentary Biography*, 300-1. Precise information concerning the genealogy and vital statistics of the Saxon royal family is presented in *Burke's Royal Families of the World*, 171-79.

The letter of Countess Caroline von Waldstein of 5 October 1787 is reproduced in facsimile in Volek and Bittner, *Mozartiana*, 32-35. This document was originally brought to light by Eva Mikanová in her "Neznámá mozartovská bohemika," 181-85.

P. 111 - For the days on which the Bondini company performed, see the note for p. 93.

The anecdote concerning Micelli is recorded in Nissen, *Biographie W. A. Mozarts*, 519.

Mozart's letter of 15 October 1787 to Jacquin is reproduced in facsimile in Volek and Bittner, *The Mozartiana of Czech and Moravian Archives*, 36-38.

P. 112 - For the precise tenures of the *Oberstburggrafen* during the time of Mozart's visits to Prague, see Schaller, *Description of the City of Prague*, vol. 2 (1795), 155.

P. 113 - The opinion of the emperor Joseph concerning the "licentiousness" of Beaumarchais's play is recorded in Da Ponte, *Memoirs*, 150.

The permission to present *The Marriage of Figaro* as an opera is preserved in the National Archive, fund ČG - Publicum, document 34/32. It is reproduced in facsimile in Volek and Bittner, *Mozartiana*, 25.

The report from the *Prague Post* of 16 October 1787 is transcribed in Berkovec, *Musicalia*, 67, and translated in Deutsch, *Mozart: A Documentary Biography*, 300.

P. 114 - The excerpt from the *Wiener Zeitung* is translated in Deutsch, *Mozart: A Documentary Biography*, 301.

The relevant excerpt from Count Zinzendorf's diary of 19 October 1787 is translated in Deutsch, *Mozart: A Documentary Biography*, 301.

P. 115 - For a brief biographical notice about Bridi, see Clive, *Mozart and His Circle*.

The notice in the *Prague Post* of 30 October 1787 is trascribed in Berkovec, *Musicalia*, 67, translated in Deutsch, *Mozart: A Documentary Biography*, 302, and reproduced in facsimile in Volek and Bittner, *The Mozartiana of Czech and Moravian Archives*, 39-40.

The notice in the *Prague Post* of 3 November 1787 is transcribed in Berkovec, *Musicalia*, 67-68, and translated in Deutsch, *Mozart: A Documentary Biography*, 303-4.

A brief notice from the Hamburg *Staats und gelehrte Zeitung des hamburgischen unpartheyischen Correspondenten* of 9 November 1787 is translated in Eisen, *New Mozart Documents* (Stanford University Press, 1991), 51. A notice of 10 November 1787 in the *Provinzialnachrichten* is translated in Deutsch, *Mozart: A Documentary Biography*, 304, which reports that the same notice published in Prague on 1 November also appeared in the *Wiener Zeitung* on 14 November.

The excerpt about the first performance of *Don Giovanni* is taken from Němeček, *Lebensbeschreibung*, 42-43.

P. 116 - The first Da Ponte excerpt is taken from the *Estratto delle memorie*, 60-62, the second one from the *Memoirs*, 178-79. The portion of the *Memoirs* that excerpts the putative letter of Mozart is partially translated in Deutsch, *Mozart: A Documentary Biography*, 302.

P. 117 - See Alfred Meissner's *Rococo-Bilder*, 2nd ed., 98-113, for a fictionalized account of the events surrounding the first performance of *Don Giovanni* in Prague.

P. 118 - The circumstances surrounding the Casanova letter written from Prague are discussed in Nettl, *Mozart in Böhmen*, 144-45.

The memoirs that document Casanova's many love affairs are collected under the title *Histoire de ma vie*. The publication of the memoirs began in the form of a German adaptation in 12 volumes under the title *Aus den Memoiren des Venetianers Jacob Casanova de Seingalt; oder, Sein Leben, wie er es zu Dux in Böhmen niederschrieb* (Leipzig, 1822-1829). A French version soon followed in 14 volumes: *Mémoires du Vénitien J. Casanova de Seingalt, extraits de ses manuscrits originaux* (Paris, 1825-1829). The first edition of the complete text in French did not appear until the 1960s: *Histoire de ma vie*, 12 vols. (Leipzig: Brockhaus; Paris: Plon, 1960-1962).

Otto Jahn's references to Dušek are found in his *W. A. Mozart*, vol. 4 (Leipzig: Breitkopf & Härtel, 1859), 282.

P. 119 - A translation of the letter of 14 October 1785 is not found in Anderson, *Letters of Mozart and His Family*. Dušek's relationship with Count Clam is discussed in some detail in Nettl, *Mozart in Böhmen*, 42-43.

The impression of the dowager duchess Anna Amalia is recorded in a letter of Schiller to Christian Gottfried Körner of 7 May 1788 transcribed in Friedrich Schiller, *Briefwechsel zwischen Schiller und Körner von 1784 bis zum Tode Schillers*, vol. 1 (Stuttgart and Berlin, 1892), 217-19. For the length of Da Ponte's stay, see the *Memoirs*, 178.

There is no mention of a tavern in Templová lane in the *Complete Description of Prague* of 1787 or Schaller's *Description of the City of Prague* from the 1790s. It is only from two guidebooks from the 1820s that references to a coffeehouse "im Tempel" start to be found: August W. Griesel, *Neuestes Gemälde von Prag* (Prague, 1823), 150, and Wolfgang A. Gerle, *Prag und seine Merkwürdigkeiten für Fremde und Einheimische* (Prague, 1825), 152. Herold, *Malerische Wanderungen*, vol. 1, 210-11, claims that Mozart visited it in the 1780s.

Casanova's *Histoire de ma fuite des prisons de la République de Venise: qu'on appelles les Plombs, écrite à Dux en Bohême l'année 1787* (Leipzig, 1788) was not yet published in 1787 - a detail apparently not known to Meissner.

The dialogues and incidents created by Meissner for the *Rococo-Bilder* invite quick mention of one of the less reliable anecdotes about Mozart that appears in the Nissen biography. Nissen's *Biographie W. A. Mozarts*, 561, claims that Mozart wrote several of the musical numbers for *Don Giovanni* while people were bowling in the garden of the Bertamka villa, an activity that did not disturb his concentration at all.

P. 120 - The best biographical summaries for Luigi Bassi and Teresa Saporiti are found in *Starší divadlo*; information is also available in Clive, *Mozart and His Circle*, and the *Cambridge Mozart Encyclopedia*. Micelli is not accorded an entry in any of these reference works. In his vignettes, Meissner indicates her given name as Maria, not Caterina.

P. 125 - For the Herold account, see the *Malerische Wanderungen*, vol. 1, 692-93. The earliest mention of the Blue Grape in Prague guidebooks is Schaller's *Description of the City of Prague*, vol. 3 (1796), 326.

Constanze's account of the composition of the overture to *Don Giovanni* is found in Nissen, *Biographie W. A. Mozarts*, 651.

P. 126 - Nettl, *Mozart in Böhmen*, 139, also quotes a short version of finishing the *Don Giovanni* overture only the night before the first performance that originates from the music critic Johann Friedrich Rochlitz in a journal of the year 1799.

For the Štěpánek account of the composition of the overture to *Don Giovanni*, see Nissen, *Biographie W. A. Mozarts*, 519-20.

For the *Don Giovanni* rehearsal anecdote, see ibid., 559.

P. 127 - For Němeček's account of the composition of the overture to *Don Giovanni*, see the *Lebensbeschreibung*, 84-85.

Svoboda's reminiscence is set forth in Wilhelm Kuhe, *My Musical Recollections* (London, 1896), 7-10. Zerlina was sung by Caterina Bondini, the wife of Pasquale Bondini. Meissner refers to the incident of Zerlina being started in his *Rococo-Bilder* (see p. 122 of the main text of this volume).

P. 128 - For the Meissner account, see his *Rococo-Bilder*, 2nd ed., 113-16.

P. 129 - For the reminiscence of Eduard Genast, see *Aus dem Tagebuche eines alten Schauspielers* (Leipzig, 1862), 3-5.

Chapter 7

P. 131 - Nissen's version of the story of the harpist is recorded in the *Biographie W. A. Mozarts*, 562.

The Němeček quotation is translated from the *Lebensbeschreibung*, 38.

P. 132 - Freisauff's discussion of the incident of the harpist is found in *Mozart's Don Juan*, 16-18.

P. 133 - This "harpist's theme" bears Köchel number Anh. C 26.10, since it was not included in the original catalog ("Anh." is an abbreviation for "Anhang," i.e., appendix).

The decree concerning harpists is preserved in Prague, National Archive, fund PŘ (Policejní Ředitelství) 1769-1823, document 323. The documents from this fund are inventoried in Ruth Ballnerová, *Městské Hejtmanství a Policejní Ředitelství Praha 1769-1855: Inventář* [The City Captaincy and

Police Administration of Prague 1769-1855: an inventory] (Prague: Archivní Správa Minsterstva Vnitra, 1960).

The so-called "New Inn" is identified in Schaller, *Decription of the City of Prague,* vol. 3 (1796), 540. According to Schaller, it had been purchased by its owner, Johann Michael Schoyer, in 1788. Nettl, *Mozart in Prag,* 109, reports that the "New Inn" is mentioned in an unidentified issue of the *Prague Post* of 1791.

P. 134 - The story from the bookseller Schenk is found in Procházka, *Mozart in Prag,* 46. The quotation from Meissner is taken from the *Rococo-Bilder,* 2nd ed., 153.

This portrait of the harpist is reproduced in Nettl, *Mozart in Böhmen,* between pp. 104 and 105.

The version of the "harpist's theme" in F major has been assigned Köchel number Anh. C 26.11.

The translation from Herold is taken from the *Malerische Wanderungen,* vol. 1, 211.

Nettl's discussion of the Inn "Zum Tempel," which includes two photographs, is found in his *Mozart in Böhmen,* 112-14.

P. 135 - For Schaller's brief notice concerning the Inn "Zum Tempel," see his *Description of the City of Prague,* vol. 3 (1796), 540.

The page citations from the guidebooks cited are August Griesel, *Neuestes Gemälde von Prag* (Prague, 1823), 100, and Wolfgang Gerle, *Prag und seine Merkwürdigkeiten* (Prague, 1825), 152.

The page citation for the earliest anecdote about the "Grape" coffeehouse is anon., *Prag in seiner jetztigen Gestalt,* 148-49. For mention of the "Blue Wine Grape," see Schaller, *Description of the City of Prague,* vol. 3 (1796), 326. See Griesel, *Neuestes Gemälde,* 100, and Gerle, *Prag und seine Merkwürdigkeiten,* 152, for its popularity in the 1820s. Its closing is mentioned in Herold, *Malerische Wanderungen,* vol. 1, 694.

For the Nissen version of the story of the harpist, see his *Biographie W. A. Mozarts,* 559-60. The Herold version is found in the *Malerische Wanderungen,* vol. 1, 217-18. See Meissner, *Rococo-Bilder,* 2nd ed., 145, for the specification of the coffeehouse "zum Sturm."

P. 136 - Lehman's letter is also translated in Deutsch, *Mozart: A Documentary Biography,* 517-18, with information about the early publication of its text.

P. 137 - Of course it is also possible that Dušek escorted Mozart from lodgings in the city of Prague itself, and not the Bertramka villa at all.

The fragmentary improvisation recorded by Lehman has been assigned Köchel number Anh. C 27.03.

The time that Mozart spent with Dušek in incidents such as the excursion to the Strahov Abbey have led some scholars to suggest that they were involved in a romantic relationship; one that is frequently cited is Maynard Solomon in his *Mozart: A Life,* 445-49, which also includes citations for other scholars' opinions about the matter. This suggestion is not supported by any direct documentation; existing information only confirms that they were friends and artistic collaborators. In this matter, one should keep in mind the ruthlessness of the "love market." If Dušek were able to attract and retain a lover as desirable as Count Clam outside of wedlock, it is very difficult to see what she would have had to gain by involvement with the physically unimpressive and financially insecure Wolfgang Amadeus Mozart. There is no reason at present to believe that his artistic collaboration came with strings attached.

P. 139 - The letter of Karl Mozart is transcribed in full in Procházka, *Mozart in Prag,* 62, and Walter Hummel, *W. A. Mozarts Söhne* (Kassel: Bärenreiter, 1956), 18-19.

P. 140 - The excerpts from Mozart's album are translated in Deutsch, *Mozart: A Documentary Biography,* 304.

Documents related to Mozart's appointment at the imperial court are translated in ibid., 305-7. A detailed explanation of the circumstances surrounding this appointment are presented in Dorothea Link, "Mozart's Appointment to the Viennese Court," in *Words About Mozart: Essays in Honour of Stanley Sadie,* eds. Dorothea Link and Judith Nagley (Woodbridge: The Boydell Press, 2005), 153-73.

The report in the *Prague Post* of 29 December 1787 is transcribed in Berkovec, *Musicalia*, 68.

P. 141 - The report in the *Prague Post* from 11 December 1787 is transcribed in Berkovec, *Muscalia*, 68, and translated in Deutsch, *Mozart: A Documentary Biography*, 307.

The Haydn letter is transcribed in Němeček, *Lebensbeschreibung*, 78-79, and translated in Deutsch, *Mozart: A Documentary Biography*, 308-9.

P. 142 - The excerpt from the *Prague Post* of 8 April 1788 is transcribed in Berkovec, *Musicalia*, 141.

The reception of *Don Giovanni* in Vienna is described in greater detail in Braunbehrens, *Mozart in Vienna*, 304-10. Reports of performances of *Don Giovanni* in Frankfurt-am-Main in May of 1789 that were greeted with indifference are recorded in Deutsch, *Mozart: A Documentary Biography*, 341. The latter also records early productions of *Don Giovanni* in Mannheim beginning in September 1789 (p. 390), with a revival in March 1791; in Berlin in December of 1790 (p. 386); in Hanover on 4 March 1791 in German (p. 387), many performances in Berlin during the spring of 1791 (pp. 390-92); a performance in Bad Pyrmont on 8 July 1791 (p. 398); and performances given at Munich on 7 and 23 August, and 27 September 1791 (p. 399). A considerable amount of information concerning early performances of *Don Giovanni* up to the 1880s is found in Freisauff, *Mozart's Don Juan*, 105-75.

See Meissner, *Rococo-Bilder*, 2nd ed., 116, for remarks paraphrased from Da Ponte, *Memoirs*, 179-80.

For the foundation and operation of the Hybernian Theater, see Teuber, *Geschichte des Prager Theaters*, vol. 2, 292-321.

Da Ponte's description of the first performance of *Don Giovanni* in Vienna is taken from the *Memoirs*, 179-80.

P. 143 - Da Ponte's payment of 100 ducats is confirmed in a document from the Imperial court translated in Deutsch, *Mozart: A Documentary Biography*, 314.

The excerpt from Count Zinzendorf's diary is translated in Deutsch, *Mozart: A Documentary Biography*, 313. The opinion of Countess zur Lippe is translated on p. 314, the opinion of the archduchess Elisabeth Wilhelmine on pp. 314-15, and the opinion of emperor Joseph on p. 315.

P. 144 - The opinion of Rochlitz is translated from Nettl, *Mozart in Böhmen*, 174.

Angermüller, *Mozart auf der Reise nach Prag, Dresden, Leipzig und Berlin*, is mainly a detailed chronology of Mozart's trip to various cities to the north of Vienna in 1789; as a scholarly resource, it is of greatest value for the visits to the German cities.

The works composed of the Prussian royal family were the string quartets, K. 575, 589, and 590, and the piano sonata, K. 576.

P. 145 - Mention of the Unicorn Inn is found in the *Complete Description of Prague*, vol. 1, 19, and vol. 2, 245.

P. 146 - Nettl, *Mozart in Böhmen*, 178, suggests that "Leliborn" might be a corruption of "Schönborn," the name of a distinguished Bohemian family, one of whose members acquired the palace that now houses the Embassy of the United States in Malá Strana (Tržiště 15, č.p. 365-III). Angermüller, in his *Mozart auf der Reise nach Prag, Dresden, Leipzig und Berlin*, 112, was even more anxious to make this identification, even pointing out the existence of a wine café with the name "U Schönbornů" located there is modern times. In fact, what is now known as the Schönborn Palace did not belong to any member of the Schönborn family until 1794 (see *Pražské paláce*, 271). Mozart had no known connections to this family.

A facsimile of the placard from 1788 is reproduced in Nettl, *Mozart in Böhmen*, between pp. 152 and 153, besides many other publications.

Guardasoni's activities in Warsaw, including an early production of *Don Giovanni* in Warsaw in 1789, are detailed in Alina Żórawska-Witkowska, "Domenico Guardasoni a Varsavia: due episodi polacchi dalla sua carriera operistica (1774-1776, 1789-1791)," in *Böhmische Aspekte*, 213-38.

A document in the National Archive in Prague, fund ČG - Publicum 34/165, dated 5 November 1789, specifically cites Bondini's departure as a reason not to grant anyone permission to produce operas in Prague any more in the absence of any impresario. The precise date of Guardasoni's departure to Warsaw from Prague is not known. The last opera given in Prague in 1789 was Paisello's *Il mondo della luna* (date unknown).

A biographical notice for Ramm is found in Clive, *Mozart and His Circle*.

The reference to an operatic commission for the autumn of 1789 helped lead the Czech musicologist Tomislav Volek to formulate what for him has been an enduring fantasy, first articulated in his essay "Über den Ursprung von Mozarts Oper *La clemenza di Tito*," in *Mozart-Jahrbuch* 1959 (Salzburg: Internationale Stiftung Mozarteum, 1960), 274-86, that the opera proposed was to be *La clemenza di Tito* and that Mozart started to compose it long before it was actually commissioned by the Estates of Bohemia in 1791. One of the most effective refutations of this notion is set forth in Sergio Durante's thorough study "The Chronology of Mozart's 'La clemenza di Tito Reconsidered," *Music & Letters* 80 (1999): 560-94. Volek's reasoning was highly flawed from the start, but even recently, he has chosen to cling to the indefensible in his diatribe "Nochmals: Über den Ursprung von Mozarts Opera *La clemenza di Tito*," in *Böhmische Aspekte*, 265-77.

As regards putative plans of the impresario Guardasoni to produce a setting of *La clemenza di Tito* in 1789, it must be pointed out how eccentric it would be for Mozart or Guardasoni to be so interested in the subject matter at that time. By 1789, the librettos of Pietro Metastasio were becoming less and less attractive to opera managers after an amazing period of dominance that lasted from the 1730s until the 1770s. *La clemenza di Tito* was not even one of the Metastasian texts that was greatly favored during the period of the poet's ascendancy. As of 1789, there had not been a single setting of it in Europe since 1774 (a version by Josef Mysliveček performed at the Teatro San Benedetto in Venice). What outstanding merit Guardasoni might have sensed in this text, or how he could have imagined that it would be an attractive offering to audiences of his day, is unfathomable. The culture of Italian opera of the late eighteenth century depended on the presentation of newer settings of newer operatic texts. The type of serious opera represented by Metastasio's texts was quite old-fashioned by 1789 (which is why extensive alterations had to be made to Metastasio's text in order to accommodate Mozart's setting of 1791). Clearly, the commission for the Mozart setting of *La clemenza di Tito* in 1791 can only be described as the result of an extraordinary coincidence in which the circumstances of a unique political event could be matched to the specific characteristics of a particular operatic text.

P. 147 - The placard in question was reproduced among the illustrations in Buchner, *Mozart und Prag*, and in Volek, *Mozart a Praha*, facing p. 33. It is partially translated in Deutsch, *Mozart: A Documentary Biography*, 393. In his essay "Über den Ursprung von Mozarts Oper *La clemenza di Tito*," 274-79, Tomislav Volek speculated that the aria accompanied by basset horn was "Non più di fiori" from *La clemenza di Tito*. He did not seem to think it of critical importance that no definite plans had been made by the Estates of Bohemia to sponsor a coronation opera or select its subject matter until after the concert of 26 April, nor did he bother to investigate whether or not Mozart ever wrote an earlier aria that included the sonority of basset horn in its accompaniment. It is remarkable how long Volek's specious theory has been given credence in the musicological community. Indeed, Landon, in his *1791: Mozart's Last Year*, 91-101, felt it necessary to include a huge digression in his work in order to find some means to lend it legitimacy, and it is also taken seriously in the article on Prague in the *Cambridge Mozart Encyclopedia* (although not in the article on *La clemenza di Tito*).

Marius Flotuis offered a convincing resolution to the matter in his article "Welche Arie sang Josepha Duschek am 26. April 1791?" in *Mitteilungen der Internationalen Stiftung Mozarteum* 37 (1989): 81-82, by pointing out that the original reference to basset horn in the German text is plural, thus it could not denote "Non più di fiori," which includes only one basset horn in its accompaniment. In light of this observation, the only likely candidate would be "Al desio di chi t'adora," K. 577 of 1789, which also conforms to the pattern of a slow-fast "rondò." Sergio Durante, in his "The Chronology of Mozart's 'La clemenza di Tito' Reconsidered," 574-75, did not necessarily endorse Flothuis' findings, but on the basis of other evidence far too complicated to present to the intended readership of this volume (principally analysis of the paper on which various portions of the opera were written), rejected the claim that "Non più di fiori" was composed before the main body of Mozart's opera during the summer of 1791. Whether or not the reference to basset horn is accurately described as singular or plural, the most important point is that the sonority of basset horn was present and that Mozart did compose an earlier aria that included it.

Some other points about the vocal piece "Non più di fiori" should also be emphasized. One touches on the fact that the text for this vocal piece is not included among the original texts that Metastasio wrote for his drama *La clemenza di Tito* of 1734, and it cannot be traced to any other poet except Caterino Mazzolà in the libretto and score for the Mozart setting first performed on 6 September 1791. If the aria had been written earlier as something to be included in a planned setting of *La clemenza di Tito* months before the summer of 1791, it would mean that Mozart (instead of a theater manager) would have had to take it upon himself to pay an Italian poet to fashion a substitute text to replace Metastasio's original text "Getta il nocchier talora" in the same dramatic theme for a production that he had no assurance would ever take place (an extremely improbable scenario).

The absence of "Non più di fiori" from Mozart's catalog of compositions is also of great significance. It is almost inconceivable that such a substantial vocal piece would not have been entered into his catalog if it was considered to be suitable for public performance as an independent composition (which it would have had to have been if it were released to Josefa Dušek for that purpose). The rondò "Al desio di chi t'adora," an additional number intended for performances of the opera *The Marriage of Figaro*, most definitely was included in his catalog. It would not have been appropriate to advertise the latter vocal piece, unlike the "grand scene" for voice "quite recently completed," as "new" in the placard printed for the concert of 26 April 1791, and indeed the vocal piece with basset horn was not specified as a new composition. If the vocal piece in question actually was "Non più di fiori," it would be strange that its newness would not be drawn attention to along with the newness of the "grand scene."

Any theory that the composition of *La clemenza di Tito* began before the summer of 1791 would have to consider the fact that eighteenth-century operas by professional composers were almost invariably written only on commission for imminent performance. There was generally nothing like the phenomenon of nineteenth-century composers such as Wagner or Debussy who completed operas on texts or stories that caught their imagination, then hoped that somebody could be found one day to sponsor a performance of the result, even if it took years. This means of creating operas was quite alien to Mozart's era of operatic composition.

Chapter 8

P. 148 - Robert L. Marshall, *Mozart Speaks: Views on Music, Musicians, and the World* (New York: Schirmer Books, 1991), which takes the form of a detailed survey of the contents of the Mozart documentation, in particular the Mozart correspondence, yields this opinion concerning Mozart's knowledge of political affairs: "Mozart's interest in the news of the day apparently was extremely limited" (p. 106).

P. 149 - For Mozart's alleged lack of education, see Němeček, *Lebensbeschreibung*, 92. The lines about the expectation of an artist to be an author, journalist, and politician are found in the first edition of the Němeček biography, not the second, and are translated here from another edition of Němeček's biography: Ernst Rychnovsky, ed., *W. A. Mozart's Leben nach Originalquellen beschrieben von Franz Niemetschek* (Prague: I. Taussig, 1905), 59, which favors the earlier version for this passage.

An excellent example of a study that regards Mozart without question (or adequate documentation) as a dedicated intellectual is Nicholas Till, *Mozart and the Enlightenment: Truth, Virtue and Beauty in Mozart's Operas* (London: Faber and Faber, 1992). In this work, Mozart's sympathy for the progressive political ideals of his day is taken as an article of faith without any direct evidence to support it, and it also assumes that Mozart tried to use operatic productions to promote progressive political ideals. A specialty of the presentation is fantastic interpretations of innocuous passages from the Mozart correspondence that are used to compensate for a lack of genuine evidence concerning the composer's reaction to contemporary political events.

Němeček's opinion that Mozart had enough general knowledge for a cultured man is expressed in the *Lebensbeschreibung*, 91, whereas his all-consuming devotion to music is described in ibid.,

89-90. The contents of the small library that Mozart left at the time of his death supports a view of him as a "man of taste," not an intellectual, for its emphasis on literature and basic instruction in a variety of academic subjects. As far as can be determined, he did not make a habit of collecting weighty tomes. See Deutsch, *Mozart: A Documentary Biography,* 587-89, 601-2.

P. 150 - The quotation of Napoléon Bonaparte is taken from Jasper Ridley, *The Freemasons* (New York: Arcade Publishing, 2001), 152. Ridley's study finds over and over again that the true function of Masonic lodges over the centuries has been to provide opportunities for social intercourse and what is referred to now as professional "networking." He made no exception for the Viennese lodges of Mozart's time. Ridley concluded that the only period in which Masonic societies truly did exist primarily to advance a political agenda was in nineteenth-century Spain (the origin of Francisco Franco's famous suspicion of Masons). Paul Nettl's study *Mozart and Masonry* (New York: Philosphical Library, 1957), makes no claims concerning the political orientation of the Masonic movement as it existed in the Austrian Empire in Mozart's day. Till, *Mozart and the Enlightenment,* esp. 117-29, offers in contrast a portrayal of the movement that attributes political activism in support of "enlightened" ideals to be an essential activity of Masonic lodges, a fashionable view among certain Mozart scholars of the late 20th century, even though it is based mainly on speculation.

Claims of Mozart's sympathy for Enlightenment philosophy are based far too much on the assumption that he shared all the ideals of certain progressive members of the Masonic movement in Austria simply because he knew them. The true nature of his interaction with these individuals remains unknown (perhaps nothing more than meeting them "to have a good time"). The Masonic tribute published in Mozart's honor after his death tends to support Ridley's view of the Masonic lodges essentially as social clubs. Translated in Deutsch, *Mozart: A Documentary Biography,* 447-50, it praises Mozart only for artistic merit, devotion to family, and congenial personal traits, but nothing having to do with intellectual prowess, stimulating conversation, or political consciousness.

Count Künigl's participation in the meetings of the Bohemian Estates is mentioned in Kerner, *Bohemia in the Eighteenth Century,* 102-3.

P. 151 - Count Ludwig von Cavriani served as supreme burgrave from 9 September 1787 until he was replaced by Count Heinrich von Rottenhan on 27 January 1791; Rottenhan was replaced on 23 November 1792 by Count Prokop von Lažanský.

The instruction of the imperial court of 2 March 1791 is detailed in Volek, "Über den Ursprung," 280.

The memorandum (*Hofrescript*) of the Estates of 20 April 1791 resolving to put on a coronation is preserved in the National Archive in Prague, fund ZV (Zemský Výbor), carton 1176, fascicle 84/1, ff. 189-89'.

The issues of the *Prague Post* cited in this chapter are all preserved in the collection of the Library of the National Museum in Prague. The issue of 19 April 1791 indicates the date of Count Rottenhan's return from Vienna as 17 April.

The coronation of Charles VI in 1723 is described briefly in Freeman, *The Opera Theater of Count Franz Anton von Sporch,* 21-22, with references to more thorough discussions.

The plans of the committee of the Estates as drawn up on 29 April 1791 are documented in Volek, "Über den Ursprung," 280. In contrast to the lavish coronation of Charles VI in 1723, Maria Theresa's coronation as Queen of Bohemia in 1743 was a rather tawdry affair. The opera performed for this event, a setting of Metastasio's libretto *Semiramide riconosciuta*, was given in a temporary theater built on the grounds of Prague Castle. The libretto that records the event does not specify a composer's name or the identity of the singers, a sign that the production was a pastiche of music thrown together hastily (whereas the production of Johann Joseph Fux's *La costanza e fortezza* for Charles VI was accompanied by the one of the greatest convocations of distiinguished musicians ever assembled in the eighteenth century). Clearly the subject of the opera was chosen to draw attention to Maria Theresa's accomplishments as a female ruler and overseer of military policy (the Babylonian queen Semiramis was one of the most famous warrior females of antiquity). The librettos for the coronation operas are listed in Sartori, *I libretti italiani.* Maur, *12.5.1743,* provides a detailed explanation of the circumstances surrounding Maria Therea's coronation as queen of Bohemia.

For the musical requirements requested from Salieri, see Landon, *1791: Mozart's Last Year*, 103.

The memorandum (*Hofdekret*) of the Estates of 25 May 1791 is preserved in the National Archive in Prague, fund ZV, carton 1176, fascicle 84/1, ff. 191-92.

Le Noble is listed among the "departing foreigners" at the New Gate (those bound for Vienna) on 17 June in an issue of the *Prague Post* of 21 June; an issue of 23 July records Le Noble's return from Vienna as of 20 July with the intent of staying in Prague Castle.

The instructions given to Wenzel von Ugarte are recorded in Landon, *1791: Mozart's Last Year*, 103.

P. 152 - The *Prague Post* of 14 June records the names of the entire Guardasoni company and the detail that they came as "arriving foreigners" through the New Gate from Warsaw and would be staying at the "Blue Star" inn ("zum Blauen Stern") in Prague. According to the *Complete Description of Prague*, vol. 2, 244, this inn was located in the New City on what is now Hybernská street, and it catered to travelers who entered Prague from the New Gate.

The arrival of the Seconda company is recorded as taking place on 3 June at the "Imperial Gate" (Reichstor), the usual gate for visitors from Saxony. The "Imperial Gate" skirted the western boundary of the Strahov complex in Hradčany, corresponding to modern Strahovská street. According to the *Prague Post*, the Seconda company planned to stay at the Thun palace in Malá Strana, just were Mozart stayed during his first trip to Prague in 1787. There is a biographical entry for Seconda in *Starší divadlo*, 526-28.

The response of Count Nostic to Count Rottenhan, dated 1 July 1791, is preserved in the National Archive, fund ZV, carton 1187, fascicle 84/43, ff. 11-11. At this time, the Estates of Bohemia were already considering acquiring the theater, as detailed in a large collection of documents in carton 1195 of the fund ZV. The first recorded proposal is dated 9 November 1790 (and signed by Count Rottenhan); however, the acquisition was not completed until 1798.

The contract with Guardasoni of 8 July 1791 is preserved in the National Archive, fund ZV, karton 1188, fascicle 84/42 without foliation. It was first transcribed in Tomislav Volek, "Über den Ursprung von Mozarts Oper *La clemenza di Tito*," and is reproduced in facsimile in Volek and Bittner, *Mozartiana*, 42-43. It is translated into English in Landon, *1791: Mozart's Last Year*, 88-89, but a much better resource for a discussion of the document is Durante, "The Chronology of Mozart's 'La clemenza di Tito' Reconsidered," 562-64.

The document of 10 July 1791 is preserved in the National Archive in Prague, fund ZV, carton 1187, fascicle 84/43, f. 46.

P. 153 - Durante, "The Chronology of Mozart's 'La clemenza di Tito Reconsidered," 576, hypothesizes the recruitment of singers in northern Italy during the third or last week of July. It would appear that he never needed to travel as far south as Bologna, only Padua and Vicenza.

The movements of pre-nineteenth-century operatic singers can be traced from listings in the singers' appendix of Sartori, *I libretti italiani*, at least in cases in which the librettos cataloged in the earlier volumes have cast lists included. Bedini was appearing in the pastiche *Didone abbandonata* in Padua in the summer of 1791, whereas In the summer of 1791, Maria Marchetti Fantozzi was appearing in the title role of Sebastiano Nasolini's *La morte di Cleopatra* in Vicenza (Rubinelli appeared as Mark Antony). Violani appeared in Nasolini's *Teseo e Stige* and Alessio Prati's *La vendetta di Nino* in Florence at the beginning of 1791, then is not traceable again until his appearance in Ferdinando Robuschi's *Attalo re di Bitinia* in Lisbon at the end of the same year. It can be established from the Sartori catalog that Bedini appeared in the pastiche *Didone abbandonata* in Padua in the summer of 1791, but his appearance in Giovanni Paisiello's *Ipermestra* during the same summer season can also be established from other sources (see Durante, "The Chronology of Mozart's 'La clemenza di Tito' Reconsidered,' 575).

The movements of Antonio Baglioni are traced meticulously in John A. Rice, "Antonio Baglioni, Mozart's First Don Ottavio and Tito, in Italy and Prague," in *Böhmische Aspekte*, 295-321.

The document of 10 July 1791 is preserved in the National Archive in Prague, fund ZV, carton 1187, fascicle 84/43, f. 46.

P. 154 - Durante, "The Chronology of Mozart's 'La clemenza di Tito' Reconsidered," 569-574, contains detailed information on the sets designed for the coronation opera by Pietro Travaglia and additional bibliography concerning their conception and discovery.

The authorization for 600 gulden dated 9 July 1791 is preserved in the National Archive in Prague, fund ZV, carton 1187, fascicle 84/43, f. 39. The final authorization for Guardasoni's travelling expenses, dated 28 October 1791, is found in carton 1188, fascicle 84/42, ff. 745-46. The latter document is reproduced in facsimile in Volek and Bittner, *Mozartiana*, 45-46. Guardasoni felt that he deserved further compensation for losses incurred by the production of *La clemenza di Tito*, and petitioned the Estates on 10 October 1791 for extra money in documents preserved in carton 1176, fascicle 84/12 (pp. 72-76).

Salieri's account of being approached about the composition of *La clemenza di Tito* is translated in Landon, *1791: Mozart's Last Year*, 86-87. Durante, "The Chronology of Mozart's 'La clemenza di Tito' Reconsidered," 565-68, provides an expanded discussion.

P. 155 - The means by which Mazzolà was approached as librettist (and his movements at the time) are discussed in Durante, "The Chronology of Mozart's 'La clemenza di Tito' Reconsidered," 568-69. While in Prague, he stayed at the "Blue Star" inn, according to the *Prague Post*, just like the Guardasoni company that arrived the following 10 June.

Travel funds for a deputation to Vienna are recorded as being approved in documents in the National Archive in Prague, fund ZV, karton 1176, fascicle 84/1, f. 200. The arrival of the delegation from the Bohemian Estates on 22 July is confirmed in Joseph Schiffner, *Neuere Geschichte der Böhmen* (Prague, 1816), 80.

The ceremonies that accompanied the return of the crown jewels at various stages of their return to Prague are documented in Johann Debrois, *Urkunde über die vollzogene Krönung seiner Majestät des Königs von Böhmen Leopold des Zweiten und Ihrer Majestät der Gemahlin des Königs Marie Louise* (Prague, 1808; repr. Prague, 1818), 4-11.

Count Chotek's memorandum is preserved in the National Archive in Prague, fund ZV, carton 1176, fascicle 84/1, f. 267'.

P. 156 - Němeček's account of the circumstances surrounding the composition of *La clemenza di Tito* is found in the *Lebesbeschreibung*, 48-50; the claim that it was written in the time frame of 18 days is repeated in another section of Němeček's biography that discusses the music for *The Magic Flute* (see the *Lebensbeschreibung*, 85). Nissen, *Biographie W. A. Mozarts*, 554-55, plagiarizes Němeček's account. Another version of the commission of *La clemenza di Tito* that originated from the critic Johann Friedrich Rochlitz in an issue of the Leipzig *Allgemeine Musikalische Zeitung* of December 1794 is translated in Landon, *1791: Mozart's Last Year*, 222-23. Durante, "The Chronology of Mozart's 'La clemenza di Tito' Reconsidered," 585, transcribes a bit more of Rochlitz's account. This version implies that the Estates turned to Mozart because they waited so long to find someone to compose the music in a hurry (with Leopold nearly ready to leave Vienna) that nobody else could be found to do it so quickly. Mozart's wife and friends supposedly were relieved that he would be setting aside his work on the depressing Requiem (in Rochlitz's version, the commission for it came from a mysterious stranger only Mozart had begun to compose it). Besides the *Prague Post* of 30 August, Mozart's arrival at the New Gate on 28 August is also recorded in the *Prager Interessante Nachrichten* of 3 September (see Deutsch, *Mozart: A Documentary Biography*, 401).

The date of 25 August 1791 for Mozart's departure is also asserted in Landon, *1791: Mozart's Last Year*, 97, for the same reason that it would take three days to travel. Durante, "The Chronology of Mozart's 'La clemenza di Tito' Reconsidered," 589, mistakenly claims 26 August.

Besides the *Prague Post* of 30 August, Mozart's arrival at the New Gate on 28 August 1791 is also recorded in the *Prager Interessante Nachrichten* of 3 September (see Deutsch, *Mozart: A Documentary Biography*, 401).

P. 157 - The intended readers of this volume would be best advised merely to glance over the main discussion of the chronology of the composition of *La clemenza di Tito* presented in Durante, "The Chronology of Mozart's 'La clemenza di Tito' Reconsidered," and skip to its conclusions on pp. 588-90. Readers with specialized knowledge of course will find the preceding discussion engrossing.

Biographical notices for Süssmayer are found in Clive, *Mozart and His Circle*, and the *Cambridge Mozart Encyclopedia*.

For Nissen's claim about Süssmayer writing recitative for *La clemenza di Tito*, see his *Biographie W. A. Mozarts*, 556 and 558.

The anonymous *Krönungsjournal für Prag*, "published by Albrecht" in 1791 (probably a reference to Johann Friedrich Ernst Albrecht, the possible author of the *Observations in and about Prague*) mentions Salieri and the seven court musicians on p. 124 (this journal also has an alternate title: *Journal der doppelten böhmischen Krönung Leopolds des Zweiten und Marien Luisens, Infantin von Spanien, in Prag im Jahre 1791*). The inclusion of the organist Albrechtsberger is indicated in Karl Pfannhauser, "Mozart's 'Krönungsmesse,'" *Mitteilungen der Internationalen Stiftung Mozarteum* 11 (1963): 5. In an Appendix found in Debrois, *Urkunde*, Salieri's lodgings and those of the musicians are indicated more precisely (see pp. 22-23). His travel with court medical personnel is confirmed in Johann Debrois, *Aktenmässige Kroenungs-Geschichte des Koenigs von Böhmen Leopold des Zweiten und Marie Louisens* (Prague, 1792), vol. 1, 58.

The reference to a stay with František Dušek is found in the *Rococo-Bilder*, 2nd ed., 140. The reference to the "Three Axes" ("zu den drei Hackeln") is found in ibid., 146. Nettl, *Mozart in Böhmen*, 215, identifies the house as No. 48 in the Königshofgasse. It can be seen from the map of Prague attached to the *Complete Description of Prague* of 1787, this would now correspond to an address on Celetná in the Old City, just to the east of the Ovocný trh (which is labeled Königsstrasse in the map in the *Complete Description of Prague* and referred to as such in the main text). This would have placed Mozart very close to the National Theater, however Meissner's indication is completely unreliable and its source is unknown.

Němeček's letter to Breitkopf & Härtel is excerpted in Wilhelm Hitzig, "Die Briefe Franz Xaver Niemetscheks und der Marianne Mozart an Breitkopf & Härtel," in *Der Bär: Jahrbuch von Breitkopf & Härtel auf das Jahr 1928* (Leipzig: Breitkopf & Härtel, 1928), 105-6.

P. 158 - The unsympathetic Count of Artois has attracted few biographers. Indeed, the last full biography in English to appear is Vincent W. Beach, *Charles X of France: His Life and Times* (Boulder, Colo: Pruett, 1971). The count's movements in central Europe are little explored in this work, just as in most research about him originating from western Europe and North America.

Albrecht's *Krönungsjournal für Prag*, 203, records a visit of the Count of Artois to Prague on his way to Pillnitz on 24 August 1791 in the company of Charles Alexandre de Calonne (1734-1802), a former Finance Minister of France whose attempts to close the budget deficit of the country before the French Revolution were so unpopular that he was dismissed in 1787. Almost immediately after the start of the French Revolution, he went into exile, then associated himself with prominent French émigrés is various parts of Europe. The Albrecht journal specifically states that the Count of Artois did not actually attend Leopold's coronation in Prague.

The site of the Dušek town house corresponds to modern Upper Malá Strana Square (Horní malostranské náměstí), nos. 14 and 15 (č.p. 203-III and 204-III). A view of the square from the eighteenth century is reproduced among the illustrations in Buchner's booklet *Mozart und Prag*. For further information on the Dušek town house, see Brauneis,"Franz Xaver Niemetschek," 497-98.

The significance of the Declaration of Pillnitz is not in dispute among political historians. Most standard surveys of the French Revolution report much the same information about it. A recent one that summarizes its effects succintly is P. M. Jones, *The French Revolution, 1787-1804*, 2nd ed. (Harlow: Longman, 2010), 52. The text of the Declaration of Pillnitz is translated into English in *From Enlightenment to Romanticism, Anthology I*, eds. Ian Donnachie and Carmen Levin (Manchester: Manchester University Press, 2003), 84-85; it is easy to understand why the French revolutionaries would feel threatened by it.

P. 159 - The Kleist *Fantasien*, published in 1792 in Dresden and Leipzig outside the reach of imperial censors, are easily accessible on the Internet website *www.kleist.org/familie/fa_reise.htm*; it is otherwise unavailable in modern edition. Portions of Kleist's account of the coronation ceremonies in Prague in 1791 have been quoted selectively in much Mozart literature with no recognition of the way that it documents the anti-Enlightenment atmosphere in Prague that surrounded this event. One of the best examples is Landon, *1791: Mozart's Last Year*, which leaves the impression that any hint of Kleist's highly negative view of Leopold's political policies was systematically suppressed.

P. 160 - See Kleist, *Fantasien*, 75-79, for a description of the entrance into Prague of Leopold II on 31 August 1791. The *Urkunde* of Debrois, 22-24, documents the travel arrangements of the entire imperial family to Prague.

P. 161 - The course of the entrance procession is documented in the Debrois *Urkunde*, 29-53.

Besides the notice in the *Prague Post* restricting the movements of Jews on the day of the procession, there is confirmation of anti-Semitic regulations in the Debrois *Urkunde*, 29.

P. 162 - See Kleist, *Fantasien*, 79-84, for a description of theatrical entertainments during the first days of the coronation ceremonies.

Tomášek's impressions are taken from his autobiography, the *Selbstbiographie*, part 1, from the journal *Libussa* (1845), 363 and 367.

The outline of the coronation ceremonies is found in Albrecht's *Journal der doppelten böhmischen Krönung*, 304-7; a less concise layout of the coronation events is also provided in the anonymous *Tagebuch der böhmischen Königskrönung* (Prague, 1792).

P. 163 - The relevant passages from Count Zinzendorf's diary are translated in Landon, *1791: Mozart's Last Year*, 106. The prominence of wind ensemble music in Prague during the time of the coronation celebrations is documented in Procházka, *Mozart in Prag*, 151-52.

See Kleist, *Fantasien*, 79-84, for impressions of theatrical entertainments recorded on 1 September 1791. His description of a performance of Mozart's *Don Giovanni* in the National Theater on 2 September 1791 is found in the *Fantasien*, 84-92, and is partially translated in Deutsch, *Mozart: A Documentary Biography*, 432-33, which contains the assertion that the Heinrich von Kleist was Franz Alexander's nephew and that he attended the coronation ceremonies. Neither claim is accurate. The precise relationship between the two authors is clarified in Peter Michalzik, *Kleist: Dichter, Krieger, Seelensucher* (Berlin: Prolyläen, 2011), 75, as third cousins. There is no reason to believe that Heinrich ever met Franz Alexander, much less attended the coronation of Leopold II in his company.

P. 164 - A short notice about the production of *Don Giovanni* is found in an issue of the *Prague Post* of 6 September 1791, partially transcribed in Jiří Berkovec, *Musicalia*, 74-75; it reports little more about the production than the theater was quite full of people.

Although Mozart's operas were the only ones given during the official period of coronation celebrations, a production of an anonymous *Pirro* on 29 August by the Guardasoni company in the National Theater is noted in Procházka, *Mozart in Prag*, 153, and Nettl, *Mozart und Böhmen*, 190. Landon, *1791: Mozart's Last Year*, 105, attributes the music unequivocally to Paisiello without explanation or documentation. No libretto survives to evaluate the question. Landon's identification is likely correct, since Paisiello's setting of 1787 was the most recent one with this title.

Fersen's relationship with Marie Antoinette is discussed in detail in many parts of Fraser, *Marie Antoinette*, esp. 110, 179, 202-6, 266-68, 313-14, 327-37, and 363-64.

Besides frequent mention in Fraser, *Marie Antoinette*, there has appeared a recent study devoted solely to Gabrielle's relationship with the queen of France: Nathalie Colas des Francs and Martial Debriffe, *Madame de Polignac et Marie-Antoinette: une amitié fatale* (Paris: Les 3 Orangers, 2008).

P. 165 - A somewhat recent biography of Bouillé is Paul Pialoux, *Le Marquis de Bouillé: un soldat entre deux mondes* (Brioude: Almanach de Brioude, 1997). Issues of the *Prague Post* from 9, 19, and 26 July 1791 record the Flight to Varennes and Bouillé's movements outside of France.

The original fifth verse of *La Marseillaise*, written by Claude Joseph Rouget de Lisle in 1792, reads as follows: Français, en guerriers magnanimes/ Portez ou retenez vos coups!/Épargnez ces tristes victimes/À regret s'armant contre nous./Mais ces despotes sanguinaires/Mais ces complices de Bouillé/ Tous ces tigres qui, sans pitié/ Déchirent le sein de leur mère! (Frenchmen, as magnanimous warriors, bear or hold back your blows! You spare those sad victims who are armed against us with regret. But [not] these bloody despots, these accomplices of Bouillé, all these tigers who pitilessly rip their mothers' breast!)

P. 166 - The first wife of the archduke Francis died in February 1790. He married his second wife, Maria Theresa of Naples, later the same year.

P. 167 - See Kleist, *Fantasien*, 92-95, for a description of his attendance at the court ball of 3 September. The reference to it as the "Spanish Hall" is found in the *Complete Description of Prague*, vol. 1, 50.

The National Archive in Prague, fund PŘ (Policejní Ředitelsví), carton 5 (Korunovační akta I), contains multiple original copies of publicly-distributed decrees with various regulations concerning the coronation events, including the regulations for the ball of 3 September 1791. In Debrois, *Aktenmässige Krönungs-Geschichte von Böhmen*, vol. 1, transcriptions of these decrees are provided in a section entitled "Aktenmässige und vollständige Sammlung der Verordnungen, welche in Bezug auf die böhmischen Krönung Leopold des II. und seiner durchlauchtigsten Gemahlin erlassen wurden."

See Kleist, *Fantasien*, 95-101, for a description of the "mass of allegiance" on 4 September 1791.

P. 168 - For one, Landon, in his *1791: Mozart's Last Year*, 111, claims Koželuch as the author of the mass performed on 4 September. Nonetheless, the catalog of the music collection of St. Vitus' Cathedral compiled in Jiří Štefan, ed., *Ecclesia Metropolitana Pragensis catalogus collectionis operum artis musicae*, vol. 1 (Prague: Supraphon, 1983), 374, indicates that a mass in D major by Leopold Hofmann (sign. 528 in the collection) was actually the one performed as the "mass of allegiance" in 1791 (then for subsequent liturgical occasions in 1792, 1794, and 1800). Landon's undocumented claim concerning Mozart's Offertorium *Misericordias Domini* is also found in *1791: Mozart's Last Year*, 111. The best biographical notice presently available for Jan Antonín Koželuch is found in *Starsí divadlo*; biographical notices for Leopold Hofmann are found in Clive, *Mozart and His Circle,* and the *Cambridge Mozart Encyclopedia*.

The liturgical compositions conducted by Salieri on 4 September are cited in Pfannhauser, "Mozart's 'Krönungsmesse,'" 5. There was also the antiphon *Ecce mitto angelum* and a *Te Deum* performed in the cathedral as part of Leopold's formal entrance ceremonies into the city on 31 August. See Kleist, *Fantasien*, 101-11 and 112-19, for his encounter with Meissner, and a description of the coronation ceremony.

Joseph never went through with a coronation ceremony, perhaps partially because he disdained the ceremonials involved, perhaps because he never wanted to be in a position of taking an oath before God to uphold the privileges of the Estates. Whatever the reason, the avoidance of a coronation ceremony for Joseph was explained in one of the coronation journals prepared for Leopold's coronation as the result of nothing more than he being too busy with pressing affairs of state to arrange it - see the *Merkwürdigkeiten der feierlichen Krönung eines Königs von Böhmen* (Prague, 1791), p. 2.

P. 169 - For Koželuh's mass, see Štefan, *Ecclesia Metropolitana Pragensis*, vol. 1, 442.

Landon's speculations are set forth in *1791: Mozart's Last Year*, 103-4, 112-14, 118. A copy of the mass K. 317 survives in the music collection of the Cathedral of St. Vitus according to Štefan, *Ecclesia Metropolitana Pragensis*, vol. 2, 52-53, however it was copied in the second half of the nineteenth century. No copy of the masses K. 258 or 337 survive in this collection. It should be kept in mind, though, that for the question of evaluating what music was used at Leopold's coronation, it would not necessarily be expected that the imperial court would permit its music manuscripts to be copied by the musical establishment at the cathedral.

P. 170 - Prague, National Archive, fund PŘ, carton 5, contains multiple original copies of publicly-distributed announcements of various regulations concerning the coronation events, including the rules for admission to the coronation opera of 6 September 1791 and traffic regulations. The texts are also transcribed in Debrois, *Aktenmässige Krönungs-Geschichte*, vol. 1, 128-33.

P. 171 - For reports of house illuminations, see the *Krönungsjournal für Prag*, 409, and an issue of the Czech newspaper *Císařské královské vlastenské noviny* [The imperial and royal homeland newspaper] for 10 September 1791 (unnumbered page reproduced in Volek and Bittner, *Mozartiana*, 44).

For ticket regulations, see the *Krönungsjournal für Prag*, 383; for arrival at 7:30 p.m., 383. For the account of Count Zinzendorf, see Deutsch, *Mozart: A Documentary Biography*, 404-5; an expanded translation is provided in Landon, *1791: Mozart's Last Year*, 115, which confirms that the theater was very crowded and difficult to leave. The *Tagebuch der böhmischen Königskrönung*, 225, reports the arrival of the court after 8:00 p.m. Berkovec, *Musicalia*, 75, transcribes only a portion of the notice from the *Prague Post* of 10 September 1791 and omits the time of arrival of the court. In spite of many contradictory claims, the Debrois *Urkunde*, 110, indicates that the royal couple arrived on time at 7:00 p.m. The time frames reported in the Czech press are found in the *Císařské královské vlastenské noviny*.

P. 172 - Kleist's impressions of *La clemenza di Tito* are found in the *Fantasien*, 119. Zinzendorf's estimation is translated in Deutsch, *Mozart: A Documentary Biography*, 405, and Landon, *1791: Mozart's Last Year*, 115. The empress's boredom is recorded in a document translated in Eisen, *New Mozart Documents*, 70. For the famous "porcheria tedesca" remark, see Meissner, *Rococo-Bilder*, 2nd ed., 141. The long translation of passages from the *Rococo-Bilder* found in Chapter 5 confirms that Meissner loved to concoct Italian phrases for the dialogue attributed to Italian characters. The empress was of Italian origins, born and raised in Naples, then resident for most of her adult life in Tuscany as Leopold's wife. But Meissner was careless, since the Italian expression assigned to her in itself renders the attribution highly suspicious, since it was customary for members of the imperial family of Austria to communicate with their courtiers and each other only in French, the international language of aristocracy in Mozart's time.

The excerpt from Meissner is translated from the *Rococo-Bilder*, 2nd ed., 136-41.

P. 174 - The article from the *Allgemeinisches europäisches Journal* was first brought to light in Christopher Raeburn, "Mozarts Opern in Prag," *Musica* 13 (1959): 158-63. Raeburn accurately reported its attribution as anonymous. Tomislav Volek, however, in his article "Repertoir Nosticovského divadla v Praze z let 1794, 1796-8" [The repertory of the Nostic theater in Prague from the years 1794 and 1796-98], *Miscellanea musicologica* 16 (1961): 5-191, tried to make a case that the article was written by František Xaver Němeček on the basis of questionable reasoning. Unfortunately, in later publications, Volek treated this speculative identification as unequivocal - for example, in the biographical notice he prepared with Milada Jonášová for the German music dictionary *Die Musik in Geschichte und Gegenwart*, ed. Ludwig Finscher, *Personenteil* 12 (Kassel: Bärenreiter, 2004), 1103. Many other scholars have followed Volek's lead, for example Landon in his *1791: Mozart's Last Year*, 109-118, in which some excerpts are translated. Many other scholars prudently regard the attribution as speculative.

In fact, the author or authors of the series of articles concerning theatrical life in Prague in the *Allgemeines europäisches Journal* are identified only with ciphers whose resolutions are not clear, specifically "K.K.," "N.k.," and "+++k." There is no compelling reason to match all of them to Němeček, and it is not obvious why Němeček would want to conceal his identity. Furthermore, the writing style of these articles does not at all resemble what is seen in Němeček's biography of Mozart. They exhibit a much more sophisticated approach to theatrical criticism than Němeček ever revealed in his biography, including caustic remarks that are not typical of the way he wrote about the cultural life of Prague. In 1794, Němeček had only recently moved to Prague from Plzeň, and it is difficult to comprehend how he would have been able to comment with such authority on theatrical life in Prague extending back for years. Why the *Allgemeines europäisches Journal* would value the opinion of a newcomer who had no credentials as a theater or music critic at the time is also unclear. The ciphers could be matched just about as easily to the venerable František Xaver Dušek, a fixture of cultural life in Prague, as to František Xaver Němeček. The latter's authorship must only be considered a possibility, nothing more.

P. 175 - The document of 28 October 1791 with Count Rottenhan's annotations (mentioned earlier) is reproduced in facsimile in Volek and Bittner, *Mozartiana*, 45-46.

For impressions recorded on 9 September, see Kleist, *Fantasien*, 119-24; for 11 September (including impressions of the balloonist Blanchard), see ibid., 124-28.

Kleist's account of the ball of 12 September is recorded in ibid., 128-35; the attendance is recorded in Albrecht's *Krönungsjournal für Prag*, 238. A fanciful account of the ball of 12 September (with lavish illustrations and much background information) is provided in Josef Petráň, *Kalendář: velký stavovský ples v Nosticově Národním divadle dne 12. září 1791* [Diary of the grand ball of the Estates in the

Nostic National Theater on 12 September 1791] (Prague: Československý spisovatel, 1988). The *Prague Post* of 17 September gave far more coverage to this ball than the coronation opera, which its reporters were unlikely to attend (see Berkovec, *Musicalia*, 76); it reported the presence of 300 musicians to provide dance music).

P. 176 - For the last ball of 15 September, see Kleist, *Fantasien*, 136-39.

The departures from Prague of Salieri and the royal couple are recorded in Debrois, *Aktenmässige Krönungs-Geschichte*, vol. 3, 12, 18, and 21.

Mozart's letter of 7-8 October 1791 is not translated in Anderson, *The Letter of Mozart and His Family*. It is transcribed, however, in Bauer and Deutsch, *Mozart: Briefe und Aufzeichnungen*, vol. 4, 157-59, and partially translated in Braunbrehens, *Mozart in Vienna*, 388.

As mentioned earlier, a concise layout of coronation events in provided in Albrecht's *Journal der doppelten böhmischen Krönung*, 304-7. Evening operatic performances for 9 September and 16 September are indicated here with the notation "Abends Spektakel," in precisely the same manner that the performance of *Don Giovanni* on 2 September is indicated. All other evenings between 1 and 22 September bear other indications or were specified as vacant. The reference in the Mozart letter of 7-8 October 1791 of the success of *La clemenza di Tito* "for the last time" it was performed, not the "second time," strongly indicates that there were more than two performances of it during the month of September.

The *Prague Post* reported the performances of Koželuh's cantata at the ball of 12 September and its repetition on 23 September in issues of 17 September and 27 September, respectively (see Berkovec, *Musicalia*, 76). As with the ball of 12 September, the canata performed on 12 September received much more attention than the coronation opera of Mozart. According to a letter of Němeček written to Breitkopf & Härtel in 1799, as excerpted in Hitzig, "Die Briefe Franz Xaver Niemetscheks," 105, Koželuh, who ordinarily resided in Vienna, was guilty of some very petty behavior during the period of the coronation ceremonies with regard to Mozart, including stalking him and spreading vicious slanders behind his back - all out of jealousy. The relevant passage is translated in Landon, *1791: Mozart's Last Year*, 121. Just a year later, Koželuh secured an appointment as composer to the imperial court at double the salary Mozart had been paid.

P. 177 - The excerpt from Meissner is translated from the *Rococo-Bilder*, 2nd ed., 145-47.

Chapter 9

P. 178 - The disagreement among physicians over the cause of Mozart's death in noted in Němeček, *Lebensbeschreibung*, 54.

The account of Mozart's last illness is taken from ibid., 50-52. It is plagiarized in Nissen, *Biographie W. A. Mozarts*, 555-56, 559, and 563-64, perhaps a confirmation that Nissen trusted its veracity on the basis of information provided by his wife. An issue of the Berlin newspaper *Musikalisches Wochenblatt* that appeared at the end of 1791, translated in Deutsch, *Mozart: A Documentary Biography*, 432, corroborates key points that Němeček made. Its report from Prague dated 12 December claims that Mozart "returned home from Prague a sick man, and continued to get worse." It also confirmed suspicions of poisoning and referred to the failure of *La clemenza di Tito* in Prague. Nonetheless, no claims of deliberate poisoning are now treated with credibility by Mozart scholars.

Nissen's biography provides two examples of humor that Mozart indulged in while apparently being so sick in Prague. One, related to his habit of playing billiards at a coffeehouse, is translated in Chapter 7. Another concerns an encounter with a pianist who gave a concert in Prague while Mozart was in the city (Nissen deliberately masked his identity). The pianist claimed in his program to have been a student of Mozart. At the end of the concert, after Mozart saw the program, he supposedly declared that "The young man certainly plays well, but I can take no credit for it; perhaps he has profited some from studying with my sister." (The other Mozart pianist, Nannerl, also gave lessons.) This highly suspicious anecdote appears in the *Biographie W. A. Mozarts*, 561, and draws attention to Němeček's claim that he suppressed many anecdotes he heard about Mozart because he did not consider them reliable (a remark found in a short section at the end of the first edition of his biography, in which he explained where his sources of information came from). The pianist is identified as Joseph Wölfl in Procházka, *Mozart in Prag,* 178, and Nettl, *Mozart in Böhmen,* 214. If the anecdote is accurate, Mozart would have known that Wölfl was from Salzburg in order to make his joke about perhaps studying with his sister.

P. 179 - The cantata mentioned by Němeček was "Laut verkünde unsre Freude," K. 623, set to a text of Emanuel Schikaneder and performed at the Masonic lodge "Zur neugekrönten Hoffnung" on 18 November 1791. Writing in the era of the repressive emperor Francis II, Němeček clearly did not want to draw attention to Mozart's activities in a secret society, thus did not identify the organization for which the cantata was written.

Exactly how much mourning there was for Mozart in Vienna, how tawdry his funeral really was, and the number and nature of commemorations in his honor is very much a matter of dispute in the Mozart literature. Deutsch in his *Mozart: A Documentary Biography,* 429, went out of his way to point out that he did not believe that a number of commemorative events that were actually announced ever took place. Nonetheless, the notice of his death that appeared in the *Wiener Zeitung* of 7 December 1791, translated in Deutsch, *Mozart: A Documentary Biography,* 418, certainly provides adequate acknowledgment of Mozart's artistic stature and expresses suitable regret at this passing. Some of the commemorative activity going on in Vienna shortly after Mozart's death is summarized in Solomon, *Mozart: A Life,* 498-99. A common excuse for the less lavish commemorations in Vienna is a personal crisis in the life of Mozart's patron Baron van Swieten, as pointed out in Clive, *Mozart and His Circle,* 151. On the very day of Mozart's death, Swieten was relieved of his duties as a prominent government official in by Leopold II. Without this setback to deal with, it is possible that Swieten would have stepped forward to arrange something similar to what took place in Prague, but it is not clear how anyone could have inspired in the Viennese populace the same sense of loss that manifested itself among the ordinary citizens of Prague. If the level of mourning in Vienna was not what one would hope for, conditions were even worse in Salzburg. Solomon, *Mozart: A Life,* xv-xvi, makes a point of explaining how indifferent the Salzburgers were to Mozart after his departure in 1781.

The translation of the report of Mozart's commemorative service in the *Prague Post* of 17 December 1791 that appears in Eisen, *New Mozart Documents,* 123, is based on a version of it that is incomplete and inaccurate. The full version is transcribed in Berkovec, *Musicalia,* 77-79. The text of a printed announcement of the commemorative service of 14 December intended for public distribution is translated in Deutsch, *Mozart: A Documentary Biography,* 424. The commemorative service in Prague was reported in the *Wiener Zeitung* on 24 December 1791 (translation in Deutsch, *Mozart: A Documentary Biography,* 427).

The musical centerpiece of the commemorative service of 14 December, a Requiem by Antonio Rosetti, cannot be identified with certainty, but was probably the same one performed at St. Nicholas church in a memorial service for a member of the Gubernium on 24 September 1789, also with Dušek as soloist. The latter performance was described in an issue of the *Prague Post* of 26 September 1789 (transcription in Berkovec, *Musicalia,* 71). The lingering patriotic sense left over from the coronation ceremonies is clear in the remark about referring Rosetti as Rössler, since this particular Bohemian composer took pains to Italianize his name after leaving Bohemia in order to conceal his ethnic origins. The patriotic feelings awakened during the period of the coronation of 1791 lingered for years in the Prague press. Reports of commemorations of Mozart's death from Prague of the 1790s are bursting with nationalistic fervor.

P. 180 - The report in the *Prague Post* of 21 January 1792 is transcribed in Berkovec, *Musicalia,* 79-80.

P. 181 - Constanze's efforts to support herself and her sons before coming to Prague are summarized in Landon, *1791: Mozart's Last Year,* 182-185, and Solomon, *Mozart: A Life,* 498-99. Sources of income included a small pension from the imperial court, the sale of compositions, the organization of musical performances, and outright gifts of money from sympathetic parties in Vienna and elsewhere.

The report in the Prague Post of 27 October 1792 is transcribed in Berkovec, *Musicalia,* 83.

Václav Mihule is accorded a biographical entry in *Starší divadlo,* 386-91.

P. 182 - The report from the *Prager Neue Zeitung* of 24 January 1794 is transcribed in Berkovec, *Musicalia*, 86-87.

The libretto for the performance of *Così fan tutte* is cited in Kneidl, "Libreta italské opery" 4: 195, along with a placard that confirms its performance on 23 November 1791. There is no evidence to support the report in Braunbehrens, *Mozart in Vienna*, 388, that *Così fan tutte* was performed during the period of coronation festivities.

The extraordinary number of performances of Mozart operatic works in Prague in 1794 is partially confirmed by the existence of librettos listed in Kneidl, "Libreta italské opery," *Strahovská knihovna* 4 (1969): 199-200 and 202-3, along with placards matched to performances of *The Magic Flute* in Italian (27 October, 10 and 26 November, and 15 December 1794), *Così fan tutte* (12 November 1794), *La clemenza di Tito* (3 and 20 December 1794), *Don Giovanni* (17 December 1794), and *The Marriage of Figaro* (31 December 1794). By coincidence, detailed lists of the daily performances given at the National Theater for the months of September - December 1794 and the entire years 1796-1798 still survive. The dramatic works involved are all cataloged in Volek, "Repertoir Nosticovského divadla." There were many more performances than just those that can be confirmed from placards, and in addition, there was a performance of *The Abduction from the Seraglio* on 9 October. The Prague public thus was able to sample all six of the Mozart operas that are best loved today within a period of weeks in the later months of 1794.

P. 183 - Tomàšek's narrative is found in his "Selbstbiographie," part 1, 365-66. Nettl, *Mozart in Böhmen*, 194-95, and Landon, *1791: Mozart's Last Year*, 110-11, placed the incident described by Tomàšek in the year 1790 (a year when Guardasoni was not present in Prague and no Italian operas were given in the city). The confusion originates with Tomàšek himself, since he placed his recollection of events between his arrival in Prague in 1790 and the coronation of 1791. Of course, by the late 1840s he may not have remembered exactly when the performance took place, but his account provides clues nonetheless. Volek, "Repertoir Nosticovského divadla," 56, indicates performances of Don Giovanni on 15 November and 17 December 1794.

No performances of Paisello's opera *I filosofi imaginari*, first performed in St. Petersburg in 1779, are documented in Prague during the entire eighteenth century, thus Tomàšek's reference cannot be explained.

The announcement of Mozart's death in the *Prague Post* of 17 December 1791 is transcribed in Berkovec, *Musicalia*, 79. Swieten was dismissed from the courst post cited in the announcement just twelve days earlier.

P. 184 - Various documents and newspaper reports that attest to the generosity of Baron von Swieten at this time are translated into Dutch, *Mozart: A Documentary Biography*, 420, 425-26, and 467. Karl's indication that he came to Prague to study with Němeček at the age of eight in the year 1792 comes from a letter written to Adolf Popelka from Milan (where he was living at the time) on 4 March 1856 (at the age of 71). The contents of the letter are transcribed in Hummel, *W.A. Mozarts Söhne*, 18-19. He said that he stayed in Prague for five years, until the end of the year 1797.

In a letter to the Leipzig publisher Breitkopf & Härtel written in 1799, Němeček claimed to have come in contact with Mozart for a brief time during his "last stay in Prague," i.e., during the coronation celebrations of 1791 (see Hitzig, "Die Briefe Franz Xaver Niemetscheks," 106). Brauneis, "Franz Xaver Niemetschek," and Tomislav Volek, "Neznámá tvář F. C. Němečka" [The unknown face of F. X Němeček], *Hudebni rozhledy* 14 (1966)" 427, have disputed the notion that Němeček ever met Mozart, in each case without confronting the evidence of this letter directly. The most important reason to doubt Němeček's claim is that he served as a schoolteacher at the Gymnasium in Plzeň between 1787 and 1793. Strangely, Volek and Brauneis did not consider the possibilitiy that he simply could have been visiting Prague from Plzeň at the time, and could have done so frequently over the years. A loophole that makes Němeček's claim more credible comes from the autobiography of Václav Jan Tomášek, who was able to flee Prague as a student during the coronation ceremonies of 1791 because they coincided with a school recess. It is quite possible that the same period of recess was observed in Plzeň, thus leaving Němeček free to visit Prague for the coronation. Němeček reported that his wife also came into contact with Mozart at this time. In 1791, he was not yet married to this woman, Theresia Schnell (they did not marry until 1798), although she was working at the time in the service of the Dušeks, hence her access to Mozart. He also claimed to know the Dušeks well. Němeček mentioned in passing his impression that Mozart's younger son had the same "spirit" that his father had.

Karl Mozart's accommodations with Němeček are likely to have been very spare, since Němeček was an ordinary schoolteacher at the Gymnasium in Mala Straná. According to a letter of 21 March 1800 sent to Breitkopf & Härtel, Karl slept in Němeček's room for the three years that he was with him (see Hitzig, "Die Briefe Franz Xaver Niemetscheks," 110). Němeček did prosper, however, after the appearance of his Mozart biography in 1798. He was promoted to the rank of professor at Charles-Ferdinand University in Prague in 1802, then moved to Vienna in 1820 to accept another university post. He died in Vienna in 1849.

Němeček's complaint about Swieten's failure to make good on promises to help support the Mozarts is found in the same letter of 21 March 1800 just cited.

P. 185 - The visit of Karl's younger brother to Salzburg in 1821 and his meeting with Nannerl (aged 69 at the time) is documented in Hummel, *W.A. Mozarts Söhne*, 142-43.

The notice from the Prager Neue Zeitung of 10 February 1794 is transcribed in Berkovec, *Musicalia*, 87-89, and partially translated in Deutsch, *Mozart: A Documentary Biography*, 469-70. The report of the same event on 7 February in the *Prague Post* of 11 February is regrettably brief: "On Friday the Legal-Musical Society celebrated the memory of the great musician Mozart in a special concert in which several virtuosos could be heard, especially the renowned Madame Dušek" (transcription in Berkovec, *Musicalia*, 90).

P. 186 - Meinert's poem is transcribed in Nissen, *W. A. Mozarts Biographie*, 697-98, and Procházka, *Mozart in Prag*, 190.

The notice from the *Prague Post* of 4 March 1794 is transcribed in Berkovec, *Musicalia*, 89.

The notice from the *Prager Neue Zeitung* of 7 April 1794 is transcribed in ibid., 90, and translated in Deutsch, *Mozart: A Documentary Biography*, 471. Salieri's *Axur*, first performed in Prague in 1788 shortly after its première in Vienna the same year, was one of the most frequently performed operas in Prague at the end of the eighteenth century.

P. 187 - Constanze's appearances in the years 1794-96 are verified in Deutsch, *Mozart: A Documentary Biography*, 471-84. She also continued to try to profit from other performances of Mozart's works and the sale of editions of his music.

The precise time that the younger son, Franz Xaver Wolfgang, was in Prague, is subject to question. In the same letter to Breitkopf & Härtel of 21 March 1800 cited earlier, Němeček claimed that he stayed in Prague with his wife for a half year when he was six years' old and his mother was traveling in northern Germany. However, the child only turned six on 26 July 1797, just a few months before Constanze left Prague permanently, certainly not just before a tour of northern Germany. Her tour of northern German cities began with a benefit concert in Leipzig on 11 November 1795 (see Deutsch, *Mozart: A Documentary Biography*, 478). Thus it would seem more likely that the child would have been left with Theresia Schnell in Prague at this time. The last of the series of benefit concerts in northern Europe was given in Dresden in May 1796, therefore confirming Němeček's time frame. Theresia Schnell was not yet Němeček's wife when his letter was written. Nonetheless, she was close to the Dušek family, so it would not be so surprising that Constanze would leave her son with her.

The notices from the *Prague Post* of 7 November 1797 and *Prager Neue Zeitung* of 10 November 1797 are both transcribed in Berkovec, *Musicalia*, 103. The program of the concert given on 15 November 1797 is translated in Deutsch, *Mozart: A Documentary Biography*, 484-85.

P. 188 - The notice from the *Prager Neue Zeitung* of 17 November 1797 is transcribed in Berkovec, *Musicalia*, 103.

Information about Josefa Dušek mortgaging the Bertramka villa for Constanze's benefit is presented in Deutsch, *Mozart: A Documentary Biography*, 485.

Constanze's announcement in the *Prague Post* of 4 May 1799 is transcribed in Berkovec, *Musicalia*, 110.

A very large number of letters of Constanze written to Breitkopf & Härtel and André between 1798 and 1893 are transcribed in Bauer and Deutsch, *Mozart: Briefe und Aufzeichnungen*, vol. 4, 212-432.

Chapter 10

P. 193 - Still useful as a comprehensive guide to Mozart's opera *Don Giovanni* in English is Julian Rushton, *W. A. Mozart: Don Giovanni* (Cambridge: Cambridge University Press, 1981). The score of *Don Giovanni* is available in the authoritative *Neue-Mozart-Ausgabe* in Series II, Bühnenwerke, Werkgruppe 5, vol. 17, as *Il Dissoluto punito ossia Il Don Giovanni*, ed. Wolfgang Plath and Wolfgang Rehm (Kassel: Bärenreiter, 1968). All of the music edited for the *Neue-Mozart-Ausgabe* is now available to view online. The autograph score of *Don Giovanni* preserved in the Bibliothèque Nationale in Paris is also available in a facsimile edition: *Wolfgang Amadeus Mozart: Il dissoluto punito ossia il Don Giovanni*, K. 527, 540a, 540c (Los Altos, California: The Packard Humanities Institute, 2009). Besides the score, this edition also includes facsimiles of the Vienna and Prague librettos printed for the première in 1787 and the first performance in Vienna. As explained in Chapter 6, the Vienna libretto of 1787 was prepared in anticipation of the visit of Prince Anton of Saxony and his bride Maria Theresa on 14 October 1787, and was dedicated to them. The production could not be arranged in time, however, so a new libretto that did not include their names was needed for the actual première of 29 October. It can be seen from the large number of typographical errors in this libretto how hurriedly it had to be prepared. The text of Da Ponte's libretto can be viewed in Italian or English translation on multiple online resources, and it is also customary for it to be transcribed with translation into English in booklets that accompany most recordings. Not surprisingly, the transcriptions and translations found with recordings usually follow the reading of the score, not the printed librettos.

P. 194 - The operation of the Sporck theater is explored in Freeman, *The Opera Theater of Count Franz Anton von Sporck in Prague*. Besides this work, the circumstances of Denzio's Don Juan production are detailed in Daniel E. Freeman, "Newly Found Roots of the Don Juan Tradition in Opera: Antonio Denzio and Antonio Caldara's *La pravità castigata*," *Studi Musicali* 21 (1992): 115-57. Commentary about the Don Juan operas in Prague before the Mozart setting is also found in Reinhard Eisendle, "Don Giovanni in Böhmen. Die Prager Don Juan-Opern vor Mozart im Kontext der europäischen Sujetsgeschichte," in *Böhmische Aspekte*, 153-164, a study that would have benefited from an acquantance with Freeman, "Newly Found Roots." The earliest citations in the musicological literature that offer a clear recognition of the significance of the Denzio adapation of the Don Juan tale are found in Daniel E. Freeman, "The Opera Theater of Count Franz Anton von Sporck in Prague (1724-35)," Ph.D. dissertation, University of Illinois, 1987, 262-63, and Tomislav Volek, "Význam pražské operní tradice pro vznik Mozartovy opery Don Giovanni" [The significance of Prague operatic traditions for the origin of Mozart's opera *Don Giovanni*] in *Mozartův Don Giovanni v Praze* (Prague: Divadelní Ústav, 1987), 24-26. Earlier citations of it in Czech scholarly literature without recognition of its signficance are detailed in Freeman, "Newly Found Roots," 115-16. The latter also includes bibliography concerning the history of the Don Juan legend in general, as does Eisendle, "*Don Giovanni* in Böhmen" (in this case with an emphasis on resources in German).

A survey in English of the Don Juan operatic settings written before the Mozart setting of 1787 is Charles C. Russell, *The Don Juan Legend Before Mozart* (Ann Arbor: The University of Michigan Press, 1993), which includes transcriptions of many of the librettos, however the author was unaware of about the Denzio libretto of 1730 and the importance of Prague is founding the eighteenth-century traditions of Don Juan operas. Stefan Kunze, *Don Giovanni vor Mozart* (Munich: W. Fink, 1972) also contains valuable commentary, but was written before important archival discoveries in the 1980s.

P. 195 - Righini was accorded a biographical notice in *Starší divadlo*, 493-95, however the elusive Porta was not. The only reference work known to the author that includes him is the "Oxford composer companion" *Haydn*, ed. David Wyn Jones and Otto Biba (Oxford: Oxford University Press, 2002), 289, which records his *floruit* as 1770-95, however makes no mention whatsoever of his period of activity in Prague. Righini was the same age as Mozart and died in 1812. His opera *Il convitato di* *pietra* is the subject of David J. Buch, "The Don Juan Tradition, Eighteenth-Century Supernatural Musical Theatre and Vincenzo Righini's *Il convitato di pietra*," *Hudební věda* 41 (2004): 295-307, another study marred by a lack of acquaintance with Freeman, "Newly Found Roots."

P. 196 - The text of the Bertati libretto is transcribed (but unfortunately not translated) in Russell, *The Don Juan Legend Before Mozart*, 408-43. The score by Gazzaniga is available edited by Stefan Kunze as *Giuseppe Gazzaniga: Don Giovanni o sia Il convitato di pietra* (Kassel: Bärenreiter, 1974).

See Chapter 6 for a discussion of the conflicting accounts of the genesis of *Don Giovanni* left by Da Ponte. Felicity Baker, in her essay "The Figures of Hell in the *Don Giovanni* Libretto," in *Words About Mozart*, 77-106, was either unaware of the Da Ponte *Extract* or simply ignored it in order to produce an interpretation of the *Don Giovanni* libretto as deeply influenced by Dante's *Inferno*. Of course this is quite an overreach. At one point (p. 79), Baker adopts the attitude that Da Ponte's remark that he "imagined reading Dante's *Inferno*" (not *actually* reading it) while working on the *Don Giovanni* libretto means that Da Ponte decided to "draw the *Inferno* into his account of the Don Juan story." This interpretation of the libretto is specious; the scenes Baker believed to be based on the *Inferno* are actually based very closely on Bertati and the earlier tradition of Don Juan dramatizations. There is no reason to believe that Da Ponte made close reference to Dante's *Inferno* while preparing his libretto for *Don Giovanni*, nor did he claim to. In addition, the Da Ponte libretto is completely dominated by polytheistic and classical pagan references that are incompatible with Dante's Christian orientation. This point is completely unappreciated as well by the author of the article on *Don Giovanni* in the *Cambridge Mozart Encyclopedia*.

P. 197 - As pointed out in Rice, "Antonio Baglioni," 299-300, there are conflicting indications in the Mozart literature about whether the tenor Baglioni performed the role of Don Giovanni in Venice or Don Ottavio. Rice favors Don Ottavio, the same role as in Prague, based on reasonable evaluation of evidence. It must be questioned, though, why Guardasoni would take such trouble to bring him to Prague from Italy just to perform a subsidiary role. It could be that Baglioni was Guardasoni's first choice for Don Giovanni, but the role was altered to suit a different voice range and the acting capabilities of the baritone Luigi Bassi (see below). The article on *Don Giovanni* in the *Cambridge Mozart Encyclopedia* claims that Baglioni may have been responsible for bringing the Bertati libretto to Prague, also a plausible hypothesis, but this would not explain how a copy ever made it to Da Ponte in Vienna.

According to the biographical entries in *Starší divadlo*, Bondini (1731-1789) had been in Prague on and off since 1760, whereas Guardasoni (1731-1806) first came in 1764. Each was present in Prague at least during part of the year 1776.

P. 198 - The erection of the stone statue as a memorial to the dead Commendatore as depicted in most Don Juan dramatizations, including Da Ponte's, would have to take place in a suspiciously short amount of time (it appears that it takes only a day to have a sculptor execute it). The rationalist Don Juan play of Carlo Goldoni (which never depicts Don Juan being dragged down to hell) provides a more believable explanation for the presence of the statue: a passage in Act I, scene 3, alludes to the order of the king of Castile to erect an equestrian statue in his honor while he is still alive.

A useful translation into English of the Don Juan plays of Tirso and Molière along with the Da Ponte libretto is found in Oscar Mandel, ed., *Three Classic Don Juan Plays* (Lincoln: University of Nebraska Press, 1971).

The Cicognini play has never been translated into English. The most useful modern edition of it is found in Georges Gendarme de Bévotte, *Le festin de Pierre avant Molière* (Paris: Cornély, 1907), 369-424. The edition found in Giovanni Macchia, *Vita, avventure e morte di Don Giovanni* (Bari: Laterza, 1966), 181-226, is less well annotated, but on the other hand, Macchia's work does provide an excellent historical overview of Don Juan dramatizations.

Braunbehrens, *Mozart in Vienna*, 304-10, documents the distaste that Mozart's *Don Giovanni* engendered in Vienna at first because its sophisticated musical setting was joined incongruously to something as vulgar as the Don Juan story.

P. 199 - For the Francis accounts of Lorenzo Da Ponte, see John W. Francis, *Old New York: Reminiscences of the Past Sixty Years* (New York, 1858), 260-69, quotation from 265-66.

P. 200 - Interestingly, Gluck was a resident of Prague in his youth at roughly the time that the Denzio drama was first performed in 1730 (certainly in the years just after). Whether distant memories of this production were responsible for suggesting the subject matter of Don Juan in 1761 is an open question. It is not by any means certain that he chose it. The large number of performances of the Gluck ballet in the eighteenth century is documented in Russell, *The Don Juan Legend Before Mozart*, 448-76. The Gluck ballet is edited by Richard Engländer with *Semiramis* of 1765 in his *Sämtliche Werke*, Abteilung II, *Tanzdramen*, vol. 1 (Kassel: Bärenreiter, 1966). An excellent explanation of the circum-stances surrounding the first performance and a facsimile of the preface distributed to the original audience members is found in Engländer's introduction (pp. X-XXVII).

P. 201 - That is, the murder appears in the interior if it is depicted at all. The Molière drama, for example, does not include it.

P. 202 - The strength of the convention of ending eighteenth-century operas (and indeed all types of theatrical works) with marriages is confirmed by Da Ponte himself in his libretto for *The Marriage of Figaro*. At a point in the "buffo finale" of Act II, Figaro expresses his faith in the certainty of his scheme to marry Susanna by saying that it will conclude "happily" with a marriage ceremony "following theatrical custom" ("all'usanza teatrale").

David J. Buch, *Magic Flutes & Enchanted Forests: the Supernatural in Eighteenth-Century Musical Theater* (Chicago: University of Chicago Press, 2008), provides a survey of theater pieces from the eighteenth century that include supernatural elements.

A valuable aid in evaluating the text of Da Ponte's *Don Giovanni* is Giovanna Gronda, ed., *Il Don Giovanni: Dramma giocoso in due atti* (Turin: Giulio Einaudi, 1995). This work collates the three principal sources of the text for the work: the Viennese libretto printed in honor of the wedding of Prince Anton of Saxony and his wife Maria Theresa; the Prague libretto actually distributed to the audience for the première of *Don Giovanni* on 29 October 1787; and the autograph score preserved in the Bibliothèque Nationale in Paris. Variants for the first production in Vienna in 1788 are also included. For the latter production, Da Ponte actually intensified pagan references. In new scenes, he has the servant Leporello invoking "gods" ("dei"), "eternal gods" ("eterni dei"), "unjust gods" ("ingiusti dei"), and the classical deity Mercury (see Gronda, *Il Don Giovanni*, 106-8).

The dialectical "oddio" as a substitute for "Oh Dio" is found in fleeting references at the very end of finale to Act I uttered by Don Giovanni and Leporello (in this case, sung in a declamation so brisk and a musical texture so dense that no audience members would be able to catch it) and later when it is quickly uttered by Masetto in Act II, scene 6, in a dialogue with Zerlina. In this context, the expression would be somewhat equivalent to the colloquial English "jeez" (for "Jesus"), which carries with it no religious intent. The very fact that Da Ponte only used this dialectical spelling for his two monotheistic utterances (never the polytheistic ones) indicates that a careful distinction was intended. As far as literary models in Italian are concerned, the dramas of Denzio, Goldoni, Porta, and Bertati all mix monotheistic and polytheistic invocations (the most usual forms of address are "Dio," "Dei," "Nume," and "Numi"), never with the spelling "oddio" used by Da Ponte.

Even though "God" is brought up only with the dialectical spelling "oddio," Da Ponte does invoke the devil explicitly in a reference to Don Giovanni being dragged down to hell by "the devil" in the final scene of Act II, when Leporello explains to his late master's victims what happened to him. This indication clearly derives from the equivalent scene in the libretto of Bertati, whose servant character refers to the demons who pull Don Giovanni down to hell as "devils." In Da Ponte's version, however, the statue of the Commendatore could never be referred to accurately as a "devil," and the "spirits" who drag him to hell are a plural entity. It is possible that Da Ponte was merely careless in making a singular reference to what the "spirits" were doing.

The use of pagan invocations for lower-class characters could have been inspired at least in part by Bertati's libretto, which has Don Giovanni's servant and the rustics of Villena, Spain, invoking the Roman gods Bacchus, Mercury, and Diana during their merry-making in scene 11 of this one-act opera. Da Ponte includes polytheistic invocations for both upper-class and lower-class characters in

The Marriage of Figaro as well, but never mention of classical deities. One might think it a slip of Da Ponte to portray his lower-class characters as so well educated, but it is a common foible of literati to forget that their erudition is not universally shared.

Among the literary models in Italian available to Da Ponte, the only one whose depictions can be reconciled with mainstream Catholicism is the play of Goldoni, which does not include a portrayal of the resurrected Commendatore and disposes of Don Giovanni by having him request "heaven" to send a thunderbolt to strike him dead.

P. 204 - The operatic "reform" of the turn of the seventeenth century is described in Robert Freeman, *Opera Without Drama: Currents of Changes in Italian Opera, 1675-1725* (Ann Arbor: UMI Research Press, 1981).

P. 205 - The "Catalog aria" is one of the most celebrated vocal pieces written by Mozart, its presence in *Don Giovanni* the result of a scenario involving the listing of sexual conquests that dates back to Tirso. Selected topics having to do with the device of the "catalog" in Don Juan operas are explored in Daniela Goldin Folina, "Alle origini del Catalogo," in *Böhmische Aspekte*, 165-85. A much more extensive study that covers all types of dramatizations is Piero Menarini, *Quante volte, Don Giovanni?: Il catalogo di Don Giovanni da Tirso al romanticismo* (Bologna: Atesa, 1984).

P. 206 - It is true that it is presently a conceit of operatic directors worldwide to have Donna Elvira appear on stage in an ostentatious state of advanced pregnancy while in pursuit of Don Giovanni. This device does add a fresh element of titillation for modern audiences, but it is impossible to reconcile it with the text of the drama. It is very difficult to believe that something as obvious as a pregnancy would never be mentioned among any of the characters. Considering the revulsion for sexual relations with women in an advanced state of pregnancy that many men profess, one wonders why Leporello would want to try so hard to make love to Donna Elvira at the beginning of Act II, or that Don Giovanni would propose it. It is furthermore inconceivable that a Spanish noblewoman would flaunt pregnancy in public, regardless of her marital status.

P. 208 - The scenario prepared by the dance master Gasparo Angiolini for the Gluck ballet also borrows "Donna Elvire" from Molière, but provides no names for peasant characters, thus it seems more likely that the origins of Bertati's character names in common with Molière were taken directly out of the latter's play.

P. 210 - Nissen's anecdote about revising the instrumentation for the recitation of the Commander in Act II by adding oboes, clarinets, and bassoons to a complement of trombones is translated in Chapter 6. Nissen indicated that this section was originally scored only for three trombones (just like the recitation of the voice of Neptune in Act III of *Idomeneo*). Nissen's other anecdote concerning the rehearsal of *Don Giovanni* (see *W. A. Mozarts Leben*, 560) claims that the trumpet and tympani parts for the finale to Act II were copied out from memory without Mozart looking at the full score at all. He told the players at a rehearsal that he knew their parts in one spot would be either four bars too early or four bars too late, and that they should pay careful attention. When they played their parts as written, it was revealed that the count was indeed out of alignment. Presumably, the musicians were able to adjust the count themselves for the actual performance.

P. 212 - Bassi's creation of the role of the Count of Almaviva in Prague is confirmed in Freisauff, *Mozart's Don Juan*, 25.

The comments of the anonymous author of the "Reports" are transcribed in Volek, "Repertoir Nosticovského divadla," 24 and 27-28. Attentive readers will recall the vignette of Meissner translated in Chapter 6 that has Bassi complaining of a lack of arias, and it is true that the effectiveness of the characterization of the role as crafted by Mozart is simply not invested in the vocal set pieces written for Bassi.

P. 213 - In his own catalog of completed works, Mozart listed *Don Giovanni* as an opera buffa (not "dramma giocoso") consisting of 24 "pezzi di musica" ("pieces of music"), precisely the same amount of musical "numbers" that is usually indicated in scores of the work. Mozart's generic designation serves as a reminder that eighteenth-century composers were now as consistent about these matters as modern music scholars would prefer.

P. 219 - See Da Ponte, *Estratto delle memorie*, 36-38, for his description of a "buffo finale."

P. 221 - The toast "Viva la libertà" has become controversial only since the late 20th century, when scholars and critics began to claim that Mozart was deeply committed to progressive political ideals. Occasionally one encounters the claim that this toast to freedom is intended to express sympathy with the political conception of freedom as later epoused by French revolutionaries. Of course, Mozart did not write the line (Da Ponte did), and it is inconceivable that imperial censors would have permitted it to be heard if there was any reasonable expectation that audience members would have interpreted it as a political appeal. Surely the freedom toasted by Don Giovanni is the freedom of the "libertine": a lifestyle unconstrained by conventional morality.

P. 222 - Otto Jahn, *W. A. Mozart*, vol. 4, 444, claimed already in 1859 that the banquet scene of Act II was only inserted during the rehearsals of the opera, an assertion noted in Procházka, *Mozart in Prag*, 86-87, and Nettl, *Mozart in Böhmen*, 132, which also mention Jahn's claim that the duet and chorus for Zerlina and Masetto, "Giovanetta che fate" from Act I, scene 7, and Masetto's aria "Ho capito, Signor, sí," from Act I, scene 8, were inserted during rehearsals as well. None of these scholars took note of the fact that the texts for the latter vocal pieces do appear in the libretto for *Don Giovanni* printed for the performance of 29 October, whereas the texts that appear to have been inserted by Mozart do not.

The specialized term *Harmoniemusik* was used in the late eighteenth century to denote music for wind ensemble of the type heard in Mozart's *Don Giovanni*. Still useful as a resource for the origins of *Harmoniemusik* in late eighteenth-century Europe is Roger Hellyer, "Harmoniemusik: Music for Small Wind Band in the Late Eighteenth and Early Nineteenth Centuries" (Ph.D. dissertation, Oxford University, 1973). Although live musicians on stage were specified in Mozart's scores, it is customary now only to use mock musicians on stage and have the music played in the pit (just as for the ball scene in Act I).

P. 224 - Da Ponte certainly based his "scena ultima" closely on Bertati, but the idea of ending with surviving characters explaining how they will continue with their lives probably descends from the Goldoni play.

For the omission of the "scena ultima" after the first performance of *Don Giovanni*, see Kuhe, *My Musical Recollections*, 10. Kuhe claimed that it was never heard again (presumably he meant in Prague, not the rest of Europe), until a jubilee performance of 1837 at which it was considered "exceedingly dull."

Chapter 11

P. 227 - The equivalent study for *La clemenza di Tito* to Rushton's study *W. A. Mozart: Don Giovanni* is John A. Rice, *W. A. Mozart: La clemenza di Tito* (Cambridge: Cambridge University Press, 1991). The score of *La clemenza di Tito* is available in the *Neue-Mozart-Ausgabe* in Series II, Bühnenwerke, Werkgruppe 5, vol. 20, as *La Clemenza di Tito*, ed. Franz Giegling (Kassel: Bärenreiter, 1970). The autograph score of *La clemenza di Tito* as preserved in several libraries is also available in a facsmile edition: *Wolfgang Amadeus Mozart: La clemenza di Tito : K. 621, Facsimile of the Autograph Score, Staatsbibliothek zu Berlin - Preussischer Kulturbesitz, Biblioteka Jagiellonska Kraków (Mus. ms. autogr. W.A. Mozart 621), The British Library London, Music Collections (Zweig 62)* (Los Altos, California: The Packard Humanities Institute, 2008).

P. 228 - A concise description of the conventions of late eighteenth-century *opera seria* is presented in Freeman, *Josef Mysliveček*, 127-33.

P. 229 - Suetonius' remarks concerning Titus can be found in Gaius Suetonius Tranquillus, *The Twelve Caesars*, translated by Robert Graves (London: Penguin Books, 1989), 292-98.

P. 231 - The operas with tragic endings in which Maria Marchetti Fantozzi appeared were Giovanni Battista Borghi's *La morte di Semiramide* (Padua, 1790, and Milan, 1791), Niccolò Antonio Zingarelli's *La morte di Cesare* (Milan, 1791), and Sebastiano Nasolini's *La morte di Cleopatra* (Vicenza, 1791). These roles are verified in Sartori, *I libretti italiani*.

P. 232 - The dalliance of the historical Titus with Berenice is well documented, but he bowed to popular pressure and repudiated her, even after living for years almost as her husband.

In his catalog of compositions, Mozart used the phrase "ridotta á vera opera dal Sig:re Mazzolá" ("reduced to a true opera by Signor Mazzolá"). The phrase has been the subject of controversy in the Mozart literature. To the present author, the phrase indicates that the reductions made to Metastasio's libretto made it more in touch with modern taste, thus "true opera" would be roughly synonymous with "modern opera."

Another evaluation of Mazzolà's role as an adapter of Metastasio's libretto for *La clemenza di Tito* is provided in Friedrich Lippmann, "Mozart, Mazzolà und Metastasio: *La clemenza di Tito*," in *Böhmische Aspekte*, 279-94.

P. 234 - The development of aria forms in the 1760s and 1770s is summarized in Freeman, *Josef Mysliveček*, 134-70, including notes on the emergence of the vocal rondò.

Chapter 12

P. 238 - This discussion does not include spurious works such as the Contredanses, K. 510/Anh. C13.02, now not believed to be authentic, or the bass aria "Io ti lascio," K. 621a, whose violin parts are the only thing probably written by Mozart. Nettl, *Mozart in Böhmen*, 211-12, 239- 45, included a description of it with the assumption that it was written in Prague in 1791 and actually included a modern edition of it in his text, however there are two studies of the composition that conclude it was mainly the work of Mozart's friend Jacquin: Stefan Kunze, "Die Arie KV 621a von W. A. Mozart und Emilian Gottfried von Jacquin," in *Mozart-Jahrbuch 1967* (Salzburg: Internationale Stiftung Mozarteum, 1968), 205-28, and Wolfgang Plath, "Zur Echtheitsfrage bei Mozart," in *Mozart-Jahrbuch 1971/72* (Salzburg: Internationale Stiftung Mozarteum, 1973), 35. The findings of these scholars emphasize the reluctance anyone should have to regard alleged Mozart works composed after 1784 as authentic if they no not appear in his own catalog of completed works.

The score of the "Prague" Symphony is available in the *Neue-Mozart-Ausgabe* in Series IV, Orchesterwerke, Werkgruppe 11: Sinfonien, vol. 8, ed. Friedrich Schnapp and László Somfai (Kassel: Bärenreiter, 1971), 63-120.

Theories concerning the original purpose for the composition of the "Prague" Symphony are aired in Zaslaw, *Mozart's Symphonies*, 409-21. There is also discussion of this question in Elaine R. Sisman, "Genre, Gesture, and Meaning in Mozart's 'Prague' Symphony," in *Mozart Studies* 2, edited by Cliff Eisen (Oxford: Clarendon Press, 1997), 27-33. A planned trip to London could have been a reason for writing, also a series of instrumental concerts that were to take place during Advent of 1786 in Vienna according to a letter of Leopold Mozart of 8 December. It is unknown for certain whether these ever took place. For what it is worth, Němeček certainly considered the "Prague" Symphony to have been written expressly for Prague, as can be seen in his account of its first performance translated in Chapter 5.

P. 239 - The symphonies composed in Vienna after Mozart's move in 1781 are No. 35 (the "Haffner"), written for Salzburg in 1782; No. 36 (the "Linz"), written for Linz in 1783; No. 38 (the "Prague"), first performed in Prague in 1787; and Nos. 39-41, all written in Vienna during the summer of 1788 (the work known as "No. 37" is actually a symphony of Michael Haydn found among his effects after his death; the only part of it by Mozart is a slow introduction to Haydn's first movement).

P. 240 - More information about the currency of three-movement symphonies in late eighteenth-century Europe is found in Freeman, *Josef Mysliveček*, 185-210 (Mysliveček was one of the greatest composers of three-movement symphonies at the time and one of the last prominent composers who cultivated them consistently). Zaslaw, *Mozart's Symphonies*, provides no coherent explanation for the highly exceptional three-movement format of the "Prague" Symphony. Sisman, "Mozart's 'Prague' Symphony," 31-32, explains one theory about how the last movement of the symphony may have been intended originally as a substitute finale for the Symphony No. 31 (the "Paris" Symphony), composed in 1778, which was also cast in three movements. Instead of using it for this purpose, the idea would be that new movements were added, thus creating a whole new symphony. The theory that the finale of the "Prague" Symphony was written earlier than the rest is based on the survival of Mozart's autograph; the last movement is written on a different type of paper than the other movements.

Of the 106 symphonies generally accepted as authentic works of Joseph Haydn, 15 are cast in three-movement format: the Symphony A (by 1762) and Nos. 1 (by 1759), 2 (by 1764), 4 (by 1762), 9 (1762?), 10 (by 1766), 12 (1763), 16 (by 1766), 17 (by 1765), 18 (by 1766), 19 (by 1766), 25 (by 1766), 26 (by 1770), 27 (by 1766), and 30 (1765).

Examples of four-movement symphonies written for Vienna while Mozart was a child include the Symphonies Nos. 6, 7, and 8 of 1767-68.

See Freeman, *Josef Mysliveček*, 57, 80-85, for documentation of the composer's relationship with Count Colloredo, the archbishop of Salzburg. The possibility that the "Prague" Symphony was suggested by Mysliveček's example is also discussed in ibid., 251-53.

P. 241 - Mozart's disappointment at J. C. Bach's reaction in meeting him for the first time since childhood (and the last time in his life) is quite evident in a letter he wrote to his father from St. Germain on 27 August 1778.

The letter in question, witten to the music publisher Boyer, is translated in H. C. Robbins Landon, *Haydn: Chronicle and Works: Haydn at Eszterháza, 1766-1790* (Bloomington: Indiana University Press, 1978), 476-77.

A letter of Haydn letter of January 1792 sent to Vienna to Mozart's friend Michael Puchberg notes indifference of the Londoners towards Mozart music. See Deutsch, *Mozart: A Documentary Biography*, 434. Under such circumstances, it is difficult to see how musicians in London would be amenable to having to learn how to play something as difficult as the "Prague" Symphony in the late 1780s.

P. 242 - The excellence of the orchestra of the National Theater led by Strobach is rarely acknowledged in the Mozart literature. Baron Riesbeck's estimation of the quality of orchestral playing in Prague in the early 1780s is quoted in Chapter 3. Zaslaw, *Mozart's Symponies*, 414, also reports the opinion of the composer Adalbert Gyrowetz that the orchestra of the National Theater in Prague in the 1780s was "excellent" (Zaslaw indicated this as an evaluation from "about 1780" not realizing that the National Theater did not even open until 1783). The striking remark of the composer Tomášek quoted in Chapter 9 (that Mozart, who knew the capabilities of all the orchestras in Germany, said "my orchestra is in Prague") finds indirect corroboration elsewhere, with the recognition that orchestral playing in Prague experienced a decline sometime in the early nineteenth century. The memoirs of Wilhelm Kuhe contain a very specific judgment that of all the orchestras in Germany, the orchestra of Prague was the best until 1830 (*My Musical Recollections*, 7). In addition, the Prague travel guide of August Griesel published in 1823 (see the *Neuestes Gemälde von Prag*, p. 104), frankly acknowledges that musical life had been in decline for a period of decades.

P. 246 - The score of the six German dances, K. 509, is available in the *Neue-Mozart-Ausgabe* in Series IV, Orchesterwerke, Werkgruppe 13, Tänze und Märsche, Abteilung 1: Tänze, vol. 2, ed. Marius Flothuis (Kassel: Bärenreiter, 1988), 23-42.

P. 247 - The score of the concert aria "Bella mia fiamma, addio"/"Resta, o cara," is available in the *Neue-Mozart-Ausgabe* in Series II, Bühnenwerke, Werkgruppe 7: Arien, Szene, Ensembles und Chöre mit Orchester, vol. 4, ed. Stefan Kunze (Kassel: Bärenreiter, 1972), 37-56. Two stimulating essays about this aria have appeared quite recently: Lucio Tufano, "'Bella mia fiamma, addio'/'Resta, o cara' tra Jommelli e Mozart: osservazioni e ipotesi sull'aria K. 528," in *Böhmische Aspekte*, 125-151, and Geoffrey Chew, "The Public and Private Affairs of Josepha Duschek: A Re-Interpretation of Mozart's *Bella mia fiamma, addio* KV528," *Early Music* 40 (2012): 639-57.

This tradition of "farewell" arias is explained in Chew, "Mozart's *Bella mia fiamma, addio* KV528," 639. The earlier arias in question are "Se al labbro mio non credi," K. 295a, set to a text from Johann Adolf Hasse's *Artaserse* of 1730 (originally composed for Venice, but revised for Dresden in 1740 and Naples in 1760), and "Ch'io mi scordi di te"/"Non temer, amato bene," K. 505, on a new text that was to be used as a substitute aria for *Idomeneo*.

Lucio Tufano, in his "'Bella mia fiamma,'" has recently established that the Jommelli aria did circulate in the north as an operatic excerpt used for concert purposes, one possible means by which

Dušek could have gotten access to it. Furthermore, that it is possible that Dušek was able to obtain a copy of it from the Bohemian singer Tekla Podleská, who was present in Naples in the year 1786, then quickly returned north. This may well explain how Dušek became interested in the text just before Mozart's second trip to Prague in the autumn of 1787. Podleská has been accorded a biographical entry in *Starší divadlo*.

P. 253 - The reductive analysis provided in Chew, "Mozart's *Bella mia fiamma, addio* KV528," makes it easy to recognize these downward-moving gestures.

P. 254 - Scores of the *Lieder* "Des kleinen Friedrichs Geburtstag" and "Das Traumbild" are available in the *Neue-Mozart-Ausgabe* in Series III, Lieder, Mehrstimmige Gesänge, Kanons, Werkgruppe 8, Lieder, ed. Ernst August Ballin (Kassel: Bärenreiter, 1963), 50-53.

Postscript

P. 258 - For the remark of Štěpánek, see Nissen, *Biographie W. A. Mozarts*, 518; for Svoboda, see Kuhe, *My Musical Recollections*, 7; for Strobach, see Němeček, *Lebensbeschreibung*, 41.

Appendix I

P. 260 - The engraving of Luigi Bassi depicts him performing the title role in the opera *Don Giovanni* in Act II, scene 3. He would be singing the canzonetta "Deh, vieni alla finestra" (No. 16) as part of an attempt to seduce Donna Elvira's maid, who is supposed to be able to hear his singing from the open window. This maid never sings anything herself, and in most productions of the opera is never actually shown. Don Giovanni is supposed to be disguised as Leporello in this scene. The mandolin with a ribbon would have been perceived as an attempt to introduce local Spanish color. Just a little later in the opera, in the aria "Metà di voi quà vedano" (No. 17) from Act II, scene 4, Don Giovanni instructs Masetto and a group of peasants to find Leporello (in disguise as Don Giovanni) by looking for a man wearing a hat with large plumes. Bassi is wearing such a hat in the engraving, even though he is supposed to be dressed in disguise as Leporello.

Select Bibliography

Angermüller, Rudolph. *Mozart auf der Reise nach Prag, Dresden, Leipzig und Berlin.* Bad Honef: Verlag K. H. Bock, 1995.

Anon. *Beobachtungen in und über Prag von einem reisenden Ausländer.* 2 volumes. Prague, 1787 (perhaps written by Johann Friedrich Ernst Albrecht).

----------. *Vollständige Beschreibung der königlichen Haupt- und Residenzstadt Prag: von den ältesten bis auf die jetzigen Zeiten, besonders für Fremde und Reisende bearbeitet.* 2 volumes. Prague and Vienna, 1787 (perhaps written by Johann Ferdinand Opitz).

Agnew, Hugh. *The Czechs and the Lands of the Bohemian Crown.* Stanford: Hoover Institution Press, 2004.

Anderson, Emily. *The Letter of Mozart and His Family.* 3rd edition. New York: W. W. Norton, 1985.

Bauer, Wilhelm A., and Otto Erich Deutsch. *Mozart: Briefe und Aufzeichnungen.* 4 volumes with additions and supplements. Kassel and New York: Bärenreiter, 1962-75.

Berkovec, Jiří. *Musicalia v pražském periodickém tisku 18. století.* Prague: Státní Knihovna ČSR, 1989.

Burton, Richard. *Prague: A Cultural History.* Northampton, Mass.: Interlink Books, 2009.

Clive, Peter. *Mozart and His Circle: A Biographical Dictionary.* London: J. M. Dent, 1993.

Da Ponte, Lorenzo. *Estratto delle memorie.* Edited by Lorenzo della Chà. Milan: Edizioni Il Polifilo, 1999.

----------. *Memoirs of Lorenzo Da Ponte.* Translated by Elisabeth Abbott. Philadelphia: J. B. Lippincott, 1929; repr. New York: Da Capo Press, 1988.

Demetz, Peter. *Prague in Black and Gold.* New York: St. Martin's Press, 1997.

Deutsch, Otto Erich, ed. *Mozart: A Documentary Biography.* Translated by Eric Blom, Peter Branscombe, and Jeremy Noble. Stanford: Stanford University Press, 1965.

Eisen, Cliff, and Simon P. Keefe, eds. *The Cambridge Mozart Encyclopedia.* Cambridge: Cambridge University Press, 2006.

Jakubcová, Alena, et al. *Starší divadlo v českých zemích do konce 18. století: osobnosti a díla.* Prague: Divadelní Ústav - Akademia, 2007.

Kerner, Robert. *Bohemia in the Eighteenth Century.* New York: Macmillan, 1932; repr. Orono, Me: Academic International, 1969.

Kleist, Franz Alexander von. *Fantasien auf einer Reise nach Prag.* Dresden and Leipzig, 1792.

Krögen, Karl Heinrich. *Freye Bemerkungen über Berlin, Leipzig und Prag.* Copenhagen, 1785; repr. as *Freie Bemerkungen über Berlin, Leipzig, Prag,* Leipzig and Weimar: Gustav Kiepenheuer Verlag, 1986.

Landon, H. C. Robbins. *1791: Mozart's Last Year.* New York: Schirmer Books, 1988.

Meissner, Alfred. *Rococo-Bilder: nach Aufzeichnungen meines Grossvaters*. Gumbinnen, 1871; 2nd ed., Leipzig and Lindau, 1876.

Němeček (Niemetschek), František Xaver. *Leben des K. K. Kapellmeisters Wolfgang Gottlieb Mozart, nach Originalquellen beschrieben*. Prague, 1798; 2nd ed. as *Lebensbeschreibung des K. K. Kapellmeisters Wolfgang Amadeus Mozart* (Prague, 1808), repr. edited by Claudia Maria Knispel (Laaber: Laaber Verlag, 2005).

Nettl, Paul. *Mozart und Böhmen*. Prague: Neumann, 1938.

Nissen, Georg Nikolaus von. *Biographie W. A. Mozarts*. Leipzig, 1828; repr. Hildesheim: Georg Olms, 1984.

Procházka, Rudolph Freiherr. *Mozart in Prag: Zum hundertjährigen Gedächtnis seines Todes*. Prague, 1892.

Rice, John A. *W. A. Mozart: La clemenza di Tito*. Cambridge: Cambridge University Press, 1991.

Rushton, Julian. *W. A. Mozart: Don Giovanni*. Cambridge: Cambridge University Press, 1981.

Salfellner, Harald. *Mozart und Prag*. Prague and Furth im Wald: Vitalis, 2000.

Schaller, Jaroslaus. *Beschreibung der Königlichen Haupt- und Residenzstadt Prag*. 4 volumes. Prague, 1794-1797.

Solomon, Maynard. Maynard Solomon, *Mozart: A Life*. New York: HarperCollins, 1995.

Teuber, Oskar. *Geschichte des Prager Theaters*. 3 volumes. Prague, 1883-88.

Index

Abel, Christian Friedrich, 55, 241
Adriatic Sea, 9
Albrecht, king of Bohemia, 10
Albrecht, Johann Friedrich Ernst, 37, 158, 163, 171, 175-176
Albrechtsberger, Johann Georg, 157
Alembert, Jean le Rond d', 13, 23
Alexander the Great, 229
Alexander Leopold, Palatine of Hungary, 166
Amsterdam, 28
Andalusia, 205
André, Johann, 184
Anna of Bohemia, 10
Anna Amalia, duchess of Weimar, 119
Anton, king of Saxony, 110-111, 113, 161, 222
Antonini, Signora, 267
Arno river, 173
Artaxerxes I of Persia, 229
Assumption in the Strahov Abbey complex, church of, 137, 272
Attilius Regulus, Marcus, Roman general, 229
Attwood, Thomas, 76, 93, 99, 102
Auersperg, Prince Karl Josef Anton von, 78
Auersperg, Prince Johann Adam von, 78-79
Auersperg family, 78
Austria, 8-9, 13-14, 16-17, 19-21, 23-25, 33, 36-39, 61, 64, 83, 86, 89, 101, 109, 139, 158-159, 164-165, 173-174, 193, 222, 246
Austria-Hungary, 25
Austrian Netherlands, 15, 19, 21, 28, 158-159, 173

Bach, Johann Christian, 55, 241
Bach, Johann Sebastian, 225, 241
Baden, 176
Baglioni, Antonio, 153, 197, 260, 268
Bakov, 56
Bambini, Eustachio, 195
Bassi, Luigi, 119-120, 122, 124, 126, 129-130, 212, 260
Bastille prison, 165
Bath, 35

Baumgarten, Countess Maria Josepha von, 252
Bavaria, 14, 67, 96, 252
Beaumarchais, Pierre-Augustin Caron de, 73, 91, 113, 208, 210
Bedini, Domenico, 153, 175-176, 268
Beer, Joseph, 67
Beethoven, Ludwig van, 17, 52, 54, 55, 79, 87, 117, 144, 243-244, 259
Belgium, 15, 158
Berchtold zu Sonnenberg, Johann Baptist Franz von, 76, 105
Berchtold zu Sonnenberg, Leopold Alois Pantaleon, 76-77
Berlin, 2, 37, 46, 48, 56, 85, 144-147, 149, 187
Bertati, Giovanni, 107, 155, 196-197, 199-202, 205, 208, 225
Bertramka villa in Prague, 85, 101, 106, 109, 118-119, 133, 137, 139, 157-158, 188
Bizet, Georges, 211
Blanchard, Jean-Pierre, 175
Blue Grape (Blue Wine Grape) coffeehouse (or tavern) in Prague, 125, 135, 146, 175
Bohemia, duchy, province and kingdom of, 118, 149, 168, 170-174, 181, 186, 261: clergy, 16-17; Germanization, 3, 12, 22-23, 47, 49-50, 83, 91-92; history, 2-3, 7-26; internal political tensions between Czechs and Germans, 3, 22-23, 25-26, 49-50; musical culture, 7, 50-59, 71, 75, 115, 182, 222, 242-244; national character, 42-43, 54-59; nobility, 10, 13-19, 21-23, 32-33, 39-42, 45, 51, 56, 63-65, 77-79, 86, 100-101, 112-114, 118, 148, 150-151, 161, 167-172, 258-259; religion, 9-13, 23, 27, 37-40; serfdom, 13, 17-22, 25, 52, 148, 150, 159, 169, 227
Bohemian Diets, 10, 21, 24, 150-151
Bohemian Society of Sciences, 39
Bologna, 68, 153-154
Bonaparte, Napoléon, 20, 64, 110, 150, 159, 165, 231

323

Bondini, Caterina, 74, 78, 120-123, 126, 128, 260
Bondini, Pasquale, 46-48, 74-75, 84, 94, 97-98, 100, 103, 106-107, 119-120, 123, 126, 129, 150, 177, 197, 212, 258
Bondy, 163, 174
Bořivoj I, duke of Bohemia, 29, 274
Born, Ignaz von, 40, 177
Botič brook in Prague, 29
Bouillé, François Claude Amour, marquis de, 165-166, 173
Bouillé, Louis Joseph Amour, marquis de, 167
Brahe, Tycho, 28
Braunschweig, 189
Breicha, Anton Daniel, 78
Bretikopf & Härtel (publisher), 153, 184, 188
Bretfeld, Baron Joseph von, 86-90
Bridi, Giuseppe Antonio, 114
Brixi, František Xaver, 51, 138
Brno, 61, 83, 118, 174, 188
Brown, Edward, 31, 38
Brussels, 28
Burgos, 205, 261
Burgtheater in Vienna, 47, 70, 72-73, 113, 154
Burney, Charles, 24, 32-33, 54-56
Bustelli, Giuseppe, 46, 196
Byron, George Gordon Byron, 6th Baron, 109, 197

Ca' Pesaro in Venice, 66
Caldara, Antonio, 155, 194, 228, 233-234, 268
Calegari, Giuseppe, 196
Calvinist religion, 10, 12
Campe, Joachim Heinrich, 257
Campi, Antonia, 188
Campi, Gaetano, 267
Canal, Joseph Emmanuel Malabaila, Count von, 39, 86-87, 93-94, 100, 145-146
Čapek, Karel, 18
Capetian dynasty of France, 8
Carinthia, 9
Carniola, 9
Casanova, Giacomo, 7, 107, 117-122, 124-125, 139, 164, 207
Čáslav, 55, 79
Cassius Dio, 229
Casti, Giovanni Battista, 122

Catherine the Great, empress of Russia, 20, 120
Catholic religion, 9-13, 23, 34, 88, 212
Cato the Younger, 229
Cavriani, Count Ludwig Franz Xaver von, 112, 133, 151
Čechtín, 83
Ceneda, 109, 119, 121
Černín, Count Humprecht von, 65
Černín, Count Jan Rudolf von, 64-66, 163
Černín, Count Prokop Vojtěch von, 64-66
Černín family, 13, 63-66
Černín palace in Prague, 66
Černohorský, Bohuslav, 51
Český Brod, 55, 83
Charles III, king of Spain, 173, 249
Charles IV, Holy Roman Emperor, 9, 28, 30
Charles V, Holy Roman Emperor, 10
Charles VI, Holy Roman Emperor, 13-14, 45, 151
Charles VII, Holy Roman Emperor, 14
Charles X, king of France (Count of Artois), 158
Charles Bridge in Prague, 30, 34-35, 145, 168, 171
Charles University in Prague, 40, 46
Charles-Ferdinand University in Prague, 24, 40, 53, 69, 88, 185
Cherubini, Luigi, 231
Chotek, Count Jan von, 155
Christian religion, 195, 209-210, 218
Churchill, John, duke of Marlborough, 173
Cicognini, Giacinto Andrea, 196, 198, 207-208
Clam, Count von Gallas, Christian Philipp, 118-119
Clam-Gallas family, 52
Collegium Virgilianum in Salzburg, 64, 77
Colloredo, Count Hieronymus Joseph Franz de Paula von, prince-archbishop of Salzburg, 44, 64-65, 67, 69, 93
Colloredo, Countess Maria Antonia von, 64
Colloredo-Mannsfeld, Count Franz de Paula Adam Gundackar von, 93
Colloredo-Mannsfeld, Countess Maria Isabella von, 93

Colloredo-Mannsfeld palace in Prague, 93
Colloredo-Waldsee, archbishop of Olomouc, Count Antonín Theodor von, 163
Congo, Belgian, 148
Copenhagen, 37
Council of Basel, 10
Council of Constance, 9
Cowper, Countess Hannah, 173
Cowper, George Nassau Clavering-Cowper, 3rd Earl, 173
Crébillon, Prosper Jolyot de, 90
Crescentini, Girolamo, 153
Crux, Marianne, 90, 92
Czech language, 2, 22-24, 40, 46, 48-49, 94-95, 170-171, 193
Czech Museum of Music, 102
Czech Philharmonic Orchestra, 49
Czech Republic, 3, 26, 65-66, 86, 95
Czechoslovakia, 2-3, 25-27, 29

Da Ponte, Lorenzo, 1, 78, 89-92, 107-110, 113, 115-122, 124, 129, 142-143, 155, 196-210, 212-214, 219-220, 223-224, 258, 261
Dante Alighieri, 108-109, 196-197
Danube river, 184
Declaration of Pillnitz, 151, 158-159
Defenestration of Prague (1618), 11, 25, 28
Demetrius II Nicator, 229
Denmark, 12, 98
Denzio, Antonio, 45, 194-197
Diderot, Denis, 13, 23
Dittersdorf, Karl Ditters von, 71
Domitian, emperor of Rome, 229
Don Juan legend, 7-8, 105, 109, 194-204, 207
Dresden, 32, 43, 46, 48, 110, 112, 114, 116, 126, 144-145, 152, 155, 158, 160-161, 187
Dublin, 7
Duchcov Castle, 118, 120
Dumas, Alexandre, 95
Durante, Sergio, 157
Dušek, František Xaver, 52-54, 67, 85, 99-100, 106, 119-121, 122-126, 136, 148-150, 157-158, 174, 176-177, 181, 182, 195
Dušek, Josefa (née Hambacher), 52-54, 67, 71, 85, 99-100, 112, 119, 113, 125, 136-139, 148, 151, 174, 176-177, 179, 181, 185, 188, 247-254
Dusík, Jan Ladislav, 54
Dvořák, Antonín, 49, 54

Edinburgh, 28
Ehrlich, Matthias, 137
Elbe river, 34
Elisabeth Wilhelmine, princess of Württemberg, 113, 143, 166
Eliška of Bohemia, princess, 9
England, 28, 31, 35-36, 54, 75-77, 92-93, 99, 102, 174
Estates of Bohemia, 7, 10-12, 15, 21-22, 24-25, 49, 51, 86, 148, 150-153, 155-156, 158, 160, 163-164, 170-172, 174-175, 227, 250
Eszterháza, 141, 196
Eszterházy, Prince Anton, 154
Eszterházy, Prince Nikolaus, 150
Eugenius IV, Pope, 10
Exeter, 32

Fantozzi, Angelo, 153
Ferdinand, duke of Parma, 62
Ferdinand I, Holy Roman Emperor, 10-11, 27
Ferdinand II, Holy Roman Emperor, 12, 23
Ferdinand IV, king of Naples, 60, 242-243
Fersen, Count Axel von, 164-167, 173
Fischer, Rudolph, 180
Flavius Aetius, 229
Flight to Varennes, 158, 164-165
Florence, 31, 106, 153, 173, 202, 228
France, 8-9, 12, 16, 19-21, 23, 31, 57, 61, 64, 67, 69, 90, 92, 158-159, 162-166, 205, 229
Francis, John W., 198-199, 205
Francis I, Holy Roman Emperor, 14-15, 19, 173
Francis II, Holy Roman Emperor (Emperor of Austria as Francis I after 1806), 20-21, 70, 110, 116, 117, 139, 143, 158, 160, 164-166, 169, 249
Frankfurt-am-Main, 16, 151, 169
Franz Josef, Emperor of Austria, 49
Frederick II, Holy Roman Emperor, 8
Frederick II the Great, king of Prussia, 14, 20, 35, 38, 120, 159

Frederick V, Elector Palatine, 11-12
Frederick Augustus III of Saxony, 110, 158, 161
Frederick William II, king of Prussia, 148-149, 151, 158, 161
Freisauff, Rudolf von, 132
Friedrich, prince of Anhalt-Dessau, 254
French Revolution, 19-20, 54, 64, 158-159, 162, 165-166, 231
Freystädtler, Franz Jacob, 94, 96
Fux, Johann Joseph, 45

Gallus, Jacobus, 51
Gassmann, Florian, 54
Gazzaniga, Giuseppe, 196
Gellert, Christian, 90
Genast, Anton, 133
Genast, Eduard, 133-134
George (Jiří) of Poděbrady, 10
Gerle, Wolfgang, 134
German Theater in Prague, New, 50
Germans in the Bohemian lands, 3, 22-23, 25-26
Germany, 3, 8-9, 23-25, 31-32, 34, 36, 38, 40, 47, 54-55, 57, 64, 67-69, 77, 121, 142, 162, 167, 183, 187, 193, 205, 240
Gluck, Christoph Willibald, Ritter von, 51, 54, 124, 140, 167, 174, 193, 200, 227, 229
Goethe, Johann Wolfgang von, 134
Golčův Jeníkov, 55
Golden Angel Inn in Prague, 133
Goldoni, Carlo, 196, 199, 208
Graz, 187
Great Britain, 35, 38, 61, 106, 159, 162, 167
Greece, ancient, 194, 202, 204, 228
Griesel, August, 135
Guardasoni, Domenico, 107-108, 110-112, 115-118, 119-122, 124-125, 129-130, 133, 145-147, 177, 182, 196-197, 212, 258; participation in coronation opera production of 1791, 152-155, 170, 174
Gubernium, Czech, 15, 24, 46, 87, 97, 111-112, 114, 163, 170
Guibert, Jacques Antoine Hippolyte de, 39

Habermann, Franz Xaver, 51
Habry, 83

Hadrian, emperor of Rome, 229
Haffner, Siegmund, 72
Hagenauer, Johann Lorenz, 62
Hamburg, 70, 77, 115
Handel, George Frideric, 7, 167, 174, 196, 214
Hapsburg dynasty of Austria (and domains), 9-15, 17, 19-21, 23-25, 27-28, 31-32, 40, 45, 51, 61-62, 69, 78-79, 86-87, 90, 112, 119, 150, 158, 228
Harant z Polzič a Bezdruzič, Kryštof, 51
Häusler (or Hofmann/Hoffmann), Josef, 131-136
Havel, Václav, 25
Havlíčkův Brod, 55, 83
Haydn, Joseph, 17, 141-142, 144, 154, 196, 240-241, 243-244
Herold, Eduard, 106, 109, 125, 134-135
Heydrich, Reinhard, 12
Hibernian Theater in Prague, 142
Hispalis, ancient city of, 205
Hispania Baetica, Roman province of, 205
Hitler, Adolf, 12
Hofer, Franz de Paula, 84-85, 92, 94-96
Hofmann, Leopold, 168, 177, 259
Holy Roman Empire, 9-12, 173, 249
Holy Savior in Prague, church of the, 93, 273
Holyrood castle, 28
Höltz, Ludwig Heinrich Christoph, 254
Hradec Králové, 52
Hungary, 10, 13, 19, 21, 25, 39, 141, 149, 166, 173
Hurdálek, Josef, 140
Hus, Jan, 9-10, 35
Hussite religion, 9-12, 23, 38

Illuminati, 20
Invalidovna in Prague, 161
Ippold, Franz Armand d', 77
Ireland, 7, 13, 142
Istria, 9
Italian Chapel in the Klementinum in Prague, 89
Italy, 16, 45, 49, 55, 57, 68, 72, 86, 90, 150, 152, 156, 193, 196-197, 204-205, 228-231, 234, 240, 243, 251

Jacquin, Franziska von, 84, 96, 112
Jacquin, Gottfried von, 84-88, 90, 94,

96, 99, 110-112, 114, 139-140
Jacquin, Joseph Franz von, 96-97, 112
Jacquin family, 84, 94, 96, 112
Jagiellon dynasty of Poland, 10
Jahn, Otto, 119
James I, king of England (James VI of Scotland), 28
Jesuit order, 12, 15, 23-24, 40, 87, 93, 273
Jewish-Roman War, First, 222
Jews in the Bohemian lands, 3, 10, 16, 25-27, 37-39, 50, 54, 119, 121-122, 161
Jihlava, 83, 162, 182
Jindřichův Hradec, 51
John of Luxemburg, king of Bohemia, 9
Johnson, Samuel, 34
Jommelli, Niccolò, 139, 242-243, 245-246, 249
Joseph (Mozart's servant), 94
Joseph I, Holy Roman Emperor, 101
Joseph II, Holy Roman Emperor, 15-19, 21-22, 24, 28, 30, 37, 39, 46-47, 58, 61-62, 69-70, 73, 101, 106, 109-110, 113-107, 109, 113, 120-121, 140, 142-143, 148, 159, 161-162, 164-165, 168-169, 172-173
Judea, 229, 232

Kaliningrad (Königsberg), 56
Kanálka in Vinohrady, Prague, 86
Karl of Austria, duke of Teschen, 165
Karl August, Crown Prince of Sweden, 164
Karlovy Vary, 160
Kaunitz, Count Wenzel von, 14
Kelly, Michael, 76, 93, 99, 102
Kepler, Johannes, 28
Khünburg, Count Ferdinand von, archbishop of Prague, 195
Kinský, Count Franz Josef von, 23-24
Kinský family, 13
Kleist, Franz Alexander von, 159-169, 171-172, 175
Kleist, Heinrich von, 159
Klementinum (Jesuit College) in Prague, 40, 56, 92-93, 140
Klyvis, Remigijus, 224
Knights Templar, 134-135
Kolín, 55, 83
Kolovrat, Count Leopold von, 20, 163
Konvikt of St. Bartholomew in Prague, 87, 100
Košíře, 106, 119-120
Kotcích (Kotezentheater) in Prague, Divadlo v, 33, 45-47, 197
Kotzebue, August von, 162-164
Koželuh, Jan Antonín, 168-170
Koželuh, Leopold, 54, 169, 175-176
Krásný Dvůr, 160
Krögen, Karl Heinrich, 37, 40-42, 46, 48, 93
Kroměříž, 51
Kuchař, Jan Křtitel, 75, 177
Kuhe, Wilhelm, 127-129, 224, 258
Künigl, Count Kaspar von, 150
Kutná Hora, 83

Ladislav, king of Bohemia, 10
Lamballe, Marie Louise of Savoy, princess de, 164
LaMotte, Baron Franz von, 87
Landon, H. C. Robbins, 168-170
Laudon, Field Marshal Ernst Gideon von, 162
Le Noble von Edlersberg, Leopold, 111, 151
Lehman, Norbert, 136-138, 247, 272
Leipzig, 37, 39, 46, 48, 129, 148-150, 157, 160, 184, 187-188
Lemberg, Count Max von, 114
Leopold I, Holy Roman Emperor, 30-32
Leopold II, Holy Roman Emperor, 19-22, 37, 110, 172-173, 229, 232-223; coronation as king of Bohemia, 16, 21-22, 66, 70, 110, 148-175, 178, 227-228, 249-250
Leopold II, king of the Belgians, 148
Lessing, Gotthold Ephraim, 47
Levý Hradec, 29
Liběň Castle in Prague, 161
Libuše, princess, 8, 29
Lichnowsky, Prince Karl von, 152
Liechtenstein-Kastelcorn, Bishop Karl von, 51
Linz, 72, 78
Lipová Castle, 101
Lippe, Countess Henriette Luise zur, 143
Lisbon, 153
Livorno, 153
Lolli, Giuseppe, 122, 260
Lombardy, 28, 139
London, 28, 31-32, 35, 39, 55, 76-77, 84, 102-103, 107, 238, 241, 243

Loučeň Castle, 110
Louis II, king of Hungary and Bohemia, 10
Louis XVI, king of France, 21, 62, 158-159, 165
Lutheran religion, 10
Lützow, Countess Antonie von, 64
Luxemburg dynasty, 9, 14
Lyon, 31

Mannheim, 71, 85, 150, 248
Mantua, 119, 121
Marchesi, Luigi, 153
Marchetti Fantozzi, Maria, 153, 172, 174, 176, 231, 268
Maria Amalia, duchess of Parma, 61-62
Maria Anna, archduchess of Austria, 61, 101, 163
Maria Anna Ferdinanda, archduchess of Austria, 163, 170, 175
Maria Carolina, queen of Naples, 61, 249-250
Maria Elisabeth, archduchess of Austria, 61-62
Maria Josepha, archduchess of Austria, 61-62
Maria Luisa, Holy Roman Empress, 162, 166, 172-175
Maria Theresa, Holy Roman Empress, 13-15, 18, 19, 29, 38-39, 46, 61-62, 101, 110, 173
Maria Theresa, queen of Saxony, 109-114, 116, 161, 222
Maria Theresa Carolina Giuseppina, Holy Roman Empress, 249
Marie Antoinette, queen of France, 62, 117, 158-159, 164-165
Marseillaise (French National Anthem), 165
Martin V, Pope, 10
Martín y Soler, Vicente, 108, 110, 116, 196, 216, 223-224
Masaryk, Jan, 66
Masaryk, Tomáš Garrigue, 25, 27
Mašek, Vincenc, 53
Masons (Freemasons) and Masonry, 20, 78, 87, 93, 96, 149-150, 177
Matthias, Holy Roman Emperor, 11, 27
Maximilian II, Holy Roman Emperor, 10-11, 27
Mazzolà, Caterino, 155, 157, 232-233, 237, 268

Meinert, Joseph Georg, 182
Meissner, Alfred, 88-89, 106, 117-119, 125, 129, 134-135, 139, 142, 157, 168, 172-174, 176
Meissner, August Gottlieb, 88-90, 168, 172, 175
Melani, Alessandro, 194
Mělník, 120
Memorial of National Literature in Prague, 146, 272
Mersch, Jean André van der, 172
Metastasio, Pietro, 153, 155, 157, 174, 201, 228-234, 236-237, 249, 252, 268
Micelli, Caterina, 111, 120-121, 124, 260
Michna z Otradovic, Adam Václav, 51
Mihule, Václav, 181
Milan, 28, 139, 216
Mnichovo Hradiště, 78
Mohács, battle of, 10
Molière (Jean-Baptiste Poquelin), 192
Montagu, Lady Mary Wortley, 32, 35, 41
Monte, Philippe de, 50
Monteverdi, Claudio, 230
Montezuma, Aztec ruler of Mexico, 229
Moravia, province of, 2, 9, 15, 18, 23, 33, 39, 53, 55, 83, 104, 106, 144
Moravské Budějovice, 83, 144-145
Mörike, Eduard, 104, 106
Moscheles, Ignaz, 54
Mosel, Ignaz Franz von, 169
Mozart, Anna Maria, 76
Mozart, Constanze (née Weber), 1, 69, 76-77, 84-85, 87-88, 92, 94, 96, 98, 104, 106, 110, 125-129, 144-147, 148, 155-156, 176-189
Mozart, Franz Xaver Wolfgang, 69, 76, 176-177, 180, 184-189
Mozart, Johann Thomas Leopold, 76, 98
Mozart, Karl Thomas, 69, 76, 85, 110, 138-139, 145, 176-177, 180, 184-189, 248, 252-253
Mozart, Leopold, 61-68, 73, 76-77, 84-85, 88, 93, 99, 102-103, 105, 119, 139, 149, 239, 249
Mozart, Nannerl (Maria Anna Walburga Ignatia), 61-63, 73, 76-77, 85, 93, 102, 104, 118, 140, 185
Mozart, Maria Anna Walburga (née Pertl), 67-68, 77
Mozart, Raimund Leopold, 76
Mozart, Theresia Costanzia Adelheid

Friederike Maria Anna, 76, 110
Mozart, Wolfgang Amadeus, 12, 15, 17, 18, 29, 30, 36-37, 40-42, 45, 56, 142-144; and Czech language, 24, 94-95; attitude toward Prague, 94-95, 111-112, 129, 144, 258-259; childhood, 61-62, 67-68, 70, 75-77, 162, 165, 240; death and burial, 1, 177-181; employment crisis of 1777-78, 44, 66-69; family, 52, 61-69, 76-77, 84-85, 87-88, 104-105, 110; move to Vienna in 1781, 44, 68; personality, 87-90, 94-96, 98, 100, 102, 104, 120-130, 126-139, 140, 143-150; plans to travel to Prague before 1787, 63-79; posthumous commemorations, 1, 179-188; trip to Moravia in 1767, 62-63; visit to Prague of January-February 1787, 41-42, 78, 83-103, 131-133, 135-139, 157, 223; visit to Prague of October-November 1787,104-130, 134, 136-140, 157; visits to Prague of 1789, 55, 144-147, 273; visit to Prague in 1791, 133, 135, 148-179

Works:
  The Abduction from the Seraglio, 47, 58-59, 69-73, 212, 217, 235, 272
  Aria "Ah, lo previdi/Ah, t'invola agl'occhi miei," K. 272, 138, 247
  Aria "Al desio di chi t'adora," K. 577, 147
  Aria "Bella mia fiamma, addio"/ "Resta, o cara," K. 528, 112, 138-139, 238, 247-254, 272
  Aria "Ch'io mi scordi di te/Non temer, amato bene," K. 505, 252
  Aria "Misera, dove son/Ah, non son io che parlo," K. 369, 252
  Aria "Vorrei spiegarvi, oh Dio," K. 418, 252
  Canon "Lieber Freystädtler, lieber Gaulimauli," K. 232, 96
  Cantata "Die Maurerfreude," K. 471, 177
    La clemenza di Tito, 21-22, 135, 148, 150, 153, 155-157, 163, 170-172, 174-176, 182, 185-187, 197, 199, 214, 227-237, 268-272
  Clarinet Concerto, K. 622, 236
  Contredanses (German dances), K. 509, 42, 100, 238, 246-247
  Contredanses (German dances), K. 536, 567, 571, 586, 600, 602, and 605, 247
  Così fan tutte, 89, 116, 182, 212, 217, 234-235
  Don Giovanni, 7, 44, 49, 59, 89, 98, 103, 104-130, 134-135, 140, 142-144, 146, 153, 161, 164-165, 167, 174, 186-187, 193-226, 235-237, 242, 259, 260-267, 272
  "Haffner" Symphony, K. 385, 72
  "Harpist's theme," K. Anh. C 26.10, 133, 177, another version, K. Anh. C 26.11, 134
  Idomeneo, 69, 78, 139, 181, 188, 199, 202, 212, 217, 227, 229
  "Jupiter" Symphony, K. 551, 186, 239, 243-244
  Lieder "Des kleinen Friedrichs Geburtstag," K. 529, and "Das Traumbild," K. 530, 239, 254-257
  "Linz" Symphony, K. 425, 72, 78, 186
  The Magic Flute, 40, 75, 85, 127, 135, 154, 176-177, 181-182, 188, 212, 217, 219, 227, 235, 237, 259
  The Marriage of Figaro, 34, 37, 59, 71-78, 83, 85, 89-91, 94, 96-98, 105-108, 111-114, 116, 131-133, 142, 182, 199, 208-210, 212, 217, 219, 223, 227, 235, 237-239
  Mass in C Major, K. 258, 170
  Mass in C Major, K. 317, 170
  Mass in C Major, K. 337, 170
  Mass in C Minor, K. 427, 141
  Offertorium *Misericordias Domini*, K. 222, 168
  Organ improvisation at the Strahov Abbey in Prague, K. Anh. C 27.03, 137-138 "Paris" Symphony, K. 297, 72, 240
  Piano Concerto, K. 246, 64
  Piano Concertos, K. 413-415, 71

Piano Concerto, K. 449-451, 72, 242
Piano Concerto, K. 453, 72, 242
Piano Concerto, K. 456, 72, 242
Piano Concerto, K. 459, 72, 242
Piano Concerto, K. 466, 72, 186, 242
Piano Concerto, K. 467, 72, 242
Piano Concerto, K. 482, 72, 242
Piano Concerto, K. 488, 72, 242
Piano Concerto, K. 491, 72, 242
Piano Concerto, K. 503, 72, 242-243
Piano Concerto, K. 595, 181
Piano Sonatas, K. 284, 309-311, 330-333, 71
Piano Sonata, K. 521, 96
Piano Sonata, K. 576, 144
Piano Trio, K. 498, 96
"Prague" Symphony, K. 504, 53, 59, 97-98, 186, 238-246, 259
"Prussian" string quartets, K. 575, 589, and 590, 144
Requiem, K. 626, 155-156, 178-179, 237
Die Schuldigkeit des ersten Gebots, K. 35, 67
Serenade "Eine kleine Nachtmusik," K. 525, 142
Serenade "The Musical Joke," K. 522, 142
Sonatas for Violin and Piano, K. 296, 376-380, 70
Symphony No. 25, K. 183, 72
Symphony No. 29, K. 201, 72
Symphony No. 33, K. 319, 72
Symphony No. 34, K. 338, 72, 186, 240, 243
Symphony No. 39, K. 543, 239, 240
Symphony No. 40, K. 550, 239, 243
Thamos, König in Ägypten, K. 345, 170
Variations for piano on "Come un agnello," K. 460/454a, 223
Vocal trio "Liebes Mandel, wo is's Bandel?", K. 441, 92
Zaide, 188
Munich, 44, 46, 67, 68-69, 71, 77, 139, 211, 240
Musicians' Society of Vienna, 72

Mysliveček, Joseph, 51, 54, 68-69, 79, 240-241, 252

Naples, 28, 68, 94, 249-250
Napoleonic Wars, 20, 54, 64, 110, 165
National Assembly of France, 159, 165-166
National Museum, Czech, 15
National Theater (Estates' Theater) in Prague, 24, 34-35, 40, 44-50, 53, 70, 73-75, 94, 98-99, 100, 105, 111-116, 125-130, 133, 135, 150-151, 152, 158, 163-164, 171, 173, 175-176, 179-181, 187, 197, 222-223, 238-239, 242, 272; orchestra under Strobach, 53, 74, 78, 80, 94, 96, 98-99, 115-116, 125-130, 175, 178-179, 238-239, 242, 258
National Theater (Národní Divadlo) in Prague, 49-50
Němeček (Niemetschek), František Xaver, 59, 69-73, 75, 78, 97-98, 102, 106, 115, 127, 131, 133, 136-139, 141, 149, 156-157, 177-178, 184, 188-189, 223, 258
New York City, 107, 190-191
Nettl, Paul, 2-3, 86, 101, 109, 118, 134-135
New Gate in Prague, 83, 154, 156
New Inn in Prague, 131-134, 132
Nissen, Georg Nikolaus von, 98-99, 106-107, 111, 125-126, 131, 133, 135, 157, 177, 185, 187, 258
Noble Ladies' Foundation in Prague, 17, 101-102, 163, 170, 175
Noot, Hendrik van der, 173
Nostic-Rieneck, Count Franz Anton von, 40, 46-47, 53, 70, 112, 114, 152
Nostic-Rieneck, Countess Maria Elisabeth von, 112
Nugent, Thomas, 13, 17, 23, 32-33, 38, 83

O'Neill, Thomas P., 160
Oehlschlägel, Jan Lohelius, 51, 136-138
Offenbach, 184
Olomouc, 51, 62-63, 163
Olomouc Cathedral, 63
Opitz, Johann Ferdinand, 36, 118
Otakar I, king of Bohemia, 8
Otakar II, king of Bohemia, 9

Otter, Joseph, 72

Pacassi, Nicolò, 29
Pachta, Count Franz Joseph von, 101
Pachta, Count Hubert Karl von, 100
Pachta, Count Johann Joseph von, 100-101
Pachta, Count Johann Joseph Philipp, 100
Pachta, Count Percival von, 100
Pachta family, 52, 68, 100-101, 145-146, 239
Pachta palaces in Prague, 100-101
Padua, 149
Paganism, 202-203
Paisiello, Giovanni, 94, 183
Palacký, František, 15
Palatinate, Rhenish, 11
Paris, 16, 28, 39, 44, 54, 68, 71-72, 77, 108, 116, 132, 149, 158, 164, 173, 222, 241
Parma, 62
Patin, Charles, 31, 38
Pergolesi, Giovanni Battista, 46
Perini, Carolina, 267
Peruzzi, Antonio Maria, 45
Petermann, Baron Karl von, 64-65
Petrarch, 104, 196
Physiocrats, 16, 19
Pichl, Václav, 54
Pillnitz Castle, 151, 158-159
Piozzi, Gabriel, 34
Piozzi, Hester Lynch, 32, 34-35, 39, 41, 48, 74, 239
Pixis, Friedrich Wilhelm, 132, 134-135
Pixis, Johann Peter, 128
Platýs Inn in Prague, 107, 109
Pleyel, Ignaz, 183
Podstatský z Prusinovic, Count Alois Arnošt, 63
Poland, 9, 23, 53
Polignac, Gabrielle de Polastron, duchess of, 164-165
Polignac, Jules, duke of, 164-166, 173
Pöllnitz, Baron Karl Ludwig von, 17, 33, 38-39
Polná, 83
Ponziani, Felice, 74-75, 260
Popelka, Adolf, 139
Porta, Nunziato, 188
Potsdam, 156
Prague, 1-4, 7, 14, 16-17, 21-22, 24-25, 44-59, 64-77, 83-177, 240-241, 247, 258-259; aid to Mozart's family, 69, 138-139, 178-189, 259; appreciation for Mozart's music, 1-2, 4, 58-59, 70-71, 73-75, 77-78, 83-84, 86, 91, 97-99, 102, 113-116, 127, 147, 181-182, 185-187, 188, 242-243, 258-259; character of residents, 42-43, 54-59; commemorations of Mozart's death, 1, 175-182; culture of balls, 33, 41-42, 48, 58, 66, 84, 86-92, 100-101, 151, 155, 163, 168, 171, 174-176, 246, 258; geography, 29-31; history, 9, 11-13, 27-43; Jewish culture, 27, 37-39, 50, 54; musical culture, 42-59, 71, 73-75, 93, 176, 186-188, 186-190, 238-243, 258-259
Prague Castle, 11, 17, 27-29, 45-46, 101, 110, 113, 157-158, 163, 168-170, 173
Prague Conservatory, 98, 128
Přemysl, 8
Přemyslid dynasty of Bohemia, 8-10, 29
Příchovský z Příchovic, Count Antonín Petr, archbishop of Prague, 163, 169, 173
Private Learned Society of Prague, 40
Procházka, Rudolph Freiherr, 3, 109
Protestant religion, 12, 15, 27-28, 51, 168-169
Provisional Theater in Prague, 49
Prussia, 9, 17, 25, 33, 37, 144-145, 151, 158-159, 161
Puccini, Giacomo, 216

Quallenberg, Elisabeth Barbara, 94, 96

Raimondi, Livia, 173
Ramisch, Anton, 181
Ramlo, Kaspar, 94, 96
Ramm, Friedrich, 145-146
Regensburg, 20, 27
Reicha, Antoine, 54
Reichardt, Johann Friedrich, 56
Riesbeck, Baron Johann Kaspar von, 18, 39-40, 57, 58, 83
Righini, Vincenzo, 195
Rochlitz, Friedrich, 144
Rome, 39, 194, 202, 228-229, 233, 237, 268
Rosenberg, Count Franz von, 139, 143

Rosenthal Theater in Prague, 101
Rossini, Gioacchino, 157, 193, 217, 219, 231, 235
Rössler (Rossetti), Antonín, 54, 179
Rott, Franz, 141
Rott House in Prague, 141
Rottenhan, Count Heinrich von, 151-152, 155, 163, 175
Rousseau, Jean-Jacques, 55
Royal Bohemian Society of Learning, 40
Rubinelli, Giovanni Maria, 153
Rudolf of Hapsburg, Count, 9
Rudolf I, king of Bohemia, 10
Rudolf II, Holy Roman Emperor, 11, 16, 27-28, 31, 37, 50-51, 167
Russia, 8, 17, 56, 165

St. Francis Serafin in Prague, church of, 93
St. George in Prague, church of, 101
St. Nicholas in Prague (Malá Strana), church of, 1, 53, 94, 140, 179
St. Paul the Apostle in Prague, church of, 134
St. Stephen in Vienna, Cathedral of, 1, 85, 168, 179, 259
St. Vitus in Prague, Cathedral of, 27, 29, 114, 138, 151, 161-162, 168-169, 172
Salfellner, Harald, 3
Salieri, Antonio, 73, 108, 116-117, 122, 151-152, 154, 157, 168-170, 176, 186-187, 196, 213, 219
Salzburg, city and archbishopric of, 44, 52, 61-69, 71-72, 77, 84, 93, 99, 102, 104, 119, 138, 141, 163, 170, 185, 239-240, 247
Saporiti, Teresa, 120-123, 260
Sarcone, Michele, 249-250, 253
Sardinia, kingdom of, 86
Sarti, Giuseppe, 223-224
Saxony, 37, 48, 55, 110, 113, 147-148, 158, 160-162
Schall, Johann Eberhard Friedrich, 254
Schaller, Jaroslaus, 101, 106, 133-134
Schebek, Edmund, 132
Schenk, Joseph Max, 133-134
Schickaneder, Emanuel, 177, 181
Shiller, Friedrich, 119
Schönbrunn palace in Vienna, 29
Schrattenbach, Count Franz Anton von, 62
Schrattenbach, Count Siegmund Christoph von, prince-archbishop of Salzburg, 62, 67
Schubert, Franz, 54, 243, 246
Scotland, 13, 28
Seconda, Franz Bartholomäus, 152, 164
Seger, Josef, 51
Semiramis, queen of Assyria, 229
Seven Years' War, 14, 24, 34-35, 43
Seville, 7, 194, 205, 261
Shakespeare, William, 231
Sicily, 249
Siena, 153
Sigismund, Holy Roman Emperor, 9-10, 14
Silesia, province of, 9, 14, 129
Slovakia, 25-26, 150
Slovenia, 51
Šluknov, 56
Smetana, Bedřich, 29, 49, 54
Soběslav I, duke of Bohemia, 29
Spain, 173, 194, 198, 205, 223, 249, 261
Sporck, Count Franz Anton von, 33, 45
Sporck theater in Prague, 33, 45, 194, 197
Stadler, Anton, 92, 94, 96, 156, 176, 236
Starhemberg, Count Josef von, 20
Štěpánek, Jan Nepomuk, 98, 106, 125-126, 258
Sternberg, Count Franz von, 180
Sternberg, Count Kaspar von, 15-17, 19-22, 24, 28, 101
Stockholm, 164
Storace, Nancy, 76, 93, 99, 102, 248
Storace, Stephen, 34
Strahov Abbey in Prague, 40, 136-138, 253
Strasbourg, 195
Strinasacchi, Teresa, 178-179
Strobach, Johann Joseph, 53, 98, 177, 179, 258
Styria, 9
Sopron, 154
Soviet Union, 3, 8, 25
Sudetenland, 23
Suetonius, 222
Süssmayer, Franz Xaver, 156-157, 174, 186, 236
Svitavy, 53
Svoboda, Václav, 122, 258
Sweden, 8, 12, 28, 164

Swieten, Baron Gottfried van, 184, 186
Sylva-Taroucca palace in Prague, 83

Tasso, Torquato, 108, 196
Tchaikovsky, Pyotr Ilyich, 211
Templová lane in Prague, 119, 123, 133-135
Thám, Karel Hynek, 24
Thirty Years' War, 11-12, 27-28, 31, 37, 50, 56, 79, 86
Three Axes house in Prague, 157, 177
Three Lions' Inn in Prague, 106, 119, 133
Thun palaces in Prague, 78, 85-86, 92, 94, 96, 99-100, 133, 142, 223
Thun-Hohenstein, Count Franz Josef, 86
Thun-Hohenstein, Count Johann Joseph Franz von, 46, 56, 78, 85-86, 92, 95-96, 99-100, 102, 110, 133, 142, 223
Thun-Hohenstein, Countess Wilhelmine von, 78
Thun Hohenstein-Salm, Count Oswald, 101
Thuringia, 54
Timur (Tamerlane), 229
Tirso de Molina, 194, 198, 207-208
Titus, emperor of Rome, 155, 229-230
Tomášek, Jakub, 183
Tomášek, Václav Jan, 54, 162, 182-183
Třebíč, 83
Tuileries Palace in Paris, 164
Turkey, 8, 10, 19, 21-22, 143-144, 205
Tuscany, 20-22, 110, 116, 153, 158, 160, 172
Tyl, Josef Kajetán, 49
Tyrol, 78

Ugarte, Wenzel von, 147
Ungar, Raphael, 93
Unicorn (or Golden Unicorn) Inn in Prague, 55, 144-145
United States of America, 3, 25, 107

Vaňhal, Jan Křtitel, 54
Varennes, 158, 163-164
Venice, 45, 66, 103, 105, 118-120, 124, 194, 196-197, 200, 211, 228, 230
Verdi, Giuseppe, 204
Vernier palace in Prague, 93
Vespasian, emperor of Rome, 222

Věžník, František Xaver, 114
Vicenza, 153
Vienna, 2, 18, 19, 20, 23-25, 27-29, 32, 34, 36, 39, 46-49, 54-55, 59, 61-64, 69-75, 77-79, 83-86, 88, 90-94, 99, 102-103, 104, 106, 108-111, 113-116, 121, 126, 129, 135-136, 140, 142-144, 147, 148, 151-152, 154-158, 161, 169, 172, 174-177, 174, 182, 196, 200, 211-212, 222, 224, 228, 238-240, 242-243, 246, 248-249, 258-259, 268; lack of appreciation for Mozart, 1, 69, 72-74, 79, 91, 114, 142-144, 179-180, 187, 258; reluctance to provide financial support for Mozart's widow and sons, 181, 184-185
Vinohrady, 39, 86
Violani, Valeriano, 153
Vitásek, Jan August, 181, 185, 188
Vitellius, emperor of Rome, 232
Vivaldi, Antonio, 45, 51, 194
Vltava (Moldau) river, 11, 29-30, 33-34, 49, 93, 168, 171
Voltaire (François-Marie Arouet), 90, 149
Voříšek, Jan Václav Hugo, 54
Vranický, Pavel, 54
Vratislav II, duke of Bohemia, 29
Vyšehrad, 29

Wagner, Richard, 89, 100, 210, 216
Wahr, Karl, 129-130
Waldstein, Albrecht von, duke of Friedland, 78
Waldstein, Count Ernst Joseph von, 56
Waldstein, Count Ferdinand von, 79, 119
Waldstein, Count Joseph Karl Emanuel von, 118, 120
Waldstein, Count Vincenz von, 78-79, 110
Waldstein, Countess Caroline von, 110-111
War of the Austrian Succession, 9, 14, 24, 38, 46
War of the Spanish Succession, 173
Warsaw, 146, 152-153
Waterloo, battle of, 159
Weber, Adelheid, 140
Weber, Aloisia, 85
Weber, Caecilia, 84-85

Weber, Carl Maria von, 23, 84, 96, 140
Weber, Edmund, 83
Weber, Franz Anton, 140
Weber, Fridolin, 84, 140
Weber, Friedrich Dionys, 132
Weber, Josepha, 85
Weber, Sophie, 85
Weigl, Joseph, 154
Weimar, 119
Weiser, Ignaz Anton von, 52, 67
Weiser, Maria Domenica Colomba, 52
Wenceslas (Václav) I, duke of
    Bohemia, 8, 16, 174
Wenceslas (Václav) II, king of
    Bohemia, 9
Wenceslas (Václav) III, king of
    Bohemia, 9
Wenceslas (Václav) IV, king of
    Bohemia, 9-10
Wendling, Dorothea, 241
White Mountain, battle of, 12-13, 21,
    51, 59, 148
Wilson, Woodrow, 25
World War I, 25, 29
World War II, 3, 9, 23, 50
Wrocław, 53
Wussin house in Prague, 41, 86-87, 100

Zach, Jan, 51
Zemlinsky, Alexander, 50
Zinzendorf, Count Johann Karl von,
    73, 114, 143, 163, 171-172
Žižka, Jan, 10
Znojmo, 83, 144